Work Inequalities in the Crisis

Evidence from Europe

Edited by

Daniel Vaughan-Whitehead

Senior Adviser, Responsible for Wage Policies, International Labour Office, Geneva, Switzerland

Professor, Sciences Po, Paris, France

Edward Elgar

Cheltenham, UK • Northampton, MA, USA

International Labour Office

Geneva, Switzerland

Published by
Edward Elgar Publishing Limited
The Lypiatts
15 Lansdown Road
Cheltenham
Glos GL50 2JA
UK

Edward Elgar Publishing, Inc.
William Pratt House
9 Dewey Court
Northampton, MA 01060
USA

In association with

International Labour Office
4 route des Morillons
1211 Geneva 22
Switzerland
ISBN 978 92 2 124885 9 (paperback)

A catalogue record for this book
is available from the British Library

Library of Congress Control Number: 2011927325

MIX
Paper from
responsible sources
FSC
www.fsc.org   FSC® C018575

ISBN 978 0 85793 750 6 (cased)

Cover design by Boroka Gergely; layout by James Patterson
Typeset by Servis Filmsetting Ltd, Stockport, Cheshire
Printed and bound by MPG Books Group, UK

Contents

Anthony Rafferty   Senior Research Fellow, Manchester Business School, University of Manchester, United Kingdom.

Wiemer Salverda   Director of the Amsterdam Institute for Advanced Labour Studies (AIAS) of the University of Amsterdam and coordinator of the European Low-Wage Employment Research Network (LoWER), the Netherlands.

Vasil Tzanov   Senior Research Fellow, Institute of Economics, Bulgarian Academy of Sciences, Sofia, Bulgaria.

Daniel Vaughan-Whitehead   Senior Adviser, Responsible for Wage Policies, International Labour Office, Geneva, Switzerland. Professor, Sciences Po, Paris, France.

Foreword

Maria Helena André

This book is important in many respects. It is essential to look at the rise in inequalities during the crisis and how we should address this issue in the post-crisis period. This leads me to a series of questions. Where should we go after the crisis and what model should we pursue? The same model or a new one? Can we even think of returning to the same kind of regulation – in fact, the lack of regulation, especially of financial markets – that put us where we are now?

Undoubtedly, this crisis will be felt for a long time. Furthermore, both the job losses and the reduction in activity in many countries mean that we will not be returning to cruising speed any time soon.

In Portugal, the crisis was exacerbated by the fact that we were undertaking structural reforms in an effort to converge with the most developed EU countries. The crisis has clearly stopped this convergence process.

Two moments in the crisis stand out. First, the focus on bailouts and second, the current situation in which we will have to resume a policy of budget deficit reduction, cutting sovereign debt in order to retain our grip on what comes afterwards. The crisis has certainly led, in Portugal, to an increase in unemployment and, as shown in this volume, different groups have been affected in different ways. Young people and women have been particularly hard hit, with substantial rises in their unemployment rates between the first and third quarters of 2010.

Although Portugal has been able to sustain economic activity and growth, especially with regard to exports, there is a large group of unemployed people who need to be taken care of. The group is heterogeneous, including the highly educated and the low skilled, young workers starting their careers and employees over 35. A whole range of policy goals is needed to meet the challenge. The priority must be job creation. This requires economic growth. The government's first concern is therefore to take the necessary steps to achieve this.

At the same time, higher levels of education and training are needed to prepare the workforce not just for the jobs of today but also for the jobs of tomorrow: greening the economy, meeting the demographic challenge, indeed everything we have been talking about for years, but which has been pushed aside due to the crisis. It is not merely the quantity of jobs that is important, but their quality. This volume proposes a number of concrete ways forward.

Minimum wages are one way of reducing inequalities. In Portugal, despite the crisis, we have been able to raise the minimum wage significantly. This was possible through an agreement signed by the government and the social partners. The minimum wage has proved to be a powerful instrument for tackling one of the main pre-crisis problems, the working poor and a general increase in inequalities in the workplace.

We also need specific policies for target groups. In Portugal, we have put in place a major austerity package, but we have also initiated as many as 50 measures to boost competitiveness and employment, addressing the functioning of the economy, exports, support for companies, the informal economy and urban renewal. This agenda is being discussed, measure by measure, with the social partners, our aim being to achieve consensus, or at least the broadest possible tripartite acceptance of how this agenda can be promoted.

We have started a debate on active labour market policy, which will be fundamental in reducing inequalities. In agreement with the social partners we are developing traineeships, opportunities for young people and, for the first time in Portugal, full social protection for trainees. We have also agreed to create 50,000 new traineeships for young people, with full protection rights for the first time in our country. We have also looked at how best we can support companies to hire those trainees but also to hire the long-term unemployed. We have produced a programme which is not as generous as it would have been in the past, but which is still fairly conducive to the hiring of the long-term unemployed and young people, reducing social contributions and offering employers a lump sum, among other things to transform short-term contracts into open-ended contracts. We think that this is also a very practical way of reducing inequalities and of helping people get back into the labour market.

Thirdly, we have launched a new micro-financing programme for long-term unemployed young people but also for small and micro-enterprises, especially in the export sector. This programme is a novelty because it not only supports people in starting up in business but also provides follow-up support to try to ensure that the mortality rate of bright ideas is not as high as in the past. Finally we will also launch a programme to reskill unemployed university graduates.

To conclude, we should do everything possible to help get people back into the labour market and to support companies in increasing their activity. It might be with regulation – such as the minimum wage – or with targeted measures, but best of all would be a mixture of the two, and with the close involvement of the social partners. Without their help, we will not be able to identify the challenges or the best ways of moving forward. Understanding where we have come from and where we are heading is probably the most important challenge today.

Maria Helena André
Minister of Labour and Social Solidarity
Portugal

Foreword

Nicolas Schmit

Inequality was not created by the crisis, although it was perhaps one of its triggers. Joseph Stiglitz and Patrick Artus in particular stress how, especially in the United States – where the crisis began – elements such as work inequality, wage stagnation and the working poor have allowed the infernal mechanism of sub-prime mortgages to develop due to the unequal and unregulated redistribution of growth between wages and capital that has been taking place for more than 20 years.

This phenomenon of increasing inequality is also affecting Europe, even Luxembourg, although here we have tried to counter such trends through a national minimum wage, tax incentives and social transfers. It is also important to identify those who have suffered most from globalization. It is the least qualified, who were traditionally employed in industry where they enjoyed fair wages and also a high degree of unionization and social protection, whose jobs started to disappear with globalization and increasing relocation. Even where they managed to keep their jobs, downward pressure on wages increased dramatically.

Globalization has thus led to a new distribution: between industrialized countries and emerging countries, on the one hand, and – within our own societies – between the highly skilled and those with low or no skills, on the other. The latter were already the most vulnerable, receiving the lowest wages.

The risk of poverty has become a reality everywhere, even in a rich society such as Luxembourg which is also under strict budgetary discipline – although its deficit remains below the 3 per cent threshold. The risk of poverty in Luxembourg in 2009 was 14.9 per cent, particularly affecting young workers and people on short-term contracts. The key element here is precariousness, although this remains undeveloped in Luxembourg. Nevertheless, we observe the same trend, with short-term contracts increasing in both absolute and proportionate terms. We are careful – notably through social dialogue – not to let this process develop further, but there are increasing external pressures. Although Luxembourg's economy is based primarily on services – banking and finance – these generally highly qualified jobs have also been under attack due to relocation. In particular those involving more mechanical tasks, such as accounting and computer processing, are coming under threat.

To these problems there is no single solution. First, Europe must return to the path of growth because this is the only way to boost employment. Germany's good employment performance has been led by export growth, but this should not be concentrated in one or a few countries but rather extended throughout Europe. This also involves proper management of budget consolidation which should not become destructive to growth and employment as this would increase inequality between European countries and, consequently, also inequalities within countries. Rights at work – such as social dialogue, decent working conditions and social protection, all part of the European Social Model – are also important. We must ensure that such minimum standards are not dismantled but rather promoted within our competitiveness model, as Jacques Delors emphasized. Coordination is important, however, because we will not be able to do it alone. If we progressively accept the dismantling of basic labour rights and let atypical forms of work dominate, one country after another will succumb.

Among these basic rights, wages are also crucial. In Luxembourg, the minimum wage is the highest in Europe, in line with higher average wages. At the end of 2010 we increased the minimum rate (increase that was applied from 1st January 2011), a decision which the employers criticized, warning of job losses. But if wages are so low that people cannot live, then what is the added value and the contribution to enhanced productivity? It is vital to ensure that proper living standards are maintained.

Some groups are more vulnerable than others, even in Luxembourg. While young people in general are not particularly vulnerable in Luxembourg, unqualified ones are. This is why the European '20–20 Strategy' is aiming to reduce, at all costs, the number of early school-leavers and to ensure that more young people go on to higher education. People with qualifications will have a better chance of finding a job. But the most vulnerable young people are often those of immigrant parents. Some 45 per cent of the Luxembourg population are immigrants. Many have no qualifications and have been mobile during the crisis in search of better employment conditions. This again has implications for wages and highlights the value of a minimum wage policy around Europe.

Education and training are key. There is a vicious circle in all European societies because inequality creates poverty, and poverty creates inequality.

We all know that children whose parents – often immigrants – are in poverty, as the Pisa study has shown for Luxembourg and France, tend to be trapped in inequality. We must ensure that there is proper access to education and training to break the inequality cycle, both at the global level and within the European context.

Nicolas Schmit
Minister of Labour, Employment and Immigration
Luxembourg

Foreword

Guy Ryder

This volume and the research project that led to its publication are important in at least two respects. The first is in respect of the organizations whose cooperation brought it about – the ILO itself and our colleagues in the European Commission. I think it is vital that we continue to work together on these issues, as indeed on many others. This second is, of course, in respect of the subject matter, the question of inequality. All three social partners – government, employers and trade unions – are clear that there is a problem.

Growing inequality needs to be addressed, first, on the moral grounds that above a certain level, inequality is socially unacceptable. Different countries and different regions have different levels of tolerance of inequality. But the degree and trends of inequality that we continue to witness are economically damaging and dysfunctional. The chronology of events is quite clear. In the years leading up to the crisis there was a long-term secular increase in inequality. Much of this, though not all, is to be traced to developments in labour markets, connected with the wider ongoing process of globalization but also to conscious decisions taken with regard to labour markets. The crisis itself exacerbated that trend and, as highlighted in this volume, while the situation deteriorated across the board, a number of particularly vulnerable groups were hit harder than others. The question that remains, leaving aside whether we are still in, on our way out of, or beyond the crisis, is where we should go next. Will the pre-crisis trends continue and even intensify, or is there a consensus among social partners and governments that inequality must be reduced, and do we have the policy instruments to hand to make this happen?

Much has been written or said about unemployment in the crisis and proposals that would allow business to return to full health, and for growth to resume. But many of these proposals would also risk entrenching or aggravating inequality. Indeed, it is often unclear whether we are discussing proposals to deal with unemployment, the sustainability of enterprises or inequality. They are not necessarily the same.

This volume shows that two areas in particular remain controversial.

The first is minimum wages. The ILO is engaged in its own debate on minimum wages and minimum wage fixing. One unresolved issue concerns the correct path – which of course can be country-specific – and the correct procedures to follow in respect of minimum wages. Their role in reducing inequality and as an automatic stabilizer is acknowledged to some degree, but other effects remain disputed. The second area of controversy is precariousness and flexibility in labour markets. These are not new debates. They closely resemble those we were having 10–20 years ago, but our current circumstances lend to them a new perspective and a new urgency.

A number of chapters in this book address the positive role of social dialogue. Social dialogue, of course, is a much vaunted comparative advantage of the ILO, but also of Europe. It is recognised as a crucial instrument for dealing with all the issues addressed in this volume, and many others as well. It should not be considered a panacea. We are all very conscious that social dialogue is merely a tool and must be used with intelligence and, above all, commitment. It can never guarantee results, but the crisis gave social dialogue – and perhaps, by extension, collective bargaining – renewed impetus and value, not just in Europe but elsewhere. The crisis presented such desperate circumstances that it concentrated the minds of all parties to find a way forward. The question is whether this boost to social dialogue will last beyond the acute crisis during which its value as a coping mechanism was self-evident.

Equally, collective bargaining is now taking place on a playing field which looks quite different in the wake of the crisis. We see in this volume that the shock has been moving on from the private sector – which has experienced some recovery in real incomes – to the public sector. In some countries, we are also witnessing levels of tension and of potential or real industrial conflict that we have not seen for many years, with all their possible consequences.

There are also a number of other important background factors. A key one of these is the sense of, at a minimum, frustration and, at worst, of acute unfairness and injustice at the fact that the burden of getting out of this crisis is being borne unevenly. The most vulnerable are in the firing line, while others appear to be unscathed. The degree of responsibility for what happened does not seem to have much of a bearing on the burden and the manner in which it is being shared.

We are also in a situation, taking a wider, global perspective, in which – with or without the crisis – we would have to deal with some fundamental issues that cannot be postponed. The need for greening of economies of has not been significantly or fundamentally changed by the advent of the crisis. That agenda is still with us and bears enormously on the way in which labour markets must evolve. Equally, there are demographic challenges which have not gone away. This affects pension reform, but also a good deal else.

It is also widely agreed that the tectonic plates of the global economy have shifted. If that was not induced by the crisis, it was certainly brought to the surface by it. This crisis looks very different viewed from South-East Asia; from China and India; and from Brazil and Argentina. I find it interesting that the two places where I have heard inequality addressed and spoken of most strongly, most explicitly and with a determination for action are China, where clearly the government has recognized inequality as a major social problem, and the revolutionary events in Tunisia, Egypt and other Arab countries which have their very roots in problems of inequality and unemployment.

To conclude, the ILO has been trying to address the crisis in a number of different ways. The tripartite Global Jobs Pact, negotiated at global level in June 2009, was an early and important response to the crisis. In addition to its content, which concerns the need for a job-rich recovery, it embodies the working method of social dialogue in a very obvious way. We believe it is an important instrument and sends an important signal. The ILO has, of course, been active within the G20 since Pittsburgh, committing itself to meet the call from the G20 leaders to put quality jobs at the heart of the recovery. We also attach very great importance – and I think there are some parallels with our cooperation with the European Commission – to our cooperation with the International Monetary Fund, following the conference that took place in 2010 in Oslo, where there was a quite new and encouraging convergence on the need for our two organizations to work together and find a consensus on the not altogether different objectives constitutionally mandated by the two organizations. The challenge for the ILO, and I would venture to say for the IMF as well, is to apply that Oslo agenda on the ground and to turn that global discourse of convergence into practical consequences.

Finally, I would like to underline again our eagerness to continue cooperating with the European Commission on these issues, and to stress – as we have in this volume – our readiness to play our part in strengthening the multilateral response to the crisis.

Guy Ryder
Executive Director, Standards and
Fundamental Rights and Principles at Work,
International Labour Office, Switzerland

1. Introduction: Has the crisis exacerbated work inequalities?

Daniel Vaughan-Whitehead*

1. INTRODUCTION

International meetings on the crisis and possible recovery have emphasized the need to address inequalities, alongside the need to generate the requisite economic conditions.

The ILO and the IMF, in a joint document presented in 2010 at a joint conference on the crisis and prospective recovery, warned about the employment and social effects of the crisis:

> In the wake of the current crisis there is an emerging view about the importance of growing inequality as one of the causes of global crises past and present. . . . it is vital to ensure that exit strategies are linked to a progressive recovery of the real economy and jobs and are fair in the sharing of the benefits and burdens of adjustment, especially in the protection of the most vulnerable. (ILO-IMF 2010: 8)

Inequalities in the world of work have unquestionably been affected by the crisis, although the effects vary from country to country and in accordance with policy responses to the crisis.

This book is aimed at providing an in-depth account of the effects of the crisis on inequalities in the world of work. Has the crisis exacerbated existing inequalities? Has it introduced new tensions and disparities to the labour market? And what types of policies, institutions and initiatives do we need to tackle such issues successfully?

We have sought to study work inequalities in a multi-dimensional fashion, looking at the effects of the crisis in a variety of complementary areas: employment, wages and incomes, working conditions and social dialogue. Another object of investigation is whether the crisis may halt Europe's progress towards higher quality jobs and better working conditions.

The present introductory chapter is aimed at providing a first comprehensive assessment of national trends in inequalities in 30 European countries. In doing so, we shall try as far as possible to distinguish between the different sources of inequality that have developed during the crisis, while also attempting to identify systematically which categories have been most vulnerable or most at risk. We shall also try to distinguish between the short-term effects of the crisis and the effects that might only reveal themselves in the longer term.

The chapters prepared by noted European specialists in this field present the inequalities story in individual countries. After providing an overview of the main issues with regard to inequality they present a series of case studies furnishing direct evidence of the concrete effects of the crisis on inequalities in individual enterprises or sectors, and on policy solutions adopted at local level to address such inequalities.

In this way, this volume is aimed at shedding light on one aspect of the crisis that has been poorly documented so far – its microeconomic effects at enterprise level – on various worker categories and the areas of work that directly concern them.

2. IS EVERYONE EQUAL IN THE ADJUSTMENTS DEMANDED BY THE CRISIS?

The first source of inequality unleashed by the crisis is the variegated impact of employment adjustments imposed on the workforce. Employment adjustments in response to the crisis differ not only between countries, but also between different categories of workers.

2.1   National Variations in the Impact of the Crisis on Employment

As shown in Figure 1.1, countries have not experienced the same employment effects. This is due, first and foremost, to the different effects of the crisis on the development of GDP, which has not been equally affected in all European countries. Harder hit have been countries such as Latvia, Lithuania, Estonia, Finland, Ireland and Hungary, while Germany and Poland have fared somewhat better. Poland, for instance, did not experience a fall in GDP in 2008–2009. Second, the timing of the crisis was also different: the impact on such countries as Hungary, Sweden and the United Kingdom was substantial and came relatively early, in 2008, while the crisis arrived much later – in 2009–2010 – in countries such as Bulgaria and Croatia. As a result, the latter are likely to continue to register poor growth in 2011, while the green shoots of recovery are already discernible in countries such as Sweden and the UK.

The pattern of employment–GDP changes presented in Figure 1.2 shows that a larger group below an imaginary 45-degree line shows fairly moderate employment losses. The countries which have performed best in

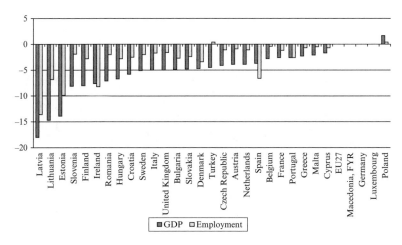

Source: Eurostat.

Figure 1.1   GDP and employment trends, 30 European countries, 2007–2009

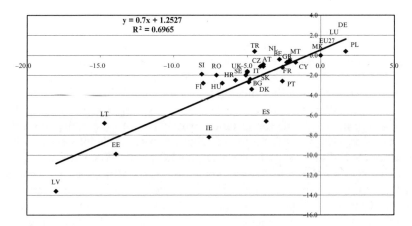

Source: Eurostat.

Figure 1.2   Correlation between GDP and employment, 30 European countries, 2008–2009

preserving employment include Austria, Germany and the Netherlands. In contrast, Estonia, Ireland, Latvia and Spain represent extreme cases of employment loss, as outliers, of a kind, in the left-hand corner. The Spanish labour market has been one of the hardest hit in the European

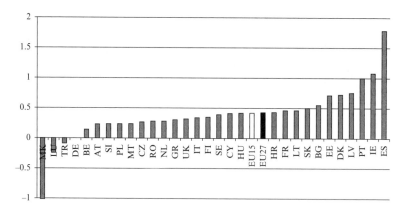

Source: Eurostat.

*Figure 1.3   Employment elasticity to GDP, 30 European countries,
            2008–2009*

Union: in December 2009, unemployment rose to almost 20 per cent.
Latvia, too, has a high unemployment rate.

Figure 1.3 on the elasticity of employment to GDP confirms these
national variations. Employment overreacted in countries such as Spain
(elasticity just below 2), but also Portugal and Ireland (above 1), while the
same elasticity was very low in Austria, Germany, Malta, the Netherlands,
Poland, Romania and Slovenia (elasticity less than 0.5).

National differences can also be explained by other factors, such as the
demographic situation: for instance, with regard to Germany, the low
entry of a new generation into the labour market explains a substantial
part of the less dramatic effects on employment and participation.

The reaction of employment to changes in GDP clearly had immediate
effects on unemployment rates. They increased dramatically – by between
6 and 10 percentage points – in the three Baltic states, Ireland and Spain,
while in the EU27 the unemployment rate increased by an average of
2 percentage points (Figure 1.4). The lowest increases were in Croatia,
Germany and the Netherlands, with a declining rate also in the former
Yugoslav Republic of Macedonia.

2.2   Inequalities Arising from Employment Adjustments

The crisis has highlighted the polarization of the labour force: workers
at the periphery of the labour force have been the first to be affected by
employment cuts, with the core labour force remaining protected, at least

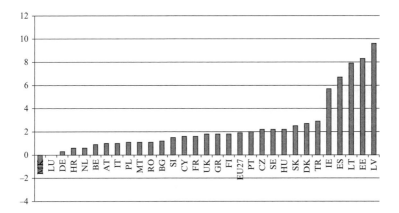

Source: Eurostat.

*Figure 1.4   Growth of unemployment rates, 30 European countries,
2008–2009 (in percentage points)*

initially. It was only when the crisis deepened that the latter started to be
affected.

The chapters on, for instance, France, Spain and Sweden in this volume
illustrate how temporary workers have functioned as a sort of employment buffer in the crisis: nearly 50 per cent of employment losses in France
concerned temporary workers, and about 90 per cent of them in Spain.

This particular group at risk of unemployment is clearly illustrated in
Figure 1.5, which shows how the share of temporary contracts in total
employment has declined rapidly in countries such as Spain, where they
represented 33 per cent of the labour force before the crisis before falling,
over a few short months, to 26 per cent. Lithuania, Poland and Sweden
have been similarly affected.

This is not to say that permanent workers have not been affected by
layoffs; nevertheless, they have been relatively protected by the nature of
their labour contracts.

At the same time, part-time contracts have increased for both men and
women (Figure 1.6, overleaf). A number of countries and enterprises have
encouraged reductions in working hours, leading to a shift of workers
from full-time to part-time work to adjust to the economic slowdown (see
Section 2.3 on working time).

Employment adjustments by gender show an interesting result, namely
that males have been more directly affected by the crisis and consequent
layoffs. In all countries for which we have data the unemployment rate
of men has increased by more than the rate for women (Figure 1.7). The

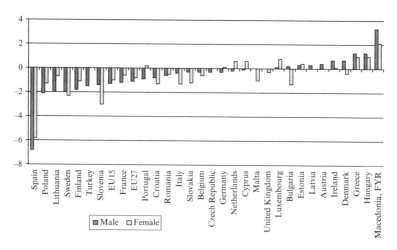

Source: Eurostat.

Figure 1.5   *Evolution of temporary work, 30 European countries,*
              2007–2009 (percentage point change in the rate of temporary
              workers in total employment)

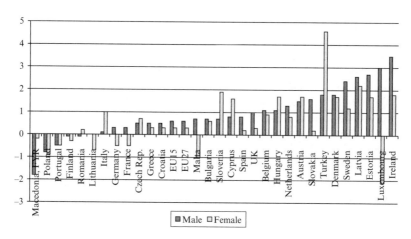

Source: Eurostat.

Figure 1.6   *Evolution of part-time work, 30 European countries,*
              2007–2009 (percentage point change in the rate of part-time
              work in total employment)

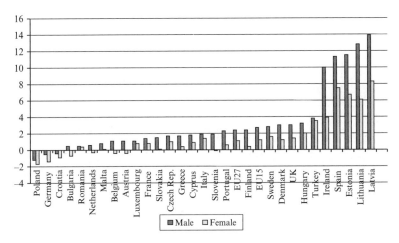

Source: Eurostat.

Figure 1.7   *Unemployment increases by gender, 29 European countries,*
                  2007–2009 (percentage points)

difference is striking, and as high as 6 percentage points or more in the three Baltic countries, Ireland and Spain.

This is mainly due to the fact that the impact of the crisis has fallen mainly on sectors such as construction and manufacturing, which traditionally are male-dominated. Women employed in less cyclically sensitive occupations have been relatively protected from unemployment to date. In some countries, this has led to a reduction in the gender unemployment gap, with a higher increase in unemployment among men, who generally enjoy lower unemployment rates. At the same time, it is important to note that women employed in male-dominated sectors have often been the first to be dismissed (Hogarth et al. 2009).

Moreover, women might be more likely to be affected later, mainly in 2011–2012, with a second wave of job losses expected in the public sector.

Young workers have been hardest hit by this process. Increasing youth unemployment has been particularly marked in the three Baltic states, Ireland and Spain, with an increase in the unemployment rate for workers below 25 years of age of 10–15 percentage points above the increase in the rate of unemployment among those above 25 years of age (Figure 1.8). This may in part reflect the principle of last in, first out – the 'seniority principle' – that has generally been applied by employers in their efforts to shed part of their labour force during the recession. The chapters of this book show that the seniority principle has been applied in many countries;

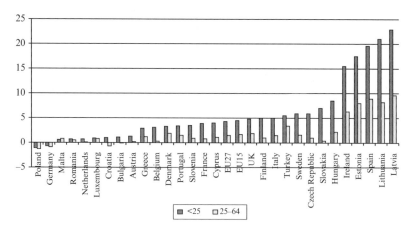

Source: Eurostat.

*Figure 1.8   Unemployment increases by age, 29 European countries,
2007–2009 (percentage points)*

in Sweden, it is even stipulated in the Labour Code.[1] This also reflects the
preponderance of young people on temporary contracts, and the fact that
employers have found it easier not to renew such contracts or to shed temporary workers. The fact that young people are also often those with less
work experience is another element increasing their unemployment risk
during the recession; employers prefer to retain their most skilled employees in order not to deplete their human capital in anticipation of an upturn.

Interestingly, while older workers – between 50 and 60 years of age – are
traditionally a vulnerable group in the labour market, they have been less
affected by employment adjustments in a number of countries. This certainly reflects – in comparison to previous crises – the lower reliance on early
retirement schemes, especially in a context of public debates on the possible
extension of the retirement age within the framework of pension reforms.

The chapters in this volume also report that long-term unemployment
has also increased during the crisis, with a higher percentage of workers
below 25 years of age remaining unemployed for more than a year. At the
same time, senior workers were found to have borne the brunt of increased
long-term unemployment because of their difficulties in finding a new job
after dismissal. In the United Kingdom, the share of older workers in long-
term unemployment has multiplied twofold during the crisis; this is likely
to get worse in the wake of the austerity plans and cuts in welfare spending
announced and taken by the new Conservative-led coalition government
in 2010–2011.

Low-skilled workers have also been in the frontline with regard to job cuts. The initial impact of the recession saw the loss of relatively high-skilled jobs, especially in the financial services sector. Subsequently, however, those losing their jobs have been mainly the less skilled. In Sweden, employment among high-skilled workers has even increased, while that of unskilled workers fell sharply. The chapter on Spain shows that, in 2009, employment adjustments were much more severe in the lowest two wage deciles. Figure 1.9 (overleaf) shows that unemployment rates have increased most among low-skilled workers in almost all European countries.

The recession has also affected the activity rates of the disabled in the UK (Hogarth et al. 2009).

Finally, the labour market situation of ethnic minority groups began to deteriorate in the recession. In the United Kingdom, their unemployment rate rose faster than that of whites. The situation was worse for Afro-Caribbean and African males in comparison to Indian, Pakistani and Bangladeshi males (Hogarth et al. 2009).

Interestingly, again in the United Kingdom some ethnic minorities have been relatively insulated from the recession because a high percentage of them live in London which, together with the South-east overall, is likely to recover relatively quickly from the recession in comparison to other regions.

People – generally men – from selected ethnic groups sometimes lose out because of their concentration in economic sectors that have suffered the most in the crisis. In the long term, minority unemployment may remain relatively high, especially after the planned employment cuts in the public sector, where ethnic minority groups are strongly represented.

2.3 Working Time Reductions to Avoid Unemployment: Core Employees at an Advantage?

Figure 1.10 clearly illustrates the extent to which changes in average working hours in most European countries have been used as an important adjustment variable. In Germany, in 2009, 1.1 million workers were affected by short-time working, complemented by other collectively agreed measures.

Figures 1.10 and 1.11 clearly illustrate how much the economic slowdown has been tackled by reducing hours instead of layoffs. Figure 1.11 in particular shows that nearly 90 per cent of the adjustment has been in the form of reduced working time. The use of such arrangements has been important in Austria, Germany, Cyprus and the Czech Republic, as well as in a wide variety of other countries. All countries have utilized this method in one way or another, and with greater or less success, in an effort to avoid putting all the burden on external adjustment of the labour force.

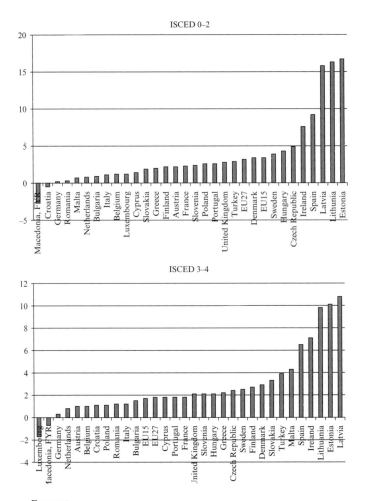

Source: Eurostat.

*Figure 1.9   Unemployment increases by skills, 30 European countries,
              2007–2009 (percentage points)*

Part-time arrangements have also increased. This type of adjustment
has affected men as much as women. In fact, more and more men have
been moving to the service sector, as well as taking on an increasing share
of part-time jobs. However, while the shift from full- to part-time contracts
might help women to avoid job losses, this move has not been enough for
men and has been accompanied by a substantial number of layoffs.

The fact that temporary workers have borne the brunt of employment

ISCED 5–6

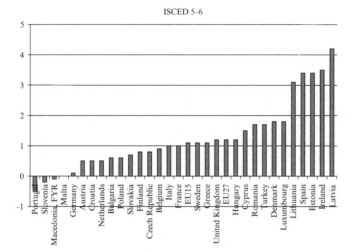

Figure 1.9 (continued)

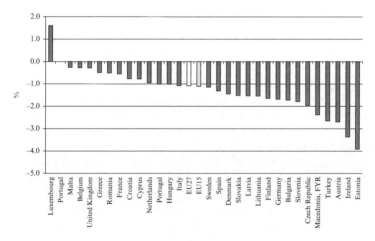

Source: Eurostat.

Figure 1.10 Changes in usual working hours by country, 30 European countries, 2008–2009 (change)

adjustments suggests that this category of workers has not really been given any other alternative, such as working fewer hours. In most countries only permanent workers – that is, the core labour force – have been able to take advantage of the subsidies provided by governments to enable work sharing arrangements.

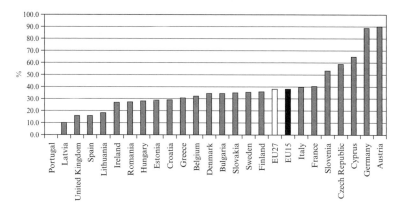

Source: Eurostat.

Figure 1.11   *The role of working hours in the reduction of labour inputs*
                without layoffs, 24 European countries, 2008–2009

2.4   Wage Inequalities Further Aggravated by the Crisis?

Wages have also been affected by the crisis in most European countries. When analysing this, it should be taken into account that the pre-crisis period was already dominated in most European countries – except the new EU member states of Central and Eastern Europe, where rapid growth was also converted into high double-digit real wage growth – by wage moderation, a decrease in the wage share and an increase in low pay and wage inequalities.

As recognized by the IMF, '[o]ver the past three decades, inequalities have widened in many countries, driven by various factors, including the diminishing share of wages in national income and increasing inequality within wage income . . . contributing to the emergence of imbalances nationally and internationally' (IMF 2010). It was thus essential to capture the situation emerging from the crisis.

Generally, a decline in real wage progression may be observed around Europe. Declines have been particularly severe in countries where not only real wages but also nominal wages have fallen during the crisis. This is the case in Estonia, Latvia and Lithuania, as well as in other new EU member states from Central and Eastern Europe.

In other countries, the picture of real wage growth provided by Figure 1.12 confirms that real wages have continued to increase despite the crisis, even if at a much more moderate pace: that is, half the real wage increase – which was already small – reported in European countries before the

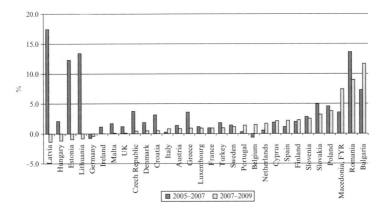

Source: ILO Wage Report database.

Figure 1.12   Annual real wage growth, 30 European countries, 2005–2007 compared to 2007–2009

crisis. The difference in annual real wage growth is particularly strong for countries that experienced rapid real wage growth before the crisis, such as the Baltic states and other Central and Eastern European countries, such as Hungary, Romania and Bulgaria, although real wage growth continued at a rapid pace in the latter two countries, mainly because the crisis started later, at the end of 2009. But this means that the fall is likely to be even more dramatic in 2010 and 2011.

The fall in the average wage is likely to be underestimated because of a composition effect, with average wages remaining artificially high in parallel with employment losses that have hit mainly unskilled and temporary employees who earn relatively lower wages; the retained labour force tends to comprise more skilled and better-paid employees. Layoffs of unskilled workers have thus induced increases in both the average wage and the median wage, but without any underlying improvement in the purchasing power of the remaining employees.

This is not true in a number of Central and Eastern European countries, however, especially the three Baltic states, but also Ireland, where wage falls have been particularly dramatic, accompanied by massive layoffs.

We should also add that the trend among employers in the crisis seems to have been to reduce bonuses rather than basic wages, which remain somewhat protected by collective bargaining. In the United Kingdom, bonuses fell dramatically in 2009, generally due to the automatic downward adjustment of profit-related payments (Hogarth et al. 2009). Similarly, in France profit-sharing schemes have been reduced systematically in parallel with

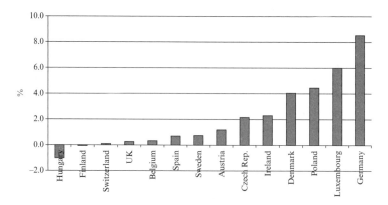

Source: ILO (2010).

*Figure 1.13   Increases in the number of low-paid workers, 14 European
            countries, 2007–2009 compared to 1995–2000*

profit declines, highlighting the use of such schemes as a sort of wage flexibility tool in an effort to limit labour costs and thus to avoid layoffs.

In general, wage declines have often been the result of a reduction in
working time; cuts in working hours applied as an alternative to layoffs are
often associated with lower wages.

It is also remarkable that, despite the composition effect – that is, the
exit of low-paid workers from the labour market – the long-term increase
(ILO 2010a) in low-paid workers (defined as those earning less than two-
thirds of the median wage) seems to have been continuing during the
crisis (Figure 1.13). This, again, is partly the result of wage moderation,
especially among the low-skilled, and freezes in the legal minimum wage
in countries such as Ireland or marginal increases, as in France and the
United Kingdom. It is also notable that the number of low-paid workers
has not increased in those European countries that decided instead to use
the minimum wage as a protective tool against the crisis for the most marginal workers, including Poland and Portugal, but also, to a lesser extent,
Belgium and a few other countries (Vaughan-Whitehead 2010). The crisis
will thus reinforce the long-term low pay and related poverty trends in
Europe. Today, 17.5 million people are experiencing 'in-work' poverty in
the EU27 (ILO 2010a).

According to Eurofound (2010) survey results, 40 per cent of workers
reported that their household had great difficulties or some difficulties
making ends meet (Table 1.1), this proportion being particularly high
among non-permanent workers and the self-employed.

Table 1.1   Percentage of workers in households having difficulties making ends meet, European countries, 2010

	Great difficulty	Some difficulty
All	12.2	26.0
Permanent contracts	9.7	24.9
Other forms of contract	19.0	31.8
Self-employed	12.3	24.1

Source: Eurofound (2010).

Alongside the increase in the number of low-paid workers in some European countries, wage differentials between those at the top and those at the bottom of the wage scale have also increased, as reported in this volume with regard to Bulgaria and Hungary. Similarly, in Sweden the crisis seems to have hit the first wage decile harder because the government has been protecting mainly the middle wage categories (see the chapter on Sweden). In the UK the recession had the effect of halting the pre-recession improvement in the relative position of the bottom decile wage.

· These increases in wage inequality are also significant with regard to the composition effect that continues to operate in the opposite direction: the fact that there are fewer workers at the bottom of the wage scale because of layoffs normally generates less, not more, wage disparity. Again, this increase in wage inequalities may be due partly to the freezing of the minimum wage in a number of countries.

At the same time, evidence provided in some chapters in this volume – for example, for the United Kingdom – seems to suggest that the crisis has contributed to halting the ongoing reduction in the gender pay gap, which remains substantial in a number of European countries. Having said that, the gender pay gap has been reduced, even reversed, in Sweden during the crisis, confirming that the bulk of employment adjustment concerns the male labour force.

Young workers also tend to have suffered more from wage declines due to their lower bargaining power, especially for the majority of them confined in temporary and low-paid employment.

The wages of disabled workers have also been adversely affected. The wage gap between disabled and non-disabled workers had narrowed before the crisis, but widened again in the wake of the recession.

Wage cuts at least in a first phase seem to have been more substantial in the public sector in many European countries, aimed at preserving employment. As a result, the wage gap, which generally favours public sector employees, has been reduced, for instance, in Bulgaria. It has been even reversed in the Baltic states, where wages in the public sector have fallen below those in the private sector. While this may be seen as a levelling effect, it may have serious detrimental effects on the motivation of public employees, and also on the overall quality of public services, with most skilled employees deciding to quit to join the private sector, especially in a context of employment cuts in this sector in 2010–2011. Budgetary cuts in public administration in most countries should lead to further wage cuts in the public sector, together with employment reductions, thereby making public employees the category most at risk.

2.5   Inequalities in Working Conditions: Deteriorating in the Crisis?

The crisis has also affected several other aspects of working conditions.

2.5.1   Stress at work – health and safety

As indicated by the IMF (2010), 'layoffs are associated with a higher risk of heart attacks and other stress-related illness in the short term. In the long term, the mortality rate of laid-off workers is higher than that of comparable workers who kept their jobs.' In the workplace, the effects of the crisis are not easy to capture. Interestingly, the number of serious accidents at work seems to have decreased during the crisis in a number of European countries. While this reflects the continuation of a general downward trend it may also be due to the new context brought about by the crisis: that is, less activity and thus also less intensity at work. Moreover, this decrease – as explained, for instance, in the chapter on the Netherlands – may also be due to a cut in the number of workers at the margin of the core labour market; that is, those on atypical short-term contracts who generally also have a higher probability of experiencing serious accidents and/or injuries at work. Similarly, the reduced activity in, for example, construction, a sector that generally generates a high proportion of accidents at work, may also contribute to this downward trend, which will have to be monitored closely during the recovery period.

There are mixed results on intensity at work. Recent results from Eurofound show that the proportion of workers estimating that their health and safety are at risk because of their work decreased from 28.6 per cent in 2005 to 24.2 per cent in 2010 (Eurofound 2010).

But this does not seem to hold for all the countries under study. The chapter on Turkey reports increasing intensity at work, as well as increasing harassment and bullying. The situation also seems to have deteriorated rapidly in Spain. Case studies in Croatia are also reporting increased intensity at work in those companies that have instigated massive layoffs and thus had to redistribute the – albeit now smaller – burden of work

Table 1.2   Health and safety risks, European countries, 2005–2010

	2005	2010
Percentage reporting health and safety at risk because of work	28.6	24.2
Percentage reporting working at very high speed almost all the time	25.4	22.6
Male	26.3	23.7
Female	24.2	21.2
Atypical contracts	27.5	25.3
Permanent contracts	25.8	23.0
Percentage reporting working between one-quarter and three-quarters of their time at very high speed	34.2	36.7
Male	36.1	38.1
Female	31.8	34.8
Atypical contracts	34.6	38.2
Permanent contracts	31.3	33.3
High-skilled clericals	33.1	36.5
Low-skilled clericals	34.8	37.4
High-skilled manuals	38.7	40.7
Low-skilled manuals	30.5	31.7

Source: Eurofound (2010).

among fewer employees. Moreover, Eurofound results also show that in 2010 one-quarter of employees – and more, one-third, among manual workers – also reported that their work negatively affected their health, a figure which is still high (Eurofound 2010).

The proportion of workers working at very high speed declined from 25.4 per cent in 2005 to 22.6 per cent in 2010 (Table 1.2). It seems, however, to have increased for unskilled workers, from 28.8 to 29.8 per cent. At the same time, the proportion of those working at high speed between one-quarter and three-quarters of their time has increased from 34.2 to 36.7 per cent. The increase is more significant among female workers than male workers, and also more important for atypical forms of contract than for those on permanent contracts. Workers of all categories are affected, although, interestingly, the increase is along the occupational scale. Although these data mainly trace long-term trends they may also indicate that the crisis may not have particularly decreased intensity at work, especially among the most vulnerable workers, such as women, the unskilled and those on atypical forms of contract.

At the same time, the recession has also increased the reported level of disability, with a notable rise in work-related disability resulting from psychological problems.

Table 1.3   *Proportion of workers experiencing discrimination at work,*
              European countries, 2005–2010 (in percentage of total workers)

	2005	2010
All workers	4.8	6.2
Permanent contracts	4.6	5.4
Other forms of contracts	6.5	9.7
High-skilled clericals	4.6	5.6
Low-skilled manuals	3.8	6.6

Source: Eurofound (2010).

Longer spells of unemployment or inactivity impact negatively on people's health, particularly in terms of psychological wellbeing. Evidence in the United Kingdom shows that psychological stress because of job losses in the crisis has affected mainly men. In Greece, people's pessimism has been growing about their personal economic situation. According to a survey carried out in May 2010 (VPRC 2010), the number of employed and unemployed people who said that their personal economic situation had worsened increased by 9 percentage points. Also, 70 per cent reported that their situation had deteriorated in the past 12 months, and more than 80 per cent were expecting their situation to further deteriorate in the future; 71 per cent also reported that they were fairly exposed to the risk of poverty.

Another source of stress at work is discriminatory practices, which have increased further over the past few years, affecting 6.2 per cent in 2010 compared to 4.8 per cent in 2005 (Table 1.3). Particularly striking is discrimination by employment status, with workers on atypical forms of contract and unskilled workers being particularly affected. National surveys also show significant gender and ethnic discrimination in the workplace, for instance in Denmark[2] and Ireland (Bond et al. 2010) but also other countries, an aspect that will need to be further documented in the crisis.

The recession is also having indirect effects on families in the sense that stress related to job loss may lead to relationship problems that affect both men and women. It may also be that women may be more affected by the impact of job loss in the household, given reports of increased domestic violence, relationship breakdowns and reduced divorce settlements, with associated longer-term concerns over children's wellbeing. In Sweden, the crisis is expected to have long-term adverse effects on fertility. This type of implication will clearly have repercussions long after the recession.

2.5.2 Work and family life

Work–life balance and diversity initiatives have also been given lower priority by employers during the current recession. This is likely to exacerbate one – not particularly encouraging – long-term trend identified by Eurofound, namely that the percentage of workers considering that their working hours fit in very well with their family commitments decreased from 31.1 per cent in 2005 to 30.1 per cent in 2010.

As a result of the crisis, although women have been less affected by employment adjustments, they have suffered from a general decrease in family-friendly arrangements. Especially where demand for labour has decreased most employers have proved to be less keen on facilitating work–life reconciliation among their employees. Women with childcare responsibilities are often at a greater disadvantage in comparison to either men or other women in continuous employment. Single mothers, older women and those with lower skills and long-standing disabilities were especially negatively affected, as in the United Kingdom (Hogarth et al. 2009).

It is also important to note that the public sector has been in the vanguard of diversity and work–life balance policies, so that the current wave of budgetary restrictions in this sector may also have a marked impact on such practices.

2.5.3 Vocational training and lifelong learning

Within the crisis there is some evidence of a reduction in training programmes carried out by individual enterprises as shown here in enterprise case studies. In a context of excessive labour supply, employers also have a tendency to recruit those employees who impose the least costs with regard to training. Country experiences, however, differ widely in this respect. The Danish model, for instance, is based on significant training for the unemployed, complemented by strong labour reallocation (activation) after the period of training. This has also been the case with regard to the Swedish flexicurity model in the crisis, as shown in Chapter 11. In contrast, Spain is characterized by a lack of vocational training and lifelong learning in individual firms, also due to a model based on temporary labour. Naturally, enterprises will not be willing to retain employees who are unskilled and do not have much enterprise-specific training.

This fall in training expenditure at enterprise level, combined with reduced training programmes financed by the state, can only have a detrimental effect on human capital and the quality of employment in the long term, well after the crisis. Interestingly, Eurofound results also show that the percentage of workers who believe that their job offers good prospects for career advancement did not change from 2005 to 2010, remaining stable, albeit at a very low 31 per cent. At the same time, this percentage has decreased among atypical workers, while slightly increasing among permanent workers (Eurofound 2010).

2.6   Inequalities with Regard to Access to Social Dialogue

Social dialogue seems to have played an important role in the crisis. It has made it possible to negotiate alternatives to layoffs in a number of companies and sectors, generally through wage or/and working time reductions. Social dialogue has also played a role in the negotiation of shorter working hours in Germany. Companies without trade unions or works councils also benefitted from national agreements on short-time working and also copied other working time measures. On the other hand, in a majority of other European countries, companies and workers not covered by social dialogue were unable to benefit from these possibilities and generally relied on immediate employment cuts to cope with declining activity.

Second, social dialogue has helped to limit the effects of the crisis on working conditions. For instance, the fact that wages are negotiated through collective bargaining in France, with also extension mechanisms to cover enterprises that were not part of the original agreement, helped to limit the adverse effects on wage growth. In contrast, in countries in which there was no wage bargaining, such as Estonia, Latvia and Lithuania, wage cuts were much more immediate and substantial, involving even falls in nominal wages.

This potential role of social dialogue means that workers who do not have access to it are disadvantaged, especially during a recession. Workers on the margins of the labour market, such as temporary workers, agency workers, domestic workers and the self-employed, are traditionally not covered by social dialogue, which has only aggravated the effects of the crisis on these more vulnerable categories. Social dialogue and its contents should be extended to vulnerable groups.

3.   EXPLANATORY FACTORS BEHIND WORK INEQUALITIES

The national and local stories presented in this volume show that a number of factors have combined to explain the variations in the employment impact of the crisis. Of course the variegated fall in GDP documented earlier provides a first explanation. But it clearly does not explain all of it and especially not why countries confronted by the same economic shock have not performed similarly on the employment front. We must therefore investigate the potential effects of a number of other factors. In particular, it seems essential to distinguish the situation that prevailed before the crisis, especially in terms of labour market models, from the responses to the crisis, especially from a policymaking angle, and finally also with regard to the role of institutions. Case studies in each chapter (listed in Table 1.4) illustrate the role of these different factors.

3.1   The Characteristics of Labour Market Models Prior to the Crisis

The ways in which employment has been adjusted to the crisis in individual European countries is obviously closely related to their labour market model.[3] These models range from the flexible numerical flexibility dominant in 'Anglo-Saxon-type' countries (Ireland and the United Kingdom) to the external (or internal) functional flexibility based on 'education-based' mobility which is dominant in Scandinavian countries, such as Denmark and Sweden, encompassing also the internal flexibility based on the use of working time arrangements practised in Austria, France, Finland and Germany and, finally, the high external and wage flexibility found in Southern European countries (Italy, Portugal and Spain) and many Central and Eastern European countries.

Not surprisingly, the impact of the macro shocks on unemployment has been highest in the Anglo-Saxon-type countries (especially Ireland), but also in Southern (especially Spain) and Central and Eastern European (especially Estonia, Latvia and Lithuania) economies.

The outcome of the crisis in a number of countries reflects their prior overreliance on the expansion of the low pay sector, and on the growth of atypical forms of contracts, as in Italy and Spain. In Spain, not only were one-third of employees working on fixed-term contracts before the crisis – most with a duration of less than six months – but 85 per cent of them did so involuntarily.

In Germany, the core labour force seems to have been better protected. While those on normal contracts benefited from working time arrangements to avoid layoffs, workers on temporary contracts – generally also on part-time arrangements, such as mini-jobs – simply did not have their contracts renewed. The dual system of vocational training somehow helped to better integrate outsiders, mainly young people (see Chapter 6).

At the same time, services and the public sector continue to be based on growth in low-paid jobs.

Table 1.4 List of case studies in the volume

	Companies/sectors	Main focus
Baltic states	• Five Estonian industrial (private) enterprises	• Different adjustment strategies through employment, wages and working time and categories concerned
	• Estonian police force (public)	• Wage cuts, unpaid leaves and effects on inequality and working conditions
Bulgaria	• Chemical company	• Negotiated alternatives to job cuts and effects on working conditions
	• Construction company	• Employment main adjustment variable to output collapse
	• Clothing company	• Adjustments on different fronts
Croatia	• T&V construction	• Categories concerned by job and wage cuts (temporary, sub-contracted)
	• FNC building materials	• Inequalities in adjustments (of working hours, etc.)
	• Electronic components firm	• Shared adjustments via social dialogue
	• ABC shipbuilding	• Subcontracted, older, and production workers most concerned
Germany	• Automobiles and machine-tools	• Use of short time
	• Collective agreements on vocational training	• Vocational training, social dialogue and role of youth employment
Hungary	• Multinational electronics company	• Hard adjustment through significant job losses and role of trade unions
	• Food processing company	• Soft adjustment through working time, wage cuts and trade strategy
Italy	• Two family firms in the South	• Adjustment mechanisms: 'Cassa Integrazione Guadagni' scheme; through temporary workers
	• Company FIAT at Pomigliano	• Flexibility schemes and industrial relations
The Netherlands	• Truck-producing firm	• Use of partial unemployment benefit
	• School of vocational education	• Impact on young people between education and employment

Table 1.4   (continued)

	Companies/sectors	Main focus
Spain	• Construction sector	• Employment shock and effects on different categories of workers
	• Three automobile companies	• Time flexibility, role of trade unions and social dialogue
Sweden	• Automobile company Volvo	• Swedish flexicurity, temporary layoffs, training, wage freeze
	• Aluminium components company Profilgruppen	• Employment but also working time adjustments, and collective agreements
Turkey	• Industrial enterprises in the region of Bursa	• Adjustment mechanisms and social dialogue
United Kingdom	• Three companies in the security sector	• Effects of intensified competition on employment, hours, wages and skills

3.2   The Influence of Policy Responses to the Crisis

The collection of national stories presented in this volume shows that European countries have been particularly active in their policy responses to the crisis. To underline this, each chapter presents a detailed table with a list of policy measures taken during the crisis, notably with regard to the labour market. Most of the 30 European countries on which we collected data first put in place packages to counter the crisis and only then recovery measures to boost demand and economic growth. Fiscal stimuli were provided and governments have been particularly imaginative on the labour market front, with a series of arrangements, generally subsidized by the state, aimed at avoiding layoffs.

The chapter on Germany shows how working time reduction schemes have been used extensively based on public funding; this policy probably explains the 'German miracle'.

Policies aimed at extending unemployment benefits have been shown to be particularly effective also on the macro side, compared to other measures, such as public works and job creation incentives (Institute Flagship Report, ILO 2010b).

Finally, most countries have implemented specific subsidies (direct job subsidies, wage subsidies or reductions in payroll taxes) to protect the groups most vulnerable to job cuts. The best performing programme against youth unemployment has been the one implemented in Sweden which offers specific measures for young people, with a direct effect on their propensity to keep a job or engage in training during the recession, thus avoiding an increase in long-term unemployment among younger workers.

At the same time, it is important to distinguish between initial anti-crisis programmes from the policy shifts that occurred most recently in 2010 in a number of countries. Most European countries at the beginning of the crisis – early and mid-2008 – implemented Keynesian-type expansionary policies in order to stimulate demand and sustain wages and incomes, notably by increasing expenditure on training and education, but also sectoral support, for instance, for construction (as in Sweden) and increases in unemployment benefits. The same countries shifted to a more restrictive policy in the second half of 2009 and early 2010 in order to limit budget deficits. This has led to a major policy reversal, in the public sector but also in services and other sectors, a process that we present in our conclusion as one of the paradoxes of the crisis.

This shift may also change the outcome in terms of inequalities. Employment cuts have generally been higher in the private sector, but the crisis recently extended to public sector employees. Many European governments are planning rationalizations and reductions of public deficits and budgetary reductions, including cuts in employment and wages in the public sector. This happened earlier in countries such as Croatia and Hungary and has emerged more recently in countries such as France, Germany, Romania and the United Kingdom.

In Germany and the United Kingdom, the public sector was less affected in 2008–2009, but has been going through a period of employment cuts in 2010, which will continue in 2011, generally due to a combination of downsizing and increased outsourcing in reaction to the crisis.

This could change the inequality outcomes of the crisis. While, as we have seen, men have been hardest hit, employment and wage cuts in the public sector and in services, which are female-dominated, will mainly impact women, thus reversing the narrowing gender pay gap and unemployment gap generated by the crisis so far. Other categories of employees, more skilled and older, but also disabled and lone parents, are also likely to be directly affected by the cuts in budgetary expenditure. Employees from ethnic minority groups will also be hit because of their concentration in the public sector.

3.3 The Role of Institutions: A European Best Practice?

We have seen that, while some European countries have experienced a steep increase in unemployment, employment in other economies has not fallen in parallel with a significant decline in GDP. Labour market institutions can explain such cross-country differences.

We have also seen that the particular policies implemented have played a role. But it is important to note in this regard that governments have generally used arrangements or schemes already in place prior to the crisis, extending or more actively supporting them. The chapter on Germany shows, however, that the short-time working or partial unemployment schemes already in place before the crisis began have been modified in several respects, for instance by increasing the maximum duration from 6 to 24 months in 2009, extending exemptions from social security contributions and also simplifying the administrative requirements facing firms wishing to take up this scheme. The same happened in France with regard to its partial unemployment, time accounts and even its profit-sharing schemes.

Spain has also tried to implement new policies in favour of working time reductions, which are seen as a better alternative to excessive external flexibility, but without much success.

This sheds light on the importance of having reputable institutional arrangements in place. The comparison between Italy and Spain is illuminating. These two countries have traditionally relied on temporary workers as an external flexibility source. Faced with a fall in GDP of a similar magnitude Italy should have experienced the same type of employment losses and unemployment increase as Spain, but thanks to the 'Cassa Integrazione Guadagni' system employment losses were halved and workers kept in the labour market. This institution was key to mitigating employment effects in both the northern and the southern parts of the country.

In the UK labour market, institutions already in place at the outset of the crisis, such as the JobCentre Plus and Rapid Response Services, achieved broader activation, with more intensive support for all job seekers.[4] Incentives for employers who recruit and train the unemployed were also introduced and extra funding provided for training.

In Sweden, focused action and funding via specific programmes to young people helped directly to limit unemployment increases among this more vulnerable category of workers whom, as we have seen, have been hardest hit in other countries. Legislation also helps to ensure that disabled people are not easy targets for job cuts.

The role of institutionalized social dialogue was also essential in a number of cases. It helped to avoid layoffs in a number of countries, and its absence led to harder adjustments in countries which lack such social dialogue institutions, as in Central and Eastern Europe. Similarly, social dialogue was key to the implementation of working time arrangements in Germany.

The national differences with regard to wage growth described earlier in this chapter can also be explained partly by institutional differences. Countries that lack collective bargaining have experienced immediate and dramatic wage falls, while countries with a tradition of social dialogue and wage bargaining – with the possible exception of Ireland – have been able to limit wage declines, as well as employment adjustments. In France, for instance, wage increases had already been negotiated so that wages remained fairly protected from the shock of the crisis, unless workers' representatives themselves decided to negotiate, trading wage cuts for maintaining employment. Even in such cases, negotiated wage decreases have been less severe than those imposed unilaterally by the management in many Central and Eastern European countries.

4.   THE PARADOXES OF THE CRISIS

The behaviour and response to the crisis of the majority of European governments is certainly encouraging. By and large, they have undoubtedly helped to mitigate the employment and social effects of the crisis. At the same time, the same combination of pre-crisis labour market models, policy responses and institutional features leaves us with a number of paradoxes which the crisis highlighted. These will have to be addressed if increasing work inequalities are to be mitigated in the future.

4.1   Paradox 1: Some Inequalities Arising from the Crisis will Become Visible only Much Later

In their analyses of the potential effects of the crisis, most of the chapters in this volume reach the conclusion that it is essential, first, to distinguish between the short-term and long-term effects of the crisis and, second, that the effects on inequality will certainly become more critical and more visible in the long term, in almost every area of the world of work covered here.

While projections suggest that most European economies will start to recover during 2011 they also predict that employment levels will not pick up until the middle of the next decade. This lag in employment – and even more in wage – adjustments will have serious effects on work inequalities.

First, in terms of the quality of jobs, employment adjustments will have an impact on the human capital side. For instance, unskilled and semi-skilled workers have been particularly affected by layoffs, which will undermine their ability, first, to find a job at all, but also to find one of the same quality or wage level. This is also why we expect the number of low-paid workers to continue to increase in the coming period. The productive capacity of young people will be devalued by an extensive period of worklessness or in precarious employment. This will also affect 'highly qualified' young people. Studies have shown that obtaining a high-level diploma in the middle of such a deep economic crisis will affect their employment and wage prospects throughout their carrier. They may miss out on getting onto the first rung of the career ladder.

Long-term employment rates in the next few years, but also other qualitative information, will help us to comprehend the long-term effects on at-risk categories, such as migrant workers and the disabled.

Second, as regards wages, they are expected to lag behind economic recovery in the coming period. Wage inequalities are also expected to grow further, precisely because of the better prospects of employees who managed to keep their jobs during the crisis than those who lost them and may now have to accept lower quality and lower paid jobs. The skill premium will thus contribute to increasing the gap between those at the bottom and those at the top of the wage scale, and also exacerbate other types of disparity. It will also depend on the employment model that countries select. We saw, for instance, that the continuous expansion of the low pay employment sector in Germany may have had direct consequences on inequalities in the world of work.

4.2 Paradox 2: Tenuous – in Contrast to Structural – Decreases in Work Inequalities During the Crisis

Related to the fact that all the effects of the crisis will be more visible in the long term is a second paradox, namely that almost all decreases in inequalities in the world of work that may have been observed during the crisis – and are reported in this volume – are mostly tenuous, in the sense that they do not seem to reflect structural changes and thus may not indicate substantial improvements in inequality. We shall look at three examples.

(i) Gender gaps. Since the crisis has tended to hit male-dominated sectors harder, it has to some extent helped to reduce the gender gap in employment and thus also in unemployment rates: women's employment rates are traditionally lower and unemployment rates higher than for men. This led some experts to highlight that the crisis may have had some good effects after all, perhaps decreasing work inequalities between men and women on the labour market.

At the same time, the fact that many men were forced to shift from full-time to part-time employment to avoid losing their jobs has also led some to believe that, for once, not only women but also men were forced into involuntary part-time working. Such decreases in inequality, however, are merely artificial and temporary phenomena and not likely to be robust.

First, the reduced gender gap in employment and unemployment is due not to the improved situation of women on the labour market – there was no greater access of women to certain jobs, especially higher level jobs – but rather to a deterioration in the position of men in the crisis, who started to face a similar situation to that traditionally experienced by women.

Second, these are only temporary reductions in the gender gap that occurred during the two years of the crisis (2008–2009). Already in 2010, the gender employment gap started to increase again, for instance in Italy and elsewhere, as reported in this volume. As soon as recovery sets in – especially in the male-dominated sectors hit hardest, such as construction and manufacturing – hirings will affect mostly men, thus immediately putting the gender gap on an upward trend.

Third, the fact that women have suffered less than men from employment adjustments does not mean that they have not faced discriminatory practices in the crisis. Evidence in this volume shows that in those sectors in which gender representation is balanced, women have been laid off more rapidly than men. Chapter 13 on the United Kingdom also highlights other forms of gender bias, for instance with regard to access to unemployment benefits, reduced entitlement of lone parents to income support without a job search requirement and the gender bias in pay systems. In other countries covered in this volume women seem also to have experienced more wage cuts than men rather than employment losses. The evidence provided in the various chapters also shows that the reduction or removal of arrangements to reconcile work and family life observed during the crisis has also increased stress at work, mainly for female workers.

Fourth, while the 2008–2009 crisis seems to have hurt women less than men, the situation has been changing rapidly in 2010–2011 alongside the second wave of reforms aimed at reducing budget deficits, involving significant cuts in both employment and wages in the public sector, in which a higher proportion of women are employed.

Overall, we thus cannot claim that the crisis has structurally changed the gender gaps that prevailed before the crisis. Both males and females have been affected – even if in different ways and with different timings – especially from the household point of view, where losses have just been accumulated, for instance with a male breadwinner losing his job, combined with a significant wage cut and increased stress at work for the woman.

(ii) Similar to the gender employment gap, the first years of the crisis seem to be showing that the crisis has affected employees in the private sector more directly, who have experienced a higher propensity to be laid off. This has not been the case everywhere, as shown for instance by the significant employment cuts in the public sector in some countries, such as Bulgaria, even in the first months of the crisis. Furthermore, the new series of reforms in the public sector instituted in most European countries will hurt public employees much more than private employees, in terms of both employment and wages.

On this last issue, many analysts have said that the significant reduction of wages in the public sector would help, after all, to reduce the wage gap between the private and the public sector since wages in the latter are above those in the former in a number of countries. This reduced gap would – generally according to the same analysts – be particularly justified, given that public sector employees traditionally enjoy better job protection and in fact have been less affected than employees in the private sector in the first two years of the crisis. But here again, the reduced wage gap has been driven by the deterioration of wages in one sector – the public sector – rather than better wages in the private sector. Moreover, we know that lower wages in the public sector may lead to a deterioration of employees' motivation and a decline in the quality of public services that in the end may affect everyone. In Bulgaria, the crisis has resulted in the wage gap which existed prior to the crisis – with lower wages in the private sector – even being reversed: wages in the public sector are now lower, a phenomenon that may lead to problems in attracting young people and better qualified employees into public sector jobs, especially since this sector also no longer – and this trend may be observed throughout Europe – enjoys its traditional employment protection due to the increasing outsourcing of former public activities to the private sector (see, for example, the police in Estonia).

(iii) Our final example is health and safety. The lower number of accidents at work or lower intensity at work within the crisis, as reported in many chapters in this volume, may be somewhat artificial, being due only to falling production rather than to structural improvements in work organization. Without deeper structural changes the sudden increase in activity as a result of economic recovery may lead once again to health and safety problems. Moreover, we have seen that the situation is not the same everywhere. While work sharing and internal flexibility in general seem to have led to improvements in health and safety, in contrast, intensity at work has been found to have increased in those countries and companies where immediate layoffs were instituted, leaving the remaining employees with an even greater burden and stress at work, as shown in the case studies presented in this volume, notably for Turkey, Croatia and Spain (for instance, in the automobile sector).

4.3   Paradox 3: Greater Use of Internal Flexibility Within an External Flexibility-based Paradigm

The chapters in this volume show that European countries have used a range of flexibility tools. Germany, for instance, stands out as a champion of internal numerical flexibility through working time reductions, whereas the United Kingdom exhibits much greater external numerical and wage flexibility.

But the crisis has shown that those countries that have relied on external flexibility adjustments, such as Spain, have experienced severe difficulties on the employment front. Massive reliance on temporary contracts for nearly 20 years has left the country vulnerable and employment has plunged in response to the economic slowdown.

Other countries that have developed such atypical forms of work, including Poland and Slovenia, have also experienced automatic adjustments of employment, with temporary contracts being used as a buffer in the crisis. The human cost of this policy should be more properly evaluated, especially in light of the long-term adverse effects on the affected employees' career and pay prospects. This led Spain to limit and better regulate companies' recourse to temporary work contracts. It also encouraged the IMF to advise implementation of a different economic model from the one used by Spain so far: 'A review of Spain's employment experience relative to that of other countries concluded that temporary contracts became the weak link in labour markets during the recent crisis, leading to large employment losses, affecting disproportionally some sectors, and making other possible shock absorbing mechanisms almost irrelevant' (IMF 2010).

Paradoxically, countries that had shifted to more liberal labour markets in the 1990s –such as Germany, by means of the Hartz reforms – have mainly had recourse in the crisis to internal flexibility measures, such as working time reductions. Similarly, several countries, including Austria, have used such arrangements – which have generally proved effective – to avoid a rapid increase in unemployment in the recession.

Compared to previous economic crises, in the current recession European enterprises have had much more recourse to internal flexibility tools. Moreover, economies able to rely on strong internal flexibility have, to date, been able to avoid major increases in unemployment. Their effects on inequality are also better. As the IMF recognizes, 'these programmes can spread the burden of the downturn more evenly across workers and employers, reduce future hiring costs, and protect workers' human capital until the labour market recovers'.

Nevertheless, despite this interesting and unexpected lesson from the crisis, several countries – as well as employers' organizations in a number of European countries – have called for an increase in the number of temporary contracts in anticipation of possible future economic crises. Temporary contracts, after declining immediately as a buffer during the tempest, have started to grow again rapidly in 2010, as shown in Figure 1.14. The figure shows that in 2008–2009 the percentage of temporary workers among the total number of employees fell rapidly, generally due to a fall in the number of temporary workers much larger than the fall in overall employment. The picture has been reversed in a majority of countries in 2009–2010, with the proportion of temporary workers this time increasing as a percentage of total employment, due to the immediate hiring of this type of employee as economic recovery gets under way, even though the general number of employees continues to decline (if at a more moderate pace than in 2008–2009). The reversal of the trend was particularly striking in Portugal, Romania, France, Italy, Cyprus, Turkey and Hungary, but also discernible in Scandinavia, for example, in Finland and Sweden.

This trend is confirmed in most other contributions in this volume. The chapter on Sweden in this volume shows clearly that Swedish managers intend to develop temporary forms of contracts in the event of another crisis. This would allow them to adjust their employment quickly to changes in production volumes. In Germany, there is also a strong probability that the trend towards the expansion of the low pay sector (mainly in services and the public sector) through more atypical forms of contract will continue, despite its use of forms of internal flexibility during the crisis. Although it is too early to draw conclusions on whether the current increase will merely compensate for the fall registered during the crisis or whether the proportion of temporary workers will in the end increase – although we have indications that this second scenario is more realistic – the figures clearly show that the crisis may well induce employers (even where they have successfully relied on internal flexibility to face the crisis) to rely much more than hitherto on temporary workers as a major mechanism of external flexibility to adjust to changes in economic activity.

Is this new trend desirable? Could it not deepen structural inequalities? And what should be the role of the state in this process?

We should try to answer such questions without entering again into a direct conflict between internal and external flexibility. A few countries – such as Germany and Italy – have tried to extend institutional arrangements, such as shorter working time, to workers under atypical forms of contract, illustrating a possible combination of internal and external flexibility. The Swedish experience has also shown a combination of training with external flexibility. Other flexibility tools, such as pay flexibility – for

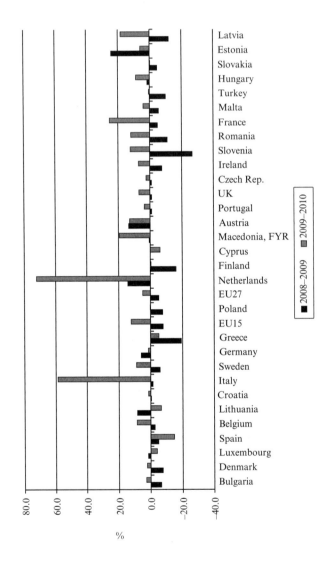

Figure 1.14   Changes in number of temporary workers, 30 European countries, 2008–2009 compared to 2009–2010

instance, through profit-sharing schemes, that seem to have played a role in the UK and France – also need to be further investigated in the future.

4.4 Paradox 4: Anti-crisis Solutions Reproducing the Inequalities of Dual Labour Markets

While some countries have launched a series of measures to limit the employment effects of the crisis, we have seen that only a fraction of the labour force has been given an opportunity to take advantage of such programmes. While Germany, for instance, has relied on working time reductions to avoid unemployment, this option has benefitted mainly the core labour force – skilled workers in manufacturing who remain covered by strong legal protection against dismissals – while another adjustment, this time external, at the margins of the labour market, has taken place, with employment losses among temporary workers (generally unskilled but also young skilled) and those with atypical forms of contract, such as those in mini-jobs or atypical part-time contracts. When the crisis began, employers started by laying off agency workers (about 300,000), so that the employment decline could basically be limited to this category of workers. The same happened through the non-renewal of fixed-term contracts.

It is important to note that such dual markets seem to have prevailed in many European countries, while others, with much more liberal labour markets – such as the Baltic countries – have relied purely on quantitative labour adjustments.

Even in countries with different labour market models, for instance the European 'champion' for temporary work, Spain, and the welfare-oriented, protective labour market of Sweden, have ultimately instituted the same type of employment adjustments, and on a similar scale, due to the existence of this dual employment system.

Similarly, in France the dual labour market led to a dual adjustment, external for temporary workers and internal for core employees. Such non-standard workers are not only disadvantaged in terms of employment stability, but also less protected by social insurance.

According to the IMF:

> one labour market policy that appears to have aggravated the pain during the recession is the dual labour market system, which was introduced to make labour markets more flexible . . . These disparities between the permanent and temporary workforce risk becoming entrenched as the temporary workforce has less access to on-the-job training and thus acquire less human capital than their permanent peers, which in turn worsens their prospective employment opportunities. (IMF 2010: 5 and 36)

Although complementary measures will be put in place for the most vulnerable groups, we shall see below that such targeted programmes have not been very effective, and certainly not sufficient to compensate for the adverse effects of the dual labour markets reported in most European countries. Certainly, the crisis is showing a need to move towards a more equal distribution of risks.

4.5   Paradox 5: The Ineffectiveness of Targeted Programmes for Vulnerable Groups

Despite some targeted actions to protect the most vulnerable groups from the impact of the crisis, inequalities have increased rapidly. Specific initiatives have been unable to impede the rapid increase in youth unemployment or the systematic laying-off of less qualified workers, not to mention discriminatory practices against immigrant workers. The increased difficulties facing disabled people trying to find jobs in the crisis also highlights the need for support programmes for them.

This lack of effectiveness might be due to the limited scale of these initiatives in terms of financial, human and administrative resources. In this regard, it is notable that where more has been invested, better results have been achieved, as shown by the favourable outcomes of the youth programme implemented by the Swedish government. The problem with many programmes aimed at helping vulnerable groups is that their coverage has been too small. The authorities at both national and local level, as well as social partners should therefore propose new approaches to improve their extent and effectiveness. However, this objective is likely to be at odds with current attempts by governments to reduce deficits.

But more generally, such limited results during – but also before – the crisis tend to show the limits of the targeted approach. For protecting vulnerable categories, especially when individual workers often cumulate several adverse features – youth, lack of skills, migrant – targeted programmes are not enough and inequalities need to be tackled on different fronts simultaneously: labour market, wages, social protection, education and tax policy. More research is needed on the variety of tools and policies available and the optimal ways to combine them to successively reduce inequalities in the world of work.

Such more comprehensive and ambitious programmes against inequality should be further legitimized by the fact that not only were work inequalities exacerbated by the crisis, but recognized as a major cause of the crisis (ILO 2010a; ILO-IMF 2010).

4.6 Paradox 6: Key Role of Education and Training in the Crisis Threatened by New Restrictive Budgetary Policies

The fact that the crisis has hit unskilled workers harder, in terms of both employment and wages, underlines the importance of education. Programmes promoting training, further supported by government subsidies, have also led to interesting and positive outcomes in the crisis, as illustrated by the case studies in the UK chapter in this volume. Nevertheless, the current policies aimed at reducing expenditure in all related sectors, such as education, health, training and also labour market measures, in a majority of European countries could halt this active policy aimed at avoiding losses in human capital. The effects of this new orientation may be seen in the short term, but will be especially apparent in the long term, since they may affect the probability of present and future unemployed persons finding jobs, particularly jobs of sufficient quality, in terms of both contents and wages.

5. CONCLUSIONS

The financial and economic crisis of 2008–2009 has been the most severe since the Great Depression, as shown by successive quarters of economic contraction in most EU countries. Its impact on the employment side has also been on a large scale. According to ILO data, global unemployment has reached 210 million, 30 million of which is the direct result of the 2008–2009 crisis. At the same time, the crisis has further aggravated wage moderation and wage inequalities which have been identified by a number of economists as a major cause of the crisis: the purchasing power of wages was curtailed to such an extent that massive household borrowing was needed to make up the difference, contributing significantly to the financial bubble that finally collapsed, generating the current financial and economic crisis. The kind of long-term adverse trends observed over the past ten years – such as wage moderation, the long-term decline in the wage share, increased wage inequality between the top and the bottom and an increase in the number and proportion of low-paid workers – may be further aggravated by the crisis. This volume documents, for instance, the increase in the number and proportion of low-paid workers, for instance in the chapters on Bulgaria, Germany and Spain.

It is for these reasons that the ILO, at recent G20 meetings, has pushed the more advanced economies to do all they can to generate employment-led, but also income-led, growth.

In this regard, the European experience within the crisis, reviewed in this comparative volume, furnishes an important lesson, namely that policies and institutions count in terms of employment and also work inequalities. More than in other regions, the combination of stimulus packages, subsidies to preserve investment and employment stability and social dialogue has helped to limit the shocks with regard to employment and social cohesion. Such lessons should be heeded when redesigning labour markets and implementing institutional reforms.

At the same time, our findings highlight a number of unexplored aspects of the crisis, potential new sources of inequality due to the crisis and the profiles of employees who have suffered the most. We have seen that those particularly hard hit include men, young people, the unskilled, employees on temporary contracts and generally those on the margins of the core labour market. We have also seen that the groups at risk can also change over time, as shown by the new risk of both employment and income losses among public sector employees, which may put additional groups of workers at increased risk, such as women and migrant workers.

Furthermore, the impact on inequalities must be analysed, not only at the point of adjustment, but also much later, since the effects on human capital, skills, career and income prospects may be revealed only in the longer term, such as the effects on health, demographics and society as a whole. This underlines the need for continuous monitoring of inequalities in the world of work.

The message of this volume can be summarized in simple terms. Not only did work inequalities contribute to generating the economic crisis, but these inequalities have only got worse as a result of it. Our general economic system will thus continue to be at risk until we properly address inequalities. This should motivate policymakers and actors on all sides to develop a powerful agenda and a full set of policies to address inequalities within the complexities of the world of work.

To be effective, such concerted action will have to go well beyond targeting programmes for this or that group or to address this or that source of inequality. Rather it must be established as the focus of our choice not only of labour market policies, but also of economic model and form of society.

NOTES

*   I would like to thank the authors of all the other chapters for their contribution to this introductory chapter through the numerous discussions we had during this project. I am also grateful to Jaan Masso and Kristen Sobeck for their precious help in preparing some of the comparative graphs.
1.   On the other hand, application of this same principle is prohibited in a number of other countries, including the Netherlands, on the grounds of non-discrimination.

2. See recent findings from the Danish Board of Equal Treatment in 2009 available at http://www.eurofound.europa.eu/ewco/2010/11/DK10110191.htm.
3. First, internal and external flexibility represent strategies which are applied inside a company or in the labour market; second, flexibility derives either from variation of workload (numerical) or from organizational adaptability (functional).
4. However, in the UK ALM services were privatized. Moreover, the gross replacement rate is one of the lowest in the EU, as is the level of ALM expenditure.

BIBLIOGRAPHY

Bond, L., F. McGinnity and H. Russell (eds) (2010) *Making Equality Count – Irish and International Approaches to Measuring Equality and Discrimination*, Dublin: The Liffey Press.

Eichhorst, W., M. Feil and P. Marx (2010) 'Crisis, what Crisis? Patterns of Adaptation in European Labour Markets', Discussion Paper Series No. 5045, IZA, Bonn.

Eurofound (2010) *Changes Over Time – First Findings from the Fifth European Working Conditions Survey*. Available at: http://www.eurofound.europa.eu/ewco/surveys/ewcs2010/results.htm, European Foundation for the Improvement of Living and Working Conditions, Dublin.

European Commission (2010) *Labour Market and Wage Developments in 2009*, European Economy series 5/2010, Directorate General for Economic and Financial Affairs, Brussels.

European Commission (2011) *Industrial Relations in Europe 2010*, Brussels ec.europa.eu/social/BlobServlet?docld=6566&Langld=en.

Hogarth, T., D. Owen, L. Gambin, C. Hasluck, C. Lyonette and B. Casey (2009) 'The Equality Impacts of the Current Recession', Equality and Human Rights Commission, Research Report 47, Warwick Institute for Employment Research, University of Warwick.

ILO (2010a) *Global Wage Report 2010–11*, Geneva: ILO.

ILO (2010b) *World of Work Report 2010: From One Crisis to the Next?*, Geneva: ILO.

ILO-IMF (2010) *The Challenges of Growth, Employment and Social Cohesion*, Joint ILO-IMF conference in cooperation with the office of the Prime Minister of Norway, Oslo.

IMF (2010) 'The Human Costs of Recessions', in ILO-IMF, *The Challenges of Growth, Employment and Social Cohesion*.

Vaughan-Whitehead, D. (2010) *The Minimum Wage Revisited in the Enlarged EU*, Cheltenham, UK and Northampton, MA, USA: Edward Elgar / Geneva: ILO.

VPRC (2010) *Greek Society's Attitudes Towards the Economic Crisis*, May. Available at: http://www.vprc.gr/uplds/File/banners/Economic%20crisis_VPRC_2010.pdf.

2. Mixed adjustment forms and inequality effects in Estonia, Latvia and Lithuania

Jaan Masso and Kerly Krillo

1. INTRODUCTION

The recent economic and financial crisis has hit the Baltic states particularly hard: their declines in annual GDP exceed even those seen at the beginning of the transition (see Table 2.1). There are several reasons for this. During the years preceding the crisis (2004–2007), all three countries experienced the highest growth in the European Union: average growth rates were 8.2 per cent in Lithuania, 8.5 per cent in Estonia and 10.3 per cent in Latvia. However, there were serious imbalances behind this growth that made it unsustainable. Wage growth – that compensated for wage fall in early transition – exceeded productivity growth, causing a loss of competitiveness in the private sector (especially in certain branches of manufacturing; Estonian Development Fund 2008). The large current account deficit (occasionally more than 20 per cent of GDP – it was around 22 per cent in Latvia in 2006–2007) was to a large extent financed by credit inflows, and so it was no longer possible to maintain external imbalances when the crisis broke out. While during 2003–2007 easy access to credit and low interest rates helped to fuel economic growth, in 2008 and 2009 bank lending contracted significantly due to banks' sharply diminished appetite for risk and fear of loan default.

Economic growth slowed in the Baltic states earlier than in the rest of Europe: Estonia and Latvia faced strong negative growth (–3.6 per cent and –4.6 per cent) as early as 2008. On the positive side, the financial institutions in the Baltic states had lower exposure to toxic US financial assets and the fact that the biggest banks are owned by Scandinavian banks has brought stability.

The crisis has been exacerbated by the use of fixed exchange rates by all three countries: Estonia and Lithuania have linked their currency to the euro, Latvia to SDR. Although at the beginning of the crisis devaluation

Table 2.1   Main macroeconomic and labour market indicators, Baltic states, 2009

Indicator	Estonia	Latvia	Lithuania	EU-25
GDP, % change	–14.1	–18.0	–14.8	–4.1
Industrial production, % change	–25.9	–15.8	–14.6	–14.5
Exports, % change	–24.1	–22.2	–21.7	–19.3
Employment, % change	–10.0	–13.6	–6.9	–1.8
Unemployment rate (LFS)	5.5 → 13.8	7.5 → 17.1	5.8 → 13.7	7.5 → 9.4
Vacancy rate*	2.5 → 0.9	1 → 0.3	1.7 → 0.5	2 → 1.4
Nominal wages, % change	–4.6	–4.0	–4.4	N.A.
Average working hours, % change	–2.0	–2.0	–1.3	–0.5
Budget deficit/GDP	–1.7	–9.0	–8.9	–6.8
Government debt/GDP*	4.6 → 7.2	19.5 → 36.1	15.6 → 29.0	62.3 → 74.3

Notes: * Change in annual average from 2008 to 2009.

Source: Eurostat, national statistical offices of the various Baltic states.

was discussed as the possible adjustment mechanism, all three countries have kept fixed exchange rates, while the currencies of many trading partners have lost value – and were even voluntarily depreciated – including Sweden, Norway, the Russian Federation and Poland. One of the main arguments for keeping a fixed exchange rate has been the large euro-denominated loan burden of the household sector.

All three Baltic countries are small open economies with foreign trade amounting to more than 100 per cent of GDP. This high export dependency also explains some of the strong impact of the crisis. Fiscal policy has not been able to balance this effect. Although there are automatic fiscal stabilizers such as unemployment insurance in place and initial levels of public debt were fairly low, these countries' ability to finance budget deficits has been limited. Their credit ratings for sovereign debt dropped and at the end of 2008 and beginning of 2009, Latvia and Lithuania in particular had limited access to sovereign debt. Latvia even had to apply for a loan from the IMF to finance government expenditure. An ambition to join the Eurozone in 2010 has motivated Estonia to keep its budget deficit below the Maastricht criterion (3 per cent of GDP). In a sense, fiscal policy has been pro-cyclical; for example, in Estonia there were tax cuts in 2006–2007 and tax increases in 2009 (OECD 2009).[1]

In this chapter we provide an overview of the effects of the crisis on the labour markets of the Baltic states and on inequalities in the world of work. Despite some differences, these three countries form a fairly homogenous group, with similar institutions, overall level of economic development and similar development paths.[2] The Baltic states' labour markets have had one of the highest levels of wage inequality among EU countries (the value of the 90th/10th wage decile ratio in some years exceeded 4.5 – European Commission 2005). That is, in part, a result of the institutional setting of the labour market, characterized by low minimum wages, low union density and low coverage of collective agreements. In such conditions, the wage gaps between particular labour market groups can also be considerable. For instance, earlier studies have documented a large gender wage gap (see Rõõm and Kallaste 2004), as well as wage gaps between Estonians and non-Estonians (Leping and Toomet 2008) and part-time and full-time employees (Krillo and Masso 2010). The Baltic states have also been characterized by fairly high labour market flexibility (Masso and Eamets 2007), not to mention low union density and collective agreement coverage, modest expenditure on passive labour market policies and flexible wages (there were wage cuts during the previous recession in 1999). Employment protection legislation has been relatively strict but low enforcement seems to undermine its importance (Eamets and Masso 2005). In such conditions, it is interesting to study how different labour market segments have been influenced by the crisis.

2.   INEQUALITIES DUE TO EMPLOYMENT ADJUSTMENTS

2.1   GDP Fall Immediately Reflected on Employment

Economic developments have directly influenced unemployment rates in all three Baltic states (see Figure 2.1). Due to strong economic growth and migration (for Estonia, see Randveer and Rõõm 2009) unemployment decreased considerably in all three Baltic states in the mid-2000s and until the beginning of the recession unemployment rates were below the EU27 average. Unemployment rates fell to levels not seen since independence was regained. This was a period of labour shortages in all the Baltic states, reflected in a substantial increase in wages (see subsection on wages).

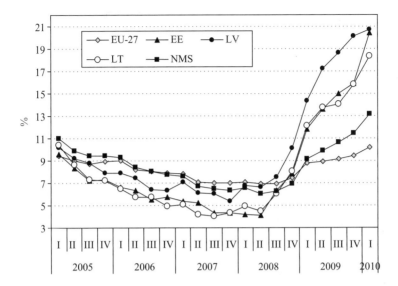

Note: The average for New Member States (NMS) has been calculated as the unweighted average of new CEE member states.

Source: Eurostat.

Figure 2.1   *Unemployment rates for persons aged 16–64 years in the EU-27, the NMS, Estonia, Latvia and Lithuania, 2005–2010*

The economic crisis hit the Baltic states quickly and painfully. The unemployment rate rose more rapidly in Latvia (to almost 20 per cent at the end of 2009) than in Estonia and Lithuania (about 15.5 per cent), reflecting the greater GDP decline there. In comparison to the end of 2007, the unemployment rates were almost four times higher in all three Baltic states at the end of 2009. While in many Western European countries the current crisis has been characterized by falls in employment which are a lot lower than the falls in GDP (in the EU15 in 2009 GDP declined by 4.2 per cent, but employment fell by only 1.8 per cent), in Estonia and Latvia in particular falls in GDP and in employment have been closely correlated (the employment reduction was 71 per cent of the GDP decline in Estonia and 76 per cent in Latvia). In Lithuania, employment has fallen relatively little compared to the GDP decline (47 per cent only). Until 2010 unemployment was a short-term phenomenon. In 2010, however, the share of long-term unemployed also increased. While in most new member states unemployment rates have not yet reached the levels of the early 2000s, this has been the case in the Baltic states.

Table 2.2   *Change in employment during the boom (2005–2007) and the recession (2008–2009) by sector, Baltic states (%)*

Sector	Employment change, 2005–2007			Employment change, 2008–2009			Percentage of total job loss in 2009		
	EE	LV	LT	EE	LV	LT	EE	LV	LT
Total economy	7.9	8.0	4.1	–9.2	–12.2	–6.8	100.0	100.0	100.0
Primary sector	–3.2	–11.9	–22.9	–5.1	–0.4	8.9	2.1	0.3	–10.3
Industry	–5.6	7.2	1.0	–14.0	–21.0	–13.3	34.9	29.8	38.3
Construction	68.2	38.8	29.0	–28.0	–39.7	–26.4	37.4	36.2	42.2
Business services	7.3	19.1	15.1	–6.3	–8.1	–4.9	23.1	24.7	25.9
Public services	5.8	–6.4	0.1	–0.9	–4.3	–1.1	2.6	9.2	3.9

Source: National statistical offices.

2.2 Losses Different by Sector and Workers' Category

Job losses have not been uniform across economic sectors (Table 2.2). Developments in the construction sector have been particularly striking. During the boom years the sector was the biggest job creator (related to the boom in the real estate market, fuelled by easy credit) and during the recession the employment decline has been enormous. It is certain that most of these jobs will not be restored in the near future. Also, the manufacturing sector has seen major employment decline. Public sector employment has decreased significantly only in Latvia, where the depth of the recession made it impossible to make adjustments in the public sector by means of cuts in wages and working hours alone. Most of the employment adjustment occurred in the relatively early stages of the crisis. In Estonia, statistics on collective dismissals[3] indicate that, at the end of 2007, the number of applications for collective redundancies started to increase; for a year (4th quarter 2007–3rd quarter 2008) the increase was fairly stable and modest, but in the last quarter of 2008 the increase in the number of applications as well as the number of employees involved was considerable – more than three times higher than in the previous quarter. The peak was in the first quarter of 2009, the figures falling off thereafter.

Labour market developments have influenced various labour market segments in different ways in the Baltic states (see Table 2.3). The recession has clearly hit the employment of males more than of females: several sectors in which males predominate have shrunk considerably. There are 'female-occupied' sectors that have been influenced by the economic cooling off, too, such as hotels and catering.

Table 2.3   Unemployment rates, various labour market groups, Baltic states, 2005–2009

Labour market group	2005	2007	2008	2009	Percentage points change, 2005–2007	Percentage points change, 2008–2009
Estonia						
Men and women	8.1	4.8	5.6	14.1	−3.3	8.5
Men	9.0	5.5	5.9	17.4	−3.5	11.5
Women	7.2	4.0	5.4	10.8	−3.2	5.4
15–24	15.9	10.0	12.0	27.5	−5.9	15.5
25–49	7.5	4.3	4.7	13.0	−3.2	8.3
50–69	5.9	3.3	4.5	10.5	−2.6	6.0
Nationals	5.3	3.5	4.2	11.0	−1.7	6.9
Foreigners	13.0	6.9	8.2	19.0	−6.1	10.7
Latvia						
Men and women	8.8	6.2	7.8	17.3	−2.6	9.5
Men	9.1	6.6	8.4	20.4	−2.5	12.0
Women	8.5	5.8	7.2	14.1	−2.7	6.9
Nationals	8.9	4	4.6	12.1	−4.9	7.5
Foreigners	NA	NA	11.1	23.5		12.4
15–24	15.7	8.2	13.4	29.2	−7.5	15.8
25–49	8.4	4.4	5.9	13.9	−4.0	8.0
50–74	7.8	3.7	5.1	10.8	−4.1	5.7
Lithuania						
Men and women	8.3	4.3	5.8	13.7	−4.0	7.9
Men	8.2	4.3	6.0	17.0	−3.9	11.0
Women	8.3	4.3	5.6	10.4	−4.0	4.8
15–24	15.7	8.2	13.4	29.2	−7.5	15.8
25–49	7.8	4.0	5.1	12.5	−3.8	7.4
50–74	6.8	3.8	4.4	10.4	−3.0	6.0

Source: Eurostat, national statistical offices.

Compared to the national majorities (Estonians, Latvians, Lithuanians), minorities (in the Baltic states mostly the Russian-speaking population) generally fared worse (in terms of both wages and employment) during the crisis since their unemployment rate increased disproportionately, probably due to poor language skills and ethnic segregation of the workforce.

During the whole period since regaining independence, high unemployment among young people has been one of the main challenges facing labour policymakers in the Baltic states. In comparison to other age groups, young people (aged 15–24) were more markedly affected by both the economic boom and the recession. Thus, it is one of the buffers that absorbed the labour shortage during the boom years and employment reductions during the crisis. Nevertheless, even during the economic boom unemployment was highest among young people. The labour market entry of the relatively large cohorts born at the end of the 1980s and the beginning of the 1990s has also contributed to the high youth unemployment.

With regard to atypical forms of employment, temporary work is not widespread in the Baltic states. While in the EU on average about 13–15 per cent of employees are employed on a temporary basis and in the New Member States the incidence of temporary work is even higher, in the Baltic states the use of temporary contracts constituted only 2–3 per cent of total employment in 2008. In Estonia and Latvia, the level of temporary contracts shows a contra-cyclical trend: for example, it decreased in 2005–2008 (in Latvia from 8.5 per cent to 3.3 per cent, and in Estonia from 2.7 per cent to 2.4 per cent), but has increased during the crisis (in the first half of 2010, it was 6.2 per cent in Latvia and 3.6 per cent in Estonia). In Estonia the new law on employment contracts introduced in the middle of 2009 has liberalized the use of fixed-term contracts. The increasing share of temporary contracts is also due to increasing demand uncertainties during the crisis; firms want more flexibility and thus hire new employees on a temporary basis. Similarly, the self-employment rate, lower in the Baltic states than in the EU15, has even decreased during 2008–2010: in Estonia from 5.3 per cent to 3.9 per cent, in Latvia from 5.3 per cent to 5.1 per cent and in Lithuania from 7.7 per cent to 4.6 per cent (which is interesting, given the increasing employment in the primary sector). Self-employment is also likely to increase if people previously in salaried employment are forced to start their own business in order to make a living; the Global Entrepreneurship Monitor data indicate something similar for Latvia (Bosma and Levie 2010). Another form of flexible employment, temporary agency work, is relatively new in Estonia, with only about 2,800 temporary agency workers in 2007 (Estonian Ministry of Social Affairs 2007). Temporary agency work during the period of economic growth was used in cases of labour shortage and a need for additional staff. Thus, it is highly likely that the sector has shrunk considerably, although no statistics are available on that.

2.3   Changes of Employment Status

One advantage of the Estonian Labour Force Survey (LFS) is that it includes detailed information on the various reasons why employment contracts have been terminated. As shown by Table 2.4, relative to 2008,

Table 2.4   *Reasons for termination of employment contract, Estonia, 2007–2009 (%)*

Reason	Percentage of all terminations			Percentage change in total number, 2008–2009
	2007	2008	2009	
1. Closure of the enterprise	6.9	5.9	10.3	194
2. Reorganization of the enterprise	2.2	1.2	0.9	22
3. Dismissal initiated by the employer	7.6	7.4	7.0	60
4. Personnel reduction	9.2	11.3	26.7	300
5. Expiry of fixed-term contract or probation period	7.8	7.5	5.1	16
6. Termination of self-employment or farming	0.2	1.3	2.3	190
7. Military service	1.2	0.5	1.1	239
8. Illness or injury	19.1	16.4	11.2	16
9. Study	0.9	2.2	0.9	−28
10. Retirement at pension age	18.4	19.0	9.8	−12
11. Early retirement	4.2	2.9	2.8	64
12. Maternity leave	8.8	14.4	10.5	24
13. Need to take care of children or adults	1.5	0.8	1.4	183
14. Other personal reasons	5.7	4.8	4.2	51
15. Other work-related reasons	5.5	4.2	5.6	125

Source: Authors' calculations based on Estonian LFS.

involuntary departures (due to personnel reductions, closure of the enterprise or termination of self-employment) have become more significant and have grown in absolute numbers. However, there is anecdotal evidence that employers are trying to achieve the termination of employment contracts by other means than redundancies in order to avoid the payment of severance pay. Maternity leave has become less important. There is anecdotal evidence that women have opted to use the crisis for child birth in order to take advantage of Estonia's fairly generous system of paid parental leave (up to 435 days and with a maximum monthly benefit of 2,260 euros).

Table 2.5   Flows between labour market states, Estonia, 2008–2010 (%)

Group	Year	EE	Ee	EO	EU	UU	UE	UO	Hiring	Separation
Males	2008	91.9	8.0	5.8	2.2	30.0	43.2	26.8	15.7	16.1
	2009	82.5	8.2	7.6	9.9	42.1	45.4	12.5	14.7	25.7
	2010	76.7	8.3	8.9	14.3	64.0	18.3	17.7	16.4	31.5
Females	2008	89.4	6.9	8.5	2.0	23.5	58.5	18.0	18.2	17.5
	2009	83.6	6.0	11.2	5.1	30.0	45.6	24.4	17.9	22.4
	2010	82.3	4.7	10.7	7.0	41.8	36.4	21.9	16.2	22.4
Estonians	2008	90.2	7.0	8.0	1.8	24.1	50.4	25.4	17.3	16.8
	2009	83.2	7.1	10.3	6.5	29.2	51.0	19.8	16.3	23.9
	2010	82.6	7.3	10.0	7.4	50.8	26.8	22.5	17.3	24.7
Non-Estonians	2008	91.8	8.5	5.2	2.9	31.6	49.4	19.1	16.2	16.7
	2009	82.8	7.1	7.2	10.0	46.7	38.9	14.4	16.2	24.3
	2010	73.3	4.2	9.6	17.2	60.4	24.2	15.4	14.0	30.9
All	2008	90.7	7.5	7.2	2.1	27.4	49.8	22.9	17.0	16.8
	2009	83.1	7.1	9.4	7.5	36.8	45.7	17.6	16.2	24.0
	2010	79.8	6.3	9.9	10.3	54.9	25.7	19.4	16.3	26.6

Source: Authors' calculations based on Estonian LFS; 2010 includes only the first quarter.

Table 2.5 (above) presents the indicators of various labour market flows. Let us denote the three labour market states 'employment', 'unemployment' and 'inactivity', respectively, as *E*, *U* and *O*, then, over a given period (in this case, over the previous year), *EU* denotes movement from employment to unemployment. Let us also use *EE* to denote constant employment with the same employer and *Ee* job-to-job mobility. The hiring and separation rates (respectively *HR* and *SR*) can thus be defined as follows (Haltiwanger and Vodopivec 1999):

$$HR = (UE_t + IE_t + Ee_t)/E_{t-1}$$
$$SR = (Ee_t + EI_t + EU_t)/E_{t-1}$$

As we can see, the separation rate increased from 17 per cent to 27 per cent, while the hiring rate decreased only slightly. That is different from, for example, Hungary, where the employment adjustment occurred mostly through reduced hiring, while separations did not change much (Köllő, Chapter 7 this volume). The relatively higher separation rate in the Baltic countries might also mean a relatively lower wage decline; for example, while in Estonia the percentage change in employment was larger than the percentage change in wages in 2009 (respectively –10 per cent and –4.6 per cent), in Hungary it was the other way round (–3.7 per cent and −5.5 per cent, respectively). The separation rates have increased relatively more for males and non-Estonians. The prospects of moving from unemployment to employment have clearly worsened, thus showing that long-term unemployment is a growing problem. Flows to inactivity have grown only slightly, at around 10 per cent, but are likely to increase in the near future if high unemployment persists. The rates of job-to-job mobility have decreased, especially for some groups (females, non-Estonians). The quarterly data show that while, during 2006–2007, 7–9 per cent of employees changed their workplace within the year, that number increased to 11.8 per cent at the end of 2008, but fell to 5 per cent in the third quarter of 2009. That may indicate that while in 2008 people being dismissed could still find work with another employer, in 2009 they remained unemployed. The recession may also have discouraged voluntary moves; that is, people chose to stay with their current employer even if they were dissatisfied. That may result in decreased job quality. Svejnar and Semerak (2009) argue that the crisis seems to have increased geographical labour mobility in New Member States: for example, people are more willing to commute or relocate to places with better employment opportunities.

3. ADJUSTMENT THROUGH PART-TIME EMPLOYMENT AND WORKING HOURS

3.1 Resort to Part-time

The Baltic states have been characterized by fairly high weekly working hours and a low incidence of part-time employment compared to the rest of the EU.[4] In the Baltic states, the adjustment through working hours has been the most extensive compared to other CEE countries (Table 2.6). This adjustment has been more extensive for males (especially in Latvia: −2.4 per cent for males and −1.4 per cent for females). In Estonia, the adjustment was more marked in manufacturing (−2.5 per cent), and in Latvia and Lithuania in construction (−3.6 per cent and −1.8 per cent, respectively). Svejnar and Semerak (2009) argue that the observed adjustment in the form of a shorter working week in New Member States could be temporary and might later translate into unemployment. Shortened working hours might be due to the higher frequency of part-time employment or forced vacations. Data from the Estonian Labour Inspectorate on firms' applications for partly paid holidays or part-time working show that, at the end of 2008, there was a sudden spectacular increase in both applications and the number of employees involved (Figure 2.2, p. 49).

Table 2.6   Reduction of working hours during the crisis, Baltic states,
2008–2009

Country	Average number of weekly working hours in main job			Share of working hours in labour input reduction (%)
	2008	2009	2008–2009 (%)	
Estonia	39.1	37.6	–3.8	29.1
Latvia	39.4	38.8	–1.5	11.0
Lithuania	39.2	38.6	–1.5	17.8
Slovenia	39.5	38.8	–1.8	45.8
Bulgaria	41.0	40.3	–1.7	35.6
Hungary	40.0	39.6	–1.0	28.0
EU24	37.3	36.9	–1.1	37.6

Note: The share of hours in the reduction of labour input was calculated by differentiating the natural logarithm of the total labour input (hours times number of employed).

Source: Eurostat, authors' calculations.

Table 2.7 presents figures on the share of part-timers in employment. While in the EU27, average part-time employment was stable in 2005–2007 and in 2008–2009 increased slightly (by 0.5 percentage points), in the Baltic states the fluctuations have been much greater. The recession not only led to a decrease in the number of employed, but also forced many companies to resort to part-time work, due to falling demand. For example, in Estonia the share of part-time work increased from 7.2 per cent to 10.5 per cent. In Latvia and, especially, Lithuania the increase in part-time employment was more modest. In the last two quarters of 2009 the frequency of part-time employment decreased in Estonia, probably due to the fact that employers, who resorted to the adjustment of working time, had either overcome their financial problems or fired the redundant workers.

As in most other EU member states, in the Baltic states the incidence of part-time is more frequent among females, young people and older workers. During the recession, the incidence of part-time employment grew in all labour market groups, but the largest increase was among young people in Estonia and Latvia. This reflects the sectoral segregation of the workforce: young people and older workers are more often employed in service sector companies where the impact of the recession has not been as great as in industry, where more middle-aged workers are employed (see LFS data). Nevertheless, emerging part-time employment is also noticeable among men. The conclusion is that part-time work has

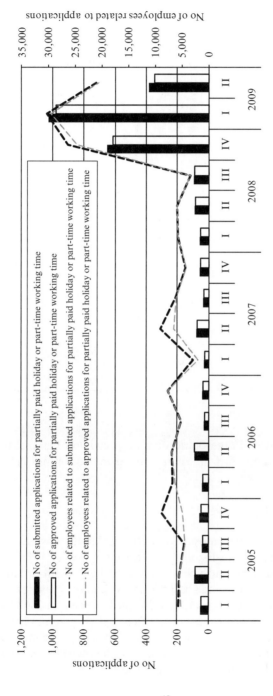

Source: Labour Inspectorate of Estonia.

Figure 2.2   Use of partly paid holidays or part-time working, Estonia, 2005–2009

49

Work inequalities in the crisis

Table 2.7   Frequency of part-time employment by gender and age, Baltic states, 2005–2009

Country	Group of workers	2005	2007	2008	2009	Percent-age point change, 2005–2007	Percent-age point change, 2008–2009
Estonia	All	7.8	8.2	7.2	10.5	0.4	3.3
	Males	4.9	4.3	4.1	7.0	−0.6	2.9
	Females	10.6	12.1	10.4	13.8	1.5	3.5
	15–24	16.9	13.8	12.9	17.7	−3.1	4.8
	25–49	5.1	5.6	4.7	7.7	0.5	3.0
	50–74	11.5	11.5	10.1	13.9	0.0	3.8
Latvia	All	8.3	6.4	6.3	8.9	−1.9	2.6
	Males	6.3	4.9	4.5	7.5	−1.4	3.0
	Females	10.4	8.0	8.1	10.2	−2.4	2.2
	15–24	9.9	12.9	9.6	15.0	3.0	5.4
	25–49	6.6	3.6	4.3	7.2	−3.0	2.8
	50–74	11.9	9.7	9.0	10.5	−2.2	1.5
Lithuania	All	7.1	8.5	6.7	8.2	1.4	1.5
	Males	5.1	6.9	4.9	6.9	1.8	2.0
	Females	9.1	10.1	8.6	9.5	1.0	0.9
	15–24	8.3	9.3	10.7	12.0	1.1	1.3
	25–49	5.9	6.9	5.4	6.7	1.1	1.4
	50–74	10.3	12.5	8.8	11.0	2.2	2.2

Source: Eurostat.

been used extensively in the Baltic states, especially in Estonia, to adjust to economic recession. Part-time employment enabled employers to avoid collective redundancies.

3.2   Forced Vacation

Another adjustment mechanism for reducing labour costs was (partly paid) forced vacations (in Estonia, at least 60 per cent of the minimum wage must be paid during such periods). The ELFS data show that, among the different reasons for being absent from work in the previous week, the frequency of forced vacations increased from 1 per cent in 2007 to 7.6 per cent in 2009. Groups of workers most often sent on involuntary vacation were construction workers, those with basic education, people employed in the primary sector, employees of domestically owned firms and males. On the other hand, this instrument was little used among young people.

3.3 An Opportunity or an Additional Risk for the Categories Concerned?

Table 2.8 (overleaf) presents the reduction in working hours for various labour market segments. Hours were reduced more often among the elderly and young employees, union members, those with basic education and public services employees, and less often in construction and some small firms. This shows us the various adjustment patterns across industries: while in construction, employment change was more important, in the public sector it was adjustment through working hours. A reduction in working hours is usually accompanied by a reduction in monthly pay (according to the LFS, this applied to 70 per cent of working hour reductions in 2009). The natural question is whether the cuts in hours have helped to preserve employment. Indeed, across various labour market segments a negative correlation was observable between the frequency of cuts in hours and the frequency of job losses.

4. GROWING WAGE INEQUALITIES AND ADJUSTMENT BY WAGE CUTS

It is worth paying particular attention to wage dynamics in the Baltic states during the crisis since past reactions to economic downturns, such as the Russian financial crisis in 1999, show that in the Baltic states, unlike in many other countries, wages were significantly decreased (Masso et al. 2007). The Baltic states are in fact characterized by weak wage-fixing institutions (modest minimum wages, weak unions, low coverage of collective agreements – see Section 1), and thus the stronger reaction of wages to adverse shocks is more likely to occur than in countries where industrial relations are better developed.

4.1 Immediate Wage Plunge

During the crisis, the inflation rates were very low or even negative in the Baltic states, and thus reductions in real wages could occur only through the cutting of nominal wages.

Table 2.9 illustrates the dynamics of annual wage increases. While during the period of rapid economic growth (2005–2007) annual wage increases could reach 20 per cent and more, at the beginning of the recession wage increases slowed down and even fell in 2009. Latvia, which was at the forefront in this respect during the growth period, also experienced the earliest and deepest decline during the recession. The wage growth

Work inequalities in the crisis

Table 2.8   Average weekly working hours for various groups of employees, Estonia, 2008–2009

Variable	Average hours, 2008	Average hours, 2009	Percentage change in average hours, 2008–2009	Percentage of reduced working hours, 2008–2009
All	39.6	38.9	−1.8	14.5
Male	40.7	40.0	−1.6	11.8
Female	38.4	37.7	−1.7	17.2
Basic education	40.6	38.9	−4.1	18.1
Secondary education	39.7	39.1	−1.5	15.4
Higher education	38.6	38.5	−0.4	11.8
Age 15–24	40.2	37.5	−6.7	32.6
Age 25–49	40.6	39.6	−2.3	10.9
Age 50–75	38.9	37.7	−2.9	18.1
State	38.5	38.5	−0.1	14.6
Foreign	40.4	39.9	−1.1	15.1
Domestic private	39.8	38.7	−2.8	14.3
1–10 employees	39.0	37.7	−3.2	14.6
11–49 employees	40.0	39.1	−2.1	14.0
50–199 employees	39.5	39.2	−0.8	17.8
200–499 employees	39.4	39.7	0.7	10.6
11–49 employees	39.8	39.2	−1.4	14.6
North Estonia	39.4	38.3	−2.7	17.0
Central Estonia	39.8	39.2	−1.5	11.9
North-East Estonia	39.7	39.4	−0.8	12.0
Western Estonia	39.5	38.9	−1.6	9.2
Southern Estonia	39.3	38.7	−1.6	15.3
Union member	39.2	38.9	−0.6	16.0
Blue-collar job	40.0	39.3	−1.9	16.3
White-collar job	39.1	38.4	−1.7	12.6
Primary	42.0	40.7	−3.2	14.7
Secondary	40.3	39.5	−2.0	14.6
Construction	41.5	40.2	−3.3	6.9
Business services	39.5	38.9	−1.6	16.0
Public services	37.9	37.7	−0.7	16.2

Source: Estonian LFS, authors' calculations.

preceding the recession was clearly unsustainable, however: real wage growth exceeded productivity growth, which undermined competitiveness, a process which continued during the recession despite large wage cuts. The turning point arrived in the last quarter of 2009 and in 2010

Table 2.9   Real wage growth and productivity growth, Baltic states, 2005–2010 (first half) (%)

Indicator	2005	2006	2007	2008	2009	2010, 1st half
Estonia						
Nominal wage growth	11.4	16.2	20.4	14.1	−4.6	−0.6
Real productivity growth	7.2	3.9	5.5	−5.2	−5.0	8.5
Real wage growth	7.0	11.2	12.8	3.1	−4.8	−2.0
Wage share	44.2	44.4	47.0	51.2	52.0	49.4
Real unit labour cost	−2.1	0.4	6.2	8.4	1.2	−9.6
Latvia						
Nominal wage growth	16.4	22.7	31.7	21.0	−3.8	−7.2
Real productivity growth	8.8	6.8	6.9	−4.5	−6.0	6.0
Real wage growth	8.9	15.1	19.7	4.9	−7.0	−4.3
Wage share	41.9	43.9	46.9	50.5	47.0	44.1
Real unit labour cost	4.2	5.0	6.0	7.0	−6.0	−12.0
Lithuania						
Nominal wage growth	10.0	16.6	19.4	19.6	−4.3	−6.4
Real productivity growth	4.6	6.1	7.3	4.1	−8.4	4.3
Real wage growth	7.2	12.3	12.9	7.6	−8.2	−6.4
Wage share	40.8	42.9	43.1	44.5	44.6	42.3
Real unit labour cost	−0.6	3.4	−1.8	0.5	0.9	−9.7

Source: Authors' calculations based on data from Eurostat and national statistical offices.

productivity growth was clearly ahead of wage growth. Thus, the Baltic states differ from other EU countries also in that the huge employment reduction was accompanied by a major reduction in aggregate productivity (Marelli et al. 2010).

4.2   Explanatory Factors

Several factors explain this wage decline. First, workers are more likely to accept wage cuts if they occur throughout the economy, thereby limiting their outside options (compare relative wage theories of wage rigidity). Another reason is certainly the low coverage of collective agreements and trade union weakness (Masso and Eamets 2007). Trade unions sometimes agree to wage reductions in order to maintain jobs, while there are also cases in which companies have introduced wage cuts without the prior agreement of the unions (for example, the Finnish-owned supermarket chain Prisma in 2010 – Osila and Nurmela 2010). It should be noted that Estonian legislation does not allow unilateral wage reductions. In each case, the employees have to sign a wage reduction agreement, but they generally agree to do so to avoid being laid off.

   Wage flexibility is also achieved through various flexible pay schemes: according to the Bank of Estonia's wage survey, about 78 per cent of enterprises used payment schemes based on either individual job perform-ance or the firm's performance (Rõõm and Uusküla 2006). In this case, a sort of in-built wage flexibility contributed to reduce wages automatically when profits went down.

4.3   Wages in the Public Sector Particularly Hit in Latvia

Table 2.10 shows that wages have declined throughout the economy, although of course there are differences across sectors. We have already mentioned the problems in the construction sector: but in comparison to the large nominal wage cuts in Estonia (–13 per cent) and Lithuania (–21 per cent), the change has been much more modest in Latvia (–1 per cent). Public administration jobs have also been hard hit (from 7.6 per cent in Estonia to 18 per cent in Latvia), reflecting cuts in the budgets of both national and local governments. While in Latvia the adjustment also took the form of employment cuts and unpaid vacation, the change in public sector employment was relatively more modest in Estonia and Lithuania. Despite the sharp decline in industrial production, the average wage has declined in manufacturing much less than in many business services branches. Comparing Tables 2.10 and 2.2 on adjustments in wages and employment, we can find evidence that the reason for the somewhat smaller wage decline in some sectors (such as manufacturing in Estonia) could be their relatively greater employment decline. The primary sector and mining and quarrying have also suffered. Almost the only sector with positive wage development is energy, which might also reflect the monopolistic position of several enterprises in this sector. The

Table 2.10   Annual wage changes by economic sector, Baltic states, 2008–2009 (%)

	Estonia		Latvia		Lithuania	
	2008	2009	2008	2009	2008	2009
Total economy	13.8	–4.6	20.6	–4.0	19.3	–4.4
Primary	17.7	–7.4	17.2	–4.6	23.4	–7.8
Industry	11.5	–3.5	13.4	–4.0	17.5	–4.2
– Manufacturing	10.8	–3.9	19.8	–2.1	17.5	–4.4
– Energy	17.0	6.8	5.6	–5.0	15.9	–0.1
Construction	8.3	–13.4	19.0	–1.1	10.3	–21.1
Business services	12.3	–4.2	21.0	–1.8	18.8	–5.2
Public services	17.4	–4.5	20.2	–9.7	22.0	–11.3
– Public administration	15.7	–7.6	16.1	–18.0	23.1	–9.7
– Education	20.4	–2.5	23.4	–9.9	25.9	7.8

Source: National statistical offices of Estonia, Latvia and Lithuania.

Table 2.11   Wage gap between the private and public sector, Baltic states, 2008–2009

Private/Public gap	Estonia	Latvia	Lithuania
2008	106	78	88
2009	96	86	84

differences in the education sector are quite significant across countries: while in Estonia the decline was modest (in fact, at the beginning of 2009 teachers even achieved some wage increases, although these were later reversed), wages in Latvia were cut drastically; from 1 September 2009 teachers' monthly gross wages were reduced by 28 per cent (Curkina 2009). In public administration, the largest contraction in public administration was also seen in Latvia: on 1 July 2009, wages below LVL 300 were cut by 15 per cent and those above LVL 300 by 20 per cent (Curkina 2009). Summarizing the differences between the public and private sectors, the wage cuts have been especially severe in the Latvian public sector. Table 2.11 summarizes the differences over time in the private–public sector wage gap in the three Baltic states. While all the above information applies to gross wages, net wages have been further reduced in Latvia due to the reduction of tax-free allowances and the introduction of progressive income tax (see Appendix Table 2A.2).

4.4   Persisting Wage Inequalities

Table 2.12 presents a range of data on wage inequalities. The rather
high inequality level has not decreased during the crisis. The main trend
in this respect seems to come from the increase in returns to education
with the wage premium of people with higher education relative to
basic education that increased from 51 per cent in 2008 to 67 per cent
in 2009. During the crisis the wage gap with the non-Estonian population has also slightly decreased. The part-time wage penalty has been
declining because of growing part-time employment among males.
Union members have been somewhat better off during the crisis compared to non-union members. The number of minimum wage recipients
decreased slightly in 2009. This is surprising, given that the minimum
wage to average wage ratio increased (the minimum wage has been
constant, but average wages have declined), but that is also because
during the crisis many low-paid employees have just lost their job. The
percentage of low-paid employees is increasing, which is consistent with
increasing inequality.

Developments with regard to the gender pay gap deserve particular
attention in the Baltic states, where it is the highest in the EU, above all
in Estonia (around 25 per cent), but also in Latvia and Lithuania (15 per
cent). One effect of the recession has been the narrowing of the gender
pay gap in Estonia and Lithuania (unfortunately no data are available on
Latvia) by almost 10 percentage points because male-dominated industries have suffered more (such as construction). However, at the end of
2009 some signs of an increase in the gender pay gap were observable
again in both countries (in Estonia from 21 per cent in the second quarter
of 2009 to 25 per cent in the first quarter of 2010), which could be due to
a recovery in industrial production and the further budget cuts in public
sector. The reduced gender pay gap was thus a very short-term phenomenon. Table 2.13 presents the results of the Oaxaca–Blinder decomposition for the gender wage gaps in various years (using the Estonian LFS
and Stata package Oaxaca written by Jann 2008). As can be seen, during
2005–2007 the proportions of the explained (due to differences in workers'
characteristics) and unexplained part attributed to discrimination were
similar to the findings of earlier studies (Rõõm and Kallaste (2004) found
for 1998–2000 that, of the total gap of 30 per cent, the explained part was
8 per cent and the unexplained part 21.3 per cent). For 2009 we can see
that the reduction in the gender wage gap took place at the expense of
the explained part (the most important factors being sectoral and occupational segregation), while the unexplained part of the wage gap did not
change.

Table 2.12   Wage inequalities according to the Estonian LFS, 2005–2010

Variable	2005	2006	2007	2008	2009	2010
Overall wage inequality, P90/P10	3.54	3.41	3.63	3.52	3.75	3.78
Wage inequality in the lower half, P50/P10	1.79	1.74	1.88	1.88	1.99	1.90
Wage inequality in the upper half, P90/P50	1.98	1.96	1.93	1.88	1.88	1.99
Percentage of low-paid employees	27.1	27.5	28.1	27.5	30.6	30.6
Proportion of employees on the minimum wage (%)	6.7	5.6	5.4	5.0	4.2	5.4
Wages of females as a percentage of males	–23	–26	–29	–28	–23	–25
Wages of non-Estonians as a percentage of those of Estonians	–18	–21	–21	–18	–20	–24
Wages of union members as a percentage of those of non-members	10	–3	–5	–3	4	11
Wages of part-timers as a percentage of those of full-timers	–2	–5	–9	–10	1	6
Wage premium of those with a higher education in relation to those with a basic education (%)	61	54	41	51	67	85
Wage premium of those with a secondary education in relation to those with a basic education (%)	4	6	4	5	10	21

Source: Authors' calculations based on Estonian LFS; data on 2010 include only the first quarter.

4.5   Probability of Wage Cuts According to Individual Features

Next we analyse wage cuts at the individual level. Estonian LFS data include data on wages and each person is observed first for two quarters, and then after a two-quarter break for another two quarters.[5] Table 2.14

Table 2.13   Oaxaca-Blinder decomposition of the gender wage gap,
*   Estonia, 2005–2007, 2008 and 2009*

Variables	2005–2007	2008	2009
Wage gap	0.29 (29.98)	0.31 (21.39)	0.26 (21.07)
Unexplained	0.24 (25.76)	0.24 (16.81)	0.28 (22.55)
Explained	0.05 (7.07)	0.08 (6.26)	–0.03 (–2.58)
Education	–0.022 (–9.59)	–0.03 (–7.23)	–0.035 (–10.07)
Sector	0.027 (5.21)	0.026 (2.93)	–0.002 (–0.32)
Age	0.014 (8.38)	0.015 (5.26)	–0.001 (–0.47)
Nationality	0.001 (1.14)	0.002 (0.79)	0.0 (–0.15)
Firm size	0.028 (4.73)	0.046 (4.84)	–0.002 (–0.23)
Ownership	0.012 (3.87)	0.021 (4.08)	0.014 (2.7)
Occupation	–0.006 (–5.35)	–0.002 (–0.99)	0.002 (1.38)

Note: Z-statistics are in parentheses.

Source: Authors' calculations based on Estonian Labour Force Survey data.

Table 2.14   Proportion of workers whose nominal hourly wages were
*   increased or cut over the year, Estonia, 2006–2010 (%)*

Indicator/group	2006	2007	2008	2009	2010, 1st quarter
Frequency of wage increase, all employees	69	77	67	33	34
Frequency of wage cut, all employees	23	15	16	42	51
Basic education	23	18	21	51	61
Secondary education	23	13	18	50	52
Higher education	26	17	16	34	45
Females	23	15	16	43	48
Males	24	15	20	50	57
Blue-collars	22	15	20	52	60
White-collars	25	15	16	40	44
Low wage	29	22	25	61	71

Source: Authors' calculations based on Estonian Labour Force Survey data.

shows that, by 2009, those whose net wages were reduced constituted 42 per cent of all people employed one year earlier. While during the period of high wage growth around 70–80 per cent of employees experienced wage increases, in 2009 the figure fell to 33 per cent. While wage cuts were somewhat more frequent among males than among females, education is fairly important and among those with a higher education the probability of a wage cut was much lower.

We also ran the probit model for the probability of wage cuts and linear regressions for the size of the wage change (Table 2.15). For comparison, the last two rows present the estimation results of a probit model for flows from employment to non-employment. As we can see, after controlling for other factors, the aforementioned conclusions still hold: wage cuts are more frequent in construction, in Northern Estonia (capital region) and for those with a lower level of education. There are no significant differences in the probability of wage reductions across firms with various owners, but if wage cuts occur, they are higher in private sector enterprises, both domestic and foreign-owned (and a bit smaller among foreign firms).[6] Wage cuts are also more frequent among small firms (11–199 employees). The noted differences between blue-collar and white-collar occupations are no longer statistically significant, once we control for other variables. Concerning flows out of employment, many patterns are similar: the probability of moving from employment to unemployment is higher for men, young people, for those in the private sector (especially foreign-owned firms) and in certain other sectors (especially construction, but also manufacturing and the primary sector). For young people, a return to education has been one response to the reduced possibilities to find a job. Employees of foreign firms have once again a higher probability of being affected by the crisis. Employment in sectors other than services (either private or public services) also has a positive impact on the probability of losing one's job. People with a higher education have a significantly lower probability of falling out of employment.

Table 2.16 (overleaf) shows the extent to which reduction in the firm's total salary payments has been achieved by cutting nominal wages, working hours or employment. As can be seen, despite the widespread wage cuts the bulk of adjustment in payroll costs was due to employment reductions (see also Latvijas Banka 2009). Wage cuts are relatively more important in sales and trade, while in other sectors, such as energy, all adjustments have taken place through employment and hours reductions.

Table 2.15	*Regression models for wage cuts and wage changes between 2008 and 2009, Estonia*

Variable	Probit model for wage cuts		Regressions for wage changes among those experiencing wage cuts		Probit model for flows from employment to non-employment	
	Marginal effect	T-stat.	Coef.	T-stat.	Marginal effect	T-stat.
Males	0.010	(0.43)	−0.024	(−2.20)**	−0.003	(−0.25)
Secondary education	−0.002	(−0.09)	0.010	(0.78)	−0.019	(−1.35)
Higher education	−0.106	(−3.05)***	−0.034	(−1.92)*	−0.047	(−2.69)***
Age 25–49	0.021	(0.87)	−0.020	(−1.75)*	−0.050	(−4.15)***
Age 50–75	0.044	(1.64)	−0.033	(−2.58)**	−0.019	(−1.36)
Foreign	−0.012	(−0.26)	−0.055	(−2.61)***	0.005	(0.20)
Domestic private	0.030	(0.81)	−0.081	(−4.34)***	0.037	(1.82)*
11–49 employees	0.074	(2.62)***	0.008	(0.54)	0.019	(1.29)
50–199 employees	0.111	(3.51)***	−0.004	(−0.23)	0.000	(0.00)
200–499 employees	−0.038	(−0.76)	−0.008	(−0.27)	0.035	(1.16)
More than 500 employees	0.083	(1.50)	0.020	(0.76)	0.010	(0.32)
Central Estonia	0.022	(0.70)	−0.011	(−0.70)	−0.003	(−0.16)
North-East Estonia	−0.073	(−1.73)*	0.026	(1.28)	−0.016	(−0.74)
Western Estonia	−0.051	(−1.57)	0.033	(2.12)**	−0.023	(−1.42)
Southern Estonia	−0.025	(−0.92)	0.007	(0.54)	−0.021	(−1.50)
Union member	−0.066	(−1.65)*	−0.002	(−0.11)	−0.046	(−2.07)**
White-collar job	0.003	(0.14)	−0.004	(−0.34)	−0.028	(−2.12)**
Primary	−0.034	(−0.68)	0.005	(0.20)	−0.008	(−0.31)
Secondary	0.038	(1.30)	0.002	(0.13)	0.011	(0.70)
Construction	0.036	(0.89)	−0.043	(−2.02)**	0.035	(1.67)*

Table 2.15 (continued)

Variable	Probit model for wage cuts		Regressions for wage changes among those experiencing wage cuts		Probit model for flows from employment to non-employment	
	Marginal effect	T-stat.	Coef.	T-stat.	Marginal effect	T-stat.
Public services	−0.016	(−0.43)	−0.020	(−1.02)	−0.005	(−0.26)
Number of observations	2553.000		1152.000		4675.000	
Log-likelihood	−1719.768		461.642		−2067.580	
R-squared			0.074			
Pseudo R-squared	0.021				0.021	

Note: The reference groups are females, young people (age less than 25), state firms, Northern Estonia, blue-collar jobs and non-unionized workers. In the probit model for wage cuts, the dependent variable is 1 if nominal wages were cut more than 3 per cent during 2008–2009. * significant at 10%; ** significant at 5%; *** significant at 1%.

Source: Estonian Labour Force Survey data.

Table 2.16 Percentage changes in various labour indicators across industries, Estonia, 2009 relative to 2008

Industry	Total payroll	Hourly pay	Average hours per employee	Number of employed
Primary sector	20.4	22.1	−0.3	−1.1
Manufacturing	−23.1	−7.4	−2.5	−14.7
Energy	−7.0	−6.4	−1.2	0.5
Construction	−38.5	−14.1	−2.0	−26.9
Business services	−16.3	−9.0	−2.1	−6.0
Public services	1.3	3.8	−0.6	−1.8
Total economy	−15.8	−5.5	−1.8	−9.2

Note: The figures on primary sector wages are not reliable and differ from the official statistics.

Source: Authors' calculations based on the Estonian LFS.

5.   INEQUALITIES DUE TO OTHER WORKING CONDITIONS

5.1   Accidents and Diseases at Work Declining but Differing by Country

This part of the report reviews developments during the crises with regard to other working conditions. First, we analysed recorded workplace accidents as indicators of health and safety in the workplace. Representatives of the Estonian Labour Inspectorate expressed the opinion that firms struggling to survive may pay less attention to the management of the work environment. The data on minor accidents exhibit a pro-cyclical pattern, while the number of fatal accidents has been trending downwards since 2006 and the number of serious accidents was fairly stable during 2005–2007 and decreased thereafter (see Table 2.17). Similar to Estonia, in Lithuania the total number of accidents decreased by 37 per cent during 2008–2009. While one explanation could be that the declining number of accidents simply reflects the decrease in employment, especially in sectors with a high

Table 2.17   Accidents at work per 100,000 employees, Estonia, 2005–2009

Indicator	2005	2007	2008	2009	Percentage change 2005–2007	Percentage change 2008–2009
Number of accidents						
All accidents	3431	3723	4073	2927	9	−28
Minor accidents	2405	2615	3105	2314	9	−25
Serious accidents	1002	1087	947	594	8	−37
Fatal accidents	24	21	21	19	−13	−10
Accidents per 100,000 employees						
Minor accidents	396	399.1	459.3	387.2	1	−16
Serious accidents	181.4	165.9	144.2	99.4	−9	−31
Fatal accidents	4	3.2	3.2	3.2	−20	0
Total economy	564.9	568.1	620.4	491.3	1	−21
Primary sector	689.4	623.8	747.0	600.0	−10	−20
Mining	813.6	981.8	716.7	625.0	21	−13
Manufacturing	977.8	1134.1	1088.9	812.8	16	−25
Electricity, gas, water	240.0	444.4	628.6	465.3	85	−26
Construction	620.1	521.3	591.4	447.7	−16	−24
Business services	431.1	411.8	469.3	390.3	−4	−17

Source: Labour Inspectorate of Estonia.

average frequency of accidents (more hazardous working conditions and higher risks of accidents, as in construction and manufacturing), that does not seem to be the case. When looking at the number of accidents at work per 100,000 employees (thus effectively controlling for sector and number of employees, but not working hours), the indicator has decreased in most sectors. The declining number of accidents is found in all sectors and may be related to less intensive work. The correlation coefficient between the changes in the value added produced in the sector and the change in accidents per 100,000 employees is 0.31, which gives some support to this proposition. Another explanation could be an increase in compliance with various regulations, but the visits of the Labour Inspectorate to enterprises indicated that the working environment was fairly similar in 2008 and 2009 (in both years in 82 per cent of enterprises the situation was considered 'Good' or 'Fairly good'). The number of different health and safety-related violations discovered grew by 21 per cent in 2009 in comparison to 2008 in Estonia, while it decreased by 10 per cent in Lithuania.

Other indicators of health and safety include registered occupational diseases and diseases caused by working. However, as the changes in this field are fairly long-term, it is not surprising to find that the number of occupational diseases diagnosed did not increase in Estonia in 2009 in comparison to 2008, while in Lithuania it decreased by 20 per cent (State Labour Inspectorate of the Republic of Lithuania).[7]

5.2   Training Falls in Latvia and Lithuania

Information on participation in training is relatively scarce in the Baltic states for the years of the crisis. According to the Estonian LFS, the proportion of those who had participated in some kind of training during the past four weeks was 2.6 per cent in 2008, 2.8 per cent in 2009 and 3.3 per cent in 2010 (first quarter). Similarly, the average number of hours in training has increased (19.9 in 2008, 24.9 in 2009 and 32.9 in 2010). However, compared to the previous year, the training was less often financed by the employer (72 per cent in 2008 and 83 per cent in 2009) and more frequently from other sources. The results of our case studies (Section 7) indicate that the situation is fairly diverse in different enterprises. According to the LFS data, participation in training decreased most in manufacturing and among blue-collars and increased among white-collars, but differences across other labour market segments were relatively small. The situation in Latvia and Lithuania is somewhat worse. While we do not have specific data on training, during 2008–2009 participation in lifelong learning in general increased in Estonia (9.8 to 10.6), but decreased in Latvia (6.8 to 5.3) and Lithuania (4.9 to 4.5).

5.3   Some Improvements in the World of Work?

One well-known phenomenon encountered in the Baltic states' labour
markets is the use of unreported wages or so-called 'envelope wages',
although a downward trend was observable before the crisis. According to
Kriz et al. (2007), while in 1999 19 per cent of all working-age respondents
received unreported wage income, by 2004 the share had fallen to 14 per cent.
Despite the economic crisis the proportion of employees receiving envelope
wages decreased from 12 per cent in 2008 to 9 per cent in 2009 (estimates
of the Estonian Institute of Economic Research). The indicator 'working
with oral employment contract' (used also by Kriz et al. 2007) decreased
also (from 1.5 per cent to 0.9 per cent – authors' calculations from Estonian
LFS data). The likely explanation for the decreasing incidence of envelope
wages is that those earning such wages (construction workers, private sector
employees, secondary jobs) have had a higher probability of losing their job.
According to the traditional view, the informal sector could expand during
downturns as it is inferior to formal employment, but there is also more
recent evidence that it may behave pro-cyclically (Tyrowicz and Cichocki
2010), and thus the direction of change cannot be taken for granted.

The Estonian LFS includes data on general satisfaction with working
conditions only for 2007 and 2008. Generally, in all four respects satisfaction with working conditions increased somewhat: the proportion of those
almost or fully satisfied increased from 52 per cent to 55 per cent in health
and safety, 51 per cent to 53 per cent in work intensity, 43 per cent to 49 per
cent in health inspection and 47 per cent to 50 per cent regarding the design
of the workplace. On the other hand, the case studies in the last section
present enterprises in both the private and public sectors at which intensity
at work and motivation have decreased. We can thus conclude that the crisis
may have brought some improvements in working conditions, such as on
the health and safety front, or reconciliation of work and family life because
working hours are fewer, but in some cases it has also brought about a deterioration in the intensity at work and also wage cuts that have led to worker
demotivation. The evidence presented in the case studies is thus mixed.

Due to the lack of data, it is not possible to say much about the impact
of the crisis on the reconciliation of work and family life.[8] Generally,
Estonia has been characterized by low levels of part-time work which, in
contrast to other countries, is not used by females for combining work
and family life, but rather among the elderly and students; thus some full-
timers cannot reduce their working hours, although they would like to do
so (Krillo et al. 2007). Concerning developments during the crisis, among
voluntary part-timers the importance of family-related reasons (taking
care of children or other family members) increased from 15 per cent in

2008 to 19 per cent in 2009 (while in 2005 it was 10 per cent). The gap between the employment rates of females with children up to 6 years of age and males decreased during 2007–2009 (from 42 to 32 percentage points during 2007–2009), indicating a somewhat improved position for females in the labour market or maybe deteriorating for men.

5.4 Drastic Increase in Labour Conflicts

Another piece of evidence on the quality of labour relations concerns labour disputes, the number of which has been clearly affected by the crisis. During the whole period, the majority (about 94–97 per cent) of claims were submitted by employees in Estonia (see Table 2.18). While from 2005 until mid-2008 the number of claims submitted by employees was fairly stable, in the third quarter of 2008 it started to increase and peaked at about 1,850 in the second quarter of 2009. Since then the number of claims has decreased gradually. The rise was probably partly due to the new Labour Contracts Act that entered into force in July 2009 and partly due to the recession. Given the growing number of lay-offs, an increase in the number of claims for unlawful termination of contract is expected; the increase in these claims (91 per cent) is more or less in line with the increase in employment contract terminations at the employer's initiative (84 per cent, according to LFS data). The number of claims for unpaid wages while the labour contract is still in force has also increased (by 50 per cent). Claims related to withholding or not paying holiday pay have also increased considerably. Given falling employment, these developments clearly indicate that during the crisis many problems have emerged in relation to the timely payment of wages.

6. POLICY RESPONSES TO THE CRISIS: EFFECTIVE IN LIMITING GROWTH IN INEQUALITY?

The tables in the appendices provide an overview of the various policy measures introduced in the three Baltic countries to stimulate labour demand. As mentioned in the introduction, the ability of Baltic state governments to pursue expansionary fiscal policies has been fairly limited because of the need to control budget deficits.

6.1 More Resources for Labour Market Policies

Despite that, expenditure on labour market policies has increased considerably during the crisis (Table 2.19), both in absolute numbers and as

Table 2.18   *Dynamics of different kinds of claims made by employees and employers to the Estonian Labour Inspectorate**

Kind of claims	2005	2007	2008	2009	Percentage change 2005–2007	Percentage change 2008–2009
Claims by employees						
Total number of claims	4 985	4 230	6 316	12 166	–15	93
Claim for unlawful termination of employment contract	677	472	681	1 304	–30	91
Claim for unlawful termination of employment contract (pregnant or person raising child below 3 years of age)	37	27	31	53	–27	71
Claim for unlawful termination of employment contract (submitted by employee representative)	4	1	6	0	–75	–100
Claim for unpaid wages while still employed	2 211	1 274	2 032	3 054	–42	50
Claim for unpaid terminal wage	0	0	0	3 034		
Compensation for withholding terminal wage	908	1 098	1 628	1 124	21	–31
Claim on compensation for withholding employment record book	23	17	11	0	–26	–100
Claim for annulment of disciplinary punishment	106	75	134	171	–29	28

Table 2.18   (continued)

Kind of claims	2005	2007	2008	2009	Percentage change 2005–2007	Percentage change 2008–2009
Claim related to unlawful withholding of wages or other compensation	109	83	110	85	–24	–23
Claim related to withholding of holiday pay	351	365	535	1 078	4	101
Claim related to the nature of the contract	44	55	70	0	25	–100
Claim related to unequal treatment of the employee	0	7	8	10		25
Breach of contract due to the employer	0	0	0	648		
Other claims	515	756	1 070	1 605	47	50
Claims by employers						
Total number of claims	155	159	125	257	3	106
Compensation for material damage caused by employee	52	58	41	76	12	85

Note: * Employees' reasons for claims are not directly comparable during the whole period due to changes in methodology.

a percentage of GDP: in Estonia from 0.2 per cent to 1 per cent and in Lithuania from 0.4 per cent to 0.9 per cent.[9] Most of the growth has come from passive measures, but spending on active policies has increased, too: from 0.04 per cent to 0.15 per cent in Estonia, and from 0.07 per cent to 0.24 per cent in Latvia. Nevertheless, even after the increase expenditure as a percentage of GDP is well below the levels of the old EU member states (EU15, in 2008: 1.7 per cent of GDP). The increasing funding from the EU structural and social funds has helped to finance active policies: for example, in Lithuania the use of EU funds in the financing of labour policies grew by 135 per cent. Expenditure on unemployment insurance has grown in Estonia particularly rapidly due to the growing average size

Table 2.19   Spending on labour market policies in Estonia before and during the crisis, 2005–2009 (%)

Indicator	2005	2006	2007	2008	2009	Change in total, 2009
Total spending, % of GDP	0.17	0.12	0.11	0.21	1.04	325.8
Spending on active measures, % of GDP	0.05	0.05	0.03	0.04	0.15	251.3
Spending on passive measures, % of GDP	0.11	0.07	0.08	0.17	0.89	341.7
Unemployment benefit	54.5	61.6	46.4	52.2	68.2	477.0
Unemployment assistance	21.6	17.2	26.8	15.1	9.6	179.5
Benefit upon collective termination of employment contract	10.1	10.6	15.0	17.2	11.3	190.6
Benefits upon insolvency of employer	13.8	10.5	11.8	15.5	10.9	211.6
New recipients of unemployment benefit	8 749	6 074	6 467	15 743	54 790	143.4
New recipients of unemployment benefit/new registered unemployed	20.5	24.1	22.7	33.1	45.3	46.2
Average unemployment benefit during first 100 days for new recipients	183	212	256	319	350	24.5
Registered unemployed/total (LFS) unemployed	49.9	37.6	42.0	51.4	70.5	37.2

Source: Unemployment insurance fund, Statistics Estonia, authors' calculations. The passive measures exclude data on early retirement.

Table 2.20 Participants in active labour market programmes, Estonia, 2005–2010

Indicator	2005	2006	2007	2008	2009	2010	Change 2009
Total participants (000s)	29.6	23.4	20.9	21.5	48.0	49.1	123.2%
Training (%)	44.6	43.0	33.8	30.6	36.1	28.7	162.8%
Job subsidies (%)	2.9	3.0	1.0	0.5	0.4	29.0	67.2%
Start-up grants (%)	1.2	1.2	0.7	0.8	1.0	0.8	205.6%
Public works (%)	1.6	1.8	4.0	2.8	3.2	2.3	163.7%
Job advice (%)	49.7	45.7	49.4	56.0	49.8	18.5	98.5%
Job club (%)	–	–	–	0.0	0.5	2.6	–
Other measures (%)	0.0	5.2	11.2	9.4	9.0	18.1	114.6%
Ratio of participation in active measures to registered unemployed (%)	44	51	57	39	35	NA	−8%

of benefits (indicating the relatively higher wages of the new unemployed people) and the growing proportion of newly registered unemployed receiving benefits; in other words, they more often have the required length of service. Probably related to the modest support for the unemployed, in the Baltic states registered unemployment has been constantly below LFS unemployment. Nevertheless, during the crisis we can see that the ratio has grown considerably in Estonia. The conditions for receiving unemployment benefits have been stable there (the foreseen increase in benefits related to the adoption of the new law in 2009 was postponed), but in Latvia the duration of benefits was increased to nine months and the eligibility criteria were loosened (Purfield and Rosenberg 2010). Table 2.20 on participation in active measures shows that the total number of participations more than doubled in 2009. The ratio of participations to registered unemployed declined slightly.

6.2 Training More Effective in Estonia?

In Estonia, the most important measures have been training and job advice. Participation has increased in all measures, but relatively more in start-up grants and job subsidies (in 2010). In Estonia, the new action plan (with a budget of around 45 million euros) to tackle the crisis was introduced in the second half of 2009, the aim of which was to create 5,000 jobs through a range of measures, such as the development of business start-up support, widening the conditions for wage subsidies and hiring more consultants to advise the unemployed. The completely new policy measure introduced in 2010 is training vouchers: with that, micro and small firms can buy training from a specified list of organizations (maximum size of subsidy is about 960 euros); for micro firms it has also been made easier to apply for funding from the other training measure by lowering the minimum amount of the subsidy. Some local governments have also initiated public work programmes: in particular the city Government of Tallinn has organized several temporary jobs in municipality-owned enterprises at the minimum wage (in transportation), but jobs have also been created in private enterprises with the wage subsidy, the upper limit of which is the national minimum wage, together with payroll taxes.

We do not have detailed statistics on active policies in Latvia and Lithuania, but they have widened there as well. In Latvia, the public works programmes have offered full-time work for 24,000 registered unemployed, while training and assistance in starting a business have been offered to job seekers. In Lithuania, the Government introduced a large-scale programme consisting of various job support schemes at a total cost of 7 per cent of GDP (Purfield and Rosenberg 2010).

6.3   Towards More Flexible Labour Markets?

The most important legislative change in the field of labour relations in the recession period in Estonia was the new Labour Contracts Act, which entered into force on 1 July 2009. The main aim of adopting the new law was to make the labour market more flexible and to increase the social security provisions for workers. While before the crisis employment protection in Estonia was generally more rigid than in other Central and Eastern European countries, it is now more comparable (based on OECD EPL index, Brixiova, 2009). The new Labour Contracts Act has in many ways relaxed the regulations on regular contracts: notice periods for redundancy were reduced (depending on the length of the previous employment contract, from 2–4 months to 1 month); severance payments were also cut (from 2–4 to 1–3 months) and payment is now shared by the employer and the Estonian Unemployment Insurance Fund. To promote the use of flexible forms of employment, the conclusion of fixed-term contracts is now allowed in all cases. In Lithuania, similar to Estonia, the reforms introduced more flexibility into employment relations, in particular relaxing the conditions on using various flexible work arrangements (part-time, temporary employment and so on) and reduced severance pay (Purfield and Rosenberg 2010).

6.4 The Limited Influence of Social Partners

The recession has halted the rise of the minimum wage. In Estonia and Lithuania, the minimum wage has remained at the same level since 2008.[10] By way of comparison, in Latvia at the beginning of 2009 the minimum wage was raised by 13 per cent to 180 lats; later in the tripartite negotiations in 2010 it was decided not to reduce the minimum wage to prevent further reductions in welfare.

In the period of rapid economic growth, the bargaining power of both employers and employees was more or less balanced and their influence remained relatively weak in Estonia. General pressure to raise wages did not originate from the trade unions; the main driver of wage increases was labour scarcity. During the crisis, we saw that trade union members did somewhat better in terms of employment and wages. Although the Estonian Trade Union Confederation expected a decline in trade union membership due to the large increase in unemployment and major collective redundancies in sectors in which trade union membership has traditionally been high (Nurmela 2009a), data from the Estonian LFS indicate that trade union membership as a percentage of salaried employees declined from 7.6 per cent in 2007 to 6.2 per cent in 2008, but then increased again in 2009 (7.6 per cent) and 2010 (9.5 per cent). Trade union membership has increased in the capital region, large enterprises and the public sector, while it has decreased in North-Eastern Estonia, the region with the highest unionization rate due to the large industrial enterprises located there.

One of the peculiarities of Estonia, in comparison to many other EU countries (and also Latvia) is that, despite the fairly radical steps taken by the Government to balance the state budget during the recession, the reaction from citizens and trade unions was less strong than one might have expected. Of course, the social partners have made recommendations to the Government and parliament on how to deal with the downturn.[11] However, to balance the state budget, governments have pushed through several changes, such as reducing social guarantees and cutting public sector wages without an adverse reaction from employees and employers. The relative weakness of both trade unions and employers' representatives in Estonia has clearly played a role here. Although the social partners have of course reacted, they have not had sufficient power to either force the Government to change its plans or to negotiate for more favourable conditions (except in Lithuania in 2009 – see Appendix Table 2A.3). For example, in February 2009 the Estonian parliament approved a state budget cut in the amount of EEK 8 billion (512 million euros), which included cuts in public sector wages (7 per cent on average) and changes in sickness benefits. While the trade unions opposed the first, employers' representatives were not satisfied with the second which represented a major financial burden (according to estimates, EEK 500 million (32 million euros) on the employers (Nurmela 2009b). However, both changes were implemented.[12]

One indicator of the relative weakness of the social partners was the increase (three times) in 2009 of unemployment insurance contributions for both employers and employees in Estonia. By the end of 2009, contributions had almost quintupled in comparison to the beginning of the year, despite the opposition of both employers and trade unions.

7. CASE STUDIES: ADJUSTMENTS IN PRIVATE AND PUBLIC ENTERPRISES AND EFFECTS ON INEQUALITIES

We present here the different forms of adjustment adopted by five private enterprises in Estonia and analyse their various effects on inequalities and on vulnerable groups. We also present a case study carried out with the Estonian Police and identify the various effects which the crisis and the policy responses to it have had on policymakers and administrative employees. The five cases are summarized in Table 2.21.

7.1 Adjustment Patterns in a Sample of Five Estonian Private Enterprises

The following comparison of five industrial enterprises in Estonia illustrates the different adjustment patterns chosen by individual enterprises due to the different initial conditions and business environment. After the outbreak of the crisis, Estonian industry has perhaps been the most dynamic sector in the economy: in 2009, industrial production declined by 25.9 per cent in comparison to 2008, but in the second quarter of 2010 industrial production was 20 per cent higher than in 2009. Information was also available on company personnel policies during the recovery. The five case studies are from very different sectors of industry and represent typical enterprises: (1) Estiko Plastar, producer of various packaging materials; (2) Sangar, a sewing industry enterprise; (3) Toom Tekstiil, a textile industry enterprise; (4) Hanza Tarkon, a mechanical industry company; and (5) Eesti Energia, the largest energy producer. The information is based on interviews with the firms' personnel managers and other members of the enterprise, supplemented by information from other sources (for example, annual reports).[13]

Table 2.21   Different reaction patterns of Estonian industrial enterprises to the crisis

	1. Estiko Plastar	2. Sangar	3. Toom Tekstiil	4. Hanza Tarkon	5. Eesti Energia
Sector	Plastics	Clothing	Textiles	Mechanical	Energy
Percentage fall in sales in 2008–2009	–11.4	–21.7	–5.0	–10.9	+1.8
Main adjustment mechanism	Employment reduction	Various (employment, hours, wages and bonuses)	Employment (and wages)	Employment reduction	Employment of unskilled Cuts in fringe benefits
Employment	Employment reduction without major redundancies	Employment reduction without major redundancies, not only due to the crisis	Around 20% of employees made redundant, later some hiring	Around 25% employment reduction through redundancies, recovery in 2010	Reduction of about 13% through terminations for various reasons
Working time	Part-time (80% of usual working-time) for about 30% of employees	Introduction of part-time work with summarized working time, around 10% of employees	No use of part-time work	Shortened four-day working week used in 2009	Part-time work has been used, as well as vacations
Wages	No cuts in basic pay	Wage cuts of between 10% (management) and 20% (production workers)	25% for whole workforce	No wage cuts	No cuts in basic pay but of bonuses

Table 2.21 (continued)

	1. Estiko Plastar	2. Sangar	3. Toom Tekstiil	4. Hanza Tarkon	5. Eesti Energia
Categories of employees most affected	Pre-retirement age employees	In production, mostly women employed. For wage cuts production workers most hit	In production, mostly women	Redundancies affected whole enterprise relatively evenly (both males and females, employees mostly with secondary education)	Pre-retirement age employees temporary workers, unskilled affected by employment cuts. Remaining employees by fringe benefits cuts and by more intensity at work
Training	Has not decreased	Decreased considerably	Not much training has been offered	Some cuts in budget, but no major reductions	Some cuts in budget, but no major reduction, more selective
Fringe benefits	Christmas fve days removed	Offered, but now mostly suspended	Not offered	Offered, mostly not reduced	Many offered, mostly suspended
Other working conditions	Work satisfaction has not changed Work–family balance improved	No major changes	No major changes	Work satisfaction has improved	Increased intensity at work; lower motivation and commitment
Other aspects of crisis	Crisis has enabled company to improve the workforce	Reduced labour turnover	No voluntary leaves of best employees, better job applicants	Reduced labour turnover	Desire to unify the conditions of collective agreements

7.1.1 Estiko Plastar: Human resources enhanced through agreed terminations and part-time work

Estiko Plastar is a producer of various packages and packaging materials and exports about 43 per cent of its production. During the crisis, the proportions of different groups of customers have changed: sales to the construction industry have declined and sales to the food industry have increased. The number of employees decreased from about 167 in 2008 to about 150 in 2010. There were almost no redundancies, however: in most cases, the employment contracts were terminated by mutual agreement. These employment contract terminations did not lead to labour disputes. The main group of employees affected was people of retirement age.[14] Labour turnover decreased significantly during the crisis (10 per cent in 2007, but only 1 per cent in 2009). The economic crisis has enabled the enterprise to improve its workforce as it is possible to select new employees from a better pool of applicants (as evidenced by the fact that they remained with the enterprise after the probation period). The latter was noticeable only in 2009, however, and no longer in 2010. Part-time work was also used in 2009 for about one-third (45) of employees (80 per cent of regular working time). The firm did not even consider reducing employees' wages, but wages have not increased either. According to the firm's personnel manager, it is possible that wages will soon need to be increased in order to retain good quality workers. The training of employees has not decreased during the crisis, partly thanks to the projects of Enterprise Estonia. The provision of fringe benefits has not decreased either (childbirth, funerals, sports, Christmas parties and so on) as the management believes that it would lower working morale: only the paid five-day holiday at Christmas was abandoned. Combining work and family life was easier during the crisis as workers have had more time and there is less work over weekends. Involuntary leave was used only in the case of a few employees, although initially the enterprise submitted the application to the Labour Inspectorate to use it for all employees in order to achieve equal treatment. The regular survey of work satisfaction indicated that it remained at the same level in 2009 as before, despite the reorganization, employment reductions and increased requirements with regard to performance. In conclusion, the crisis had a relatively positive impact on the firm's human resources. The relatively early response to the crises was beneficial both to the firm and the employees leaving the firm as the latter were able to find a new job in the early phase of the crisis. The reorganization within the enterprise and the treatment of each employee on a case-by-case basis were also important.

7.1.2   Sangar: Wages and bonuses cuts to face declining orders

Sangar is a clothing industry enterprise located in the city of Tartu, whose
main products are shirts for men and blouses for women. Subcontracting
accounts for 75 per cent of sales and the rest is sold under its own brand. A
reduction in orders was noticed only in the second half of 2009 with regard
to advance sales; it was more noticeable in relation to subcontracting.
Sales to some markets have decreased more (Iceland, Latvia, Lithuania),
while the share of others has increased (Netherlands). The number of
employees decreased from 308 in 2009 to about 250 in 2010. The greatest
proportion of the employees concerned were women. However, according
to the management, that was inevitable and not related only to the crises,
but also caused by the folding of two production lines. There have been
few redundancies and the reduction in the number of employees is mainly
voluntary. Labour turnover has decreased significantly (from 10 per cent
down to nil). In 2009, wage cuts were introduced: 20 per cent for office
workers and 10 per cent for production workers (due to their lower wage
levels) through reductions in bonuses. It was easier to explain the need
for wage cuts to office workers as they knew the enterprise's situation.
According to management, due to the wage cuts there have been no wage
arrears. The collective agreement specified various fringe benefits (for
marriage, funerals, workers with long tenure and so on) that have now
mostly been suspended. The enterprise also started to use part-time work
(30 hours a week, which in case of need can be increased to 40 hours) with
summarized working time calculations that make possible working during
weekends (although this has not been resorted to so far). This flexible
working time arrangement applies to about 30 employees and is the result
mainly of the fact that demand has become less predictable. Involuntary
leaves have also been used to a very limited extent. The provision of training has decreased considerably (at some points to nil): in autumn 2010 the
first training for two years was held. Despite the crisis, it is still not possible
to hire good seamstresses.

7.1.3   Toom Tekstiil: Restructuring and wage cuts leading to voluntary
quits

Toom Tekstiil is a textile industry enterprise with units in various towns
(Viljandi, Abja) that produces mostly mattresses, bedding products and
non-woven products. Most sales (70–80 per cent) are exports to EU countries on a subcontracting basis, while the rest is sold in Estonia under the
company's own brand. The wide customer base has helped to achieve
stability of sales. The reduction in sales in 2009 in comparison to 2008
was not large, but competitive pressure has increased, mark-ups have
decreased and more work needs to be done to get orders. The number

of employees was reduced due to the reorganization of production: in Viljandi, two production units were merged, as a result of which 50 employees were made redundant. Currently, there are about 250 employees in the various production enterprises of the group. Due to the lengthy redundancy procedure it was also necessary later to hire people again as demand recovered. Wages were decreased for all employees by 25 per cent in mid-2009. There were discussions about the wage cut but it was decided that there was no alternative, something that has certainly demotivated best employees especially since there are several textile industry enterprises in the region. There have been no other fringe benefits due to the lack of a collective agreement. The firm has also used fixed-term contracts in case of extra need for working hours (currently about 10–15 per cent of all employees); part-time work or involuntary leaves have not been used. The crisis has been positive as it is now possible to be more selective when hiring employees, but there are now problems because some of the best employees are leaving voluntarily.

7.1.4 Hanza Tarkon: Preference given to external flexibility
Hanza Tarkon is a mechanical industry enterprise situated in Tartu doing subcontracting for various industries (telecommunications, automotive, energy and so on). The firm's revenues decreased in 2009 by about 11 per cent, but the relatively higher share of sales in the telecommunication industry has helped to stabilize revenues. The number of employees was reduced from 570 in 2008 to 400 in 2009, mostly through redundancies (about 150 employees). Redundancies were used because the firm aims to be transparent in its dealings. During the process the firm cooperated with the Estonian Unemployment Insurance Fund and external subcontractors. During 2010, due to the recovery of demand, half of the people made redundant were hired again. The training budget was reduced, but it cannot be said that the amount of training has decreased: on average, each employee participates annually in three to four training courses, also thanks to the help of Enterprise Estonia, Tartu City Government and the Ministry of Education and Research. In 2009, part-time work (in the form of a four-day work-week) was also used, but employees were not sent on involuntary leaves. The company did not undertake (and did not consider) wage cuts despite the increased competitive pressure, because the accompanying risks (reduced loyalty, motivation) would outweigh the benefits. But there were no wage increases either. Several fringe benefits for employees have also not been cut. Demand has always been fairly uncertain, especially after the outbreak of the crisis, and thus there is considerable need for flexibility in employment relations. Since 1 July about 20 per cent of employees have been employed on temporary (civil)

contracts (*tööettevõtuleping*); especially during 2010 most new employees have been on temporary contracts.

7.1.5   Eesti Energia: Pre-retired, unskilled and temporary workers the buffer in the crisis

Eesti Energia is the largest energy producer in Estonia. It is a state-owned and vertically integrated company engaged in power production, trans-mission, distribution and sales, and other related activities. An expanding area of activity is the production of fuel. Despite the reduction in energy sales to the domestic market the company managed to increase its profit-ability (net income increased by 65 per cent in 2009 in comparison to 2008) thanks to the sale of energy in other markets, the sale of shale oil and cost savings. However, competitive pressure is increasing due to the liberaliza-tion of the energy market. The number of employees was reduced from 8,501 to 7,351. During 2009, among the 1,229 employment contract termi-nations there were 500 lay-offs and 300 contracts were terminated based on mutual agreement. Employment reduction occurred in many areas, mainly employees close to retirement age and people employed on fixed-term contracts. Part-time work has also been used (by giving days off), both in the mines and among white-collar workers. Many people also took unused vacation days. Partly paid vacations were also used: for example, in summer 2009 one of the power stations (Balti elektrijaam) halted pro-duction for three weeks during the period of low demand and around 200 people were on holiday.

Thanks to the crisis, the firm has been able to release less capable employees and to replace them with more skilled workers. Unskilled workers, therefore, were the victims in this adjustment process. During 2008–2010 wages have remained at the same level; wage negotiations with the trade unions were relatively easy (job preservation was more impor-tant to them), but now people are worried about the fact that wages have stayed the same for two years and a certain pressure for wage increases can be felt. Perhaps the most important means of adjustment during the crisis was the freezing of several fringe benefits foreseen in the collective agreements. However, family-related benefits have been retained. The presence of nine different collective agreements makes reorganization more difficult (for example, when moving employees between different enterprises of the group). The goal is therefore to make uniform the condi-tions of the various collective agreements. It is also intended to abandon bonuses unrelated to work performance and to replace them with bonuses based on results and value added. All this is not entirely the result of the crisis, but the latter has brought things to a head. Although training was not a priority area for savings, the training budget was reduced and now the company selects training more carefully: it avoids so-called 'luxury' products, but has retained professional training. Concerning the availability of people for vacant positions, at least for positions requiring less skill, only the quantity, not the quality of applicants has increased. Among the negative impacts of the crisis, people are less committed and loyal; they are often tired due to more intensive work; and, in case of dissatisfaction, they do not leave.

It is evident that adjustment patterns differ considerably. Several changes were not due to the crisis, but the downturn did increase the management's motivation to introduce them. The variations in the main adjustment mechanism across the enterprises contribute to work inequalities – some people are affected by wage cuts, others are not, and both the size and the differentiation of wage cuts differs: some enterprises have been able to maintain employment, but not others. This should explain the growing wage inequality that we noted in the LFS data. While earlier we referred to the impact of the crisis on young people and males, in particular, the case studies demonstrate that in certain cases females (in textile company 3, Textiil, and in clothing company 2, Sangar) and pre-retirement age workers (in plastics company 1, Estiko Plastar, and in energy company 5, Eesti Energia) were also heavily affected. Thus the picture is more complicated and there are emerging inequalities within various age groups, as well as between males and females.

7.2   Wage Cuts and Other Adjustments in the Estonian Police Force[15]

The Estonian Police (hereafter the Police) is one of the largest public sector organizations in Estonia. At the end of 2009, it hired approximately 4,230 people (police officers and civil servants).[16] At the beginning of 2009, it was clear that the Police would have to economize. Faced by the need to cut staff costs by EEK 110 million in 2009 due to reductions in the state budget, there were basically three options to consider: (1) wage reductions, (2) holidays without pay and (3) redundancies. The Ministry of the Interior chose the first option. In July 2009, the Government changed the decree regulating the wage rates of police officers. The nature of the wage cut is permanent, not temporary.

7.2.1   Across-the-board wage cuts despite trade union opposition
The decision to cut wages was made at ministry level, although both the Police Board and the Association of Trade Unions of Employees of State and Local Government Agencies (ROTAL) would have preferred other solutions (namely, the use of obligatory leave without pay). In the opinion of Ele Nuka, representative of the Estonian Police Officers Trade Union,

the negotiation process was difficult and lasted for several months since the retirement benefit of former police officers is related to wage rates and the trade union demanded that the wage rate at the bottom of the wage scale not be cut. Nevertheless, the trade union eventually abandoned this claim.

Wages were decreased by 8 per cent at all levels (there are 10 wage levels altogether, with wage rates from EEK 8,280 to EEK 28,440). The same rates were agreed between the Ministry of the Interior and the trade union on 10 December 2009, when a new collective agreement was concluded (Press Release No. 239). The trade union proposed differentiating between different wage levels and, as already mentioned, not to cut wages at the first salary level; this option was not considered by the Ministry.

7.2.2   Increased wage inequality

Although the decree regulates the wage rates of police officers, several prefectures cut the wages of all staff, in other words including civil servants. In the Northern Police Prefecture wages were cut by 8 per cent for both police officers and other officials. In the Southern Police Prefecture the wages of other officials (excluding police officers) were cut by 4 per cent. In the Eastern Police Prefecture only the wages of policy officers were cut, while those of others were not decreased. Therefore, in some sub-units of the Police wage inequality between police officers and other civil servants increased as a result of the wage decrease. Another effect of the wage cut was the decrease in retirement benefit of former police officers since their retirement benefit is related to the minimum salary level.

However, in October 2010 it was widely discussed in the media that, although it was stated that the wage cut was uniform, in fact at the beginning of 2010 management wages were increased. The Director General of the Police and Border Guard Board argued that the wage increase was due to the increase in workload and responsibility due to the merging of the two institutions. As a result of this, wage inequality increased during the crisis. We can conclude that, although it was emphazised that wages were cut on the solidarity principle, this was not in fact the case.

7.2.3   Second step: The use of unpaid holidays

At the beginning of 2010, when it was clear that it was necessary to save another EEK 200 million in staff costs, the administration of the Police (now the Police and Border Guard Board) faced the same difficult question: from what sources should the budget savings come? The decision was made at the administration level (and approved by the Ministry of the Interior) not to apply wage cuts or redundancies, but to use more unpaid holiday leave.[17] Although at first the Ministry of the Interior took the view that it is necessary to cut wages, both the Director General of the Police and Border Guard Board and the trade union insisted on the use of unpaid holiday leave instead. This was the least bad option because it made it possible to maintain jobs for all and the indirect loss of wages was compensated in the form of free (although not paid) days. Moreover, while wage adaptation must take place at the national level, which means that rates are likely to increase only after a number of years, the number of unpaid holiday leave days can be changed much more flexibly.

In addition to wage cuts and unpaid leave days, other measures to cut staff costs have been used. In 2009, the Police administration decided not to hire additional employees unless it was absolutely necessary.

7.2.4 Increasing quits due to wage cuts and higher intensity at work

The workload of the employees who left the organization was generally distributed between other employees, whose burden had already increased due to the use of statutory unpaid holiday leave.

The main concern of the Police with regard to human resources is certainly voluntary departures by employees because of wage cuts especially since wages are already higher in the private sector. According to the head of the Estonian Police Board labour relations department, Janne Pikma-Oovel, there were two categories that did leave after wage cuts: (1) men on low wages who had to support their families and (2) high-ranking officers (although the latter have tended to leave the Police during both the economic boom and the recession).

However, Janne Pikma-Oovel believes that this process is expanding to other categories. The first signs appeared in summer 2010, when she observed that the current situation had negatively influenced working morale. The same conclusion was drawn by the trade union representative. While at the beginning of the adaptation period people understood that wage cuts and unpaid holiday leave were absolutely necessary to avoid redundancies and there was a sense of solidarity, their patience is now fraying. The incidence of departures due to low wages and demands for pay increases are growing, now that in several areas the economy has begun to recover. It is difficult to distinguish between effects of organizational change and wage cut effects since some departures are due to the merger of the Police and the Border Guard, which is not acceptable to everybody. However, it is clear that reorganization would be easier to tolerate if the Government was dealing with the economic recession better.

In summary, wages and working condition have rapidly deteriorated and the Government has now put in place appropriate policy measures.

Among other savings measures directly related to human resource management, training has also decreased. There are two main reasons for this:

Table 2.22   Expenditure on training and number of participants in the Estonian Police, 2006–2009

	Cost (thousands of euros)			
	2006	2007	2008	2009
Form of training				
Open training	60.8	201.9	66.2	46.1
Tailor-made training	84.1	241.6	159.1	82.9
In-house training	60.3	132.4	226.3	182.6
Other	72.6	35.6	0.2	0.4
Total	277.7	611.5	451.8	312.1
Annual increase, %	–	120	–26	–31

Source: Police and Customs Board.

budgetary and reorganizational. When facing the need to cut costs, training costs were cut first. In addition, according to Ms Pikma-Oovel, in 2010 another reason was the launching of the new merged organization. There simply is not enough time to organize internal training seminars and those that have been carried out are related mainly to the new systems now in place (training seminars for users of the new SAP system that came into use in January 2010). The most important change made due to the recession is the abandonment of external training and motivational and teamwork training. In sum, although participation in training even increased in 2008 and 2009, the cost of training decreased in those years by one-quarter and one-third, respectively (Table 2.22).

In the opinion of the head of the labour relations department and the trade union representative, the recession has not influenced the incidence of working accidents and absence from work.

To conclude, the measures taken by the Estonian Police to meet the demand of the Ministry of the Interior to cut personnel costs were uniform nominal wage cuts (of 8 per cent) and unpaid leave. Wages were cut uniformly for senior and junior officers, without exceptions based on gender, tenure and so on. Different prefectures used different numbers of unpaid leave days because their need to save on labour costs was different. No redundancies have been imposed for budgetary reasons. In 2009, this was avoided because there was no money to pay compensation, while in 2010 there is no need for it (other measures, such as decreasing training costs and applying unpaid leave have been used instead). Staff workload has clearly increased, however. Moreover, recently it has been observed that people have started to leave. This cannot be attributed to wage cuts alone; the merger of the Police Board, the Citizenship and Migration Board and the Border Guard has also played a role. It is clear that people are tired of the situation and welcome new challenges if they appear.

8. CONCLUSIONS

The Baltic states are an interesting case for the study of inequalities during the crisis because the latter has hit them harder than any other EU member states. The Baltics have been characterized by fairly flexible labour markets and major labour market inequalities. As we have seen, various adjustment mechanisms have been combined during the crisis: by international comparison, fairly large falls can be seen in both employment (around –10 per cent in 2009), working hours (–2 per cent), wages (5–7 per cent) and fringe benefits. Overall, employment reductions have been the most important instrument. Part-time employment has grown, especially in Estonia, from fairly low levels. Employment reduction has occurred mainly due to increased job losses (separations), while the hiring rate has decreased only slightly. Declining job-to-job mobility is expected as people are afraid to change jobs. During the past 15 years expenditure in the Baltic states on both active and passive labour market policies has been relatively modest in comparison to the old EU15 (Masso and Paas 2007). However, during the crisis expenditure on both passive and active measures has grown significantly, also thanks to the use of EU funds.

Large wage cuts merit particular attention because usually there are many reasons for downward wage rigidity and in some previous crises (for example, in Sweden during the 1990s) wage cuts have affected only a small proportion of the population. In the case of Estonia, we have seen that, according to the LFS data over a year, about 50 per cent of employees had their monthly wage reduced. Although this number includes both basic pay and bonuses, there is also much evidence of cuts in basic pay, too. These adjustments can be seen not only in the private, but also the public sector (especially in Latvia), originating in the need to cut budget expenditure to keep the budget deficit down (2.7 per cent of GDP in Estonia in 2009). Nevertheless, expenditure is below the levels of the EU15.

The combination of different forms of adjustment might be the result of the high flexibility of Baltic labour markets, but since the crisis has been so deep (annual GDP decline in 2009: 14–18 per cent) it is probably not possible to make the necessary adjustments with employment alone (that is, without wage cuts). But we have also seen different adjustment patterns at the enterprise level, although the crisis has affected almost all sectors severely. Despite widespread wage cuts there are companies that did not plan to cut wages, despite economic difficulties and massive

Work inequalities in the crisis

unemployment. It seems that, among the various forms of expenditure on personnel, fringe benefits (with the possible exception of those related to families and children) were the first savings option (for firms that had them). On the other hand, although training expenditure was not unaffected, it was not hit hard. There is some evidence that the crisis seems to have stimulated more flexible work arrangements at enterprise level: the use of fixed-term contracts, flexible working time arrangements and pay schemes dependent on performance. It seems that many developments that we can see are not due solely to the crisis; rather the latter tipped the scales. Concerning health and safety, despite some warnings that firms struggling to survive may try to cut corners in this area, there do not seem to be negative developments; the same applies also to reconciling work and family life. Concerning the positive impacts of the crisis, firms have indicated that they have been able to be more selective in choosing among job applicants and to improve their pool of employees.

The different adjustment patterns at the level of individual enterprises contribute to work inequalities. Concerning the diverse impact of the crisis on various labour market segments, some aspects are similar to other European countries, such as the strong decline in manufacturing and the resulting employment decline among males. The other groups that have suffered particularly hard from the crisis are young people and Estonia's and Latvia's considerable non-native (Russian-speaking) populations. Estonia's high gender pay gap has decreased somewhat during the crisis, but only due to the component related to the different labour market characteristics of males and females. Wage inequality has increased somewhat during the crisis, which seems to be due primarily to the increasing premium for education and the differences in wage reductions across sectors and firms. The different labour market segments have also been affected by different means of adjustment and to different effects. For instance, in the public sector in Estonia and Lithuania employment cuts have been few and far between, with adjustments being made via wage cuts and working time reductions.

We can conclude that the current crisis has hit the labour markets of the Baltic states earlier and more severely than most other EU countries. The response of the three economies to the crisis has been relatively successful. The level of public debt has remained relatively modest in 2010 and the GDP growth rate in the second quarter of 2010 was one of the highest in the EU (3.1 per cent). The crisis is likely to have a relatively long-term impact on the labour market, however, not only because the high unemployment is likely to persist for a while and lead to an increase in structural unemployment, but because of its effect on other labour market developments. Due to the previous overheating of the economy certainly it has also had some positive consequences (for example, the moderation of wage growth is needed to restore competitiveness). But the burdens it has imposed will be difficult to cope with. Given the previous growth in unemployment and Estonia joining the Eurozone, labour market developments remain a key challenge with regard to ensuring future growth.

NOTES

1. For an analysis of macroeconomic developments in the Baltic states and the boom–bust cycle, see also Brixiova et al. (2009) and Purfield and Rosenberg (2010).
2. For an overview of past labour market developments in the Baltic states, see, for example, Paas and Eamets (2007).
3. In Estonia, firms need to present applications for collective redundancies to the Labour Inspectorate. Under the Law on Employment Contracts, collective redundancies are defined as follows: employment contracts terminated within 30 calendar days of at least (a) 5 employees in enterprises employing up to 19 employees, (b) 10 employees in enterprises employing 20–99 employees, (c) 10 per cent of employees in enterprises employing 100–299 employees and (d) 30 employees in enterprises employing at least 300 employees.
4. For instance, in 2008 average weekly working hours in Estonia, Latvia and Lithuania were 39.5, 40.1 and 39.1 hours, respectively (compared to EU average of 37.8, Eurostat).
5. For wages we have only one figure, thus we cannot say whether the wage cut is due to a cut in basic pay or a reduction in bonuses.
6. Foreign firms' stronger orientation towards international markets could make them more responsive to global crises. On the other hand, foreign firms might also have more internal reserves while domestic firms need to react immediately to declining revenues with cost cutting.
7. The opinion of the Labour Inspectorate is that too few occupational diseases are diagnosed in Estonia (Tööinspektsioon 2009). It believes that the declining number of diseases caused by working is related to the fact that the employers do not direct employees to take part in mandatory health examinations.
8. At the time of writing only the Estonian LFS was available, while earlier studies (Anspal and Karu 2007) used working life barometer data for 2000, 2003 and 2005.
9. Sources: Estonia – Unemployment Insurance Fund; Lithuania – Lithuanian Labour Exchange.
10. Similar to the national minimum wage, in Estonia several collective agreements aimed at increasing wages at sectoral level (for example, in road transport, initially a 37 per cent increase was foreseen – Nurmela and Karu 2008) and at firm level (at the largest shipping company Tallink, a 9 per cent wage increase was foreseen in September 2009 but postponed by one year) have been halted.
11. For example, in September 2008 the Estonian Employers' Confederation forwarded its proposals on how to manage the economic downturn to the Government (Nurmela and Karu 2008). The list of actions covered such areas as public sector expenditure and fiscal policy, public administration and e-government, taxation, investment, labour market and education. With regard to the labour market, the employers proposed increasing flexibility by adopting the hotly debated draft Employment Contracts Act negotiated between the social partners earlier in 2008 and promoting the use of flexible forms of work (fixed-term employment, part-time work, teleworking). The employers also called on the Government to change the pension system to increase incentives to take up retirement, improve the availability of childcare facilities and make the regulations on

parental benefit more flexible. The trade unions have also attempted to initiate dialogue – in 2008, EAKL and the Estonian Employees' Unions' Confederation expressed their dissatisfaction in a letter to the Prime Minister in which they claimed that 'with regard to the basic issues of working life, the Estonian authorities have repeatedly tried to avoid dialogue with the employee representative bodies' and that 'several draft acts that are important to employees . . . have been drafted without including the social partners' (Nurmela and Karu 2008).

12. The system of sickness benefit was also changed. Until July 2009, from the second day of illness, sickness benefits were paid by the Estonian Health Insurance Fund at a rate of 80 per cent of the employee's average wage. From 1 July 2009, the period not covered by sickness benefits was increased to three days. For the subsequent five days of illness, sickness benefits are paid by the employer at a rate of 70 per cent of the employee's average wage. The Health Insurance Fund pays sickness benefits (70 per cent of the employee's average income subject to social security contributions) only from the ninth day of illness.

13. The interviews were conducted with Anne Ladva (Estiko), Jaan Rosenthal (Sangar), Aivar Talvet (Toom Tekstiil), Anu Ulp (Hanza Tarkon) and Riina Varts (Eesti Energia). The authors are grateful to them for their assistance.

14. These employees had a lower retirement age (by five years) due to their work (thermo-processing of plastics). They were therefore entitled to both pensions and unemployment insurance.

15. We would like to thank everyone who provided input to the case study. The following were interviewed: Janne Pikma-Oovel (head of labour relations department, Police and Border Guard); Vilve Kalda (head of administration, Police and Border Guard), Ele Nuka (representative of Estonian Police Officials Trade Union) and Riho Tamm, Veronika Remsel and Ketlin Nurk (labour relations specialists in the prefectures until the end of 2009).

16. In August 2010, the number of employees was 6,260 (about one-quarter of all civil servants in Estonia), but it is not directly comparable due to structural changes carried out in the organization. On 1 January 2010, the Police Board, the Citizenship and Migration Board and the Border Guard merged into one institution, named the Police and Border Guard Board (PPA).

17. However, facing the need to cut budgets, police prefectures applied other budget saving measures, even before the decision to cut wages was made at government level. The Eastern Police Prefecture applied obligatory unpaid holidays to balance the budget of the prefecture as early as May 2009; the Southern Police Prefecture had been doing so since June. The number of statutory unpaid leave days varied between different units, depending on the extent of the necessary cuts. For reasons of confidentiality, it is not possible to go into more detail here.

BIBLIOGRAPHY

Agell, J. and Bennmarker, H. (2003) 'Endogenous wage rigidity', CESifo Working Paper No. 1081.

Anspal, S. and Karu, M. (2007) 'Paindlikud töövormid Eestis ja Euroopas', in B. Vahter and K. Seeder (eds), *Töö ja pere. Paindlik töökorraldus ja lastevanemate tööhõive*, Eesti Tööandjate Keskliit, pp. 119–62.

Babecky, J.P.D.C., Kosma, T., Lawless, M., Messina, J. and Rõõm, T. (2009) 'Downward nominal and real wage rigidity: survey evidence from European firms', ECB Working Paper No. 1105.

Bosma, N. and Levie, J. (2010) *Global Entrepreneurship Monitor 2009*. Executive Report.

Brixiova, Z. (2009) 'Labour market flexibility in Estonia: what more can be done?', OECD Economics Department Working Papers No. 697, OECD Publishing.

Brixiova, Z., Vartia, L. and Worgotter, A. (2009) 'Capital inflows, household debt and the boom–bust cycle in Estonia', William Davidson Institute Working Paper No. 965.

Curkina, I. (2009) 'Wide-scale cuts in salaries and social benefits', European Industrial Relations Observatory. Available at: http://www.eurofound.europa.eu/eiro/2009/07/articles/lv0907019i.htm (accessed on 11 September 2010).

Eamets, R. and Masso, J. (2005) 'The paradox of the Baltic states: labour market flexibility but protected workers?', *European Journal of Industrial Relations*, Vol. 11, No. 1: 71–90.

Estonian Development Fund (2008) 'The Estonian economy. Current status of competitiveness and future outlooks', *Estonia in Focus* No. 1/2008.

Estonian Ministry of Social Affairs (2007) *Temporary agency work survey*, Klaster Research Center, University of Tartu, Tartu.

European Commission (2005) *Employment in Europe 2005 – Recent Trends and Prospects*, Luxembourg: European Commission.

Haltiwanger, J.C. and Vodopivec, M. (1999) 'Gross workers and job flows in a transition economy. An analysis of Estonia', World Bank Policy Research Working Paper No. 2082.

Jann, B. (2008) 'A Stata implementation of the Blinder–Oaxaca decomposition', ETH Zurich Sociology Working Paper No. 5.

Krillo, K. and Masso, J. (2010) 'The part-time/full-time wage gap in Central and Eastern Europe: the case of Estonia', *Research in Economics and Business: Central and Eastern Europe*, Vol. 2, No. 1: 47–75.

Krillo, K., Philips, K. and Masso, J. (2007) 'Osaajaga töötamine – oht või võimalus Eesti tööturul?', in *Eesti pärast Euroopa Liiduga ühinemist: Eesti sotsiaalteadlaste VII aastakonverents*, 23–24 November, Tartu. Tartu: Tartu Ülikooli Kirjastus, pp. 68–70.

Kriz, K.A., Meriküll, J., Paulus, A. and Staehr, K. (2007) 'Why do individuals evade payroll and income taxation in Estonia?', University of Tartu, Faculty of Economics and Business Administration Working Paper No. 49.

Latvijas Banka (2009) *Macroeconomic Developments Report*, 3/2009.

Lauringson, A. (2010) 'Disincentive effects of unemployment insurance benefits: maximum benefit duration versus benefit level', University of Tartu, Faculty of Economics and Business Administration Working Paper No. 70.

Leping, K.-O. and Toomet, O. (2008) 'Emerging ethnic wage gap: Estonia during political and economic transition', *Journal of Comparative Economics*, Vol. 36, No. 4: 599–619.

Marelli, E., Signorelli, M. and Tyrowicz, J. (2010) 'Crises and joint employment–productivity dynamics: a comparative perspective for European countries', 11th Bi-Annual Conference of the European Association for Comparative Economic Studies. Available at: http://ec.ut.ee/eaces2010/.

Masso, J. and Eamets, R. (2007) 'Macro-level labour market flexibility in the Baltic states', in T. Paas and R. Eamets (eds), *Labour Market Flexibility, Flexicurity and Employment: Lessons of the Baltic States*, Nova Science, pp. 101–42.

Masso, J. and Paas, T. (2007) 'Social protection systems and labour market policies in the Baltic states', in T. Paas and R. Eamets (eds), *Labour Market*

Flexibility, Flexicurity and Employment: Lessons of the Baltic States, Nova Science, pp. 143–81.

Masso, J., Eamets, R. and Philips, K. (2007) 'Job flows and worker flows in the Baltic states: labour reallocation and structural changes', in T. Paas and R. Eamets, *Labour market flexibility, flexicurity and employment*, Nova Science, pp. 61–99.

Nurmela, K. (2009a) 'Impact of global crisis on labour market and industrial relations', European Industrial Relations Observatory. Available at: http://www.eurofound.europa.eu/eiro/2009/02/articles/ee0902059i.htm.

Nurmela, K. (2009b) 'Debate on further cuts in state budget for 2009', European Industrial Relations Observatory. Available at: http://www.eurofound.europa.eu/eiro/2009/02/articles/ee0902049i.htm.

Nurmela, K. and Karu, M. (2008) 'Employers offer solutions in managing downturn'. Available at: http://www.eurofound.europa.eu/eiro/2008/11/articles/ee0811029i.htm.

OECD (2009) *OECD Economic Surveys: Estonia 2009*.

Osila, L. and Nurmela, K. (2010) 'Salaries continue to decline', European Industrial Relations Observatory. Available at: http://www.eurofound.europa.eu/eiro/2010/06/articles/ee1006019i.htm (accessed on 11 September 2010).

Paas, T. and Eamets, R. (eds) (2007) *Labor Market Flexibility, Flexicurity and Employment: Lessons of the Baltic States*, Nova Science.

Purfield, C. and Rosenberg, C. (2010) 'Adjustment under a currency peg: Estonia, Latvia and Lithuania during the global financial crisis 2008–09', IMP Policy Discussion Paper WP/10/213.

Randveer, M. and Rõõm, T. (2009) 'The structure of migration in Estonia: survey-based evidence', Bank of Estonia Working Paper No. 2009/1.

Rõõm, T. and Kallaste, E. (2004) 'Naised-mehed Eesti tööturul: palgaerinevuste hinnang', Poliitikauuringute keskus PRAXIS, Poliitikaanalüüs No. 8/2004.

Rõõm, T. and Uusküla, L. (2006) 'Palgakujunduse põhimõtted Eesti ettevõtetes', Eesti Panga toimetised 5/2006.

Svejnar, J. and Semerak, V. (2009) 'New member countries' labour markets during the crisis', University of Michigan, CERGE-EI. Available at: http://ipc.umich.edu/policy-briefs/pdfs/BEPA-NMS-labor-markets.pdf (accessed on 18 October 2010).

Tööinspektsioon (2009) *Aasta töökeskonna ülevaade*. Available at: http://www.ti.ee/public/files/2009_a_ylevaade.pdf (accessed on 18 October 2010).

Tyrowicz, J. and Cichocki, S. (2010) 'Employed, unemployed? On shadow employment in transition', University of Warsaw, Faculty of Economic Sciences Working Paper No. 2010-05.

APPENDIX

Table 2A.1   *Policy responses and recovery measures in Estonia*

Policy area	Description of measure(s) taken	Implemen-tation	Objectives
Increasing aggregate demand	Increased funding in the amount of EEK 264 (ca €16.9) million of transportation and entrepreneurship as a result of restructuring EU structural aid	In force since October 2009	Sustain employ-ment
	Supporting enterprise start-up: • Increased subsidies to start a business (from EEK 50,000 to 100,000) and growth support (from EEK 200,000 to 500,000) • Extension of range of eligible applicants, activities supported and eligible expenditure Decrease in self-financing rate (from 50% to 35%)	In force since September 2009	
	Entrepreneur starting a business (or a business already operating up to three years) gets a subsidized start-up loan of up to EEK 1,000,000 (previously up to EEK 500,000)	In force since October 2009	Creation of new compa-nies
Increase demand for labour	Increased funding in the amount of EEK 750 million (€48 million) of entrepreneurship (EEK 650 million) and employment (EEK 100 million) as a result of restructuring EU structural aid. Priorities in subsidizing entrepreneurship are promoting exports and investment in technology and R&D As regards employment promotion, additional funds were targeted to increase wage subsidies, trainee subsidies, remuneration of labour market training, and so on According to the estimates made in February 2010, 1,000 new jobs were created as a result of wage subsidies and practical training in January 2010. The Ministry of Social Affairs forecasts that by the end of 2010 the number of persons employed due to these measures will be up to 10,000. In total, the government has channelled an additional 2.3 billion kroons to support entrepreneurship and improve the labour market situation	In force since December 2009	Counter-cyclical employ-ment measure

Table 2A.1   (continued)

Policy area	Description of measure(s) taken	Implementation	Objectives
	Simplified conditions to obtain a wage subsidy. According to new regulations, a wage subsidy (50% of the wage, but at most the minimum wage) is paid to an employer for a maximum of 6 months if they hire:	In force since January 2010	Increase employment of longterm unemployed
	• an unemployed person who has been registered with Töötukassa at least six months and has not found a job		
	• an unemployed person aged 16–24 who has been registered with Töötukassa at least three months and has not found a job		Reduce youth unemployment
	In the case of non-permanent jobs, the wage subsidy is paid for half the duration of employment, but up to a maximum of six months		
	Until 1 January 2010 it was possible to pay a wage subsidy only in the case of permanent jobs		
	For employees or public sector workers who were unemployed for at least six months out of the past 12 months before getting a job, social contributions are paid on wages: that is, the general minimum limit on social contributions does not apply in such cases	Since 1 July 2010	Increasing employment for longterm unemployed
	Until this change employers had to pay social contributions from the statutory minimum (in 2009 and 2010 equal to EEK 4,350), whatever the gross wage was EEK 2,500 or EEK 4,350		Promoting part-time employment
	Summarized calculation of social contributions for employees with several part-time jobs; until 1 July employer had to pay social contribution at least from the minimum wage (in 2009 and 2010 equal to EEK 4,350)[1]		
	According to estimates, the number of part-time employees whose wage is less than the statutory minimum for the social contribution is 18,000. Their average wage is EEK 2,700; 8% of them have more than one part-time job (1,400 people)		

Table 2A.1   (continued)

Policy area	Description of measure(s) taken	Implemen- tation	Objectives
	It is estimated that these changes will affect 41,900 people; 3,000 new part-time jobs will be created; the cost of these changes will be EEK 10 million and the amount of additional social contributions paid will be EEK 32 million a year		
Increasing employment of people (and family members) with social and economic subsistence problems	An employer who hires a disabled person or a person with long-tem health problems may receive up to 100% of the adaptation costs of work rooms and work instruments.	In force since January 2010	Reduce unem- ploy- ment of disabled
	Labour market services and training targeted on people (and their family members) with social and economic subsistence problems (part of the programme 'Social work measures supporting employment': • subsistence consultation services to people with special needs and their families; consultation on technical aid to adjust home and workplace rehabilitation programmes (for at least 250 persons) • consultation for disabled youth who have left the family or substitute home (for at least 100 persons) • training provided by National Institute for Health Development to care workers (50 persons), psychiatric special needs workers (125 persons) and home care workers (75 persons) • training in how to use social services data register targeted on local government employees and service providers (500 persons) • technical aid technician training (60 persons) • debt consultation (15 persons) • training for experts and consultants assessing quality of rehabilitation services	In force since January 2010	

Table 2A.1   (continued)

Policy area	Description of measure(s) taken	Implemen-tation	Objectives
Promoting use of tele-working	Training in teleworking for unemployed persons in different areas in Estonia, developing Estonia-wide teleworking network	In force since January 2010	Promoting tele-working
Training	The training card pilot project is aimed at better training of the unemployed based on their needs. The personal approach is used and training is targeted to increase the qualifications of the unemployed and their chances of getting a job.	In force since September 2009	Increase the skills of the unem-ployed
	Supporting the continuation of suspended studies	In force since January 2010	Increase the number of people with profes-sional skills and know-ledge

Table 2A.2   Policy responses and recovery measures in Latvia

Policy area	Description of measure(s) taken	Implemen-tation	Objectives
Social policy	Increasing the period during which unemployment benefits can be received (to 8 months, previously 4 months for persons who have been made redundant and have accumulated up to 9 years of service, and to 6 months for persons who have been made redundant and have amassed between 10 and 19 years of service. For persons who have been made redundant and whose length of service is 20 or more years, unemployment benefit was granted for 9 months)[2] Source: http://www.eurofound.europa.eu/eiro/2009/06/articles/lv0906019i.htm	1 July 2009– 31 December 2011	Increasing social insu-rance
	Decreasing old-age pensions and long-service pensions by 10% for non-working and 70% for working pensioners Source: http://www.eurofound.europa.eu/eiro/2009/06/articles/lv0906039i.htm	Since 1 July 2009	Decrease costs of state budget
Tax policy	Reducing tax-free allowance on personal income tax to LVL 35 (€50) (up to 1 July 2009 LVL 90 (about €129)). Source: http://www.eurofound.europa.eu/eiro/2009/06/articles/lv0906039i.htm	Since 1 July 2009	
	Increasing personal income tax to 26% (previously 23%)	Since 1 January 2010	Increasing tax revenues
	Increasing the tax rate on self-employed persons (on income from economic activity) from 15% to 26% Reducing tax-free allowance of peasants and fishermen from LVL 4,000 to LVL 2,000 Sources: http://www.riganewstoday.com/2009/12/in-final-reading-of-saeima-has-been.html		
Decreasing state budget imbalances	Cutting state sector salaries Salary fund was reduced by 15% Monthly salaries below LVL 300 (€430; affecting 21% of employees in ministries and subsidiary institutions) were reduced by 15% Wages above LVL 300 were cut by 20% The salary decrease was projected to reduce state expenditure by about LVL 90 million (€129 million)	January 2009 Since 1 July 2009	Decrease costs of state budget

Table 2A.2 (continued)

Policy area	Description of measure(s) taken	Implementation	Objectives
	Source: http://www.eurofound.europa.eu/ eiro/2009/07/articles/lv0907019i.htm Decreasing teachers' monthly gross wages from LVL 345 (€494) to LVL 250 (€358) Source:http://www.eurofound.europa.eu/ eiro/2009/07/articles/lv0907019i.htm	Since 1 September 2009	Decrease costs of state budget
	Implementing reform in the health care sector and decreasing the number of employees in the Ministry of Health by 43% (from 155 employees to 89) Source: http://www.eurofound.europa.eu/ eiro/2009/07/articles/lv0907019i.htm	Since September 2009	Decrease costs of state budget
Training	Implementing three projects to promote training: • vocational training for employees at risk of unemployment; • unemployed persons' and jobseekers' training in Latvia; • promoting vacancies in local government in order to develop and maintain work skills[3] • professional training using vouchers[4] Source: http://www.eurofound.europa.eu/ eiro/2009/11/articles/lv0911019i.htm	Since September 2009	Increase skills of unemployed
Promoting employer-side flexibility	Shortening notification terms in case of collective redundancies. The notification obligation in the case of collective redundancies was decreased to 45 days (previously 60 days); collective redundancies could also now be imposed 45 days (instead of 60 days) following notification: the right of the State Employment Agency to extend the term of notification to 60 days (instead of 75 days) prior to redundancies Source. http://www.labourlawnetwork. eu/national_labour_law/legislative_ developments/prm/109/v_detail/ses_id_ dab6d80bdb6c97c055d02bc1083c4d70/ id_947/category_19/size_1/index.html For more information about changes in Latvian labour law, see: http:// www.sorainen.com/legal/newsflash/ lv-employment-april-2010/en.html	25 March 2010	Decreasing protection of workers in case of collective redundancies

Table 2A.3   Policy responses and recovery measures in Lithuania

Policy area	Description of measure(s) taken	Implemen-tation	Objectives
Decreasing state budget imbalances	Without consulting with trade unions, the government decided on 17 June 2009 to cut the basic monthly wage[5] in the public sector. The basic weekly wage was to be reduced from LTL 128 (about €37 as at 30 July 2009) to LTL 115 (€33). The pay cut was due to enter into force on 1 August and would have affected about 230,000 public sector employees, most of whom are already relatively low paid		Decreasing public sector wages
	Dissatisfied with the government's decision, the Lithuanian Trade Union Confederation (Lietuvos profesinių sąjungų konfederacija, LPSK) adopted, on 19 June, a 'Declaration regarding the inconsiderate and unreasoned policy implemented by LRV'		
	As the government ignored LPSK's warning, the trade union confederation launched a hunger strike initiative on 2 July at Independence Square in front of the parliament buildings. During the hunger strike, a meeting was held between the government and the trade unions' working group which ended in a number of joint decisions		
	In the end, it was agreed with the trade union representatives that the government would cancel its decision to reduce the basic monthly wage with effect from 3 July. Taking into account the government's promise, LPSK stopped the hunger strike on 3 July. In turn, the government submitted alternative proposals to the parliament (Lietuvos		

Table 2A.3 (continued)

Policy area	Description of measure(s) taken	Implemen-tation	Objectives
	Respublikos Seimas, LRS) on how to reduce state spending. The proposals were accepted by the LRS on 16 July		
	As promised, the main burden of the wage decrease was imposed on the highest paid public sector employees, including lawyers and state officials		
	Pay rises for civil servant qualification grades were cut on a temporary basis from 1 August 2009 to 31 December 2010: more specifically, by 10%–15% for the third (lowest) qualification rating and by 30%–50% for the first (highest) qualification rating. Officers of the country's Special Investigation Service (Specialiųjų Tyrimų Tarnyba, STT), the State Security Department (Valstybės Saugumo Departamentas, VSD) and other civil servants have also been subject to similar changes		
Promoting flexicurity	Providing for additional security of workers employed under fixed-term employment contracts. Fixed-term employees should not receive less favourable employment conditions or opportunities to improve their qualifications and receive promotion than those employed on regular employment contracts	1 August 2009	Regulating fixed-term employment
	Developing procedures for the termination of fixed-term employment contracts prior to expiry. An opportunity was provided in a collective agreement to reach agreement on cases when an employer is entitled to pay lower severance pay than the abovementioned		

Table 2A.3 (continued)

Policy area	Description of measure(s) taken	Implemen- tation	Objectives
	in case of termination of a fixed-term employment contract during the crisis. In no case may such severance pay be less than one month's average wages.[6] Effective until 31 December 2010 Source: http:// www.eu-employment- observatory.net/resources/ reports/Lithuania- LabourCodeAmendments.pdf		
	Allowing employers and employees to come to terms in a collective agreement on conditions more favourable to employers as compared to those set out in the Labour Code. Matters with which collective agreements may deal include the following:	Since 1 August 2009	
	• Shorter dismissal notice period. Under the Labour Code, employers are required to notify employees in writing of the termination of employment (without employee fault) two (and in certain cases – four) months in advance. Henceforth, collective agreements may provide for shorter time-limits, that is, up to one or two months, respectively		
	• Shorter notice period for change in remuneration terms and conditions. Under the Labour Code, employees must be notified one month in advance of new payment conditions. The amendment allows a two-week term to be included in the collective agreement		

Table 2A.3   (continued)

Policy area	Description of measure(s) taken	Implemen-tation	Objectives
	• The amendment allows restrictions on dismissal from work to individuals with three years (rather than five, as in the Labour Code) until entitlement to old-age pension • Under the amendment, a fixed-term employment contract may, along with other grounds, be terminated with severance pay in the amount of one month's average salary • The amendment allows employers to pay a lower salary for time off granted for looking for a new job (stipulating a minimum hourly pay for time spent searching) These changes remain in force until 31 December 2010 Source: http://www.sorainen.com/ legal/newsflash/employment-law-july-2009/en.html		
	Introducing the possibility for the employer to settle with a redundant employee within a term of three months (rather than on the date of dismissal as was formerly the case), but only if the employee is eligible for severance pay amounting to at least five months' average wages Effective until 31 December 2010 Source: http://www.sorainen.com/ legal/newsflash/employment-law-july-2009/en.html	1 August 2009	
	Revision of the procedure applied to pension-age employees in case of termination of employment contracts on their initiative. This amendment was sought by the GRL to take into consideration the requests of social partners and to avoid cases of abuse often	1 August 2009	

Table 2A.3   (continued)

Policy area	Description of measure(s) taken	Implemen-tation	Objectives
	encountered when pension-age employees enter into successive fixed-term employment contracts with new employers and become entitled (irrespective of the length of service with a particular enterprise) to termination of the employment contract under the simplified procedure (that is, by giving three days' notice to the employer) and receiving severance pay in the amount of two months' average wages. Expected to remain valid for an unlimited period Source: http://www.eu-employment-observatory.net/resources/reports/Lithuania-LabourCodeAmendments.pdf		
	Providing the possibility of concluding fixed-term employment contracts for work of a permanent nature for newly created jobs. Employers will be able to take advantage of this option for two years but no longer than for the period until 31 July 2012. If after this date an employment relationship continues under such a fixed-term contract, it will become a regular contract Source: http://www.deloitte.com/view/en_LT/lt/insights/publications/	1 August 2010	
	Introducing summary recording of working time in any enterprise, if necessary after considering the opinion of the employees' representatives or in other cases established by the collective agreement	1 August 2010	Regulating working time

Table 2A.3 (continued)

Policy area	Description of measure(s) taken	Implemen-tation	Objectives
	Previously, this right was granted only to enterprises that engage in uninterrupted activity and meet the established criteria Source: http://www.deloitte. com/view/en_LT/lt/ insights/publications/ e6e73363ce71a210Vgn VCM100000ba42f00aRCRD.htm		
	Changing overtime work conditions. Now employees may work four hours overtime daily (previously four hours overtime was allowed every two working days). The annual overtime norm of 180 hours was not changed Source: http://www.sorainen.com/ legal/newsflash/employment-law-july-2009/en.html	1 August 2009	
	Introducing more flexible procedures for determining overtime. As was previously the case, the employer will be able to resort to overtime only in exceptional cases. However, in other cases overtime may also be organized with written consent or at the request of the employee Source: http://www.deloitte. com/view/en_LT/lt/ insights/publications/ e6e73363ce71a210Vgn VCM100000ba42f00aRCRD.htm	1 August 2010	
	Establishing employees' right to suspend an employment contract for no longer than three-month period if the employer for more than two consecutive months does not pay wages or fails to comply with their other obligations to the employee. If the employee on reasonable grounds suspends the employment contract, the	1 August 2010	

Table 2A.3   (continued)

Policy area	Description of measure(s) taken	Implemen-tation	Objectives
	employer shall pay him not less than one minimum monthly wage compensation for each month. An employee who suspends the contract with no justification is responsible for the damage caused to the employer. During the suspension of the employment contract state social insurance contributions must be paid Source: http://www.deloitte. com/view/en_LT/lt/ insights/publications/ e6e73363ce71a210Vgn VCM100000ba42f00aRCRD.htm	1 August 2010	
	Establishing a new type of employment contract – distance work, which also covers former employment contracts with home workers. A distance work employment contract may establish that an employee will perform his job functions in other places than a workplace, as long as it is acceptable to the employee, using IT. It is expected that distance work employment contracts will allow more flexible work organization. The details of such employment contracts will be established by the government and collective agreements Source: http://www.deloitte. com/view/en_LT/lt/ insights/publications/ e6e73363ce71a210Vgn VCM100000ba42f00aRCRD.htm	1 August 2010	

NOTES

1. For example, assume that the person has two part-time jobs: the first employer calculates the income tax exemption and pays EEK 2,500, the second employer pays EEK 1,500. Until 1 July 2010, the first employer had to pay social contributions from the statutory minimum (in 2010 EEK 4,350), that is, EEK 1,436, the second employer from the actual wage, that is, EEK 495. According to the new regulation, tax obligations can be summed. The second employer still pays social contributions from the actual wage, that is, EEK 495, but the first employer pays the contribution from the part lower than the statutory minimum (EEK 941 (4,350 – 1500) × 0.33). The only requirement is that employees must inform the first employer of wages in other jobs.

2. Until July 2009, in order to receive unemployment benefit in Latvia, a person had to fulfil certain conditions: they had to obtain unemployed status; their length of service had to be at least one year; and they had to have paid compulsory social insurance contributions for no less than 12 months out of the past 18 before obtaining the status of an unemployed person. As of 1 July 2009, however, the period of compulsory social insurance contributions for eligibility to receive unemployment benefits was changed: all employees have to pay social insurance contributions for at least 9 months over a period of one year.

3. Under this programme, local governments provide vacancies for non-commercial purposes in the structural units of local government, institutions and agencies, and state social security centres. An unemployed person participating in the programme 'Training for developing and maintaining work skills if the employer is a local government' receives a grant of €142 (about LVL 100 as of 23 December 2009). An unemployed person who participates in the programme is insured against accidents at work as long as the employment does not exceed six months a year.

4. Employees working in the private sector who, due to the reduction of production capacity, are now part-time workers, can avail themselves of training vouchers under certain circumstances: if they are employed for more than six months in the company and as long as their working hours were reduced a month before applying for the programme. The voucher is a guarantee for an employee at risk of unemployment, enabling them to choose an educational programme relevant to their work. The training expenses will be covered by the government up to €711 (LVL 500) for a vocational training programme and €427 (LVL 300) for a professional postgraduate training programme. The minimum duration of training is six months. The programme aims to involve at least 11,000 employees at risk of unemployment up to 2013. This includes about 2,000 employees in 2009.

5. The basic monthly wage is applied as a reference to determine the wages of public sector employees, such as teachers, social workers, librarians and cultural workers.

6. Previously, the Lithuanian Labour Code provided that an employer shall be entitled to terminate a fixed-term employment contract before expiry only in exceptional circumstances if the employee cannot, with his consent, be transferred to other work, or upon the payment of the average wage to the employee for the remaining period of the employment contract.

3. Inequality at work emerging in the current crisis in Bulgaria

Vasil Tzanov

1. INTRODUCTION

The effects of the economic crisis on the Bulgarian economy began to reveal themselves from the second half of 2008. From the beginning of 2009, the economy entered into recession which deepened throughout the year and was prolonged to early 2010. Bulgaria began to come out of the recession in the second half of the year but the crisis was not over at the beginning of 2011. The negative effects spread over the entire economy, including the labour market, the public finances, fiscal policy and social protection. Naturally, different branches, firms and social groups are affected in different ways and this is reflected in different developments with regard to inequality.

The significant fall in GDP has had a strong negative impact on the labour market. The key labour market indicators have deteriorated during 2009–2010. Total employment has declined significantly and unemployment has gone up. Since the crisis is concentrated in particular economic branches the effects on the labour market are focused on specific segments. This implies inequalities with regard to employment and unemployment adjustment and structure. Furthermore, the crisis is affecting to different degrees not only employment and unemployment, but also other aspects of work, such as working time, compliance with health and safety regulations, working conditions, training, social dialogue and so on. The overall outcome is increased inequalities in respect of all working conditions.

The impact of the crisis on working conditions depended not only on economic circumstances but also on policy responses to the crisis. Policy decisions at national and firm level had a significant effect on the development of inequality. The measures taken by the government in response to the crisis were directed mainly towards consolidating the budget by curbing public expenditure and this has affected labour market inequality accordingly.

The aim of this chapter is to analyse the effects of the crisis on the Bulgarian labour market. We shall investigate a broad range of working conditions. The focus will be on the assessment of inequality in employment, unemployment, wages and other working conditions. The effects of government policy on inequality are also analysed. The case studies illustrate the issues under consideration at enterprise level.

2. GENERAL ECONOMIC EFFECTS: BULGARIA SEVERELY HIT BY THE CRISIS

2.1 Sharp Decline in Economic Activity: The Sectors Most Affected

The Bulgarian economy underwent substantial development before the crisis. GDP growth rates were relatively high (Figure 3.1). During the past five years GDP has grown at a stable rate of about 6 per cent a year. The recession that started in 2009 has strongly affected output. GDP contracted significantly and at an accelerating rate. As a result, GDP fell by 5 per cent in 2009. The recession has continued into 2010, and GDP fell by 4 per cent in the first quarter in comparison to the same quarter of the previous year. The positive growth of GDP in the next two quarters (by 0.5 per cent in the second and by 1 per cent in the third) suggested that the recession was over.

The economic crisis has affected different sectors to different degrees. Agriculture appears to have been less affected by the crisis since the end

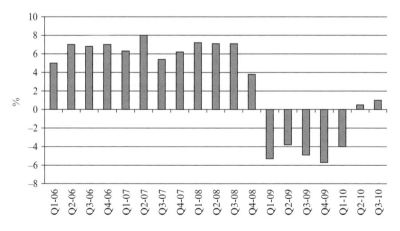

Source: National Statistical Institute.

Figure 3.1   GDP growth rates, Bulgaria, 2006–2010

Table 3.1   Labour market situation, Bulgaria, 2005–2010 (%)

	2005	2006	2007	2008	2009	Q1 2010	Q2 2010	Q3 2010
Employment rate, increase	2.7	3.3	2.8	3.3	–2.9	–7.3	–6.5	–5.0
Employment rate	55.8	58.6	61.7	64.0	62.6	58.8	60.2	60.6
Unemployment rate	10.2	9.0	6.9	5.7	6.9	10.2	10.1	9.6
Participation rate	62.1	64.5	66.3	67.8	67.2	65.5	66.9	67.1

Source: National accounts, Labour Force Survey.

of 2009. Gross value added (GVA) in agriculture declined only by 3.3 per cent in 2009. Industrial output (mainly in manufacturing) has been hardest hit: gross value added in industry contracted by 8.5 per cent in 2009, while before the crisis it was growing. Total manufacturing output decreased by 14.5 per cent during the period December 2008–December 2009. The manufacturing branches most strongly affected were furniture (–35.7 per cent), machine production (–27.6 per cent), textiles (–24.5 per cent) and clothing (–19.5 per cent).

Construction was also hard hit by the crisis. Gross value added fell by 7.2 per cent in 2009 in comparison to 8.5 percentage points growth in the previous year. The fall in domestic demand has had a negative effect on trade turnover. Value added in trade fell by 6.2 per cent, while trade turnover has been reduced by over 12 per cent.

2.2   Labour Market Situation Deteriorating Rapidly

The negative impact of the crisis on the labour market refers to all indicators (Table 3.1). Most affected are employment and unemployment. Employment fell by 2.9 per cent (112,000 workers) in 2009 after prolonged and stable growth over the past few years. As a result, the employment rate fell from 64 per cent in 2008 to 62.6 per cent in 2009. The deterioration in the employment situation was not as marked as that of GDP, mainly due to inertia and the protective measures that have been taken (reduction of working time, unpaid leave and so on).

Unemployment started to increase from the second half of 2008 and continued to grow throughout 2009. According to data from the Labour Force Survey, the number of unemployed in 2009 increased by 38,300 in comparison to 2008, and now affected 9.6 per cent of the labour force.

The other negative effect on the labour market is the fall in the participation rate. Some people quit the labour market (mainly discouraged

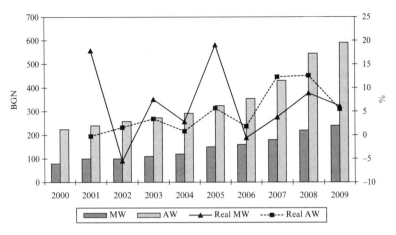

Source: National Statistical Institute.

Figure 3.2   Nominal and real wage dynamics, Bulgaria, 2000–2009

workers) because of their difficulties finding a job. The participation rate
fell by 0.6 percentage points in 2009. This is relatively modest given that the
number of inactive people aged 15–64 grew by 15,600 in 2009. Obviously,
the crisis forced a significant part of the unemployed to stay in the labour
market, looking for a job. Also, a proportion of inactive people re-entered
the labour market because of their dwindling financial resources.

   The positive economic development since the recession has had a negligible impact on labour market performance. Nevertheless, all labour
market indicators have started to improve, including the employment and
participation rates.

2.3   An Impact on Real Wage Dynamics but Limited So Far

Alongside the economic and labour market deterioration, nominal and
real wages have experienced lower growth than in previous years (Figure
3.2). Both the minimum wage (MW) and the average wage (AW) continued to increase in nominal terms: the average wage rose by 8.4 per cent in
2009, while the minimum wage rose by 9.1 per cent. These rates of growth
are much lower than those achieved in the pre-recession years (22.2 per
cent in 2008 and 12.5 per cent in 2007 for the minimum wage and 26.5 per
cent and 21.8 per cent for the average wage).

   In real terms, the minimum wage and average wage have also increased,
but by a lower proportion than in the previous year. The real minimum
wage grew by 6.1 per cent in 2009 in comparison to 8.8 per cent in 2008.

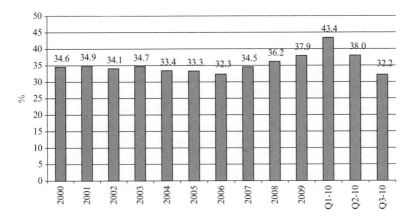

Source: National Statistical Institute.

Figure 3.3   Wage share in GDP, Bulgaria, 2000–2010

The increase in the real average wage was below that of the minimum wage, at 5.5 per cent, so that the ratio between the minimum wage and the average wage increased slightly, from 40.4 per cent in 2008 to 40.6 per cent in 2009.

This growth is only half that registered in 2008. At the same time, there has been an increase in the proportion of low-paid workers (see Section 5.3).

Wage development during the recession has been determined by many circumstances. First, the slow adjustment of wages to economic output. Wages are fixed and changes require time to take effect. Second, there is a trade-off between employment and wages. Wage increases were compensated by job reductions (see Section 5.4). Third, most dismissed workers were low skilled and low paid. This automatically increases the average wage in the firm.

2.4   Missing Link Between Wages and Productivity Confirmed

Since wage trends during the crisis have not deteriorated as much as the contraction in output, this has led to an increase, at least temporarily, in the wage share in GDP (Figure 3.3), rising by 1.7 percentage points in 2009. Such a disconnection between wages and GDP also in a period of crisis cannot be interpreted as an improvement in the linkage between earnings and economic performance that had already been observed in the pre-crisis growth period.

Evidence for this conclusion is provided by the total disconnection between real wage growth and productivity over the past ten years. Real wage dynamics did not follow productivity development after 2000. Annual changes in the real average wage differ significantly from productivity changes for all years during the period and especially in the past three years. In 2007 and 2008, the average real wage increased by much more (by 12.1 per cent and 8.2 per cent, respectively) than productivity (3.3 per cent and 2.7 per cent, respectively). In 2009, productivity fell by 2.2 per cent, while the real average wage grew by 5.5 per cent. All this suggests a weak relationship between them and, consequently, low economic efficiency and competitiveness. Unit labour costs and total production costs have grown. This negatively affected the functioning of the market which, in the current crisis, is highly inadequate.

The relationship between wages and productivity started to improve at the beginning of 2010. Productivity increased significantly (by 7.5 and 6.4 per cent in the second and third quarters, respectively) due to the further reduction in employment, and in practical terms balanced real wage growth.

2.5   The Rise of the Budget Deficit

The recession has brought about a strong deterioration in the balance of payments in 2009 and 2010. Budget revenues have declined dramatically and for this reason the government has decided to cut public expenditure in all areas. Wages in the public sector were frozen at the end of 2009 and the government postponed all payments to firms carrying out public projects. Despite these restrictive measures, in 2009 the budget balance became negative for the first time for a number of years. The budget deficit for 2009 was BGN 3.21 billion (1.64 billion euros), or 4.7 per cent of GDP. In response, cuts in public expenditure were also made in the 2010 budget. The budget was revised again in the middle of the year, leading to further reductions in government expenditure (of about 10 per cent). This restrictive budgetary policy has had a strong negative impact not only on particular segments and social groups in the labour market (employment and wages in the public sector; unemployment and active labour market policy; low-paid workers), but also on working conditions overall.

3.   POLICY RESPONSE TO THE CRISIS

The economic crisis in Bulgaria has hit economic output, the labour market, foreign trade and the public finances very hard. In these circumstances, the Government has implemented a package of measures (2009 and 2010) aimed at reducing the negative effects of the recession. These measures concern a number of areas of economic policy. Most are oriented towards supporting fiscal policy and reducing the budget deficit. The measures directed towards the labour market and social protection are summarized in Table 3.2.

To meet the ongoing decrease in budget revenues during the recession the Government enforced a restrictive public spending policy from the second half of 2009. That policy has continued in 2010. Most government spending was cut to the bone. Budget expenditure was reduced, first, by cancelling the envisaged growth in wages financed from the budget (public administration, teachers, doctors and so on) from July 2009 and, second, by removing all additional year-end payments to workers in public administration. Further reductions in public expenditure were carried out from the middle of 2010. The budget subsidies of all public organizations were cut by 10 per cent until the end of the year. In some public organizations, this reduction will severely affect the wage bill and wages.

The reduction in public expenditure was supplemented by restrictions on wage growth. The minimum wage and wages in the public sector were frozen for 2010. This is aimed at reducing the pressure on increased labour costs and lowering the budget deficit. This was expected to stimulate economic activity and preserve employment. It might also have had an adverse effect on global consumption while also reducing the quality of public services.

The effects on workers can be summarized as follows. First, the minimum wage and wages in the public sector fell in real terms. This affected a considerable proportion (almost one-third) of employment. Second, the minimum wage freeze had an effect on workers at the bottom with a consequent increase in the proportion of low-paid workers.

Third, the wage gap between the public and private sectors has declined but not because of wage increases in the private sector or a shrinking shadow economy but rather a strong decline in public sector wages. Fourth, decreasing the purchasing power of a sizable part of the employed will reduce consumption and total domestic demand, which in crisis conditions is undesirable.

With regard to the minimum wage, the Government announced its intention (in April 2010 on the basis of an agreement with the trade unions and employers' organizations) to create a new mechanism for its determination which would be based on the development of economic and social indicators. The idea is to link minimum wage growth with the official poverty line, productivity and wage development.

Labour market support measures deal primarily with maintaining

Table 3.2   Policy response recovery measures, Bulgaria, 2009–2010

Policy area	Description of measure taken	Implemen-tation	Objectives
Cutting public expenditure	1. Abolish envisaged increases in wages financed by the budget	July 2009	Reducing the budget deficit
	2. 10% reduction of public expenditure in all budget organizations except for education and social care	In force since July 2010	
Restrictive wage policy	1. Freeze the minimum wage	Since 2010	Reducing labour costs and maintaining employment
	2. Freeze all wages financed by budget	Since mid-2009	Reducing the budget deficit
	3. Intention of creating a mechanism for minimum wage fixing	From the beginning of 2010	Increasing the minimum wage in relation to social and economic parameters
Preservation of employment	1. Complex of measures maintaining employment in the hardest hit enterprises through:	Since June 2010	Maintaining employment
	– introduction of flexible working time;	Since 2009 Since 2009	
	– specific leave for economic reasons;	Since 2009	
	– compensation for short-time working	Since July 2010	Maintaining employment
	2. Restrict access to the labour market for low-skilled foreign workers.	Since 2010	Maintaining employment and increasing incomes
	3. Reduction of social insurance contributions by 2 percentage points		
Reduction of unemployment	1. Creating mechanisms to help young people find their first job	Since July 2010	Reducing youth unem-ployment
	2. Additional resources for subsidized employment	Since July 2010	Reducing unem-ployment

Table 3.2   (continued)

Policy area	Description of measure taken	Implemen-tation	Objectives
Supporting household income	1. Removal of the ceiling on unemployment benefit All unemployed persons must receive 60% of their income before job loss	Since July 2010	Increasing incomes of the unemployed
	2. Removal of the quota principle in the distribution of food vouchers	Since July 2010	Supporting real incomes of workers
	3. Temporary restriction on increases in prices regulated by the Government	Since July 2010	Supporting real incomes
	4. Additional financing of soup kitchens	Since July 2010	Supporting the poor
Strengthening social protection	Increase resources for social assistance. Ministry of Labour and Social Policy received BGN 142 million for social assistance programmes	Since July 2010	Supporting the poor

employment. Most were initiated in 2009 and prolonged in 2010. The Government introduced a compensation scheme for short-time working and other measures of flexible working time and specific forms of leave. Many affected firms took advantage of this opportunity, but most implemented unpaid leave. To protect the employment of low-skilled workers, the Government restricted the access to the Bulgarian labour market of foreign low-skilled workers. The effect of this measure will not be strong because pressure on the labour market is not intense. Measures related to subsidized employment and the reduction of pension-related social insurance contributions (by 2 percentage points from the beginning of 2010) will probably have more impact on maintaining employment. The aim is to reduce labour costs and thus maintain employment. The expected effects on employment are questionable because there are no controlling mechanisms ensuring that the resources saved would be used for employment protection. The positive effect on real wages is obvious because workers have to pay lower pension contributions.

Particular attention is being paid to youth unemployment; young people are one of the most at-risk groups in the labour market. The

Government needs to create mechanisms by which school leavers can find their first job.

The other group of government measures focuses on improving household incomes. The unemployed in principle could receive the full amount of benefits (60 per cent of income before losing their job) after the removal of the ceiling from July 2010. Real wages are supported by the abolition of the quota principle in the distribution of food vouchers (enabling the purchase of food free of charge). The effects of this measure are expressed in the increase in the number, amount and coverage of vouchers, but not in terms of inequality. A stronger effect on real incomes can be expected from the restrictions imposed on prices. The prices of electricity, gas, water and heating are regulated by the Government and their temporary freezing or slight increase should support real household incomes.

4. INEQUALITY IN THE FACE OF EMPLOYMENT AND UNEMPLOYMENT RISKS

4.1 Employment Adjustments

The effects of the crisis on employment have not been distributed equally across sectors and branches, types of labour contract, gender, educational attainment and so on. Inequalities might arise depending on employment status and the extent to which the recession has hit enterprise performance. We shall analyse employment inequality within this framework. Our objectives are to analyse the effects on different categories of employment and to identify the most vulnerable groups of workers.

4.1.1 Employment inequality by sector

The development of employment across economic sectors was different before and during the crisis (Figure 3.4). Before the crisis, several sectors (construction, finance, trade, hotels and restaurants) experienced high employment growth. New jobs in construction and the financial sector increased by 50 per cent and 30 per cent, respectively, during 2005–2008. Employment in trade experienced a similar trend. Employment in other sectors (industry and agriculture) changed at moderate, stable rates and did not exhibit any specific development tendency. This picture suggests unequal employment development by sector before the crisis.

The impact of the recession on jobs has also been uneven across sectors. The financial sector in Bulgaria has not been strongly affected by the global financial crisis. Employment in this sector remained stable during 2009 and employment increased, albeit at a low rate (1.1 per cent).

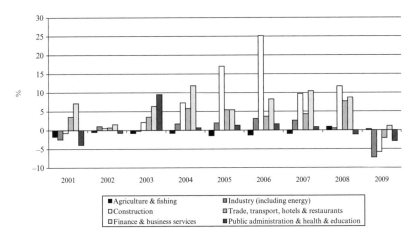

Source: National Accounts.

Figure 3.4 Employment growth rates, Bulgaria, 2001–2009

Employment in agriculture did not change despite the fall in output in 2009. Most affected by the crisis have been jobs in industry, construction and services (trade, transport and tourism). In construction, employment fell by 5.8 per cent (15,000), while in services job losses totalled 20,700 (about 2.1 per cent).

Workers in industry faced the highest risk of unemployment. The number of dismissed workers was 59,900, a contraction of 7.3 per cent in comparison to 2008. This concerned mainly manufacturing: the number of employees in manufacturing fell by 84,000 (14.2 per cent) during the past five quarters of the recession (2009–2010). Most affected are export-oriented branches (base metals, machine products, textiles and clothing).

4.1.2 Inequality by occupational status and type of contract
The structure of employment with regard to occupational status (employ-ees and self-employed) did not differ significantly prior to and during the crisis. Both occupational groups developed positively before the recession but with different rates of growth (the number of self-employed increased at a lower rate). The share of employees represents over 70 per cent of total employment and has exhibited a tendency to grow since 2005. This trend continued in 2009, despite the higher number of lay-offs.[1] Thus the crisis neither halted nor accelerated this development. The impact of the reces-sion on employees and the self-employed differ notably across economic sectors. Job reductions prevail in industry, construction and services, while the number of self-employed declined mainly in industry and services.

Table 3.3   *Share of employment by type of working time and educational attainment and permanency of job, Bulgaria, 2006–2009*

	Employed by type of working time		Employed by level of education			Employees by permanency of job	
	Full-time	Part-time	Higher	Upper secondary	Lower secondary and lower	Perma-nent job	Tempo-rary job
2006	93.8	1.9	25.5	58.2	16.3	88.6	5.9
2007	94.7	1.6	25.5	60.0	14.5	91.5	5.1
2008	97.7	2.3	25.5	59.6	14.9	95.0	5.0
2009	97.7	2.3	26.4	59.2	14.4	95.3	4.7

Note: Not included: the category 'Unspecified' for 2006 and 2007.

Source: Labour Force Survey.

The Bulgarian labour market is dominated by typical forms of employment, most workers being hired on full-time contracts. The proportion of full-time workers increased before the crisis and reached 97.7 per cent of total employment in 2008, while in 2006 it was 3.9 percentage points less (Table 3.3). The share of part-time workers also increased from 1.9 per cent in 2006 to 2.3 per cent in 2008. The effect of the recession was evenly distributed among full- and part-time workers. Employment in both groups fell by the same percentage, –3.2 per cent and –3.5 per cent, respectively, for full- and part-time workers. Consequently, their shares remained unchanged in 2009. Moreover, the flows between full- and part-time contracts were limited. The estimates suggest that 0.6 per cent of full-time workers moved to part-time contracts during the recession (Beleva 2010). The opposite movement (from part- to full-time contracts) changed little during the crisis (falling by 1 percentage point). Generally, the impact of the crisis on full-time and part-time employment was negligible.

The workers on temporary contracts represent a small part of employees in Bulgaria. Their share declined to 5 per cent in 2008 from 5.9 per cent in 2006 and 5.1 per cent in 2007 (Table 3.3). This tendency accelerated in 2009, rising to 4.7 per cent. The number of workers in temporary jobs declined by 9.4 per cent (13,900), while permanent job losses amounted to 2.9 per cent (82,300). Temporary workers have thus been one of the buffers in the crisis, despite their small numbers.

The crisis gave rise to higher inequality among workers with different levels of education. The typical employer sought to retain high quality

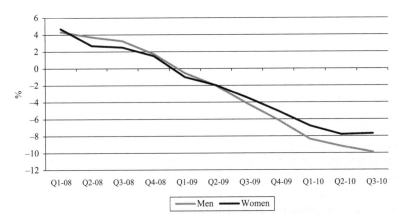

Source: Labour Force Survey.

Figure 3.5   Changes in male and female employment, Bulgaria, 2008–2010

jobs and skilled workers. This is confirmed by all case studies. Low-skilled workers faced a much higher risk of unemployment. The number of workers with a primary education (lower secondary and lower) decreased by 6.2 per cent (31,300) during the recession. As a result, their share declined to 14.4 per cent (Table 3.3). Workers with a secondary education were also strongly affected by the crisis. Their number fell by 3.8 per cent (from 2,002,500 in 2008 to 1,924,700 in 2009). Employees with a higher education were less affected by the recession: the total number of employees with a higher education increased and this raised their relative share in total employment.

4.1.3   Effects on gender inequality in employment
Employment dynamics for men and women show considerable inequality during the crisis. Men experienced a more negative impact than women (Figure 3.5). Male employment declined at a higher rate than female employment during the whole recession and the gap between them became wider in 2010. For the period between the fourth quarters of 2008 and 2009 male employment decreased by 6.1 per cent, or 107,900 workers. During the same period, female employment fell by 5 per cent (51,800). There was a greater reduction of male employment in 2010: employment for men fell at an increasing rate (from –8.4 per cent in the first quarter to –9.9 per cent in the third quarter) and for women by an almost constant rate (around –7.78 per cent).

This inequality contributed to reducing the difference between the male

Table 3.4   Employment rate by age, Bulgaria, 2005–2009

Age group	2005	2006	2007	2008	2009
15–24	21.6	23.2	24.5	26.3	24.8
25–34	69.4	72.2	76.2	78.2	75.1
35–44	77.1	79.6	82.8	84.6	82.6
45–54	72.1	74.8	78.4	80.6	79.0
55–64	34.7	39.6	42.6	46.0	46.1
65+	2.5	2.7	3.0	3.8	3.3

Source: Labour Force Survey.

and female employment rates. The employment rate for men declined by 6.9 percentage points between the first quarters of 2009 and 2010 (from 69.2 per cent to 62.3 per cent). The female employment rate went down by only 4 percentage points, reaching 55.3 per cent at the beginning of 2010. As a result, gender inequality in employment narrowed. The improvement of the economic situation since the recession provoked a rise in the employment rates of both groups and further shrinkage of gender inequality.

4.1.4   Young people hardest hit by the crisis

Employment among young people showed positive development before the crisis. The number of employed young people (aged 15–24) increased by 15.8 per cent in the period 2005–2008, yielding an employment rate of 26.3 per cent (Table 3.4). This development of youth employment was the result of the special programmes and measures implemented in recent years (2006–2008). Employment in other age groups also showed progress, in particular, among older people, whose employment increased by 117,000 or 34.8 per cent.

The crisis affected employment in the first two groups (young people aged 15–24 and 25–34) most strongly. Employment in the age group 15–24 declined by 8.6 per cent or 22,600. As a result, the employment rate in this group decreased by about 1.5 percentage points. In the age group 25–34, the fall was about 6.3 per cent (46,300) and the employment rate fell by a higher magnitude (3.1 percentage points). In total, the crisis reduced youth employment by 68,900.

4.2   Inequalities in Unemployment Risks

The effects of the crisis on unemployment were also not distributed equally among groups. Some groups were more affected than others, leading to

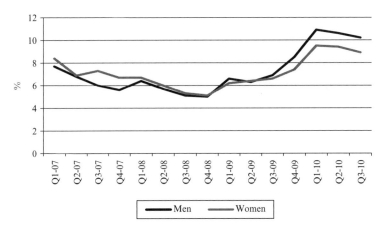

Source: Labour Force Survey.

Figure 3.6   Unemployment rate by gender, Bulgaria, 2007–2010

higher inequality between them and changing the structure of unemployment in a number of respects (gender, age, level of education and duration).

4.2.1   Stronger unemployment growth among men

The higher reduction of male employment (the crisis strongly affected
branches with predominantly male employment) was translated into
higher unemployment among men. Before the crisis (2008), unemployment was almost equally distributed between men and women, with
female unemployment slightly higher (Figure 3.6).

Gender inequality started to emerge from the first quarter of 2009. The
male unemployment rate increased from 6.5 per cent in the first quarter of
2009 to 10.9 per cent in the same period of 2010 and declined to 10.2 per
cent in the third quarter, while the female unemployment rate grew from
6.2 per cent to 9.5 per cent and dropped to 8.9 per cent. The gender gap
in the unemployment rate, calculated as the difference between men's and
women's unemployment rates, grew from 0.4 to 1.1 throughout 2009 and
decreased slightly in 2010 (from 1.4 in the first quarter to 1.3 in the third
quarter). Therefore, the crisis significantly increased gender inequality in
unemployment. This situation differs strongly from the pre-crisis period
when gender inequality declined in favour of women.

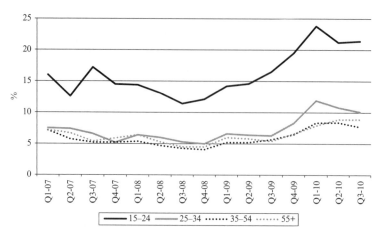

Source: Labour Force Survey.

Figure 3.7   Unemployment rate by age, Bulgaria, 2007–2010

4.2.2   Youth unemployment at a peak

Young people aged 15–24 typically faced a higher unemployment rate than older workers. The unemployment rate for this age group declined significantly during the period 2007–2008 (from 16.0 per cent in the first quarter of 2007 to 11.4 per cent in the third quarter of 2008). Consequently, the gap between the unemployment rate of young people and that of the other age groups was reduced. The impact of the recession totally changed this tendency. The unemployment rate of young people climbed from 14.2 per cent in the first quarter of 2009 to 23.8 per cent in the same period of 2010 and slightly decreased after the recession (Figure 3.7). At the same time, the unemployment rate of older workers (aged 35–54) also increased, but to a smaller extent (from 5.2 per cent in 2009 to 8.4 per cent in 2010). The effect was to increase the ratio between unemployed young people and unemployed older people from 2.7 in 2008 to 2.8 in 2010. This small difference suggested that the crisis caused a moderate increase in unemployment inequality by age.

The other group particularly hard hit by the recession is persons aged 25–34. Before the crisis, the unemployment rate of this group decreased in parallel with older groups and there were no major differences between them. The recession caused a rapid increase in unemployment among this group during the fourth quarter of 2008 and the first quarter of 2010. In this period, the unemployment rate jumped by 6.9 percentage points (from 5.0 to 11.9 per cent) and declined to 10.1 per cent in the third quarter of 2010.

Table 3.5   Unemployment by duration, Bulgaria, 2008–2009 (in '000s)

	Up to 5 months	6–11 months	Over 12 months
Q1-08	82.4	30.3	116.2
Q2-08	69.7	32.4	105.1
Q3-08	65.2	31.4	97.5
Q4-08	58.5	24.6	94.6
Q1-09	93.8	30.7	97.6
Q2-09	81.4	41.4	99.7
Q3-09	88.9	46.8	98.7
Q4-09	100.0	55.2	117.6

Source: Labour Force Survey.

A more modest increase in unemployment was observed among older workers (aged 35–54 and 55+). The unemployment rate of the 35–54 age group increased by 3.2 percentage points during the recession, while that of the 55+ group rose by about 1.9 percentage points. In contrast to the other age groups, the unemployment rate of the oldest workers (aged 55+) continued to rise in the period after the recession (from 7.9 per cent in the first quarter of 2010 to 8.9 per cent in the third quarter). Evidently, economic development in this period did not affect the oldest workers.

4.2.3   Increase in long-term unemployment
Unemployment started to increase from the second half of 2008, when the Bulgarian economy experienced the first symptoms of the crisis. The small number of new unemployed did not influence the structure of unemployment by duration. The number of persons unemployed for up to five months continued its downward trend to the end of the year (Table 3.5). Also, the number of long-term unemployed declined by 21,600 during 2008. The proportion of those unemployed for 6–11 months remained stable throughout the first three quarters and sharply declined at the end of the year.

The recession significantly increased the number of short- and long-term unemployed. The first significant rise appeared in the first quarter of 2009 and hit short-term unemployment (less than six months). In comparison to the previous quarter the number of those unemployed for less than six months increased in the first quarter of 2009 by 60 per cent (35,300) and of those unemployed for 6–11 months by 25 per cent. The number of long-term unemployed rose by only 3 per cent because a part of those unemployed for 6–11 months (3,000) entered this group. The augmentation of unemployment in 2009 caused a further and higher increase in short-term than in long-term unemployment. The effect on long-term unemployment was revealed after four quarters in which the number of those unemployed for more than 12 months rose by 19 per cent: 2009 has thus been characterized by growth in long-term unemployment.

5. EFFECTS ON WAGE INEQUALITY

The overall impact of the recession on wage dynamics was characterized by reductions in the nominal and real rates of growth, although they remained positive during the period 2009–2010. This effect was not distributed evenly among economic sectors, form of ownership, occupations, professions and so on. As a result, wage inequality has changed in these respects.

5.1 Wage Inequality Between Public and Private Sector

Average earnings in the public sector in Bulgaria are traditionally higher than those in the private sector. Average wages in the public sector from 2000 were higher (anything between 27 per cent and 48 per cent). However, the inequality between wages in the public and private sectors has shown a downward trend since 2002. The wage gap[2] fell from 32.5 per cent in 2002 to 23.7 per cent in 2007 and then 23.5 per cent in 2008 and

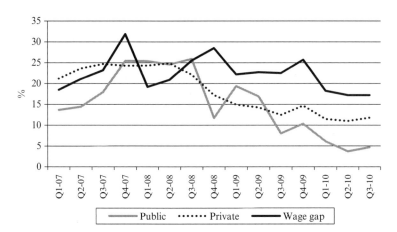

Source: National Statistical Institute.

Figure 3.8   Changes in gross wages in the public and private sectors and the wage gap, Bulgaria, 2007–2010 (percentage change between current quarter and same quarter of previous year)

23.1 per cent in 2009. The recession to some extent contributed to further reduce this disparity. The restrictions on wages financed by the budget, initiated in 2009 and 2010, caused a lower rate of wage growth in the public than in the private sector (Figure 3.8), especially after restrictive measures were introduced (second half of 2009). Figure 3.8 shows a decline in both sectors from mid-2008, but with the decline in the public sector being more significant. The average gross wage in the public sector increased by 10.4 per cent in the fourth quarter of 2009 (in comparison to the fourth quarter of 2008), while wages in the private sector rose by 14.7 per cent. The difference was bigger at the beginning of 2010 when the gross average wage in the public sector went up by 6.1 per cent, in contrast to 11.5 per cent in the private sector.

Due to the crisis, the difference between earnings in the public and private sectors has declined. The wage gap calculated on the basis of quarterly data clearly confirms this. During 2008, the wage gap increased significantly, reaching over 30 per cent at end of the year, while in 2009 it remained almost stable and in 2010 it declined. The wage gap in the first quarter of 2010 fell by 4 percentage points on an annual basis, reaching 18.2 per cent, and further decreased to 17.2 per cent in the third quarter. This trend is likely to continue until the end of 2010 because of the restrictive wage policy in the public sector.

5.2 Wage Inequality by Sectors: Public Employees Hardest Hit

Wage development across economic sectors during a recession is different depending on firms' adjustment to the crisis. All sectors experienced a progression of average nominal wages but the overall tendency is downwards (Figure 3.9). The average wage in manufacturing increased at fairly stable rates of around 10 per cent on an annual basis during the recession. In the first quarter of 2010, the average wage in manufacturing rose by 9.1 per cent in comparison to the same period of 2009. In contrast, wages in construction experienced higher rates (over 20 per cent) in 2009 and fell significantly (to 4.1 per cent) in the third quarter of 2010. Wages in the financial sector also grew, but with very low rates in comparison to the pre-recession period.

Employees in the public administration appeared to be most affected by the crisis. The wage restrictions caused a strong decline in nominal wage growth which became negative at the end of 2009. Compared to the pre-recession period, the average wage in public administration in the last quarter of 2009 decreased by 15 per cent.

These differences in wage dynamics across economic sectors lead to changes in relative wages and inequality. Generally, the recession has had an equalizing effect on wage inequality among economic sectors.

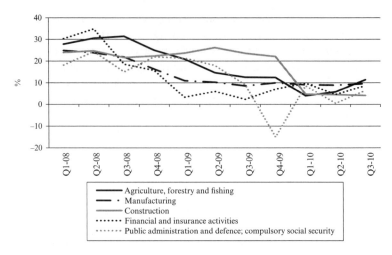

Source: National Statistical Institute.

*Figure 3.9   Wage dynamics in selected economic sectors, Bulgaria, 2008–
2010 (percentage change between current quarter and same
quarter of previous year)*

The following evidence supports this conclusion. First, wage dynamics in
high wage sectors were lower than in low wage sectors. For example, the
average wage in the financial sector increased by 7.1 per cent in the fourth
quarter of 2009, while wages in hotels and restaurants increased by 14.0
per cent and in agriculture by 12.5 per cent.

Second, there was reduction in the wage differential between the highest
and lowest wage branches. The difference between the sectors with highest
and lowest average wages declined from 3.6 in the first quarter of 2008 to
3.2 in the same quarter of 2009 and further to 3.1 in 2010.

Third, the coefficient of variation, that measures the variability of sectoral wages in relation to the average wage, based on quarterly data for
the period 2008–2010, presents a clear downward tendency. This means
a lower deviation of sectoral wages from the average, indicating decreasing wage inequality by sectors. It declined steadily from 0.51 in the fourth
quarter of 2008 to 0.46 in the first quarter of 2010.

5.3   Effect on Low-paid Workers

The impact of the crisis on low-paid workers in Bulgaria could be analysed by comparing the dynamics of the minimum wage and low pay (LP)
threshold. There is no statistical information on wage distribution which

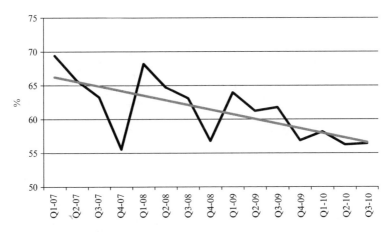

Source: National Statistical Institute.

Figure 3.10   Dynamics of the minimum wage/low wage ratio, Bulgaria, 2007–2010

would enable us to analyse the changes in the proportion of workers below the minimum wage and low pay. The effects on low-paid workers in the crisis differ from those in pre-recession years. It was found before the crisis that there was compression of the wage distribution from the bottom and the distance between low and average wages narrowed (Tzanov 2010a).

During the recession, the Government froze the minimum wage and public sector wages for 2010. This led to an increasing gap between the minimum wage and the low pay threshold, the latter increasing more since it is measured as two-thirds of the median or average wage. The low pay threshold rose by about 9.9 per cent, while the minimum wage remained unchanged throughout 2010. As a result, the minimum wage/low wage ratio shows a downward trend (Figure 3.10). This means that the pressure for higher wages on the bottom of the wage distribution began to relax in comparison to previous periods (2005–2006, when the minimum wage increased faster than the average wage) and the protective power of the minimum wage declined. In practical terms, this means more low-paid workers because the low pay threshold increased and the minimum wage remained unchanged.

5.4   Varying Wage–Employment Trade-offs by Sector and Enterprise

Firms' adjustment to the crisis includes different patterns, depending on the extent to which the recession affected economic performance. In the hardest hit firms, a combination of employment adjustment, working time

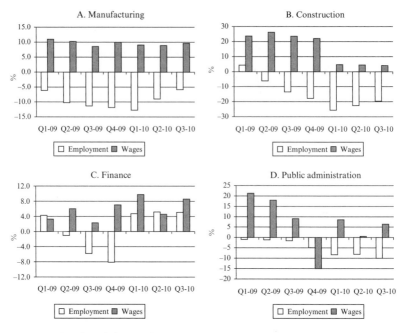

Source: National Statistical Institute.

Figure 3.11 *Wage and employment dynamics in some sectors, Bulgaria, 2009–2010 (percentage change between current quarter and same quarter of previous year)*

reduction and wage cuts was applied. In less affected firms, reductions in wages and hours worked were often sufficient and made it possible, in particular, to retain skilled workers. The case studies confirm the range of company approaches to adjustment. Generally, the trade-off between wages and employment appeared to be a frequent arrangement for adapting to the crisis. Across economic sectors, the wage–employment trade-off was applied differently, although the general practice consisted of a reduction of employment while maintaining positive, albeit reduced wage growth (Figure 3.11).

In the hardest hit sectors (manufacturing and construction), employment decreased faster than wages. The positive wage development in manufacturing was made possible by growing rates of employment reduction (Figure 3.11, panel A). The number of employees has declined at a growing rate, quarter by quarter (from 6.1 per cent in the first quarter of 2009 to 12.7 per cent in the same period of 2010). This implies a strong downward

Table 3.6   Changes in the Gini coefficient and quintile share S80/S20, Bulgaria, 2004–2009 (%)

	2004	2005	2006	2007	2008	2009
Gini	26.4	24.9	24.1	25.3	26.3	26.2
S80/S20	4.0	3.7	3.5	3.7	3.9	3.9

Source: National Statistical Institute.

replacement between wages and employment. At the beginning of the recession, 1 per cent wage growth corresponded to a 0.6 per cent decline in the workforce, while in the same quarter of 2010 this ratio was 1:–1.4 (that is, 1 per cent wage growth corresponded to a 1.4 per cent decline in the labour force). Thus, a reduction in employment allowed positive wage growth.

A more severe decline in employment and wage growth was observed in construction (Figure 3.11, panel B). Wage dynamics decreased by 19 percentage points during the period 2009–2010 (from 23.7 per cent to 4.7 per cent in the first quarters of the two years), while employment contracted by 25.6 per cent. A 1 per cent increase in wages coincided with a 5.4 per cent decrease in employment. This indicates that in construction there was not a strong relationship between changes in wages and employment and thus employment adjustment prevailed. The situation in the financial sector, which has not been so affected by the recession, is different. The positive wage growth is not always accompanied by the reduction of employment and the trade-off appears only in some quarters (third and fourth quarters of 2009).

The adjustment of the public administration to the crisis was accomplished by reductions in both wage growth and employment. The ongoing reform in the public administration (2009–2010) optimized employment by cutting redundant jobs. In particular, this was observed at the end of 2009 and the beginning of 2010. In addition, the wage restrictions strongly reduced the rates of growth and the peak of the reduction was observed in the fourth quarter of 2009; wages in that quarter declined by 15 per cent in comparison to the same period of the last pre-recession year (2008) because all annual bonuses were cut.

5.5   Income Inequality and Impoverishment

The equalization effect on sectoral wages was also revealed with regard to household incomes but to a much lower extent (Table 3.6). Income inequality, measured by the Gini coefficient, decreased slightly in 2009 after a 1 percentage point growth in 2008.

Table 3.7   At risk of poverty rate among different households, Bulgaria, 2004–2009 (%)

	2004	2005	2006	2007	2008	2009
Working poor	6.8	5.9	5.5	5.0	5.0	5.7
Inactive poor	19.3	19.5	20.2	20.5	21.4	20.4
Employees	6.9	5.6	5.7	4.9	4.5	5.3
Self-employed	6.1	8.7	2.8	5.9	10.0	9.8
Men	13.0	12.8	11.8	11.3	12.7	12.8
Women	17.4	15.4	15.7	16.6	15.8	16.4

Source: National Statistical Institute.

Also, the burden of the recession was equally distributed among low and high income households. Disparity between the incomes of the highest 20 per cent of households and the bottom 20 per cent did not change in comparison to the pre-recession year.

The effect of the crisis on impoverishment has been quite different among different social groups. The disappearance of incomes from work for those who were forced to leave the labour market led to an increase in poverty among workers (Table 3.7). The percentage of working poor increased by 0.7 percentage points in 2008, halting the downward tendency since 2004.

In contrast to working people, inactive people (pensioners and so on) are characterized by a declining poverty rate. Not all inactive groups have experienced a reduction of poverty. The poverty rate among the unemployed went up from 43.3 per cent in 2008 to 44 per cent in 2009, while among pensioners it dropped from 17 per cent to 15.5 per cent due to the increase of all pensions from the middle of 2009.

Among working people, employees are in a more disadvantageous position than the self-employed. The poverty rate has risen by 0.8 percentage points for employees, but for the self-employed it decreased slightly (–0.2 percentage points). Generally, budgetary restrictions have had a negative impact on household incomes and have caused an increase of poverty.

With regard to the impact of the crisis on gender impoverishment, there are also differences. The poverty rate for women increased more (0.6 percentage points) than for men (0.1 points). This is probably due to the higher income differences between them because inflows into unemployment affect men more than women.

6.   INEQUALITY WITH REGARD TO OTHER WORKING CONDITIONS

6.1   Reduction of Working Time: An Option for All Workers?

The most popular reaction to the crisis among firms was to reduce working time. To protect employment the Government introduced a compensation scheme at the beginning of 2009. In the firms with a trade union, the decision on a working time reduction was taken through negotiations (see case study 1). This scheme allowed workers to receive compensation for short-time working. However, the coverage of the compensation scheme remained limited: only a relatively small number of employees (19,485) and firms (531) received compensation for short-time working in 2009. The number of workers obtaining compensation fell further to 6,188 in 2010.

The total number of hours worked by all workers declined at a growing rate in parallel with the depth of the recession. While total working hours dropped by 0.5 per cent in the first quarter of 2009, at the beginning of 2010 they shrank by 7.5 per cent. A higher contraction of working time is observed among employees than among the self-employed. The hours worked by employees fell by 8.6 per cent in the first quarter of 2010, but those of the self-employed decreased much less (by –3.3 per cent). Most self-employed work as shopkeepers and have no reason to reduce working time.

The reduction of working time is unequally distributed across economic sectors but has been present nearly everywhere (Figure 3.12). A higher reduction has been observed in sectors harder hit by the recession. Construction is the sector with the highest reduction. During the second half of 2009 and the first quarter of 2010, hours worked decreased by over 15 per cent each quarter. Industrial firms are also reducing working time, but at a lower rate. Working time in industry has declined less than 10 per cent each quarter since mid-2009, so over the whole period of the recession it has been reduced by 9.6 per cent. The lowest decrease in working time has been in services (trade, transport, hotels and restaurants). In this sector, the total number of hours worked declined by between 4 and 9 per cent during the same period. An exception is the financial and business services sector. Working time in this sector has increased, following its overall tendency to rise during the past few years.

Differences in working time reductions also appeared between types of contract. According to LFS data, average weekly working hours fell from 40.5 hours in 2008 to 40 hours in 2009. The contraction of working time affected both full-time and part-time workers, but to different extents. For full-time employees the weekly fall in working time was 1.2 per cent (from

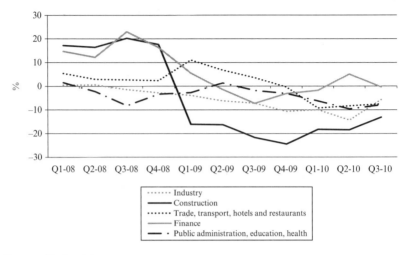

Source: National Accounts.

*Figure 3.12   Quarterly changes of hours worked in selected economic
             sectors, Bulgaria, 2008–2010 (percentage change between
             current quarter and same quarter of previous year)*

40.8 hours in 2008 to 40.3 hours in 2009), while for part-time employees
the contraction was much greater (4.7 per cent).

6.2   Health and Safety: Mitigated Effects of the Crisis

The impact of the crisis on health and safety presents a mixed picture.
Some basic risk factors (stress, accidents, noise, dust, toxicity and so on)
improved, while other remained unchanged or deteriorated. According to
the data from the Annual Reports of the Labour Inspectorate, the share
of employees working under unfavourable conditions has declined over
the past few (from 2007) years, continuing in 2009. The share of workers
with poor working conditions fell from 17 per cent in 2008 to 12 per cent in
2009. The improvement in the working environment mainly affects firms
in mining and electricity supply. However, the share of workers with unfavourable working conditions remained high (over 53 per cent) in firms in
metal extraction, electricity supply, coal mining, production of paper and
metal founding.

In the case of particular risk factors the Labour Inspectorate found that
the highest percentage of workers were exposed to unfavourable microclimates (dust, lighting and so on). Almost 52 per cent of the workers (66,410

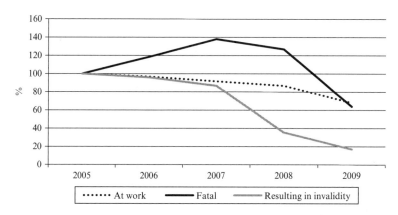

Source: National Insurance Institute.

Figure 3.13   *Dynamics of accidents at work, Bulgaria, 2005–2009 (Index 2005=100)*

in 2009) worked under such conditions. This share remained almost unchanged in comparison to the pre-recession year. Workers in construction, cement, glass and wood are most seriously affected by inappropriate microclimates.

The other widespread risk factor is noise in the workplace. About 40 per cent of the workers inspected have to work in conditions which breach the standards (50,387 in 2009). Noisy workplaces are concentrated in specific branches, where technological processes are characterized by intensive noise (metal construction, timber and wood-processing industry, electricity supply, textile industry and so on). There was no reduction in noisy workplaces during the recession.

Among risk factors, only accidents at work had a tendency to decline. This concerns not only the total number of accidents but also the number of accidents ending in fatalities and accidents leading to invalidity (Figure 3.13). The total number of accidents at work has decreased by about 39 per cent since 2005 (from 3,638 cases in 2005 to 2,476 cases in 2009). A higher reduction has been observed in accidents that cause invalidity. Their number fell significantly, from 76 cases in 2005 to 13 cases in 2009 (about 83 per cent). Accidents ending in fatalities also decreased. It is worth noting that the economic crisis did not impact negatively on accidents at work. It is notable that during the recession (2009) the number of accidents at work declined at the highest rates. Compared to 2008, their total number fell about by 21.6 per cent, while fatal accidents went down by 49.6 per cent and accidents causing invalidity by 51.9 per cent. This general downward tendency continues in 2010. While this mainly reflects the continuation of a long-term trend that started in the early 2000s, it might also reflect lower working hours.

6.3 Difficult Work and Family Life Balance in the Crisis

Analysis of the reconciliation of work and family life before the crisis shows that work appeared to be a priority in people's living strategies (Beleva and Tzanov 2006). Most families tried to compensate low labour incomes by increasing working time, taking a second job or postponing the birth of children. The difficulties that families face in balancing work and family were supplemented by the lack of social infrastructure for child care, insufficient use of flexible working time and so on.

The worsening of economic and labour market conditions caused by the crisis influenced arrangements of work and family life in different ways. The interaction of positive and negative impacts on families' decisions makes them more difficult to assess. On the one hand, the crisis provides an opportunity for better reconciliation of work and family in the sense that it left more time for family life; on the other hand, the high risk of unemployment has led to higher competition for jobs and less attention to family responsibilities.

Another positive effect on work–family life reconciliation was the forced reduction of working time. In the Bulgarian model, where work dominates family responsibilities, shorter working time provides an opportunity to increase the time devoted to the family. This effect is not strong, however, given that average weekly working hours fell by only 0.5 hours per week and benefited men more than women (0.7 hours for men versus 0.4 hours for women).

Work–life reconciliation depends strongly on government support for family dependents (children and dependent elderly). This should be considered in terms of two aspects: first, protection of maternity within the family (ensuring maternity benefits and leave), and second, providing support outside the family for child care and care for the elderly (crèches, kindergartens, homes for elderly people and so on). Analysis of social protection indicates that resource provision with regard to the social protection of maternity has tended to increase during the past few years, including the year of recession (Tzanov 2010b). In 2009, the level of maternity compensation rose by 31 per cent, accompanied by an increase in the duration of benefits (from 315 to 410 calendar days).

Resource provision for child care outside the family also rose during the recession. The number of places in crèches grew by 1,861 (7.4 per cent) in comparison to the pre-recession year. In general, all these figures suggest that government support for maternity and child care during the crisis improved conditions for the reconciliation of work and family duties.

6.4 Vocational Training as a Response to the Crisis

One of the most effective answers to the crisis, and one that will have long-term effects on economic restructuring, is investment in human capital. Support for vocational training in particular will increase the quality of the labour force and jobs. The measures taken by the Government and employers will have both short- and long-term effects on economic development.

During the recession, the Government continued to implement training programmes launched in previous years and introduced new ones, but the budgetary restrictions imposed sharply reduced the coverage of these programmes. The number of unemployed who started vocational training declined by 16,053 (about threefold) in the period 2008–2009. A further reduction is expected in 2010. The number of unemployed participants in training has declined by 6,934 in 2010 compared to 2009, a 79 per cent fall. This considerable contraction of vocational training coverage suggests that the Government's restrictive budgetary policy does not provide sufficient support for those who have lost their jobs and require re-qualification.

The willingness of particular unemployed groups to participate in training programmes did not change during the recession. Traditionally, young people (up to 29 years of age) make up the highest proportion of participants. They account for 30.8 per cent (2,670 persons) of the total number of training participants. Older unemployed people (above 50 years of age) also show high interest in vocational training. Compared to 2008, their share has increased by 3.2 percentage points to 24.1 per cent. This shows that both risk groups among the unemployed participate strongly in training.

The situation is particularly unfavourable with regard to the educational level of participants in training courses. Low-skilled unemployed persons are poorly represented in training programmes, due to a lack of interest. The proportion of unemployed persons with a primary and lower education participating in training in 2009 was the smallest (15.8 per cent) compared to higher skilled groups, despite the fact that it increased by 3.6 percentage points in relation to 2008. Next come people with a lower secondary education (16.4 per cent). Nearly one-fifth (19.7 per cent) of participants have higher education. Their share increased by 4.1 percentage points during the recession. It seems that inequality with regard to training increased in relation to educational level.

Depending on the type of training course the expected effects might emerge in the near or distant future. Training courses that offer new professions or new skills will have long-term effects. Most of the courses offered to the unemployed have such a character. The other type of training is aimed at upgrading existing skills (accounting, basic computer skills, information technology and so on). Such courses have short-term effects.

A particular problem facing vocational training in Bulgaria is its relatively low coverage at company level. A study of lifelong learning (Atanasova 2010) shows that about 30 per cent of the enterprises offered vocational training in 2007. During the recession, this share probably decreased due to the limited financial resources of the firms, as shown by the case studies. Only a relatively small proportion of enterprises (in construction, trade, transport and manufacturing) organized training (between 25 and 35 per cent). In other sectors (finance, mining and electricity) about 50–70 per cent of the firms offered vocational training. Inequalities in training also appeared between small/medium-sized and large enterprises. Small and medium-sized firms have been found to conduct training only rarely.

6.5   Social Dialogue – Reinforced During the Crisis

The negative effects of the recession on the economy and the need to take adequate anti-crisis measures to overcome them strengthened social dialogue at all levels. Depending on a given level's degree of competence a number of different issues were discussed, in particular, dismissals, wage adjustment, short-time working and unpaid leave.

National social dialogue has traditionally discussed the issues of national minimum wage fixing, minimum insurance thresholds and other industrial relations issues of national scope. Besides these traditional issues, the National Council for Tripartite Cooperation (NCTC) discussed measures initiated by the social partners to combat the impact of the severe economic crisis. In September 2009, the NCTC accepted 32 anti-crisis measures, including a national information system for job search, an increase in the maximum payment to which workers are entitled in the case of enterprise bankruptcy, the creation of mechanisms and procedures to accelerate the reintroduction of VAT, reducing corporate debt and so on. The trade unions accepted these measures, but expressed their disappointment at the rejection of their proposed precautionary measures with regard to the incomes of employees and the unemployed (increase the minimum wage and unemployment benefits, introduce a tax free minimum income and so on).

In March and April 2010, the new round of negotiations discussed 64 measures proposed by the Government. The social partners reached an agreement on four groups of measures in support of fiscal policy; (i) limitation of public expenditure and recovery of financial discipline; (ii) ensuring additional financial resources; (iii) supporting household incomes and domestic demand; and (iv) measures to support the labour market and the social insurance system.

Social dialogue at national level also covers measures related to changes in labour and insurance legislation, the pension system, untaken paid leave and patient's charters. In May 2010, the NCTC approved the changes in the state budget for 2010. All these activities of the National Council for Tripartite Cooperation suggests an increasing role for national social dialogue in solving the problems emerging from the crisis.

Social dialogue at branch and firm level has also become stronger in response to the crisis. Many new collective agreements have been signed that reflect the new circumstances. Efforts are being directed towards reaching agreement on employment, wages and working time, among other things.

7. CASE STUDIES: DIFFERENT CRISIS ADJUSTMENTS AND DIFFERENT IMPACTS ON WORKING CONDITIONS AND INEQUALITIES

The sectors most affected by the crisis are manufacturing and construction. For this reason, the case studies focused on enterprises from these sectors. The effects of the crisis on working conditions varied substantially between companies. Firms producing for export were hardest hit. Depending on the economic situation and management objectives workers in some companies faced multiple negative effects, while in others the workers were less affected. The aim of the case studies was to analyse the impact of the crisis on working conditions and work inequalities at enterprise level and to discover the extent to which our earlier conclusions are supported by the facts.

The case study covered three enterprises from different branches: chemicals, clothing manufacturing and construction (industrial buildings). For the sake of comparison, we chose both large and smaller and medium-sized enterprises, and both with and without trade unions. Table 3.8 (overleaf) summarizes the main features of the companies and their main adjustment mechanisms in the crisis, which obviously led to a differentiated impact on both working conditions and work inequalities.

Table 3.8   Main characteristics of case-study companies

	Case 1: Sviloza	Case 2: FFCP	Case 3: Robsov
Sector	Chemicals	Construction	Manufacturing
Employment	540	228	135
Employment reduction in the crisis	50 employees or 9%	78 employees or 34%	75 employees or 44%
Main form of adjustment	Wages: basic wage cuts Bonus cuts Working time reduction	Employment: strong reductions	Employment: employment reduction Wages: basic wage cuts by 44% Bonus cuts Working time reduction Shift from permanent to temporary contracts
Main advantages in terms of inequalities	No lay-offs, so no inequality in employment	No wage cuts and no wage inequality	No advantages in terms of inequality
Main drawbacks interms of inequalities	Severe wage cuts led to declining purchasing power; trade unions helped to make time and wage cuts equal for all	Negative effects of a restrictive budgetary policy on employment	Deterioration of all working conditions led to higher inequality; absence of social dialogue impeded any possible negotiated trade-offs

7.1   Case Study 1: Marked Wage Decline in Chemical Company

7.1.1   High output contraction during recession

'Sviloza' is a private joint-stock company in the chemical industry and consists of four holdings. The basic enterprise is 'Svilocell' producing cellulose and carboxymethyl cellulose for the paper industry. The firm also produces viscose silk and wood briquettes. Svilocell is the only producer of these products in Bulgaria and the Balkans. There has been considerable investment in technological modernization. Nearly 95 per cent of production is exported, to a number of EU countries (including Germany, Italy, Greece and Austria).

The world economic crisis hit the company hard. The world prices of cellulose collapsed dramatically (by nearly 50 per cent) and, at the same time, the prices of wood pulp rose in Bulgaria. As a result, sales in the Bulgarian market fell and exports stalled. In the face of this severe deterioration in economic conditions Svilocell slowed down production in February–December 2009.

7.1.2 Modest effect on employment: a key priority in the firm

Sviloza is a large company. The total number of employees was 540 in 2008. The number of temporary workers was negligible (below 10). All employees worked full-time. There were no part-time or seasonal workers. The age structure of the personnel was favourable because nearly 25 per cent of all workers were under 35 years of age. The educational attainment of employees was also fairly good: about 14 per cent of workers had a higher education, 81 per cent had a secondary or specialized secondary education and only 5 per cent were low-skilled workers. The total number of workers decreased only slightly during the recession (by about 50 employees or 9 per cent), compared to 2008. The main management objective was to preserve employment and particularly that of skilled employees. Most of those dismissed were low-skilled workers in services. During the recession the other employment conditions (type of contracts) did not change. There were no cases of transition from permanent to temporary contracts and also there were no shifts from full-time to part-time. The employment structure also remained stable by education and age. In general, the workers experienced only a modest negative impact on employment.

7.1.3 Considerable wage reductions

The firm's deteriorating economic situation led to a marked reduction in wages. The employer did not disclose the firm's wage levels and the change in the average wage (due to confidentiality), but did comment that the wage reduction had been significant. All workers received much lower wages than in the pre-recession period. This concerns not only the basic wage but also additional payments, such as bonuses.

During the period of short-time working, all employees received compensation not exceeding 120 BGN (60 euros) per month. Individual compensation was calculated on the basis of hours worked and did not affect wage disparity in the firm. Also, the sharp reduction in all wages during the recession did not significantly influence inequality, which remains almost unchanged. The minimum wage in the firm (290 BGN or 145 euros) was 20 per cent above the national level and did not change during 2009.

7.1.4 Mixed effects on other working conditions

Reduction of working time The other negative effect on working conditions was the temporary reduction of working time. All workers, including executives, worked a four-hour day during April–July 2009. This short-time working was compensated by the Government under the abovementioned compensation scheme. Reducing working time in the firm had a positive effect on employment: relatively few workers were dismissed. To protect employment, the management also made it possible for workers to take unpaid leave. About 50 workers did so, some of them taking up secondary employment elsewhere.

Maintenance of health and safety Investment in technology during the period 2005–2008 improved job quality considerably. Most technological processes were automated and this created healthier and safer working conditions. Besides this, spending on maintaining health and safety remained unchanged.

Reduction of expenditure on training The firm, however, reduced expenditure on training. Only a limited number of workers attained further qualifications in 2009. The requirements of the newly introduced technological processes for qualified workers were met in the years before the recession.

7.1.5 Strengthening social dialogue in the firm
There are two trade union organizations in the firm: the Confederation of Independent Trade Unions of Bulgaria (CITUB) and CL 'Podkrepa'. Both organizations evaluated social dialogue in the firm positively. During 2009, there were negotiations on employment, wages, working time and maintaining social benefits, among other things. The agreements reached aimed at preserving employment in the firm, shifting to short-time working, use of unpaid leave and cutting wages, while maintaining all social benefits. The trade unions agreed that the firm's priority task was to save employment.

The trade unions expressed satisfaction that social benefits were not reduced. Workers were given additional paid leave (five days), monthly food vouchers, free food and transport to the workplace. Free medical services, provided by the employer, continued despite the difficult economic situation in the firm during the crisis.

7.1.6 Concluding remarks
The case study illustrates the different ways in which the crisis influenced working conditions in the firm. Most affected were wages, working

time and training, while employment, types of contract and social benefits fared better. Social dialogue in the enterprise was strengthened and helped, in fact, to avoid large employment adjustments, while preventing serious deterioration of working conditions, although wages were used as the main adjustment variable. Workers participated in negotiations on working conditions. This enterprise is a good example of a strong trade-off between employment and wages. To maintain employment, wages were reduced sharply. This made it possible to retain qualified technological staff in the hope of better times to come.

7.2 Case Study 2: Considerable Reduction of Employment in a Construction Firm

7.2.1 Why the construction sector?

Construction has been hit hard by the crisis. Industrial building and house building were affected to different extents. Firms oriented towards house building after the rapid development of the past few years faced a sharp decrease in demand and production in 2009. In contrast, enterprises specializing in industrial buildings suffered from low demand during the entire period of transition and firms were constantly under pressure to restructure. The chosen firm belongs to this category.

7.2.2 Dramatic shrinkage of output

The Factory for Ferroconcrete Constructions and Products (FFCP) is one of the best known firms in construction. It was founded in 1961 and has undergone significant changes in production and technology. Starting with the production of ferroconcrete traverses for railways the company's product range widened over the years and the firm is now able to produce all ferroconcrete elements for industrial buildings. FFCP was privatized in 1999.

Before and during the recession the firm limited its range to two groups of products: first, ferroconcrete traverses for overground and underground railways, and second, ferroconcrete poles for electro transmission networks. All production is directed towards the domestic market where the company enjoys a monopolistic position.

During the recession output fell significantly. Sales and production of ferroconcrete traverses ceased, while the production of ferroconcrete poles declined strongly. The enterprise now produces mainly marginal products (elements for road and railway building).

7.2.3 Restrictive budgetary policy further worsened economic activity

As a construction firm FFCP is heavily dependent on public contracts. Most orders are from the Government and concern large construction projects (electrification of the railways, building of the metro in Sofia and so on). The Government appears to be the main source of the firm's revenues. During the recession, the financial situation worsened significantly because the Government postponed (in practical terms, halted) all payments. In this way, the restrictive budgetary policy directly harmed the enterprise.

7.2.4 Considerable negative effect on employment

The FFCP is a medium-sized enterprise. All workers are employed on permanent and full-time contracts. There are no workers on flexible contracts (fixed-term, seasonal or part-time workers). The educational structure of the workforce is normally distributed. Most have completed a secondary education. A relatively small part (17 per cent) are low-skilled.

Employment in the firm started to decline much earlier than the advent of the recession that started in Bulgaria in early 2009. The number of employees fell by 7.9 per cent in 2008 (from 228 workers in 2007 to 210 persons in 2009). In 2009, the firm dismissed about 60 workers (29 per cent), which means that the workforce now numbers 150. Most of the workers made redundant were low-skilled and engaged in auxiliary activities.

According to the employer, this was the only solution in the current situation. Output had fallen dramatically (traverse production had practically ceased) and thus the firm could not use these workers. There is no short-term prospect of production resuming.

7.2.5 No changes in wages and other working conditions

The substantial reduction in employment made it possible to maintain the wages of those remaining at the pre-recession level. The minimum and average wages in the firm are above the respective national levels. Also, there was no change in wage disparity.

In these circumstances, the firm has not used flexible forms of employment. Working time remains unchanged; labour contracts remain as they were; unpaid leave has not been resorted to.

The firm's policy in relation to training and qualifications remained encouraging, even in the recession. The technical staff are obliged to take periodical training courses and the firm provides the necessity resources. Spending on health and safety has been maintained. In addition, the firm provides medical services.

7.2.6 Concluding remarks

This case study presents a limited number of negative effects on working conditions. The substantial reduction in employment to some extent limited the deterioration of other working conditions. The particular conditions in the construction sector forced the management to dismiss surplus workers. This case study also shows the negative effects of a restrictive budgetary policy on the business climate. Non-payment of government liabilities for public orders has further worsened the economic situation in many supply firms.

7.3 Case Study 3: Deterioration of all Working Conditions in Clothing Company

Textiles and clothing was found to be one of the branches of manufacturing hardest hit by the crisis. Production is strongly connected with international markets. The effects of the crisis in this sector have been mainly negative with regard to employment, wages and all other working conditions. Typical in this respect is the company 'Robsov Ltd', a medium-sized private company.

7.3.1 Strong decline in output
Production is mainly for export. The company works with materials supplied by foreign clients and depends on commissions from abroad. For this reason, the effects of the world crisis on the firm's output showed up earlier than in the country as a whole. During the recession the firm lost a significant part of its foreign markets and output contracted by around 60 per cent. In addition, the company faced problems with financing because credit conditions in Bulgaria deteriorated. This situation negatively affected working conditions in the firm.

7.3.2 Strong negative effect on employment and wages
The total number of employees in 2008 was 135 workers. Most were on permanent contracts (80 per cent) and the rest on temporary contracts. New workers are engaged on temporary contracts with a duration of six months. All work full-time. In relation to educational status, most workers have completed secondary and elementary education. The company experienced shortages of qualified staff both before and during the recession.

The negative impact of the recession on employment has been proportionate to the fall in output. From the beginning of 2009, employment started to decline, falling as low as 75 workers in the most difficult period. Over a period of a few months the number of employees decreased by over 44 per cent. Most of those dismissed were low-skilled workers.

Wages decreased for all categories of workers. In comparison to the pre-recession period, the average wage in the firm declined by 44.4 per cent (from 450 BGN in 2008 to 250 BGN in 2009). In this period, the starting wage in the company also declined due to part-time work (from 240 to 150 BGN). Changes appeared in the wage structure. All additional payments, such as bonuses, were also cut.

7.3.3   Deterioration of other working conditions

To save the remaining part of the workforce the company used flexible working time and unpaid leave. In the period January–June 2009, all workers shifted to short-time working (four hours a day) and received wage compensation. The management also encouraged low-skilled workers to take unpaid leave, up to a maximum of 45 days. According to the management, all these measures could not prevent employment and wage reductions.

Although the problem of low qualifications persists, the management did not make any attempt to solve it. Spending on training and recruitment was cut. Health and safety provisions were at the required minimum because the available resources had been reduced.

7.3.4   Concluding remarks

The case study show that firms hardest hit by the crisis have generally allowed working conditions to deteriorate. Workers in this clothing company suffered from multiple negative effects due to the crisis. There were no trade-off effects between working conditions. The absence of social dialogue impeded any possible negotiated trade-offs. All working conditions deteriorated to different extents and this brought with it greater inequality.

8.   CONCLUSIONS

The research presented here illustrates a number of key issues in Bulgaria's experience of the crisis and its impact on labour market inequalities. A substantial decline in total output worsened working conditions. The unequal distribution of negative production effects by sector and enterprise caused the emergence of inequality in employment, unemployment, wages and other working conditions. The other source of inequality in the labour market has been the restrictive budgetary policy. Imposing restrictions on public expenditure (including public sector wages) has multiple effects on the augmentation of inequality in employment, unemployment and wages. With limited resources, the firms were forced to reduce employment or cut wages, generally both.

The deterioration in labour market conditions concerns all key indicators. Employees in manufacturing and construction faced the highest risk of job losses during the recession. The restrictive government policy also put workers in administration, health and education at risk. The crisis has provoked raising inequality among workers in accordance with educational and occupational levels: higher skilled employees and professionals have been less affected by the recession, while elementary occupations and low-skilled workers have been hard hit and form a particularly disadvantaged group of the unemployed.

Young people also represent a particular risk group in the Bulgarian labour market. Their share in employment is relatively small and their share of unemployment is correspondingly high. The measures taken by the Government in the pre-recession years significantly improved their situation in the labour market, but the crisis halted this positive trend. The recession hit youth employment and unemployment hard. The Government's programmes appear to have been ineffective in counteracting the crisis.

The effects of the crisis on wage dynamics and inequality are more modest. The evidence suggests positive dynamics in nominal and real terms, but at low rates. This positive growth of wages is compensated by employment decline. The case studies identified a strong trade-off between employment and wages, particularly in the hardest hit branches (manufacturing and construction). Wage inequality among economic sectors and type of ownership has also changed. The data show a process of wage equalization during the recession. The equalization effect is also revealed with regard to household incomes, but to a much lower extent.

Adaptation to the crisis correlates strongly with the worsening of other working conditions. Most companies used short-time working, not always with compensation. Moreover, the reduction of working time has not been distributed equally across economic sectors. It is not surprising that higher reductions are observed in the most affected sectors. Also, many firms are not able to ensure health and safety conditions in accordance with the relevant standards. Vocational training has been severely limited at both national and company level. The Government has reduced the resources made available for training despite the obvious need for the re-qualification of the unemployed (a situation worsened by the qualification structure of the crisis).

In contrast to working conditions, the crisis has had a positive impact on social dialogue, which has been strengthened at all levels. At national level, the anti-crisis measures applied to reduce the negative effects of the crisis were discussed and consensus was reached. Social dialogue at branch and firm level was also strengthened in response to the crisis.

Government policy in response to the crisis includes a package of measures related to different parts of the economy. Most are aimed at reducing the budget deficit and thus have a restrictive character. Their effects on the labour market and inequality in many cases have a twofold character. Freezing the minimum wage has increased wage inequality between workers on the minimum wage and other workers. On the other hand, freezing wages in the public sector has reduced wage inequality in relation to the private sector. The reduction of public spending and the postponement of government payments to firms with government contracts have contributed to a deterioration in working conditions in all organizations and firms dependent on the budget. In general, the restrictive public policy as a response to the crisis has generated more inequality in the labour market rather than solving the problems.

NOTES

1. The number of employees declined by 3.7 per cent and that of the self-employed by 0.7 per cent.
2. Calculated as the percentage difference between average gross earnings in the public and private sectors.

BIBLIOGRAPHY

Atanasova, M. (2010) 'Complex lifelong learning strategy on the Bulgarian path to flexicurity and segmentation in the labour market', in *Flexicurity in the Labour Market in Bulgaria – Situation and Prospects*, MLSP, pp. 40–63.
Beleva, I. (2010) 'Flexicurity in labour relations (labour agreements and working time arrangements) and risk segments', in *Flexicurity in the Labour Market in Bulgaria – Situation and Prospects*, MLSP, pp. 5–39.
Beleva, I. and V. Tzanov (2006) 'Bulgaria: towards a better balanced world of work?" in F. Eyraud and D. Vaughan-Whitehead (eds), *Evolving World of Work in the Enlarged EU. Progress and Vulnerability*, ILO, pp. 53–90.
Ministry of Labour and Social Policy (MLSP) (2008 and 2009) *Annual Report*, Safia.
Tzanov, V. (2010a) 'Bulgaria: A shift in minimum wage policy', in D. Vaughan-Whitehead (ed.), *The Minimum Wage Revisited in the Enlarged EU*, Cheltenham, UK and Northampton, MA, USA: Edward Elgar Geneva: ILO, pp. 57–84.
Tzanov, V. (2010b) 'Social protection and security on the labour market', in *Flexicurity in the Labour Market in Bulgaria – Situation and Prospects*, MLSP, pp. 93–112.

4. Croatia: Prolonged crisis with an uncertain ending

Vojmir Franičević

1. INTRODUCTION: 2008–2010 – LEAVING THE PATH OF GROWTH[1]

After a 'difficult' 1990s, the period 2000–2008 saw improvements in many economic and social indicators, but a number of important 'hard realities' remained (Franičević 2007a). A deep recession had set in by the second half of 2008, with no clear prospect of coming to an end. Underlying these cyclical phenomena are a number of structural issues and institutional deficits, but also the need to meet the conditions for EU accession.

The economy overall presented an attractive picture: high growth; increased investment, consumption and FDI; price and exchange rate stability; moderate fiscal consolidation; and increasing international reserves. However, increasing trade and current account deficits, heightening the country's external vulnerability with growing foreign debt will be major limiting factors. External vulnerability was not limited to the state alone, however: 'at the end of 2008, around 90 per cent of total corporate debt and about 70 per cent of household debt was external or foreign currency denominated' (World Bank 2009). Widespread corruption, a weak judiciary and low capacity for reform will be major barriers to timely reforms, but also to speedier EU accession. Table 4.1 illustrates some basic macroeconomic trends of the period.

The impact of the global recession in 2008 was stronger and more durable than expected. Throughout South East Europe during the first half of 2008 'there was a feeling that SEE would be able to escape the worst of the contagion from the crisis' (Sanfey 2010: 2). However, in 2009 the economy entered full recession. All components of GDP turned negative, except government spending, which continued to grow, leading to emergency government measures in summer 2009 and a series of budget revisions. Particularly hard hit were industry, construction, trade, hotels and restaurants and transportation.

GDP forecasts for 2010 have had to be revised downwards: to between

Table 4.1 Selected macroeconomic indicators, Croatia, 2000–2010

	2000	2001	2002	2003	2004	2005	2006	2007	2008	2009	2010 (to July)
GDP growth, real %	3.0	3.8	5.4	5.0	4.2	4.2	4.7	5.5	2.4	−5.8	−2.5
Private consumption, real, year-on-year %	3.6	4.9	8.3	4.8	4.3	4.4	3.5	6.2	0.8	−8.5	−3.3
Public consumption real, year-on-year %	−1.7	−6.5	4.4	1.3	2.6	1.2	2.2	3.4	1.9	0.2	−1.5
Fixed investment real, year-on-year %	−3.8	7.1	13.9	24.7	5.0	4.9	10.9	6.5	8.2	−11.8	−13.6
Industrial production growth rate	1.7	6.0	5.4	4.1	3.7	5.1	4.5	5.6	1.6	−9.2	−2.0
Retail trade growth rate	14.4	10.0	12.5	3.7	2.6	2.8	2.1	5.3	−0.5	−15.3	−5.4
Construction volume growth rate	−9.1	3.6	12.8	22.8	2.0	−0.8	9.3	2.4	11.8	−6.5	−17.8
Registered unemployment rate	21.1	22.0	22.3	19.1	18.0	17.9	16.6	14.9	13.2	14.9	17.7
LFS unemployment rate	16.1	15.8	14.8	14.3	13.8	12.7	11.1	9.6	8.4	9.1	11.8
Real wage, gross, year-on-year %	1.6	−0.8	4.1	2.6	4.2	1.1	2.9	3.2	0.9	−0.2	−1.7
Consolidated general government deficit, % of GDP	−6.5	−5.9	−4.3	−5.4	−4.2	−3.5	−2.6	−2.0	−1.8	−4.1	−2.2
Public debt, % of GDP	34.5	35.5	34.9	35.7	37.9	38.5	36.0	33.4	29.3	34.8	37.0
Current account deficit, % of GDP	−2.5	−3.2	−7.5	−6.3	−4.4	−5.5	−6.9	−7.6	−9.2	−5.2	−7.6
Foreign debt, % of GDP	53.0	53.3	53.9	66.3	70.0	72.1	74.9	76.9	82.6	98.3	97.9

Sources: Croatian Bureau of Statistics (CBS), Croatian National Bank (CNB), Ministry of Finance.

–1.5 and –2.0 per cent. The sustainability of the public finances may come into question, with a major impact on public sector employees, farmers receiving subsidies, pensioners and others dependent on social welfare.

2.   IMPACT OF THE CRISIS

2.1   Labour Market Conditions Prior to the Crisis

The 2000s brought increasing employment and falling unemployment. But beneath the favourable trends, a number of shortcomings have remained. First, activity/employment rates remained comparatively low. Both rates have fallen, but unemployment increased in 2009 and Q1–Q2/2010, particularly for males, due to the differential sectoral impact of the crisis (Table 4.2).

Second, inactivity and dependency remained high. In the presence of high inactivity (in 2009 it increased by 2.5 per cent, and the increase continued in 2010), a further lowering of activity/employment rates increases pressure on the pension system and the budget (in 2009, only 56 per cent of revenues were from social insurance contributions) (Bađun 2010). The number of pensioners is increasing, while the number of contributors is falling. The ratio between insured persons and pensioners fell from a low 1.40 in 2006–2008 to 1.30 in 2009 and 1.27 in June 2010 (Croatian Social Insurance Institute data). The low share of average pensions in average net wages (40 per cent in 2009) will be hard to sustain. However, firms' adaptation and restructuring, and the Government's intention of increasing 'penalization' for early retirement and extending the female retirement age encouraged earlier retirement: in 2009, early retirement increased by 20 per cent, and in January–June 2010 by 76 per cent (annual) (ibid.).

Third, long-term unemployment rates (5.3 per cent in 2008; 5.2 per cent in 2009) are much higher than the EU25 average. Increased inflows to unemployment have reduced the share of long-term unemployment, particularly for males (Figure 4.1). However, males' share in long-term unemployment increased from 35.7 in 2008 to 36.5 in 2009 and 38.1 per cent in 2010 (March, Croatian Employment Service – CES – data). Nevertheless, a recovery in employment should not be expected before 2012, particularly among older workers, making some people unemployable.

Fourth, the functioning of the labour market has been leading to flexibilization 'at the margin' – with a protected 'core' of workers on permanent contracts and those at the margin relegated to the unofficial economy or temporary employment and vulnerable to numerous risks (Franičević 2007a). The available data, the case studies presented below and trade

Table 4.2 Employment and unemployment, Croatia, 2007–2010 (quarterly data)

	2007				2008				2009				2010	
	Q1	Q2	Q3	Q4	Q1	Q2	Q3	Q4	Q1	Q2	Q3	Q4	Q1	Q2
GDP growth	7.0	6.7	4.8	3.5	4.3	3.4	1.6	0.2	-6.7	-6.3	-5.7	-4.4	-2.5	-2.5
Employment total (registered)	1480	1519	1544	1524	1524	1561	1580	1555	1512	1511	1507	1464	1420	1425
Employment (LFS, thousands)	1563	1609	1661	1625	1591	1638	1681	1633	1608	1611	1608	1594	1563	1534
Employment rate, LFS, 15–64	55.2	56.7	58.8	57.4	56.0	57.6	59.7	57.8	56.5	56.5	57.0	56.4	54.9	53.5
Unemployment (registered, thousands)	297	264	245	252	259	233	220	234	261	257	253	283	316	297
Unemployment (LFS, thousands)	197	162	151	174	176	140	126	155	167	157	153	162	197	216
Unemployment rate, LFS 15–64	11.4	9.3	8.6	9.9	10.2	8.1	7.1	9.0	9.7	9.1	8.9	9.6	11.5	12.7
– males	9.5	8.5	7.5	8.4	8.6	6.8	6.0	7.2	8.0	8.3	8.5	8.2	10.8	12.4
– females	13.7	10.4	9.9	11.8	12.1	9.7	8.6	11.1	11.8	10.1	9.4	11.2	12.4	13.1
Unemployment rate, registered	16.7	14.8	13.7	14.2	14.5	13.0	12.3	13.1	14.7	14.5	14.4	16.2	18.2	17.2
– males	12.5	10.9	10.0	10.4	10.7	9.3	8.7	9.3	10.9	11.0	11.3	13.1	15.5	14.9
– females	21.3	19.1	17.7	18.4	18.8	17.1	16.2	17.3	19.0	18.4	17.8	19.6	21.2	19.9

Source: CBS.

146

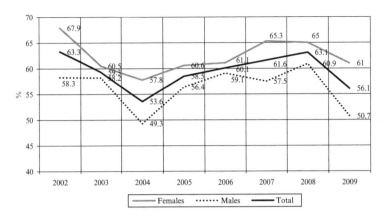

Source: LFS.

Figure 4.1 *Long-term unemployment shares by gender, Croatia, 2002–2009*

union evidence point to a particularly precarious position for temporary workers. They are the first to suffer from employment cuts. Flexibility at the margin, affecting young people in particular, is likely to intensify, as evidenced by an increase in the share of temporary contracts in new registered employment.

There was an end to positive labour market developments in 2009. A closer look shows significant unevenness and inequalities with regard to labour market outcomes (Section 2.2) and working conditions (Section 2.3).

2.2 The Period 2007–2010 in More Detail

Table 4.2 illustrates the trend of falling GDP coupled with falling employment, falling employment rates, increasing unemployment and unemployment rates by the end of 2008. To date, males have been hit harder than females and the private sector harder than the public sector. The gap between LFS and administrative unemployment rates, particularly in 2009Q4 and 2010Q1, may be indicative of relative growth in the informal economy, but also of discouragement. In the period 2008–2010, total administrative employment decreased by −7.8 per cent, while according to the LFS it fell by −4.0 per cent. The gap between administrative and LFS employment, after decreasing in 2008 by −16.8 per cent, increased in 2009 by 36.5 per cent and in 2010 by 28.6 per cent (first halves of years

Table 4.3   *Employed persons according to employment status, Croatia,*
             2008–2010 (%)

	Annual change (%)	
	2009/ 2008	2010 1st/ 2009 1st
All employed	–1.9	–3.8
Employers	–8.0	–6.5
Self-employed without employees	0.0	–0.4
Helping family members	3.5	5.2
Private sector – employees	–1.5	–7.0
State sector – employees	–2.5	–0.4

Source: CBS–LFS.

compared). The strong increase in the number of 'helping family members'
(Table 4.3) also points to that effect. However, due to the high margin of
statistical error, no firm conclusion on informality increase can be drawn,
and the relevant research is lacking.

Substantial job losses in an economy suffering from low job creation is
worrisome. When comparing 2009Q4 (administrative data) with 2008Q4,
and then 2010Q2 with 2008Q4, those mainly affected were legal entities
(by 5.3 per cent and 7.8 per cent, respectively), crafts and free trades (8.0
per cent and 10.3 per cent) and insured farmers (7.8 and 12.2 per cent).
Employment losses were particularly high in some sectors: December
2008/2009 job losses were as follows: manufacturing, –10.9 per cent; trade,
–8.2 per cent; and construction, –7.3 per cent. It was much worse in the
private sector (Table 4.3). Lower or no loss of employment in the public
sector will become a major public issue.

Self-employment has also been affected. This is indicated by data on
crafts, professions and farmers, as well as by LFS data on employment
status, showing a strong increase in 'helping family members' and a fairly
stable number of self-employed persons without employees, but a strong
decrease in employers. Some craft businesses closed down, but continued
informally (Chamber of Crafts expert).

2.2.1   Unemployment – many workers at risk

The increase in unemployment inflows in 2009 was considerable (35.2 per
cent or 70,464), primarily fed by the previously employed (43 per cent
increase) and to a lesser extent by first job seekers (10.8 per cent increase).

Average registered unemployment increased in 2009 by 11.2 per cent.

2010Q1 brought a further increase in monthly inflows, with the unemployment rate peaking. However, due to strong seasonal effects, in 2010Q2 and 2010Q3 unemployment rate decreased. Nevertheless, with the end of the tourist season in September, unemployment growth resumed. It is expected that the unemployment peak will be reached in February/March 2011, with 330,000 registered unemployed and 19 per cent unemployment rate (CEOQ 2010: 44).

Men have been harder hit than women. Average 2009 unemployment increased by 19.6 per cent for males and 6.0 per cent for females. In December 2009 compared to December 2008, unemployment increased by 39.6 per cent for males and 10.2 per cent for females. The gender structure of unemployed has changed: from 61.8 per cent (2007) and 62.5 per cent (2008), females' share fell to 56.5 per cent 2009 (year end); in 2010 it was 54.8 per cent (for January–August) (CES data). This reflects sectoral trends in unemployment, but this may change due to pressure to reform the public sector, which is widely considered to be bloated, which may affect females disproportionally.

Those below 34 years of age have also been hit hardest. Annual averages show that all groups below 34 years of age increased in 2009 by more than 11.2 per cent (that is, total increase); all age groups between 35 and 59 increased by 2.5 per cent to 10.6 per cent, but 60+ year-olds by 13.5 per cent. Older males in particular were hit hard by recession cutbacks (see case studies). Males' share in 50+ registered unemployment increased from 47.7 per cent by 2008 to 50.3 by 2009, and to 52 per cent by June 2010. In 2007, 2008 and 2009, there was a strong increase in the number of workers affected by collective dismissals registered with the CES: 1,504, 2,642 and 6,199, respectively. This affects mainly older workers: 39.2 per cent are 50–59 years of age and 24.0 per cent are between 40 and 49, mostly from male-dominated sectors (manufacturing, transportation) (CES 2010a). Many will end up as long-term unemployed, followed by retirement on low pensions.

All educational groups suffered in 2009 from a strong increase in unemployment inflows of between 29 and 38 per cent (between 36.7 and 45.5 per cent for those previously employed). However, absolute numbers, and consequently shares, are still much lower for those with a higher education. Among those without previous experience unemployment increased strongly also among those with higher (non-university or university) qualifications – by 29.4 and 22.8 per cent, respectively – which points to increased difficulties in finding jobs for those with a higher education (Matković 2010).

The recession has strongly affected workers on temporary contracts but increasingly those on permanent contracts, too. The share of newly

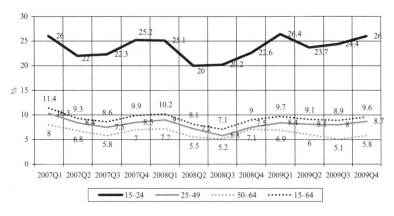

Source: CES.

Figure 4.2   Unemployment rates by age, Croatia, 2007–2009

registered unemployed from employment increased from 60.6 per cent in 2007 to 64.7 per cent in 2008 and to 69.9 per cent in 2009: that is, by 46.2 per cent in 2008/2009. Data on reasons for employment termination show that those on temporary contracts bear the heaviest burden (in 2008, 46.2 per cent and in 2009, 43.0 per cent of all those newly registered as unemployed). However, the entry into unemployment of those previously employed on permanent contracts doubled, increasing their share from 17.5 per cent to 26.5 per cent. As the crisis deepened, firms had to cut permanent positions, too.

Age differences point to the influence of the 'last in, first out' (seniority) principle on the relative risk of unemployment. Younger people are more likely to lose their jobs. Younger workers predominate among the new unemployed (Figure 4.2). Out of 263,000 unemployed in 2009 (annual average, registered), 30.6 per cent are 15–29 years of age. The LFS 2009 unemployment rate for 15–24 year-olds increased to 25.1 per cent from 22.0 per cent in 2008 – that is, by 14.1 per cent. Even when young people are employed, they tend to end up on temporary contracts: their share in total temporary employment in the 15–59 age group for 2007–2009 was 30.8 per cent, 31.3 per cent and 29.5 per cent, respectively, far above their share in total employment for the same age group, which is 10.2 per cent, 10.3 per cent and 10.1 per cent, respectively (CBS, Croatia–Europe Statistical Reports). The precarious position of young people is a typical feature of the Croatian labour market.

However, in the second half of 2009 the situation of the 25–49 group also clearly deteriorated. The crisis penetrated to the very 'core' of the workforce. The proportions of men and blue-collar workers 'becoming unemployed increased by some 5 percentage points'; 'a newly unemployed person is more likely to be a prime-age skilled blue-collar male worker' (World Bank 2010: 8; Matković 2010). This is putting an increasing number of households at a higher risk of poverty because 'the crisis disproportionally hit primary earners (prime-age men) who are likely to be household heads', which differs from the pre-crisis period when 'predominantly secondary earners (youth, women) . . . bore the brunt of labour market adjustment' (World Bank 2010: 24, 38). A simulation (based on absolute poverty line and HBS data) points to a 'new poor' who are 'predominantly persons who lost their jobs in the wake of the crisis' (World Bank 2010: 36).

The study argues that for the 'new poor' their condition is likely to be difficult, but 'transitory'; once job prospects improve they stand a better chance of re-employment (being younger and better educated) (ibid.: 9). However, with a delay in the recovery of the Croatian economy many may end up in long-term unemployment and find the transition back to work very difficult indeed; jobs in some sectors may not be recovered at all (for example, construction, textiles and ship-building).

The seniority principle is also in operation. Particularly in firms where the crisis is used as an opportunity to restructure the workforce, older workers are very vulnerable (see case studies). For older workers, however, vulnerability to poverty is much higher as age discrimination is the most widespread type of discrimination faced by the unemployed (Franc et al. 2010).

Job opportunities have been reduced considerably. With the unemployment/vacancies ratio increasing from 1.41 in 2008 to 2.64 in 2009 (due to seasonality it was 1.76 in 2010Q2, but 3.37 in 2010Q3) (CES data), for most unemployed persons, the chances of finding a job are slim. Even when an opening is available, it is increasingly temporary in nature (Figure 4.3).

Demand is not only much weaker, but more uncertain. With falling GDP in 2010, a recovery of employment hardly can be expected to start before 2012, with substantial consequences for job-seekers and households. This is strongly reflected in the 2010 European Working Conditions Survey, in which Croatian workers perceive a much higher job loss risk than in the EU15/EU27, but much lower chances of finding a comparable job (Table 4.4).

Importantly, manual workers perceive a higher than average job loss risk, combined with lower than average chances of finding a comparable job. The same is true for industry workers if compared with services, for males when compared with females and for those under 30 and/or on

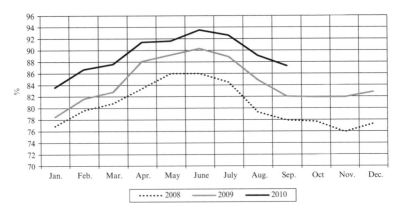

Source: CES, Monthly bulletins.

Figure 4.3   Share of employed (from the register) on temporary contracts, Croatia, 2008–2010

non-permanent contracts (however, they are less pessimistic concerning job finding, similar to the self-employed). On the other hand, some groups (50+, those on permanent contracts), while perceiving a lower than average risk of losing their job, are quite pessimistic about finding one. No doubt, the costs of losing one's job in Croatia are perceived as very high, with potentially profound but uncertain effects on changing working conditions and industrial relations.

3.   CHANGING WORKING CONDITIONS: COST CUTTING IN THE CENTRE

Employers have tended to focus their adaptation measures in response to the crisis on cost cutting. In a survey (non-representative; more than one answer was allowed) of 1,500 employees conducted in January 2010, 82 per cent reported that the crisis had taken its toll in the firm they work for, in the following ways: a freeze on new employment (52 per cent); wage reductions (43 per cent); cuts in training (38 per cent) and departmental (37 per cent) budgets; redundancies (35 per cent); a freeze on wages (34 per cent) and new projects (25 per cent); and closure (5 per cent).

Importantly, 'instead of focusing on growth, cost cutting will remain the main problem' and reorganization of the workforce in 2010 will become even more important as an anti-crisis measure (while true for 93 per cent of surveyed Croatian firms, it is much higher than in Western Europe and

Table 4.4   Job loss risk, Croatia, 2005–2010

	'I might lose my job in next 6 months' – agree	'I might lose my job in next 6 months' – agree	'If I were to lose or quit my job, it would be easy for me to find a job of similar salary' – disagree
	2005 (%)	2010 (%)	
Croatia total	19.3	26.7	61.6
High-skilled clerical	8.3	20.3	48.8
Low-skilled clerical	17.6	25.6	62.4
High-skilled manual	25.0	32.6	65.4
Low-skilled manual	23.6	29.0	67.9
Males	20.1	29.5	64.9
Females	18.6	23.2	59.9
Under 30	25.2	36.0	49.7
30–49	18.2	26.5	60.6
50+	17.7	21.8	72.0
Industry	23.2	29.5	60.2
Services	16.3	23.2	59.9
Permanent contracts	15.4	21.3	64.7
Other contracts	45.9	54.5	54.1
Self-employed	9.0	26.5	50.7
EU15	11.3	14.6	47.2
EU27	13.7	16.4	48.3

Source: http://www.eurofound.europa.eu/ewco/surveys/ewcs2010/results.htm.

CEE, where the figures are 43 per cent and 62 per cent of surveyed firms) (RolandBerger 2010).

In unionized firms, this often resulted in changes to collective agreements. Most of this was applied unevenly to various sectors and groups of employees.

3.1   Temporary Contracts and Part-time Employment

Many employers, in adjusting their workforce, targeted those on temporary contracts first. At highest risk of dismissals/non-renewals were younger workers: temporary contracts are more prevalent in the 15–24 age group than in other age groups, and, for both genders, they were hardest hit in 2008–2009, as indicated by Table 4.5. However, the increase in the

Table 4.5   Temporary employees as a percentage of given age group, by gender, Croatia, 2007-2010

Percentage

	Total				Males				Females			
	2007	2008	2009	2010H1	2007	2008	2009	2010H1	2007	2008	2009	2010H1
15–64	12.6	12.1	11.6	12.2	12.1	11.9	11.4	11.9	13.2	12.3	11.9	12.6
15–24	39.5	37.9	35.0	36.5	34.8	34.8	32.6	32.9	46.9	43.3	39.3	41.8
25–49	11.6	11.0	11.6	11.8	11.2	10.7	10.0	11.5	12.0	11.3	12.0	12.1
50–64	4.3	4.3	4.5	4.5	4.8	4.5	5.4	4.6	3.6	4.0	3.5	4.3

Annual percentage change

	Total			Males			Females		
	2008/2007	2009/2008	2010H1/2009H1	2008/2007	2009/2008	2010H1/2009H1	2008/2007	2009/2008	2010H1/2009H1
15–64	-4.0	-3.9	4.3	-1.7	-4.2	3.5	-6.8	-3.3	5.9
15–24	-4.1	-7.7	8.5	0.0	-6.3	3.3	-7.7	-9.2	14.5
25–49	-5.2	0.0	4.4	-4.5	-6.5	11.7	-5.8	6.2	-1.6
50–64	0.0	4.6	3.5	-6.3	20.0	-20.2	11.1	-12.5	n.a.

Source: Eurostat–LFS.

share of the temporarily employed in the first half of 2010 indicates that new employment is based increasingly on temporary contracts (as confirmed by Figure 4.3). Some employers are reorganizing their workforce in order to achieve greater flexibility. This may also indicate sectoral restructuring, with an increasing share of new openings in sectors with a high share of temporary employment (tourism, services, retail and so on), resulting in an increase in the overall share of temporary employment in years to come. Temporary contracts will remain a contested issue between unions and employers in the future, too.

Another avenue of adjustment is offered by part-time employment. It is comparatively low and it did not change markedly in 2009, nor in 2010H1: for the 15–64 age group, the respective rates in 2007–2010 (first halves) were: 6.0 per cent, 6.6 per cent, 7.3 per cent and 7.5 per cent. The share of part-time workers is particularly low among males and there was no significant change in the crisis period (4.3, 5.0, 5.3 and 5.0), while for females there has been an increase: 8.3 per cent, 8.7 per cent, 9.7 per cent and 10.3 per cent (Eurostat–LFS). While the share of involuntary part-time workers aged 15–64 in total part-time changed slightly (from 21.1 per cent in 2007 to 21 per cent in 2008 and 21.4 per cent in 2009), it decreased for females (from 16.2 per cent to 15.1 per cent and 14.1 per cent, respectively) and increased for males (from 28.0 per cent to 28.8 per cent and 32.0 per cent). This may be indicative of males' increased difficulties in finding full-time jobs but overall numbers are too small for firm conclusions.

The CES employers' survey confirms that full-time employment is the norm: reported new employment in 2009 was 95 per cent on a full-time basis, and new employment planned for 2010 is 96.1 per cent full-time (CES 2010b). This is indicative of the low flexibility of employers in offering more versatile working time arrangements. The 2009 European Company Survey shows that 87.9 per cent of Croatian companies do not employ part-timers at all, and only in 0.5 per cent of companies do they make up 20 per cent or more of the workforce (respective shares for private companies are 84.6 per cent and 1.1 per cent). This is considerably below the figures for the EU27, and groups Croatia together with Bulgaria, the former Yugoslav Republic of Macedonia and Turkey (EFILWC 2010) However, the institutional and social barriers are also considerable (Franičević 2008).

3.2 Limited Use of Working Time Adjustments

The adjustment of working time in 2007–2010 has been limited, but has clearly been affected by the crisis. It is important to note that the crisis was being strongly felt by the second half of 2008. Nevertheless, over

Table 4.6   *Changes in actual/usual working time rates, Croatia, 2007–2010 (%)*

	2008/2007		2009/2008		2010(1st half)/ 2008(1st)	
	Actual	Usual	Actual	Usual	Actual	Usual
Total employment	−0.8	0.0	−0.8	0.0	−1.9	−1.0
Full-time employment	−0.7	0.0	−0.8	0.0	−0.7	−0.1
Full-time employees	−0.5	0.0	−0.5	0.0	−0.7	−0.1
Self-employed	−0.9	0.3	−1.2	0.0	−4.1	−1.4
Full-time employees, private sector	0.3	−0.1	−0.4	0.0	n.a.	n.a.
Full-time employees, state sector	0.2	0.0	1.2	0.3	n.a.	n.a.

Notes: Usual working time relates to hours 'usually' worked; actual to hours really worked in a reference (the previous) week. Last two rows: author's calculation from database.

Source: Eurostat–LFS.

the two-year crisis period a picture of limited adjustment, except for the self-employed (thus influencing total employment too), clearly emerges (Table 4.6). As the last two rows indicate (our calculation from the LFS database), the adjustment was mostly confined to the private sector, with many firms experiencing a strong fall in demand (see also case studies). Unfortunately, administrative data for 2009 based on firms' reporting, which could shed more light on working time adjustments, including over-time, are still not available.

Sectoral data also show unevenness of adaptation. Actual working time in the main job for all those in employment fell by –1.6 per cent in agriculture, by –0.7 per cent in industry and by –0.2 per cent in services. The respective two-year decrease from the first half of 2008 to the first half of 2010 was: –6.9 per cent (agriculture), –0.5 per cent (industry) and –0.5 per cent (services), and –1.8 per cent overall (CBS–LFS). Selected sectoral data for all in full-time employment and full-time employees (Table 4.7) show for most sectors a shortening of working time both over 2007–2009 and the two-year period between the first six months of 2008 and the first six months of 2010.

Behind the limited working time adjustments are typical manage-rial rigidities, but also policy failure. The European Company Survey (EFILWC 2010) shows the low internal flexibility of Croatian companies: concerning the share of firms offering 'flexitime arrangements' Croatia is at the bottom of 30 EU and candidate countries surveyed; it is also

Table 4.7   Changes in actual working time rates, selected sectors, Croatia, 2007–2010

	2008/2007		2009/2008		2010(1st half)/2008(1st)	
	FT employed	FT employees	FT employed	FT employees	FT employed	FT employees
	actual %	actual %	actual %	actual %	actual %	actual %
Agriculture, forestry and fishing	-2.5	-0.7	-0.9	-0.2	-0.9	-0.5
Manufacturing	-1.2	-1.0	-0.6	-0.7	-0.4	-0.5
Construction	-1.4	-1.6	-1.6	0.0	-1.6	-0.7
Trade	0.2	0.2	-1.2	-1.0	-2.3	-2.1
Public administration, defence and social security	-0.7	-0.7	-0.8	-0.7	-1.1	-1.1
Education	0.8	0.8	-0.8	-0.5	-1.3	-1.3
Health and social work	-0.2	-0.2	0.0	-0.5	0.5	0.1

Source: Eurostat–LFS.

157

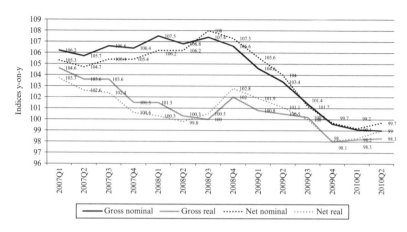

Source: CBS, First releases 9.1.1. 9.1.2 and 9.1.3.

Figure 4.4   Wages, Croatia, 2007–2010 (quarterly data, year-on-year)

ranked low with regard to employees entitled to flexi-time (EFILWC 2010: 5–7). While with regard to overtime it is closer to the EU27 average and concerning atypical hours it is above the EU27 average, again it is at the bottom with regard to the number of establishments using part-time work and 'marginal part-time jobs' (ibid.: 11–14). On the other hand, policy measures to support a shorter week failed, despite the strong interest of employers and unions in them in some sectors (particularly manufacturing). Union evidence shows that a shorter working week has been quite common since the second half of 2008 in manufacturing, particularly affecting production workers. Nevertheless, the case studies indicate that it is a short-term measure, usually preceding a return to normalcy, or (if bad conditions persist) to worker dismissals. An ad hoc programme of subsidized short-time introduced by the end of July 2009 upon joint demands from employers and real sector unions, but far from their preferred design, proved to be a complete failure. Due to its restricted eligibility, administrative requirements and the low financial incentives offered (World Bank 2010: 18), in the period 14 August to 31 December 2009 only four firms applied (for 236 persons) and two were found eligible, receiving a subsidy for 27 workers (information from CES on 15 March 2010).

3.3   Wages: Decreasing Unevenly

The impact of the crisis on employees' incomes was felt through two major channels:[2] the reduction in employment and the reduction in wages (accompanied by an increase in net-wages taxation). In addition, workers were hit by the non-payment and/or delayed payment of wages (however, there are no reliable data, but only indicative and/or anecdotal evidence), as well as decreasing fringe benefits and in-kind payments. Wages have been more resistant than employment, particularly in 2009: while the average nominal gross wage in 2009 increased by 2.2 per cent, and the real one hardly changed (–0.2 per cent), employment decreased by –3.6 per cent (in legal entities –3.3 and crafts –4.9 per cent) (CBS data). However, with the prolongation of the crisis, a downward adaptation of both nominal and real wages set in. Figure 4.4 clearly shows the slowing-down of both gross and net real wage growth in 2008 and 2009, as well as the fall in both nominal and real wages by the end of the period and continuing in the first half of 2010. However, this is unevenly distributed across sectors.

Affected particularly strongly in 2009 were agriculture, mining, manu-facturing, construction, trade and administrative services, with real wages falling by between 1.1 and 2.0 per cent. Behind the sectoral data there are important sub-sectoral differences. In January–June 2010, there was a decrease in (annual) wages in most sectors, including the public sector, but particularly in electricity and gas supply, construction and some services. Wage flexibility 'has thus emerged as an important crisis impact mitigation mechanism, which is a notable new phenomenon' in an economy char-acterized by pervasive high wage pressures and no experience of falling nominal wages. The World Bank study finds this a positive evolution because 'the reduction of wage pressure helped to cut labour costs and thus to limit layoffs' (World Bank 2010: 7). There are numerous examples of wage moderation and wage cuts in the private sector, often based on firm-level social dialogue (see the GC case study). A special 'solidarity' tax (the so-called 'crisis tax'), introduced as an emergency device to stabilize public finances, on net earnings (that is, on net wages, pensions and other incomes), with two rates, 2 and 4 per cent, and exemption for incomes below 3,000 kuna (409 euros) (July 2009) affected sectors differently, depending on sectoral wages and workforce composition. For example, in December 2009, net wages were affected by between 1.8 and 3.4 per cent. Importantly, the above data on net wages do not take into account the 'crisis tax' impact. This coupling of falling employment and falling average net wages, together with a 'crisis tax', certainly had a strong impact on households' disposable income, estimated at around –6 per cent by early 2010 (annually) (CEOQ 2010: 43), hurting many families and increasing the risk of poverty.

The number of firms facing bankruptcy also increased. By the end of 2009, 29,997 businesses/institutions with legal personality (that is, incor-porated businesses and public sectors) (a one-third increase) and 37,031

craft businesses (a 15.6 per cent increase) had become insolvent. This led
to an increase in the number of employees potentially affected: a rise to
72,980 (48,454 in businesses with legal personality, that is, by some 50
per cent and 24,526 in craft businesses, in other words, by some 20 per
cent). By the end of July 2010, there were 30,500 firms and 39,718 craft
businesses employing 42,909 and 25,867 workers, respectively (Croatian
Chamber of Commerce data). These employees are at much greater risk
of receiving their wages with considerable delays or sometimes not at all,
of social contributions not being paid on their behalf (even tolerated for
some larger firms by the Government for longer periods). Furthermore,
many are likely to end up unemployed. Most exposed to the non-payment
of wages risk are employees in construction, trade, manufacturing and
real estate (HGK/FINA data). While reliable data do not exist, construction and manufacturing union data confirm that in a number of unionized
firms such problems do exist. A number of desperate protests have been
reported by the media. Risk is comparably higher for employees in small
and/or craft businesses hardest hit by the crisis. As the LFS shows, for
full-time employees, the share of those 'not receiving pay', after falling
in 2008 (to 0.13 per cent) increased in 2009 to 0.24 per cent, but for all
persons in employment (that is, including self-employed and helping
family members) from 5.33 to 5.61 per cent.

3.3.1   Gender wage gap decreasing – private vs. state sector wage gap increasing

The unadjusted gender wage gap, while comparatively not very high,
narrowed in 2009 (Figure 4.5). This should be attributed primarily to the
relatively high share of females in the public sector, with little or no cuts in
employment and wages in 2006–2009. However, this may be temporary,
due to increasing pressures on the public sector to cut both employment
and wages. On the other hand, to get a more precise picture, adjustments
for labour-market characteristics (and they are higher for females, particularly in education) should be made: when comparing 1998 with 2008 Nestić
finds 'that due to differing rewards the gap exceeds 20 percent on average
– twice the size of the unadjusted gap'. Furthermore, while the unadjusted
figure decreased, the adjusted one 'increased somewhat between 1998 and
2008' and 'the gap is found to be the highest at the lower-to-middle part of
the wage distribution' (Nestić 2010a: 83–84).

The unevenness of adaptation processes has increased pressures and
conflicts along the private/public sector divide (Figure 4.6). After reaching
its relative (to manufacturing) peak in 2000, in 2001–2006 the public sector
relative wage decreased. However, between 2006 and 2009 the trend was
reversed. In 2009, the public sector 'was faring better than manufacturing'

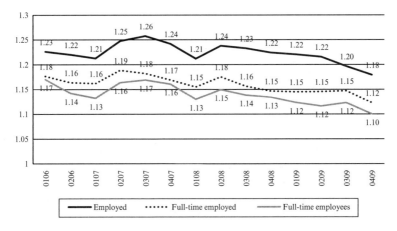

Source: LFS.

Figure 4.5 Gender wage gap: average net wages, Croatia, 2006–2009

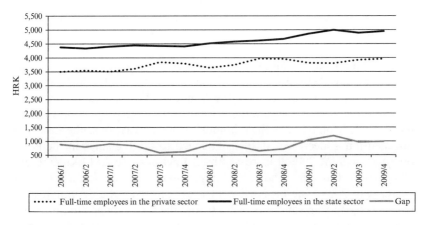

Source: LFS.

Figure 4.6 Public vs. private sector wages, Croatia, 2006–2009

(Nestić 2010b), although public sector wages, after being raised by 6 per cent (by the start of 2009, in line with the collective agreement), fell back to their 2008 level in spring due to the compromise reached between the Government and the unions and successful union resistance to any further nominal cuts. Calculations based on LFS data on state vs. private sector wages confirm that the gap increased considerably in 2009: the ratio between state sector and private wages, after falling from 1.24 in 2006 to 1.20 in 2007 and 2008, increased in 2009 to 1.27 – that is, by 5.8 per cent.

In 2010, however, there will be a fall in both nominal and real net wages in public administration (98.3/97.5 per cent), education (99.2/98.4 per cent) and health and social work (98.0/97.3 per cent) (CBS, January–June 2010/2009 indices). Public sector average net wages fell marginally relative to manufacturing and trade, but increased relative to construction in the first half of 2010. However, it is not to be expected, particularly with regard to the parliamentary elections in 2011, that the overall picture of the public sector faring better during the crisis will change soon. While cost-cutting pressures on private sector firms (in the face of a prolonged crisis) will very likely dominate in 2011 too, and perhaps for even longer, it is very unlikely that the Government will risk major confrontations with public sector unions. Recent agreement on a prolongation of the wage freeze into 2011, but no nominal cuts and with symbolic cuts in fringe benefits, attest to that. In the medium term, however, it is unlikely that public sector wages will improve their relative standing either, rather the contrary: while pressures on public finances will remain (most likely, increase), restructuring will proceed in the private sector as the private economy starts picking up again.

3.3.2   More details on low, below average and high wages

Minimum wage legislation was introduced *de facto* in March 1998 and *de jure* in July 2008 by the Law on the Minimum Wage, resulting in a considerable increase in the minimum wage and in the proportion of those receiving it. Moreover, as the minimum wage increase (and the Law does not mention a 'decrease' at all) is attached to GDP change in the previous year, in June 2009 it increased by 2.4 per cent (to 2,814 kuna, gross; 383 euros). However, it has not changed since then, despite a real GDP decrease in 2009. The proportion of those receiving the minimum wage has increased, from some 3 per cent before the Law changed to more than 5 per cent in March 2009 (Table 4.8, approximation based on net wages in legal entities only). It is certainly due to the minimum wage increase and freeze, but also due to crisis dynamics; the effects, with the available data, are hard to disentangle. REGOS (Central Registry for Insured Persons) data on gross wages, while giving the proportion of those at (or below) the minimum wage in January–November 2009 at around 7 per cent, shows a decrease in December–January 2009/2010 – at 4.70 per cent. While in February 2010 it was 4.9, in March–September it varied between 4.5 and 4.7 per cent. Available data do not allow us to conclude whether behind this are greater job losses among those on very low pay (due to job cuts, bankruptcies and/or a move to informality).

Table 4.8   Workers at different wage levels, Croatia, March 2007–March 2009 (% of all workers)

	Average	60% of the average	60% of median	Minimum wage
2007	65.5	25.3	14.1	2.7
2008	65.7	25.8	14.4	2.7–3.7
2009	70.1	26.2	14.6	4.6–5.8

Source: CBS First Release 9.2.5. Note: approximations from wage brackets shares (even distribution inside the brackets assumed).

While data do not allow for firm conclusions, one thing is certain: the minimum wage is certainly acting as an important anti-poverty tool, so that its freezing may have had some effect.

Estimates (Table 4.8) of the proportion of those on/below average wages and on low wages in legal entities only (60 per cent below the average and 60 per cent below the median) indicate that the share of those paid low wages has somewhat increased, on two alternative measures, to 26.2 /14.6 per cent (an increase which should be treated cautiously due to possible error built into the estimation), while the share of those earning below the average net wage has risen to 70.1 per cent. REGOS (January) data on 2003–2010 gross wage shares, based on social insurance registrations, shows the percentage of those registered as receiving average gross wages and below at around 65 per cent in 2003–2009. Moreover, consistent with Table 4.8 data is their high increase in January 2010, to 70 per cent. In February–September 2010, the average share remained close to 70 per cent, except in April and May when it was considerably lower (60.5 and 55.5 per cent) (only part of it may have to do with payments of holiday bonuses above the untaxed limit; but it remains to be explained). These increases reflect strong downward pressures in the formal private sector, while public sector wages remained largely intact in 2009.

LFS data on full-time employees' net wages consistently show lower values for average wages than administrative data, which is due to the inclusion of those employed by crafts, that is, by the self-employed, both formally and informally. Interestingly, while from 2005 to 2008 the ratio of the two averages (net wage CBS, legal entities/net wage LFS, all full-time employees) increased from 1.16 in 2005, to 1.22 in 2006, 1.24 in 2007 and 1.28 in 2008, in 2009 it did not change. It seems that with the crisis the advancement of wages in the formal sector (including the public sector) came to a halt. As Figure 4.7 also shows, the LFS-based shares of those below the average net wage are, accordingly, lower than those concerning

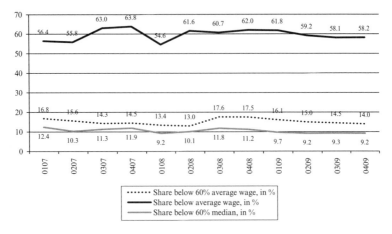

Source: LFS.

Figure 4.7 Average and below average net wages, Croatia, 2007–2009

legal entities only (Table 4.8), and fell somewhat in 2009. The proportions of those paid 60 per cent below the average/median wage have changed, but not significantly: from 15.3/14.1 in 2007 to 15.4/14.4 in 2008 and to 14.9/14.6 in 2009. In relative terms, however, when comparing administrative data with survey data, it seems that the impact of the crisis on the formal sector of the economy (more connected to the global economy) has been stronger, pushing a greater proportion of employees below the average wage and/or below 60 per cent of the average/median wage. Of course, behind some of these differences may be underreporting in the administrative data (workers registered on lower pay than what they really receive); but the extent of this (and its direction) cannot be inferred from the available sources. There are also fears that the number of persons who are highly paid may be underrepresented in the LFS.

REGOS data provide further important information: the proportion of those receiving very high gross wages (determined as six times the average gross wage, as the highest base for social contributions) has been falling during the crisis period and in particular fell from January 2009 to January 2010 (from 0.27 to 0.17) to remain between 0.18 and 0.19 from February to October 2010. The crisis certainly affected highly paid workers, but also relations between high and low wages.

3.3.3 Wage and income inequalities have decreased
Workers on the lowest wages were hit hard by employment losses but less by wage cuts (due to the impact of the minimum wage). This, together with

Table 4.9   Gini coefficients by gender, Croatia, 2007–2009

	2007	2008	2009
Employment	0.305	0.309	0.310
Males	0.294	0.285	0.288
Females	0.338	0.332	0.331
Full-time employees	0.235	0.232	0.227
Males	0.237	0.227	0.223
Females	0.241	0.232	0.227

Source: LFS.

decreased higher wages and the progressive nature of the 'solidarity tax' (with net wages below 3,000 kuna [409 euros] exempted), led to a more even distribution of wages, which is shown in the reduction of the 90/10 ratio: from 4.79 in 2007 to 4.66 in 2008 and 4.13 in 2009 (LFS). However, the male 90/10 ratio decreased more markedly in 2009: by –2.9 per cent in contrast to –1.7 per cent for females, which reflects the higher proportion of females in the public sector, where there were few or no changes in wages in 2009. However, this may change: in 2010, there were some cuts in high wages in the public sector; but by the year's end the 'solidarity tax' was removed. The impact of the 2010 income tax reform is unclear (see policy section below) because it benefits both those at the lowest and the highest end of the wage distribution.

With the above developments, not surprisingly, the Gini coefficient for net wages shows considerable stability with regard to employment, with slight decreases in 2009 for full-time employees. It decreased slightly for full-time employees of both genders and even more slightly for females in total employment but increased in 2009 for males, albeit remaining below 2007 values (Table 4.9).

The slight decrease in wage inequality among employees may be attributed to the increase in public sector employees' share (with typically lower wage differentials), the decrease in the share of those on the highest wages and the impacts of the minimum wage increase and the 'solidarity tax'. It may be also due to the destruction of the lowest paid jobs, but clear evidence is lacking.

The stability and 'rather low' level of income inequality over the entire transition period (between 0.28 and 0.30) was explained by the public sector's large presence in the economy and the state's role in transfer payments (Leitner and Holzner 2009). The most recent data, based on household incomes (HBS), show that, after an increase in 2008, both the Gini

Table 4.10　Income inequality, Croatia, 2005–2009

	2005	2006	2007	2008	2009
Quintile share ratio S80/S20	4.5	4.2	4.3	4.6	4.3
Gini	0.29	0.28	0.28	0.29	0.27

Source:　CBS, Poverty indicators 2009.

Table 4.11　Financial situation in households, Croatia, 2007–2009

	Full-time employees		Employment		Unemployed	
	Mainly bad	Bad	Mainly bad	Bad	Mainly bad	Bad
2007	25.2	15.0	25.6	16.7	16.5	64.3
2008	25.6	15.3	25.5	17.9	24.2	62.5
2009	24.8	17.1	24.7	19.4	23.4	64.6

Source:　LFS.

coefficient and the 80/20 ratio decreased, in line with the abovementioned wage data (Table 4.10).

However, behind this relative stability is an increase in the numbers and proportion of households whose financial situation worsened in 2009 (Table 4.11).

In a Gfk survey in April 2010 (representative, n = 800), 71 per cent said they felt the crisis directly or in the household: 37 per cent through wage cuts, 16 per cent due to delayed wages and 14 per cent through dismissals; 57 per cent report that life was harder, but still 'normal', while 18 per cent said that life was now 'very hard' and could hardly make ends meet.

3.3.4　Poverty risk has increased

As may have been expected, the poverty risk increased in 2009, albeit unevenly. Behind the increase in the national at-risk-of-poverty rate (19.0 in 2007, 18.9 in 2008 and 20.2 in 2009) are major differences. While the risk has increased both for the employed (4.2, 4.1 and 5.2) and the unemployed (35.8, 33.8 and 42.0) (without income in kind), to be sure of having (and keeping) a job is a fundamental insurance against poverty. Particularly for the unemployed and the self-employed, income in kind significantly reduces the poverty risk (from 42.0 to 37.4 and 26.7 to 19.5, respectively; overall, from 20.2 to 18.0) – pointing to the importance of diverse 'coping strategies',

which include gardening/smallhold farming and help from relatives (as confirmed by interviewed workers in the case studies), but also in-kind social
services.

The recession has increased poverty-related uncertainties for older
workers in particular. The crisis increased people's vulnerability to ending
up with lower pensions, not only because of previous low wages (and therefore low contributions), but also due to the pension system's dependence
on the state budget. Data on pensioners' high poverty risk only add to the
uncomfortable prospects facing too many pensioners of being supported
by the (low) productivity of current employees, whose number has been
reduced by the crisis. The poverty risk rate for pensioners in 2007–2009 was
around 24.5 per cent (24.8 per cent in 2007, 24.7 per cent in 2008 and 24.3
per cent in 2009). Looking at 2009, however, the pension system managed to
prevent an increase in poverty risk among retirees: 'pensions were regularly
indexed and grew in real terms by 2.2 per cent' (World Bank 2010: 35); and
all pensions below 3,000 kuna were exempted from July 2009 'solidarity
tax'. Despite the freeze on pension 'indexation' for 2010, it is not likely that
the poverty-risk impact will be considerable as long as the system remains
viable.

Social transfers also reduce poverty risk: without them the 2009 rate
would have been 25.8 and 27.2 (with/without in-kind) (CBS, First releases,
14.1.2). Despite the numerous shortcomings of social welfare systems in
Croatia with regard to their adequacy, coverage, targeting and efficiency
(for more detail see Franičević 2008; also World Bank 2010: 49–55), 'inactive persons', as the World Bank study concludes, 'have not been affected
by the labour market contraction in 2009, and their incomes increased
(pensions, social assistance benefit) in 2009, explaining their lower exposure to the current crisis' (ibid.: 36–37). However, if negative economic
and public finance trends persist, this may also easily come into question.

3.4 Health and Safety: Higher or Lower Risks in the Crisis?

Exposure to health and safety risks is high, above the EU15/27 averages and, with regard to a number of indicators, higher than the NMS10
average (EFILWC 2007; Franičević 2008; also 2010 European Working
Conditions Survey). However, it is hard to distinguish the immediate
effects of the crisis with regard to risk. The sick leave rate and related indicators decreased in 2009. This may be due to real improvements, including more stringent regulation and monitoring, but also employees' fear
of taking sick leave because it might lead to their dismissal (Poslovni.hr
(news online) 14.10.2009).

According to one leading expert (personal communication), the

Table 4.12   Accidents at work, Croatia, 2005–2009

	Total number	Per 100,000 of employed ***	Accidents at work leading to fatalities
2005	22738*/17885**	1568*/1233**	62*/55**
2006	24843/19503	1650/1295	76/62
2007	23914/18907	1545/1222	77/59
2008	25285/19979	1663/1314	80/58
2009	19566/14917	1279/975	38/32

Notes:

*   includes travel to/from job; **   at workplace.

Source: Croatian Institute for Public Health.

recession has not led to worsening of physical working conditions, but has had an adverse effect on workers' health due to psychosomatic disorders. Research that could substantiate this is lacking. However, in the case studies most workers report crisis-related stress and worries.

The case studies indicate that the crisis has not increased accident risk at the firm level. As Table 4.12 shows, the fall in the number and rates of accidents in 2009 was significant. This is due to decreasing activity and sectoral variations – the cumulative fall in just four sectors (manufacturing, construction, trade and transportation) accounts for 80.5 per cent of the total decrease.

According to safety inspectors, fatigue and overwork are major causes of accidents: shorter working time and restrictions on overtime may have helped to reduce them. However, enforcement problems remain, as the State Inspectorate's 2009 annual report shows, pointing to still low (labour relations and safety) inspection monitoring capacities (despite some improvements) and not sufficiently credible enforcement of regulations (see also Franičević 2007a and 2008).

3.5   Training: Not a Priority in the Crisis

Participation in lifelong learning is very low in Croatia, but the LFS does not show a crisis-related decrease. The percentage of those aged 25–64 who participated in education and training was 2.4 per cent in 2007 and 2.2 per cent in 2008, before increasing slightly in 2009, to 2.3 per cent (Eurostat–LFS). However, surveys and the case studies indicate that firms' resources for training were reduced. In 2008, 29.8 per cent of surveyed employers expressed a need for additional staff training; in 2009 and 2010, the figures were 24.5 per cent and 22.7 per cent, respectively (CES 2010b), which is consistent with the abovementioned findings on cost cutting still being the focus of Croatian firms. In another survey on adaptation to the crisis, among 1,519 surveyed employees, 38 per cent reported training budget cuts (MojPosao 2010). Recent 2010 EWCS shows that only 20.8 per cent of those surveyed responded affirmatively to the question of whether 'over the past 12 months' they have undergone paid training; this is less than in 2005 (22.9 per cent) and considerably below the figures for the EU15/27 in 2010 (34.8/33.7, which is much higher than in 2005: 27.3/26.1). In two of the companies in the case studies, training budgets were also reduced (T&V and ABC).

While data training cost cuts in the hardest hit sectors and workers' groups are not available or sufficient to make firm conclusions, cuts certainly affected the unemployed too: (i) due to reduced new employment by firms that would have required re-training, but also due to (ii) limited and certainly insufficient funds for (re)training from the CES.

3.6 Job Satisfaction is High, But. . .

The effects of the crisis were also felt by workers subjectively. Plečaš and Galić (2010) found that most of the nine work characteristics[3] surveyed in previous 'job satisfaction' research (reported in Šverko and Galić 2009; also in Franičević 2007a) were judged (on a 1–5 scale) by surveyed workers as being worse in 2009 than in 2008 for all three educational groups (basic school, secondary school, college/university). This continued in 2010 for those with basic schooling, with a particularly strong fall with regard to good (that is, enabling a decent life) and fair pay and security of employment (against dismissal). For the other two groups a slight increase was registered, but still below pre-crisis values. The differences are much more marked for the first group than for the other two. Overall, differences, while indicative, are quite small. Nevertheless, with the crisis, the long-term trend of increasing attainment on all nine job-satisfaction variables (both extrinsic and intrinsic) registered between 1993 and 2008 (Šverko and Galić 2009) was reversed.

However, 'general' job satisfaction is high and quite stable; around 65 per cent are satisfied with their job. In phone survey carried out by Hendal (August–September 2010, n = 498) 65.5 per cent were 'satisfied', but the figures were 64.1 per cent in September 2008, 64.7 per cent in March 2009 and 67.1 per cent in March 2010. However in the last survey, satisfaction with 'good pay' (42.1 per cent), 'fair pay' (39.9 per cent) and 'job security' (49.4 per cent) was much lower, as well as with 'participation in decision making' (39.8 per cent). With another five work characteristics satisfaction was between 56.8 and 64.3 per cent (Galić 2010). The fact that extrinsic aspects of work came to the forefront with the crisis is indicated by 2010 EWCS, too: 33.2 per cent agree that they are 'well paid for the job' they do (25 per cent highly skilled and 26.2 per cent low-skilled manual occupations). The survey also shows that, 'on the whole', 72.7 per cent are satisfied with working conditions (72 per cent in 2005), but this is lower than in the EU15/27 (85.6/84.3).

In my interviews for the case studies, in all four firms, stress and fear of losing their job was reported by the majority as their main fear. Some reported having a family member affected by the crisis, too, with a significant impact on family income. Particularly those on lower wages and supporting larger families had major difficulties making ends meet.

4.   EFFECTS OF THE CRISIS ON SOCIAL DIALOGUE

The crisis has contributed to conflicts between actors, but has also exerted pressure towards cooperation. It has been an important learning experience for the social partners, in particular at the firm level. The crisis may change the balance of forces for an extended period, due to its strong effects on all actors.

4.1   Unions: Between Conflict and Cooperation

The crisis has contributed to trade union fragmentation and conflicts, particularly between private and public sector unions, especially concerning who is going to bear the costs of the crisis and how. Data on the crisis's impact on union density are not available, but it may plausibly be expected that it decreased, however asymmetrically.[4] The unions are largely limited to larger firms and/or formerly publicly owned ones (with little coverage of small or new firms) and to workers on permanent contracts; density is higher among workers with longer tenure and among public sector employees. Trade union experts agree that it is likely that the crisis will strengthen the asymmetry between the public and private sectors. The share of private sector trade union membership in total trade union membership (about 30 per cent – Bagić 2010: 160–61) is likely to further decrease, thus negatively affecting their ability to influence national-level policymaking.

Fragmentation has been reinforced by conflicts between unions with regard to particular issues: for example, the law on the minimum wage

(2008) and more recently (in 2009) the changes to the Labour Code, and particularly the 'crisis tax' and VAT increase in summer 2009. These two measures were opposed (unsuccessfully) by real sector unions as 'pro-recessionary' (in that respect allied with employers, particularly industrialists). However, the measures were strongly supported by public sector unions, who demanded that the burden of the crisis should be shouldered by all. Personality conflicts are also present: 'it is not the interests of members and of private and public sector employees that are at the centre of things, but problems between the union leaders' (union expert). On the other hand, there are also attempts at cooperation, some of which are successful, particularly concerning the Government's attempt in May 2010 to change the Labour Code without consultation, resulting in the unions leaving the tripartite Economic and Social Council (ESC) and seeking public support for a national referendum. Despite some recent easing of tensions, unity between the major unions seems fragile.

4.2 Social Dialogue Entered Into in a Period of Conflict

While sectoral dialogue has typically been weak, at the enterprise level employer/union relations have ranged between cooperation and conflict. As the union leader said in our interview: 'we had to learn to negotiate defensively'. Cooperation tends to prevail when there are incentives on both sides (Marginson 2010: 362) to retain the core workforce until 'better times'. The GC case study attests to that. However, the capacity to mobilize workers and sustain strikes (on the firm and wider level) is low; unions' financial and logistic capacities are weak. There are no statistics on strikes, but there has been an increase in failed mediations in collective disputes, rising from 27 in 2007, to 43 in 2008 and 53 in 2009. When more radical actions (strikes, walk-outs and so on) do take place, they are often coupled with acts of desperation (occupation of premises, hunger strikes), and often they 'tend to be defensive in their objectives' (Hyman and Gumbrell-McCormick 2010: 366), including the payment of wages and the resumption of production.

Formal coverage by collective agreements is significant, at about 60 per cent (Bagić 2010: 219). While, nominally, coverage does not seem to have decreased lately, most private sector collective agreements are old and merely formal; those signed or renewed since 2007 cover only 10 per cent of employees (and 57 per cent are in the public sector) (ibid.: 210). However, high decentralization of collective bargaining has helped a number of firms to adapt via firm-level social dialogue, unconstrained by national/sectoral unions.

With the crisis, the employers' commitment to collective agreements, and their renewal, decreased. In an attempt to confront the public sector unions' refusal to agree to further cuts, the Government put before the Parliament changes to the Labour Code concerning the removal of the unlimited extension of collective agreements and making their cancellation easier. Fearing that many private sector collective agreements would also be cancelled, the five confederations, after episodes of disunity, united and called for a national referendum. An extremely prohibitive clause demanding 450,000 signatures was easily satisfied in June 2010 with more than 800,000 signatures (710,000 valid) which turned into a vote of confidence in the Government. The Government's attempt to deny the legitimacy of signatures met with public outrage. This represents a significant boost for the unions' shaken reputation. This was attested by the September agreement on the basic public sector collective agreement, which kept wages and most benefits intact. However, increasing pressures to reform the public sector may eventually result in more decisive cuts.

In October 2010, the Constitutional Court controversially decided against the legitimacy of the referendum. The decision was based on the Government's withdrawal of its proposal from the Parliament. Most recently, but also controversially, a compromise agreement was reached between the unions and the Government. Instead of the expected referendum on changes to the Labour Code there should be a referendum on changing the referendum law, reducing the number of required signatures to 200,000.[5] The public reaction was unfavourable, and some commentators saw this as a favour by the unions to the ruling party which is likely to end up in opposition, but also as a 'politicization' of unions and their leaders. With all this, both the Government's and unions' credibility suffered.

The virtual standstill of tripartite dialogue in the ESC in 2010 signifies a severe crisis for tripartism which was at least formally functional until the crisis. However, unions were increasingly dissatisfied with being regularly outvoted (by employers and the Government) and with being given too short a time to consult on the Government's measures and proposals. When the Government decided unilaterally to submit to Parliament's changes to the Labour Code, the dissatisfied unions withdrew from the Council. Despite ongoing negotiations on the unions' return to the ESC this has still not happened. Despite attempts at 'rapprochement', the future of tripartism remains uncertain. And the crisis of tripartism, if it continues, will certainly undermine the legitimacy of any future reforms, as well as the unions' capacity to protect workers' rights.

Table 4.13   Policy measures, Croatia, 2008–2010

Policy area	Measures	Implementation	Objectives
Fiscal policy	Budget revisions	April 2009, July 2009, Aug. 2010	Fiscal stability and deficit, sustaining social spending
• Public expenditure	Public investment cuts	July 2009	Reducing expenditure
	Cost cutting in ministries and state companies	Nov. 2008, Feb. 2009	
	Revoked free textbook and transportation for pupils	July 2009	
• Revenues	Solidarity tax on wages, pensions and other income (2% and 4% rates)	August 2009	Increasing revenues
	Charges on GSM services VAT increase: 22% to 23%		
• Debt financing	Issuance of bonds; bank loans	May 2010	Reduction of corporate tax burden
• Tax reform	Four rates (15, 25, 35, 45%) to three: 12, 25, 40%	July 2009	Redistribution of tax burden
	Removal of income tax deductions	May 2010	Revenues, redistribution
	25% reduction of some non-tax levies		Corporate tax burden decrease
Monetary policy (CNB)	Decreased reserve rate	Dec. 2008	Increasing liquidity
	Increasing reserve requirement	End 2008/Jan. 2009	Alleviating depreciation
	Reducing required foreign currency claims	Feb. 2009	pressures
			Facilitating financing of domestic economy, government
	Revoked compulsory purchase of CNB bills	Nov. 2009	Removal of restrictions on bank loans
	Lower reserve requirement	Feb. 2010	Increasing liquidity/ loans

Table 4.13   (continued)

Policy area	Measures	Implementation	Objectives
Subsidized credit	Co-funding venture capital funds	Dec. 2009	Investment/ restructuring
	Subsidized loans (model A)	Jan. 2010	Alleviating firms' liquidity
	State guarantees (model B)	April 2010	Investment/ employment
	Subsidies for troubled companies (model C)		Restructuring
Wage policy	Cuts of 6% for public sector and state employees	April/May 2009	Controlling expenditure
State officials	Cuts of 10%	April 2009	
	Cuts of 5%	July 2009	
Management of state companies	Ceiling put at 3.2 x April average net wage	July 2009	
Pensions	Freeze on pensions	July 2009	Controlling
State officials	Decrease by 10%	July 2010	expenditure
'Privileged' pensions	Decrease by 10%		and increasing legitimacy
Pension reform	Later retirement for females, penalization of early retirement	Autumn 2010	Increasing sustainability
Labour market policies	Decreased employment benefits	July 2009	Controlling expenditure
	Increased benefits	November 2010	Income support
Shorter working time	Employer's subsidy	July 2009	Preventing dismissals
ALMP	Employment subsidies, training, public works	2008–2010	Supporting employment (133 million KN in 2008, 93 million in 2009)
Income support	Removal of 2% 'crisis tax'	July 2010	Lower incomes support
	Removal of 4% 'crisis tax'	November 2010	Supporting demand

5. POLICY RESPONSES: TOO LATE AND TOO LITTLE

From the start of the crisis,[6] economic policy focused on short-term measures related to fiscal and monetary stability. The policy response to increasing unemployment 'has been very limited' (World Bank 2010: 13) and not sufficiently timely. February 2009's anti-recession measures were based on budget revisions and state/public sector cost cutting, thus commencing a series of confrontations with the unions. In spring 2009, public sector employees' accepted 6 per cent wage cuts (returning to 2008 levels). Unable to prevent the surge in the budget deficit by cutting expenditure radically, the Government added to the private sector's pains: in August 2009 it introduced a 'solidarity tax' ('crisis tax') (on personal incomes) and increased VAT from 22 per cent to 23 per cent. Due to its progressivity (2 per cent and 4 per cent rates and exemption for workers earning below 3,000 kuna), the first measure should have had the effect of reducing after-tax net wage inequality. The second, due to its supposedly regressive nature, may have acted in the opposite direction. Research that would confirm both effects, however, is lacking.

A mid-2009 ad hoc programme of subsidized short-time working was, due to its restrictive nature, as explained earlier, a complete failure.

In April 2010, a Programme for Economic Recovery was presented as a set of measures, intentions and 'wishes' to be realized over time.[7] This includes a reform of personal income tax: from July 2010 numerous deductions were removed and income tax brackets were reduced from four (15–45 per cent) to three (12–40 per cent), which benefits those on the lowest incomes, but also those on the highest – for those in particular whose rates were lowered from 15 to 12 per cent and from 45 to 40 per cent, after-tax disposable incomes should have increased. The 'crisis tax' was withdrawn too: in July 2010 its lower rate, in order to support those on lower incomes, and in November 2010 the higher rate of the 'crisis tax', benefiting those on higher incomes. Finally, the pension system was modified in Autumn 2010 by the introduction of higher penalties for earlier retirement and a higher retirement age for women.

Spending on labour market policies has been very low – about 0.4 per cent of GDP – and their reach has been extremely limited: they covered about 4 per cent of the labour force in 2007 (World Bank 2010: 43). Expenditure on active labour market policies is low, with limited impact. Their coverage rate, just above 3 per cent prior to the crisis, fell to 2.5 per cent in 2009. In simple terms, the numbers are too small to make a significant difference.

Unemployment benefits have been the main policy instrument

throughout. Data on the high poverty risk of the unemployed is consist-ent with data on low coverage of unemployed by unemployment benefits. Despite increased coverage – from 22.6 per cent in 2007 to 24.2 per cent in 2008 and 26.2 per cent in 2009 (28.2 per cent in March, but 25.3 per cent in June 2010) (CES data) – too many are left out. As many as '57 per cent of the short-term unemployed do not receive unemployment benefit' (World Bank 2010: 40).

The wage replacement rate is also low. The substantial increase in benefits in July 2008 soon had to be revised, thus hurting many eligible newcomers to the unemployment register. At present, the unemployed are under three regimes and a fourth will be applied from November 2010, with the majority under the third. For an 'average worker' (earning an average gross wage before unemployment and receiving benefits over the whole year), the first regime (up to 1,200 kuna or 163 euros) gives an net replacement rate of 0.20, the second (tied to the average wage) 0.55 and the third, with the minimum wage as a ceiling, 0.32.[8] This creates inequalities even between the recipients themselves, depending on the regime which was in force at the time they applied for the benefit.

The Government responded favourably to suggestions that the present rules should be relaxed and coverage increased from November 2010 (Matković 2010; World Bank 2010: 57), leading to an increase in the net replacement rate to 0.44. In addition, the long-term unemployed (more than 12 months) are entitled to an extension of between 30 and 120 days. The real challenge is not only to increase coverage and replacement rates but to integrate protection of the unemployed with re-employment policies. In both respects, Croatia is lagging behind, risking a major increase in long-term unemployment, unemployability and social exclu-sion. Nevertheless, too many unemployed – and their families – are without adequate income support, with the informal economy being their only alternative. Inequalities between employed and unemployed are high, but hard to resolve; with the prolongation of the crisis they should become central to policy and to both social and political actors.

6.   CASE STUDIES

Among the sectors which have been hardest hit by the crisis, two stand out: construction and manufacturing. Four firms were surveyed: a large construction firm; a medium-sized manufacturing firm supplying the construction sector; an export-oriented firm producing electrical compo-nents and the state-owned shipyard. The section ends with a conclusion, including a summary table.

6.1 Large Construction Company T&V: Cutting Back to Survive?

T&V specializes in low-level construction. Large infrastructural investments helped the firm to stabilize after the transition and war-related difficulties. T&V was visited for this case study in April 2010,[9] followed by
interviews with employees in July 2010 at the construction site: Matko,
a profit centre manager; Jozo, a foreman; Pero, a carpenter; Ivan, a carpenter; Ante, an assistant manager; Veljko, a steel-bender; and Marko, a
security guard.

The atmosphere of the crisis was tangible. The Government's decision
on drastic reductions in public infrastructural investments of August
2009 was 'shocking': KN 1.5 billion (around 202 million euro) of signed
contracts were 'called into question', creating huge capacity surpluses
(Filip). Seven hundred workers were sent home on a kind of forced
paid leave ('waiting'[10]) on the minimum wage. Despite the fact that in
September some 200 million kuna (27 million euros) in contracts, concerning one project, was allowed to proceed, after pressures from large
construction firms, urgent reductions in T&V's employment and costs
were necessary.[11]

There are two unions at T&V: the Independent Union (330 members)
and a branch of SGH (250 members). Members are largely permanent
workers with a long tenure with T&V. The interviewed workers found that
the unions' capacity to protect them and to organize collective action was
low; they did not have a good word to say for either the unions or the works
council. Cooperation with the works council, whose members are mostly
from the firm's head office (well under management control, according to
Matko), has been the management's main instrument in employment cuts,
while the unions were thrust aside. Marija and Goran found social dialogue worse than before; at T&V there was no special agreement or annex
to the collective agreement concerning crisis adjustments, despite union
demands. Both Marija and Goran felt that the unions are sidestepped by
management, and personally feel resigned and 'powerless' (Goran), but
very loyal to the firm and ready to help.

6.1.1 From shock to adjustments

Employment cuts started in mid-2009. As of 31 July 2009, there were
2,090 workers; by 31 March 2010, this had fallen to 1,562, including
400 considered to be 'surplus' (Table 4.14). The management's assessment was that, under new business conditions, a viable workforce would
number 1,100 (Filip). Targeted first were those on temporary contracts
– there were about 400 of them (making close to 20 per cent of the
workforce before the crisis shock). Those among them who were what is

Table 4.14   Employment at T&V, 2007–2010

2007	2008	2009, July	2009	2010, March	2010, June	2010, September	2010
1998	2068	2090	1692	1562	1496	1405	1366

Source: T&V.

called 'waiting' did not receive a renewal, while those on building sites were laid off as soon as the construction work was finished. This was the most regrettable: 'we cut the green branch' because among them were 270 workers with badly needed skills (Zlatko). However, Ljubica, works council chair, considered it 'necessary': 'they are young and they will find their way'. The second group to be targeted were those eligible for retirement. By the end of 2009, 368 had ended their fixed-term contracts, 94 had retired and 18 had left. There was no new employment. However, with a bad start to 2010 further cuts ensued. To those eligible for earlier retirement, 10–15 per cent above legal severance pay was offered. A programme of laying off a group of employees who were surplus to requirements ('technological surplus') (approved by the Croatian Employment Service – CES) was accepted, encompassing 62 workers but reduced to 52 under union pressure (in order to protect the most vulnerable). Third, subcontracting was reduced from 30 per cent in 2009 to 10 per cent, also affecting workers from Bosnia and Herzegovina. The remaining 'surplus' (at the time of the interview) totalled 380 workers 'waiting', including 29 in managerial positions (Zlatko).

Sending workers home to 'wait' is a useful way of achieving employment cuts; 'waiting' workers receive the legal minimum wage (2,814 kuna gross, around 2,200 net (300 euros).[12] While 46 have already signed up for retirement, a further 38 will do so soon. For some 150, 'no bigger problems should be expected' (Zlatko). A new technological surplus programme covering 164 workers was recently approved by the CES. Ljubica finds it 'difficult' but, again, 'necessary'. She does not expect conflicts: the 'workers have adapted . . . it will pass like a short bura' (cold wind). By the end of the year, T&V will be employing 1,366 workers instead of the initial 2,090 – a 35 per cent decrease. The CEO's statement that priority would be given in new employment to those registered with CES ('even if we might prefer to chose younger workers who would work on a fixed-term basis'), Zlatko regards as 'political', and intended to 'sell the programme more easily'.

6.1.2 Earnings hit hard, and their fairness contested

At T&V, workers' take-home earnings for years depended very much on overtime and additional supplements/benefits, which were particularly important for workers on construction sites and largely used as a sort of hidden (in material costs) payment (Franičević 2007a). First, overtime was curtailed; where necessary it was compensated by 'free days' (but Marko and Luka doubt that they will ever be given their free days).

Next, wages were reduced progressively (gross wages of 4,000–6,000 kuna were reduced by 2 per cent, 6,000–8,000 kuna by 4 per cent, 8,000–12,000 by 6 per cent and 12,000+ by 8 per cent). Take-home pay is also affected by reductions of various supplements to their legal minimum given by the sectoral collective agreement (for example, field supplements). Also Christmas, Easter and holiday bonuses have not been paid since 2008.

Most of the workers I talked to had experienced wage/earnings cuts of some 20–30 per cent. However, workers on construction sites are more strongly affected than those at headquarters. Marija (financial department) explained: 'while my wage is reduced by 4 per cent, my husband's earnings are reduced by some 30 per cent; he is working at the tunnel, and he lost overtime and his field supplement has been reduced'. Similarly, Ljubica experienced a 2 per cent wage cut but her husband, an engineer at T&V, lost 20 per cent. Zlatko, whose pay was reduced by 18 per cent (8 per cent plus loss of overtime) added: 'people do not argue, they understand, they are resigned'.

Marija and Goran complained that the sectoral collective agreement was not being fully respected in these cuts, but also concerning the low pay of those 'waiting' (denied by Zlatko, but see note 10). However, the union did not react 'in order to help our employer'. And the 'workers wouldn't strike for this, they accept the situation . . . there is no money and that's it' (Goran). Indeed, most interviewees were realistic. However, the majority also argued that workers on construction sites were hit harder and found it 'unfair'. Some had harsh words for head office: 'it is no solution to fire people; they are firing only those from the construction sector and not those from Green Square' (address of head office) (Pero and Matko).

Clearly, being too dependent on state-financed projects, but hardly ready and restructured enough to absorb major shocks, T&V was hit by severe employment and wage cuts, well above the sectoral ones. Particularly affected were those on temporary contracts and subcontractors; production workers were harder hit and among permanent employees older aged ones emerge as particularly vulnerable. T&V badly needs to increase its competitiveness and reduce dependency on state projects. It is uncertain that it will succeed. T&V's future is still not assured – all the employees may lose their jobs eventually.

Table 4.15   Employment at FNC, 2007–2010

	2007	2008	2009	2010 June	2010 September
1. FNC	134	139	132	124	120
• 'city'	35	35	35	34	32
• factory in the 'region'	99	104	97	90	88
Plant-production only	89	94	89	82	81
FNC: Fixed-time	28	21	15	5	4
2. Student contracts	2	3	0	0	0
3. Cooperating firm workers (cleaning, security, help in plant) (calculated on the basis of hours of work)	24	20	1	1	1
Total: 1+2+3	160	162	133	125	121

Source: FNC.

6.2   Medium-size Construction Supplier FNC: Employees Without Employment Alternatives

FNC is part of a multinational family-owned group. It produces building materials. Those employed at FNC's factory, located not far from a small town in a war-affected region with high unemployment and scarce job opportunities, are considered 'lucky'. In autumn 2008, exports fell and domestic market conditions deteriorated. In 2009, sales dropped by 14 per cent and continued to drop in 2010. There is a lot of uncertainty with regard to 2011. In April 2010, I interviewed Milan, the firm's director. On 1 July I visited the factory, where I talked to the factory manager (Željko) and six workers (Mladen, a warehouse worker; Ivo, a shift leader; Branko, a quality control worker; Tvrtko, a shift leader; Tonči, a maintenance worker and Ljubo, a lathe worker).

Milan regards FNC as nurturing 'family-like relationships'. Every year, there is a Christmas dinner for all, and meetings are occasionally organized with factory employees. FNC provides regular pay. In February 2010, average net wages – before the cuts in 2010 – were 5,931 kuna (808 euros) and 4,867 kuna (663 euros) at the factory (the manufacturing average was 5,157 kuna or 702 euros). However, workers agree that they have few opportunities to exert influence or make themselves heard. They have no organized voice. There is no works council. An attempt to unionize in 1999 failed. Some 15 workers got a Construction Union of Croatia membership card (Ljubo showed it to me), but 'it was not received well by the firm'. The limits of paternalistic governance were clearly exposed in the crisis.

6.2.1 When reaching the core became reality

Following the construction boom, employment at FNC peaked by 2008 (Table 4.15). With workers on 'student' contracts and provided by subcontractors by the end of 2007 there were 160 and by the end of 2008 162 employees; 28 workers were employed on fixed-time contracts in 2007 and 21 in 2008. Both in 2007 and 2008 reliance on outside workers (auxiliary workers and security jobs) was high: 24 and 20, respectively. However, with the crisis the picture changed dramatically; 'now this is all done by our own people' (Željko).

Outside and temporary workers were the first to go in the employment cuts – both at headquarters and in the factory. By the end of 2009, the total workforce had been reduced to 133, that is, by 18 per cent, and outside workers were reduced to just one. The reduction in temporary employees continued into 2010, finally numbering only four in September. In addition, overtime was radically cut: in 2008 there was 7.5 per cent of overtime at FNC, and in the factory only about 10 per cent; at the start of 2009 it was suspended.

However, with the production fall in 2010, further adaptation was necessary, particularly at the factory, also involving permanent jobs. At a factory meeting (early 2010) workers were offered two options: to reduce FNC employment to (targeted as optimal in the given conditions) 108 (from 127 at that time) through a technological surplus programme (that is, collective dismissals) or to share the pain through solidarity-based reductions in working time and wages by 25 per cent until full capacity was restored. The second option was chosen: 'within three days, 99 per cent signed an annex to their work contract' (Milan). FNC applied for 'the government's subsidy, but we didn't meet the conditions' (making profits in 2008 and losses in 2009). In spite of that, the short-time programme started in March 2010. However, it was not enough to prevent further employment cuts, thereby reaching deeper into the core workforce.

In July 2010, 79 workers were employed in the plant (and 90 altogether at the factory, including sales and management), but 'ten are still surplus to requirements'. If the present level of production continues, the introduction of two 12-hour shifts and workforce reductions will be necessary, since there are 'three teams' which are not 'fully used' (Željko). September 2010 data show that cuts in employment are proceeding: resulting in a 14 per cent decrease in FNC employment from the end of 2008 to September 2010 (24 per cent if outside workers and students are included).

6.2.2　Was it just and fair?

Being on a special contract ('there are 7 or 8 of us') Željko has not experienced any earnings reductions. However, for production workers on shortened working time, wages were reduced by 25 per cent, even when they were working more than 75 per cent of their regular hours ('really it was 85 per cent'): 'it negatively affected workers' satisfaction, they became nervous and . . . it became more difficult to manage'. Discipline was beginning to fray. Workers were getting together, asking for explanations. The FNC's reputation in the region was also damaged: people were talking in bars and cafés and local press were unfavourable. Željko acknowledges that 'the system was unjust' and 'tactless' (he would have preferred a linear reduction for all). The interviewed workers considered the management of the crisis 'unfair', particularly in the March–June period: 'it isn't right that only those in production suffered wage cuts . . . we should have shared the burden, including managers and those from the city' (Ljubo); 'they reduced workers' wages but not their own' (Tvrtko).

Željko alerted head office and in June an hourly wage was introduced. But no one is permitted to exceed the 85 per cent limit of full-time working time. Workers welcomed the change ('now wages will depend on hours worked . . . the previous solution put everyone in the same basket, both good and lousy workers; now workers are more satisfied and less nervous' – Ivo). However, their take-home pay has been significantly reduced – the elimination of overtime is particularly significant. Namely, it could add some 15 per cent to workers' wages. Reported reductions are between 15 and 25 per cent. Having said that, while pay is low for many, it is at least regular and everyone receives a Christmas bonus and travel expenses.

6.2.3　Organized voice lacking

FNC provides decent working conditions and cares for its employees – within limits inevitably exposed by the crisis. The lack of an organized workers' voice makes crisis management more difficult. Whether this will lead to conflicts, particularly if further workforce reductions come onto the agenda, remains to be seen. Most of those interviewed would now support the union, but they fear exposure: 'people are afraid of losing their job; there is nowhere else to go . . . and they pay wages regularly' (Ljubo). 'It was an issue among us, but nobody wants to make the first move' (Ivo). 'Everybody is in debt and we are afraid of the sack; we want things to remain as they are' (Branko). FNC is a sound firm, with good products, and important both to its employees (who can hardly find alternative employment) and to the local community (both for employment and contributions to the local budget). However, there is no guarantee that further cost and employment reductions, if it comes to that, will not result in open

Table 4.16   Employment at GC, 2007–2010 (period ends)

2007	2008	2009	2010 June	2010 September
1226	1176	1091	1089	1071

Source: GC.

conflict. Prolonged crisis in the construction sector, with a bleak outlook for 2011 and even 2012, is putting a lot of strain on all involved: foreign owners, local managers and, particularly, employees. This is certainly a firm whose employees could have benefited a lot if successful policies on subsidized short-time had been put in place in time. On the other hand, it well illustrates some typical features of the Croatian story: after temporary and subcontractor workers took the first hit, permanent employees suffered increasingly, too.

6.3   Electrical Company GC: Managed the Crisis Well – with Luck

GC is a major producer of electrical components. After long cooperation, OGC, a multinational concern, bought a majority share in GC in 1992. This brought new investment and technological upgrading; 75 per cent of sales are made through OGC. I visited GC in July 2010 and interviewed Vlatko (CEO), Petar (union president), Mario (works council president), Igor (foreman) and four shop-floor workers (Ines, Sanja, Daria and Martina).

GC has been a 'family-like firm' for decades, with children of GC employees always having priority in getting a job, explains Petar. This is reflected in the high unionization rate – around 80 per cent in 2008–2010 ('younger people are harder to recruit', he added). The GC union was established in 2001 as an independent union (previously it was a branch of SMH). Close relations between the management and the union resulted in the union, as well as the works council, being included in crisis management from the start. This will prove important in the firm, in which long-tenured employees predominate. In October 2008, there was a meeting with Vlatko, and twice monthly thereafter, explains Petar, who has a high regard for his handling of the crisis. Vlatko concurs: social dialogue is 'developed and trust-based'.

6.3.1   GC affected early – but made a rapid but soft response
GC felt the effects of the global crisis early (by September 2008), as first US, then EU orders fell. This resulted in falling sales and revenues in

2008 and even more so in 2009. An operating profit in 2008 turned into a loss, although this was reduced in 2009, due to a good end of year. On 1 October 2008, 'we announced that the crisis was coming' (Vlatko). Management reacted quickly by implementing a set of measures (for example, reduction in night work, suspension of overtime, capacity and investment reductions, including moving some production to subcontractors) and developing alternative crisis scenarios. As Table 4.16 shows, the major employment effect was in 2008 and 2009: cuts were achieved with incentives offered for earlier retirement, and with regular retirement and/or workers leaving GC without being replaced.

By the end of 2007 there were 28 on temporary contracts. Unusually, with the advent of the crisis, all 'temps' received permanent contracts. In 2008, when a 20 per cent reduction in production was expected, incentives for early retirement led to 54 employees accepting it, followed by another 30 in 2009/2010. However, 'there were no crisis-related dismissals' (Mario).

By 2009Q1, while stocks were building up, a 'dilemma emerged: either fire 20 per cent of the workforce or reduce working time'. The first option was 'unfair . . . the whole burden would have fallen on those made redundant' (Vlatko). The second option was chosen. In agreement with the union, an annex to the collective agreement was signed on 31 March 2009, allowing management to reduce workers' wages by up to 25 per cent, while allowing workers to reduce their working time until 31 December. However, while applied to all employed at GC, this lasted until September 2009 only, when full working time was restored.

Namely, while orders fell more than expected in January–June 2009, GC prepared to make around 200 employees redundant. 'The parameters for dismissal were drawn up' (Petar): workers with poor disciplinary records and those eligible for retirement (with severance pay). If orders had fallen by 60 per cent, GC would even have moved part of its production to its plant in Bosnia-Herzegovina, where labour costs are lower. Fortunately, export markets recovered sooner than expected, in autumn 2009. At the same time, GC benefited from OGC's restructuring: 'the production of electrical switches was transferred to us [from Switzerland], ensuring full employment for the next three to four years' (Vlatko).

There has been a continuous trend of average wage increases, accompanied by widening wage differences, agreed with the unions (from 1:2.8 in 1992 to 1:8 today). The 2010 average net wage is 5,400 kuna (736 euros), close to the national average. The only exception was a period of shortened working time (April–September 2009) when wages fell by 20 per cent (but by more for some employees, due to overtime restrictions). Wages are always paid on time, and other rights have been fully complied with during the crisis. The Christmas bonus, uncharacteristically for Croatia, is tied to profits: it was 4,500 kuna (613 euros) in 2007, but 1,500 kuna (204 euros) in 2008 and 1,250 kuna (170 euros) in 2009. The Easter bonus of 400 kuna (54 euros) was reduced in 2009, as was the holiday bonus (from 2,500 kuna to 2,000 kuna – 340 to 272 euros).

The crisis at GC did not last long. By the end of 2009, GC was out of the woods and by 2010 'business as usual' had been restored. This also applies to working time and wages. Production was growing, but not employment. And the 2010 Christmas bonus has been increased – to 2,000 kuna (272 euros). Not surprisingly, most have a good word for the management. Daria: 'We were worried, but we trust our management, we can see that our director cares. They got things right and took the least painful path'. Sanja agreed: 'We should be grateful to Vlatko'. But Igor added: 'fortunately, Germany recovered quickly', aware that a soft approach was time-limited. In the crisis period, a shorter week and reduced wages were 'applied to everybody . . . up to the CEO'. Most interviewees seemed to agree that 'reduced wages are better than firing people . . . we prayed God that no one would be fired' (Sanja). However, while Daria was positive about the management, she thought that the burden was not shared fairly: 'I can't explain it . . . [but] restrictions on the shop-floor came earlier, and they were heavier than among the management'. Ines added: 'No, it wasn't fair – those on lower earnings suffered more', showing that fairness is a contestable but subjective notion. Even if restrictions are applied evenly to all employees, as seems to be the case at GC, some feel it harder than others. Simply, those on lower wages (and/or family earnings) are more vulnerable to crisis-related risks.

6.3.2 Uncertainties remain

Many would say that GC is a 'special case' in Croatian manufacturing: it suffered less than many, and for a shorter time. However, decent working conditions and path-dependent governance modes are under pressure from global competition and the globalized OGC, which owns GC. And fortunes may be reversed – while in this recession GC profited by taking over the 'Swiss programme', in the future GC programmes might be shut down or taken over. Moreover, Vlatko is a charismatic leader, strongly attached to the firm and its workers; he is GC's child in whom the workers trust. But he feels he cannot stay forever. And once he leaves, instead the idiosyncratic management which has eased GC's way through recession, the OGC's ways may prevail. The presence of OGC consultants in GC, 'who think that there is a surplus of 120 employees, while we think that we need an additional 110 in order to increase production' (Vlatko) adds to workers' fears and incessant speculation.

GC is strategically responding to the abovementioned pressures by technologically upgrading, optimizing capacity and developing its network of subcontractors to which older production lines based on low-skilled jobs are moved. Taking into account such a strategic orientation and the already low share of those not working in production (close to 90 per cent are engaged in direct production), it seems that further adjustments will most likely be borne by unskilled workers, among whom women predominate, but also by subcontractors whom Vlatko described as 'our flexibility buffer'. While the GC case shows that a proper and timely management response and good social dialogue, based on transparency and inclusivity, are important, the 'happy ending' may also be attributed to the rapid recovery of its export markets. For many firms, such a recovery came much later, at a higher cost, or not at all. In addition, this case shows that even in firms where no noticeable inequalities characterized the adjustment, subjective perceptions of fairness may conflict.

6.4   State Shipbuilding Company ABC: Restructure or Perish

For decades, shipbuilding has been an important industry and a major exporter. The industry's output is mostly the product of five loss-making state-owned shipyards, which are dependent on state subsidies, with one partial exception. Shipyards are major employers, directly and indirectly (through their suppliers); however, with the crisis their employment has declined.

The most significant reductions were in shipbuilding, particularly in the cooperating firms: overall employment fell from 15,435 in 2005 to 11,753 in 2010, that is, by 24 per cent (Table 4.17). Shipbuilding is a political 'hot potato' due to its huge economic and social impact, but also emotional (this is a long tradition) and a major issue in Croatia's EU accession negotiations on the Competition chapter. The opportunity to restructure while order books were full was lost. Nevertheless, removing untenable subsidies (forbidden under the EU rules) is a *sine qua non* for the European Commission, thus requiring their fundamental restructuring (making them viable without the present subsidies) or liquidation. The coming together of a global shipbuilding crisis, the fiscal crisis of the state and the finalization of EU negotiations brought things to a head.

6.4.1   Shipyards: continuing privatization plans despite the crisis
After the first unsuccessful privatization tender for four troubled shipyards in autumn 2009, the second tender, launched in spring 2010, brought four offers, including two for ABC.[13] The investor was supposed to offer a viable

Table 4.17   Employment in five state-owned shipyards, 2005–2010

	2005	2006	2007	2008	2009	2010
Shipyard 1 (group)	2783	2798	2761	2808	2796	2779
Cooperation	1833	1583	1387	1259	1342	1289
Shipyard 2 (group)	4096	4019	3930	3820	3742	3658
Cooperation	1540	1682	1622	1240	1061	719
Shipyard 3 (group)	3016	2997	2829	2734	2687	2661
Cooperation	1353	1410	1196	1178	395	512
Shipyard 4	561	557	505	486	521	526
Cooperation	424	308	164	186	327	352
ABC	1265	1254	1174	1152	1134	1247
Cooperation	624	656	623	632	380	203
Total group/shipyards	11721	11625	11199	11000	10880	10871
Total shipyards	9661	9298	8910	8689	8628	8678
Total cooperation	5774	5639	4992	4495	3505	3075

Source: Prepared by Hrvatska brodogradnja – Jadranbrod d.d.

restructuring programme, to be approved by the Government (Competition Agency) and the European Commission. Special committees were set up for each shipyard, which included the trade unions. The European Commission's request that the shipyards did not sign any new contracts before decisions were taken alarmed managements, employees, their representatives, but also local communities. 'This is dangerous – it would mean "turning the key in the lock"', commented Jure (union representative at ABC): 'we reacted strongly – we were ready to protest'. In shipyards with empty order books this would mean sending workers home to 'wait', with their wages reduced to the minimum, explained Vedran, president of the metalworkers' union (SMH). Unions threatened strikes and other forms of protest, calling on the Government to intervene if it wanted to avoid the explosion of a 'social time bomb' (Vedran in *Vjesnik*, 28 August 2010).

6.4.2   Two privatization options at ABC

In 2006, when I first visited ABC (Franičević 2007b), the management was preparing the restructuring plan in order to get ready for imminent privatization. The 2006 restructuring programme envisaged a 10 per cent reduction of the workforce by 2009 and later to 900 through regular retirement. It also envisaged a technological and human capital upgrade, but also the introduction of new profitable activities. Despite the Government's delays the programme has been continuously updated and will remain key to the management's activities.

In July 2010, I visited ABC again. I talked to Drago, restructuring manager, the two union leaders (Ivo and Jure) and four employees (Luka, Toni, Nikola and Dino). I focused on the two offers: one promising continuity in shipbuilding through restructuring and developing additional businesses; the other turning attractive land occupied by the shipyard into a tourist resort. The first bidder publicly expressed a readiness to align his offer with ABC's restructuring programme and to sign a social compact on labour and social rights which the trade unions had offered bidders. This bidder is favoured by both management and unions. The local community is also hoping for this outcome, as shown by a petition in October 2009 asking for the Government's assurance that the shipyard would continue, signed by 1,020 workers and 1,789 citizens. However, the voices and interests backing the second option are also strong, both locally and in the wider business community.

6.4.3   Core employees replacing subcontractors

Due to restructuring and crisis management (2009/2010 was particularly difficult), the number of ABC employees fell from 1,254 in 2006 to 1,134 in 2009 (year ends), mostly through regular retirement. However, in June 2010 numbers were back up again to 1,247. Behind this increase, however, is a considerable decrease in overall employment at the shipyard, which used to total as many as 2,000 when the workers of subcontractors on the shipbuilding sites are included.

Difficulties in financing production (the Government's reluctance to issue guarantees) in 2009 and 2010 ('the water was up to our neck' – Ivo) resulted in idle workers being sent home to 'wait' or sent on annual leave. However, the management's and the unions' focus was on preserving permanent jobs. Overtime was suspended and outsourced activities replaced, if possible, with the company's own workers. This resulted in a radical reduction in cooperation with subcontracting companies, from more than 600 workers in 2006–2008 to 203 by June 2010. Simultaneously with these cuts, around 100 workers who were working for subcontractors were instead invited to join ABC and employed on fixed-term contracts. Since some cooperating firms are likely to go out of business, ABC will have to take greater care of its own workforce: 500 are leaving over the next 10 years, making 'sustainability' and 'renovation' of the workforce 'the central issue' (Drago). However, this is the issue only if the first bidder wins the tender. If the second bidder wins, then the workforce will be reduced to '200 . . . strongly affecting the local population' (Drago).

For years, wages at ABC have been regular but highly dependent on overtime (Franičević 2007b). The crisis period led to earnings reductions in spite of the fact that in 2009 there was no decrease in the basic wage. Due to the suspension of overtime, take-home pay for many workers, particularly those in production, decreased by 10–20 per cent. However, fringe benefits have been fully respected. In addition, all 'contract wages' (managerial ones) were reduced by 10 per cent. Throughout 2010 wages have been below the national average (by some 10–12 per cent) but close to the manufacturing average. While some agree that the burden has been shared fairly (Luka, Toni and Ivo), some harsh words were spoken, too: 'While I have to go to the soup kitchen, management protected themselves with contracts, while the firm is making losses' (Dino); 'those on managerial wages do not bring new business or new technologies – something is wrong' (Nikola).

6.4.4 A window of opportunity, even though a narrow one

At present, the situation is serious and the window of opportunity is narrow: in crisis conditions, proving the long-term viability of the shipyard is difficult, while bidders' calculations look less credible in the presence of great uncertainty and depressed conditions in global (European in particular) shipbuilding. Will the five shipyards' story have a happy ending? Will we witness the end of shipbuilding in some of them, accompanied by difficult local economic and social adaptation, but also conflict? Whatever the outcome will be, many will lose their jobs and many should prepare to retrain for jobs outside shipbuilding which will certainly provide a critical test for the CES's capacities. ABC's restructuring, which includes the development of new activities, will also require internal retraining. The continuance of shipbuilding will also demand greater enrolment in local vocational schools for a number of occupations – at present, this is extremely low (Drago).

On the same day I interviewed Vedran (2 September 2010), the Government had given the 'green light' to continue the privatization of three shipyards, including ABC. Importantly for ABC, the first bid has been accepted. However, one should remain cautious; and particularly in the cases of two other shipyards in which the bidders do not enjoy the unions' support (due to their bad reputation, lack of experience, weak support from the banks and so on). Many fear the realization of the worst-case scenarios, leading to bankruptcy and liquidation. This may be the outcome for the shipyards whose restructuring programmes (offered by bidders) are rejected. Nevertheless, with the Government giving priority to 'putting this problem behind it' (as Vedran put it) and fulfilling the EU conditions, thus removing one of the major barriers to EU accession, one uncertain process is going ahead. And certainly, the Government's fiscal capacity to continue subsidizing loss-making shipyards is greatly reduced. On 22 September, up

Table 4.18 Case studies, Croatia, 2010 – summary

	Case 1: T&V	Case 2: FNC	Case 3: GC	Case 4: ABC
Sector	Low-level construction	Building materials	Electrical components	Shipbuilding
Ownership	Private/managerial	Private/Foreign	Private/Foreign	State ownership
Unions/Employees Council	Two unions/Yes	No/No	Enterprise union/Yes	Two unions/Yes
Employment change	7/09 to End 2010: −35%	2008 to 9/2010: −14%/−24% (with outside workers)	2007 to 9/2010: −13%	2007 to 6/2010: 6.2/−19.3 (with subcontractors)
Main targets of employment cuts	Temporary contracts; subcontracting; aged workers	Outside workers; temporary contracts; permanent	Aged workers	Subcontracting reduction; aged workers
Wage reductions	All (2–8%); with overtime reduced for many around 20–30%	Production workers 15–25% (overtime and shorter week)	For all by 20% in March–Sept 2009 period; also overtime reduction felt	Due to overtime wage cuts (10–20%); for Managers: wages by 10%
Benefit reductions	Yes	No	Yes	No

Working time adjust ments	No overtime; re-organization of working time; 'waiting'	No overtime; from March 2010 25% working time reduction	No overtime; from 3–9/2009, 25% reduction of working time	No overtime; some 'waiting'
Social dialogue on adjustments	Formal, but weak	No formal dialogue; meetings with workers	Strong, and regular	Strong, unions involved
Inequalities	Permanent workers vs. temporary and outside workers; production vs. non-production; younger vs. aged	Outside and temporary workers vs. permanent ones; Headquarters vs. factory	Pain shared by all; perception of greater share taken by the shop-floor	Permanent vs. subcontractor workers; Production vs. non-production
Current vulnerability of firm	High; barely restructured, too dependent on the state	Low; solid firm, with good and competitive production	Low, the crisis is 'behind'; vulnerable to vagaries of global markets	(i) Moderate if restructuring plan is accepted; (ii) otherwise extreme
Present workers' vulnerability	High; further cuts quite possible	Production workers at highest risk if recession deepens	Low, risk relocated to subcontractors	In case of (i) low in case of (ii) very high

to 3,000 shipyard workers (organized by the three unions) in Split went on a warning protest march through the city. They asked for the Government's guarantees that contracting new ships would not stop and their 'right to work' respected (as the media reported). Others may follow. Even in the case of ABC, where presently hopes are high, liquidation is still possible if the restructuring plan is not accepted by Brussels. In that case 'there are few who could change their careers (many are too old), opportunities to get jobs in foreign shipyards are much reduced, and our town could barely function (due to tax income loss)'. But Jure is realistic: 'it is high time that we cease our dependence on the state and the current model of governance'. So far, at ABC, the crisis adjustments put the heaviest burden on sub-contracting workers. However, if the restructuring plan of the first bidder does not receive the final 'go ahead', it would hurt the great majority of permanent employees, but particularly the older ones.

6.5   Lessons from the Case Studies: Vulnerable Firms, Vulnerable Employees

The case studies illustrate some of many paths firms have taken in the course of the recession (Table 4.18).

What do they point to? First, two categories of workers have had to bear the heaviest burden: temporary workers and outside workers from cooperating firms (T&V, FNC and ABC). They were first in line when it came to employment cuts; they had no voice.

Furthermore, the severity and duration of the recession forced firms into further adaptation and restructuring. The core workforce has also been affected, by reductions in employment and wages, but also fringe benefits (T&V, FNC). This particularly concerns production workers, and among them older workers, who are given incentives (GC) but also pressurized to take early retirement or register as unemployed (T&V).

Working time measures – typically the elimination of overtime (in all four firms) and/or the introduction of a shorter week (FNC, GC) – have a strong effect on wages: again, production workers suffered more (as in FNC) (even if all employees suffered cuts to some degree) (ABC, T&V).

Another important issue in managing the crisis is fairness: even though they are aware of the need for cuts, production workers tend to perceive their situation as unfair: they complain characteristically about those not engaged in production not taking on their 'fair share' of the burden (FNC and T&V in particular, ABC and GC to some extent).

Workers' adaptation strategies are diverse. In all four firms, faced with low or reduced family earnings they seek additional sources of income (moonlighting, small farming and so on) or of food (gardening), or simply depend on the help of relatives. Some are reaching into the unofficial economy in order to survive, but find it difficult there too, due to the recession (as some ABC and T&V workers complained).

Adaptation is an ongoing process: the crisis is still bottoming out and many uncertainties remain (for ABC in particular). For many firms and employees, it may continue for a long time (T&V, FNC, ABC), and for those so far unaffected, such adaptations might become necessary at some point in the future (GC). Lack of proper or any social dialogue (T&V, FNC) made the adaptation more difficult.

7. CONCLUSION

Throughout the 2000s, the Croatian labour market has experienced persistent problems, major vulnerabilities and inequalities, with structural issues and institutional deficits affecting job creation, unemployment risks and particular groups and regions. The crisis added to these problems and created new ones. The impact of the crisis on inequalities has been complex.

In the shorter term, the crisis has particularly affected – with regard to both employment and wages – some sectors (for example, construction, industry, trade and tourism) and related groups of workers (for example, males, prime-age, but also very young and older workers; those on temporary contracts and subcontractors' employees, but also 'core' workers). Most of this is supported by the case studies, too. It has created some characteristic inequalities: between production and non-production workers at the enterprise level (for example, T&V and FNC), but also between private and public sector workers more widely (where the gap has increased). Both have contributed to frequent use of 'us and them' discourse on inequalities, which reflects the actors' perceptions of unfairness in sharing the burden of the crisis.

Importantly, the chapter shows that temporary – and other sorts of 'flexible' – employment has not been the only one providing necessary adjustments in firms: the crisis has increasingly affected the core workforce with strong effects on their households too – overall, poverty risk has increased. This is still ongoing: pessimistic views of the crisis dominate. A December 2010 survey on business expectations by Privredni vjesnik (437 firms, employing 12 per cent of workers in the business sector) graded Croatia's general economic conditions a low 1.99 (on a scale of one to five), which is even lower than December 2009 (2.24) and December 2008 (2.82). Significantly, 41 per cent of firms expect reduced employment and 39 per cent that it will remain unchanged. Economic recovery is unlikely to come soon; further cuts seem imminent and not only in the private sector. However, the ability of public sector unions to protect workers is much greater that that of the private sector unions, which are shrinking. Existing inequalities due to workers' protection from social dialogue (large firms vs. small firms; new firms vs. old, privatized ones; permanent jobs vs. temporary jobs; older workers vs. younger workers) are only increasing in the crisis.

Gender inequalities have been somewhat reduced, due to the differential sectoral impact of the crisis, disproportionally affecting male-dominated sectors. However, it is unlikely that this will remain the long-term effect, as economic recovery resumes and pressure for public sector cuts increases. The same applies to the somewhat reduced wage and income distribution inequalities. Importantly, it has been shown in this chapter that some policies contributed to that too: particularly the minimum wage and protected pension and social welfare expenditure. In the long run, however, due to the fiscal vulnerability of the state and the pension system, this may change, particularly affecting older workers.

While both employment and wage adjustments were strong, working-time adjustments have been much weaker and the use of part-time arrangements modest. Firms' failure to manage working time more flexibly, policy failures to promote shorter working time, when needed (FNC case), and institutional inertia have contributed to that. Even more worrisome, for future working conditions, is that already very low expenditure on (re)training has been reduced even further. Cost cutting remains at the centre of Croatian firms' policy, with potentially further negative effects on workers and their working conditions, but even more on the increasing numbers of unemployed – with many at risk of unemployability, social exclusion and poverty.

In the longer term, structural issues will again come to the fore. If long-term unemployment has decreased for the time being, it is likely that it will increase again, putting skills mismatches in focus, but also shortcomings with regard to active policies aimed at the most vulnerable. From job losses, the focus will shift to job creation. Enhanced company competitiveness and increased activity are necessary if Croatia is to embark on a higher growth path. Problematic and worrisome is the lack of a social strategy and consensus on achieving that without compromising workers' security, employability and living conditions in the future. The crisis of national social dialogue is also worrisome. Employer pressure for radical reform of the labour market and industrial relations has been strong and is likely to remain so. Employers are demanding greater flexibility of employment, with easier 'firing and hiring', with labour cost reductions the key. Pressure to reduce public spending and guarantees (to vulnerable groups and sectors) is also strong and social policy reforms seem imminent. Unions' and other stakeholders' ability to confront such pressures, to protect workers' security in a changed and globalized (via the Single Market) context is highly uncertain, as is political actors' capacity to produce social consensus on a more inclusive and equitable growth path. In an uncertain situation, policies affecting the world of work will certainly come to the fore, particularly with regard to the distribution of the costs of reform. The eventual outcome, however, is anything but clear: whether inequalities will be consolidated and new ones emerge.

NOTES

1. I would like to thank Mr Jurica Zrnc for assisting me greatly with work on the LFS database.
2. I would like to thank Danijel Nestić for helpful comments and suggestions concerning this section.
3. Good pay, just pay, good working conditions, safe job, able management, pleasant co-workers, advancement opportunities, participation and interesting job.
4. In November 2009, 545 unions were registered, the majority of which are 'in-house unions' (that is, unions whose members are all employed in the same place of employment). There are around 50 sectoral unions and a large proportion of unions – 26 per cent – organized along occupational and professional lines (Bagić 2010: 134–37). Trade union density is comparatively high, at around 35 per cent (Kohl 2009; Bagić 2010). In Bagić's sample (n = 693 employees, stratified sample), private sector union density is 16.8 per cent and that in the public sector 68.1 per cent (Bagić 2010: 169).
5. Agreement was reached also on future changes to the Labour Code concerning cancellation of collective agreements (their duration may be prolonged by up to one year after expiry) and the organization of specialized labour courts (an old union demand).
6. I would like to thank Sandra Švaljek for helpful comments and information used in this section.
7. For example, among four subsidized credit schemes (Table 4.13) only model A has achieved notable results.
8. I would like to thank Darko Oračić of CES for the net replacement rate calculation.
9. Persons interviewed in April 2010 were: Filip, the CEO; Zlatko – the personnel director; Ljubica – president of Employees Council; Marija – president of the Independent Union; and Goran – representative of the Construction Union of Croatia in T&V.
10. In contrast to earlier regulations the Labour Code does not have a specific paragraph on 'waiting' (that is, being sent on forced paid leave). During the recession (as explained in a written communication by the SSSH union expert) employers are instead using an institution regulating 'interruptions of work not caused by the workers'. However, the practice of sending employees to 'wait' has remained in place, and legal dilemmas abound. It can be regulated by collective agreement; in the 2008 collective agreement for the construction sector, compensation for workers during a non-working period is determined in the amount of the basic wage (according to the tariff scale) to which one is entitled. While, until 2009, this was applied mostly in accordance with the collective agreement (for example, bad weather conditions), in the recession it became a major employers' tool. However, compensation does vary: from those who pay in accordance with the collective agreement to, 'increasingly', those who pay 'below that amount,

that is, either around 50–80 per cent below or in the amount of the legal minimum wage' (which is the case at T&V). The expert warns that the situation is particularly difficult in non-unionized firms where employers often make one-sided and illegal moves. In some cases, at otherwise solid but distressed firms, the unions turn a blind eye.

11. In December 2010, in a phone conversation Filip informed me that one of the suspended contracts (300 million kuna or 41 million euros) is finally 'going ahead' in spring 2011.

12. This practice (applied at other firms too) is controversial (see note 10). In our December 2010 phone conversation Marija informed me that some of the affected workers were suing T&V for this (confirmed by legal adviser from SSSH).

13. In October 2010, after the European Commission agreed, there was a third tender for the shipyard which had not received a bid in the second tender; three bids were received. The fifth one – which is better performing – is exempted from mandated privatization and allowed to tender autonomously.

BIBLIOGRAPHY

Bađun, M. (2010) 'Hrvatski mirovinski sustav i gospodarska kriza', Institut za javne financije, *Aktualni osvrti*, 21.

Bagić, D. (2010) *Sustav Industrijskih Odnosa u Republici Hrvatskoj: Hrvatski Sindikati Između Društvene Integracije i Tržišnog Sukoba*, PhD dissertation, University of Zagreb, Faculty of Philosophy.

CES (2010a) 'Annual Bulletin 2009', Zagreb: Croatian Employment Service.

CES (2010b) 'Anketa Poslodavaca 2010', Zagreb: Croatian Employment Service.

Croation Economic Outlook Quarterly (CEOQ) (2010) Zagreb: Institute of Economics.

EFILWC (2007) *Fourth European Working Conditions Survey*, Dublin: European Foundation for the Improvement of Living and Working Conditions.

EFILWC (2010) *European Company Survey 2009*, Dublin: European Foundation for the Improvement of Living and Working Conditions.

Franc, R., I. Ferić, S. Rihtar and J. Maričić (2010) 'Raširenost i obilježja diskriminacije na hrvatskom tržištu rada: Izvješće na temelju ankete među nezaposlenim osobama i ankete među poslodavcima', Zagreb: Institut društvenih znanost Ivo Pilar.

Franičević, V. (2007a) 'Croatia: Between EU normalisation and persistent hard reality', in F. Eyraud and D. Vaughan-Whitehead (eds), *Evolving World of Work in the Enlarged EU: Progress and Vulnerability*, Geneva: ILO, pp. 91–139.

Franičević, V. (2007b) 'Being at risk: Institutional and structural uncertainties in Croatian labour markets', in *Enterprise in Transition, Seventh International Conference on 'Enterprise in Transition', Split – Bol, 24–26 May 2007*, Faculty of Economics, Split.

Franičević, V. (2008) *Decent Work Country Report – Croatia*, ILO: Regional Office for Europe and Central Asia. Available at: http://www.ilo.org/public/english/region/eurpro/geneva/download/events/lisbon2009/dwreports/dw_croatia.pdf.

Galić, Z. (2010), 'Kvaliteta radnog života u RH: Jesmo li sretni na poslu?', presentation for the conference 'Može li se živjeti bez rada?', Zagreb, 24 November.

Hyman, R. and R. Gumbrell-McCormick (2010) 'Trade unions and the crisis: A lost opportunity?', *Socio-Economic Review*, 8: 364–72.

Kohl, H. (2009) *Freedom of Association, Employees' Rights and Social Dialogue in Central and Eastern Europe and the Western Balkans*, Berlin: Friedrich-Ebert-Stiftung. Available at: http.//library.fes.de/pdf-files/id/06606.pdf.

Leitner, S. and M. Holzner (2009) 'Inequality in Croatia in comparison', WIIW Research Report No. 355, June.

Marginson, P. (2010) 'New forms of co-operation, new forms of conflict', *Socio-Economic Review*, 8: 360–364.

Matković, T. (2010) 'Utjecaj ekonomske krize na tržište rada', Zagreb: UNDP Hrvatska. Available at: http://www.undp.hr.

MojPosao (2010) 'Djeca krize' (Children of the crisis), survey, January 2010, Zagreb. Available at: http://www.moj-posao.net/download/istrazivanja/DjecaKrize.pdf.

Nestić, D. (2010a), 'The gender wage gap in Croatia – estimating the impact of differing rewards by means of counterfactual distributions', *Croatian Economic Survey*, 12(1): 83–119.

Nestić, D. (2010b) 'Plaće u Hrvatskoj: Trendovi, problemi i očekivanja', presentation, mimeo, Zagreb.

Plečaš, M. and Z. Galić (2010) 'Quality of working life in time of crisis: perceptions of Croatian workers', Zagreb, unpublished manuscript.

RolandBerger (2010) 'Studija o restrukturiranju – Hrvatska 2010', Roland Berger Strategy Consultants. Available at: www.rolanberger.hr.

Sanfey, P. (2010) 'South-eastern Europe: Lessons from the Global Economic Crisis', EBRD Working Paper No. 113, February.

Šverko, B. and Z. Galić (2009) 'Kvaliteta radnog života u Hrvatskoj: subjektivne procjene tijekom posljednjih 15 godina', in V. Franičević and V. Puljiz (eds), *Rad u Hrvatskoj: Pred Izazovima Budućnosti*, Zagreb: Centar za demokraciju i pravo Miko Tripalo i Pravni fakultet Sveučilišta u Zagrebu, 197–223.

World Bank (2009) Programme document for a proposed development policy loan – DPL, 30 November.

World Bank (2010) *Social Impact of the Crisis and Building Resilience*, World Bank Report No. 55111-HR, Zagreb: World Bank and UNDP Croatia.

5. France: Protecting the insiders in the crisis and forgetting the outsiders?

Jérôme Gautié*

1. INTRODUCTION

Like many other countries, France was seriously hit by the recent crisis. Gross domestic product (GDP) fell sharply from the second quarter of 2008, and 300,000 jobs were lost during 2008–2009. The unemployment rate jumped from 7.2 per cent at the beginning of 2008 to 9.5 per cent at the beginning of 2010, the highest level since 1999. But the loss of jobs was not the only consequence of the crisis: many workers saw their wages reduced, because of a reduction in their working time and/or hourly compensation. All workers were not affected the same way. At first sight, an economic crisis should exacerbate inequalities – between the 'losers' who have lost their job or experienced a wage drop – and the 'lucky ones', who have not. But assessing the detailed impact of the crisis on inequalities is a quite complex matter.

The first reason for this is the difficulty of clearly identifying outcomes with appropriate data. If data on employment are easily and rapidly available, data on wages and outcomes and, even more, on working conditions, may not be available without delay, or in sufficient detail. But, even when data are available, difficulty arises from the timing of the different impacts of the crisis. One must differentiate between the short-term and medium- or long-term effects of the crisis. In the long term, the so-called 'hysteresis' effects should in particular be taken into account. The employability of the long-term unemployed, but also of new entrants to the labour market, may be lastingly affected by the crisis, and this may help to exacerbate inequalities for years to come. A second source of complexity is related to the difficulty of identifying the various factors at play that may contribute to influencing and 'shaping' outcomes in terms of inequality. The same economic shock may have different consequences across countries – in terms of employment, wages and incomes, or working conditions – depending on national institutional contexts.

Regulatory institutions play an important role. French wage-fixing mechanisms, with a legal national minimum wage (the so-called 'SMIC' – see Gautié 2010), which is relatively high compared to the median wage, as well as the legal extension of collective agreements, limit the possibility for firms to adopt 'social dumping' strategies based on wage cuts. Employment protection legislation (EPL) is also important, because it shapes firms' choices in terms of hiring and dismissals. According to the OECD index, EPL is at a fairly high level in France in comparison to many other countries. This may explain why the (short-term) elasticity of employment to economic activity is lower than in more 'liberal' countries, such as the United States or the United Kingdom. But a high level of EPL is also usually correlated with a high proportion of temporary workers (OECD 2004) and, therefore, a higher degree of dualism between 'insiders', on relatively protected permanent contracts, and 'outsiders', on temporary contracts which play a role as an adjustment variable during economic downturns. Indeed, the share of temporary workers among all employees amounted to about 13 per cent in France at the beginning of 2008, and during the first fourteen months of the crisis (April 2008–June 2009) more than half of all job losses were concentrated on temporary agency workers.

But France is also characterized by a high level of 'social protection' – including labour market policies – and this should limit the social impact of the crisis in terms of employment and, above all, income. But one must scrutinize the coverage and entitlement rights of different categories of people to assess the degree of inclusiveness of the social protection system.

Social dialogue may also play a role in the way the crisis affects inequalities, depending on how unions and employers take into account the interests of different categories of workers. Unionization is low in France (about 5 per cent in the private sector), and unions are weak and often divided at the firm level. Social dialogue is usually more vivid at industry and national levels, and unions also play a role in the social protection system, in particular in the governance of the unemployment insurance system. France is also characterized by a complex interplay between the social partners (unions and employers' organizations) and the state, which impacts notably on labour market policies and regulations, as well as on social policies.

All these features may contribute to an explanation of the outcomes of the crisis in terms of employment and incomes.

Section 2 presents the main symptoms of the crisis, in terms of growth and employment (at both global and industry levels). Section 3 assesses its impact on employment and unemployment inequalities, as well as on job quality – although the latter is harder to assess, because of lack of data. Section 4 turns to inequalities in wages and incomes, and Section 5 assesses the role of public policy and social dialogue. In Section 6 I present two case studies that illustrate the unequal impact of the crisis in terms of employment and compensation: the first focuses on short-term compensation schemes, the second on measures taken in favour of temporary agency workers. Section 7 presents some concluding remarks.

2.   ANATOMY OF A CRISIS: THE BASIC FACTS

2.1   Then Came the Storm

After the slowdown of 2002–2003, France recovered and experienced annual growth of about 2 per cent, on average, during the next four years.[1] This recovery induced a fairly large increase in employment: about 850,000 jobs were created between the beginning of 2005 and the beginning of 2008, and unemployment fell to its lowest level since 1983 (7.2 per cent).

France was hit by the crisis from the second quarter of 2008, and the bottom was reached during the first quarter 2009. Overall, GDP collapsed by –3.4 per cent during the downturn (from the peak 2008 Q1 to the bottom 2009 Q1), which was less than in Germany (–6.7 per cent from peak to bottom), Italy (–6.5 per cent) and the United Kingdom (–5.7 per cent). During the whole period covered here (beginning of 2008–beginning of 2010), household demand remained fairly stable during the period, limiting the negative impact on GDP, whereas household investment (about –14 per cent between 2008 Q2 and 2010 Q2), exports (about –14 per cent between 2008 Q2 and 2009 Q4), and private sector investment (about –10 per cent between 2008 Q2 and 2010 Q2) collapsed.

The impact on unemployment was significant: the unemployment rate rose from 7.2 per cent at the beginning of 2008 to 9.5 per cent at the beginning of 2010 – see also below – and the number of unemployed increased by 690,000 during this period (2008 Q1–2010 Q1, that is, a 34 per cent increase).

2.2   Impact on Different Sectors and Firms

The manufacturing and construction sectors were the hardest hit by the crisis in terms of employment in annual terms. Cumulated job losses in the manufacturing sector from the beginning of 2008 to the end of 2009 amounted to about 255,000 – that is, about 8 per cent – with a peak in job losses during the second and third quarters of 2009. In the construction sector, employment continued to increase until the fourth quarter of 2008, then declined continuously until the end of 2009 – there were more than 45,000 job losses during that year, about 3 per cent. Eventually, in the service and trade (competitive) sector, the decline in employment was less pronounced – about 231,000 job losses, less than 3 per cent – and the level of employment started to rise again during the last quarter of 2009.

It should be noted that, in these figures, temporary agency work is not counted in the utilizing sectors, but in the 'temporary work agencies' sub-sector, which is included in the service and trade sector. As a consequence, the effective decline in the actual number of employees was higher (and faster) in the manufacturing and construction sectors – where the number of temporary agency workers was particularly high before the crisis (see also Section 3.1) – than indicated here.

The negative impact of the shock was also differentiated according to firm size. The number of bankruptcies was higher among small and medium-sized firms: it increased by 52 per cent between 2008 and 2009 among firms with 50 to 200 employees, while it decreased (–28 per cent) in firms with more than 200 employees (Jeanneau 2010).

3. IMPACT ON EMPLOYMENT AND UNEMPLOYMENT INEQUALITIES: THE CONSEQUENCES OF A DUALISTIC LABOUR MARKET

3.1 Inequalities in the Risk and Manner of Losing One's Job

3.1.1 Temporary work as adjustment variable
Since the mid-1990s, the proportion of temporary agency work has increased continuously and dramatically (up by about 120 per cent in the whole economy, full-time equivalents – see Figure 5.1).[2] Even though their number increased most in the trade and service sector, temps are concentrated mainly in the manufacturing and construction sectors, the sectors hardest hit by the crisis. In 2007, the shares of the manufacturing sector and the construction sector, respectively, in temp agency employment was about 45 per cent and 21 per cent, while their shares in total employment in the competitive sector were only about 20 per cent and less than 9 per cent, respectively. Overall, the share of temps among employees amounted to about 7.5 per cent of the whole workforce in the manufacturing sector, and up to 8.8 per cent in the construction sector in 2007 (see Table 5.1).

The increasing use of temporary agency work is the result of changing company strategies and human resource management practices in the

Source: National Institute of Statistics and Economic Studies (INSEE), France.

Figure 5.1   *Evolution of temporary agency work, France, 1995–2007 (full-time equivalents, in thousands, upper figure, 1995 = 100, lower figure)*

past 20 years (Liégey 2009). Many firms decided to concentrate on their core activity and to externalize other activities. The subcontracting rate – measured by the share of the expenses of subcontracting in the turnover of firms – doubled between the mid-1980s and the mid-2000s, from about 4 per cent to 8 per cent. Even small and medium-sized firms were affected: the share of firms with fewer than 100 employees that subcontract part of their activity grew from 56 per cent to 86 per cent during the period.

Table 5.1   *Share of temporary agency work in total employment, France*
                2007 (%)

Agriculture	1.4
Manufacturing	7.5
Construction	8.8
Trade and services (competitive sector)	1.7
All	3.6

Source: INSEE.

Subcontractors bear the blunt of flexibility and therefore use more temporary contracts. At the same time, many firms adopted 'just-in-time' and 'lean' production processes, which require higher reactivity and therefore more flexibility. As a result, dualism did not increase only between firms – between (larger) firms and their (often smaller) subcontractors – but also within firms, between the core workforce and the peripheral workforce, usually younger and less skilled.[3]

As a result of the various forms of externalization, firms were able to decrease the volatility of both their value added and profits – while the volatility of their activity did not decline: according to Liégey (2009), since the beginning of the 1990s, at the macro level, there has been a fairly good correlation between the decline in volatility of value added and profits, on the one hand, and the increase in temp agency work on the other.

Due to all these changes, temporary agency work served as a buffer when the crisis came. Firms, especially in manufacturing and construction, reacted to the crisis by rapidly cutting the number of temps (see Figure 5.2) which accounted for more than half of the total employment decrease between the beginning of March 2008 and the end of June 2009.

3.1.2   Internal flexibility for permanent workers

Many firms tried to implement internal flexibility devices. The short-time compensation scheme, so-called 'partial unemployment', is one of them (for the French experience in a comparative perspective, see Bosch 2009 and Erhel 2009) – that is, a reduction in working time and wages, partially compensated by a public subsidy.[4] In order to facilitate the use of partial unemployment, a new tripartite national agreement was adopted at the beginning of 2009 (see Section 5.2, and also case study 1 in Section 6.1). To get the subsidy, a firm must seek authorization from the Ministry of Labour, which fixes the number of hours compensated. The number of authorized hours to be compensated by the state (Figure 5.3)[5] and the number of workers concerned (Figure 5.4) increased dramatically from

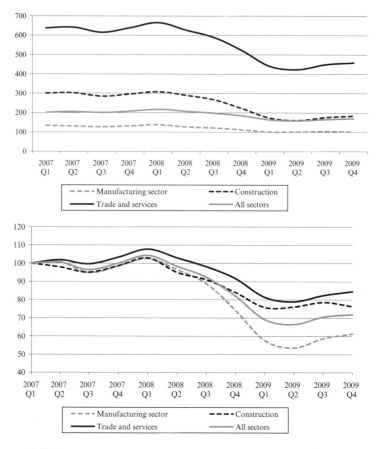

Source: INSEE.

Figure 5.2   *Quarterly evolution of temporary agency work, France, 2007–
              2009 (full time equivalents, in thousands, upper figure, 2007
              Q1 =100, lower figure)*

mid-2008 to mid-2009. When the peak was reached (second quarter of
2009), about 1.1 per cent of the total employed workforce was affected, as
compared to only 0.1 per cent at the beginning of 2008 (2008 Q1).

Working time flexibility opportunities and some schemes introduced
by the '35 hours law' at the end of the 1990s – such as annualization
of working time and time-saving accounts – were also intensively used
in many firms (see also Section 6.1, case study 1). Paradoxically, while
reductions in working time were implemented in many firms, the average

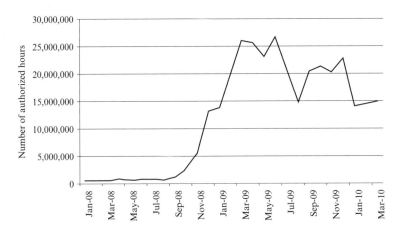

Figure 5.3   Partial unemployment: number of authorized hours, by year, France, 2008–2010

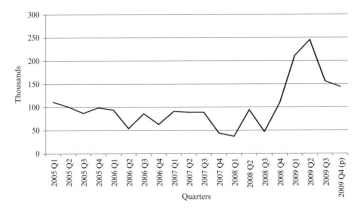

Figure 5.4   Partial unemployment: number of workers concerned, France, 2005–2009

number of overhours per employee in the private sector[6] did not decline, and even increased by more than 8 per cent between the second and the fourth quarter 2008. It then declined by 12.5 per cent during the first quarter of 2009, but increased strongly again from then onwards (+18.9 per cent between 2009 Q1 and 2009 Q4), while the number of employees was still declining. There is indeed a strong incentive for both the employers and the employees to use or do overhours, because since the adoption of a new law in 2007, the former benefit from employers' social contribution reductions, and the latter from income tax exemptions. Overall, it

Work inequalities in the crisis

Table 5.2   *Entry flows in the jobseekers list of the Public Employment*
            Service according to the previous employment status and the
            form of exit from the firm, France, 2007–2009 (in thousands
            and percentages)

	2007	2008	2009	% Change 2007– 2008	% Change 2008– 2009	% Share in 2008	% Share in 2009
End of fixed term	1341	1383	1481	3.1	7.1	25.6	24.6
End of temp agency contract	469	528	449	12.6	–15.0	9.8	7.5
Dismissal for economic reasons	197	185	266	–6.1	43.8	3.4	4.4
Other dismissal (mainly 'dismissal for personal motives')	701	693	643	–1.1	–7.2	12.8	10.7
Quits	270	266	225	–1.5	–15.4	4.9	3.7
First entry in the labour market	362	342	403	–5.5	17.8	6.3	6.7
Re-entry in the labour market	346	388	472	12.1	21.6	7.2	7.8
Others* (including 'termination by mutual agreement')	1661	1619	2081	–2.5	28.5	30.0	34.6
Total	5347	5404	6020	1.1	11.4	100.0	100.0

Note: * Mainly unknown.

Source: Ministry of Labour, DARES.

seems that many firms preferred to cut employment while maintaining overtime for their core workforce – that is, favouring external flexibility over internal flexibility, and therefore increasing inequalities between those who kept their jobs and those who lost them.

3.1.3   Inequalities also in the conditions of dismissal

Beyond temp agency work, analysis of the entry flows in the jobseekers list of the Public Employment Service shows that the great majority of new jobseekers were the least protected in terms of employment status, as well as in terms of conditions of dismissal (see Table 5.2).

Resulting from the specificities of the French EPL, the most protective form of dismissal for the workers is 'dismissal for economic reasons', even more so in the case of collective dismissals.[7] Workers dismissed for economic reasons can benefit from three schemes. The first, the '*congé de reclassement*' (outplacement scheme), is mandatory for firms with more than 1,000 employees. The duration is between four and nine months, during which the worker can benefit from specific follow-up and training measures. He or she keeps all his or her social security rights (in terms of pensions and so on), and receives from his or her firm 65 per cent of his or her former gross hourly compensation (85 per cent in the case of a minimum wage earner). Firms with fewer than 1,000 employees have to implement the CRP scheme ('*convention de reclassement personnalisée*') or the CTP scheme ('*contrat de transition professionnelle*') – the CTP being experimented with in only a few regions. Those schemes provide the jobseeker with a higher replacement rate than the standard unemployment benefit and with a reinforced follow-up and job search assistance provided by the Public Employment Service.[8] But to benefit from a CRP, an employee must have tenure of at least two years and a long enough employment record to be entitled to unemployment benefit. Recently hired workers (including many young people) are therefore excluded. Middle-aged skilled male workers make up a large proportion of the beneficiaries.[9]

Even though their number increased notably during the crisis, monthly entry flows for dismissals for economic reasons made up only 4.4 per cent of total entries in 2009, against about 7.5 per cent for entries due to the end of a temporary agency work contract and 24.6 per cent for those due to the end of fixed-term contracts.

But the most striking fact is the big jump in the entries due to 'other reasons'. This includes 'termination by mutual agreement' ('*rupture conventionnelle*'), which is not legally considered as a quit nor a dismissal, *stricto sensu*. This new legal way of terminating a labour contract was introduced at the beginning of 2008, and no data are yet available on the content of agreements (in terms of effective severance pay, accompanying measures and so on). They numbered 128,000 in 2009 (Jeanneau op. cit.).

3.2 Outcomes in Terms of Unemployment: Inequalities in Terms of Age, Gender and Skill

Because women are less concentrated in the manufacturing and construction sectors than men, their unemployment rate did not rise as much (see Figure 5.5).

Young people and older workers were severely hit by the crisis: between the first quarter of 2008 and the second quarter of 2009, the number of unemployed increased by 39 per cent among 16–24 year olds and 32 per cent among 55–64 year olds, as compared to 'only' 24 per cent among 25–49 year olds. But from then on, whereas youth unemployment stabilized and even decreased slightly, the number of unemployed aged 50 years and over continued to increase sharply, as did the number of middle-aged unemployed (see Table 5.3).

This indicates that, in fact, the negative impact on adult and senior workers may have been only delayed, with young people, often on temporary contracts, serving as a buffer. The significant increase in the declared unemployment of older workers results not only from dismissals but also from an increase in their participation rate. Two reforms adopted before the crisis have played a role here. First, the pension reform of 2003 acted as an incentive to postpone retirement. Second, unemployed workers of 57 years of age or over could receive, under some conditions, their unemployment benefit without being required to search actively for a job under the DRE (*Dispense de Recherché d'Emploi*) scheme. As a result, they were not considered as officially unemployed (that is, according to ILO criteria), but instead, as being out of the labour force. But the DRE scheme was reformed in 2008 and the minimum entry age was progressively increased (to 58 in 2008 and 59 in 2009), as a result of which the number of new entrants in the scheme fell from 155,000 in 2007 to only 77,000 in 2009. As a consequence, many workers who would have entered the DRE scheme before the reform were now on unemployment benefit (and considered as unemployed according to ILO criteria).

The most dramatic effects are perhaps yet to come, especially for low-skilled workers of age 50 or over, with long tenure in their previous job, who are particularly hard to place once unemployed. But long-term effects may also impact young workers – more particularly, the 2008 and 2009 cohorts of school leavers. According to the CEREQ (2008) such a 'scarring' effect on a cohort of school leavers was observed after the 2003 recession.

Long-term unemployment – and the resulting potential 'hysteresis' effect – may be a significant problem in the coming months, and even years. The share of unemployed who have been seeking a job for one year or more decreased notably during the first months of the crisis, due to the great number of new entrants resulting from cuts in employment. But it started to rise rapidly from the first quarter of 2009 – jumping from 32.2 per cent in 2009 Q1 to 37.9 per cent in 2009 Q4.

3.3   A Substantial Impact on Job Quality?

If the rise in unemployment is the most obvious symptom of the crisis, the consequences for the workers that remain employed (or find a new job) should also be taken into account. Indeed, one should expect some deterioration in average job quality. Beyond pay, on which we will focus in

Table 5.3 Unemployment rate by gender and age, France, 2005–2010 (last quarter of each year)

	Men				Women				All			
	Age			Total	Age			Total	Age			Total
	15–24	25–49	>49		15–24	25–49	>49		15–24	25–49	>49	
2005	20.1	7.1	5.9	8.1	23.5	9.8	6.2	10.2	21.6	8.4	6.0	9.1
2006	21.7	6.8	5.8	8.0	21.7	8.4	5.8	8.9	21.7	7.5	5.8	8.4
2007	17.7	6.3	4.8	7.1	19.0	7.6	5.2	8.0	18.3	6.9	5.0	7.5
2008	21.4	6.1	4.9	7.4	19.7	8.0	5.3	8.4	20.6	7.0	5.1	7.8
2009	25.3	8.2	6.4	9.4	22.9	9.1	6.7	9.7	24.2	8.6	6.5	9.5
2010 (*)	22.0	8.3	6.0	9.1	24.7	8.6	6.2	9.4	23.3	8.6	6.1	9.3

Note: * 2nd quarter.

Source: INSEE.

209

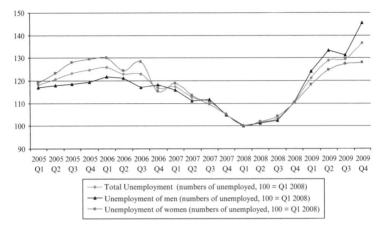

Source: INSEE.

Figure 5.5   Unemployment, France, 2005–2009 (2008Q1 = 100)

the next section, 'job quality' covers all the employment terms and working conditions attached to a job: job security (contractual basis of the employment relationship), social entitlements (such as health insurance, pension, paid vacation, parental leave, paid sick days and other non-wage compensation), training and career opportunities, work schedules (imposed or desired), work pace, health and safety conditions, and many other things.

Assessing the impact of the crisis on job quality is particularly complex, not only because of the numerous dimensions to be taken into account, but also because of the lack of detailed data on many of them. For many aspects, one has to rely on case studies.

One of the indicators of the deterioration in job quality may be the rise in the share of part-time jobs, notably among young women (Figure 5.6), and, beyond that, the increase in under-employment, covering 'involuntary part-time' and partial unemployment (see Table 5.4).

Case and field studies may provide some interesting empirical evidence on the evolution of job quality. According to the Alpha (2009) report,[10] in the manufacturing sector, the crisis has induced reallocation of jobs from large firms to smaller ones, with lower job quality (in terms of pay, working time and other working conditions). Some displaced workers have also had to take a job in the personal service activity (caring and so on), which is also characterized by lower job quality. In some sectors, such as big retailers, if the negative impact on employment was fairly limited, the crisis has accelerated the introduction of new work organizations intending to cut costs, with an impact in terms of work intensification.

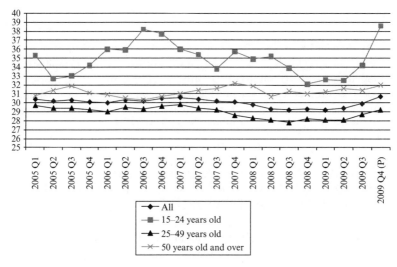

Source: INSEE.

Figure 5.6 *Evolution of part-time work among female employees (in %), France, 2005–2009*

Table 5.4 *Under-employment (in thousands), France, 2008–2010*

	2008 Q1	2009 Q2	2010 Q2 (p)	Evolution 2008 Q1- 2010 Q2 (%)
Part-time workers, wishing to work more hours, and looking for another job (1)	283	311	311	+ 9.9
Part-time workers, wishing to work more hours, and not looking for another job (2)	860	911	1046	+ 21.6
Workers on 'partial unemployment' or functional equivalent (3)	32	275	126	+ 293.8
Total (= 1 + 2 + 3)	1175	1497	1483	+ 26.1
Underemployed women	924	1061	1087	+ 17.6
Underemployed men	251	436	396	+ 57.8

Source: Ministry of Labour (DARES).

Another consequence of the crisis is an increase in the violations of labour law, especially for temporary work. This may be an important element, especially in the French context. Indeed, in a comparative perspective, the French labour market may appear highly regulated, but because unions are often weak or absent at the workplace level, and because the number of labour inspectors is relatively low, law violations are numerous, especially in sectors intensive in low-skilled/low-paid work (Caroli and Gautié, 2008; Gautié and Schmitt, 2010).

4. IMPACT ON WAGES AND INCOME INEQUALITIES: SO FAR RATHER LIMITED, THE WORST MAY BE TO COME

4.1 Wage Inequalities: Limited Impact of the Crisis

4.1.1 Basic wages little affected by the crisis

To assess the impact of the crisis on worker's earnings, one must differentiate between the basic wage, on the one hand, and bonuses and premiums on the other.

The average monthly basic wage (MBW) was apparently little affected by the crisis. Its growth did decelerate – from an annual rate of about 3.1 per cent between June 2005 and June 2008, to 2.2 per cent between June 2008 and June 2009 – but as inflation also decelerated, and at a faster pace, on average the purchasing power of basic wages increased. Moreover, the inequalities between occupational skill levels tended to be stable (or even to decrease slightly) during the period (see Table 5.5).

The limited impact of the crisis on the basic wage is confirmed by a survey[11] on wage policies during the first year of the crisis (Horny et al., 2010 – see Table 5.6). Cuts in basic wages were implemented in only 1 per cent of firms. One must remember that, according to French labour law, a basic wage cut requires a written modification of the labour contract, which must be officially approved by the worker. Moreover, more than 90 per cent of workers in the private sector are covered by a collective agreement because of the legal extension mechanism.[12] Those agreements usually fix a minimum wage level for every skill level. Nevertheless, restrictions due to legislation do not seem to be the main reason for not decreasing the basic wage. More than 80 per cent of firms declared that such a wage cut would have had a negative impact on motivation and effort, and more than 60 per cent feared they would have lost their best workers; results which are in line with basic models of efficiency wage theory. Nevertheless, those considerations did not prevent about 30 per

Table 5.5   Evolution of the monthly basic wage according to occupational level, France, 2005–2009

	Evolution June 2005– June 2006 (%)	Evolution June 2006– June 2007 (%)	Evolution June 2007– June 2008 (%)	Evolution June 2008– June 2009 (%)	Evolution June 2009– Dec 2009 (%)	Evolution June 2005– Dec 2009 (%)
Blue-collars	3.1	2.9	3.3	2.2	0.7	12.8
Clerks	3.1	2.8	3.1	2.2	0.7	12.5
Intermediate occupations	2.6	2.5	2.9	2.2	0.7	11.5
Managers, executives, engineers	2.5	2.5	2.8	2.0	0.6	10.8

Source: INSEE.

Table 5.6   Wage policies during the crisis, France, 2009 (% of firms)

	Basic wage		Other components of compensation
	Decrease	Freeze	Decrease
Total	1	81	30
Manufacturing sector	2	80	39
Trade and services	0	82	28
Small and medium-sized firms	1	78	28
Large firms	1	86	36

Source: Banque de France, survey on a representative sample of firms of more than five employees in the manufacturing, trade and service sectors, summer 2009. Horny et al. (2010).

cent of firms cutting components of compensation other than the basic wage (see Table 5.6).

4.1.2   Bonus cuts but potentially affecting more skilled employees

Indeed, bonuses and premiums are more sensitive to the economic downturn, especially performance-based individual and collective bonuses, as well as earnings from profit-sharing (see below).

The share of premiums and bonuses (other than profit-sharing) in compensation increases with the compensation level (and is higher for full-time than for part-time workers) (Table 5.7), so their decline in the

Table 5.7   Structure of compensation, France, 2006 (earnings from profit-sharing schemes not included)

	Basic wage	Over hours	Bonuses and premiums	Total
All	86.3	1.3	12.4	100
Quartile of compensation level:				
Less than Q1	91.7	1.6	6.7	100
Between Q1 and Q2	88.4	1.8	9.8	100
Between Q2 and Q3	85.8	2.0	12.2	100
More than Q3	84.4	0.6	15.0	100

Source: Bignon and Folques (2009).

Table 5.8   Structure of bonuses and premiums, France, 2006 (earnings from profit-sharing schemes not included)

	Seniority	Work constraints	Individual performance	Collective performance	Other	Total
All	16	12	27	5	40	100
Quartile of compensation level:						
Less than Q1	22	13	13	5	47	100
Between Q1 and Q2	22	15	15	6	42	100
Between Q2 and Q3	22	18	17	5	38	100
More than Q3	11	8	35	6	40	100

Source: Bignon and Folques (2009).

crisis should have affected more high wage workers. This is confirmed by a more detailed analysis of premiums and bonuses (Table 5.8). The seniority premium – which cannot be cut – represents a higher share at lower wage levels, whereas it is the reverse for individual and collective performance-based pay, which is more sensitive to the economic situation of the firm. Note that other kinds of bonuses were affected by the crisis, such as night work premiums (included in 'work constraints bonuses and premiums'), which affect more blue-collar workers. With a decrease in activity, many firms in the manufacturing sector suppressed night shifts, and many young low-paid blue-collars, in particular those who had accepted night work to increase their earnings, were affected (Alpha 2009).

Table 5.9   Earnings from profit-sharing, France, 2006

	Share of employees benefiting from profit-sharing (%)	Surplus in earnings provided by profit-sharing schemes (%)
All	43	7.8
Quartile of compensation level:		
Less than Q1	29	8.6
Between Q1 and Q2	39	7.7
Between Q2 and Q3	42	7.8
More than Q3	57	7.7

Source: DARES, Ministry of Labour, Bignon and Folques (2009).

4.1.3   Profit-sharing schemes as a flexibility tool in the crisis

Profit-sharing schemes are widespread in France, in comparison to other European countries. According to a European survey, 35 per cent of French establishments implement a profit-sharing scheme (called *'intéressement'*), the highest level in the EU27.[13]

The share of earnings from profit-sharing schemes in the total compensation of the employees that benefit from such schemes is on average (slightly) higher for low-paid workers – that is, those in the first quartile of the wage distribution (Table 5.9) – but only 29 per cent of them were affected, in comparison to about 40 per cent of the employees in the second and third quartiles of distribution, and up to 57 per cent in the highest quartile.

In some sectors, such as the automotive industry, which has been hard hit by the crisis, bonuses, premiums and gain-sharing represent a share of total compensation much higher than the average indicated in Tables 5.8 and 5.9. Cuts in those components of compensation were important in many firms in these sectors (see Section 6.1, case study 1 for some evidence on the automotive industry). But the share of low-wage work is fairly low in these sectors (in 2006, for instance, only about 4 per cent of the workers in the automotive industry earned the SMIC as their basic wage, as compared to 11.3 per cent in the manufacturing sector as a whole, and 14.6 per cent in the private sector as a whole).

Overall, cuts in bonuses and premiums and gain-sharing earnings may have affected more middle- and high-paid workers than low-wage workers. But at the time this chapter was written, no detailed data for 2008 and 2009 were available concerning the effective impact of the crisis on bonuses and premiums.

4.1.4   Working time reductions: inequalities in terms of compensation

We may assume that the employees who suffered the biggest drop in earnings were those who experienced 'partial unemployment'. The reform of the partial employment scheme adopted during the crisis significantly increased the compensation of hours not worked (see Section 6.1). In some branches and/or firms, collective agreements have introduced more generous compensation or specific advantages, as in the chemical industry and the automotive industry, for instance (see Section 6.1). Overall, there may be significant inequalities concerning the situation of workers in partial unemployment, depending on industry and firm. While large firms in the manufacturing sector, especially in sectors where the average wage is relatively high, were often able to limit the reduction in compensation, many other firms were not able to do so.

4.2   Impact on Income Inequalities and Poverty

4.2.1   Buffer role of the income maintenance scheme: crucial, but unequal

As the French social protection system is one of the most developed in the world, income maintenance schemes have played a crucial role. Nevertheless, some vulnerable groups are less protected than others, so the crisis has increased some inequalities.

Even if unemployment insurance benefit became more generous in terms of access, after the February 2009 reform (see Section 5.2), the coverage is still rather low: at the end of 2009, less than 75 per cent of the jobseekers registered at the Public Employment Service in Category A (covering those who have not worked a single hour during the month) were receiving the benefit. There is also an income support form of unemployment benefit (that is, a means-tested allowance), for those who have an insufficient employment record to be covered by the unemployment insurance system, or who have exhausted their insurance allowance. But one must have worked at least five years during the past ten years to be entitled. As a consequence, many unemployed persons are excluded – and in particular young people – and the coverage rate is only about 10 per cent of all jobseekers. Overall, about 40 per cent of job seekers do not receive benefit. In 2010, more than one million unemployed were expected to fully exhaust their unemployment insurance benefit by the end of the year, of whom 360,000 were not entitled to unemployment assistance or minimum income benefit.

The minimum income benefit, the RSA (*Revenu de Solidarité Active*), replacing the former RMI (*Revenu Minimum d'Insertion*), which is also a means-tested allowance and was reformed at the beginning of 2009, functions as a safety net (460 euros a month for a single person). But one must be 25 years of age or above to be entitled: once again, young people are excluded. At the end of 2009, a reform was introduced to facilitate the access of young people (see Section 5.2), but its expected impact is limited.

Overall, because of the gaps in the social safety net, young people and workers with sparse employment records are the most vulnerable groups. The measures targeted on them adopted in 2009–2010 (see Section 5.1) have not been sufficient to countervail the increase in poverty.

4.2.2 Poverty: is the worst yet to come?

Beyond the expected evolution of wage inequalities, the impact of the crisis on income inequalities and poverty was not easy to assess at the time this chapter was written (end 2010), as the requisite data were not yet available. The Gini index of income inequalities was not known for 2008 and 2009 and, as regards the poverty rate, the last data published by the National Institute of Statistics were for 2008. Other poverty indicators may be taken into account, such as the number of beneficiaries of the minimum income benefit (RMI, RSA since mid-2009). This number was decreasing until the end of 2008, but started to increase during the first quarter of 2009 (+1 per cent).

This timing is the result of a well-known phenomenon: the delay between the increase in unemployment and the increase in poverty. The delay may be even longer in the current crisis, due to the emergency measures that were targeted at low-income workers and households (and also measures decided before the crisis – see next section). Correlated with the expected decline – or at least stagnation – of median income following the economic downturn, these measures may even induce a decrease in the poverty rate (measured at 60 per cent of the median income threshold) in the short run, which would be a truly paradoxical outcome of the crisis (Observatoire de la Pauvreté 2010). But other forecasts are much more pessimistic: according to the OFCE (2009), the elasticity of the number of poor to the number of unemployed should be about 45 per cent between 2007 and 2010 – each increase of 100 unemployed leading to an increase of 45 in the number of poor.

When objective indicators are lacking, one may turn to subjective ones. One of the most striking results of the Flash EuroBarometer (2010) on perceptions of the crisis is that the French were among the most worried and pessimistic about the evolution of poverty – especially in relation to comparable countries in terms of GDP per capita. In the survey conducted in May 2010, 35 per cent of French respondents declared that they had the feeling that poverty 'had strongly increased' during the past 12 months in the area where they live – close to Italians (37 per cent), but higher than in Spain, Latvia and Lithuania, for instance, where the crisis was much

Table 5.10   *Perceived changes in the level of poverty in the past twelve*
months in the area where the respondents live, May 2010
(% of respondents declaring they had the feeling that poverty
had 'strongly increased')

BG	HU	IT	FR	LV	LT	EU27	DE	UK	NL	DK	SE
52	41	37	35	33	27	24	11	9	7	6	4

Source: Flash EuroBarometer (2010).

deeper, and well above Germany, the UK, the Netherlands, Denmark and Sweden (Table 5.10).

5.   TACKLING THE SOCIAL CONSEQUENCES OF THE CRISIS: THE ROLE OF PUBLIC POLICY AND SOCIAL DIALOGUE

5.1   The Main Measures Adopted

The main measures adopted to cope with the economic and social consequences of the crisis are summarized in Table 5.11 (see also Erhel, 2009; Freyssinet, 2010; Zemmour, 2010).

A first set of policy measures was introduced at the end of 2008. This initial recovery plan was based mainly on financial aid given to firms and public investment. There were few measures to sustain household consumption, and the modest 200-euro one-shot allowance targeted at social assistance recipients was conceived rather as an emergency measure to alleviate poverty. Overall, the recovery plan was fairly limited. This was the outcome of a number of factors.

First, the public deficit was already high in 2007 (almost 3 per cent of GDP), so the government's room to manoeuvre had already been reduced when the crisis arrived. Second, concerning social policies, important measures had been taken or agreed just before the crisis and were expected to have a significant positive impact on low-income households. They included the reform of the minimum income benefit, with the introduction of the RSA (see above), which is also an in-work benefit, and therefore should contribute to lowering working poverty. A major increase in a number of other means-tested allowances had also been decided. Eventually, following a small peak in inflation in 2008 (2.8 per cent), it had been decided to increase (in 2009) two of the main social allowances

– family allowances and housing allowance – by 3 per cent. It should be noted that their share in the disposable income of households in the first quintile of the distribution of the standard of living amounts to 26 per cent. As inflation strongly decelerated in 2009, the planned increase had a significant positive impact on the purchasing power of low-income families.

On the social partners' side, the main outlines of reform of the unemployment insurance system had been decided in January 2008 (before the crisis). The reform was adopted in February 2009 (following a national collective agreement in December 2008), modifying the rules on unemployment benefit in order to better cover the unemployed with poor employment records. The employment record required to be entitled to the unemployment insurance benefit – that is, funded by the Unemployment Insurance System (called UNEDIC, see below) – was decreased, and the maximum duration of benefit was extended.[14]

Due to the political pressure exerted by left-wing parties and the unions (with major demonstrations in the first quarter of 2009 – see below), and growing public anxiety, the Government was forced to adopt new measures from the start of 2009 (tripartite 'social summit' in February, tripartite agreement in April), including: a special allowance for some unemployed persons not receiving unemployment benefit; an increase in those involved in active labour market schemes; reform of the 'partial unemployment' scheme to improve coverage and income replacement; and specific measures targeted at young people. Measures to sustain household consumption were also applied, such as a cut in income tax and the distribution of vouchers to buy household services.

From the end of 2009, social emergency measures were also introduced, for young people (in September) and for the long-term unemployed whose unemployment benefit entitlement had expired (tripartite agreement of April 2010).

Overall, the public deficit rose sharply, to about 8 per cent of GDP in 2009. With regard to government spending, however, in comparison to other OECD countries, the cumulated budgetary stimulus for 2008, 2009 and 2010 was below the Eurozone and the European zone averages (5.2 per cent, as against 6.0 per cent and 6.3 per cent, respectively). Moreover, most of the budgetary impulse resulted from automatic stabilizers – in other words, from the decrease in fiscal resources and the increase in social expenditure mechanically induced by the economic slowdown. In 2009, according to National Institute of Statistics (INSEE) estimates, the impact of the discretionary measures of the recovery plan amounted to only about 0.7 per cent of GDP.

Table 5.11   Overview of the main anti-crisis measures, France, 2008–2009

Measures	Respective role of state and social partners	Categories of workers/ households targeted and/ or impacted
Recovery plans • Public investment/ measures targeted at firms or specific sectors (recovery plan of December 2008): – increase in public investment (infrastructure, such as new high speed train lines) – special measures for the automotive industry – tax credits for firms • Consumption/measures targeted at households: – 200 euros for social assistance recipients (recovery plan of December 2008) – reduction in income tax ('social summit' of February 2009) – subsidies for purchase of household services (vouchers) ('social summit' of February 2009)	Government policy, but unions put considerable pressure on the government to adopt the measures announced during the 'social summit' of February 2009	The 200 euro 'one-shot' premium affected 3.8 million *low-income households* Vouchers for the purchase of household services benefit *low and intermediate households* Reduction in income tax benefits the *middle class* (as almost 50% of households in France are exempted from income tax)
Unemployment benefit • Reform of insurance benefit (national collective agreement of December 2008): – reduction of minimum employment record required for unemploy- ment insurance benefit (from 6 to 4 months) – extension of benefit duration	The reform of unemployment insurance was initiated by the social partners that govern the Unemployment Insurance System (UNEDIC)	All these reforms result in better coverage of the least vulnerable groups, such as unemployed with a poor employment record (among them numerous young people) and long-term unemployed

Table 5.11   (continued)

Measures	Respective role of state and social partners	Categories of workers/ households targeted and/ or impacted
• Specific measure for unemployed with low employment record: ('social summit' of February 2009): 500 euro premium for those not entitled to insurance benefit, but who have worked between 2 and 4 months in the previous 28 months (and who are therefore not eligible for unemployment insurance) • Specific measure for long-term unemployed (LTU) not entitled to unemployment benefit (insurance or assistance) (tripartite agreement of April 2010): special allowance of 6 months duration	The special allowance for LTU results from an agreement between the state and social partners and is funded half by the government, half by UNEDIC	
Active labour market policy (ALMP) • Special employment subsidies for firms of fewer than 10 employees (recovery plan of December 2008): total exemptions from employers' social contributions for all new workers earning less than 1.6 × SMIC • Increase in number of subsidized jobs in private and public sector (2009 and 2010)	Both the government and the social partners participated in the reform of partial unemployment; specific tripartite agreements were also adopted at industry and firm levels Measures for long-term unemployed also resulted from a tripartite agreement, and UNEDIC	Several measures are targeted at the most vulnerable groups, in terms of both employability and of income replacement (long-term unemployed with no unemployment benefit, low-skilled unemployed young people) Other measures, such as partial employment and, to a lesser extent, the CRP for displaced workers (dismissed for 'economic reasons'),

Table 5.11   (continued)

Measures	Respective role of state and social partners	Categories of workers/ households targeted and/ or impacted
• Reform of partial unemployment (national collective agreement December 2008, 'social summit' of February 2009, tripartite agreement April 2009) – increase in the maximum number of authorized hours – increase in replacement rate • Reform of specific ALMP measure (CRP) for displaced workers (national collective agreement, December 2008) – extension of the duration (from 8 to 10 months) – increase in replacement rate (80% during whole duration) • Specific measures for long-term unemployed not entitled to unemployment benefit (insurance or assistance) (tripartite agreement April 2010) – subsidized jobs in the private and public sector – specific training measures • Specific measures for unemployed young people (Emergency Plan for Youth Employment, April 2009)	participates in funding Allowance of CRP scheme funded by UNEDIC, but state participates through follow-up of beneficiaries implemented by PES	benefit better protected workers

Table 5.11 (continued)

Measures	Respective role of state and social partners	Categories of workers/ households targeted and/ or impacted
– subsidized jobs in the private and public sector – specific training measures		
Other measures • Specific measures for unemployed young people ('Action for Youth Plan', September 2009): – young people below 25 years of age can benefit from minimum income benefit (RSA), from which they had previously been excluded, if they have worked at least two years out of the past three – specific training measures • Creation of the Social Investment Fund (FISO) ('social summit', February 2009): this Fund, created for two years, is intended to coordinate and participate in the funding of projects concerning employment, follow-up measures for the unemployed and vocational training	Measures for young people were adopted by the government Unions (especially the reformist CFDT) initiated the FISO project; it is funded by both the social partners (through UNEDIC and funds from the vocational training system they govern) and the state	The FISO intervention may apply to any type of unemployed worker or workers at risk of losing their job

5.2 Expected Impact on Various Groups in Society

To understand the measures adopted by the state and the social partners, and how they did or did not take into account the interests of various social groups, one must take into account, as pointed out by Freyssinet (2010), the complex interplay between the relevant players.

Oversimplifying somewhat, because of the mixed Bismarkian–
Beveridgian tradition, it may appear that, in France, the social partners usually take care of 'insiders' through the social insurance system,
while the state takes care of 'outsiders' by implementing several income
maintenance schemes based on the social assistance (in other words,
means-tested) principle. The best illustration of this is probably the unemployment benefit system. Since the early 1980s, it has relied on two separate
systems: the unemployment insurance system, funded by workers' social
contributions and governed by the social partners (through an institution
called UNEDIC), and unemployment assistance benefit, a means-tested
allowance funded by the state (in other words, the tax-payer). However,
this example also illustrates that, in fact, it is not easy to separate the
responsibilities and prerogatives of the state and the social partners. At
the end of 2009 and the beginning of 2010, there was growing concern
about the 360,000 unemployed who were to lose their unemployment
insurance benefit. The first reaction of the main employers' organization,
MEDEF, which plays a central role in UNEDIC, was to declare that only
the Government should intervene, whereas the Minister of Employment[15]
stated that 'unemployment benefit is above all a matter for the social partners' (quoted by Freyssinet 2010: 10). Eventually a solution was found
(see above, and Table 5.11), due to the pressure exerted by both the social
partners and public opinion.

The complex strategic interactions between the state and the social
partners rely on many channels. Unions may influence government policy
by staging major demonstrations: this was the case at the beginning of
2009 (between one and two million people demonstrated on 29 January),
when the Government was forced to propose a tripartite 'social summit'
and to announce the new measures already mentioned. As pointed out by
Zemmour (2010), this summit was considered a turning point in government policy (even if the unions were far from satisfied). Indeed, policy
measures adopted during the first half of 2009 were targeted more at
middle-income, better protected (also in terms of entitlements to unemployment benefits) workers and/or households. Middle-aged, semi-skilled
or skilled male workers, with long employment records, often working
in manufacturing sectors where wages are relatively high, were indeed
prominent among the beneficiaries of the 'partial unemployment' scheme
or of the special 'CRP' scheme for displaced workers (see Section 3.1),
which were reformed to improve coverage of workers. Middle-income
households also benefited more from the fiscal measures adopted (see
Table 5.11).

But does this mean that, overall, unions promoted the interests of
'insiders' and rather neglected 'outsiders' (in other words, the most vul-

nerable groups)? Following Freyssinet (2010), we might consider this criticism unfair. First, as detailed in Table 5.11, many measures adopted by the social partners, either alone (national collective agreements) or with the state (tripartite agreements), were intended to improve the situation of the most vulnerable groups, through unemployment benefits or active labour market schemes. The unions also urged the Government to intervene more in favour of temporary workers when they lose their job. However, financial constraints mean that policy towards these workers has remained modest (see Section 6.2, case study 2).

Second, the distinction between 'insiders' and 'outsiders' must be approached very cautiously. Workers in large firms in the automotive industry benefiting from partial unemployment (see Section 6.1, case study 1), may appear privileged in some respects, but they may also be considered 'vulnerable' workers, since, for many of them, the chances of finding a new job if dismissed are not high. The focus of the unions on such supposed 'insiders' may therefore be considered as a strategy for the development of preventive measures rather than merely curative ones for those who are already 'excluded'.

Overall, even if they have benefited from specific measures, the long-term unemployed and low-skilled unemployed young people again turned out to be the most vulnerable groups. The extension of the minimum income benefit (RSA) to young people, so far excluded from it, was symbolic. But the conditions are so restrictive (working two years out of the past three) that this extension can be expected to benefit very few unemployed young people.

6.   CASE STUDIES: CONFIRMING THE DUAL SYSTEM

As already mentioned in Section 3, a stark contrast has been discernible during the crisis between, on the one hand, the protective measures implemented in many sectors and firms in favour of the core workforce – the so-called 'insiders' – and, on the other hand, the fairly brutal buffer role played by temporary workers. The following case studies focus on this contrast. As seen in the previous sections (for example, Section 3.1) there has been intensive use of the short-time compensation scheme called 'partial unemployment' in France during the crisis, encouraged by the Government and the social partners. It is a good example of internal flexibility used to protect the core workforce, and we will illustrate this by analysing the reaction to the crisis of the two main firms in the French automotive sector, Renault and Peugeot (Peugeot Société Anonyme –

PSA). This sector was chosen because it was among those hardest hit by the crisis. Conversely, the second case study analyses what happened to 'outsiders' – temporary agency workers. As already mentioned, they suffered considerably in terms of job losses during the crisis. We will analyse what measures – if any – were implemented to help them during this period.

6.1 Internal Flexibility to Limit Job Losses: The Use of Short-time Compensation Schemes in the Automotive Industry

6.1.1 Role of social dialogue in reform of short-time compensation schemes

The main short-time compensation scheme known as 'partial unemployment'[16] (*chômage partiel*) was introduced in 1968 by a national collective agreement. Partial unemployment is intended to help firms coping with a temporary fall in activity due to a short-term economic downturn or exceptional circumstances – including disaster (fire and so on), significant building work and restructuring, or supply difficulties.

The scheme was modified several times between the end of 2008 and the end of 2010, and a new scheme was introduced in April 2009, 'Reduced Activity of Long Duration' (*Activité Réduite de Longue Durée* – ARLD).[17] The various features of the schemes are presented in Table 5.12.

All the parameters of the partial unemployment scheme were modified in order to facilitate its use: the eligibility criteria concerning the restriction on part-time work were suppressed, and the maximum duration and the maximum number of annual hours authorized were increased, as were the replacement rate of the allowance received by the employee and the amount of public subsidy.

One important concern was training, which was prohibited during the partial unemployment period. The restriction was abolished, however, and in the new ARLD scheme, training is strongly encouraged. Beyond the replacement rate, which is more generous than that of the partial unemployment scheme, ARLD innovates in the nature of the funding of the subsidy for firms: UNEDIC, which is governed by the social partners and funded by social contributions, participated, taking over the additional subsidy (of 3.90 euros, on top of the 3.33/3.84 euros provided by the state) from the fiftieth hour of inactivity.

The role of social dialogue has been crucial in these reforms, and it has long been one of the most consensual issues. The social partners first agreed (by a national collective agreement in December 2008) to increase the replacement rate of the allowance paid by the employer, and then asked the state to increase its subsidy, and also to increase the maximum duration and hours authorized, which it did immediately. As for the introduction of ARLD, it was a government initiative, and a tripartite national agreement was reached in April 2009, defining the contribution of UNEDIC.

But social dialogue also played an important role at the industry and firm levels – as illustrated below – where the detailed implementation modalities had to be determined.

In a way, all these changes – and in particular the introduction of the ARLD – benefit workers, who gain from higher compensation while on 'partial unemployment'. But at the same time, they favoured potential inequalities as the use of the most 'generous' scheme (the ARLD) – because it is more costly for the employer, despite the higher public subsidy – is in fact restricted to large firms in (relatively) high wage sectors. Another source of potential inequalities is that these schemes are just a regulatory framework, and their precise modalities of implementation have to be fixed at industry and firm level and therefore depend on the bargaining power of the workers affected.

6.1.2 Internal flexibility tools available in France

Since the mid-1990s, partial unemployment in France has been strongly affected by the introduction of the working time reduction (WTR) scheme (Calavrezo et al. 2007).[18] WTR not only involves reducing legal weekly working time from 39 hours to 35 hours, but has also introduced significant working time flexibility. Firms are now legally required to use this tool rather than partial unemployment. Most firms have adopted the 'annualization' of working time,[19] as well as, in many cases, individual and collective 'time-saving accounts'.

The working time reduction scheme has tended to replace partial unemployment as a flexibility tool since the end of the 1990s. The number of days of partial unemployment authorized by the administration[20] has strongly decreased, being cut almost by six between 1996 and 2005 (Calavrezo et al. 2007).

During the 2008–2009 crisis, the increase in the use of partial unemployment was much higher among large firms, as well as in the manufacturing sector (Tables 5.13 and 5.14).[21] More than 91 per cent of the authorized hours were concentrated in this sector at the end of 2008 – as against 65 per cent in January of the same year – and the figure was still 85 per cent at the end of 2009. Conversely, employees in the tertiary sector, and especially in small firms, were much less affected, also simply because their sector was not hit by the crisis to the same extent. Note that the decline of partial unemployment from mid-2009 is partly due to the introduction of ARLD.

Table 5.12 Short-time compensation schemes, France, 2008–2010

	PU in 2008 (before the crisis)	PU, end of 2009	ARLD (since April 2009)
Eligibility criteria	*Employees*: Low-paid part-time workers excluded (that is, partial unemployment restricted to employees earning more than the 18-hour minimum wage rate a month)	Restriction on part-time workers abolished	No restriction on part-time workers
Maximum duration (in case of total inactivity)*	4 weeks per employee	6 weeks per employee	6 weeks per employee
Maximum hours per year	600 per employee	800, and even 1,000 for some sectors: textiles, clothing and leather, automotive	1,000 hours in all sectors
Short-time allowance as a percentage of monthly wage	50% of hourly gross wage (that is, about 63% of wage net of social contributions), with a minimum of 4.42 euros per hour	60% of hourly gross wage (that is, about 75% of hourly wage net of social contributions) with a minimum of 6.84 euros per hour	75% of hourly gross wage (that is, about 90% of the wage net of social contributions) with a minimum of 6.84 euros per hour
Assessment base for short-time allowance	Paid vacations are not taken into account	Paid vacations are taken into account	Paid vacations are taken into account

Public subsidy and remaining wage costs for employers	Lump-sum public subsidy (funded by the state): – 2.42 euros for firms with fewer than 250 employees – 2.13 per cent for firms with more than 250 employees Short-time allowance may be partially exempted from employers' social contributions	Lump-sum public subsidy (funded by the state): – 3.84 euros for firms with fewer than 250 employees – 3.33 euros for firms with more than 250 employees Short-time allowance may be partially or totally exempted from employers' social contributions	Lump-sum public subsidy (funded by both the state and the Unemployment Insurance System): – 3.84 euros + 1.90 euros (3.90 euros from the 50th hour) for firms with fewer than 250 employees – 3.33 euros + 1.90 euros (3.90 euros from the 50th hour) for firms with more than 250 employees Short-time allowance exempted from employers' social contributions
Other conditions	Employees benefiting from partial unemployment cannot be trained during the relevant period	Employees benefiting from partial unemployment cannot be trained during the relevant period	The firm must sign an agreement for 3, 6, 9 or 12 months, maximum, with two mandatory commitments: – the employer must offer each employee on ARLD a skills evaluation and/or a training programme – the employee cannot be dismissed during a period double the length of the agreement**

Notes: * That is, if the employee does not work at all (if the establishment is closed, for example); ** For instance, if the agreement between the firm and the Ministry of Labour has been signed for a six-month period, the employee cannot be dismissed during the subsequent 12 months.
PU = Partial Unemployment; ARLD = Reduced Activity of Long Duration.

Table 5.13   Number of authorized hours by size of establishment, France,
2008–2009 (100 = January 2008)

	Establishments of below 20 employees	Establishments of 20–50 employees	Establishments of 50–249 employees	Establishments of 250 employees or more	Total
January 2008	100	100	100	100	100
December 2008	444	706	2,132	5,536	2,186
December 2009	1,838	2,302	5,347	5,727	3,761
Share in December 2009	12.7%	15.4%	33.7%	38.1%	100.0%

Table 5.14   Number of authorized hours by sector, France, 2008–2009
(100 = 2008)

	Manufacturing sector	Construction	Trade and Services (private sector)	Total
January 2008	100	100	100	100
December 2008	3,108	689	636	2,485
December 2009	4,868	2,450	2,461	4,258
Share in December 2009	85%	3%	11%	100%

6.1.3   Initial adaptations in the automotive sector: Peugeot-Citroën and Renault

As the automotive industry was one among the most severely hit by the crisis (sales plunged in Europe by 25 per cent between mid-2008 and mid-2009), it may be interesting to take it as an illustration. In particular, we will focus on the large firms Peugeot-Citroën (PSA) and Renault, to analyse how the short-time compensation schemes were implemented and how they complemented other flexibility tools.

When the crisis hit from mid-2008, the first reaction of all the firms in the sector was to cut the number of temporary agency workers and workers on fixed-term contracts. About 4,000 temporary workers were employed by PSA before the crisis, and about 3,000 by Renault. These numbers were reduced almost to nil at the beginning of 2009, with no accompanying measures for temps. As for permanent workers, working time flexibility tools were used.

First, there has been some wage flexibility. The share of bonuses and premiums in the automotive industry, which amounted to 13.3 per cent of average compensation (profit-sharing not included) in 2006, is slightly higher than average (12.4 per cent – see Table 5.7, Section 4.1). Both the share of the seniority premium (28 per cent of all bonuses and premiums, as compared to 16 per cent in all sectors) and the work constraints premiums (32 per cent in comparison to 12 per cent) are particularly high. Premiums for shift work and night work may represent up to 25 per cent of total compensation (gain-sharing not taken into account) for some workers. At Renault, for instance, the hourly rate for shift work is about 40 per cent higher than the normal hourly rate for the lowest paid workers. As in the other firms, the hourly overpay for night work usually amounts to 20–25 per cent of the basic (hourly) wage. But the number of shifts (especially night shifts) has decreased considerably due to the crisis. Blue-collar workers were therefore particularly hard hit, in contrast with white-collar workers who are not affected by these premiums.

Profit-sharing also plays an important role. There are two profit-sharing schemes at Renault, for instance: one at the enterprise level, the other at the plant level. The gain is proportionate to the basic wage. In 2007, profit-sharing for the lowest-paid workers amounted to between 3,220 euros and 3,700 euros (2,500 euros coming from the central level, 720 euros to 1,200 euros depending on the plant) – that is, the equivalent of 2 to 2.5 monthly basic gross wages (which amounted to 1,390 euros for the great majority of the lowest-paid workers). In 2008–2009, profit-sharing at the enterprise level was reduced to zero, and it was strongly reduced at plant level. There is some inequality between workers according to the plant they belong to, as the adjustment depended on the plant.

Internal flexibility tools were also used. Both Renault and PSA had introduced, at the end of 1999, when the 35-hour working week was implemented, individual and collective time-saving accounts for employees. Collective time-saving accounts are used as flexibility tools;[22] whereas employees are free to use the time accumulated in their individual time account as they want.

At PSA, each hour of overtime (that is, above 35 hours) goes towards the collective account, up to 35 hours. After that, every additional hour of overtime goes towards the individual account. When the workload is low, the firm can ask workers to stay at home, deducting the corresponding hours from their collective time account. The balance of the collective account can even be negative, with a maximum 35-hour deficit.[23] In case of a deficit, employees must compensate by working more hours in the future, when the firm asks them to do so, but not proportionally: for example, if they have a 35-hour deficit – that is, corresponding to five days' work – they will have to work only 21 hours (that is, three more days), within a two-year period, to compensate. At Renault, the time-saving account system is different: working time is annualized, and the reduction in working time to 35 hours a week was implemented by increasing the number of days off (ten more days holiday during the year) instead of reducing weekly working time. Seven out of these ten additional days off go towards the collective time-saving account, and the other three towards the individual account. But the use of collective time accounts is decentralized: each establishment has its own 'local agreement on flexibility'. For instance, in some establishments, workers can work even on Saturdays, and up to 48 hours a week during certain periods. In this case, the hours worked during the weekend and/or over 37 hours a week go towards the collective time-saving account, which also serves as a flexibility tool for the establishment, as at PSA.

6.1.4   The reliance on partial unemployment

But these tools turned out rapidly to be insufficient to cope with the plunge in activity, and both enterprises had to use the partial unemployment scheme from the end of 2008, and the new ARLD scheme from mid-2009.

At PSA, in December 2008, for instance, some workers were asked to stay at home for the entire month, *de facto* exceeding the fixed maximum deficit authorized for their collective time-saving accounts (−35 hours). At the end of the first semester of 2009, the global deficit of all collective saving accounts amounted to three million hours. The firm therefore resorted to the partial unemployment scheme. During the first semester of 2009, the total amount of hours of partial unemployment amounted to the equivalent of 3,000 full-time jobs. Instead of an allowance amounting to 60 per cent of the gross wage – that is, about 75 per cent of net wage (which was now the legal requirement) – PSA maintained the full wage, but with a corollary: employees had to compensate for it in the future by working 12 more days for each period of 25 days on partial unemployment. Partial unemployment and collective saving accounts (with no more limits on the deficit) were used as complementary tools. From April 2009, as made possible by the new regulation, the firm asked for a quid pro quo: training during the partial unemployment period. About 700 workers were trained in 'lean production' methods between April and July 2009. Then, in early September 2009, the new ARLD was introduced, following a collective agreement signed by all the unions (six of them are represented at the central level). Executives and managers were not affected – in other words, they were exempted from any form of partial unemployment. The short-time allowance amounted to 75 per cent of gross compensation or about 90 per cent of the net wage (but work constraints premiums, such as premiums for shift work and night work, were not included). If an employee on ARLD wanted to maintain 100 per cent of their net wage, they could increase their deficit hours on their collective account (under certain conditions), or use the surplus hours on their individual account. Those who agreed to be trained while on ARLD benefited from a 100 per cent replacement rate.

The story was similar at Renault, although with some important differences. Executives and managers (*les 'cadres'*) were also affected by the short-time compensation scheme, but with a 100 per cent replacement rate. As a quid pro quo, for every five days on partial unemployment or ARLD, one day was taken from their individual time-saving account and went into a specific fund, the 'crisis solidarity fund', which was introduced when the first 'crisis social collective agreement' (*accord social de crise*) was signed in March 2009. This fund was used to increase the allowance of other workers (blue-collars and clerks) on partial unemployment or ARLD. There was therefore some solidarity between higher- and lower-paid workers. Moreover, for blue-collars and clerks, unlike at PSA, the allowance was based on total compensation (with replacement rates of 60 per cent in the case of partial unemployment and 75 per cent in the case of ARLD); that is, including premiums. Employees could also complement their allowance up to 100 per cent of their net wage by using their individual time-saving account – using one day for every 10 days on partial unemployment. As at PSA, social dialogue played a crucial role at Renault: the agreement introducing the ARLD (December 2009) was signed by all the unions (five at the central level).

6.1.5 Concluding remarks

In many ways, the permanent workers at Renault and PSA appear to be privileged. First, they were partially protected by a 'peripheral workforce' of temporary agency workers – used intensively in this sector – who lost their jobs without any accompanying measures. Second, they benefited from fairly generous short-time compensation schemes with high public subsidies. Nevertheless, there were some inequalities among the workers at the two firms. Concerning compensation, blue-collars were hit harder overall, as many of them lost a number of premiums, such as the night shift bonus, and they were more affected by 'partial unemployment'. At PSA, executives and managers were exempted. At Renault, the inequality between blue- and (high wage) white-collars was reduced by the introduction of a 'solidarity fund'. This shows that the way in which a general

Table 5.15   Evolution of temporary agency work by occupation, France, 2008–2009 (full-time equivalents)

	Percentage change in 2008	Percentage change in 2009	Share in 2009
Executives, managers	−11.0	−15.8	1.8
Intermediate occupations	−2.2	−19.4	8.0
Clerks	+2.3	−18.6	14.4
Skilled blue-collars	−6.6	−26.0	39.5
Unskilled blue-collars	−6.5	−30.1	36.2
Total	−5.0	−25.7	100

Source: Ministry of Labour (DARES).

scheme (such as the ARLD) is implemented at firm level – and therefore, social dialogue – impacts on potential inequalities.

6.2   Caring for Outsiders: Were There any Specific Measures for Temporary Agency Workers?

6.2.1   The youngest and least skilled are the most vulnerable among temporary workers

As seen in Section 3.1, temporary work was severely hit by the crisis; and temporary workers were revealed to be the most vulnerable groups during the first year of the crisis. It is striking that inequalities are also strong among temporary workers, as some groups (the youngest and the lowest skilled) are more vulnerable than others.

The decline was the sharpest among blue-collar workers, and in particular unskilled blue-collar workers (see Table 5.15). The number of temps (in full-time equivalents) aged below 25 decreased by 31 per cent in 2009, in comparison to 24 per cent for those aged between 25 and 49 years old, and 21 per cent for those aged 50 and over. Note that the distribution of hours worked throughout the year is very uneven as, in 2009, 50 per cent of temps did only 10 per cent of total hours of temporary work. The crisis does not seem to have affected this dimension of inequality, as the distribution was almost exactly the same in 2007 – that is, before the crisis (Domens 2010).

6.2.2   Some initiatives at industry level, but of limited impact

While the government was fairly active in the protection of permanent workers through short-time compensation schemes (see Section 6.1), in sharp contrast, almost no policy measures were targeted at temporary workers. At the end of 2008, the unions asked the Government to extend the CRP follow-up measure (restricted to permanent workers laid off for 'economic reasons' – see Section 3.1),[24] but their request was rejected because the cost was considered too high. As a consequence, only a few measures were taken at the industry level, besides some local initiatives, but with limited impact.

It must be remembered that the regulation of temporary agency work in France is among the strictest in Europe. Firms are not allowed to use temporary agency work as a substitute for permanent work. The maximum duration is 18 months, and a 'precarity premium' amounting to 10 per cent of the basic wage must be paid to temporary workers. Moreover, social dialogue is alive and well rooted in the temporary work agencies sector, and many collective agreements have been signed in the past decade, in particular on vocational training. A specific mutual fund for training exists at the industry level, the 'FAF-TT' (*Fonds d'Assurance Formation du Travail Temporaire*), which collects a mandatory contribution amounting to 2 per cent of the total wage bill of temporary work agencies. At least 50 per cent of these funds must be dedicated to the training of temporary workers (that is, not the permanent workers employed by temporary work agencies). In local areas, several temporary work agencies can decide to work together to outline a training programme to meet the needs of the local labour market, and seek funding from the FAF-TT. These 'collective' training programmes are called 'OPALs'.

As the funding of the FAF-TT is based on temporary work agencies' payroll – in other words, permanent employees in the agencies and temporary workers contracting with the agencies – it was severely affected by the crisis, experiencing a 30 per cent fall between 2008 and 2009. The Ministry of Employment therefore decided to react, not only on a short-term basis (by increasing the number of training schemes for unemployed temporary agency workers), but also in the medium term, aiming also to train temporary workers for allocation to, supposedly, the most promising sectors in terms of job creation after the crisis. An agreement to this end was signed between the Ministry of Employment and the temporary work industry. The FAF-TT received a special public subsidy for a two-year period (2009–2010). This subsidy was allocated mainly to training schemes targeted at the most vulnerable groups: low-skilled workers, young people below 26 years of age without experience, jobseekers of 45 or over and social assistance recipients. Note that for the latter (young people, older jobseekers and social assistance recipients), no condition was imposed in terms of work experience as a temporary agency worker before they could benefit from a training scheme. The agreement was signed in May 2009. One year later (April 2010), the total number of beneficiaries throughout the period amounted to fewer than 2,000 persons, which is very low, reflecting the very low public subsidy allocated to this programme (6.7 million euros for the two years).[25] Overall, even if there was some attempt to implement specific schemes for temporary agency workers, the public investment in those schemes was so low that their impact was very limited.

6.2.3 Local responses: The '*Pôle Position*' scheme in Northern France

At the local level, a number of initiatives emerged to provide temporary workers with follow-up services. The most important during 2009–2010 was the '*Pôle Position*' scheme, which was introduced in northern France. This region is highly specialized in the automotive industry: automotive constructors and their subcontractors employed about 55,000 workers at the beginning of 2008, and almost 25 per cent were temporary agency workers. Almost half of them (about 5,000) lost their jobs between September 2008 and March 2009. Note that temporary workers in the automotive industry constitute a specific population: they usually have long-term contracts (up to a year, or even more in some cases);[26] and their hourly wage is relatively high.

This region was one of the few in France in which the CTP (*Contrat de Transition Professionnel*)[27] was experimented with. The local branch of the public agency for adult vocational training, the AFPA (*Association pour la Formation Professionnelle des Adultes*), which was in charge of the CTP, decided to introduce a similar scheme for unemployed temporary workers who, like all other temporary workers, were not entitled to the CTP or any other follow-up scheme. The first step was to establish a partnership with other institutions, such as the local branch of the Public Employment Service and the institution in charge of the training of temps at the industry level (FAF-TT – see above), but also five local temporary work agencies. The funding – with an initial budget of 3 million euros or so – was provided mainly by the regional authorities, as well as the European Social Fund, which provided almost 1.3 out of the 3 million euros.

In April 2009, the '*Pôle Position*' scheme was introduced. It was restricted to low-skilled temps (that is, with a high school diploma or less) who had worked at least four months out of the past 18 in the automotive industry (including all subcontractors). The scheme was implemented in four municipalities in the region, in specific local agencies with dedicated counsellors from one of the participating partners (AFPA, Public Employment Service and temporary work agencies). The scheme consisted of a one-year follow-up, with interviews once a week with the referring counsellor, and provided beneficiaries with different kinds of services: collective thematic workshops, skill assessment, in-depth personal competency assessment, active job search assistance, assistance in outlining a professional project, and so on. However, the main purpose of the scheme was to provide temps with a vocational training diploma and/or a permanent job in other activities than automotive manufacturing – such as construction, logistics and transportation (bus or truck drivers) – in which there were some job vacancies in the local labour market.

From April 2009 to August 2010, up to 3,700 unemployed temporary workers received a proposal to join, and about 35 per cent did so. One of the reasons for this relatively low take-up rate is that the '*Pôle Position*' scheme did not provide a specific allowance. As a consequence, among the temps who were not entitled to unemployment benefit, many preferred to continue to search for temporary jobs, or to benefit from other labour market policy schemes which could provide them with some income replacement. In other words, the most 'precarious' temps were those who could not afford to benefit from the '*Pôle Position*' scheme. Nevertheless, the average age of beneficiaries was 29, and more than 50 per cent were below 25 years of age.

Even at the time this chapter was written it was too early to assess the success of the scheme,[28] although the first indications are fairly positive. In August 2010, among the first five monthly cohorts of beneficiaries (April–August 2009) – about 800 persons – more than 67 per cent had managed to get a permanent job or a vocational training diploma. From an institutional point of view, the coordination between the different institutional partners functioned rather well. But, according to the organizers, the scheme would have been even more efficient if both the social partners and the employers in the automotive industry had taken part in the experiment.

6.2.4 Concluding remarks
Overall, we may conclude that, both at industry and local level, the impact of the several initiatives taken for the benefit of temporary workers was very limited – as the number of beneficiaries remained very low. Moreover, the most vulnerable temps were less affected, as local initiatives were focused mainly on temporary workers in large companies (such as in the automotive industry). The '*Pôle Position*' scheme was intended to target the least-skilled temporary workers, but in fact, many of them (especially young unskilled workers with a poor employment record – that is, with no entitlement to unemployment benefit) did not take up the measure because it offered no income replacement.

7. CONCLUSION

Two years after the beginning of the crisis, what conclusions can be drawn concerning its impact on inequalities in France? To summarize, this impact seems to reflect the characteristics of the French employment regime: fairly inclusive[29] in terms of pay, but dualistic in terms of employment.

Inequalities in terms of wages – as measured by interdecile ratios – are relatively low in France in comparison to many other OECD countries. Strong wage-setting institutions – such as the legal minimum wage and collective agreements – prevented firms from cutting the basic wage. The variable part of compensation – in which profit-sharing earnings play an important role in many sectors – probably played a buffer role. But as its share tends to be positively correlated with wages, overall adjustments in compensation may not have increased inequalities notably – except in some sectors where blue-collars benefited from night shift premiums (as night shifts were often suppressed).

As for employment, the impact of the crisis may have been much more unequal. Temporary work clearly functioned as a buffer, as more than half of job losses during the first year of the crisis were due to cuts in temporary agency work. While some initiatives were launched at the industry and local levels to help temporary agency work, as presented in case study 2, they remained very limited. In sharp contrast, permanent workers were more protected, benefiting from internal flexibility devices, such as the short-time compensation schemes that were reformed to facilitate their use (see case study 1), as well as follow-up measures for displaced workers, more generous in terms of replacement rate and more intensive in terms of job search assistance. One may conclude that both institutions – the employment protection legislation – and public and social actors (including unions) favoured 'insiders', while neglecting 'outsiders'. But this conclusion needs some qualification. As described in Section 5.1, several measures were targeted at the most vulnerable groups, and the social partners adopted some reforms of the unemployment benefit system to better cover those with low employment records and/or with exhausted entitlements. Furthermore, the distinction between 'insiders' and 'outsiders' may be of limited relevance in a dynamic perspective. Many middle-aged male workers in the manufacturing sector, benefiting from short-time compensation schemes with high replacement rates (with almost no loss in compensation) may appear to be the best illustration of such 'insiders'. But in fact, many of them were low- or semi-skilled workers, and would have experienced great difficulties finding new jobs if they had been displaced, especially in the French context, where the share of long-term unemployment is high.

The French social safety net is one of the most developed among OECD countries. There are several social assistance allowances, the main one being the minimum income benefit (the RSA scheme), which was reformed in 2009. We may therefore expect it to play a crucial role in the prevention of intensifying poverty and social exclusion. But there are still some holes in the safety net; the first victims being young people, most of whom are excluded from the RSA, despite a reform to extend its coverage.

Among the most vulnerable groups in the crisis, we find the 'usual suspects': young people, the least-skilled workers and older workers. Young people may indeed appear at first sight as the most vulnerable group, for several reasons: they are overrepresented among temporary workers, they have fewer entitlement rights in terms of unemployment and social assistance benefits and, as new entrants in the labour market, they suffer the most from the freeze in recruitment. But older workers have also been hit by the crisis, with those 50 years of age and over experiencing the highest increase in unemployment. As the retirement age was to be increased at the end of 2010, and as the access to early retirement schemes or functional equivalents has been restricted by recent reforms, there may be a strong risk of increasing poverty among this population in the coming years.

As a consequence, the worst is still to come in terms of inequality and poverty. The 2008–2009 crisis may have long-lasting effects in terms of earnings and employment – the so-called 'scarring' effect – for young new entrants in the labour market, as well as for displaced workers.[30]

NOTES

*   I would like to thank Gurdal Aslan for research assistance. I am very grateful to Sébastien Archi, Béatrice Delay, Jacques Freyssinet, Fabien Gache, Arnaud Hentz, Ricardo Madeira, Jean-Christophe Toutlemonde and Alain Wagmann.
1. Real GDP growth was 2.4 per cent in 2004, 1.9 per cent in 2005 and 2.2 per cent in 2006 and 2007.
2. Note that some categories of workers were affected more than others by the large increase in temporary agency work. While the total number of temporary workers (full-time equivalents) increased by 148 per cent among men between 1995 and 2007, it rose by only 109 per cent among women. The rise was also dramatic among young people (below 24 years of age) (+223 per cent) and even more among older workers of 50 and over (+319 per cent) – as compared to +119 per cent for all the workers. While the highest increase was among skilled and highly skilled occupations (intermediate occupations, managers, executives and engineers), 80 per cent of temps were still blue-collars in 2007, and 12 per cent were clerks.
3. Although not all temps are unskilled: in 2007, 39 per cent of temps were skilled blue-collars.
4. Note that, because their labour contracts are maintained, workers on 'partial unemployment' are considered to be employed (see also Section 6.1).
5. On average, only between one-third and one-half of the authorized hours are effectively used by firms.
6. For firms with 10 employees or more.
7. Firms of more than 50 employees which lay off ten workers or more for economic

reasons during a 30-day period are legally required to implement a 'social plan' (*plan de sauvegarde de l'emploi*), which includes specific follow-up measures for workers.

8. Before its reform in April 2009 (see also Section 5.1), the duration of the CRP was eight months, and the beneficiary received 80 per cent of the gross wage during the first three months, 70 per cent during the following five months; after the reform, the duration was extended to 12 months with an 80 per cent replacement rate during the whole period. Duration and replacement rate are the same for the CTP scheme.

9. The number of beneficiaries of these two schemes jumped from about 30,000 at the beginning of 2008 to more than 90,000 at the end of 2009. Of these, 60 per cent were men, 72 per cent were aged between 25 and 49 (against only 6 per cent of below 25 years of age) and 56 per cent were skilled blue-collars or clerks (against only 16 per cent unskilled blue-collars); see Goarant and Minni (2010).

10. This report is based on enterprise case studies and also on evidence (from interviews and statistical data) provided by a consulting group specializing in outplacement activity (for workers who were dismissed for 'economic reasons', see above), and which is also a subcontractor of the Public Employment Service for the following-up of hard-to-place jobseekers.

11. And also by case studies: for instance, none of the firms studied by Alpha (2009) in several sectors (construction, automotive, logistics and retail chains) implemented cuts in basic wages.

12. Collective agreements signed at the industry level are usually extended by law to all the firms in the industry, even if they are not members of the employers' organizations that approved the agreement.

13. The second highest being the Netherlands, with about 27 per cent. The proportion is much lower in the other large European countries: about 17 per cent in Spain, 14 per cent in Germany, 8 per cent in the UK and 3 per cent in Italy (Eurofound 2010).

14. The new required employment duration is four months during the previous 28 months for workers below 50 years of age (instead of six months during the previous 22 months), and four months during the past 36 months for workers of 50 years of age and over; the maximum duration of insurance benefit was extended to 28 and 36 months, respectively.

15. Note that since 2007, the Ministry of Employment and the Ministry of Labour and Social Affairs are two separate entities.

16. Note that, as mentioned above, the labelling is misleading, as beneficiaries are not unemployed (in the ILO meaning). In most of the cases, employees still work, but their work duration has been reduced and is lower than the legal working time duration (35 hours a week for full-time workers). Even in the case they do not work at all during a period – if their establishment shuts down temporarily, for instance – according to the law, the labour contract still holds, and only its 'implementation is suspended'.

17. ARLD does not replace the standard partial unemployment (PU), but firms are strongly encouraged to opt for the new scheme from May 2010, even those that already have an ongoing PU agreement.

18. The WTR was introduced by two laws, named after the Minister of Labour at that time, 'Aubry I' (1997), and 'Aubry II' (1998).

19. Employees work 35 hours a week, on average, throughout the year, but can work, for instance, up to 42 hours in some weeks and 30 hours in other weeks, depending on the workload, without being paid overtime.

20. An establishment must apply to the local administration of the Ministry of Labour for authorization of a given number of days of partial unemployment and for a given number of employees; it must also declare the average duration of partial unemployment per employee.

21. Assessing the use of short-time compensation schemes by firms during 2008–2009 runs up against a serious data problem. First, at the time this chapter was written, the only data available on the number of hours were on 'authorized hours' (not effective hours) for the partial unemployment scheme, and no data were available for the

ARLD scheme. Note that, according to some estimates, before the crisis, on average, only between one-third and half of the authorized hours were effectively used by firms.

22. Because the firm chooses when workers take their days off accumulated in this account.

23. The firm can force workers to take days off, even if they have no 'credit' accumulated in their collective account. Each day off is in this case counted as a debit on the collective account.

24. This scheme (as well as the CTP, see also below) provides the jobseeker with a higher replacement rate than the standard unemployment benefit and with a reinforced follow-up and job search assistance provided by the Public Employment Service. See note 8 for more details.

25. There is also a Social Fund at the temporary agency work industry level, which provides temporary workers with some financial aid (for child care or renting a car to facilitate taking up a job, for instance). Those measures were also extended during the crisis.

26. They are often labelled 'permanent temps'.

27. The CTP is a follow-up scheme for permanent workers laid off 'for economic reasons' – see Section 3.1.

28. The '*Pôle Position*' scheme was to last until December 2010.

29. Following Gautié and Schmitt (2010), a national wage system can be considered 'inclusive' if it relies on formal – and sometimes informal – mechanisms that extend the wages and benefits negotiated by workers in industries and occupations with high bargaining power to workers in firms and occupations with low bargaining power. These mechanisms include, for instance, the legal minimum wage and the legal extension of collective agreements.

30. As emphasized by the ILO-IMF (2010) discussion paper on the consequences of the crisis, there is some empirical evidence showing that in the United States earnings losses of displaced workers following a recession persist over a 15–20 year period (and may total up to 20 per cent).

BIBLIOGRAPHY

Alpha (2009) 'Crise et pauvreté: une analyse sectorielle qualitative', October. Available at: http://www.groupe-alpha.com/fr/toute-actu/analyses/crise-pauvrete-analyse-sectorielle-qualitative, 60.html.

Bignon, N. and D. Folques (2009) 'La structure des rémunérations en 2006', *DARES Premières Synthèses*, 31.4 (July). Available at: http://www.travail-solidarite.gouv.fr/IMG/pdf/2009.07-31.4.pdf.

Bosch G. (2009) 'Dismissing hours not workers: work-sharing in the economic crisis', Working Paper.

Calavrezo, O., R. Duhautois and E. Walkowiak (2007) 'The effect of working time reduction on short time compensation: a French empirical analysis', CEE Working Paper No. 88. Available at: http://www.cee-recherche.fr/fr/doctrav/working_time%20reduction_doc88.pdf.

Caroli, E. and J. Gautié (eds) (2008) *Low Wage Work in France*, New York: Russell Sage Foundation.

CEREQ (2008) 'Génération 2004, des jeunes pénalisés par la conjoncture', *Bref*, 248, January. Available at: http://www.cereq.fr/pdf/b248.pdf.

Domens, J. (2010) 'L'intérim en 2009: repli sans précédent du travail temporaire', *DARES Analyses*, No. 034 (June). Available at: http://www.travail-solidarite.gouv.fr/IMG/pdf/2010-034-2.pdf.

Erhel, C. (2009) 'Les politiques de l'emploi en Europe: le modèle de l'activation et de la flexicurité face à la crise', CES Working Papers No. 2010-02. Available at: http://hal.archives-ouvertes.fr/docs/00/46/08/67/PDF/10002.pdf.

Eurofound (European Foundation for the Improvement of Living and Working Conditions) (2010) *European Company Survey 2009*. Available at: http://www.eurofound.europa.eu/pubdocs/2010/05/en/1/EF1005EN.pdf.

Flash EuroBarometer (2010) 'Monitoring the social impact of the crisis: public perceptions in the European Union (Wave 4)' (June). Available at: http://ec.europa.eu/public_opinion/flash/fl_289_en.pdf.

Freyssinet, J. (2010) 'Les négociations collectives et les politiques publiques face aux conséquences sociales de la crise économique', Working Paper.

Gautié, J. (2010) 'France: towards the end of the active minimum wage policy?', in Daniel Vaughan-Whitehead (ed.), *The Minimum Wage Revisited in the Enlarged EU*, Cheltenham, UK and Northampton, MA, USA: Edward Elgar / Geneva, Switzerland: ILO.

Gautié, J. and J. Schmitt (eds) (2010) *Low Wage Work in the Wealthy World*, New York: Russell Sage Foundation.

Goarant, C. and C. Minni (eds) (2010) 'Emploi, chômage, population active: bilan de l'année 2009', *DARES Analyses* No. 050 (July). Available at: http://www.travail-solidarite.gouv.fr/IMG/pdf/2010-050_-_Emploi_chomage_population_active_-_bilan_de_l_annee_2009.pdf.

Horny, G., J. Montornès, J.-B. Sauner-Leroy and S. Tarrieu (2010) 'Les politiques salariales des entreprises pendant la crise: résultats d'enquête', *Bulletin de la Banque de France*, No. 179, 1er trimestre. Available at: http://www.banque-france.fr/fr/publications/telechar/bulletin/etu179_1.pdf.

ILO-IMF (2010) 'The challenge of growth, employment and social cohesion', Joint Discussion Paper, Oslo conference (September). Available at: http://www.osloconference2010.org/discussionpaper.pdf.

Jeanneau, L. (2010) 'La bombe sociale', *Alternatives Economiques*, No. 290 (April).

Liégey, M. (2009) 'L'ajustement de l'emploi dans la crise: la flexibilité sans la mobilité?', *La Note de Veille*, No. 156, Conseil d'Analyse Stratégique (November), Available at : http://www.strategie.gouv.fr/IMG/pdf/NoteVeille156.pdf.

Observatoire National de la Pauvreté et de l'Exclusion Sociale (2010) *Observing Poverty and Social Exclusion for Ten Years: An Assessment in a Time of Crisis (2009–2010 Report)*. Available at: http://www.onpes.gouv.fr/IMG/pdf/Onpes_2010_GB_BAT2_Rapport_chap_1.pdf.

OECD (2004) *Employment Outlook*, Chapter 4.

OFCE (2009) 'L'impact de la crise sur la pauvreté', in *Les Travaux de l'Observatoire de la Pauvreté, 2009–2010*. Available at: http://www.onpes.gouv.fr/IMG/pdf/Partie2Cahier2.pdf.

Zemmour, M. (2010) 'Trois approches du lien entre pauvreté et crise en 2009', in *Les Travaux de l'Observatoire de la Pauvreté, 2009–2010*. Available at: http://www.onpes.gouv.fr/IMG/pdf/Partie2Cahier1.pdf.

6. The German labour market after the financial crisis: Miracle or just a good policy mix?

Gerhard Bosch

1. INTRODUCTION

In the wake of the financial crisis, the German economy experienced its most severe slump since the Second World War. However, the effects on the labour market were different from those experienced in all previous economic crises. Employment did not decline as expected and unemployment did not rise. Moreover, youth unemployment did not increase, in contrast to experience in virtually all other European countries. This chapter sets out to investigate this German employment 'miracle'. It will be shown that state-subsidized short-time working arrangements were not alone in preventing a collapse in unemployment but that a key role was also played by several other working time instruments incorporated into collective agreements concluded between trade unions and employers. The role of the parties to collective bargaining in avoiding an increase in youth unemployment should also be emphasized. It will also be shown that not only core workers but, through the dual system of vocational training, also young workers benefited from internal labour markets. Some categories of workers – mainly agency workers – were, however, the victims of external adjustments. In the economic upswing after the crisis German firms are mainly recruiting temporary agency workers, thus further increasing the dual structure of the German labour market.

The main body of the chapter begins with an analysis of the very particular path taken by Germany's economy, which differs considerably from that taken by other industrialized countries (Section 2). The various instruments for redistributing work and their deployment in the crisis are then described (Section 3). We then investigate why in this crisis, in contrast to previous ones, firms have relied almost exclusively on internal flexibility (Section 4). The measures taken to stabilize the dual system of vocational training in the crisis are then described (Section 5). The evolution of income distribution and the controversial issue of minimum wages are briefly outlined (Section 6). Finally, two case studies – one on the use of short-time working in the automobile and machine-tool industries and the other on collective agreements and vocational training and the employment of young people – will illustrate two important policy measures in the crisis (Section 7).

2. THE GERMAN JOB MIRACLE

The financial crisis has affected different countries in different ways. In late 2008 and early 2009, the steepest declines in GDP were seen in the countries in which the manufacturing industry accounts for a high share of employment, such as Germany and Japan. As far as incoming orders are concerned, it is those industries that produce consumer durables and capital goods – such as machines, ships or cars – the purchase of which can be easily postponed during a period of recession, that have seen particularly sharp declines. Demand for non-durable consumer goods (such as food) has proved to be less elastic, as has that for services, including financial services which, in the wake of government bailouts, have even seen renewed growth in employment. Figure 6.1 shows the particularly sharp decline in GDP in Germany and Japan, two exporting countries with high

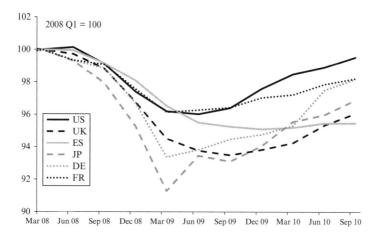

Source: Reuters-EcoWin: OECD; GDP Data national statistical offices; calculation by IMK Düsseldorf.

Figure 6.1   Evolution of gross domestic product, Germany compared to five other countries, 2008–2010 (1st quarter 2008 = 100)

shares of employment in the manufacturing industry, and the visibly less sharp decline in the other countries.

In order to stabilize the economy, the German government launched two economic stimulus packages and two additional relief packages, together worth some 100 billion euros (Table 6A.1). Among other things, this money was used in 2009 and 2010 to fund public investment and a car scrappage scheme designed to encourage the purchase of new cars, to reduce taxes, to improve firms' ability to write down their investments and to support labour market policy measures, such as short-time working, training and the recruitment of additional placement officers in job centres. These two stimulus packages were effective in helping to prevent employment collapsing in certain industries, such as the automotive and construction sectors. All economic indicators point to a surprisingly fast recovery in the second half of 2009 and 2010, due mainly to increasing exports (SVR 2009). After a decline in real GDP of 4.7 per cent in 2009, the German economy is forecast to grow by 3.7 per cent in 2010 and by 2.2 per cent in 2011. Output is expected to reach and then overtake its pre-crisis level in 2011 (SVR 2010).

Companies can react in very different ways to shrinking order books. They can reduce, firstly, the number of employees, secondly, the number of hours that employees work or, thirdly, labour productivity per hour worked. Most German experts expected firms to opt for a mix of external and internal flexibility. The joint spring prognosis of the big German economic research institutes forecast a substantial decrease in employment (–500,000) in 2009 and an increase in unemployment (+450,000) (Projektgruppe Gemeinschaftsdiagnose 2009). This pessimistic prognosis did not come true. In contrast to most other countries, employment and unemployment in Germany remained stable. However, a more dynamic perspective, which looks not only at stocks but also at flows, shows that the number of temporary agency workers dropped substantially. This was compensated for by employment growth, mainly of part-time jobs, in the service sector.

Figures 6.2 and 6.3 show the considerable differences between countries in terms of companies' reactions to the recession. Although the United States, France and Spain recorded considerably lower declines in GDP than Germany, employment in these three countries decreased and unemployment rose quickly after the crisis. In Germany, however, both parameters evolved completely differently from the path set out in every textbook. In the most severe economic crisis since 1929, employment remained largely stable, while unemployment actually declined. In the United States and the United Kingdom, the lower level of dismissal protection makes it easier to adjust the size of the workforce more quickly

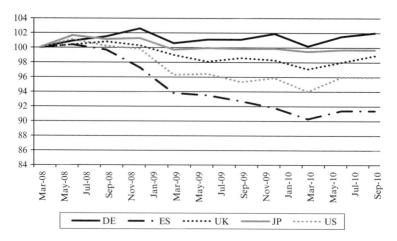

Source: Reuters-EcoWin: OECD; GDP Data national statistical offices; calculation by
IMK Düsseldorf.

*Figure 6.2   Evolution of number of employees, Germany compared to four
other countries, 2008–2010 (1st quarter 2008 = 100)*

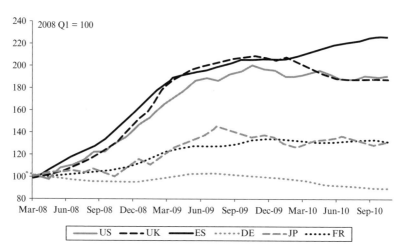

Source: Reuters-EcoWin: OECD; GDP Data national statistical offices; calculation by
IMK Düsseldorf.

*Figure 6.3   Evolution of unemployment, Germany compared to five other
countries, 2008–2010 (1st quarter 2008 = 100)*

Table 6.1   Employment, Germany, 2008 (3rd quarter)–2010 (2nd quarter)

Sector	3rd Quarter 2008	2nd Quarter 2010	Change in thousands
Manufacturing, excluding construction	8 048	7 580	–468
Wholesale and retail trade, hotels and restaurants, transport	10 080	10 008	–72
Financial intermediation, real estate, renting and business activities	7 079	7 031	–48
Public and private services	12 107	12 559	+452
Construction	2 224	2 203	–21
Agriculture	894	877	–17
Total	40 310	40 192	–118

Source: Statistisches Bundesamt (2010).

to the order situation. In Spain, the high share of employees on fixed-term contracts encourages firms to make use of external flexibility. Germany appears to be the exception, since the effects of the recession appear so far to have been absorbed by most firms internally, despite massive declines in orders in manufacturing industry. The dominant reaction of German companies was to use internal flexibility. In an allusion to the German 'economic miracle' of the post-war period, the contradictory evolution of GDP, on the one hand, and unemployment, on the other, has been dubbed the German employment miracle.

Aggregate figures, however, may be misleading. A closer look at the evolution of employment in different sectors reveals a slightly more differentiated picture and the use of external flexibility in at least some industries and companies. Between the third quarter of 2008 and the second quarter of 2010, employment in manufacturing declined by 468,000, while in public and private services it grew by almost the same amount (Table 6.1). Employment in the strongly cyclical construction industry almost remained stable because Germany had not had a housing boom before the crisis, in contrast to many other European countries whose economic stimulus packages were used largely to support construction projects. The greatest decrease in employment in a single sector was in temporary agency work (a subsector of private services), which provides workers mainly for manufacturing industry. As demand picked up, employment in temporary

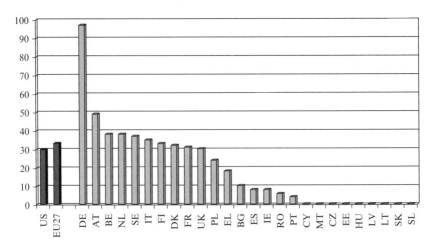

Source: Eurostat (2010a).

*Figure 6.4   Percentage of fall in total labour input due to fall in working
hours per employee, Germany compared to other countries,
2008–2009*

agency work had already reached its pre-crisis level of 800,000 by March
2010 and reached 900,000 in October 2010 (IW Zeitarbeitsindex 2010).
Since manufacturing industry is the temporary employment agencies'
main customer, it can reasonably be assumed that some jobs have shifted
out of the manufacturing sector into the temporary employment agencies,
which for statistical purposes are included among private services.

3.   WORK SHARING IN THE CRISIS

Almost all industrialized countries sought to ease the impact of the crisis
to some extent by reducing working time. Some countries, such as France,
Belgium, the Netherlands and Austria, have long-established, subsidized
short-time working schemes, the conditions for which were relaxed in
the crisis. Many firms also reduced overtime and offered their employees
sabbaticals or other forms of working time reductions, with or without
wage compensation (Eurofound 2009). Only in Germany, however, was
the reduction in labour input almost completely absorbed by a redistribution of work (Figure 6.4). German companies used various instruments
of work redistribution which had been developed prior to the crisis
(Section 3.1). It will be shown which mix (3.2) and which sequence of these

instruments (3.3) helped to avoid dismissals. Then the use of short-time working by industry and size of company, the employment impact and timing is analysed (Section 3.4).

3.1 Instruments of Work Redistribution Before the Crisis

The high level of employment stability in 2009 was the result of a wide-ranging effort to flexibilize working time in Germany that has been going on since the early 1990s and has spread across the entire economy. Almost half of German companies have introduced working time accounts since the early 1990s (Groß and Schwarz 2009). Furthermore, virtually all German industry-wide collective agreements have given the actors at firm level opportunities to reduce collectively agreed working time temporarily in order to avoid dismissals, with accompanying wage losses.

The showcase for use of this instrument is Volkswagen. In 1993, the company withdrew its plan to dismiss 30,000 employees because of restructuring and low demand in the aftermath of the economic boom after German reunification and negotiated a collective agreement[1] with the metal workers' union IG Metall that reduced weekly working hours from 35 to 28.8, cutting the working week from five to four days with corresponding wage cuts. White-collar workers, who continued to work five days a week, also took a wage cut for solidarity reasons. The annual wage declined but the monthly wage remained constant since the annual bonus was now distributed over 12 months instead of being paid in two instalments (summer and Christmas). Since wages at Volkswagen were already above average, skilled employees did not leave despite the lower annual wage. In 2006, a new collective agreement was negotiated that introduced a so-called working time 'corridor', within which working hours could range between 25 and 33 hours for blue-collar workers and between 26 and 34 hours for white-collar workers. Workers are paid extra only for hours worked in excess of the 33/34 hour threshold. This further refinement of the 1993 work-sharing model has given Volkswagen the benefit of highly flexible working hours. New shift systems with shorter hours were introduced and operating hours could be increased from 3,000 hours in 1992 up to 5,000 hours a year when orders increased. This flexibility was combined with constant marginal wage costs, since the overtime supplement is paid only when weekly working time exceeds 35 hours.

After German unification, temporary working time reductions were used widely in East Germany in order to cushion the effects of economic restructuring. Virtually all the major German industry-wide collective agreements now include provisions for temporary working time reductions. The extent of the possible reductions ranges from 6.75 per cent

Table 6.2   Provisions for possible temporary working time reductions in German collective agreements, conditions in 2009

Industry	Standard working time	Working time reductions
	In hours	*To ... hours*
Banking	39	31
Printing industry	35	30
Iron and steel industry	35	28
Wood and plastics, Westphalia/Saxony	35/38	32/30
Motor trade and repairs, Lower Saxony	36	30
Metalworking industry, Baden-Württemberg/Saxony	35/38	30/33
Local government, East	40	80–75% of standard working time
Paper processing	35/37	30/32
Travel agencies	38.5	30
Textile cleaning services	38.5/40	33.5/35
Insurance	38	30
Clothing, West	37	6.75
Textile industry, Westphalia/East	37/40	6.75
German old-age insurance	39	X
Energy NRW (GWE)/ Used (AVEU)	38	X
Confectionery industry, West/ Used	38/39	X
Transport industry, NRW	39	X

Source: Bispinck and WSI Tarifarchiv as at April 2009.

to 25 per cent of normal working time, that is between 2.5 and 10 hours calculated on the basis of the working week. The room for manoeuvre employers enjoy as a result means that jobs can be safeguarded to a considerable degree when the need arises. Table 6.2 provides an overview of the opportunities for working time reductions in various industries, as they were in 2009. In other collective bargaining areas, a working time corridor has been agreed that allows for deviations from standard working time, both upwards and downwards (Table 6.3). When working time is increased within these working time corridors, no overtime supplement has to be paid. In the case of reductions, there are generally corresponding wage cuts. Only in a small number of collective bargaining areas is there

Table 6.3 *Provisions for possible working time 'corridor' in German*
collective agreements, conditions in 2009

Industry	Standard working time in hours	Working time corridor in hours
Chemical industry, West	37.5	35–40
Refractory industry, West	38	36–40*
Rubber, West/East	37.5/39	35–40/36–40
Papermaking, West/East	38	35–40
Non-metallic mineral processing industry, Bavaria	38	34–42
Volkswagen – production		25–33
– support services		26–34
Housing sector	37	34.5–39.5
Cement industry, North-west Germany	38	35–40
Brickmaking industry, West (excluding Bavaria)/East	38/40	35–40

Note: * Two additional hours in each case in order to safeguard jobs.

Source: Bispinck and WSI Tarifarchiv as at April 2009.

partial wage adjustment to compensate from the wage cuts due to the reduction in normal working hours. In some areas, it has been agreed that, in the event of temporary working time reductions, the annual bonuses should be distributed evenly over the year, so that employees' monthly pay remains unchanged or is reduced only slightly. In all areas it has been agreed that temporary working time reductions have to be negotiated amicably with works councils and that no redundancies may be announced while agreed working hours are reduced.

In the crisis, the already extensive range of instruments for implementing temporary working time reductions was further extended. The most significant changes were made to short-time working. The short-time scheme has undergone frequent changes in recent decades. In severe economic crises, such as the one that followed German reunification, as well as in serious recessions, the conditions have been relaxed and then tightened up again once the crisis has passed its peak. Before the recent financial crisis, short-time working was intended primarily as a buffer for short-term reductions in orders but not as a response to a deep, long-term crisis. The subsidies (67 per cent of monthly net income for hours not worked) were paid only for six months and only for substantial shortages of work (over 10 per cent reduction of orders). Moreover, the subsidies did not cover employers' social insurance contributions which amounted to about 20 per cent of the wage bill. As a result, these programmes were attractive mainly to firms anticipating only a temporary decline in orders and wishing to retain their workers during a relatively short period of reduced activity. They also gave firms whose prospects for the future were uncertain some breathing space before they had to take any decisions on dismissals.

As the depth of the crisis was revealed, it quickly became apparent that mass redundancies could not be avoided by recourse to measures designed to deal with a wholly different set of economic circumstances. The financial crisis gave rise not only to sharp declines in orders but also, because of the banks' difficulties in obtaining finance, to considerable liquidity shortages as well. Even for healthy companies, it became increasingly difficult to obtain credit, so that immediate cost reductions became the main focus of company policy. In Germany, where short-time working had been subsidized since 1924, policymakers reacted by extending the period over which subsidies were paid, relaxing the regulations governing claims and reducing the employers' share of the costs until the end of 2010. The maximum period for claiming subsidies for short-time working was increased from six to 24 months. From the seventh month onwards, employers' social security contributions were reimbursed. Furthermore, the short-time allowance was paid for every period of reduced activity and not just for substantial reductions of activity (10 per cent and more). Working time credits had to be used up before applications could be made for short-time working. Companies that provided training were exempted from social security contributions from the very first month. The social partners also further negotiated improvements in the short-time working allowance. In some collective bargaining areas, particularly in the metalworking and chemical industries, an agreement on topping up the allowance of the employment office from 67 to 90 per cent of the previous net wage was concluded.

Despite the reimbursement of employers' social security contributions, the costs to firms of keeping the labour force but on reduced working hours remained not inconsiderable, since they were still responsible for holiday pay, all fixed costs and company social benefits. In the metalworking and engineering industry, in particular, which was very severely affected, both employers and trade unions feared there would be redundancies and offered an additional solution that was less costly for firms. In February 2010, the social partners in the engineering industry signed an agreement on what they called a 'collectively agreed short-time scheme' (*tarifliche Kurzarbeit*) with options for two phases. In the first phase, companies can incorporate the holiday and Christmas bonus into the monthly wage. This increases the assessment base for the short-time allowance because it increases the monthly wage which is the reference base for employment office subsidies and reduces wage costs for companies availing themselves of the employment service's short-time scheme. In the second phase, companies may reduce the standard working week to a minimum of 26 hours until June 2012. Partial wage compensation will be paid for those working 31 hours or less. One noteworthy provision is that works councils will be able to enforce the changeover from the first to the second phase by appealing to the arbitration committee provided for in the German Works Constitution Act (*Betriebsverfassungsgesetz*). The employers' associations have accepted this increase in influence for works councils only because the reduction in agreed time is very cost-effective for them. The employment office accepted the increase in the assessment base for the short-time allowance. This relatively complex agreement was concluded in order to open up another possibility for reacting to a long-lasting crisis in engineering that was expected at the beginning of 2009.

3.2 The Use of the Various Instruments of Work Redistribution

Beyond a combination of different forms of working time reduction, as well as labour hoarding, the decoupling of employment from the economic situation was also achieved by the overwhelming majority of firms (and not only a few large companies) through the use of the various instruments of work redistribution.

The volume of work fell from 57,450 million hours in 2008 to 55,985 million hours in 2009, a fall of 1,465 million hours. This equated to an average reduction per employee of 41.3 hours per year. The IAB (Institut für Arbeitsmarkt- und Berufsforschung/Institute for Employment Research) has estimated the contribution of individual components of the working time reduction (Figure 6.5) and come to the surprising conclusion that government-subsidized short-time working was responsible for rather less than one-third of this reduction. A reduction in the normal weekly working time made roughly the same contribution, followed in more or less equal proportions by the increase in part-time working, the reduction in overtime and the withdrawal of working time credits from working time accounts.

Company surveys show that only firms with fewer than 10 employees adopted dismissals as their main instrument for dealing with a decline in orders; those in other size categories had recourse primarily to short-time working and other forms of working time reduction, as well as recruitment freezes, cost cutting and searches for new customers and markets (Figure 6.6). It should be noted, of course, that firms were questioned only about their use of the various measures, not on the extent to which each one was deployed.

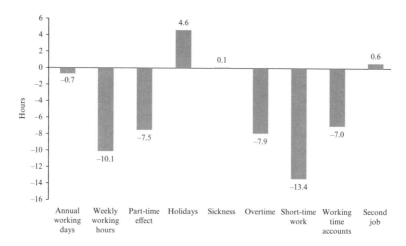

Note: Total reduction of annual working hours in hrs. 41.3 hrs (–3.1%).

Source: Fuchs et al. (2010: 2).

Figure 6.5   Contribution of different components to the development of annual hours per employee, Germany, 2008–2009

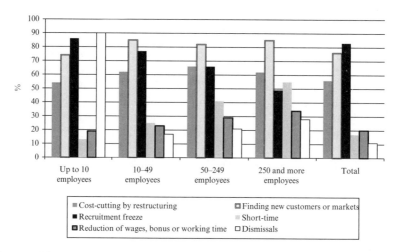

Source: IAB (2009c).

Figure 6.6   Reaction of companies to the crisis: company survey, Germany, 2009

3.3   The Sequence

The expanded 'tool box' of instruments was used by many companies in a typical sequence. At the beginning of the crisis, companies used the cheapest forms of working time reductions: in other words, reductions in overtime and use of working time accounts. This applied particularly to export-oriented segments of the manufacturing sector, which in the export-driven boom years between 2005 and 2008 had filled the accounts with some of the overtime hours worked when order books were full. In the first quarter of 2009, the overall impact of these measures on the decline in the volume of paid work was in fact considerably greater than that of short-time working, largely as a result of the use of working time accounts (IAB 2009b). However, the elimination of surplus hours on working time accounts, the reduction in overtime and the bringing forward of annual leave are one-off measures that become less significant over time. When these measures were exhausted companies started to rely on short-time work or temporary working time reductions without accompanying wage losses. Data are relatively scarce on temporary reductions in weekly working time. The examples that have become well known show that such reductions were implemented mainly by economically weak firms seeking to avoid the wage costs that continue to be incurred by firms using short-time working.

Short-time working is not without costs for companies. In the first six months, they have to pay employers' social security contributions, as well as wages on public holidays and during annual leave. The IAB (Institute for Employment Research 2009a) put the total cost of short-term working for 2009 at 14 billion euros, of which the Federal Labour Agency paid 6 billion euros, firms 5 billion euros and employees 3 billion euros. If the opportunity costs of redundancies and new hires are included, it is not difficult to understand why, if staff requirements are expected to be at similar levels again in the future, short-term working is attractive to firms. With average redundancy payments at 12,000 euros, 1 million redundancies would cost firms around 12 billion euros. And with the average cost of hiring a skilled worker at 32,000 euros, the re-employment of 1 million skilled workers would cost firms 32 billion euros.

3.4   The Use of Short-time Working

The use of short-time working reached a peak in May 2009, when 1,516,000 workers were affected. This figure fell rapidly in subsequent months (Figure 6.7) and by July 2010 had sunk to just 288,000 persons because of the economic recovery (BA 2010b). Taking as a basis for

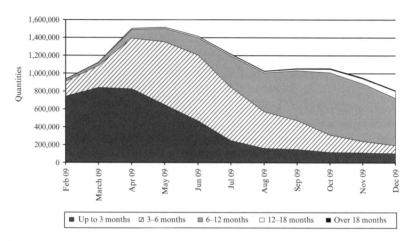

Source: Bundesagentur für Arbeit, Berechnungen des DIW Berlin, 2010.

Figure 6.7   Short-time working by duration in months, Germany, February 2009–December 2009

calculation an average decline in short-time hours worked per worker of around 31 per cent in June 2009, the number of employees on short time equated to a total of 448,004 workers (BA 2010a: 9).

However, the statistics on short-time working provide detailed information – albeit with a delay of several months – on the number of employees affected, the duration of the short-time working, size of firm, industry and the gender of the short-time workers, all on a monthly basis. The figures show that most companies used short-time working for up to six months, although others used it for considerably longer (Figure 6.7). In contrast to France, for example, there was no restriction on the volume of short-time working per employee per year, so that in theory firms could be on 100 per cent short-time working with its whole workforce for up to two years. However, for the vast majority of firms, short-time working was used only for part of the workforce and only for a part of their annual working hours. Figure 6.7 shows that, in 2009, in more than 50 per cent of firms making use of short-time working, less than 25 per cent of the work-force was on short time, while in 80 to 90 per cent of firms less than 50 per cent of the workforce was on short time. Works councils were careful to ensure that short-time working and the accompanying income losses were distributed as equally as possible among all employees.

It was not only larger firms that used short-time working. In May 2009, when short time was at its peak, almost 600,000 of those affected were employed in firms with fewer than 100 employees (Figure 6.8). Short-time

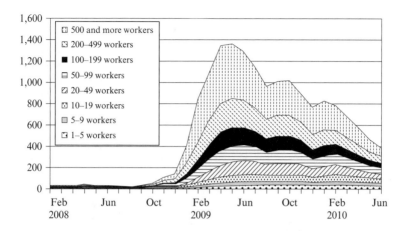

Source: Bundesagentur für Arbeit (BA) (2010b).

Figure 6.8   *Short-time workers and firms using short-time working by size, Germany, January 2008–June 2010*

working was concentrated mainly in the manufacturing sector, which saw the sharpest drops in orders. However, Table 6.4 also shows that in December 2009 around 200,000 of the 800,000 workers then on short-time working were employed in other sectors. Obviously, short-time working has now become an important instrument of personnel policy also in some service-sector companies.

4. WHY HAS INTERNAL FLEXIBILITY BEEN PRIORITIZED IN THIS RECESSION?

In the 'varieties of capitalism' literature, the German model is often regarded as the reference model for the coordinated market economy, which is characterized by long-term relationships between workers and employers and strong reliance on internal flexibility (Erlinghagen 2004; Lehndorff et al. 2009). Compared to market economies such as the United Kingdom or the United States, average job tenure is much higher in Germany. It has, however, often been overlooked that companies may behave differently even in similar institutional environments, depending on their past experience and future expectations, which may vary between recessions. Figure 6.9 shows that in the 1979–1982 downturn which, with a decline in GDP of less than 1 per cent was of course considerably less severe, employment remained stable. In the two downturns before the

Table 6.4   Short-time working by industry, Germany

	Establish-ments	Short-time workers	Short-time workers per establish-ment	Share of short-time workers[1]	Reduction in short-time workers compared to peak level in 2009	Month with highest level of short-time workers
			December 2009			
Agriculture	268	1 227	5	0.6	0	December
Mining and energy	381	3 948	10	0.7	–49	April
Manufacturing	22 090	616 503	28	9.8	–49	April
Construction	5 560	23 476	4	1.5	–49	May
Trade and repairing	8 847	56 853	6	1.4	–30	June
Transport	2 382	22 785	10	1.6	–48	April
Hotels and restaurants	553	2 889	5	0.4	–20	April
Information and telecoms	1 946	12 223	6	1.5	–36	June
Financial services	257	1 190	5	0.1	–11	November
Services to business	8 907	56 341	6	1.6	–26	May
Public administration	28	1 649	59	0.1	–30	June
Education	259	1 532	6	0.1	–17	September
Health and social services	241	1 004	4	0.0	–51	June
Other services	737	3 513	5	0.3	–27	June
Total	52 939	809 680	15	2.9	–47	May

Note: [1] Share of short-time workers of socially insured employees.

Source: Brenke, Rinne and Zimmermann (2010).

financial crisis: 1991–1993 and 2001–2005, however, during which GDP declined to roughly the same extent, employment fell considerably. Thus German companies could almost be said to have alternated in the past between internal and external flexibility.

How can the sudden shift from largely external to largely internal flexibility in the past three downturns be explained, particularly in an environ-

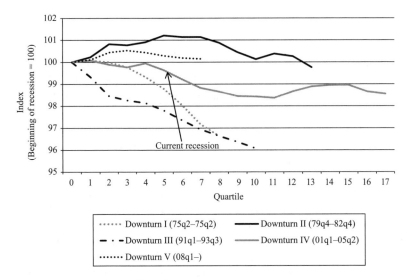

Source: Herzog-Stein and Seifert (2010).

Figure 6.9   Evolution of employment in four downturns, Germany

ment in which the Hartz Acts and the deregulation of temporary agency work have created new sources of external flexibility (Bosch and Kalina 2008)? I would suggest the following explanations:

- In the 1990s and at the beginning of 2000, in the wake of the deep disenchantment that set in at the end of the reunification boom, German companies assumed that their staffing requirements would be permanently reduced, as a result of which they rapidly shed labour. By dismissing many employees, principally younger skilled workers, firms became so lean that in the 2005–2008 upturn they found themselves short of skilled workers (Fischer et al. 2007), who had to be recruited at considerable cost. They have no desire to repeat this formative experience.
- Because of increased skill requirements and specialization in high-quality products (Lehndorff et al. 2009), companies that in the past tended to rely on external flexibility have built up their core work-forces, which they wish to retain during the downturn.
- In response to the collectively agreed reductions in weekly working time of the 1980s and 1990s, firms have introduced flexible forms of working time that have increased their opportunities for internal flexibility (Groß and Schwarz 2009). German firms, particularly in

the manufacturing sector, had high volumes of overtime and credits in their working time accounts after the export boom of recent years.

- Policies introduced in the 1980s, such as early retirement pro-grammes, provided relatively inexpensive opportunities for job cutting which no longer existed in 2008. Instead, alternatives to redundancy were offered by extending short-time working and reducing its cost.

- There was considerable political pressure from government and trade unions to use short-term working. As a result of the large-scale bailout of the banking industry, the state could have been at risk of losing its legitimacy if it had not also moved to support employment in the manufacturing sector, the cornerstone of the German economy. The imminent general election certainly helped to convince the political parties of the wisdom of this approach.

- Short-time working is an instrument for subsidizing firms hit by a downturn which, unlike direct subsidies, is not subject to EU competition legislation. The regulations on short-time working were regarded as a means of helping to save the country's industrial fabric in an exceptional situation. Short-time working was the most important support instrument for the capital goods industry, while the stimulus packages were mainly of assistance to the construction industry.

In view of countries' different responses to the crisis, it might well be asked whether a workforce stabilization policy based on short-time working is indeed a sensible long-term reaction. Mainstream economists tend to take a somewhat sceptical view of short-time working. In longer crises, they argue, short-time working acts as an impediment to structural change, leading in the longer term to reduced growth (Eichhorst and Marx 2009; Snower 2009; OECD 2010). This argument is immediately convincing when expanding firms are unable to find sufficient personnel because of short-time working (Bosch 2010a).

However, there are no indications that this was the case in 2009, and all the growth forecasts up to the end of 2010 and 2011 suggest that the situation is unlikely to change. Employment increased only slightly and the number of vacancies has decreased sharply. A labour market policy that relies on the rapid placement of workers in a recession and intensifies the pressure on the unemployed will come up against its limits because of the shortage of new jobs. Therefore the government decided to continue the short-time scheme under slightly changed conditions. Companies starting short time in 2010 can now make claims for a maximum period of only 18 months (instead of 24 months). In April 2010, the government decided to extend this scheme until March 2012. On the other hand, measures to promote training during short-time working were not particularly successful, even though firms were still able to apply for grants for the training programmes. Of the annual average of 1.43 million workers on short time, only 9,370, on average, took part in further training measures, most of which lasted only a few days (BA 2010c). The flow figures look somewhat better. In 2009, around 124,000 workers on short time embarked on a training programme. There are three main reasons for the low take-up of training grants. First, few firms had a sufficiently well-developed further training plan with an adequate supply of scheduled courses. Second, the rules governing short-time working stipulate that work takes precedence over training. Thus, there was always a risk that longer training programmes would have to be interrupted when new orders were received. To understand this it is important to know that the short-time subsidies stopped at once when there was enough work, due to new orders. Third, the grant application procedure was very bureaucratic. Training was financed by the European Social Funds and short-time working by the German Employment Office. The match between these two programmes proved to be difficult. Only larger companies with their own human resource departments had the capacity to cope with the bureaucratic barriers.

5. AVOIDING AN INCREASE IN YOUTH UNEMPLOYMENT

5.1 The Virtues of Initial Vocational Training

Young people constitute a vulnerable group. In an economic recession they are often the group most affected by unemployment since the first reaction of companies to a decline in orders is to halt recruitment. In addition, in most countries younger workers have a much higher share of temporary contracts than core workers and are the first to be dismissed. As outsiders, young people leaving the education and training systems do not benefit from employment protection. Bell and Blanchflower (2010) and Kahn (2010) have shown that the labour market consequences of graduating from college in a recession include large, negative and persistent effects on wages. Life-time earnings are substantially lower than for graduates entering the labour market in good times. Bell and Blanchflower (2010) also found for the United Kingdom that youth unemployment leads to worse health and lower job satisfaction even 25 years down the line.

BOX 6.1   THE DUAL SYSTEM OF VOCATIONAL TRAINING IN GERMANY

Entry to a training programme is dependent on the conclusion of a training contract with a firm. On the basis of such contracts, apprentices become employees of the firm until the end of their training programme. They are paid a wage, which is set by collective bargaining and rises as they become more productive in the course of their training. Apprentices in the dual system take courses in the workplace, as well as at public vocational schools, where both general subjects (languages, economics, mathematics) and the theoretical basics of their chosen trade or occupation are taught.

  The corporatist structure comes from the delegation of responsibility for the content and control of training to the social partners and to the self-governing chambers of industry and commerce and the craft chambers. According to the Vocational Training Act (Berufsbildungsgesetz 1969), vocational training for young people under 18 years of age can be provided only in one of the approximately 350 (2010) recognized occupations for which formal standards are laid down. New occupations in the service industry, such as IT, have recently been developed.

Many studies show that vocational skills acquired in apprenticeship systems with generally recognized standards make transitions to the labour market easier than skills acquired in school-based systems (Müller and Gangl 2003). The difficulties of the transition to the first job also depend on the structure of the labour market. Most of the literature on young people's transitions to the labour market differentiates between occupational and internal labour markets: in the former, allocation relies predominantly on occupations with generally recognized qualifications, while in the latter it relies mainly on seniority and experience (Marsden 1990). As outsiders, young people have difficulties entering internal labour markets, while occupational labour markets may be open to them as soon as they acquire the necessary certificates. Germany has often been taken as an example where the rapid transition experienced by the majority of young people is facilitated by the apprenticeship systems, which are closely linked to occupational markets. Most young Germans enter the labour market through the dual system of vocational training (Bosch 2010b).

  The proper functioning of the dual system depends on the readiness of firms to provide training. In spite of the strong unions and 'patient capital' of stable owners who are interested in maximizing long-term profits – which, until recently, characterized the German employment model – short-termism has increasingly played an important role, endangering the proper functioning of the dual system. The main drivers of short-term corporate strategies are new forms of corporate governance (shareholder value) and labour market deregulation, especially the deregulation of temporary agency work and the weakening of collective bargaining. Firms may seek to reduce costs in a crisis. Their first target is often training costs since training only has benefits in the medium and long terms, beyond the planning horizon of such companies (Bosch 2004).

Over the past 25 years, the dual system has been through several major upheavals due to a decline in training in economic crises. The trade unions proposed a compulsory levy to finance training to reduce its costs and stabilize it over the economic cycle. Because of the fierce opposition of employers' associations to a compulsory levy to finance training, both conservative and social democratic governments have proposed voluntary 'training pacts' as an alternative.

The effect of the training pacts of the 1980s and of today can be seen in the training rates (share of apprentices of all employed). In 1985, a training rate of 8.8 per cent was recorded. This figure has fallen to slightly over 6 per cent today. Without the pacts, however, training rates would probably have fallen even lower in the economic crisis of 2002–2005. The training pacts and public subsidies for training provide the only possible explanation for the survival of the dual training system in eastern Germany after the fall of the Berlin Wall and the collapse of the eastern German economy, even if considerable subsidies were also required. In the other Eastern European countries that suffered an economic collapse comparable to that in eastern Germany, firm-based vocational training was reduced to a minimum after 1990, when the large state enterprises were dismantled and the newly founded small firms had not accumulated the resources required for training.

5.2 Risks in the Crisis: Approaching the End of the Dual Training System?

There was much concern that the success story of the dual apprentice-ship system would come to an end in the severe crisis in 2009, since it was difficult enough for companies to retain their workforce. In contrast to developments in most other European countries, youth unemployment did not rise very much or faster than unemployment among prime-age workers (Figure 6.10). In 2009, around 566,000 training contracts were

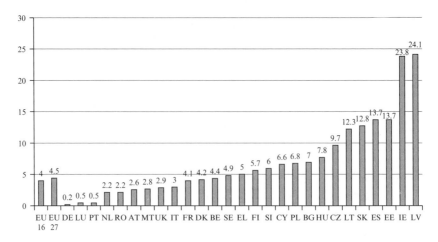

Source: Eurostat (2010b).

Figure 6.10   *Increase in youth unemployment rates in percentage points,*
Germany compared to other countries, December 2008–
December 2009

concluded, 8.2 per cent or 50,000 fewer contracts than in 2008, so there
was a significant decline. Because of the fortunate coincidence that the age
cohort entering the labour market in 2009 also declined by around 50,000,
the situation for young people looking for an apprenticeship did not deteriorate (BMBF 2010). Despite the economic difficulties most companies
consider that they have a social obligation to provide training. In addition,
they expect to encounter skill shortages in future because of a decline in
the size of the age cohorts coming into the labour market and training is
still seen as the most effective recruitment mechanism.

6.   INCREASING INCOME INEQUALITY IN THE CRISIS

In 2009, collectively agreed wages rose by 2.6 per cent. Many of the
agreements had been concluded just before the recession and came
into effect in 2009. Actual gross wages, however, fell in nominal terms
by 0.4 per cent (and in real terms by –0.8 per cent), mainly because
of short-time working but also because of wage cuts instituted, for
example, by companies making use of derogation clauses in collective
agreements or by employers not covered by an agreement. However, the

wage bargaining rounds in late 2009 and early 2010 were characterized by wage moderation. Some of the trade unions went into the negotiations without a percentage wage demand and were just proposing 'an appropriate pay increase' (chemical industry, banking) or an 'appropriate real-terms increase with a social component'. The unions agreed to forgo wage increases and to concentrate on job security and support for apprentices. The metalworkers' union accepted a single payment of 320 euros for 2010 and negotiated a wage increase of 2.7 per cent in March 2011, despite the economic recovery. The Chemical Workers Union negotiated a wage agreement until the end of 2010 with a single payment of 550 euros (715 euros for workers in continuous shift systems) and a 'cyclical' bonus of 260 euros for workers in companies not affected by the financial crisis.

However, the metalworkers' union, IG Metall, succeeded in making a breakthrough in the collective negotiations in the steel industry in September 2010, during which equal pay for temporary agency workers in this industry was agreed. This principle, laid down in the European directive on agency work, is circumvented in Germany by lower, collectively agreed wage rates. A small Christian trade union that is neither representative nor in possession of members in the employment agency sector agreed low wage rates for temporary employment agencies that are well below the collectively agreed rates in the steel and metalworking industry. This 'dumping' agreement concluded by a trade union without members in the relevant sector forced the trade unions of the German Trade Union Confederation to conclude a collective agreement with low wages as well. It is questionable, however, whether the trade unions will succeed in implementing the new agreement on equal pay for agency workers in other industries in which they are less well organized.

In attempting to curb the use of temporary agency workers on low wage rates by concluding collective agreements, the trade unions are reacting to the rapid expansion of the low-wage sector in Germany since 1995 and the refusal of the federal government to introduce a national minimum wage and to put equal pay for temporary agency workers on a statutory footing. It has been shown by Bosch and Kalina (2010) that, since the mid-1990s, wages in Germany have become widely dispersed and the low-wage sector has grown considerably. This has affected both full-time and part-time employees (including workers with mini-jobs). It is not only specific groups of persons who are affected by low wages, such as young people or the low-skilled, but increasingly also the middle age groups and skilled workers. The redistribution of wages has not been restricted to the lowest income group, but also extends into middle income groups. The middle level in terms of income distribution has been greatly thinned out. There have been marked increases in wage differences between large enterprises and smaller enterprises, and between the industries more and less bound by collective agreements. The reason for this is that the binding effect of the German system of collective agreements, which has always been vulnerable to outsider competition, has been further weakened by political interventions, such as the deregulation of temporary agency work. Growing from the mid-1990s onwards, the low-wage sector has created knock-on effects even for highly unionized companies. Coverage by collective agreements has declined, especially in eastern Germany. The wage differentials in the economy increasingly offer an incentive to outsource previously well-paid jobs to enterprises and industries with lower wages. Collective agreements are, with a few exceptions, not declared generally binding as in France or the Netherlands, so that outsourcing to low-wage jobs even takes place in industries with high trade union density and coverage by collective agreements. This trend has been strongly supported by political interventions. Outside competition obtained a great boost from changes in European competition rules. Freedom to provide services means that workers can be posted to Germany under the wage terms and conditions of their country of origin in all industries without statutory minimum wages. Only in a few industries, such as construction, were collectively agreed minimum wages declared to be generally binding under the Posting of Workers Directive. The EC directives opening up the product markets of former public services (for example, postal services, telecommunications or local transport) have had even more far-reaching effects. The lack of a minimum threshold in Germany, either through generally binding collective agreements or a national minimum wage, encourages companies to adopt business models that are no longer based on innovation, but instead rely on pushing down wages. In 2009 and 2010, only a few new industry minimum wages were introduced (care services, industrial laundries, security services, waste management, mining specialists). Some major industries with high shares of low-wage work, such as the retail trade, remain unregulated.

The small number of new minimum wages has not altered the upward trend in low-wage work in Germany (see Figure 6.11).[2] Despite the impressive employment stability, income inequality has increased further in the crisis. The share of low wage earners (two-thirds of median wage), which slightly decreased in the economic upswing in 2006–2008, increased again in 2009 (see Figure 6.12). The same trend could be observed at household level. Households with a low income (less than 70 per cent of the median) rose from 19 per cent to 22 per cent between 2004 and 2009. There was an increase of 2 percentage points between 2008 and 2009 (Goebel et al. 2010: 4). This increase of low wage earners is surprising since temporary agency workers with high shares of low wage earners were the first to be

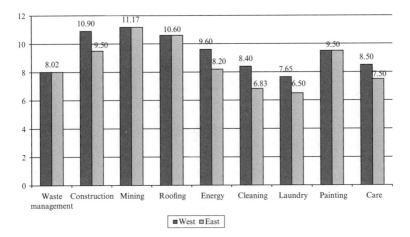

Note: * The graphic shows the lowest minimum wage levels; in the construction (West Germany only), mining and commercial cleaning industries there is an additional, higher wage bracket for skilled activities.

Source: WSI (2010).

Figure 6.11 *Level of minimum wages,* Germany (€ per hour September 2010)*

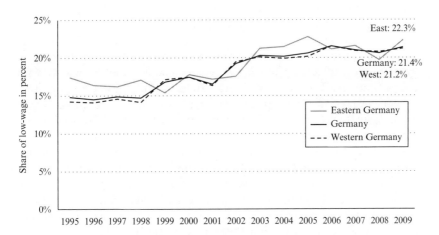

Source: German Socio-Economic Panel Study (SOEP) 2009, Thorsten Kalina, IAQ.

Figure 6.12 *Share of low-wage employees among dependent employees, Germany, 1995–2009 (excluding pupils, students, pensioners and part-time jobs)*

dismissed, and well-paid core workers remained employed. This effect, however, has been compensated by an increase of low-wage jobs in the service sector, which expanded in 2009.

7. CASE STUDIES

7.1   Case Study 1: The Use of Short-time Working in the Automobile and Machine-tool Industries

The machine tool and automobile industry used short time more intensively than other industries. Both industries are flagships of German exports and had full order books before the crisis. The sharp decline in orders in November 2009 affected production differently in the two industries. In the automobile industry, the impact on production occurred almost immediately because of the short throughput time. The credit hours on working time accounts were used up in January and the number of short-time workers reached its peak in February 2009 at around 280,000 workers, which corresponded to about 30 per cent of the workforce in this industry. Because of the car-scrappage scheme the number of short-time workers decreased slightly in March, but peaked again at 280,000 in April 2009. After that, it went down continuously to around 57,000 in May 2010. The time-lag in the machine-tool industry was much longer and extremely varied within the industry. Producers of simple machines had short throughput times, while the completion of an order in plant engineering and construction may take two years or more. The crisis therefore affected production in many machine-tool companies with a long time-lag. The number of short-time workers in the machine-tool industry peaked in June 2009 at 240,000 (25 per cent of the workforce in this industry) and remained high until April 2010, when it started to fall rapidly (Figure 6.13).

The simple fact that an economic crisis is impacting on production with very different time-lags has far reaching implications for short-time policies. If short time can be claimed only for a short period after the crisis, as in the Netherlands, this will have a selective impact. Companies with complex products and a long throughput time may not benefit from these schemes, although they are very sensitive to the economic cycle. Together with fears of a double-dip recession this was an important reason why the German government with the support of the social partners and all political parties in parliament agreed to prolong access to the post-crisis short-time scheme with the improved conditions until March 2012.

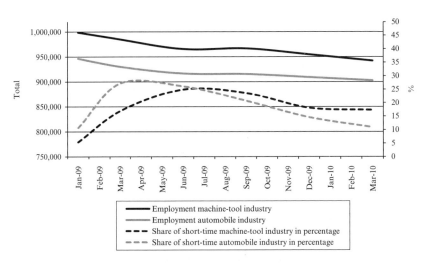

Source: Statistisches Bundesamt, Bundesagentur für Arbeit, author's calculations.

Figure 6.13 *Employment and short time in machine tool and automobile industries, January 2009–March 2010, Germany*

7.2 Case Study 2: Collective Agreements on Vocational Training and the Employment of Young People

Unions and employees supported the integration of young people into the labour market. In 2009 and 2010, the second focal point of collective bargaining (besides avoiding dismissals) was the recruitment of new apprentices and the continuation of employment after the completion of training. In spring 2010, the social partners in the metal industry agreed to continue employing all young journeymen for at least one year after the completion of their apprenticeship. In addition, going on to short time is regarded as an alternative to dismissal. Finally, young journeymen can choose a 'Future Training Contract'. They receive two-thirds of their wage for four years, work two years full-time, go on a further training programme for 12 months and then return to full-time work in the fourth year. Another good example is found in the chemical industry. In April 2010, the social partners signed an agreement with the following provisions:

- The employers undertake to recruit 9,000 apprentices each year until 2013. This equates to the numbers recruited in previous years. The industry had been able, through previous collective agreements, to

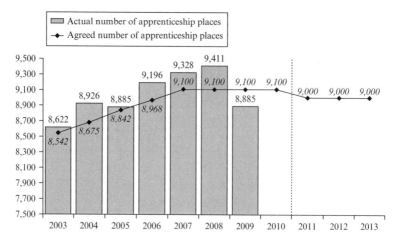

Source: Bundesarbeitgeberverband Chemie e.V. (BAVC).

Figure 6.14   *The 'Future through Vocational Training' collective agreement in the German chemical industry, 2003–2013*

raise the number of apprentices recruited annually to over 9,000 (Figure 6.14).

- The employers set up a fund that helps companies in economic difficulties to continue employing apprentices who have completed their training for up to one year. These companies will receive 1,000 euros per month per person for up to one year. Companies in the chemical industry have undertaken to pay 25 million euros – equivalent to 1 per cent of the gross wage bill – into the fund in two instalments (2010 and 2011).

- To avoid deadweight, a commission with equal representation of unions and employers will decide upon this subsidy. Only companies which are members of the employers' association and are covered by the agreement and trade union members will get the subsidy.

The aim of recruiting 9,000 apprentices in 2009, despite the crisis, was almost achieved (Figure 6.14). Only around 150 small and medium-sized firms claimed money from the fund for the training of 225 skilled workers. Because of the industry's rapid recovery, the figure of 1,000 that was originally assumed was not reached. The remaining monies from the fund will be used in the next few years to finance pre-training programmes for less able school leavers wanting to take up an apprenticeship in the chemical industry.

In concluding these agreements, and similar ones in other industries, the social partners were signalling that they do not regard apprentices as outsiders but as future insiders with similar rights to the present workforce.

8. CONCLUSIONS

The strategy of riding out the crisis by redistributing work has borne fruit for the German government, employees and companies. The government has not inhibited structural change by subsidizing short-time working; rather it has, in an exceptional situation, maintained production capacity in core areas of the German economy. Firms were able to retain their skilled workers, whom they would not otherwise have been able to recruit so quickly again after the crisis, even at high replacement prices. In anticipation of a shortage of skilled workers in the next few years because of a demographic trend towards smaller cohorts of young people, provision was made for initial vocational training even in the crisis.

Many workers were spared a visit to the job centre and the scarring effects of a lengthy period of unemployment. Income losses – which accompanied reduced working time – were inevitable, but the fact that workers kept their jobs meant that the losses were time-limited and bearable. At the same time, income inequality has increased further. This suggests that it is not only the labour market but also labour market policy that is divided. On the one hand, short-time working in the primary segment is being supported. On the other hand, the German government is refusing to introduce equal pay for temporary agency workers and a minimum wage, which would protect employees in a crisis: that is, precisely when they are in a particularly weak bargaining position. The sharp increase in poorly paid temporary agency work and service jobs in the current upturn is an indication that, after the crisis, employment is shifting into the secondary labour market.

This dualization of the German labour market was not so evident in the crisis, but may become more visible in the recovery. The traditional German model of a coordinated market economy with strong social partners and a government that lays down the general framework for internal flexibility is still dominant in the manufacturing sector, which was particularly badly hit by the crisis. However, it should not be forgotten that low-wage work has grown more rapidly in Germany in the past decade than in other countries and that this growth has been encouraged by deregulation of the labour and product markets (Bosch and Weinkopf 2008). This segment of the labour market has grown further in this crisis.

This dualization of the German labour market has made it possible to protect workers in the primary segment against dismissal and, at the same time, to lower wages in the secondary segment.

The German government and the social partners chose a good policy mix to bridge the crisis and avoid an increase in unemployment. But this policy worked only because of the rapid economic recovery in Germany, which depended entirely on rising exports, mainly to countries less affected by the financial crisis, such as the BRIC economies. The German employment miracle is therefore not only the outcome of a good policy, but also of a lot of luck. It is also questionable whether the employment miracle can be repeated. With rising numbers of temporary agency workers and smaller numbers of core workers companies may prefer cheaper external flexibility in the next crisis.

NOTES

1. Volkswagen is the only German automotive company that has its own company agreement with the union. All the other companies are covered by the industry agreement of the engineering industry.
2. The German government refuses to introduce a minimum wage. It argues that minimum wages should be determined for separate industries: employers and unions can conclude collective wage agreements for their respective minimum wages. If these agreements cover 50 per cent of employees and are concluded at the national level, the government can declare them to be generally applicable and binding on the basis of the Law on Posted Workers. However, these conditions were met only by some industries (for example, construction and cleaning). At the same time, other industries with a high proportion of low wages, such as the meat industry, have no nationwide collective wage negotiation mechanism in place, with the result that such agreements cannot be concluded (Bosch and Kalina 2010).

BIBLIOGRAPHY

BA (Bundesagentur für Arbeit) (2010a) *Der Arbeit- und Ausbildungsmarkt in Deutschland January 2010*, Nuremberg. Available at: http://www.pub.arbeit sagentur.de/hst/services/statistik/000000/html/start/monat/aktuell.pdf (accessed on 12 February 2010).
BA (Bundesagentur für Arbeit) (2010b) *Der Arbeit- und Ausbildungsmarkt in Deutschland September 2010*, Nuremberg. Available at: http://statistik.arbeit sagentur.de/Statischer-Content/Arbeitsmarktberichte/Monatsbericht-Arbeits-Ausbildungsmarkt-Deutschland/Monatsberichte/Generische-Publikationen/Monatsbericht-201009.pdf (accessed on 24 October 2010).
BA (Bundesagentur für Arbeit) (2010c) *Arbeitsmarkt 2010*, Nuremberg. Available at: http://statistik.arbeitsagentur.de/Statischer-Content/Arbeitsmarktberichte/Jahresbericht-Arbeitsmarkt-Deutschland/Generische-Publikationen/Arbeitsma rkt-2009.pdf (accessed on 26 October 2010).

Bell, D. and Blanchflower, D.G. (2010) 'Youth unemployment: déjà vu?', IZA DP No. 4705, January.

Bispinck, R. and WSI-Tarifarchiv (2009) *Tarifliche Regelungen zur befristeten Arbeitszeitverkürzung. Eine Untersuchung von Tarifverträgen in 26 Wirtschaftszweigen und Tarifbereichen,* Elemente qualitativer Tarifpolitik Nr. 67, Düsseldorf. Available at: http://www.boeckler.de/547_95548.html (accessed on 23 November 2009).

BMBF (2010) *Bundesministerium für Bildung und Forschung, Berufsbildungsbericht 2010,* Berlin. Available at: http://www.bmbf.de/pub/bbb_2010.pdf (accessed 5 May 2010).

Bosch, G. (2004) 'Brauchen wir eine Ausbildungsplatzabgabe?', in D. Haubner, E. Mezger and H. Schwengel (eds), *Wissensgesellschaft, Verteilungskonflikte und strategische Akteure,* Marburg: Metropolis, pp. 217–233.

Bosch, G. (2010a) Schriftliche Stellungnahme zur öffentlichen Anhörung von Sachverständigen in Berlin am 19. April 2010 (Ausschussdrucksache 17(11)110) zum Antrag der Fraktion der SPD [. . .]. In: *Materialien zur Zusammenstellung der schriftlichen Stellungnahmen zur öffentlichen Anhörung von Sachverständigen in Berlin am 19. April 2010 zum Antrag der Fraktion der SPD 'Beschäftigte vor Arbeitslosigkeit schützen - Konditionen für Kurzarbeit verbessern'* (BT-Drucksache 17/523), Berlin: Deutscher Bundestag.

Bosch, G. (2010b) 'The revitalization of the dual system of vocational training in Germany', in Gerhard Bosch and Jean Charest (eds), *Vocational Training, International Perspectives,* London: Routledge Studies in Employment and Work Relations in Context, pp. 136–161.

Bosch, G. and Kalina, T. (2008) 'Low-wage work in Germany: An overview', G. Bosch and C. Weinkopf (eds), *Low-wage Work in Germany,* New York: Russell Sage Foundation, pp. 19–112.

Bosch, G. and Kalina, T. (2010) 'Germany: What role for minimum wages on low-wage work?', in D. Vaughan-Whitehead (ed.), *The Minimum Wage Revisited in the Enlarged EU,* Cheltenham/Geneva: Elgar/ILO, pp. 185–212.

Bosch, G. and Weinkopf, C. (eds) (2008) *Low-wage Work in Germany,* New York: Russell Sage Foundation.

Brenke, K., Rinne, U. and Zimmermann, K.F. (2010) 'Kurzarbeit: Nützlich in der Krise, aber nun den Ausstieg einleiten', in *Wochenbericht des DIW* 16/2010, pp. 2–13. Available at: http://www.diw.de/documents/publikationen/73/diw_01.c.355425.de/10-16-1.pdf (accessed on 20 October 2010).

Eichhorst, W. and Marx, P. (2009) 'Kurzarbeit – sinnvoller Konjunkturpuffer oder verlängertes Arbeitslosengeld', *Wirtschaftsdienst* No. 5: 322–328.

Erlinghagen, Marcel (2004) *Die Restrukturierung des Arbeitsmarktes: Arbeitsmarktmobilität und Beschäftigungsstabilität im Zeitverlauf,* Wiesbaden: VS Verlag für Sozialwiss.

Eurofound (European Foundation for the Improvement of Living and Working Conditions) (2009) *Restructuring in Recession,* ERM Report 2009, Dublin. Available at: http://www.eurofound.europa.eu/publications/htmlfiles/ef0973.htm (accessed on 21 December 2010).

Eurostat (2010a) *The Conference Board Total Economy Database.* Available at: http://www.conference-board.org/data/economydatabase/ (accessed on 3 November 2010).

Eurostat (2010b) Newsrelease euroindicators 59/2010 and 153/2009. Available at: http://epp.eurostat.ec.europa.eu/cache/ITY_PUBLIC/3-30102009-AP/EN/

3-30102009-AP-EN.PDF; http://epp.eurostat.ec.europa.eu/cache/ITY_PUBLI
C/3-30042010-BP/EN/3-30042010-BP-EN.PDF (accessed on 3 November 2010).
Fischer, G. et al. (2007) 'Langfristig handeln, Mangel vermeiden: Betriebliche
Strategien zur Deckung des Fachkräftebedarfs, Ergebnisse des IAB-
Betriebspanels 2007', in *IAB-Forschungsbericht* 03/2008, Nuremburg, pp. 83ff.
Fuchs, J. et al. (2010) 'Prognose 2010/2011. Der Arbeitsmarkt schließt an den
vorherigen Aufschwung an', IAB-Kurzbericht 18/2010, Nuremberg. Available
at: http://doku.iab.de/kurzber/2010/kb1810.pdf (accessed on 24 October
2010).
Goebel, J., Gornig, M. and Häußermann, H. (2010) 'Polarisierung der Einkommen:
Mittelschicht verliert', DIW-Wochenbericht No. 24, pp. 2–8.
Groß, H. and Schwarz, M. (2009) *Arbeitszeitarrangements, Altersstrukturen und
Corporate Social Responsibility in deutschen Betrieben*, Wiesbaden.
Herzog-Stein, A. and Seifert, H. (2010) 'Deutsches "Beschäftigungswunder" und
flexible Arbeitszeiten', WSI-Diskussionspapier No. 169, February, Düsseldorf.
Available at: http://www.boeckler.de/pdf/p_wsi_diskp_169.pdf (accessed on 5
May 2010).
IAB (2009a) *Kurzarbeit: Betriebe zahlen mit – und haben was davon*, IAB
Kurzbericht 17/2009.
IAB (2009b) 'Vollzeitbeschäftigte sind stärker von der Krise betroffen als
Teilzeitbe-schäftigte', Presseinformation des IAB, 9 September 2009. Available
at: http://www.iab.de/1439/section.aspx (accessed on 27 November 2009).
IAB (2009c) 'Erhebung des gesamtwirtschaftlichen Stellenangebots II/2009', IAB-
Kurzbericht No. 18.
IW Zeitarbeitsindex (2010) BZA-Umfrage November 2010 (Welle 40) – JW
Fortschreibung. Available at: <http://www.bza.de/fileadmin/bilder/2009/2010/
BZA-Bericht_Oktober_Welle_40_20101209.pdf> (accessed on 22 December
2010).
Kahn, L.B. (2010) 'The long-term labor market consequences of graduating from
college in a bad economy', *Labour Economics*, 17 (2), 303–316, April.
Lehndorff, S., Bosch, G., Haipeter, T. and Latniak, E. (2009) 'From the "sick
man" to the "overhauled engine" of Europe? Upheaval in the German model',
in *European Employment Models in Flux: A Comparison of Institutional Change
in Nine European Countries*, Basingstoke: Palgrave Macmillan, pp. 105–131.
Marsden, D. (1990) 'Institutions and labour mobility: occupational and internal
labour markets in Britain, France, Italy and West Germany', in R. Brunetta and
C. Dell'Aringa (eds), *Labour Relations and Economic Performance. Proceedings
of a Conference held by the International Economic Association in Venice*, pp.
414–438.
Müller, W. and Gangl, M. (eds) (2003) *Transitions from Education to Work in
Europe. The Integration of Youth into EU Labour Markets*, Oxford: Oxford
University Press.
OECD (2010) Schriftliche Stellungnahme zur öffentlichen Anhörung von
Sachverständigen in Berlin am 19. April 2010 (Ausschussdrucksache 17(11)110)
zum Antrag der Fraktion der SPD [. . .]. In: *Materialien zur Zusammenstellung
der schriftlichen Stellungnahmen zur öffentlichen Anhörung von Sachverständigen
in Berlin am 19. April 2010 zum Antrag der Fraktion der SPD 'Beschäftigte
vor Arbeitslosigkeit schützen - Konditionen für Kurzarbeit verbessern'* (BT-
Drucksache 17/523). Berlin: Deutscher Bundestag.
Projektgruppe Gemeinschaftsdiagnose (2009) *Im Sog der Weltrezession*, IMK

Report No. 37, April. Available at: http://www.boeckler.de/pdf/p_imk_report_37_2009.pdf (accessed on 1 February 2011).

Sachverständigenrat (SVR) (2009) *Die Zukunft nicht aufs Spiel setzen*, Jahresgutachten 2009/10.

Sachverständigenrat (SVR) (2010) *Chancen für einen stabilen Aufschwung*, Jahresgutachten 2010/11. Available at: http://www.sachverstaendigenrat-wirtschaft.de/aktuellesjahrsgutachten-2010-11.html (accessed on 18 December 2010).

Snower, D. (2009) 'Kurzarbeit schadet langfristig', *Handelsblatt* (12 November 2009). Available at: http://www.handelsblatt.com/politik/konjunktur-nachrichten/top-oekonom-dennis-snower-kurzarbeit-schadet-langfristig;2482648 (accessed 20 October 2010).

Statistisches Bundesamt (2010) *Erwerbstätige im Inland nach Wirtschaftsbereichen, Volkswirtschaftliche Gesamtrechnung*. Available at: http://www.destatis.de/jetspeed/portal/cms/Sites/destatis/Internet/DE/Content/Statistiken/Zeitreihen/WirtschaftAktuell/VolkswirtschaftlicheGesamtrechnungen/Content100/vgr010a,templateId=renderPrint.psml (accessed on 20 October 2010).

WSI (2010) *WSI Tarifarchiv September 2010*. Available at: http://www.boeckler.de/pdf/ta_mindestloehne_aentg.pdf (accessed on 3 November 2010).

APPENDIX

Table 6A.1 *Overview of the main anti-crisis packages in Germany, 2008–2010**

	Billions of Euros		Total
	2009	2010	
1. Relief package of 7 October 2008			
Increase in child benefit and tax allowance for dependent children	2.3	2.2	
Reduction in unemployment insurance contribution rate to 2.8%	4.0	4.0	
Increase in tax allowance for health and nursing care insurance contributions	–	8.4	
Sub-total I	6	15	21
2. Economic stimulus package I, November 2008			
Bringing forward transport investment	1.0	1.0	
Degressive write-offs of capital assets/ accelerated depreciation for SMEs	2.2	4.7	
Vehicle tax exemption for new cars	0.4	0.1	
Payments to craft workers made tax deductible	–	1.0	
Additional funding for programmes (modernization of building insulation, KfW development bank programmes, improvement of regional economic structure)	0.3	0.4	
Extension of period of entitlement to short-time working allowance up to 24 months[1]	–	–	
Sub-total II	4	7	11
3. Economic stimulus package, January 2009			
Federal investment (transport/construction/ infrastructure)	2.0	2.0	
Investing for the Future Act: support of investments of local authorities	6.7	6.7	
Tax rate reduction and child bonus	4.9	5.6	
Reduction in contribution rate for statutory health insurance	3.2	6.3	
Safeguarding jobs: social contribution for short-time workers, further training in companies, 5000 additional placement officers in employment offices	3.3	2.6	

Table 6A.1   (continued)

| | Billions of Euros | | Total |
	2009	2010	
Increase in standard benefit for children	0.2	0.3	
Motor vehicle tax exemption and environmental premium	5.0	0.2	
Central Innovation Programme for medium-size firms	0.4	0.5	
Mobility research (power train engineering)	0.2	0.3	
Replenishment of credit guarantee programme for companies in economic difficulties ('Business Fund Germany')	0.3	0.7	
Re-introduction of full commuter tax relief	5.4	3.1	8.5
Temporary corporation tax reliefs	0.8	0.9	2.0
Farm diesel tax reliefs time limited			0.6
Sub-total III	26	25	51
4. Growth Acceleration Act, November 2009			
Increase in child benefit and tax allowance for dependent children		4.3	
Adjustments to loss carry-over/interest limitation/write-downs		0.7	
Adjustment to inheritance tax/bio-fuel promotion		0.3	
Reduction in VAT rate for hotel industry		0.8	
Sub-total Growth Acceleration Act		6	6
Overall total	43	57	100

Notes:
* Including financial contributions from *Länder* and local authorities.
[1] Additional expenditure cannot be quantified because even without prolongation of short-time allowances this instrument would have been used heavily.

Source: Federal Ministry of Economics, available at: http://www.bmwi.de/BMWi/Navigation/Wirtschaft/Konjunktur/konjunkturmassnahmen,did=380790.html (last accessed 8 March 2011).

7. Hungary: Crisis coupled with a fiscal squeeze – effects on inequality

János Köllő*

1. INTRODUCTION

This chapter summarizes the available evidence on how the global crisis affected the labour market and social inequalities in Hungary in the first years of the crisis. Most of what is presented is based on longitudinal micro data covering firms and individuals observed in 2008 and 2009.

The effect of labour market developments on social inequality was ambiguous. In the public sector, real wages fell by more than 10 per cent in 2009, while employment remained practically unchanged (it even grew thanks to increased inflows to public works schemes). Given that public sector employees are better educated and older, on average, than private sector workers, the cutting of their wages diminished rather than augmented inequality of earnings. At the same time, their better prospects of remaining in their jobs had an inequality enhancing effect.

In the private sector, employment was cut by almost 7 per cent in 2009, while real wages fell only marginally. Once compositional changes are controlled for, we find no statistically significant links between firm-level average wage changes and firm characteristics (size, sector, ownership, unionization), apart from an effect of a rise in the basic minimum wage in January 2009. Likewise, the individual panel data suggest that the distribution of earnings remained virtually unchanged except for the shift of minimum wage earners from the old to the new mandatory floors. Monthly working time was slightly shortened by a magnitude of about 1 per cent. Working time reductions probably did not extend beyond some national and local programmes providing job retention subsidies, which typically required that firms classify their subsidized employees as part-timers. The data suggest that enterprises reacted to the crisis by bringing hiring to a halt rather than by substantially increasing lay-offs – this provides part of the explanation of why 'hard adjustment' prevailed in the private sector. The contraction of labour demand affected the less educated and younger workers slightly more than others, implying an increase in inequality.

At the same time, men were worse affected than women, which had an equality-enhancing effect.

Government policies were aimed at minimizing job losses, on the one hand, and creating socially useful jobs, on the other. The eligibility and entitlement criteria pertaining to unemployment insurance did not change. Thanks to the improving composition of the flows to unemployment in terms of benefit eligibility and labour force attachment, the share of those losing their job receiving unemployment benefit increased, while the fraction receiving some kind of financial assistance did not fall. While unemployment insurance at least partly fulfilled its function as an automatic stabilizer, the huge amounts spent by the government on saving a relatively small number of jobs reduced the resources available for unemployment relief. The budgets for active labour market policies and employment services were markedly cut and the absolute number of unassisted prime-age people out of work increased substantially.

The available data suggest that income inequality did not change significantly until the end of 2009. The relative position of the poorest quintile deteriorated but the magnitude of change was far less dramatic than it was during the post-communist transformational recession. At the same time, growing energy bills and debt servicing brought many low-income households to the edge of financial ruin, which contributed to a feeling of desolation and despair unprecedented since the hardest years of the transition.

2. THE CRISIS IN BRIEF

2.1 Magnitudes of the Downturn

Hungary, as a small open economy deeply integrated in European product and financial markets, has been hit hard by the crisis since October 2008. Already before the crisis the country had been struggling with fiscal imbalances and political distrust for several years. After several years of irresponsible fiscal policies (on both sides), in 2006 the budget deficit came within reach of 10 per cent of GDP, forcing the government to instigate an austerity programme. Economic growth was slowing before the crisis and fiscal imbalances made the economy particularly vulnerable to outside shocks.

As shown in Table 7.1, in 2008, real GDP increased slightly – by 0.5 per cent – but fell by 6.3 per cent in 2009. Industrial output and exports decreased substantially: by 17.7 and 12.2 per cent, respectively. Despite the starting of several EU-sponsored development programmes, investment fell by 9 per cent. The shock was magnified by a dramatic depreciation of

*Table 7.1   Selected economic indicators, Hungary, 2008–2009
            (percentage change)*

	2008	2009
GDP	0.5	–6.3
Industrial output	–1.1	–17.7
Exports	4.2	–12.2
Investment	0.4	–9.1
Budget deficit/GDP (%)	3.4	> 3.6

Source: Online databases (Stadat, Statinfo) of the Hungarian Central Statistical Office:
http://ksh.hu.

the forint (at the extremes: 235 HUF/euro in August 2008 and 320 HUF/
euro in March 2009), which proved insufficient to effectively support
exports but gave rise to sometimes unmanageable problems for firms and
households indebted in hard currency.[1] At the brink of financial collapse,
Hungary had to apply to the IMF, the World Bank and the EU for loans
amounting to a total of 20 billion euros. The government, committed to
keeping the budget deficit below 4 per cent in 2009 and to push it down
further in 2010, introduced a series of austerity measures, which included
the abolition of 'thirteenth-month' wages and pensions, the abolition of
the Swiss indexation of pensions, scenarios for increasing the retirement
age from 62 to 65 years and shortening paid leave for mothers from three
to two years, the cutting of the flat rate per child family allowance and
the curtailing of subsidies and allowances for housing, heating, transport
and farming. As a result of the austerity measures, the increase in the
budget deficit could be kept to a mere 0.2 percentage points. This fiscal
success, however, also meant that the Hungarian government had limited
resources to counteract market forces.

2.2   Institutions Conditioning the Response

The government's inclination to react to the crisis by across-the-board
wage cuts in the public sector (via abolition of the 'thirteenth-month'
salary and the freezing of further wage increases) is easy to justify. On the
one hand, severance payments and procedural rules make firing costly
and time-consuming in the public sector, while wage cuts are relatively
easy to pass, given the limits of skill transferability (for example, in the
case of doctors and older teachers), and considering that the public sector
historically has attracted workers ready to trade off wages for increased
job security.[2]

In the private sector, the optimality of staff reductions as opposed to wage cuts and hours reductions is far less obvious. In a monopoly trade union setting or in the case of efficient bargaining we expect that the burden of adjustment will fall predominantly on employment (McDonald and Solow 1982; Brueckner 2001). Similar conclusions follow from the theories of implicit contracts (Azariadis 1975; Feldstein 1976, 1978; Rosen 1985) and intertemporal substitution (Lucas and Rapping 1969). Despite the theoretical predictions of strong cyclicality in employment and less in wages, both the macroeconomic and the micro evidence are mixed. In a recent study of the cyclicality of manufacturing employment and wages between 1960 and 2004, Messina, Strozzi and Turunen (2009) find substantial cross-country variations, even after controlling for type of data and methods used in measuring cyclicality. They identify positive correlation between the cyclicality of real wages and the cyclicality of employment, but identify groups of countries with different positions along these dimensions. The available data on the current crisis also suggest strong diversity across countries. While comprehensive wage statistics on 2009 are not yet available, the data on changes in GDP, employment and working hours show high cross-country dispersion in the responses of employment to GDP, as well as in the relative importance of employment adjustment versus hours reductions (Verick and Islam 2010, 25–27.)

In a transitory downturn, cutting hours and wages can prove to be attractive options if hiring and firing costs are high or large, firm-financed investments in firm-specific skills are yet to be recouped. When plant utilization is temporarily low, firms may also prefer training their workers since the costs of accumulating firm-specific skills are lower. Reacting to a negative shock in ways other than dismissals is easier if some institutions supporting the adjustment of hours and wages are at hand, as emphasized in Bellmann and Gerner (2010). One institution of this kind is working time accounts, which enable employees to work longer or shorter hours than usual and thereby collect working time credits or debits in an individual account, which are later compensated for by additional leisure or work. Similarly, softer measures can be encouraged by pacts on employment and competitiveness, in which employees accept lower wages and reduced working time and employers guarantee jobs and training, and offer financial participation (Bellmann, Gerlach and Meyer 2008). Profit sharing can also make wage adjustment easier since it establishes an automatic link between workers' pay and the fluctuations of business fortunes.

The institutional features of the Hungarian labour market make the adjustment of both employment and wages relatively easy, but there are few formal agreements and legal institutions which explicitly encourage a heterodox reaction to a negative shock.

Trade union coverage is low and has been declining since the start of the transition. According to the Labour Force Survey, the share of union members was 20 per cent in 2001, 17 per cent in 2004 and 12 per cent in 2009. The proportion of workers employed in unionized firms fell from 38 per cent in 2001 to 33 per cent in 2004 and 28 per cent in 2008. The share of workers covered by any kind of collective agreement declined from 25 per cent in 2004 to 21 per cent in 2009 (Fazekas et al. 2010, no similar data are available for 2001). The agreements are typically concluded with a single employer and are not extended. Furthermore, the unions seem to be relatively weak, as suggested by estimates of a small (0–2 per cent) regression-adjusted union wage gap (Neumann 2002; Rigó 2008).

There are few legal constraints on employment and wage setting, the most important being the minimum wage. The minimum wage/average wage ratio (34.7 per cent just before the crisis) cannot be considered high by international comparison but the real minimum wage has been constantly growing in the past ten years. The adjustment of the minimum wage is negotiated annually by employer organizations and unions, permitting careful policies in hard times, but unions generally start negotiations with very ambitious goals and usually achieve at least modest increases in real terms.[3] This was the case at the beginning of the recent crisis, too, as discussed below.

Only a single estimate of adjustment costs is available (Kőrösi and Surányi 2003), suggesting that the costs of hiring and firing are relatively low by international comparison. Training costs probably do not play an important role in firms' decisions since the fraction of Hungarians participating in adult training is one of the lowest in Europe and on-the-job training is particularly infrequent (Bajnai et al. 2009). Hungary's employment protection (EPL) index is the lowest in Central and Eastern Europe and one of the lowest in the EU (Cazes and Nesporova 2007).

Institutions encouraging the combination of employment, hours and wage adjustment are undeveloped in Hungary. Formal agreements similar to the pacts for employment and competitiveness do not exist, to the best of the author's knowledge. Working time accounts have not been established as a legal institution, in contrast to the Czech Republic and Germany, for instance, where about half of the medium-sized and large companies are covered (Bellmann and Gerner 2010). The fraction of workers covered by profit-sharing agreements is one of the lowest in Europe, with Hungary above only Portugal and Cyprus (Eurofound 2007). However, it would be wrong to conclude that such practices do not exist. We have ample anecdotal evidence that working time accounts are applied informally. Profit sharing does exist informally, as suggested by a relatively high wage elasticity with regard to productivity (Commander and Faggio 2003; Köllő

Table 7.2   Changes in employment, hours and wages in the public and private sectors, Hungary, 2008–2009

	Public sector[a]	Private sector[b]	Total
Employees[c]	3.6	–6.6	–3.7
Monthly gross real wage[d]	–10.7	–1.6	–5.5
Average monthly paid working hours per employee[e]	–1.3	–1.1	–1.1

Note: [a] Non-profits included. [b] Firms employing five or more workers. [c] 'Number of individuals participating in the organization's activity'. This figure includes all individuals on the payroll and may deviate from the number of employees. [d] The consumer price index was 1.042 on a year-on-year basis. [e] Percentage change in the average of the four quarterly figures.

Source: http://statinfo.ksh.hu/Statinfo/haViewer.jsp, July 2010.

and Mickiewicz 2005). Informal agreements on saving jobs through soft measures may also exist and we hope to find traces of such agreements when we look at how firms actually combined staff reductions, wage cuts and hours reductions during the current crisis.

2.3   First Look at the Response

The monthly gross real wage fell by 10.7 per cent in the public sector, while employment grew by 3.6 per cent (Table 7.2). This increase was explained entirely by inflows to public works programmes. Excluding public works, employment fell marginally, by 0.4 per cent. The data on the private sector mirror what happened in the public sector. Employment fell dramatically by 6.6 per cent, while the average wage was only slightly affected, with a decline of 1.6 per cent in real terms.

Wage developments were affected markedly by the rising minimum wages. In 2008, the regulations distinguished three mandatory minima: the base minimum wage (MW), the skilled minimum wage (SMW = 1.25MW) and a reduced minimum for younger skilled workers with fewer than three years' experience (YSMW = 1.2MW). In September 2008, the unions started negotiations with a demand for a 15.9 per cent rise in the MW, a 14.7 per cent rise in the YSMW and a 10.1 per cent rise in the SMW, starting from January 2009. Given a consensus inflation forecast of 4.2 per cent at the start of the negotiations, these hikes would have implied 11.2, 10.0 and 6.3 per cent increases in the minima in real terms, respectively. Even at the end of November, two months after the beginning of the crisis, the unions demanded a 10.9 per cent rise in the base MW in nominal terms,

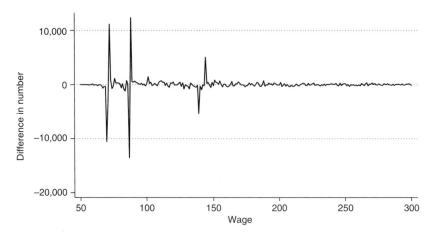

Note: The chart relates to 52,400 workers observed in the 2008 and 2009 waves of the Wage Survey and identified across waves on the basis of their employer's ID, date of birth, gender, education and 4-digit job classification code. Wages in both 2008 and 2009 were rounded and expressed in 1,000 forint units (100 denoting a wage of 100,000 forints, for instance). Denoting the number of workers earning w thousand forints with $N^{08}(w)$ and $N^{09}(w)$, respectively, the curve depicts $DN(w) = N^{09}(w) - N^{08}(w)$ for each integer value of w.

Figure 7.1   *Changes in the distribution of gross monthly earnings,*
Hungary, 2008–2009 (private sector)

and insisted on their original claims regarding the SMW.[4] Finally, under the pressure of the crisis and following a revision of the inflation forecast (3.1–3.4 per cent)[5] the parties agreed a 3.6 per cent increase in the MW, a 5.1 per cent rise in the YSMW and a mere 0.8 per cent rise in the SMW in nominal terms.[6] The effects of these – ultimately minor – hikes can be clearly observed in Figure 7.1, which shows the difference between the wage distributions of 2008 and 2009 – the negative and positive spikes show how workers shifted from the old to the new minima.

It is easy to check that, apart from the effect of the minimum wage, the density functions of 2008 and 2009 had virtually identical shapes. The stability of the wage distribution is also indicated by small movements in the inequality measures presented in Table 7.3. The Gini and the Theil indicators remained virtually unchanged, while the CV – which is sensitive to changes at the top of the wage distribution – indicates a minor decrease in earnings inequality.

Average hours fell slightly, by 1.3 per cent in the public sector and 1.1 per cent in private firms, according to the establishment-based statistics, presented in Table 7.2. The LFS data also hint at a fall of 1.1 per cent (0.4 hours) in the same target population. Furthermore, they suggest that the

Table 7.3   Inequality of gross monthly earnings, Hungary, 2008–2009

	Whole economy		Private sector	
	2008	2009	2008	2009
Coefficient of variation (CV)	1.00	1.00	1.14	1.11
Gini	0.36	0.37	0.38	0.39
Theil's mean log deviation	0.21	0.22	0.24	0.25

Note: The data relate to all workers in the Wage Survey in 2008 and 2009 (156,914 and 148,756 observations). Wage concept: base wage plus regular supplements in May minus non-regular bonuses in May plus the monthly average of non-regular bonuses received in the previous year.

Table 7.4   Selected working time indicators, Hungary, 2008–2009

	2008	2009	Change
Part-timer by type of contract			
All employees, LFS data[a]	4.6	5.5	0.9
Firms employing 5 or more workers + public sector			
• Establishment-based data[b]	8.7	10.4	1.7
• LFS data[c]	6.1	7.3	1.2
Other indicators of working time (firms > 5 and budget), LFS data)[c]			
Temporarily absent from an existing job in the reference week[d]	10.7	9.7	−1.0
Usual working time highly variable[e]	3.8	3.6	−0.2
Actual working time in the reference week: 1–19 hours[f]	1.6	2.4	0.8
Actual working time in the reference week: 20–39 hours[f]	8.8	9.3	0.5
Mean hours in the reference week[f]	38.1	37.7	−0.4

Note: [a] http://portal.ksh.hu/pls/ksh/docs/hun/xstadat/xstadat_eves/tabl2_01_07i.html; [b] http://portal.ksh.hu/pls/ksh/docs/hun/xstadat/xstadat_eves/tabl2_01_20_02ib.html; [c] author's calculation; [d] employed or temporarily absent = 100. [e] employed = 100. [f] working at least 1 hour in the reference week = 100.

fraction of employees working 1–19 and 20–39 hours increased by 0.8 and 0.5 percentage points, respectively (Table 7.4). Other indicators, such as complete absence from a job during the reference week or the incidence of highly variable hours, do not hint at working time reductions or more frequent breaks in the workweek.[7]

The deviation of firm-based and self-reported statistics on the share of workers with part-time contracts (percentage point changes of 1.7 versus 1.2) is probably explained by participation in the government-assisted 'four days work + one day training' schemes.[8] The official working time of employees in the 4+1 programmes fell because the affected workers had to be reclassified as part-timers. At the same time, the self-reported hours of such workers did not necessarily change: most probably, many of them interpreted training on the fifth day as work. According to the establishment-based statistics,[9] the number of part-time employees in firms employing five or more workers increased by 36,800 in 2008–2009, while job retention subsidies affected 52,000 workers. These data lead us to believe that working time reductions outside the subsidized firms occurred infrequently, if at all.[10]

3. FIRM-LEVEL CHANGES IN EMPLOYMENT, HOURS AND WAGES IN 2008–2009

In this section, we look at variations in the changes of employment, hours and wages using longitudinal firm-level data covering May 2008 and 2009. We shall be particularly interested in the influence of institutions potentially moderating or enhancing the effects of the crisis: state ownership, union cover-age and the minimum wage.

The available data are insufficient for an estimation of a full causal model, explaining how the crisis affected firms' decisions on the level and skill composition of employment and wages. Most importantly, we do not have, as yet, firm-level data on changes in output or other variables capturing the size of the shock to which firms had to respond. This will be approximated with two-digit industry-level data on changes in output which, admittedly, is second-best solution. Equally important, the identification of causal effects in a system with several endogenous variables (employment, hours, skill composition and wages) would require several exogenous variables having impact on a particular outcome without affecting other outcomes. Such instruments are not available in the data set. The available variables, such as firm size, industry, ownership, union coverage, exposure to the minimum wage and skill composition are likely to affect employment, hours and wages simultaneously. Therefore we shall have recourse to a descriptive three-equations model explaining the log change of employment (L), monthly working hours (H) and average hourly wages $\bar{w}$.

$$\Delta \ln L_i = X_i \beta + u_i \qquad (7.1a)$$

$$\Delta \ln H_i = X_i \gamma + v_i \tag{7.1b}$$

$$\Delta \ln \overline{w}_i = X_i \delta + \omega_i \tag{7.1c}$$

The equations have the same set of explanatory variables (X), so the coefficients and the standard errors are the same as if the equations were estimated one by one with OLS. By estimating (7.1a–7.1c) jointly as a system of seemingly unrelated regressions we can benefit from looking at the correlations between the residuals u, v and ω and test whether the three equations are independent.

In a second step, we will show that the changes in average wages were strongly affected by changes in firms' skill composition. By regressing Dlnw on changes in the demographic and skill composition of the workforce and taking the residuals $\xi - X_i$ as in equation (7.2) we can get a measure that is controlled for compositional effects. (In the equation, AGE stands for average age, EDU denotes average years in school and MALE relates to the share of men.) Then, after replacing $\Delta \ln \overline{w}$ with ξ in equation (7.1c), we can check how the residual wages were affected by the Xs.

$$\xi = \Delta h \overline{w}_i - \beta_1 \Delta AGE_i - \beta_2 \Delta EDU_i - \beta_3 \Delta MALE_i - c \tag{7.2}$$

3.1 Data

The analysis relates to 5,173 firms observed in 2008 and 2009 in the Wage Survey (WS). The WS is carried out by the Public Employment Service (PES) annually, each May. All Hungarian firms employing more than 20 workers are obliged to fill in the WS questionnaire, while in the case of smaller firms a 20 per cent random sample is selected and obliged to report. The firms provide enterprise-level data (size, industry, ownership, employment) and individual data on their workers. Firms employing fewer than 50 workers report on all employees, while the larger ones report on a (roughly 10 per cent) random sample of their workers. The firms can be linked across waves directly, while workers can be identified indirectly, with a margin of error, using data on their firm ID, date of birth, gender, education and job classification.

Out of the 9,054 enterprises reporting data in 2008, 5,428 were observed in 2009. Selection to the panel was mainly affected by the sampling design of the survey, but firm exit and non-response could also play a role. A medium-sized or large firm can vanish from the WS if it goes bankrupt or drops below the 20 workers limit and is not selected for the next year's randomly chosen small-firm sample. The probability that a small firm observed one year will also be observed the next year is 0.2 if it continues

*Table 7.5   Changes in the firm panel versus the whole private sector,
Hungary*

	Private sector 2009 Q2/ 2008 Q2	Firm panel 2009 May/ 2008 May
Employment	−7.6	−8.9
Average monthly working hours per worker	−2.6	−2.3
Real gross monthly earnings	1.4	–
Real gross monthly base wage	–	1.5
– Regular supplements and bonuses included	–	0.0
– Monthly value of previous year's non-regular bonuses included	–	−0.9

Note: Data on the entire private sector are drawn from the Statinfo database, available on
the Central Statistical Office's home-page www.ksh.hu.

to employ fewer than 20 workers, and 1.0 if it grows large enough to be
included in the 'medium-sized and large' category. In fact, out of the
base period sample 39.5 per cent of the small firms and 71.7 per cent of
the larger ones were observed in May 2009. Selection to the panel was
analysed with probit and the inverse of the estimated survival probabilities were used as weights in the calculations (see Köllő 2010a for the
estimation results).

The most important indicators related to firms in the panel are compared to the closest available figures of the CSO in Table 7.5. We do
not expect exactly the same indices since the published figures relate to
April–June, while the WS data compare May 2008 and 2009 and the
wage concepts are slightly different, too. In the firm panel, compared to
the published figures, employment fell more and hours fell slightly less.
In the firm sample, the observed rates of change in real earnings vary in a
range between −0.9 and 1.5 per cent, depending on whether bonuses are
included or not. Furthermore, the sample-based estimates differ from the
published data because of a difference in the reference periods (Q2/Q2 in
case of the published data versus May/May in the firm sample). The data
of the firm panel nevertheless follow the same pattern as the CSO data in
suggesting a considerable loss of jobs, minor downward adjustment of
working hours and slightly changing real wages.

Before turning to the estimations, we identified heavy outliers using
a procedure proposed in Hadi (1992). The procedure looks for one or
more sub-populations where the linkages between some key variables

Table 7.6   Changes of employment, hours and wages with outliers and non-outliers, Hungary

	Mean log change of		
	Employment	Hours	Hourly wage
Non-outlier (5,173)	–0.058	–0.013	0.038
Outlier (255)	–0.467	–0.136	0.165

Note: Outliers were identified with Stata's *hadimvo* procedure in the space of the log changes of employment, hours and hourly wages.

follow a pattern sharply different from the one characteristic of the whole population. Search for such a sub-population in the space of ΔlnL, ΔlnH and Δln$\bar{w}$ resulted in 255 outliers. As shown in Table 7.6, these firms lost almost half of their staff in a year, their average working hours fell ten times faster than those of the non-outliers and their hourly nominal wages went up by 16.5 per cent as opposed to 3.8 per cent in the case of the non-outliers.

The outliers were more likely to be in construction and administrative services, and less likely to be state-owned and agricultural companies than the non-outliers were, while other variables (size, ownership, union coverage, exposure to the minimum wage, industry and region) had no statistically significant effect. The outliers seem to be collapsing firms and/or companies whose structure changed considerably. In any case, their inclusion in a model looking at adjustment on the margins would hinder rather than help the analysis.[11]

In the estimations the hourly wage figure relates to total monthly remuneration (last row in Table 7.5) divided by paid hours during the month. The data on industrial output (sales revenues deflated with the producer price index in the tradable sectors and the consumer price index elsewhere) relate to 82 two-digit sectors and have 33 distinct values.

3.2   Regression Results

In the model presented in Table 7.7, industry output has a significant positive effect on both employment and hours and has no effect on wages. The elasticity of the firms' employment with respect to its industry's real sales revenues is fairly weak, at 0.06. The estimates are probably downward-biased since the industry's change of output measures the firm-specific shocks with a wide margin of error. Unfortunately, firm-level data and

Table 7.7   Changes of employment, hours and wages – multivariate regressions, Hungary (firm panel)

	Dependent: log change of					
	Employment		Working hours		Hourly wage	
	β	T	β	T	β	T
Log change of industry's output	0.0551	2.06	0.0265	4.00	−0.0198	−1.17
Share of men	−0.0289	−2.23	0.0029	0.91	−0.0256	−3.11
Average years in school	0.0047	1.69	0.0008	1.23	−0.0069	−3.90
Average age	−0.0002	−0.45	−0.0001	−0.83	−0.0009	−2.58
Fraction paid the base minimum wage	0.0039	0.22	−0.0054	−1.22	0.0418	3.65
Fraction paid the skilled minimum wage	−0.0400	−2.67	−0.0112	−3.03	0.0003	0.04
Covered by collective agreement	0.0196	2.24	−0.0003	−0.18	0.0081	1.46
Majority state-owned	0.0361	2.24	0.0057	1.44	0.0001	0.04
Majority foreign-owned	−0.0027	−0.24	−0.0049	−1.77	0.0030	0.42
0–10 employees	0.0845	5.27	0.0069	1.76	−0.0007	−0.07
11–20 employees	0.0431	2.59	0.0027	0.67	0.0161	1.53
21–50 employees	0.0235	1.47	0.0068	1.73	0.0036	0.35
51–300 employees	0.0188	1.33	0.0071	2.05	−0.003	−0.42
Personal services	0.1004	3.07	0.0028	0.35	−0.0165	−0.80
Water	0.0836	3.69	0.0072	1.30	0.0025	0.18
Health (private)	0.0758	3.38	0.0202	3.65	−0.0275	−1.93
Agriculture	0.0692	4.40	0.0122	3.15	−0.0058	−0.59
Energy	0.0594	2.08	0.0127	1.79	0.0155	0.86
Mining	0.0568	1.28	0.0069	0.63	0.0380	1.35
Finance, insurance	0.0535	2.35	0.0175	3.12	0.0050	0.35
Professional services	0.0529	2.57	0.0093	1.84	0.0240	1.85
Communication	0.0513	2.13	0.0075	1.26	0.0213	1.40
Transport	0.0428	2.50	0.0026	0.63	−0.006	−0.64
Culture (private)	0.0346	1.06	−0.0243	−3.00	0.0202	0.98
Hotels & restaurants	0.0299	1.49	0.0088	1.78	−0.0066	−0.52
Real estate	0.0227	0.89	0.0034	0.54	−0.0032	−0.20
Trade	0.0225	2.01	0.0057	2.10	−0.0108	−1.53
Construction	0.0129	0.91	0.0060	1.71	−0.0075	−0.84
Administrative services	−0.0016	−0.09	−0.0011	−0.25	−0.0042	−0.36
Education (private)	−0.0807	−2.26	0.0098	1.12	0.0313	1.38
Constant	−0.1336	−2.99	−0.0248	−2.25	0.1606	5.68
R^2	0.0376		−0.0072		0.0173	

Table 7.7   (continued)

Notes:
Correlation of residuals: Employment-hours: 0.0117. Employment-wage: –0.0072. Hours-wage: –0.3107.
Breusch-Pagan test of independence: chi^2 = 500.185 (0.0000).
Number of observations: 5,173.
Reference industry: manufacturing. Industries are ordered by the size of the coefficients in the employment equation.

three- or four-digit sector level data were not available at the time of writing.

Male-dominated firms lost more jobs and had worse than average wage records. Firms in which the proportion of males was higher by one standard deviation (31 per cent) in the base period lost more jobs – about 1 per cent – and in terms of average wages (0.7 per cent). Average skills also seem to matter: a one standard deviation (1.5 year) difference in average years in school implied about 1 per cent higher employment and 1.1 per cent lower wages in 2009 relative to 2008. Average age had no effect on employment and hours, but it affected wages marginally: a workforce older by 6.3 years (one standard deviation) implied that wages grew more slowly by 0.6 per cent.

Firm size has a marked effect on employment and some impact on hours, while its effect on wages is insignificant. Small and medium-sized firms lost fewer jobs than large ones (300+ employees) by 8, 4, 2 and 2 per cent, respectively, as we move from the bottom to the top of the SME size categories. This pattern is probably explained by differences in exposure to exports: we find the advantage of the smallest firms to be much greater (12 per cent) in manufacturing, where larger firms tend to be either export-ers or suppliers of exporters, than in the rest of the economy (5 per cent).

As far as industry effects are concerned, the employment records of man-ufacturing, construction and real estate appear to be statistically identical, while the retail trade and hotels and restaurants seem to have lost fewer jobs. Three groups of sectors stand out: (i) water, energy and transport, (ii) personal services, finance and insurance and (iii) agriculture. In these sectors, employment fell by less relative to manufacturing (5–9 per cent in comparison to 12.2 per cent), even after controlling for the changes in sales revenues. Inelastic domestic demand for some of the aforementioned services, market power and a high share of self-governing firms (family businesses, partnerships of friends and relatives) are factors potentially explaining why employment suffered so much less in these industries. Trade-offs between employment and hours and/or wages do not seem to

play a role: the changes of employment and hours were positively correlated, while the industry wage effects were statistically insignificant, with
only two exceptions.

State-owned firms lost fewer jobs than did domestic private ones by 3.6
per cent and maintained average hours at a higher level by 0.6 per cent.
In terms of wages they did not differ from their private counterparts. The
estimates relating to foreign firms are insignificant and hint at negligible
differences between them and domestic private enterprises.

Exposure to changes in the minimum wage is measured by the fraction
earning the base minimum wage (MW±1,000 Ft or 4€ a month) and the
skilled minimum wage (SMW±1,000 Ft). More workers paid the MW
in the base period predicts faster average wage growth, but having more
SMW earners has no wage effect because the SMW barely increased in
2009. A firm with only MW earners increased the average wage faster
by about 4 per cent in comparison to a company with no MW earners,
consistent with the fact that the base MW grew by 3.6 per cent. At the
same time, we do not observe larger-than-average employment and hours
cuts in firms with more MW earners. Firms with many SMW workers did
lose more jobs and also cut working hours more than did their otherwise
similar counterparts, but these cuts are hardly explained by the tiny rise in
the SMW. We conclude from these data that, while firms exposed to the
minimum wage regulations increased wages faster and destroyed more
jobs, these developments were explained by factors other than the modest
hikes in the MW and the SMW.

Finally, the estimates suggest that firms covered by collective agreements kept the level of employment higher by about 2 per cent in comparison to their observationally similar counterparts. The estimates relating
to working hours are insignificant. It seems that wages grew slightly faster
than elsewhere, but the coefficients are not significant at conventional
levels.[12]

To summarize the regression results, the employment effects of the
variables in equation (7.1a) are mainly significant and often fairly strong.
The variations in average working hours seem much smaller, while wage
evolutions were largely unrelated to the variables in the model. Apart
from the variables depicting the base-period composition of the workforce
and the share of MW earners, other variables in equation (7.1c) – such as
sector, ownership, firm size and unionization – did not exert statistically
significant effects on wage evolution.

Re-estimating the wage equation with ξ rather than $\Delta \ln \overline{w}$ on the left
hand yields a single significant coefficient: a fraction paid the MW, a
coefficient of 0.0525 significant at the 1 per cent level. Since ξ captures
the change in the cost of labour much more precisely than $\Delta \ln \overline{w}$ we con-

clude that wage developments were unrelated to industry, firm size, ownership, union coverage and region.[13] On closer inspection, the same seems to apply to the effect of skill composition. The employment and wage equations (7.1a, 7.1c) give the impression that firms with a skilled labour force adapted to the crisis by cutting wages, but keeping employment relatively high – an outcome consistent with expectations grounded in the theories of quasi-fixed costs and firm-specific skills. The re-estimated equation suggests that the cost of labour actually did not fall in these enterprises – this is a statistical illusion generated by the changing composition of the staff. Firms employing many skilled workers dismissed more skilled workers, even in relative terms, which led to lower average wages.

The close-to-zero correlations between the residuals u, v and ω of equations (7.1a–7.1c) suggest that the firm-specific changes of employment and hours, and employment and hourly wages, were independent of each other. By contrast, the residual changes in hours and hourly wages are relatively strongly correlated (–0.31). This result arises for two reasons. On the one hand, monthly earnings do not fall proportionately when working hours are cut, therefore falling hours are associated with rising hourly earnings. On the other hand, errors in the reporting of hours can establish spurious correlation between ΔW and ΔH.[14] In view of this risk I estimated a system similar to (7.1) by dropping the hours equation and working with monthly rather than hourly wages. The residual correlation between the changes of employment and monthly wages amounted to –0.02 in this case, too, and the Breusch-Pagan test did not reject the independence of the two equations.

4. JOB LOSS, JOB FINDING AND ACCESS TO SUPPORT

What happened to the workers who lost their jobs during the crisis is the subject of the remainder of the chapter. The discussion is primarily based on panels built from the quarterly waves of the LFS. The Hungarian LFS follows workers for 1.5 years – households are interviewed six times and then replaced with a randomly selected new cohort. Utilizing the rotating panel structure of the LFS we can address the issues of job loss and job finding with some precision. We start by looking at the dynamics of job loss and job finding, continue with a study of benefit receipt and close by summarizing what the available data tell us about active labour market policies (ALMP).

4.1   Job Loss and Job Finding

The LFS panels make possible the study of transitions from and to employment with some precision. Although we do not observe all flows in and out of employment we can observe whether an individual was employed in quarter t and not employed in quarter $t + 1$, and vice versa. Many of the short spells of employment and non-employment remain unobserved with such data at hand – a deficiency we cannot avoid. Following Jenkins (1995), we estimate discrete time duration models, in which members of a risk group are followed over time. The conditional job loss and job finding probabilities are estimated using constant and time-varying characteristics (X and Z) and time spent in the risk group (t) as explanatory variables. In equation (7.3), the term $f(t)$ stands for a set of dummy variables denoting that the person was employed (not employed) for 1, 2, . . ., T periods. In the case of employment, t is measured in years of tenure in the current job as a continuous variable, while in the case of non-employed individuals, t is measured with dummies standing for the months of joblessness. The function $g(\tau)$ collects the parameters of a set of dummies measuring calendar time (quarters).

$$\Pr(\text{exit between } t \text{ and } t + 1) = \beta X + \gamma Z_t + g(\tau) + f(t) \qquad (7.3)$$

Model (7.3) is estimated for a pool of 1.12 million observations from 2006.Q1–2009.Q3. The 2010.Q1 wave of the LFS was not available at the time of writing, so we do not know the direction of exit from the populations observed in 2009.Q4. The observed period was split into two overlapping parts: one from 2006.Q1 to 2008.Q2 and another from 2008.Q2 to 2009.Q3. Splitting the period in this way has the advantage of observing whether the parameters are the same before and during the crisis and ensuring that the calendar time effects can be connected using 2008.Q2 as the reference wave in both periods.

Detailed estimation results are available in Köllő (2010a). Here we start with the calendar time effects (Figure 7.2). Surprisingly, we do not see a large increase in the job loss rate during the crisis: it jumps high in 2008 October–December but a similar hike could be observed one year earlier. The job loss rate followed an increasing trend throughout 2006–2009, and the period of the crisis seems to fit the trend. By contrast, the job finding rate followed a decreasing trend in 2006–2008 and deteriorated markedly during the crisis.

We observe a dramatic slump in the job finding rate in July–December 2006 that was probably associated with the announcement of a strict austerity programme in June and the outbreak of political unrest and

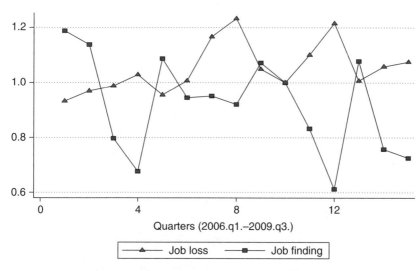

Note: Logit odds ratios; reference period: 2008.Q2.

Figure 7.2 *The impact of calendar time on the probabilities of job loss and job finding, Hungary*

escalation of violence on the streets of Budapest in September–October. Similarly to 2006, in 2009 enterprises reacted to the crisis by drastically cutting hiring. In October–December 2008, the probability of escape from unemployment fell to an exceptionally low level. It seems that some of the vacancies left open at the end of 2008 were filled in January–March 2009, when the job finding rate jumped high temporarily. If we smooth the zigzag by taking the average of the 2008.Q4 and 2009.Q1 values, for instance, the widening gap between the rates of job loss and job finding becomes readily observable.

The growing difficulty of escaping from unemployment within a short time is demonstrated by changes in the baseline hazard (Figure 7.3). The baseline hazard captures how the risk of exit is affected by the duration of joblessness, holding other observed characteristics constant.[15] The anti-clockwise shift of the curve at $t = 4$ indicates that workers in the first–fourth month of unemployment found it harder to get back into employment after July 2008. At longer durations, the two curves fall close to each other – the novelty brought about by the crisis was the deteriorating position of the new job losers. Data from the LFS thus suggest that, while the rate of job losses further increased during the crisis, the rise of unemployment in 2009 was explained mainly by the cutting of hiring rather than a large increase in firing. Less hiring meant that the chance of leaving

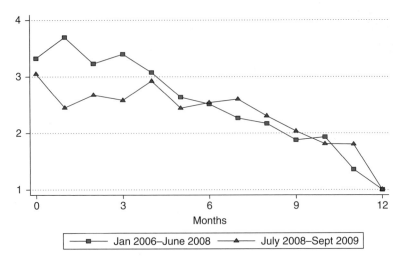

Figure 7.3 *The baseline hazard of exit to employment before and during the crisis, Hungary, January 2006–June 2008, July 2008–September 2009*

unemployment within a short time deteriorated markedly: the short-term unemployed were less likely to return to employment and more likely to slip into long-term joblessness.

4.2 Access to Passive Support

As a result of the dismissals and a slump in hiring, ILO–OECD unemployment grew from 7.8 to 10 per cent among males and from 8.1 to 9.4 per cent among females between July and December 2008 and January and June 2009 (Table 7.8). Rates calculated using other definitions of unemployment followed a similar time path, and all the rates continued to grow in the second half of 2009. The ILO–OECD unemployment rate reached its peak at 11.8 per cent in the first quarter of 2010.[16]

The 'improving' composition of flows out of employment implied that a relatively large part of the new unemployed were entitled to benefits. The fraction of the short-term non-employed receiving insurance-based benefits (UI) or unemployment assistance benefits (UA) increased by 10 percentage points, while in the same period the share of those receiving pensions or childcare fell by a similar magnitude.[17] The proportion registered at a labour office also grew by about 10 percentage points (Table 7.9).

Table 7.8   *Unemployment rates calculated using alternative definitions of unemployment, Hungary, 2006–2009*

	2006		2007		2008		2009	
	I	II	I	II	I	II	I	II
Definition of unemployment								
Male								
Looking for a job	7.3	7.2	7.2	7.2	7.6	7.8	10.0	10.8
Registered	7.6	7.2	7.4	7.3	8.3	8.3	10.1	10.5
Wants a job	12.5	11.8	12.0	11.8	12.6	12.6	15.1	15.7
Female								
Looking for a job	7.7	8.1	7.4	8.0	8.2	8.1	9.4	10.2
Registered	8.8	8.9	8.6	8.4	8.9	8.9	10.2	10.9
Wants a job	15.1	15.1	14.5	14.5	15.2	15.0	16.6	17.2

Source: LFS, author's calculation. The data relate to the population aged 15–62 (the mandatory retirement age), excluding full-time students.

Despite relative improvements in the receipt of unemployment compensation the share of job losers receiving no assistance at all (in the form of UI, UA, pension or childcare benefit) remained high: about 40 per cent of the job losers got no financial support throughout 2008–2009. The absolute number of the unassisted non-employed grew substantially, especially in July–December 2009 when many UI recipients exhausted their benefits (Table 7.10). Furthermore, the proportion of people who either wanted a paid job or were actively searching for one increased substantially among the unassisted unemployed. The fact that an increasing number of jobless people did not get any assistance obviously increased inequalities, first between those in work and those out of work, but also between different categories of persons out of work.

4.3   Access to Active Support

The direction of change in active labour market policies (ALMP) is easy to check in Table 7.11: resources were directed from the existing schemes to the provision of job retention subsidies and the extension of public works schemes. These programmes involved an additional 110,000 workers, while all other programmes were cut and the staff of the PES was curtailed by 5 per cent. The government's efforts were visibly directed at keeping employment as high as possible, even at the cost of reducing active support for the unemployed.

Work inequalities in the crisis

Table 7.9   *Registration and transfers received by workers not employed*
for 0–3 months at the time of the LFS interview (LFS),
Hungary

	2006		2007		2008		2009	
	I	II	I	II	I	II	I	II
Registered at the PES	49.7	49.6	49.5	48.0	47.2	51.2	54.5	58.7
UI, UA	38.3	38.8	39.6	38.7	37.6	40.5	44.1	47.3
Pension, childcare	19.5	20.5	26.2	21.9	22.3	17.2	14.5	12.0
None of the above	42.2	40.7	34.2	39.4	40.1	42.4	41.4	40.8
	100.0	100.0	100.0	100.0	100.0	100.0	100.0	100.0

Table 7.10   *Selected indicators of the unassisted non-employed, Hungary*

	2008		2009	
	I	II	I	II
Average stock of the unassisted non-employed (thousand)	452.8	460.0	495.5	544.7
Wants a job/unassisted, by duration categories (per cent)				
Duration: 0–3 months	76.7	76.0	86.1	86.7
Duration: 0–6 months	77.8	77.3	84.9	86.7
All duration categories	61.7	60.2	63.4	64.9
Looks for a job/unassisted, by duration categories (per cent)				
Duration: 0–3 months	53.0	52.8	61.9	61.9
Duration: 0–6 months	53.9	55.4	62.4	64.5
All duration categories	36.8	36.8	39.4	42.1

Note: Unassisted: received no UI, UA, pension or childcare benefit. The data relate to the population aged 15–61, excluding full-time students.

Source: LFS.

The costs of the job retention and public works programmes are difficult to assess. According to the data summarized in Table 7.12, about 19 billion HUF (70 million euros) was spent on job retention subsidies. The stock of workers in public works grew by 30,000 in 2008–2009 (CSO 2010), while the monthly cost of a job – assuming that the take-home pay was equal to the minimum wage – was estimated to be 89,000 HUF. This

Table 7.11   *Flows to ALMP*[a] *and staffing of the PES, Hungary, 2006–2009*

	2006	2007	2008	2009	Change in 2009
Job retention subsidies	7 390	3 843	3 040	52 027	48 987
Public works	66 403	63 098	63 100	123 754	60 654
Wage subsidies[b]	58 931	43 501	52 349	41 677	–10 672
Training, retraining	56 883	47 735	79 080	74 308	–4 772
Start your own business	5 667	4 861	7 127	5 607	–1 520
Other	7 235	4 336	13 764	3 354	–10 410
PES staff	4 306	3 931	4 017	3 825	–192
PES local office staff	3 946	3 624	3 688	3 518	–170

Notes:
a)   The figures relate to cumulative annual inflows to the given programme. Data on stocks and/or the duration of support are not available, except for public works.
b)   These subsidies are targeted at the long-term unemployed, mothers returning from childcare leave and school leavers.

Sources: CSO (2010, 27), data provided by the PES and the Treasury. Data on the PES staff were provided by the Budapest Institute of Public Policy Research and are based on the annual budgets of the Republic of Hungary.

adds up to a total cost of at least 32 billion HUF. The additional costs of the two programmes together thus amounts to a minimum of 51 billion HUF – a substantial amount equal to almost 2.5 times the total annual operative and development budget of the PES.

How many additional jobs were financed from this substantial amount? On the one hand, we have an additional stock of 30,000 workers in public works at the cost of about 32 billion HUF. On the other hand, we have an unknown stock of workers staying in their jobs thanks to the job retention subsidies. The amount spent on the job retention programmes could have financed about 18,000 person-years paid at the minimum wage. This is a lower-bound estimate of the 'saved' jobs since many jobs could be saved at the cost of relatively small subsidies. The number of jobs planned to be 'saved' by the enterprises receiving job retention subsidies (53,461) is definitely an excessive upper-bound estimate. Accepting this figure and adding the number of affected workers in other programmes, we come to a naïve upper-bound estimate of 75,000.

Putting the pieces together, and assuming away the deadweight loss and crowding-out effects inherent in such programmes, we get the result that job retention subsidies and public works together may have reduced

Table 7.12   Programmes for job retention, Hungary, 2009

Programme	Budget (billion HUF)	Firms affected	Workers affected	'Jobs saved'[a]	Expenditure per workers affected (thousand HUF)
Saving Jobs[b]	10.0	921	30365	53461	329
TÁMOP (EU)[c]					
Entire programme	30.0	–	–	–	–
Until February 2010	8.3	–	16757	–	495
Ministry of Labour	0.7	23	2201	–	318
PES Regional Centres	–	418	3473	–	

Notes:
a) As claimed by the applying firms. b) Launched by the government in February 2009.
c) Part of an EU-assisted programme for the development of human resources ('Social Renewal Operative Programme'). Pro memo: 10 billion HUF ≈ 3.7 million €. The average monthly cost of employment amounted to 254 thousand HUF in May 2009.

Source: CSO (2010, 25–27).

the loss of jobs by about 50–100,000. At the same time, the registered unemployment stock increased by 140,000 (between 2008.Q3 and 2009.Q3), and the budget for assisting the actual job losers was significantly held back by the huge amounts spent on employment subsidies. The effect of active labour market policies on overall equality is difficult to assess. The concentration of resources to save a relatively small number of jobs (together with the cutting of other active programmes) obviously created inequalities among potential job losers and adversely affected the position of the unemployed in comparison to those in work. At the same time, letting the jobs at risk die would have entailed even higher unemployment and higher income disparity. The balance is impossible to draw without knowing how many jobs were actually saved by means of the job retention subsidies.

5.   A NOTE ON INDEBTED HOUSEHOLDS

In this chapter we have concentrated on the channels through which the contraction of final demand and the spread of uncertainty affected income inequalities. The data and the findings suggest that low-income families were likely to lose more during the crisis: the unskilled were more likely to lose their jobs, many marginal workers were left without financial support after job loss and several social transfers were curtailed. At the same time, the cutting of public sector wages, the growing difficulties of finding a job within a short time and some of the austerity measures (such as the abolition of the thirteenth-month pensions and family allowances) affected middle and high income groups, too, and thereby acted against a large increase in inequality. Consistent with these expectations, in a recently published report based on the biannual Tárki Monitor Survey, Tóth and Medgyesi (2010) find that the overall measures of income inequity, such as the Gini, changed marginally in 2007–2009, but the position of the lowest income decile got worse: its share in total income fell from 3.5 to 3.1 per cent and the P10/P50 ratio fell from 55 to 51 per cent in 2007–2009.

However, in order to understand the nature and severity of the crisis in Hungary, one must consider factors beyond earned income and pecuniary transfers. Despite a relatively small increase of income inequity, the proportion of households reporting financial hardship and deprivation grew substantially, from 23 per cent in 2007 to 30 per cent in 2009 (Tóth and Medgyesi 2010). This increase reflects the inability of a growing number of households to pay their bills and make their monthly payments to banks. The rising price of gas, water and electricity, on the one hand, and the skyrocketing payments to banks (due to the depreciation of the forint and rising domestic interest rates), on the other, entailed insurmountable difficulties for many households, including those with unchanged monetary income. The implications for families indebted in hard currency (accounting for 70 per cent of all debtors) was and still is particularly severe. In the years preceding the crisis, the large interest rate differential stimulated hard currency borrowing, while the inherent risks were unclear for many – perhaps the majority of – borrowers. The government, the financial supervisory authority and the central bank did not warn debtors, or did so ineffectively. Tóth and Medgyesi estimate that in January 2010 debt payments amounted to 24 per cent of the total income of households with some debts (35 per cent of all households), with the debt service to income ratio being only 15 per cent in the upper income quintile, but as high as 43 per cent in the lowest quintile. The fraction of households unable to pay their forint debts (at least once) amounted to only 4 per cent in the upper quintile, but 33 per cent in the lowest quintile. The respective figures were 10 and 47 per cent, respectively, among households with hard currency debt. Several plans have been worked out in order to prevent these households from losing their homes but few of these have been put in practice, so far.

6. TWO CASES OF ADJUSTMENT TO THE CRISIS, HUNGARY

6.1   A Case of Hard Adjustment

The Firm belongs to a multinational electronics company, with divisions in a dozen countries in Europe and overseas. The Hungarian factory, one of the corporation's largest production units, delivers electronic appliances as a subcontractor – orders are received and managed by the company's centre located in another EU member state. About half of the multinational company's output is sold in Europe, with the rest going to North America and Asia.

Within three years of its establishment – by greenfield investment – the Firm became one of the largest employers in its region. In the past eight years, the level of employment has fluctuated in a wide range, between 4,000 and 8,000, in response to the rise and fall of orders. During upswings, up to 40 per cent of the workforce was made up of temporary workers, who were typically employed on 30-day contracts, and were the first to be released during downturns. Labour turnover has always been high among the Firm's own employees, too. Overall, the annual turnover rate was close to 30 per cent. While the factory is located in a medium-sized industrial and administrative centre, a large part of its workforce is recruited in high-unemployment villages and transported to work by buses operated by the Firm. The wages of regular employees are 20 per cent below the level paid by firms of similar size and 33 per cent below the level paid by foreign-owned firms of similar size.

The firm has been unionized since the beginning, and the local union is a member of a large industrial federation, in contact with its counterparts in the company's branches abroad. Unsurprisingly, the union's bargaining power has always been weak, given the highly competitive environment of the business, the firm's ability to relocate its activities and the possibility of hiring temporary workers. Failure to resist the firm's 'textbook capitalist' policies, as well as rival union leaders' competition for a shrinking membership resulted in the break-up of the original union and the founding of a second one in 2010.

The crisis started earlier in the firm's industry than elsewhere in Hungary. Output at constant prices fell by 2.7 per cent as early as 2008, which was followed by a dramatic decline of 14.5 per cent in 2009.[18]

The multinational company lost 15,000 jobs worldwide, 60 per cent of its pre-crisis workforce, and closed its factories entirely in four European countries. The Hungarian factory continued to operate, but the management cut the level of employment from close to 8,000 at the beginning of

2008 to 4,200 in the spring of 2010. The redundancies affected temporary workers disproportionately, but even so more than a quarter of the Firm's regular employees were dismissed. After the redundancies, temporary workers accounted for 25 per cent of the total workforce.

Compared to the magnitude of the job losses, working hours and wages did not change significantly. In May 2008–2009, average paid monthly hours fell by 1.5 per cent and monthly earnings went down by 0.7 per cent, implying a marginal (0.7 per cent) increase in the nominal earnings per hour of regular employees. In real terms, their monthly and hourly wages fell by 4.2 and 2.8 per cent, respectively.

Negotiations between the management and the unions could not influence the magnitude of the job losses, but imposed constraints on the selection of workers and the redundancy procedure. The protected groups included the members of consultative bodies (*üzemi tanácsok*), union leaders, labour safety inspectors, older workers expected to retire within five years and single parents. The management guaranteed that it would not fire two or more members of the same family within 30 days. The parties agreed on a 30-day notice period and full payment for this period without the obligation to work, thus allowing workers to start their job search and to register as unemployed as soon as notice was given.

The unions also accepted the postponement of wage increases in both 2009 and 2010, but managed to achieve a rise in the welfare fund, which provides support for children starting school, lunch coupons and access to sports and cultural facilities. Unions also achieved agreement that the firm would not (immediately and openly) shift the tax burden imposed on payments in kind in 2010 onto net wages.[19]

At the time of writing, the Firm seems to have overcome the hardest period of the crisis – it is preparing for a modest expansion of output and the introduction of some new products – but it is unlikely to regain the thousands of lost jobs in the near future.

The case of the Firm nicely illustrates some of the economic and institutional conditions leading to the prevalence of 'adjustment on the extensive margin' in Hungary. It operates in a highly competitive and fully globalized industry, subject to large fluctuations of demand, as do the majority of Hungarian industrial producers. It is a subcontractor competing with other suppliers within the corporation for orders, as do many of its counterparts in Hungary, where 40 per cent of the industrial workforce is employed in foreign-owned firms (mostly) of similar character. It satisfies orders without accumulating output inventories and it has been customarily adjusting the level of employment to the fluctuations of product demand. Similar to the majority (75 per cent) of the firms in its size category the Firm has a union and has always had collective agreement, but wages, non-pecuniary benefits, labour safety and redundancy rules, rather than the level of employment, have been the focus of collective bargaining. Institutions encouraging soft adjustment such as 'pacts on employment and productivity' or working time accounts are unlikely to develop, given the Firm's strategic choice of adjusting to cyclical fluctuations via massive firing and hiring. Finally, although importantly, this strategy practically excludes the absorption of job retention subsidies, which typically require a guarantee of the continued employment of subsidized workers and/or a promise to maintain a certain level of total employment over a protracted period.[20]

6.2   A Case of Soft Adjustment

The meat processing industry, in which the Firm is engaged, was adversely affected by the financial developments preceding and accompanying the crisis. The strong appreciation of the forint in 2007–2008 and the resulting shift of demand towards imported food had a strong negative impact on the sales prospects and liquidity of Hungarian producers. (Apart from the long-term tendency of appreciation in a catching-up economy, the forint's exchange rate was strongly affected by a shift to free floating in February 2008, high and repeatedly increased interest rates, high inflows of foreign capital and the shift of domestic demand from forint-denominated to hard-currency-based credit.) In 2007–2008, real sales revenues fell by 6.7 per cent in the food industry as a whole,[21] while the number of meat processing firms under liquidation procedure increased by 24 per cent and the number of liquidated companies rose by 17 per cent.[22] The crisis brought a further, albeit less dramatic, contraction in 2009, with real sales falling by a further 2 per cent. The further decline in demand for processed meat and the credit crunch led to considerable labour shedding in the meat industry (3.5 per cent in 2007–2008 and 5 per cent in 2008–2009 in the firm panel analysed elsewhere in the chapter), and resulted in the financial collapse of several medium-sized and large producers, including Herz, one of the leading companies in the sector.

The Firm under investigation had more than 800 employees in 2003, but several waves of restructuring brought personnel numbers down to 340 by the beginning of the crisis. Even so, it remained a key player in the Hungarian meat market and an important exporter. Over half of the firm's employees do unskilled and semi-skilled manual work, one-third are employed in skilled manual jobs and about 10–15 per cent in white-collar positions. Until recently, the vast majority of the employees have been working full-time and nearly all of them have had open-ended contracts.

The company is owned by a Hungarian industrialist, who owns several other companies in the sector. The enterprise is unionized, with a very high rate of coverage: 80 per cent as opposed to only 12 per cent in the Hungarian private sector as a whole.

The management had to respond to three major challenges during the crisis: (i) accommodating the unavoidable contraction of demand for its existing products, (ii) finding ways of entering more prosperous markets and (iii) maintaining the firm's access to short-term credit – vitally important for a producer working with very high material costs.

The Firm's choice of reaction was clearly influenced by its owner's confidence in the long-run viability of the Hungarian meat industry, as was expressed in several interviews he gave during the crisis.[23] The management did its best to minimize the loss of jobs, applied soft forms of adjustment in agreement with the union and used the available government and EU funds extensively in order to avoid significant downsizing. A list of the most important actions (and non-actions) is given below:

- The firm's level of employment did not fall; it even increased from 341 in May 2008 to 356 a year later.
- At the end of 2008, the firm was granted a government-financed job retention subsidy, amounting to about 7 per cent of its total monthly wage bill and lasting for nine months. The subsidy financed 25 per cent of the wage costs of 110 workers for a period of nine months on condition that (i) the selected workers were employed full-time, (ii) the firm's level of employment was preserved and (iii) quitters were replaced within 30 days by unemployed applicants registered at a labour office.
- In May 2009, the worst period of the crisis, the management and the union agreed upon a 2.5 month-long period of working time reductions. The agreement gave the management the right to reduce the workweek of individual workers or groups by one or more days a week, up to a maximum of five days a month, without paying compensation for the days off. This regulation applied to all employees except the 110 subsidized workers. The arrangement became effective and actually meant a shift from a five-day to a four-day workweek. In exchange for the working time reduction, the management guaranteed that collective dismissals would be avoided.
- The working time reductions implied a 20 per cent wage cut for salaried employees and somewhat less for workers paid by piece-rate, for a period of 2.5 months. On top of that, base wages and salaries were held constant throughout 2009. Overtime pay was disbursed with a delay, after making sure that total hours exceeded

the contracted limit in a longer period. Non-pecuniary benefits and smaller side payments in kind were also curtailed.

- While before the crisis, most workers had open-ended contracts, workers hired during the recession were offered a three-month trial period and fixed-term contracts for six months. By July 2009, the fraction of fixed-term contracts exceeded 10 per cent.

- In search of new markets, the firm opened a new product line in the spring of 2009. This operation was assisted by the New Hungary Regional Development Programme (an operative programme set up to allocate EU Structural Fund assistance) in the form of a lump-sum subsidy of 172 million HUF (about 570,000 euros). Furthermore, a state-owned development bank provided a subsidized capital investment loan of 179 million HUF (600,000 euros) and a working capital loan of 71 million HUF (240,000 euros). The owners added 150 million HUF (500,000 euros). The company hired 13 additional workers for the new division.

By July 2009, the Firm seemed to have overcome the crisis. Its market position was improved by the unprecedented depreciation of the forint and its expansive strategy seemed to pay off. The five-day workweek was restored, none of the 110 subsidized workers has been dismissed and the level of employment was stabilized at about 350. The Firm even opened a new trade division in Budapest.

We can identify several factors explaining why the Firm chose soft means of adjustment, and why its strategy proved successful. Among these conditions were its owner's faith in the future of the business, the presence of a strong and cooperative union, substantial contributions by the Hungarian government and the EU Structural Funds, and changes in the market position of Hungarian food producers due to an unexpected depreciation of the forint – a series of unusual conditions smoothing the way to an uncommon response to the financial and economic crisis.[24]

7. CONCLUSION

The picture emerging from the data and the preliminary results draws attention to two traits of the 'Hungarian way' of adapting to the crisis: strong bias towards employment adjustment in the private sector, and strong bias towards job protection in the government's actions: the burden of adjustment in the private sector fell almost entirely on employment, while government actions were primarily aimed at keeping employment as high as possible. These actions included a two-digit, all-embracing real wage cut in the public sector, the preserving of the pre-crisis levels of employment in state-owned enterprises, the provision of job retention subsidies and the creation of public works opportunities. Apart from financing the benefits of a growing number of entitled job losers, the government cut all other programmes aimed at assisting those who actually became unemployed.[25]

The decision to try to reduce job losses and directly create state-financed jobs rather than extend unemployment benefits was deeply rooted in the spirit of employment policies followed in the decade preceding the crisis. In 2007, as much as 26 per cent of the registered unemployed receiving some kind of ALMP support were given wage subsidies and 37 per cent participated in public works (CSO 2010, 27). Workers in government-sponsored jobs thus outnumbered the participants in all other ALMP programmes, including training, retraining, start-your-own-business schemes, rehabilitation and job search assistance (63 versus 37 per cent). A large programme designed just before the crisis (Pathway to Work) announced a further significant expansion of the public works scheme. Extending 'passive support' was unequivocally ruled out by policymakers and the withdrawal of resources from unemployment relief was regarded as a price that must be paid for the reduction of job losses.

Despite creating and saving somewhere between 50,000 and 100,000 jobs, according to the most optimistic and naïve scenario, registered unemployment grew relentlessly from 424,000 in September 2008 to 659,000 at its peak in February 2010 – an increase of 235,000. In the same period, employment (as measured by the LFS) fell from 3.924 million to 3.719 million – a decline of 205,000. It seems that the majority of those at risk of job loss did lose their jobs and have poor prospects of finding new ones because of a slump in hiring. Extending the duration of UI, loosening the entitlement and eligibility criteria of UA, expanding the existing ALMP programmes and increasing the capacity of the PES were probably unavailable options in a period of tight fiscal policies and large-scale expenditure on job retention and public works. The policies chosen by Hungarian policymakers finally helped the lucky few rather than the unlucky majority.

The outlook for the near future seems uncertain. The economy is expected to grow by somewhere between 2 and 3 per cent in 2011, and employment is already on the rise (it grew by 1 per cent between October 2009 and 2010). The government that came to power in April 2010 will probably evade large employment cuts in the public sector by means of special taxes imposed on several 'high-income' industries (banks, telecommunications, energy and retail) and the confiscation of the savings of 3 million members of private pension funds. Although many analysts regard this kind of stabilization as unsustainable in the medium term, it is likely that 2011 will not see further downward adjustment as a direct consequence of the financial and economic crisis.

NOTES

 * The author is grateful for the comments of participants in workshops in Geneva, Budapest and Beijing, and gratefully acknowledges the assistance of Balázs Reizer, Noémi Imre, Zsófia Jenei, Annamária Meszlényi and Dániel Mester.

1. The forint partly recovered by July 2009 with the exchange rate settling in the range of 265–280 HUF/euro.
2. Until 2001, the public sector paid significantly lower wages than the private sector for similar, jobs (Kézdi 2002). Huge hikes in public sector wages in 2001–2002 temporarily created a positive gap which had gradually closed by 2009.
3. The real net minimum wage increased in all years between 1998 and 2008.
4. See: http://nol.hu/gazdasag/20090919-a_nyolcvanezres_minimalber_a_tet 2008. szeptember 19 and http://www.hrportal.hu/hr/oet-76-500-forintos-minimalber-20081 121.html.
5. See: http://www.mnb.hu/Engine.aspx?page=mnbhu_inflacio_hu&ContentID=11801.
6. The negotiations resulted in the elimination of YSMW and the setting of a uniform SMW equal to 87,000 HUF, which implied the percentage changes quoted above.
7. This contradiction is apparent in the international comparative statistics, too. In terms of changes in the incidence of part-time employment in the early stages of the crisis, Hungary ranked thirteenth out of 36 countries compared in ILO (2009, 5), while in terms of changes in the average number of hours worked per employed person it ranked thirty-first, with a very small decline, falling short of 1 per cent.
8. The programme granted wage subsidies to selected firms, which reduced the workweek of their employees from five days to four and provided training for them on the fifth day. The competitive grant programme was conditional on the classification of the subsidized workers as part-timers for the duration of the subsidy.
9. See: http://portal.ksh.hu/pls/ksh/docs/hun/xstadat/xstadat_eves/tabl2_01_20_02ib. html.
10. Note that the Hungarian regulations do not distinguish short-time work from part-time employment unlike, for instance, the German rules (Kurzarbeit versus Teilzeitbeschäftigung).
11. The probit used to predict the probability of being an outlier and the regression results on all firms are available on request.
12. In Köllő (2010b), where the firm panel is examined in more detail, the employment effects of collective agreements are further analysed with propensity score matching, following Rosenbaum and Rubin (1983) and Becker and Ichino (2002). Nearest neighbour matching suggested a statistically insignificant effect of 1.7 per cent, while the stratification method and the kernel matching model resulted in significant effects of 1.9 and 2.0 per cent, respectively. The paper also addresses the issue of endogeneity, that is, the possibility that good business prospects simultaneously imply favourable employment records and better conditions for concluding a collective agreement. The available data suggested that enterprises (probably) foreseeing that their industry's sales would fall faster were more likely to conclude collective agreements for 2009. Collective agreements were stimulated by hardship rather than expected improvements

in the firm's prospects, which calls into question whether the gains estimated with OLS and propensity score matching are illusory.

13. The regional variables (NUTS-3 dummies, NUTS-4 unemployment rates) were insignificant in all specifications and dropped from the models.
14. Assume that all firms cut working hours but only some of them report it. Assume further that all firms hold genuine hourly wages constant. In the non-reporting group, the estimated hourly wages (monthly pay/observed hours) fall and observed hours remain constant. In the reporting group the calculated hourly wage rises and observed hours fall. At the end of the day we observe negative correlation between the observed changes of hours and hourly wages.
15. The hazard is also affected by unobserved attributes resulting in a gradually growing share within an unemployed cohort of people with poor chances of exit. Therefore, the exit rate falls with the duration of joblessness, even in the absence of 'true' duration dependence.
16. See: http://portal.ksh.hu/pls/ksh/docs/hun/xftp/gyor/fog/fog21003.pdf.
17. The growth in benefit receipt came entirely from growing flows to UI. The absolute number of flows from employment to retirement and childcare did not fall in 2009.
18. Available at: http://portal.ksh.hu/pls/ksh/docs/hun/xstadat/xstadat_eves/i_oia008a.html.
19. Since January 2010, non-pecuniary payments have been subject to personal income tax in Hungary.
20. This description is based on interviews carried out and a summary written by Dániel Mester (Institute for Social Policy and Labour, Budapest).
21. Database of the Central Statistical Office: ww.ksh.hu/stadat.
22. Available at: http://www.tozsdeforum.hu/i/c-valsagban_a_magyar_husipar-menu-cimlap-submenu-onearticle-news_id-398699-red-ka.html.
23. In order to preserve anonymity I shall not reveal the sources of these interviews.
24. This description is based on interviews carried out and a summary written by Noémi Imre, Zsófia Jenei and Annamária Meszlényi (Corvinus and Pázmány Universities).
25. Cutting expenditure on training was all the more painful as enterprises cut their own outlays anyway. There was much talk about the need for training and retraining during the crisis, but the number of people actually participating in training fell substantially. According to the LFS, the annual average stock of participants in adult training fell from 92,000 to 73,000, while the number of those recieving on-the-job training fell from 53,000 to 37,000.

BIBLIOGRAPHY

Azariadis, C. (1975) 'Implicit contracts and underemployment equilibria', *Journal of Political Economy*, 83: 1183–1202.
Bajnai, B., Sz. Hámori and J. Köllő (2009) 'The Hungarian labour market – a European perspective', in K. Fazekas and J. Koltay (eds), *The Hungarian Labour Market – Review and Analysis*, Budapest: OFA and MTA KTI.
Becker, O.S. and A. Ichino (2002) 'Estimation of average treatment effects based on propensity scores', *The Stata Journal*, 2, 4: 358–377.
Bellmann, L. and H.D. Gerner (2010) 'Reversed roles? Wage effects of the current crisis', paper prepared for the IZA/OECD Workshop: Economic crisis, rising unemployment and policy responses, Paris, 8–9 February.

Bellmann, L., K. Gerlach and W. Meyer (2008) 'Company-level pacts for employment', *Journal of Economics and Statistics*, 228: 533–553.

Brueckner, J.K. (2001) 'Prior restrictions on bargaining contract curves', *Economics Bulletin*, 10, 1: 1–7.

Cazes, S. and A. Nesporova (2007) *Flexicurity – A Relevant Approach in Central and Eastern Europe*, Geneva: ILO.

Commander, S. and G. Faggio (2003) 'Labour market reallocation in Central Europe, Russia and Ukraine during the 1990s: A review of the evidence', London Business School, mimeo.

CSO (2010) *The Impact of the Crisis on the Labour Market* (in Hungarian). Available at: http://portal.ksh.hu/pls/ksh/docs/hun/xftp/idoszaki/pdf/valsagmu nkaeropiacra.pdf. Accessed on 15 April 2010.

Eurofound (2007) *Financial Participation of Employees in the European Union: Much Ado About Nothing*, Dublin: European Foundation for the Improvement of Living and Working Conditions.

Fazekas, K., A. Lovász and Á. Telegdy (2010) *The Hungarian Labour Market – Review and Analysis*, Budapest: Institute of Economics and National Employment Foundation.

Feldstein, M. (1976) 'Temporary layoffs in the theory of unemployment', *Journal of Political Economy*, 84: 937–957.

Feldstein, M. (1978) 'The effect of unemployment insurance on temporary layoff unemployment', *American Economic Review*, 68: 834–846.

Hadi, A.S. (1992) 'Identifying multiple outliers in multivariate data', *Journal of the Royal Statistical Society*, Series (B), 54: 761–771.

ILO (2009) *World of Work Report 2009: The Global Jobs Crisis and Beyond*, Geneva: ILO.

Jenkins, S.P. (1995) 'Easy estimation methods for discrete-time duration models', *Oxford Bulletin of Economics and Statistics*, 57, 1: 129–138.

Kézdi, G. (2002) 'Business sector and budgetary institutions', in K. Fazekas and J. Koltay (eds), *The Hungarian Labour Market – Review and Analysis*, Budapest: OFA and MTA KTI: 92–101.

Köllő, János (2010a) 'Enterprise responses to the economic crisis, 2008–2009' (Vállalati reakciók a gazdasági válságra, 2008–2009, available at: http://www. econ.core.hu/file/download/bwp/bwp1005.pdf), in Hungarian, Budapest Working Papers on the Labour Market, Institute of Economics and Corvinus University, 2010/05.

Köllő, János (2010b) 'Enterprise responses to the economic crisis, 2008–2009' (Vállalati reakciók a gazdasági válságra, 2008–2009, http://www.econ.core.hu/ file/download/bwp/bwp1005.pdf), in Hungarian, *Közgazdasági Szemle*, Vol. LVII. No. 12., December, pp. 1045–1064.

Köllő, J. and T. Mickiewicz (2005) 'Wage bargaining, privatisation, ability to pay and outside options in Hungary', *Post-Communist Economies*, 17, 4: 465–483.

Kőrösi, G. and É. Surányi (2003) 'Dynamic adjustment' (in Hungarian), in K. Fazekas (ed.), *Munkaerőpiaci Tükör 2002*, Budapest, OFA and MTA KTI: 157–160.

Lucas, E.R. and L.A. Rapping (1969) 'Real wages, employment and inflation', *Journal of Political Economy*, 77: 721–757.

McDonald, I. and R. Solow (1982) 'Wage bargaining and employment', *American Economic Review*, 71: 896–908.

Messina, J., C. Strozzi and J. Turunen (2009) 'OECD Evidence from the time and frequency domains', European Central Bank Wage Dynamics Network, WP 1003 February.

Neumann, L. (2002) 'Does decentralized collective bargaining have an impact on the labour market in Hungary?, *European Journal of Industrial Relations*, 8: 11–31.

Rigó, M. (2008) 'Estimating union–non-union wage differentials in Hungary', Central European University, manuscript, June.

Rosen, S. (1985) 'Implicit contracts: a survey', NBER Working Paper No. W1635, June.

Rosenbaum, P.R. and D.B. Rubin (1983) 'The central role of the propensity score in observational studies for causal effects', *Biometrika*, 70: 41–55.

Tóth I. Gy. and M. Medgyesi (2010) 'Income distribution and financial hardships amidst the consolidation packages and crises in Hungary' (in Hungarian), in K. Fazekas and Gy. Molnár (eds), *Munkaerőpiaci Tükör 2010*, Budapest: OFA and MTA KTI.

Verick, S. and I. Islam (2010) 'The Great Recession of 2008–2009: Causes, consequences and policy responses', IZA Discussion Paper No. 4934, May.

APPENDIX

Table 7A.1   Summary table of major anti-crisis policy measures taken in Hungary, 2008–2010[a]

Target	Measures	Costs, savings (expenditure and/or revenue loss in 2009)
Income support	Several low-budget programmes	HUF 2.7 billion
Labour demand	Reduction of social security contribution	HUF 60 billion[b]
	Job retention subsidies provided as contribution to labour costs	HUF 45 billion
	Providing additional public works opportunities	HUF 51 billion
Measures to support job search and reemployment	No	0[c]
Training of employees and apprentices	No	0
Austerity measures to avoid further increase in budget deficit and public debt		Savings in expenditure in 2009
	Abolition of 13th month pay in the public sector	HUF −100 billion[d]
	Abolition of 13th month pension	HUF −80 billion[d]
	Abolition of Swiss in dexation pensions	n.a.
	Cutting paid parental leave from 3 to 2 years	n.a.
	Curtailing family allowance	HUF −12/−15 billion[d]
	Curtailing subsidies for housing, heating, travel and farming	n.a.
	Reduction of ALMP programmes other than job retention subsidies and public works	n.a.

Table 7A.1 (continued)

Notes:
a The table contains only crisis-related measures, over and above regular provisions for the unemployed. Training measures combined with reduced working hours are classified as measures for preserving labour demand. In the last column, the revenue loss caused by the social contribution reduction is calculated after consolidation with contributions paid by the government. All data, unless otherwise indicated, were provided by the Budapest Institute for Policy Analysis and the Office of Labour and Social Affairs.
b OFA Preservation programme (7.3 billion HUF in 2009), OFA Back To Work programme (0.7 billion HUF), central programmes (10.8 billion HUF), SROP 2.3.3. programmes (6.3 billion HUF) and extension of SROP 1.1.2. (20.2 billion HUF).
c OFA's New Prospects programme launched at the end of 2009 would belong to this category but no payment was made from it until the end of 2009. The OFA's Back To Work programme also aims at increasing labour demand. These programmes subsidize firms for hiring employees who were laid off elsewhere.
d Rough estimates available at http://www.origo.hu/uzletinegyed/valsag/20090402-bajnai-gordon-csomagjanak-erteke-koltsegek.html.

8. Italy: Limited policy responses and industrial relations in flux, leading to aggravated inequalities

Niall O'Higgins*

1. INTRODUCTION

Italy was hit hard by the global financial and economic crisis and there is little sign that the situation in the country is likely to improve significantly in the immediate future. As elsewhere, young people as a whole and prime-age adult men were particularly severely affected and, surprisingly, since the effects of the crisis were largely concentrated in industry, the impact was felt much more strongly in the less industrialized Southern part of the country, thereby further exacerbating territorial differences in employment and income which were already very marked.

In contrast to many other countries in Europe which reacted through the introduction and/or expansion of substantial macro- and microeconomic measures to counter the effects of the crisis, the response in Italy has been very limited. Discretionary fiscal stabilization has been almost entirely absent, which, given the relative lack of automatic stabilizers – such as unemployment benefits and, above all, social security benefits – has undoubtedly contributed to the relatively poor recovery. The main labour market programme was the temporary short-time working/layoff scheme, the Cassa Integrazione Guadagni. This income support scheme was mainly available to regular employees in industrial firms and although this undoubtedly relieved some of the worst effects of the crisis on incomes of workers, particularly in Northern Italy, and despite the fact that CIG was broadened in 2009 to apply to other sectors and forms of employment, the relatively limited application of the programme undoubtedly contributed to the territorial imbalance in the effects of the crisis.

All this has contributed to form a picture of growing multidimensional inequality: particularly between North and South, between the young and prime-age adults and between the poor and non-poor. In this chapter, Section 2 looks briefly at the overall characteristics of the crisis as it has manifested itself in Italy; Section 3 then looks in more detail at some of the aspects of inequality in the crisis. Section 4 examines the response of the Italian government to the crisis and considers the extent to which such actions have mitigated or indeed worsened the differential effects of the crisis. Section 5 provides two case studies of the approaches of firms to deal with the crisis-induced fall in product demand and their effects on inequalities. The final section considers some of the implications for the future.

2.   SHARP FALL IN GDP WITH UNEQUAL EFFECTS ON DIFFERENT CATEGORIES OF WORKERS

Despite fairly extensive reforms in the labour market, initiated in the second half of the 1990s, Italy's growth performance has been relatively weak in comparison to the EU average or, indeed, the United States (Figure 8.1) since 2001.[1] In contrast to the overall picture in which it was the previously strongest performers – Ireland and the Baltic states – which suffered the greatest falls in GDP, Italy had a relatively poor pre-crisis growth record and was (slightly) more severely hit in GDP terms by the

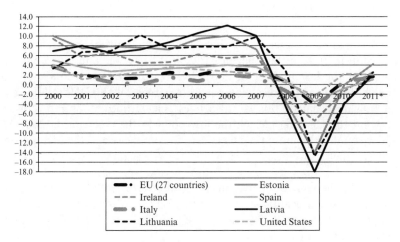

Note: 2010 and 2011 are Eurostat estimates.

Source: Eurostat National Accounts database (http://epp.eurostat.ec.europa.eu/portal/page/portal/statistics/).

Figure 8.1   Annual real GDP growth rate in Italy and elsewhere, 2000–2011

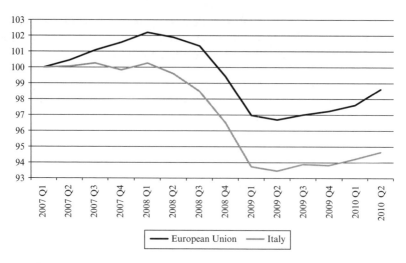

Note: Data are seasonally adjusted.

Source: Eurostat National Accounts database (http://epp.eurostat.ec.europa.eu/portal/page/portal/statistics/).

Figure 8.2 Quarterly GDP (in constant prices), Italy and EU, 2007–2010 (2007Q1=100)

crisis than the EU average or that of similar countries, such as Spain. Recession in Italy in fact began early, with signs of faltering economic growth in the last quarter of 2007 (Figure 8.2). In the second quarter of 2008, however, the recession began in earnest, with GDP falling fast. Looking at the data in this way also gives a clearer idea of the gap between Italy and the EU average. At the low point in the recession in 2009Q2, GDP had fallen by more than 6 per cent in comparison to the first quarter of 2007, whereas in the EU as a whole, the recession led to a fall in GDP of a little over 3 per cent over the same period. In both Italy and the EU as a whole, the recovery began in the third quarter of 2009, although the recovery was significantly stronger in the EU as a whole, with GDP rising by 2 per cent between 2009Q2 and 2010Q2; in Italy, the corresponding rise was of the order of 1 per cent.

The crisis hit first and foremost industry (as in other countries), although it is also interesting to note that banking was hardly affected at all (Figure 8.3). Signs of recovery are clear in all sectors save construction, although industrial output in the second quarter of 2010 was still more than 15 per cent below its pre-crisis level.

The crisis has had significant effects on employment. However, as one

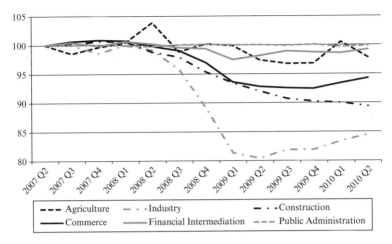

Note: Data are seasonally adjusted.

Source: Eurostat National Accounts database (http://epp.eurostat.ec.europa.eu/portal/page/portal/statistics/).

Figure 8.3   *Value added by sector (constant prices), Italy, 2007–2010 (2007Q2=100)*

would expect, these were not as immediate or as strong as the effects on output. Between the second quarter of 2008 and the second quarter of 2010, employment among Italians fell by a little over 929,300 or 4.3 per cent of the Italian workforce (Anelli and Basso 2010b).[2] Employment in industry fell particularly sharply, along with employment in commerce (Figure 8.4). Neither of these as yet show any signs of recovery. Employment in construction fell during the crisis but then recovered, which contrasts with the sectoral figures on value added.

Turning to the issue of different contractual forms of employment, in recent years there has been much discussion of the potential role of temporary contracts in facilitating entry to employment.[3] In Italy, there has been a progressive, albeit fairly gradual, move towards the increased use of temporary employment contracts (see Box 8.1), particularly for young people, since the late 1990s. Indeed, most of the employment gains observable in Italy since 1995 were due to the expansion of so-called 'atypical' employment forms: temporary and part-time employment. Between 1995 and 2007, the share of temporary employment rose from 7.2 per cent of all employment to 12.4 per cent, and the share of part-time employment from 10.5 per cent to 15 per cent (Schindler 2009).

In a recession, one would expect the initial effects of changes in

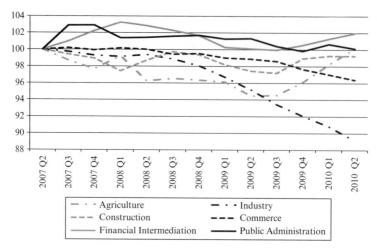

Notes:
1) Data are seasonally adjusted.
2) The figures report an index of the total number of jobs (2007Q2=100).

Figure 8.4   Employment by sector, seasonally adjusted, Italy, 2007–2010
            (2007Q2=100)

temporary employment to be negative, temporary workers being cheaper to fire. In the longer run, if the notion of the beneficial effects of temporary employment on hiring practices has some validity, one might expect temporary employment contracts to pick up more quickly than permanent ones. In Italy, as in most EU countries, temporary employment fell during the recession. Indeed, the reduction in aggregate employment in Italy was heavily concentrated among those on fixed-term and short-term contracts, as well as, to a lesser extent, self-employed workers (Table 8.1). Moreover, looking at longitudinal data on the issue, the percentage of workers on temporary contracts who managed to move from temporary to permanent contracts within one year fell from a little under 30 per cent to around 25 per cent between 2007/8 and 2008/9. This difference is accounted for by an increase in the numbers moving from temporary contracts to unemployment or inactivity, while those remaining in temporary contracts remained virtually unchanged (CNEL 2010). At the same time, over two-thirds (68.2 per cent) of new hires in non-agricultural firms expected for 2010 will be on temporary contracts. Perhaps of more significance, fewer than one in ten (9.7 per cent) of new permanent contracts concern the hiring of workers who were previously employed in the same firm on a temporary contract (Unioncamere 2010). Thus, adjustment of employment levels in

BOX 8.1   INDUSTRIAL RELATIONS AND EMPLOYMENT PROTECTION LEGISLATION IN ITALY

According to the OECD index of the strictness of Employment Protection Legislation (EPL), at 2.58 (in 2008), Italian workers are slightly more protected than the OECD average of 2.23. This is lower, however, than many other OECD countries; much lower than Spain (3.11), Luxembourg (3.39) or France (2.90), for example. However, it is relevant here that the index regarding protection against collective dismissal, at 4.88, is by far the strongest in the OECD.

There are also well-established industrial relations. The current collective bargaining system was established in 1993, and postulates a two-tier bargaining structure:

1. collective bargaining at the national (sectoral) level, to determine the terms and conditions of employment (renegotiated every four years) and basic wage guarantees (*minimi tabellari*, renegotiated every two years); and
2. bargaining at the second (regional or firm) level, allowing the bargaining partners to supplement national contracts (valid for four years).

In 1997, the then Minister of Labour, Tiziano Treu, formally introduced temporary contracts and incentives for part-time employment with the so-called Treu Law (No. 196/1997). The stated purpose of the law was to introduce 'flexibility at the margin'. In the same year, the public monopoly on employment services was abolished (Law No. 469/1997). In 2003, the 'Biagi' Law (No. 30/2003) further deregulated the use of 'atypical' work arrangements, such as temporary agency work (staff-leasing) and part-time work, and introduced some new forms, such as on-call jobs (*lavoro intermittente*), job sharing and occasional work (*lavoro a progetto*).

Source: OECD (www.oecd.org), Schindler (2009) and CNEL (2010).

Italy was mainly through reductions, and subsequent increases in temporary contractual forms, accompanied by increases in temporary short-time working or temporary unemployment under the Cassa Integrazione Guadagni (CIG) scheme for those on permanent contracts (in industry).

Work inequalities in the crisis

Table 8.1   Change in employment, by type of contract, Italy, 2008–2010

Type of contract	2008Q2 (million workers)	2010Q1	Change	% change	% of total reduction in employment
Permanent	15.053	14.942	–0.111	–0.7	–13.5
Fixed-term	2.443	2.047	–0.396	–16.2	–48.1
Short-term	0.471	0.396	–0.075	–15.9	–9.1
Self-employed	5.614	5.373	–0.241	–4.3	–29.3
Total	23.581	22.758	–0.823	–3.5	–100.0

Source: Calculated from Annelli and Basso (2010a), based on Italian Labour Force Survey data.

There is little sign, for the moment, of temporary contracts acting as stepping stones to a more stable employment relationship.

Due to the reductions in overtime and the extensive use of subsidized temporary short-time working (CIG), which will be discussed further below, hours were also significantly reduced. Between 2007Q1 and 2010Q1, hours worked fell by 4.9 per cent. It is important to observe that those entering the CIG programme are included among the employed, even if the short time is at zero – that is, the workers affected are not actually working – as is very often the case. Interestingly, the proportion of those in part-time employment fell by 9.6 per cent between 2008 and 2009, while at the same time the proportion of such employment accounted for by involuntary part-time employment increased from just under 50 per cent to just over 55 per cent for men and from 37 per cent to 43 per cent for women. This reflects two phenomena: (a) workers on part-time employment, being cheaper and easier to fire, were more likely to be laid off than full-time workers; and (b) to a limited extent, full-time workers were being forced into part-time work as an alternative to being laid off.

Informal employment[4] also rose during the crisis throughout Italy. In Italy as a whole, the rate of informal employment is estimated to have risen from 11.9 per cent in 2007 to 12.2 per cent in 2009.[5] In the North-Centre, the increase was from 9.4 per cent to 9.7 per cent and in the South from 18.4 per cent to 18.7 per cent (CNEL 2010). Perhaps the most notable issue here is the pre-existing territorial imbalance in informality, with the South having an incidence which is almost twice that of the North.

The consequences of the crisis have, of course, also been felt in terms of increased unemployment (Figure 8.5). Between its lowest point in April 2007 and March 2010, unemployment rose by 3 percentage points, from 5.8 per cent to 8.8 per cent, although if workers in CIG

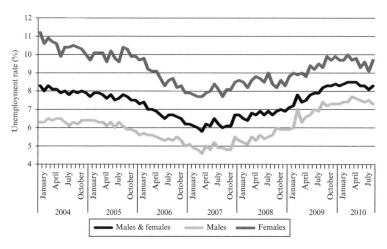

Notes:
1) Seasonally adjusted.
2) Data for September 2010 are provisional.

Source: ISTAT database (www.istat.it).

Figure 8.5   *Unemployment rates, by sex, seasonally adjusted, Italy, 2004–2010*

were included in this calculation, the unemployment rate would have risen to 11.6 per cent, almost doubling the increase (Anelli and Basso, 2010a). Unemployment had already begun to rise during 2007, before the main effects of the international crisis hit. Although the upward trend in unemployment rates was steeper for men than for women – reflecting, of course, the sectoral impact of the crisis which affected industry first and foremost, where the incidence of female employment is lower – this simply narrowed the gap between men and women. In April 2007, the low point of unemployment, the female unemployment rate was 67 per cent higher than the male rate. By April 2010, when unemployment reached its maximum, this had fallen to 26 per cent. In the summer/autumn of 2010 signs began to emerge that rising unemployment had stabilized and for men even started to fall very slightly; however, this has led to the re-emergence of a growing gender unemployment gap, which in September 2010 stood at 33 per cent.

Although average incomes fell as a consequence of the reduced employment and working hours, so far, the recession has had little impact on hourly wage rates, with adjustment having been undertaken in employment and hours (Figure 8.6) rather than in the hourly rate at which labour

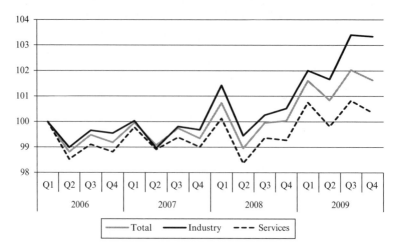

Source: Calculated on the basis of wage and CPI data from the ISTAT database (www. istat.it).

Figure 8.6   *Gross real hourly wage rates, Italy, 2006–2009 (2007Q1 =*
100)

was remunerated. Some caveats are in order. The data on wages are taken from tax and social security records and so do not record changes due to informal activity and practices. More importantly, the slightly increased wage rates observable in Figure 8.6 are largely the result of a composition effect in employment. That is, the crisis reduced the proportion of lower wage workers in employment and thus led to a rise in average wage rates due to the larger proportion of higher wage earners in employment. Analysis of employment changes and wages in firms with at least 20 workers (ISTAT 2010a) shows that industrial blue-collar employment fell by 3.9 per cent in 2008 and by 12.7 per cent in 2009 (net of CIG), while industrial white-collar employment actually rose in 2008 (by 0.5 per cent) and fell by only 2.2 per cent in 2009 (net of CIG).

As regards family and individual incomes, information from the Bank of Italy's Survey on Household Income and Wealth (Banca D'Italia 2010) suggests that, between 2006 and 2008, average real household income fell by 4 per cent and the per person equivalent income by 2.6 per cent. Self-employed people saw their incomes drop by 7 per cent between 2006 and 2008, while for employees the corresponding fall was 4 per cent. Although these data precede the main impact of the crisis, they do suggest that the effects on incomes of the crisis are likely to be substantial. We shall return to this below.

3. INCREASING SOURCES OF INEQUALITY WITH THE CRISIS

3.1 Age and Sex

The figures already presented illustrate one fairly universal differential effect of the crisis throughout Europe: it hit men harder than women because it affected sectors with a higher incidence of male employment. In the Italian case, however, this simply reduced the substantial gender gap in unemployment rates that existed before the crisis. Moreover, as noted above, in the latter part of 2010, the gender gap has risen once again, albeit not to its pre-crisis levels.

One may go into this in a little more detail. Looking at percentage changes in overall employment by age and sex (Figure 8.7), one may observe that the pattern of changes observable in Italy is fairly close to the European average; however, in Italy both positive and negative changes are accentuated compared to the EU as a whole, particularly for females. That is, in Italy employment has fallen more among young people and risen more among older workers than in the EU as a whole. Also observable from the figure is the trend towards greater participation in the labour force of older workers – this again is part of a longer-term trend which is also observable to a lesser degree in other countries in the EU.

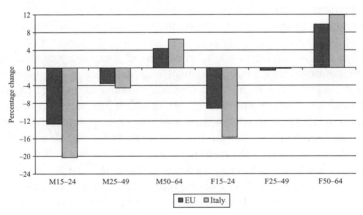

Note: From 2007Q2 to 2010Q2.

Source: Eurostat European Labour Force Survey Statistics database (http://epp.eurostat. ec.europa.eu/portal/page/portal/statistics/).

Figure 8.7 Percentage change in employment by age (15–64) and sex, Italy, 2007–2010

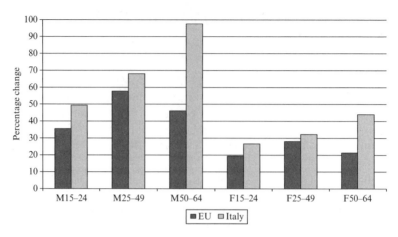

Note: From 2007Q2 to 2010Q2.

Source: Eurostat Statistics database (http://epp.eurostat.ec.europa.eu/portal/page/portal/statistics/).

Figure 8.8   Percentage change in unemployment by age (15–64) and sex, Italy, 2007–2010

Looking at the change in unemployment (Figure 8.8), one may observe the apparent paradox that, in Italy, it is the oldest age groups that have suffered most in terms of the increase in unemployment and 'gained' most in terms of employment (Figure 8.7). Indeed, unemployment among older men has almost doubled over the crisis period. The main explanation for simultaneous increases in employment and unemployment among older workers lies in the general trend towards greater labour force participation among older workers in recent years which has been encouraged by reforms in the pension system. It is also true that unemployment among this age group was very low prior to the crisis and so the denominator is very small. The increase in unemployment for older workers in absolute terms was less than for young or prime-age workers. Finally, some part of this may also be due to older workers returning to work as part of a household income generating strategy in light of prime-age (main) wage-earners' reduced income.

3.2   Education

One aspect of the crisis which has raised concerns has been the emergence of educated unemployment;[6] it is not just the low-skilled who have been affected. Among young people in high income countries, although there is

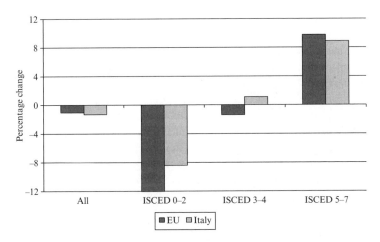

Note: From 2007Q4 to 2010Q4.

Source: Eurostat Statistics database (http://epp.eurostat.ec.europa.eu/portal/page/portal/statistics/).

Figure 8.9 Percentage change in employment by educational level (ISCED 0 to ISCED 7), Italy and EU, 2007–2009

a fair amount of cross-country variation, it appears to be those with higher levels of education who have been hardest hit (O'Higgins 2010). For the working age population as a whole, however, this is not the case. In both Italy and the EU as a whole, employment and employment rates have fallen most sharply for those with the lowest levels of education (Figure 8.9). Indeed, looking at the percentage change by education, employment of tertiary graduates in Italy has actually increased by over 8 per cent (which indeed is very similar to the average in the EU as a whole).

3.3 Temporary Contracts by Age

Although, as already noted, the fall in aggregate employment in Italy was heavily concentrated among those not on permanent employment contracts, during the recession, the incidence of temporary employment actually rose quite significantly among younger people and particularly young men (Figure 8.10). For males as a whole, temporary employment remained virtually unchanged as a percentage of total male employment, rising by just 0.3 percentage point from 11.1 per cent to 11.4 between 2007Q2 and 2010Q2. Among females, temporary employment fell from 16.6 per cent of employment to 14.8 per cent. Among young men,

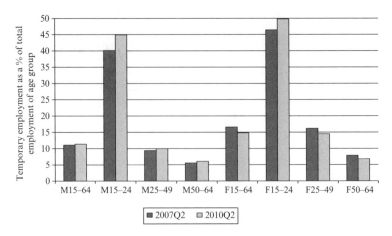

Source: Eurostat Statistics database (http://epp.eurostat.ec.europa.eu/portal/page/portal/statistics/).

*Figure 8.10   Incidence of temporary employment by age (15–64) and sex,
Italy, 2007–2010*

temporary employment rose by nearly 5 percentage points, from 40.1 per cent to 44.9 per cent, while the corresponding increase for young women was well over 3 percentage points from 46.4 per cent to 49.8 per cent. Here too, then, the gap between the sexes in terms of the incidence of temporary employment was narrowed – slightly – by the crisis. Since temporary employees were the first to be fired in the crisis, the fact that the incidence of temporary employment among the young actually increased reflects the fact that almost all new employment of young people during the crisis has been under temporary contractual forms.

3.4   Territorial Inequality: Reflecting Institutional Imbalances

Italy has the highest territorial variability in employment rates in the EU. The coefficient of variation on regional employment rates is 16.3, while in Germany it is 4.8, in France 6.6 and Spain 7.5 (CIES 2010). The crisis has clearly had the effect of widening gaps in employment and income. Perhaps surprisingly, given the relatively low industrial concentration in Southern Italy, it was precisely the less developed South which bore the brunt of the crisis in employment terms (Figure 8.11). This has much to do with the territorial distribution of production, in particular the concentration of industrial production in the North, and the nature of the CIG scheme which applies principally to industrial workers in firms with

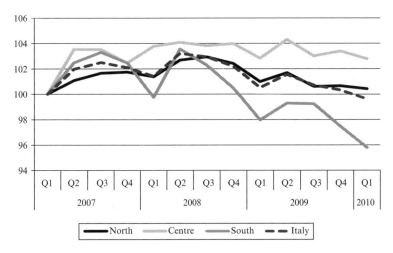

Note: Data are not seasonally adjusted.

Source: ISTAT database (www.istat.it).

Figure 8.11 Employment by broad geographical area, Italy, 2007–2010 (2007Q1=100)

a minimum of 15 employees. As a consequence, adjustment of employment in the North was more oriented towards reductions in working time through the CIG scheme, whereas in the South such adjustment manifested itself through direct reductions in employment. Interestingly, in the Central area of the country employment has actually increased by nearly 3 per cent since the beginning of 2007. Between the first quarter of 2007 and the first quarter of 2010, employment in Italy as a whole had fallen by less than 1 per cent, and by a little over 2 per cent since the first quarter of 2008. In the South, however, employment had fallen by 4 per cent since the first quarter of 2008. If one compares forms of employment in the North and South, one may observe that, while the percentage reduction in the numbers employed on temporary contracts was broadly similar for the North-Centre (–7.5 per cent) and South (–7.0 per cent) between 2008 and 2009, as was the percentage reduction in the self-employed (–3.6 per cent in the North-Centre and –3.3 per cent in the South), in the North-Centre, the number of workers employed on permanent contracts actually increased slightly (by 0.7 per cent) between 2008 and 2009, but fell in the South by 2.0 per cent.

Table 8.2 reports the variations in average hours in the industrial and service sectors in different parts of Italy, based on ISTAT's annual survey

Table 8.2   Average hours worked per worker, by area, Italy, 2008–2009

		2008	2009	% change
Industry	North-West	1625	1483	–8.74
	North-East	1639	1526	–6.89
	Centre	1664	1590	–4.45
	South	1679	1601	–4.65
	Total	1640	1523	–7.13
Services	North-West	1641	1614	–1.65
	North-East	1580	1554	–1.65
	Centre	1637	1589	–2.93
	South	1712	1718	0.35
	Total	1636	1606	–1.83
Total		1638	1564	–4.52

Source: Author's calculations from ISTAT (2010b), table B5.

of firms (ISTAT 2010b). In the North-West, the reduction in average hours in industry was almost double the reduction in the South (and Centre). Hours worked in services in the South even increased slightly between 2008 and 2009. The origin of the differing patterns of response to the crisis – falling hours in the North and reduced employment levels in the South – are to be sought in the application of the CIG programme for temporary short-time working or layoffs,[7] discussed in more detail below. The programme is applicable mainly to industrial firms and, since industrial employment is heavily concentrated in the North of the country, this meant that application of the scheme was also much more common in the North.

3.5   Wages, Incomes and Poverty

Interestingly, given the territorial pattern in employment changes over the period, between 2006 and 2008, average per person equivalent income fell by 4 per cent in both the South and the Centre of the country, while in the North, it fell by around 1.6 per cent. Again, the explanation for this can largely be sought in the greater use of the CIG scheme which, inter alia, implied a smaller loss of income associated with short-time working or temporary layoffs than would be the case for workers who were made redundant. Unsurprisingly, the Gini index also rose, albeit slightly, between 2006 and 2008, from 0.349 to 0.353 on household income and from 0.323 to 0.327 on per person equivalent income. Simulations undertaken by Addabbo and Maccagnan (2010) suggest that the effects

Table 8.3   Simulation of the effect of the crisis on per person equivalent incomes by income quintile, Italy, 2010

Income quintile	Average annual (quintile) income (€)		% change
	Before the crisis	After the crisis	
Lowest 1	8 556	8 402	−1.80
2	14 158	13 848	−2.19
3	18 826	18 328	−2.65
4	24 222	23 696	−2.17
Highest 5	39 437	38 805	−1.60
Average	21 037	20 613	−2.02

Note: The simulation refers to families with heads of household under 65 years of age.

Source: CIES (2010), table 2.12.

of the crisis on per person equivalent income distribution are of a similar order in the North and South of the country, although it is worth noting that the income distribution was significantly less equal in the South prior to the crisis.

The Commission on Social Exclusion (CIES 2010) has estimated (by simulation) the effects of the crisis on incomes and income distribution in Italy. Looking first at the effects of the crisis at different points in the distribution on a national basis (Table 8.3), the simulation suggests that the effects of the crisis (including the effects of passive income support measures) were fairly evenly spread across pre-crisis incomes. The main losers in income terms seem to be placed in the middle of the distribution with a fall of 2.65 per cent in income. This is consistent with the effects of the crisis primarily affecting males in industrial employment. One might also observe that, in line with the slight increase in the Gini index, the ratio between average incomes in the fifth and first quintile widened slightly with the crisis. Turning to the effects of poverty by area (Table 8.4), one may observe significant differences in the territorial impact. The table estimates the effects of the crisis on absolute poverty rates – defined as the proportion of those earning less than 60 per cent of national median income – on a territorial basis. One may observe first of all the huge differ-ence between North and South in terms of the pre-crisis poverty rates. One may also observe, however, that the crisis, notwithstanding the extensive use of passive income support measures, significantly raised poverty rates throughout the country, with the rise being more marked in the South (over 2 percentage points) than in the North (1.3 percentage points) or the Centre (less than 1 percentage point). The differences between North

Table 8.4   Simulation of the effect of the crisis on poverty rates by area, Italy, 2010

Area	Poverty rates (%)		Change
	Before the crisis	After the crisis	
North	8.5	9.8	1.3
Centre	10.8	11.6	0.8
South	33.3	35.4	2.1
Total	17.7	19.2	1.5

Source: Calculated from CIES (2010), table 2.16.

and South are once again to be sought in the greater use of passive income support through the CIG scheme in the North.

4.   POLICY RESPONSES: FAILURE TO ADDRESS TERRITORIAL INEQUALITY

4.1   Macroeconomic Measures: Lack of Expansionary Policy

The most notable feature of the response of the Italian government to the recession has been its absence in terms of macroeconomic measures aimed at counteracting the impact of the financial crisis on economic activity. Indeed, some commentators note the introduction of pro-cyclical measures – which, of course, in a recession tend to reinforce the downward trend in GDP – initially reacting to the crisis with measures designed to increase the overall incidence of taxation (Boeri 2009). Certainly, the reaction in Italy was modest compared to other advanced economies – European and non-European (IMF 2010). In 2008, total public intervention to support the financial system came to 0.8 per cent of GDP compared to, for example, 3.7 per cent in Germany, 7.5 per cent in the United States and 18.9 per cent in the United Kingdom (Ministero dell'Economia e della Finanza 2009). The argument was that the Italian financial system was relatively independent of the international banking system and therefore less exposed to the direct effects of the financial crisis. Less obvious is the justification of the lack of discretionary expansionary fiscal policy. In 2008 and 2009, public consumption in Italy rose by 0.8 per cent and 0.6 per cent, respectively, in comparison to 2.2 per cent and 2.1 per cent in the Euro area as a whole and 3.0 per cent and 2.8 per cent in the United States. At the same time, investment fell by 4.0 per cent in 2008 and 12.1 per cent in 2009 in Italy, a little above the Euro-area average of 0.4 per cent in 2008 and 11.1 per cent in 2009 (IMF 2010). The expansion of discretionary fiscal policy was modest, of the order of 0.2 per cent of GDP in 2009 and 2010 (Ministero dell'Economia e della Finanza 2009), which is around one-tenth of the level of estimated discretionary increase in fiscal policy in G20 countries as a whole of 2.0 per cent and 1.5 per cent of GDP in 2009 and 2010, respectively (IMF 2009). Even taking into account automatic stabilizers, the reduction in taxes and increase in expenditure amounted to around 0.7 per cent of GDP in Italy in 2009 and 2010, that is, around one-third (for 2009) and one-half (in 2010) of discretionary measures adopted in G20 countries on average (IMF 2009 and Ministero dell'Economia e della Finanza, 2009). The main argument offered in defence of the lack of expansionary fiscal policy was the substantial size of public debt. However, despite – or possibly in no small part because of – this cautiousness and the consequent prolonging of the recession, public debt increased by about 10 percentage points of GDP in 2009, reaching almost 116 per cent of GDP.

Perhaps the most important intervention measures adopted by the government have been those taken to try to counteract the immediate restriction of credit by financial institutions following the onset of the financial crisis by making funds available to banks that extended credit to SMEs and strengthening the existing guarantee fund for SMEs.

4.2 Micro-level Measures: Passive Labour Market Policies

The distinction between micro and macro measures is a little blurred, particularly since the bulk of the 'discretionary' fiscal expansion has comprised increased use of labour market policies (LMPs). In general, however, the main response of the Italian government in terms of labour market policy measures involved the expansion in January 2009 of the applicability of the CIG (Cassa Integrazione Guadagni) fund – essentially a combination of subsidized short-time working arrangements and temporary unemployment – to a broader class of workers (apprentices and temporary workers) on a discretionary basis. Indeed, the CIG scheme in various forms has been the most important income support measure utilized during the crisis in Italy and deserves further discussion.

4.2.1 Cassa Integrazione Guadagni scheme
First introduced at the end of the Second World War, the CIG scheme now exists in three mutually exclusive forms, each of which involves income support for workers who are 'temporarily' laid off or who are working reduced hours.

Cassa Integrazione Guadagni Ordinaria (CIGO)   This is the basic scheme that allows industrial (including construction) firms with more than 15 workers to introduce short-time (including zero hours) working for some or all of its workforce in the face of reduced production due to temporary (including seasonal) factors not attributable to the behaviour of the firm or its workers. The maximum duration is one year. Workers, who must be on permanent contracts, are paid up to 80 per cent of their base (not including any overtime) salaries by the INPS (the State Social Security and Pension Fund).

Cassa Integrazione Guadagni Straordinaria (CIGS)   This form has a broader applicability. It can be requested in more general circumstances – in the case of firm restructuring or reorganization, and/or in the case of a firm crisis – and is applicable also to agricultural and service sector firms. It also lasts longer, depending on the circumstances and the motivation of the request, up to four years. It also applies only to permanent workers. As before, workers are paid up to 80 per cent of their base salaries.

Cassa Integrazione Guadagni in Deroga (CIGD)   Introduced in January 2009, this form of CIG was introduced with the aim of further broadening the coverage of the CIG, including in particular those in apprenticeships and other non-permanent contractual forms. It differs from the other forms in that it is administered at a regional (not national) level and its application and form vary somewhat from region to region according to specific agreements drawn up between regional and central governments. Once again, the maximum compensation allowed is fixed at 80 per cent of the employee's previous base salary.

The CIG scheme as a whole is by far the most significant income support measure in Italy. By its nature it applies to established workers on permanent contracts, thereby further widening the gap between the protection available to permanent as opposed to temporary workers, although this has been modified somewhat with the introduction of the CIGD scheme. As the recession has worn on, both CIGS and CIGD schemes have become increasingly important (Figures 8.12 and 8.13). In part, this depends on the relatively short-term nature of CIGO as compared to CIGS, the former being of only one year's duration compared to the four years (in certain circumstances) of the latter. The growing importance of the CIGD depends in part on the fact that it was only introduced in January 2009, but its rapid growth during 2010 perhaps also reflects the increasing impact of the crisis on sectors outside manufacturing and construction.

As noted above, the geographical distribution of the CIG scheme in

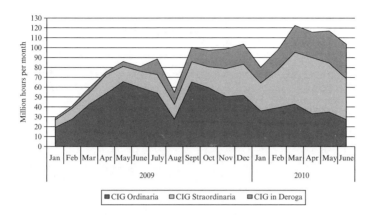

Sources: INPS (2010); ISTAT database www.istat.it.

Figure 8.12   *Usage of CIG (million working hours), Italy, 2009–2010*

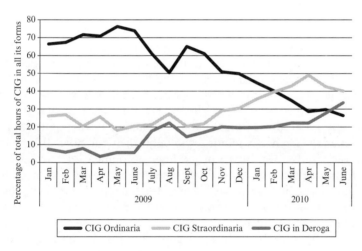

Source: INPS (2010).

Figure 8.13   *CIGO, CIGS and CIGD as a percentage of total CIG hours, Italy, 2009–2010*

its various forms is heavily weighted towards firms in the more indus-trialized North (Figure 8.14). This largely accounts for the difference in reaction in terms of hours and employment observable in the North and South and has remained true even with the growing importance

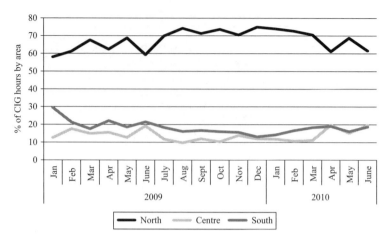

Source: INPS (2010).

Figure 8.14   CIG schemes by geographical area as a percentage of total CIG hours, Italy, 2009–2010

of the broader CIGS and CIGD forms of the scheme. In March 2010, Northern firms accounted for 70.5 per cent of the total hours covered by the CIG scheme, 70.1 per cent of the hours covered by CIGO (the first scheme), 75.3 per cent of CIGS (second scheme) hours and 61.9 per cent of CIGD (the latest scheme) hours. So, although the CIGO scheme has slightly reduced the North–South imbalance in the application of the scheme, the change is minor, especially when one notes that in that month the CIGD form of the programme accounted for only 22.2 per cent of total CIG hours. With the first signs of recovery and the conse-quent gradual reduction in the usage of the scheme visible since March 2010 (see Figure 8.12), the percentage of CIG hours accounted for by Northern firms had fallen from a high of above 70 per cent to close to 60 per cent by June 2010. In the Centre and South, the usage of the programme has increased in more or less equal measure from around 15 per cent in each of these areas to 20 per cent by June 2010. Nevertheless, the geographical distribution of the application of CIG does not vary greatly between forms of the scheme. In June 2010, Northern firms accounted for 66.7 per cent of CIGO hours, 63.5 per cent of CIGS hours and 55.4 per cent of CIGD hours. Thus, the reduced weight of Northern firms in total CIG hours is to be attributed to recovery rather than to the broadening of the scheme per se.

4.2.2 Increased eligibility for mobility lists and unemployment benefits
On completion of the CIGS eligibility period, in the case of mass layoffs or firm failure, qualifying firms' – essentially those which qualified for CIGS assistance – laid-off workers enter the 'mobility lists' where they may stay for a maximum of one (for workers under 40), two (workers aged between 40 and 49) or three (for workers over 50) years. For the first year, the payment is equivalent to that paid under the CIGS scheme (80 per cent of the person's normal full-time wage), after which those still eligible for payment receive 80 per cent of that amount. As a consequence of the crisis, eligibility for the mobility lists was broadened (*Mobilità in Deroga*) to include some laid-off workers not otherwise eligible for the payment.

Two different unemployment schemes exist for agricultural and non-agricultural workers, respectively. The agricultural scheme essentially compensates workers for seasonal unemployment, whereas the non-agricultural scheme is payable for a maximum of 8 months (12 months for workers over 50). Apart from some exceptional cases, the scheme envisages payments of between 40 and 60 per cent of the previous wage.

Firms who hire workers either in the mobility lists or on unemployment benefit receive a reduction in required tax and social security contributions payable on employees.

4.3 Active Labour Market Policies: Training but Mainly in the North

At the beginning of 2010, the social partners, along with regional and central governments, agreed on the importance of improving the usefulness of passive income support measures, and in particular 'mobility' and unemployment benefits by combining them with active measures largely involving vocational training. A sum of 250 million euros has been set aside to fund this initiative. Thus far, courses have been instituted on a limited basis, mainly in the Northern regions of the country.

Prior to the crisis, the main form of ALMP was, and remains, apprenticeship. Since a reform of the system in 2003, this takes essentially three forms: (a) apprenticeship for the completion of the duty and right to education – open to those between 15 and 18 years old for the purpose of ensuring that all those under 18 can access some form of education and training; (b) professional apprenticeships aimed at young people aged between 18 and 29 and allowing them to obtain a professional qualification through on- and off-the-job training; and, (c) apprenticeships for higher qualifications, again aimed at those between 18 and 29 – this form envisages the obtaining of a higher professional qualification. At the time of writing, the system of apprenticeships is under review and is expected to be reformed in the near future. In each case, firms receive tax and social

Table 8.5   Estimated impact of the crisis on incomes, with or without passive income support measures, Italy

Income quintile	% change in income due to the crisis	% change in income in the absence of PIS	% of income loss made up by PIS
1	–2.3	–4.0	43
2	–3.3	–4.7	30
3	–3.5	–4.9	27
4	–2.6	–3.7	28
5	–1.9	–2.4	21
Average	–2.6	–3.6	28

Note: The simulation refers to families with heads of household under 65 years of age.

Source: CIES (2010), table 2.12.

security exemptions to give them an incentive to participate. They are also not obliged (as they would be with a regular working contract) to guarantee a permanent employment contract to apprentices.

4.4   Passive Income Support Measures: Positive Effects on Incomes and Poverty

Although it is a little early to get a full picture of the likely effects of active and, above all, passive incomes policies on employment and incomes in Italy during the crisis, a simple simulation undertaken by the Commissione di Indagine sull'Esclusione Sociale (CIES, Commission for the Investigation of Social Exclusion) on the basis of the It-SILC 2007 sample[8] estimates the remedial effects of passive income support measures on incomes. In the first place, Table 8.5 reports estimates of the impact of the crisis with and without passive income support measures on average quintile income. The first column estimates the change in income arising as a consequence of the crisis on the basis of changes in employment and the usage of income support measures. The second column excludes from the estimation changes arising from income support measures to arrive at an estimate of what would have happened in the absence of intervention.[9] The final column reports the percentage of the estimated income loss without passive income support (column 2) which was recouped by the application of such measures for each income quintile.[10] The table is somewhat encouraging in that the income support measures have clearly mitigated the effects of the crisis and have done so in a progressive manner,

Table 8.6   Estimated impact of the crisis on poverty rates, with or without passive income support measures, Italy

Area	Effect of the crisis on poverty rates		Mitigating effect of PIS	
	With PIS	Without PIS	Percentage points	Percentage
North	1.3	2.4	−1.1	−45.8
Centre	0.8	1.3	−0.5	−38.5
South	2.1	3.1	−1.0	−32.3
Italy	1.5	2.4	−0.9	−37.5

Source: Calculated from CIES (2010), table 2.16.

reducing the income loss to a greater extent (in percentage terms) among those with lower incomes; the estimated loss made up ranges from 43 per cent of the 'no intervention' income loss for the lowest income quintile to 21 per cent for the highest quintile. Having said that, given the substantial differences in average incomes between the lowest and highest quintiles, if one looks at the effects of intervention in absolute terms, the benefits of passive income support were largest for the highest quintile who gained on average 210 euros per person (or 21 per cent of average fifth quintile income), whereas those in the poorest quintile received an average gain of only 143 euros per person (corresponding to 43 per cent of the lowest quintile average income) as a result of intervention.

Analysis of the territorial dimension is also instructive. In this case (Table 8.6), the table reports the change in poverty rates (defined as the proportion of those receiving less than 60 per cent of median pre-crisis income) arising with and without income support measures (estimated in the same manner as before). The table reports the mitigating effects of passive income support both in percentage point terms (column 3) and, in column 4, as a percentage of the change in poverty rates which would have occurred in the absence of intervention (column 2). In absolute (percentage point) terms the effect of passive income support measures was to mitigate more or less in equal measure the effects of the crisis in both the North and South of the country. However, if one sees these figures in terms of the proportion of the increase in poverty mitigated, the intervention measures operated more than proportionately in favour of Northern regions since the increase in poverty rates was more marked in the South. This is to be explained by the heavy reliance on CIG measures in providing income support and its predominance in the North. One may further note that the pre-crisis poverty rates were already extremely imbalanced, with a pre-crisis poverty rate of 33.3 per cent in the South and 8.5 per cent in the North. Thus, largely as a consequence of the territorial application of remedial income support measures, the crisis had the effect of further widening the already substantial difference in poverty rates between Northern and Southern Italy.

5. CASE STUDIES: ADJUSTMENT STRATEGIES AND IMPACT

This section looks at the approaches adopted by various firms operating in Southern Italy to deal with falling final product demand.

5.1 Family Firms in Southern Italy

5.1.1 Company A: Using the CIG scheme to address the crisis

Difficult context even before the crisis Company A is a family group currently comprising seven operational plants, employing a little under 200 workers and producing (principally) components for domestic appliances. It grew out of a cement plant founded in 1969. In the new millennium, the group expanded operations, opening factories in Slovakia, the Russian Federation and the United Kingdom. Already in 2007, the firm faced difficulties due to rising oil prices with the consequent effect on the price of plastics and rubber and the profits of the group remained virtually unchanged between 2007 and 2008, while in 2009 profits fell by 40 per cent. Employment in the group fell by 6 per cent in 2008 and by a further 21 per cent in 2009.

Restructuring through Naples plant closure In the face of the crisis, the family sought to reorganize and restructure the group and one of the Italian plants, in Naples, stopped production, with the workers entering into CIGS, even though it was clear to all – workers, unions and the A family who own the group – that the plant in Naples would not resume operations. Such a use of the CIG scheme – which in principle is limited to temporary layoffs – is widespread in Italy and is agreeable to all those directly involved since it is the least painful way of effectively laying off workers. Workers (and their representatives) accept it because it ensures a longer period of relatively highly paid unemployment. The alternative – plant closure – would see all the workers enter directly into the mobility lists with the prospects of shorter eligibility for income support. If workers enter first into CIG (and the plant remains formally operational, although it is producing nothing) and then, when eligibility is exhausted, the plant closes and the workers enter into the mobility lists, workers effectively receive up to four additional years of unemployment benefits (under a different name). For the A family, such a solution means that they have less opposition from the workers' representatives to the plant closure. At the same time, as a relatively small family operation (at least in Italy), as a consequence of which they feel a moral obligation towards their Italian workers, they can feel that their actions are less damaging to the workers. It moreover postpones for up to four years the strategic choice as to whether to definitively close the plant or not. Workers at the Naples plant were offered relocation to a plant in the Avellino Province some 50km to the south-west, but most refused due to the transport and/or relocation costs involved.

Clear preference for temporary workers   Until 2008, all the workers in the group's Italian plants were on permanent contracts. However, in the face of the crisis, the Italian parts of the group are hiring new workers on temporary contracts (of six months) as an experimental strategy and an alternative to taking them from mobility lists of unemployed workers. In part, the use of such temporary contracts – a new practice for the group – is due to the current market uncertainty, but it also effectively allows a longer trial period for workers (under Italian legislation the trial period for workers hired on permanent contracts is 30 days). Employment of new workers on temporary contracts means effectively taking on younger, less experienced employees, but at the same time increases flexibility for the firm by enabling it to fire them without further significant additional expense after six months. The alternative, hiring workers from mobility lists, means that the company is obliged to issue a permanent contract, but benefits from more experienced workers, as well as from a reduction in tax and social security contributions paid by the firm (from 32 per cent of the wage to 5.5 per cent) and so labour costs on these workers. Both strategies have advantages but the group feels that the current market uncertainty makes the additional flexibility associated with temporary contracts more valuable.

Shifting production to Slovakia   A second strategy adopted by the group has been to shift production, to some extent, to the Slovakian plant. Here the workforce is much more easily adjusted, given the much weaker employment protection available to workers in that country. In fact, the Slovakian operations in 2009 accounted for over half (57 per cent) of the group's workforce and 43 per cent of the group's sales.

   In terms of its usage of CIG for its stated purpose – temporary short-time working – the firm has been able to coordinate with the firms it supplies, in order to introduce short-time working in its Italian branches in correspondence with the application of short-time working by its clients to cope with short-term lulls in production.

5.1.2   Company B: Adjusting through temporary workers

A company hit by price increases   Company B is a manufacturing firm producing iron and steel components, such as wire, tubing and so on. Prior to the crisis, the firm had been planning to expand production. They had already moved to a two-shift working day and had been looking to increase this to three. The crisis essentially put this process on hold. The major problem arising for this firm, too, was the very strong increase in the price of raw materials, and in particular steel, during 2008. Between 2007 and 2008, the price of raw materials rose by around 20 per cent. The consequences of this were felt in 2009 when production fell by 35 per cent.

Firing and hiring back temporary workers   The firm had already been using temporary contracts for some time and the reaction to the contraction of production essentially meant laying off of such workers. Prior to the crisis, out of a total workforce of around 65, around 20 per cent were on nine-month temporary contracts. Although it did not actually lay off any workers during the crisis, the firm did not renew contracts that expired. From May 2009, production was returning to 'normality' and the firm started hiring back the temporary workers it had let go during the period of low demand. Thus, Company B used variations in temporary workers – as opposed to CIG – as a means of varying employment (and production) levels.

Neither of the firms interviewed make use of apprenticeship contracts.

One of the major points arising from the case studies concerns the importance of CIG as a means of regulating the workforce and laying off workers, even where there is no intention of restarting production. Used in this way, the scheme has the effect of providing relatively generous income support for a relatively long period, but, as it stands, it does little or nothing to actually support either productivity growth among retained workers, or the relocation of (effectively) dismissed workers – indeed, the CIG scheme prevents workers on *de facto* unemployment benefit from seeking work elsewhere – apart from in the informal economy, since they would otherwise lose their right to the CIG payment. At the same time, as yet, although there is agreement that it should be done, little attempt has been made to utilize periods of down time to encourage training and retraining among the workforce in view of their return to work with the same employer.

The implications of the illustrations provided by these firms on the usage of either CIG or temporary contracts underline the notion, already evident from the analysis above, that labour market policy is effectively reinforcing a two-tier labour market and that 'flexibility at the margin' means buttressing an insider-outsider labour market.

5.2 Fiat at Pomigliano: Imposed Flexibility a New Way Forward?

5.2.1 A symbol of Italian industrial success

The Fabbrica Italiana Automobili Torino – Fiat, for short – is the most important automobile producer in Italy and one of the best known car-makers in the world. The company and its principal owners, the Agnelli family, have been symbolic representatives of Italy for generations. These days, Fiat also owns Maserati and holds an 85 per cent share in Ferrari, along with the Alfa Romeo and Lancia cars which were subsumed into the Fiat car-making operations in the last century. In addition, the Fiat group also comprises commercial vehicle and agricultural machinery construction, as well as component manufacture. These days only a minority – albeit substantial – of the operations of the Fiat group take place in Italy. In 2009, around one-third (64 out of 188) of the group's manufacturing plants were in Italy, accounting for 42.3 per cent (or around 80,400) of its workforce of 190,000.[11] The merger with the bankrupt Chrysler in 2009 will further extend the group's overseas operations.

5.2.2 Also hit by the crisis

As with other car-makers, Fiat was significantly affected by the global crisis with after-tax profits falling from 1.7 billion euros in 2008 to a loss of 0.8 billion euros in 2009. At the same time, between the end of 2008 and 2009 the total workforce was reduced by 4.2 per cent from 198,348 to 190,014.

In this context, Fiat is planning its future strategy and, of central interest in Italy, the extent to which the production of new models – and consequently new investments in plant and employment – will be based in Italy or transferred elsewhere in Europe. Reflecting its symbolic as well as its substantive importance, discussions on the future of Fiat operations, as well as on aspects of its current practices have involved the President of Italy and even the Pope, as well as the Italian government and the leaders of Confindustria (the Italian employers federation).

5.2.3 'Anti-crisis' proposal passed via referendum (after failed agreement with unions and threat of relocation)

It is in this context that, in June 2010, a referendum was held in Fiat's Giambattista Vico plant in Pomigliano d'Arco. The purpose of the referendum was, in the absence of agreement from workers' representatives, to get workers to sign new contracts involving shorter breaks, compulsory overtime on request, penalties for excessive absenteeism and limits on strike action. Fiat's CEO Sergio Marchionne announced to the workers that, if they did not agree to the new working conditions, the production of the new Panda cars planned for the Pomigliano plant would be moved abroad (to Poland or Serbia). The justification cited for the new contracts was essentially the relatively low productivity of Italian plants. In Poland, Fiat produces 77.6 cars per worker per annum, in Brazil 53.2 and in Italy only 29.4. However, it is a little difficult to compare the production processes and the comparison is not like with like. Production in Italy is more heavily oriented towards medium range cars, whereas Poland produces exclusively small economy cars. Moreover, Italian plants tend to produce older models; no new production lines have been introduced in Italy for over two years. Moreover, as Marchionne himself has noted, labour costs account for only 8 per cent of total production costs, so it is a little difficult to see how agreements such as those presented to the Pomigliano workers will significantly affect any real productivity gap that may exist.

In the event, a significant but not overwhelming majority (62 per cent) of the workforce of 5,200 workers in Pomigliano voted in favour of the agreement, in the face of opposition from the FIOM, the union representing the bulk of the workers in the plant. However, it was not until November 2010 that Fiat, or rather the Minister of Welfare (and Labour), Maurizio Sacconi, announced that the investment would be forthcoming for the new Panda model to be produced in Pomigliano, and that production of the model would begin in late 2011. In the meantime, workers at the plant would remain in CIGD (as opposed to CIGS), as had been announced by Fiat in the run up to the June referendum. In doing so, a new company will be formed, FIPO (Fabbrica Italiano Pomigliano), the purpose of which is to ensure that the new contracts do not run foul of existing collective agreements since the workers will effectively have a new employer and will therefore not be bound by national collective agreements to which FIAT is subject.

5.2.4   A precedent for future flexibility?
The referendum and events surrounding it raise a series of issues concerning the future of Fiat, but more generally, the future of industrial relations in Italy. In September 2010, Marchionne extended his 'Pomigliano Strategy', announcing that he would be prepared to invest 20 billion euros in Italy, to double vehicle production in the country by 2014, but that at the same time the workers must accept more flexible 'US-style' contracts. If they refused, the company would pull out altogether from the country.

Thus Pomigliano may be seen as an opening move in a longer-term strategy of the company. Some have seen the confrontation between Fiat and the unions as some sort of 'Thatcher' moment, comparable to the British government's confrontation with the National Union of Mineworkers in 1985. Maurizio Landini, the Secretary of FIOM, has argued that Fiat is leading efforts to divide the union movement and dismantle or weaken the system of collective bargaining in place in Italy since 1993.[12] Moreover, Sergio Brancato (FIOM) suggests that other companies, such as Finmeccanica and Indesit, intend to follow Fiat's approach in introducing greater workforce flexibility, should Fiat succeed. Moreover, the financial and global crisis has seen significant disagreements emerging between the principal workers' confederations – exemplified by the case of Fiat[13] – which are likely to have repercussions for the entire system of industrial relations in the country. In particular, the strategy of the company raises the issue of how contractual agreements can be enforced under current legislation in the face of disagreements among the contracting parties.[14]

6.   CONCLUSIONS AND IMPLICATIONS

The global financial and economic crisis has had serious repercussions for the labour market in Italy. As yet, there is little sign of improvement and it is likely that the crisis will also have important repercussions for the country's system of collective bargaining. In general, the effects of the crisis, which have, as elsewhere, been concentrated in industrial firms, have been, somewhat paradoxically, more strongly felt in the poorer and less industrialized Southern regions of the country. This has had the effect of worsening the already very marked territorial differences that exist in employment and income in Italy. In part, the reasons for this are to be found in the labour market policy 'response', or rather in the pre-existing labour market institutions which have not been substantively modified since the crisis began. Labour market policy has been based almost exclusively on passive income support measures and, in particular, the Cassa Integrazione Guadagni scheme which provides income support for 'temporary' short-time working or layoffs. In the face of the crisis the CIG scheme was extended through the introduction of a new scheme, the Cassa Integrazione Guadagni in Deroga. This has extended the application of the measures to a broader range of firms and categories of workers, including apprentices and temporary workers. In principle, this should also provide more equal geographical coverage, but since the CIGD form is reliant on regional activation and financial support, so far, the increasing importance of the CIGD (and CIGS) forms of the programme have had very little effect on the geographical coverage of income support measures.

The heavy reliance on passive income support measures and, despite stated intentions to the contrary, the integration of short-time working and measures to combine passive with active measures to promote the acquisition of human capital among temporarily laid-off workers, has so far been extremely limited and does not bode well for Italy's long-term recovery. This is likely to be further exacerbated by the rapidly expanding use of temporary contractual forms, as evidenced by the growing proportion of young workers employed on temporary contracts despite the crisis and the case studies which illustrate the use of temporary contracts as a relatively new way to regulate labour demand at the firm level. The expansion of temporary employment forms may well, as its proponents suggest, facilitate the expansion of employment, but, given that such contractual forms discourage the investment of firms in workers' human capital, may also damage long-term productivity and therefore the competitiveness of Italian firms.

The crisis has once again worsened the position of young people in the Italian labour market. They have been particularly severely hit and, at the same time, the lack of career-oriented employment opportunities threatens to have severe long-term consequences. The increasingly marked distinction between heavily protected insiders and vulnerable outsiders has led to increasing age-based inequalities in the quantity and quality of employment and there is the danger of the creation of a 'lost' generation of current new labour market 'entrants'. More generally, there are indications that the quality of work, as exemplified by growing involuntary part-time work and informal employment has decreased and wages – although not wage rates – have fallen.

Clearly, there is a need to rethink labour market policy in Italy with a view to dealing with the longer-term structural issues. At the same time, the emerging industrial relations crisis in the country – as exemplified by the Fiat case study – suggests that the collective bargaining system also needs to be re-examined. As things stand, the absence of constructive structural intervention bodes ill for the country's future prosperity.

NOTES

*   I would like to thank participants in the workshops in Geneva for their useful comments, and Francesco and Roberto Amitrano, Paolo Coccorese, Mauro Maccauro, Ernesto Pappalardo and Paolo Piciocchi for their support in the preparation of the case studies.
1.   Indeed, the IMF argues that the poor overall productivity performance in Italy which

underlies the relatively low trend growth in the country is at least partly attributable to these labour market reforms which were accompanied by a reduction in unemployment rates from 11 per cent in 1997 to 6.1 per cent in 2007 (IMF 2010). The types of employment (temporary and part-time) encouraged by the reforms were fairly naturally in lower skilled work.

2. The authors' calculations exclude foreigners working in Italy. Including foreigners, the fall in employment is reduced to 574,336 or 2.4 per cent of the workforce. Anelli and Basso (2010a) argue that excluding foreigners gives a more accurate impression since the figures for the employment of non-Italians, which have risen significantly over this period, reflect various measures legalizing illegal immigrants and formalizing informal employment rather than any real increase in the demand for foreign labour.

3. See, for example, the collection of papers in the *Economic Journal*, vol. 112, no. 480. It might be observed that, of the four substantive papers in the collection, three find negative effects of temporary employment (Blanchard and Landier 2002; Booth et al. 2002 and Dolado et al. 2002), with only one (Holmlund and Storrie 2002) suggesting a (partially) positive role. In Italy, the view appears to be somewhat more positive with several studies (for example, Ichino et al. 2005, 2008; Barbieri and Sestito 2008) finding a weak positive effect of temporary employment on the chances of finding permanent employment, although Gagliarducci (2005) finds that the intermittence of work experience associated with temporary work tends to impede the transition to permanent employment and Berton et al. (2008), while noting that the probability of the transition to permanent employment is higher from temporary employment than from unemployment, also observe the existence of strong state dependence or persistence in temporary employment. That is, for young people in particular, there is a tendency towards 'permanent precariousness' with new labour market entrants becoming trapped in repeated short-term contracts.

4. The estimates of informal employment are based on the definitions used by the Italian National Statistical Agency (ISTAT) which follow the guidelines laid down by the OECD (2002). Estimates of the size of the informal economy are derived from Italian national accounts which are then used to estimate informal employment. Here the percentages of employment are defined in terms of working days, rather than jobs.

5. In practice, the changes in informal employment reported here are entirely due to changes between 2008 and 2009. Between 2007 and 2008 there was no change in informal employment as a percentage of total employment at these levels of aggregation.

6. See, for example, European Commission (2009).

7. Note that, even if workers were effectively unemployed – that is, employed on zero hours – under the CIG, they continued to be counted for the calculation of official statistics among the employed, not the unemployed.

8. For a more detailed description of the underlying methodology, see CIES (2010, pp. 81–94).

9. Obviously, these are partial equilibrium estimates which do not take account of any macro economic demand effects. In this sense one may think of the figures reported, excluding passive income support measures, as upper bounds of the estimates since, in the absence of income support measures, the aggregate demand effects of lower average incomes would have been negative.

10. That is, the difference between column 1 and column 2 as a percentage of column 2.

11. Although, of course, substantial additional employment is dependent on the presence of Fiat in Italy. Estimates of the derived employment from Fiat operations in Italy vary, but could reasonably be as high as an additional 250,000 workers.

12. Cited in 'Fiat: Marchionne's gamble', *Financial Times*, 29 September 2010.

13. See, for example, 'Tute blu contro tute blu così si divide in fabbrica', *La Repubblica*, 4 October 2010.

14. This issue has been stressed in particular by Tito Boeri in two recent newspaper articles, 'L'anomalia del Lodo Marchionne', *La Repubblica*, 16 June 2010, and 'Quegli errori da evitare', *La Repubblica*, 25 August 2010. In January 2011, divisions sharpened

following a referendum – similar to the referendum in Pomigliano – at the Mirafiori plant in Turin, which produced a 50–50 result. As well as encouraging divisions among the different unions involved, the referendum has also fed emerging divisions between workers' representatives in the various Fiat plants.

BIBLIOGRAPHY

Addabbo, T. and A. Maccagnan (2010) 'The impact of the crisis on unemployment and income distribution: the case of Italy', paper presented at the annual AIEL Conference, Pescara, September 2010.

Anelli, M. and G. Basso (2010a) 'I Numeri del Lavoro', *La Voce*, 25 June. Available at: www.lavoce.info.

Anelli, M. And G. Basso (2010b) 'La parola ai Numeri: Lavoro', *La Voce*, 24 September. Available at: www.lavoce.info.

Banca D'Italia (2010) 'I Bilanci delle Famiglie Italiane nell'anno 2008', *Supplementi al Bolletino Statistico*, No. 8, Rome, Banca D'Italia.

Barbieri, G. and P. Sestito (2008) 'Temporary workers in Italy: Who they are and where they end up', *Labour*, Vol. 22, No. 1: 127–166.

Berton, F., F. Devicienti and L. Pacelli (2008) 'Temporary jobs: port of entry, trap or unobserved heterogeneity?', Working Paper, No. 79, Turin: Laboratorio Riccardo Revelli.

Blanchard, O. and A. Landier (2002) 'The perverse effects of partial labour market reform: Fixed-term contracts in France', *Economic Journal*, Vol. 112, No. 480: F214–F244.

Boeri, T. (2009) *La Crisi non è Uguale per Tutti*, Milan: Rizzoli.

Booth, A.L., M. Francesconi and J. Frank (2002) 'Temporary jobs: stepping stones or dead ends?', *Economic Journal*, Vol. 112, No. 480: F189–F213.

Commissione di Indagine Sull'Esclusione Sociale (CIES) (2010) *Rapporto Sulle Politiche Contro la Povertà e l'esclusione Sociale, Anno 2010*, Rome.

Consiglio Nazionale dell'Economia e del Lavoro (CNEL) (2010) *Rapporto sul Mercato del Lavoro 2009–2010*, Rome: CNEL.

Dolado, J.J., C. García-Serrano, and J.F. Jimeno (2002) 'Drawing lessons from the boom of temporary jobs in Spain', *Economic Journal*, Vol. 112, No. 480: F270–F295.

European Commission (2009) *Employment in Europe 2009*, Brussels: European Commission.

Gagliarducci, S. (2005) 'The dynamics of repeated temporary jobs', *Labour Economics*, Vol. 12, No. 4: 429–448.

Holmlund, B. and D. Storrie (2002) 'Temporary work in turbulent times: The Swedish experience', *Economic Journal*, Vol. 112, No. 480: F245–F269.

Ichino, A., F. Mealli and T. Nannicini (2005) 'Temporary work agencies in Italy: A springboard toward permanent employment?', *Giornale degli Economisti e Annali di Economia*, Vol. 64, No. 1: 1–27.

Ichino, A., F. Mealli and T. Nannicini (2008) 'From temporary help jobs to permanent employment: What can we learn from matching estimators and their sensitivity?', *Journal of Applied Econometrics*, Vol. 23, No. 3: 305–327.

International Monetary Fund (IMF) (2009) *Crisis and Recovery: World Economic Outlook*, April 2009, Washington DC.

International Monetary Fund (IMF) (2010) *Staff Report for the 2010 Article IV Consultation*, Washington DC.

Istituto Nazionale di Previdenza Sociale (INPS) (2010) 'CIG – Cassa Integrazione Guadagni: Ore autorizzate per trattamenti di integrazione salariale', FOCUS June 2010, Rome.

Istituto Nazionale di Statistica (ISTAT) (2010a) *Retribuzione pro Capite nelle Grandi Imprese: Effetti di Composizione dell'Occupazione*, Rome.

Istituto Nazionale di Statistica (ISTAT) (2010b) *Indagine sulle Imprese Industriali e dei Servizi, Anno di Riferimento 2009*, Rome.

Ministero dell'Economia e della Finanza (2009) *Documento di Programmazione Economico Finanziaria: 2010–2013*, Rome.

O'Higgins, N. (2010) *The Impact of the Economic and Financial Crisis on Youth Employment: Europe and North America*, Geneva: ILO.

Organization for Economic Cooperation and Development (OECD) (2002) *Measuring the Non-Observed Economy – A Handbook*, Paris.

Schindler, M. (2009) 'The Italian Labour market: recent trends, institutions and reform options', Working Paper No. 09/47, Washington DC: IMF.

Unioncamere (2010) *Sintesi dei Principali Risultati del Sistema di Monitoraggio sui Fabbisogni Occupazionali e Formativi delle Imprese Italiane nell'Industria e nei Servizi*, Sistema Informativo Excelsior, Vol. 2, Rome.

APPENDIX

Table 8A.1   Overview of the main-crisis measures, Italy, 2008–2009

Policy area	Description of measure	Implementation	Results (expected)
Financial crisis measures	A number of measures were introduced to stabilize the financial system including: (a) government guarantee for the deposit insurance fund; (b) state guarantee for new bank liabilities; (c) bank recapitalization scheme; (d) funds made available for banks extending credit to SMEs; and (e) a bank loan moratorium.	From October 2008	Only four banks took advantage of the recapitalization scheme (with a take up of €4.05 billion from the €10 billion available), mainly because the recovery of the global financial system was already under way by the time the scheme was implemented. €9 billion in loan repayments suspended.
Fiscal policy	Discretionary fiscal expansion was very limited, comprising: (a) access to credit for SMEs; (b) a car scrappage programme.	2009	One of the smallest stimulus packages among G20 countries, of the order of 0.2% of GDP in 2009 and 2010, i.e. around one-tenth of the level of the estimated discretionary increase in fiscal policy in G20 countries as a whole of 2.0% and 1.5% of GDP in 2009 and 2010, respectively. Despite (and/or because of) this, the fiscal situation worsened considerably, with public debt increasing by about 10 percentage points of GDP in 2009, reaching almost 116% of GDP.
Income support and training	A Government Decree (DL 185/2008) transformed into law in January 2009	Applied from January 2009	The effects of the broadened application have been modest. By mid 2010, the new CIGD scheme

Table 8A.1 (continued)

Policy area	Description of measure	Implemen- tation	Results (expected)
	(Law 2/2009) widened the field of application of 'discretionary' unemployment benefits (the Cassa Integrazione Guadagni scheme). Coverage was extended to include workers on temporary contracts and apprentices. The same law extended the application of insured unemployment benefits to apprentices and those on temporary contracts by reducing the contributions required for eligibility.		accounted for around 30% of hours in the CIG scheme as a whole. The scheme remained concentrated in the North and the mitigating effects of CIG have mainly been felt in Northern Italy where the crisis was least acute. The new CIGD scheme envisaged the incorporation of training but thus far the take-up by regions has been limited and concentrated in the North.
Subsidized employ- ment and training	The PARI programme was introduced to subsidize training and employment for persons not eligible for CIG or unemployment benefits. The programme involved an interview and subsequently a subsidy of up to €1,000 for training costs and up to €4,500 in income support (spread over 10 months).	2008	Around 10,000 workers obtained employment contracts (70% of which were temporary) out of 36,000 persons involved. Almost the same number left the employment office lists at the same time without participating in subsidized employment and training.

9. The Netherlands: Is the impact of the financial crisis on inequalities different from in the past?

Wiemer Salverda

1. INTRODUCTION

The times have been turbulent since the start of the new century. GDP fell during the ' dotcom crisis' – after the dotcom equities bubble burst in the year 2000 – and declined again much more substantially in 2008 and 2009 as a result of the current ' financial crisis' (Figure 9.1). Between both were four years of considerable growth. The unemployment rate has also been fluctuating, but not fully in sync with GDP. It increased after the

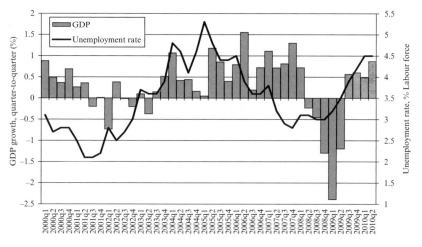

Source: GDP/capita: 2000–2007 from OECD Economic Outlook No. 87, 2008Q2–2010 from CBS/Statline, Quarterly National Accounts and Quarterly Labour Force Statistics; Harmonized unemployment rate from OECD, Main Economic Indicators.

Figure 9.1 Quarterly GDP per capita volume growth and unemployment rate, Netherlands, 2000Q1–2010Q1 (seasonally adjusted)

first GDP decline in 2001 from a minimum level of 2 per cent to a peak of 5.3 per cent in 2005. GDP continued to grow and the unemployment rate fell to 2.5 per cent in 2008, even after GDP had already started to decline. Unemployment increased quickly until early 2010 and, for now, seems to have stabilized at around 4.5 per cent, below the previous peak. Per capita GDP showed a new decline in the third quarter of 2010.

The aim of this chapter is to unravel the inequality effects of the financial and economic crisis in a long-term perspective. This perspective helps to understand the current situation and assess expectations for the near future. Needless to say, the effects on inequalities may differ in the short and the long term. That being the case, we first consider in Section 2 the economics of the current recession, comparing it to five preceding downturns, to determine its timing, depth, significance and scope. Next, we examine in Section 3 the labour market outcomes of (un)employment, wages and working conditions and their effects on inequalities mainly in terms of jobs and earnings, and we discuss some of the explanations. Such analysis is indispensable for exploring future expectations: is the worst over or is it yet to come? It is equally natural to scrutinize the role that policy – restricting ourselves to labour market policies as much as possible – has played so far, but also for the near future. Section 4 then elaborates on the inequalities that have been exacerbated in the current crisis, identifying the most vulnerable groups of workers. In Section 5, two case studies illustrate these trends and some relevant policy issues. Section 6 concludes.

2. THE CURRENT CRISIS: HOW DIFFERENT FROM PREVIOUS DOWNTURNS ?

2.1 How to Measure the Start and Ending of a Recession?

The first question concerns how the recession can best be timed. It is a matter of principle that goes beyond the Dutch outcomes. CBS (Statistics Netherlands) dates the Dutch recession as lasting for five quarters from the second quarter of 2008 until the second quarter of 2009.[1] It focuses exclusively on GDP growth and misses a vital aspect that concerns the effect of population growth – first matter of principle. Krueger and Pischke (1997: 6), discussing its importance for labour demand, suggest that the effect comes close to Say's Law, implying that a significant part of economic growth relates directly to the level of population growth. Ignoring this effect may seem reasonable in a very short-term – say, quarter-to-quarter – inspection of economic growth, but beyond that, important differences occur that should be accounted for in comparisons over time, as well as cross-section, particularly when it comes to the significance of economic growth for the labour market. The current average quarterly growth of the Dutch working-age population (+0.03 per cent) is 10 times less than in the early 1980s (+0.31 per cent) or five times less than current US population growth (+0.16 per cent).[2] Accounting for population growth is imperative also for comparing the effects of recession across age groups: over the past two years in the Netherlands, the growth of the young (15–24 years of age: +1.5 per cent) and of the older (50–64 years of age: + 3.1 per cent) popula-tions contrasts with the decline in the prime-age population (25–64 years of age: −2 per cent).

Dating the beginning of the recession is one thing, dating its ending quite another – a second matter of principle. Present cycle dating is no more than a classification of subsequent periods of expansion and con-traction that disregards how the current level compares to the economic accomplishments before the recession set in: the peak. That comparison seems more relevant to an economy's labour-market effects: as long as the economy has not returned to its initial level, labour demand will remain depressed.[3] Therefore, the period of growth after the trough until the pre-ceding peak level has been reached again should be included in the timing of the recession.[4]

Third, it is important to realize that GDP is an aggregate measure of economic performance, resulting from diverse and sometimes conflicting types of economic behaviour, such as firm investments and household consumption. GDP has no forward-looking significance in and of itself. By contrast, firm investments are directly linked to the behaviour of eco-nomic actors and mirror expectations about the future of the economy in a way that GDP cannot.[5] A lower level of investments may impair the maintenance of existing productive capacity, the installation of new capac-ity or both, and therewith the level of employment and the development of productivity. Therefore, we use here primarily investments[6] as an indi-cator of performance which, during the recession, is revealing also about (expectations of) the future.

2.2   The Extent of the Current Crisis: Comparison with the Past

We turn now to a comparison of downturns in the Netherlands, taken per capita and, naturally, in real terms after deflation, and over the full period until recovery to the initial peak level. A seasonally-corrected quarter-based approach suggests itself not only because economic problems are still unfolding and each quarter adds important new information, but also because annual data unduly smooth out fluctuations leading to an underes-timation of the extent of the downturns – or, in other words, because they overlook much of the within-recession evolution. In the current recession, Dutch GDP declined by 3.9 per cent annually between 2008 and 2009,[7] while the quarterly peak-to-trough drop amounted to 5.5 per cent (per capita).[8]

Before proceeding it is important to discuss which recessions to consider, in addition to the financial crisis. The dotcom crisis is an indisputable candidate, for both its proximity in time (implying maximum resemblance of the workings of the economy and the labour market) and its origin in financial markets (implying resemblance of the nature of the crisis). However, its effects were clearly less abrupt and severe. This motivates looking also at earlier downturns that seem more comparable in terms of severity. Evidently, going all the way back to the 1930s is beyond the purpose of this chapter. Instead, I consider the downturns that have occurred since 1970. This provides an important set for drawing parallels to the financial crisis. As a result, three more downturns are added to the comparison, one for each of the preceding decades: 1970s, 1980s and 1990s. The five recessions are brought together in Table 9.1.

Panel A indicates for GDP and investments the durations of the five recessions (traditional peak-to-trough durations between brackets). Clearly, the timing by investments leads to much longer durations. The five beginnings are roughly similar but the endings vary significantly. GDP decline usually lags investment somewhat, up to a notable four quarters in 2000/2001, except, interestingly, for the current recession: this time investment lagged GDP (by one quarter). This seems to illustrate how the recession took firms in the real economy by surprise. Differences in the endings are particularly striking for the 1970s and 2000s. These recessions took only ten and five quarters, respectively, if measured by GDP, but they stretch out very long, basically until the next recession, when using investment. For the 1970s, some caution is required as investments showed a double dip long after GDP had returned to normal. However, the long duration better represents the prevailing feelings of pessimism during and about that decade. By contrast, for the 2000s the investment measure casts doubt on the prevailing optimism; doubt which seems in line with the hindsight caused by the financial crisis. Actually, both recessions lasted longer than the more virulent one of the early 1980s, where the investment measure adds relatively little to the length. From the GDP measure the dotcom crisis would seem to resemble that of the 1990s, which was the most benign of the five recessions according to both indicators.

Panel B elaborates on the depth of the declines from three different time perspectives. The fall in investment is always much stronger than in GDP[9] and GDP usually grows substantially before the investment level is restored.

First, the panel compares for the traditional peak-to-trough measure the durations and how GDP and investment have developed for each recession;

Table 9.1 *Durations and depths of five recessions in the Netherlands since 1970 (volume of GDP and investment per capita indicators)*

	Early and mid-1970s	Early 1980s	Early 1990s	Early 2000s	Current (up to 2010Q2)
A. Durations until recovery to initial level (in quarters; from first quarter of decline)					
GDP	10 quarters 1971Q4, 1973Q2– 1973Q3, 1974Q4– 1976Q2	25 quarters 1980Q1– 1986Q1	7 quarters 1992Q2– 1993Q4	11 quarters 2001Q3– 2004Q1	9+ quarters 2008Q2–...
Investment	33 quarters 1971Q2– 1979Q2*	28 quarters 1979Q3– 1986Q2	15 quarters 1992Q1– 1995Q3	32 quarters 2000Q1– 2007Q4	8+ quarters 2008Q3–...
B. Quarter-to-quarter level changes in percentage terms					
Time measure 1. Peak-to-trough decline: extent and duration (quarterly averages in brackets)					
GDP	−0.6 in 3Q (0.2)	−7.4 in 12Q (−0.7)	−0.9 in 1Q (−0.9)	−1 in 8Q (−0.1)	−5.5 in 5Q (−1.1)
Investment	−16.9 in 6Q (−2.8)	−26.9 in 13Q (−2.1)	−12.7 in 10Q (−1.3)	−22.1 in 12Q (−1.8)	−24.0 in 6Q (−4.0)
Time measure 2. Change over the same first number of quarters as currently available (8 or 9)					
GDP (9Q)	+5.7	−1.9	+0.4	+2.9	−2.9
Investment (8Q)	−3.7	−22.0	−11.9	−9.8	−19.8
Time measure 3. Speediest four-quarter decline during the period (quarters since start of recession)					
GDP	−2.9 (Q15–Q18)	−3.7 (Q10–Q13)	−0.2 (Q1–Q4)	−0.6 (Q3–Q6)	−5.6 (Q1–Q4)
Investment	−15.8 (Q1–Q4)	−13.4 (Q7–Q10)	−9.9 (Q5–Q8)	−13.6 (Q9–Q12)	−20.0 (Q2–Q5)
C. Working-age (15–64) population change in percentage terms (between brackets: quarterly averages)					
Population	+11.9 (0.36)	+8.7 (0.31)	+1.8 (0.12)	+3.4 (0.08)	0.2 (0.03)

Notes: GDP and investment: volume figures, seasonally adjusted; population is for working age: 15–64 years. Durations 'in nQ' expressed in quarters.
* Not recovered before next recession.

Source: Calculations from OECD, Economic Outlook No. 87 for first four recessions; from CBS/Statline, National Accounts, quarterly values, for financial crisis.

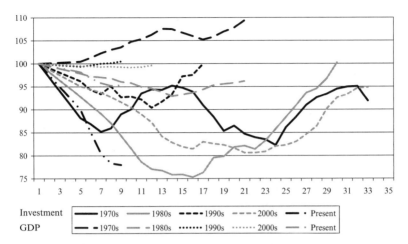

Investment | ——1970s ——1980s ■■■■1990s ----2000s ——•Present
GDP | —•1970s —•1980s ●●●●●●1990s ••••••••2000s ~~~•Present

Notes: Four-quarter moving averages (all starting from 100 in first quarter); 1971Q1, 1979Q2, 1991Q4, 1999Q4 and 2008Q2 = 100. * Solid lines for Investment, dashed lines for GDP.

Source: See Table 9.1 unemployment rate from OECD, Main Economic Indicators.

Figure 9.2   Five Dutch recessions: evolution of investment and GDP* per capita per quarter since start of each recession

obviously, we cannot be sure that the current trough has already been reached. Although ultimately the decline of the 1980s is somewhat larger, it is also clear that the current decline has been significantly steeper so far, falling almost twice as fast as GDP decreased by more than 1 per cent for five consecutive quarters, and investment by almost 4 per cent for six quarters in a row. Second, over the same number of quarters (eight) that is now available for the current recession, the 1980s went as deep as the current recession. The financial crisis beats the other four with by far the speediest one-year decline, the third time perspective. Note that for the financial crisis that year is already behind us while during the recession of the 1980s it followed only much later. This confirms the surprising decline in investments (see also Figure 9.2).

Coverage of the three recessions between 1970 and 2000 clearly improves the comparison. Given previous experiences, it cannot be taken for granted that the bottom of the financial crisis is already behind us or even within reach. It would not be the first time that quarters of decline are interspersed with a few others showing growth (for example, 1983Q1–Q3). Therefore it cannot be excluded that to date we have observed for the financial crisis only the speediest start, while the steepest one-year decline and a long aftermath may still be ahead. The least one can say from its

Table 9.2   *Scope of five Dutch recessions*: cumulative change in inflation, consumption, savings, international trade and balance over first eight quarters*

	Early and mid-1970s	Early 1980s	Early 1990s	Early 2000s	Current (up to 2010Q2)
A. Prices (%)					
GDP	+20	+10	+5	+9	+2
Consumption	+17	+13	+2	+9	+2
Exports	+6	+30	–4	+4	–1
B. Volume changes per capita (%)					
Government spending	–2.2	+0.3	+3.6	+6.0	+5.9
Consumption	+1.7	+2.8	+3.7	+4.7	+5.9
Investment	–17.4	–15.1	+2.9	+15.4	+4.4
Private consumption	+6	–6	0	+5	–2.9
Imports	+7	–6	3	+3	–4
Exports	+20	–3	+9	+3	–6
C. Other					
Current account balance	+4 pcpt	+2 pcpt	+3 pcpt	+2 pcpt	–0.7 pcpt
Net savings			+0.3 pcpt	–1.4 pcpt	–2.0 pcpt

Notes: Imports, exports and consumption: levels are seasonally adjusted volume figures, but the trade balance to GDP is based on current-value figures. Imports and exports are after deduction of re-exports; 1970–1995 using annual ratio in current values, 1996–2010 using quarter values after deflation; note that the correction for re-exports leads to much lower outcomes for both the 1970s recession, the dotcom crisis and the financial crisis. Current account balance: per cent of GDP at current prices. Net savings: change as a percentage of NNI.
* Based on investment per capita, see Table 9.1.

Source: Calculations from OECD, Economic Outlook No. 87 and Main Economic Indicators, except for financial crisis: CBS/Statline; savings from OECD Quarterly National Accounts including current recession.

abrupt start and very deep fall is that this time things are very different quantitatively. Linking the recessions to labour market outcomes in the next section will tell us more.

2.3   Aggregate Economic Performance: Different Features this Time

Before turning to that, we consider the scope of the Dutch recessions and the parallels to other countries for the financial crisis. Table 9.2

forays into aspects of aggregate economic performance beyond GDP and investment, such as inflation, consumption, savings, international trade and current account balance for the first eight quarters. Clearly, things appear, once again, to be very different this time compared to the preceding declines:

- inflation is almost absent for both GDP and private consumption, while it was rampant in the 1970s and very substantial in the 1980s; export prices fell slightly, on balance, as they also did during the 1990s recession;
- the level of private consumption has changed little after its a uniquely fast 3.2 per cent decline over the first year, thereby diverging from the 6 per cent decline of the 1980s which was largely concentrated in that recession's second year – this may still await us if austerity starts to bite;
- the total of private and government consumption has remained stable only thanks to a 6 per cent increase in government consumption, which exceeds all earlier recessions, though less for the dotcom crisis (4.7 per cent);
- government investment registered a modest growth – much less than during the dotcom crisis but radically more than in the 1970 and 1980s;
- substantial national dissaving occurred during the first year of the financial crisis (−5 pcpt), but – though still larger than on previous occasions – it has become more comparable now to the dotcom crisis;
- uniquely, import and export volumes[10] plunged by no less than 10–11 per cent in the first year (not shown), in particularly sharp contrast to their large increases over the dotcom crisis; thus far, imports have made up for half of the lost ground, while export volumes are still significantly down at −6 per cent;
- the current account balance of trade became less favourable, again in contrast to previous recessions; however, quarterly volatility is too large to safely conclude to a structural turnaround of the trade balance after the strong upward trend for almost 25 years (gaining 8 percentage points of GDP[11]).

The significant differences to previous recessions across the variables raise the important question if this time things are not different qualitatively as well, and also what the role of government policy has been.

Finally, we summarily compare the evolution of the financial crisis for the Netherlands and the four major countries: the United States,

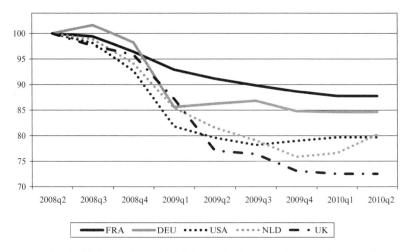

Source: For the Netherlands see Table 9.1; for all other countries, OECD Economic
Outlook No. 87 up to 2001Q2.

Figure 9.3   *Financial crisis: quarterly evolution of investment per capita in*
France, Germany, Netherlands, the United Kingdom and the
United States, 2008–2010 (2008Q2 = 100)

the United Kingdom, Germany and France (Figure 9.3). In all these
countries, investments have declined rapidly and deeply but there seems
to be a dichotomy between, on the one hand, France and Germany, where
the decline is less (between 10 and 15 per cent), and the United Kingdom
and the United States on the other hand, where it exceeds 20 or even 25
per cent. Intriguingly, the Dutch evolution seems closer to the United
Kingdom and the United States than the Continental countries. One may
speculate if this can be due to a larger role of financial markets in the
Netherlands compared to Germany or France. The investment picture
seems to capture local moods, which seem gloomier in the United States
than in Germany.

It seems only natural to conclude that, for the moment, we find ourselves in uncharted waters. The long durations and late accelerations of
labour market decline during previous recessions warrant little optimism
for the coming years. The combination with tightening credit markets
and massive shifts of debt from financial markets onto governments
can serve only to make things worse. The present relief may be temporary and relies strongly on investment demand from China and similar
countries.[12]

3. LABOUR MARKET OUTCOMES: EMPLOYMENT, EARNINGS AND WORKING CONDITIONS

3.1   Employment: Little Decline in Heads, Significant Reduction in Hours

The unemployment rate is a simple result of labour supply and demand, but behind each lurks a variety of factors which can differ significantly over time, including over the seasons, and across countries. Supply can be very volatile because of the seasonal variance in school-leavers' supply and in certain productive activities, and the possible discouragement of job seekers. The demand side is also not a simple given. Its full-time/part-time structure is shifting significantly and inflates the denominator over which the unemployment rate is calculated leading to a comparatively lower rate. The employment level may also be increased for the good reason that more people in the population have a job. If so, the same number of unemployed implies a lower unemployment rate, although the social problem of unemployment remains the same. Thus, when considering the labour outcomes of recessions, we attempt here to account for time structure and employment participation, naturally again on a per capita basis. Aggregate outcomes are the focus, while further detail is discussed in Section 5 as an important component of work inequalities.

Notably, seasonal effects do not disappear in recession and are critical for an up-to-date quarterly approach. For the current crisis seasonally adjusted data are still few, but fortunately most variables are now available for the second quarter of 2010, which can be compared directly to the starting quarter (2008Q2) without much worry about the seasonal effects.

Figure 9.4 shows the importance of these distinctions for the current recession, all on a per capita basis. Three approaches to employment show diverging effects, ranging from a 1 to a 5 per cent decline. First, the number of persons in employment, including the self-employed, changes little over the two-year period, –1.1 per cent. The number of employees (that is, excluding self-employed) falls slightly more, –1.5 per cent. The gap widens considerably, however, if their working hours are accounted for, generating a fall in all hours worked in the economy by 2.6 per cent over the first four quarters and 5.2 per cent over the two years taken together, thus showing no sign of slowing down during the second year. Apparently, employees who remained in work now tend to work almost 3.5 per cent fewer hours, on average, compared to the peak. Hours are a crucial issue that we discuss in more detail below.

Clearly, a singular focus on head-count numbers would suggest that not much is happening. This can explain the feeling harboured by many that labour market effects are astonishingly gentle, given the abrupt fall

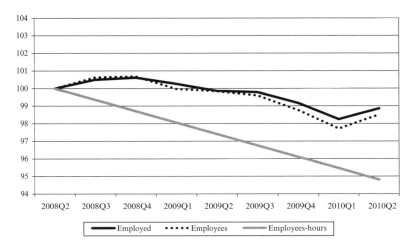

Note: Straight grey line for employee-hours indicates seasonally adjusted trend.

Source: Author's estimates from European and CBS/Statline LFS and Labour Accounts.

Figure 9.4   *Quarterly employment change in the Dutch financial*
              crisis: persons in work and hours worked, 2008–2010
              (2008Q2 = 100)

in GDP. However, from an economic point of view the hours-count approach is the most appropriate indicator of realized productive labour demand. Figure 9.5 portrays this over the five recessions. Clearly, its decline at the start of the current recession was as strong as in the 1970s and much stronger than in the 1980s, although it is gradually changing track from the former to the latter. The 1990s recession was shallow also in terms of its labour-market effects. Surprisingly, the dotcom crisis lacks a clear-cut decline in employment; to the contrary, it tended to grow. The financial crisis is distinctly different.

The fact that the employment effects remain negative far beyond renewed growth of GDP underscores the relevance of choosing the investment indicator for measuring a recession's duration. The volume of employment hours fell all the way during the long drawn-out recession of the 1970s and during the short-lived 1990s recession, and it fell for most of the time during the 1980s. In addition, the depth of employment declines of the 1970s and 1980s goes beyond GDP and matches the fall of investment much better. Only the dotcom crisis seems an exception. However, given the very severe fall in GDP in the first year of the financial crisis (−4.3 per cent), even the large decline in hours-count employment (−2.6

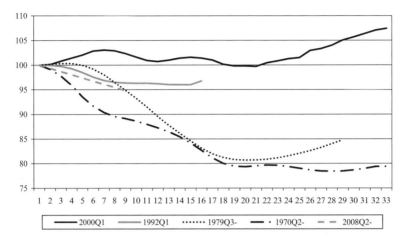

Note: 4-quarter moving averages; 1971Q1, 1979Q2, 1991Q4, 1999Q4, 2008Q2 = 100.

Source: Estimated from OECD Economic Outlook No. 87, except financial crisis: see Figure 9.4.

Figure 9.5   *Five Dutch recessions: employee-hours per capita, seasonally adjusted, per quarter since start of each recession; peak = 100*

per cent) seems relatively modest. Again, in comparison to the other four countries, the Dutch decline over two years (−5 per cent) seems to follow the United Kingdom and the United States more closely (−4 to 7 per cent), than France or Germany (−2 to +1 per cent).

The main issue to consider further is the time structure of employment. The shifting weights of full-time and part-time jobs can help explain the widening gap between head-count and hours-count (full-time equivalent[13]) employment. The gap increased secularly until 2002 and then declined by 2 percentage points until 2006. The financial crisis increased the gap again, from 16 to 18 per cent. Thus the labour market has enhanced the person-intensity of the volume of employment. The renewed increase has certainly contributed to mitigating the current unemployment effects but at the same time it should be said that the current pace does not differ significantly from previous recessions.

Three developments have contributed to enlarging the gap. First, a general shortening of the full-time working week – from 2,000 hours in 1970 down to a steady 1,700–1,750 hours since the mid-1980s (CPB) – has lowered the general number of hours by 14 per cent. Second, the equally secular growth of the share of part-time jobs, from less than one-third to more than half of all jobs, has brought average hours per job down. Third,

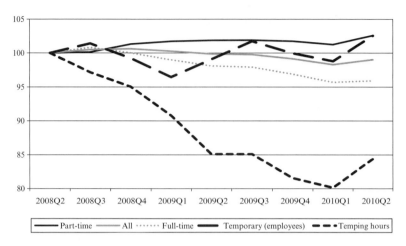

Note: Part-time is defined as less than 35 weekly hours, full-time as more, regardless of the labour contract.

Source: European LFS, seasonally unadjusted – Q2 points indicate seasonally neutral changes; temping hours from CBS/Statline, seasonally adjusted.

Figure 9.6   Dutch financial crisis: employment changes by working time and types of contract, 2008–2010 (2008Q2 = 100)

much of the growth of part-time employment was concentrated in small jobs; consequently, the average part-time jobs now counts 40 per cent fewer hours than before. This has reinforced the downward effect of part-time employment on total hours worked in the economy.

The absolute number of full-time jobs has changed very little since the 1970s; thus its percentage of the working-age population has fallen significantly, from 46 per cent in 1970 to 35 per cent recently.[14] The decline in full-time occupations is clearly visible also during the financial crisis.[15] Figure 9.6 shows a 4 per cent decline in full-time employment (−180,000) over the eight quarters into this crisis. It contrasts with a 3 per cent growth of part-time jobs (+100,000); as a result, overall employment decreased by only 1 per cent. Basically, all full-time jobs were lost by men, who at the same time gained 50,000 part-time jobs. Unfortunately, we cannot say how many full-time jobs were turned into part-time jobs individually (the 50,000 just mentioned seems the possible maximum), or that the former got lost here while the latter were created elsewhere. It is clear, however, that part of the new part-time workers are doing so involuntarily. The Netherlands has a very high rate of part-time employment but by international standards only few of the occupants (between 3 and 4 per cent in recent years) are involuntary part-time workers. However, the increase in part-time jobs from 2008 to 2009 entailed a much higher involuntary share (18 per cent) than before, but it remains clearly a minority.

Full-time jobs risk becoming an endangered species. The high and increasing level of part-time employment seems to be also at odds with the needs and preferences of the unemployed, who are mostly looking for substantial jobs.[16] During the financial crisis, the number of full-time jobs fell by 4 per cent while the number of unemployed looking for full-time employment swelled by 58 per cent, twice as fast as the rate (30 per cent) for those who were looking for less than full-time hours. This added to the similar developments during the dotcom crisis[17] and risks exacerbating the unemployment problem. The shift towards part-time jobs has important implications for inequality effects by gender and age to which I will turn in Section 5.

It is unfortunate that we do not know the role of individual transitions from full-time to part-time, as that might help establish the direct contribution of working-time flexibility to keeping people in work. Nevertheless, it is clear that the full-time/part-time shift adds significantly to the flexibility of the aggregate volume of hours worked. In spite of large seasonal fluctuations, contractual flexibility grew at the same pace as part-time employment (+3 per cent) over the eight quarters though less absolutely: 67,000 as against 106,000 (Figure 9.7). Overall temporary growth contrasts strongly with the hours worked by temp agency workers. The latter reached an all-time high of 5 per cent of employee hours in 2008, but dropped by one-fifth up to early 2010, while at the same time other, non-temping temporary jobs continued to expand. The latter can be hired on an array of different contracts, varying from zero-hours call contracts to the probationary period for a full-time permanent contract. Together with temp workers they currently comprise 19 per cent of employees. Note that temping declined similarly during the dotcom crisis, but this time the decline was twice as fast. Very recently, temps have seen their numbers starting to grow again. Clearly, temps act as an increasingly important buffer in times of crisis (see also Case study 1).

One underlying question with regard to why employment is not falling more strongly, given the extent of the downturn, is whether the structure of GDP itself may have shifted so that employment problems become less pressing in case of a downturn. The productive composition of the economy can affect the nature of labour demand, directly or indirectly. Evidently, the strong shift from producing goods towards services is an important factor contributing to a (relative) increase in the labour intensity of production and the demand for labour, and specifically also to the rise of part-time employment.

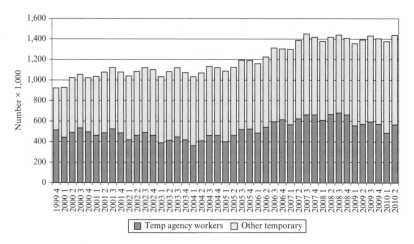

Source: CBS/Statline for temp agency statistics and Labour Accounts, and European LFS for temporary workers.

Figure 9.7   Temp agency workers and other temporary employees, ×1000, Netherlands, 1999–2010

Services production may also generate a different attitude on the part of employers towards investment and hiring, as human capital tends to play a more important role for the productive organization. However, human capital investment – for example, through firm spending on the training of its workers – is not captured by investment statistics. Also, in services the capital intensity of production is less and the firing of a worker affects productive capacity more directly. In addition, the volatility in labour demand for services may be less than for goods – not necessarily for each and every service, but in the aggregate. Among services, the strongest decline in employment has been in hotels and catering (–8 per cent between 2008 and 2009). However, this is no comparison to, for example, truck and car production, which fell by 32 per cent (see first case study).

3.2   Earnings: Less Immediately Affected than Before?

Employment and unemployment are one element of labour market outcomes, wages and labour costs are their evident complement. How do they behave over time? Table 9.3 compares between recessions for actual earnings as received by the individual worker and per hour of work respectively. Earnings are deflated for the 2 per cent consumer price rise (Table 9.2). Both show a rise since 2008, largely concentrated in the

Table 9.3   Five Dutch recessions*: cumulative changes in wages and labour costs over first eight quarters

	Early and mid-1970s	Early 1980s	Early 1990s	Early 2000s	Current (up to 2010Q2)
Earnings per person		−1.5	+1.5	+1.8	+1.4
Earnings per hour		+0.0	+5.1	+2.7	+3.6
Unit labour costs	−1.5	−0.5	+0.3	−0.3	+3.1
Labour productivity	+12.6	+1.6	+1.9	+0.2	−0.9
Wage share in GDP		−0.3 pcpt	+0.1 pcpt	−0.1 pcpt	+1.5 pcpt

Notes: Earnings are compensation of employees deflated by consumption prices, divided by employees and employees times annual hours worked respectively; unit labour costs deflated by GDP prices (see Table 9.2). Wage share based on current values of compensation and GDP.
* Timing based on investment per capita, see Table 9.1.

Source: calculations from OECD, Economic Outlook No. 88.

first four quarters, that clearly exceeds the early 1980s but is comparable to the 1990s and the dotcom crisis. Hourly earnings do better (+3.6 per cent) than individual earnings (+1.4 per cent), which is consistent with the stronger decline in hours worked than in the number of employees. The 3.6 per cent rise is slightly higher than in Germany, France or the United States (2.7–2.9 per cent) but comparable to the United Kingdom.

Dutch collectively negotiated wage scales, which lay the basis of wage formation for most workers, increased by 2.2 per cent in real terms during the financial crisis, largely during the first four quarters. The lower increase of earnings than of negotiated wages may imply that the latter were not fully endorsed or they can reflect composition effects, or both. Still their role for the earnings increase seems to be non-trivial. To some extent the Dutch Polder model, in spite of its long history of negotiated wage moderation (Salverda, 2008b), seems to have been taken by the same surprise as firms for their investments (compare Case study 1). Before the start of the financial crisis wage increases had been collectively agreed on the basis of economic forecasts provided by the Central Planning Bureau.[18] Growth forecasts turned out to be radically mistaken.[19] This affected productivity negatively. At the same time, consumer prices increased much less than expected (a 1.5 pcpt difference), affecting real wages upwards. The evolution of unit labour costs presents a different picture. These result from labour costs (gross wages including employer contributions), on the one hand, and the evolution of labour productivity, on the other. It turns out that the substantial wage growth of the 1970s was almost entirely compensated for by (strong) productivity growth. The next three recessions also show unit labour costs that hardly changed. Only the present recession sees a striking growth in unit labour costs by 3.1 per cent over the two years since the start in 2008, as a result of a 7 per cent rise over the first four quarters followed by a 3.6 per cent decline over the second four quarters. The 3.1 per cent rise is slightly higher than in Germany and France (+2.7 per cent), and the United Kingdom (+2.2 per cent), and diverges largely from the United States (−2.7 per cent) (OECD, Economic Outlook No. 88). Labour productivity is responsible for a part of this as it declined this time (−0.9 per cent) in contrast to the previous recessions – the result, again, of a decline over the first four quarters (−4 per cent) followed by a rise over the second four quarters (+3 per cent). Unsurprisingly, the wage share in GDP, which closely resembles real wages over productivity, registers a 1.5 percentage-point growth during the current crisis (+3.4 pcpt and −1.9 pcpt over the first and second four quarters), in contrast to the stagnation of the three preceding recessions. However, it is important to realize that the current increase started from the lowest level of the wage share (49 per cent) attained for decades. A secular decline since the 1970s, that has been stronger in the Continental countries than in the United States or the United Kingdom, has beefed up capital income, creating financial room for manoeuvre for firms and therewith potentially reducing their urge to lower wages or fire workers at the very first sign of productivity decline.

3.3　Other Working Conditions: Mixed Findings

Findings on the effects of the crisis on other working conditions have led so far to mixed evidence. On the one hand, the annual working-conditions survey[20] shows, first and foremost, a decline in the negative aspects of physically demanding work between 2008 and 2009: the number of accidents per 100,000 employees fell by 9 per cent, and the percentages of employees having to exert physical force, or experience vibrations, loud noise, repetitive work or difficult postures during work all declined by a few per cent. Plausibly, this reflects a decline in employment in the relevant types of work. Interestingly, the shares of employees facing pressure and intimidation rose in relation to clients and fell in relation to management and colleagues. On the other hand people also report an increase in the work that is emotionally demanding and a decrease in own initiative and decision autonomy. Taken together, the share of workers satisfied with working conditions, which had significantly expanded from 69 per cent in 2005 to 76 per cent in 2008, declined in 2009 to 74 per cent. Unfortunately, no data are readily available for analysing the causes or consequences.

Additional reporting by TNO (2010) also indicates a declining satisfaction with pay but increased satisfaction with the possibilities of working part-time. Percentages of employees reporting organizational downsizing rose significantly in 2009, from 8 per cent to 13 per cent at workplaces that had shrunk without dismissals, and from 5 per cent to 12 per cent if there had actually been dismissals.

Summarizing, we can say that the financial crisis deviates from previous recessions in several important respects not only regarding the extent of the downturn itself as was shown previously, but also with regard to its labour-market effects:

- Lower head-count employment adjustments;
- Strong working-time reduction;
- A concomitant, continued shift away from full-time to part-time jobs;
- A rise in involuntary part-time work;
- Excessive adaptation of temp agency work;
- A continued growth of employees on temporary contracts;
- Relatively benign wage developments during the first year into the crisis, largely based on a lower than expected increase in prices, followed by a downward adaptation during the second year;
- An unexpectedly rapid initial increase in unit labour costs based on growing hourly wages and falling productivity;
- A corresponding increase in the wage share in GDP, starting from the lowest level for 40 years.

Full-time jobs, and the men occupying them, and temp agency workers have borne the brunt of employment adaptation. Their important declines remain hidden in the aggregate level of the number of persons in employment as long as working hours are not accounted for. It is the small declines in employment numbers that may explain the popular feeling that unemployment growth and employment decline are significantly less than anticipated.

4. EFFECTS ON INEQUALITIES

4.1 The Complexity of the Issue

The effects of the financial crisis on inequality are not easy to verify, for both theoretical and practical reasons. Theoretically, the concept of inequality needs discussion for a host of reasons. First, it can be approached from two different perspectives: opportunity and outcome. For example, inequality of opportunity is relevant for those who cannot get a job because they are new entrants (young school-leavers) or have been made redundant (older workers). The role of part-time jobs is another example underlining the complexity of the issue: to the extent that working fewer hours is an individual decision the lower income that results is also an individual choice. However, such a 'choice' is difficult to verify, and even though voluntarily made in the short term, it may have undesired consequences in the long term. Second, inequality can be found in different domains: for example, in employment as such – as a source of life satisfaction – or in earnings and income. Because paid labour is of such overwhelming importance for citizens and society, it is not trivial where the world of work ends and other domains begin. For example, work and pay is an individual matter, but cannot be fully understood without accounting for the individual's household environment, which has a dynamic of its own but at the same time may itself be sensitive to the situation of work and pay. Third, both lead on to the dynamic aspect of inequality 'formation' which may take time to unravel: one may have to wait a long time before inequalities start to settle, and, in addition, a longer recession may in itself worsen the effects. Fourth, certain inequalities may increase, while others decrease. Improved female job chances illustrate this. Fifth, inequality may increase at the aggregate, societal level even while no individual is worse off – for example, as top incomes grow more. Sixth, not unrelated to this, inequality can be conceived of – and measured – on the basis of the full distribution of a given variable or on the basis of specific parts, for example, the tails (low-wage employment, poverty or top incomes) or the middle (polarization). Finally, inequalities are not a natural phenomenon but also depend on the character of the policies being applied. These can either counteract or stimulate their growth, and even if they counteract them they may do so outside the world of work proper (for example, by redistribution via taxes and benefits); that world may take these effects into account, however.

In practically determining current trends in inequality, we are trying to see what is going on in the middle of a storm in which bits and pieces of information are flying around and are difficult to catch and interpret, and precise, up-to-date, relevant information is not always available. Many findings presented below depend crucially on the fact that much-needed data for guesstimating trends have become available for the same season of the year that the downturn began, diminishing the worry about seasonal effects which can be very significant.

Let us see how far we can get when discussing employment chances and earnings outcomes successively. Employment and unemployment should come first, as the lack of a job usually implies a simultaneous lack of earnings; it can also have a lasting opportunity effect, even after a job has finally been obtained, as careers and later earnings may be affected by an initial 'scarring'. Employment shifts may also help us then to evaluate possible changes in wage inequality in the absence of proper wage data. In addition, it should be observed that wage inequality concerns only those who actually have a job; it cannot capture the effects of no earnings. It is one of the purposes of studying employment to acquire information about that – without it, the picture of inequality effects would be fundamentally incomplete.

4.2 Employment Opportunities: Pitting Generations Against Each Other

We have already noted that the response of employment figures to the financial crisis has been surprisingly muted, falling by only 1 per cent despite the brutality of the recession. However, taking into account four key aspects: age, gender, ethnicity and education – which often overlap and reinforce each other – the situation appears to be much less reassuring in terms of inequality. The gender distribution of the population is stable, but there have been strong changes in the age structure, also over the past few years. Ethnic minorities have grown to a sizeable presence over recent decades. Finally, the educational performance of the population has expanded tremendously.[21]

Table 9.4 breaks down the development of the population, employment and labour force since the peak before the financial crisis in the second quarter of 2008. Men appear to have lost a significant 2.7 per cent of their employment rate, while women have gained 1.1 per cent, strengthening the existing gender shift. Men lost particularly – almost 5 per cent – in full-time employment. Women also lost there, but less, and this was also of less significance to them because of their much lower incidence of full-time jobs. Male part-time employment gained relatively more, but theirs is much less important than for women, and it was insufficient to prevent a decline in the male participation rate by 1.2 per cent. In the FTE count men lost almost 7 per cent; however, women also suffered a surprising 3 per cent loss as part-time jobs also lost hours.[22]

4.2.1 Increase in part-time

Basically, part-time employment increased over the two years for all categories of workers. Youths and prime-age workers suffered a similar 3.5 per cent decline in employment numbers but as population growth diverged there is a clear difference on a per capita basis: a 5 per cent loss for youth and a 2 per cent loss for the prime-age population. For youths,

Table 9.4   *Dutch financial crisis: population, types of employment and labour-force participation by gender, age, nationality and education**

	Numbers		Per capita ratios				
	Population	Employ-ment	All	Full-time	Part-time	FTE**	Labour force
All 15–64	+0.2	–1.0	–1.1	–4.2	+2.4	–5.2	+0.3
Men	0.0	–2.7	–2.7	–4.9	+4.7	–6.8	–1.2
Women	+0.3	+1.1	+0.8	–1.4	+1.5	–3.0	+1.9
Minorities***	+2.6	–3.4	–5.9	–14.3	+5.8	–12.1	–5.3
Age							
15–24	+1.5	–3.4	–4.8	–19.6	+1.3	–14.0	–2.5
25–50	–1.9	–3.5	–1.6	–3.8	+1.6	–5.3	–0.2
50–64	+3.1	7.0	3.9	+2.6	+5.2	–0.2	+4.6
Educational attainment							
Low	–3.0	–6.0	–3.1	–6.6	0.0	–7.8	–0.9
Medium	–0.9	–2.4	–1.5	–7.3	+5.0	–6.8	0.0
High	+5.6	+5.2	–0.4	–1.0	+0.4	–4.3	+0.4

Notes:
* All figures are seasonally unadjusted but comparison of two similar quarters is assumed to compensate for that.
** FTE (full-time equivalent, put at 1,840 hours per year) approximated from a breakdown of jobs by four bands of weekly hours, normalized on the Labour Accounts total.
*** Non-Western only.

Source: European LFS, except minorities: CBS/Statline, Dutch LFS and Labour Accounts (European LFS data are based on formal nationality, CBS data refer to immigrants and their offspring, regardless of nationality).

this includes a calamitous fall in full-time employment by 20 per cent that largely spills over into an FTE decline by 14 per cent. The modest part-time growth was far from enough to compensate for the fall in full-time jobs, and, as we will see, part-time employment does not provide an adequate starting point for school-leavers for a future career. Importantly, the youth labour market participation rate declined by 2.5 per cent, or 50,000. In other words, employment decline and unemployment growth did not cancel one another out and youth labour supply has been leaking away. This has prevented a significant rise in the youth unemployment rate that otherwise might have shot up to 9.4 per cent, instead of the actual 7.8 per cent. Over the financial crisis the youth unemployment rate has grown by 40 per cent, significantly less than average (+50 per cent) or prime-age workers (+64 per cent). With an unchanged participation rate the pace would have been similar to the prime-age group.

4.2.2 Minorities most hit
Minorities'[23] employment numbers fell as strongly as those of young people (−3.4 per cent). This is no surprise as youths and minorities overlap significantly as do the low skilled and minorities.[24] On a per capita basis their fall exceeded that of all other categories, in terms of both head-count (−6 per cent) and hours-count employment (−12 per cent). On balance their labour force participation rate did fall, by 5.3 per cent, which is also more than for any other category.

4.2.3 Vulnerability by level of education
The three often-used levels of educational attainment: low (junior secondary or less), medium (senior secondary) and high (tertiary) also show diverging trends that, although they are in line with common expectations, are still worrying. For the low skilled part-time employment did not increase and could offer no compensation for the severe loss of full-time jobs (−6.6 per cent). At the medium-skill level the loss of full-time occupations was somewhat larger – one in 16 – but so was the growth of part-time jobs. Even for the high educated employment growth has been lagging slightly behind population growth and their full-time employment has fallen by 1 per cent on a per capita basis.

As to the shift to part-time jobs, we happen not to know, unfortunately, whether the individuals stayed on in employment on a part-time basis. FTE effects by level of education are found in a narrower range than might be expected. It implies that at higher educational levels the growth of part-time jobs offered the possibility to stay in employment but in exchange for fewer hours.

4.2.4 Diverging effects for the generations
Youth developments contrast with those of older workers, aged 50 to 64. The latter's numbers in employment grew strongly by any standard (+7 per cent), despite the recession. This was partly driven by population growth but even on a per capita basis they managed a favourable 4 per cent growth. Positive developments for both full-time and part-time employment underlie this. Older workers' FTE employment remained unchanged. It confirms a trend of significant employment growth for older workers that began in the early 1990s before the intense policymaking to increase older workers' participation took off (OECD, 2005), on the one hand, and a deep-seated transformation of the youth labour market, which is considered below. Prime-age workers are in the middle, with a

Table 9.5   *Dutch financial crisis: youth (15–24) population, types of*
            employment and labour-force participation by gender, age and
            education

	Numbers		Per capita ratios				
	Population	Employment	All	Full-time	Part-time	FTE	Labour force
15–24	+1.5	–3.4	–4.8	–19.6	+1.3	–14.0	–2.5
Men	+1.4	–6.2	–7.6	–19.4	–0.4	–15.9	–4.7
Women	+1.5	–0.3	–1.8	–20.1	+2.5	–11.7	–0.1
Educational attainment							
Low	–3.9	–20.7	–7.0	–25.0	–2.3		–4.2
Medium	+7.3	+2.3	–4.6	–22.8	+4.8		–2.3
High	+8.5	+5.8	–2.5	–2.3	+3.4		–1.9

Note: See Table 9.4.

significant 4 per cent loss of full-time jobs and an FTE loss of more than 5 per cent. Thus, Dutch employment trends are clearly diverging between the generations.

4.2.5   The plight of youth

The picture is more complex when we pursue a further breakdown of youth employment by gender and educational level (Table 9.5). Female young people appear to do better overall because of the much lower incidence of full-time work among them, so that the equally strong relative decline they underwent for the latter is less significant. The decline in full-time jobs for youth is colossal, in relative terms, especially for low-educated and medium-educated youths who have lost roughly one-quarter. The least-educated youths also lost part-time jobs. These changes are clearly much worse than average and seem hidden from view partly by the favourable trend among older workers and partly by youths' own withdrawal from the labour market.

There is good reason to worry about the inequity of this outcome. The above is only half the story because the Dutch youth labour market has been changing fundamentally in recent decades and has become split into two segments because of the country's uniquely high overlap between education and the labour market. Out of almost 2 million young people in 2009, two-thirds or 1.35 million held a job; some 560,000 of those jobs were for fewer than 12 hours per week, and many were micro jobs (4 hours or less). At the same time, 1.46 million young people were in education, with close to two-thirds or 920,000 of them holding a job. Putting the two together, also close to two-thirds of all 1.35 million youth jobs are held by persons who are simultaneously still in education. This overlap covers virtually all small jobs: 540,000 out of the above 560,000 for all youths. These small jobs comprise more than 40 per cent of all youth employment. This is clearly not a labour market of any interest to school-leavers who go looking for a career nor to the majority of 100,000 unemployed youths who aim to find a job of 35 hours or more. The first implication is that the common calculation of the youth unemployment rate as the number of employed over all who are in employment, notably including the 40 per cent who are simultaneously in education and a small job, leads to a strong underestimation of the unemployment problems of youth. If the 40 per cent were left aside the youth unemployment rate would be found at a much more serious level of 13–14 per cent instead of the official figure just below 8 per cent. It is important to note, in addition, that by far the majority (85–90 per cent) of the small jobs are in low-skill occupations. It is here that some sinister feedback occurs from one part of the youth labour market to the other. This has two aspects. First, most of the national total of low-skill jobs are now available in a small part-time format only which is utterly unattractive for low-skill school-leavers who (have to) try to start a professional career in low-skill jobs. Second, there is strong competition for those jobs from a better educated labour supply (the above students but also second earners in a household) who are also eager to work part-time. This finds confirmation in an OECD finding for the non-student Dutch work force (aged 15–29): a good 30 per cent of which who work part-time do so involuntarily (OECD, 2010, Table C3.6; figures for 2007), which is seven times the average. Another illustration is that the involuntary part-time share among the Dutch low-educated non-student work force (12 per cent) is more than twice the corresponding OECD average and that the Netherlands has the lowest employment rate among this category (67 per cent as against an OECD average of 77 per cent).

Thus, the severe cut in full-time jobs for young people poses a major problem for them. Two recent policy measures are reinforcing this. First, the government effectively stimulates small-job growth as it has recently freed employers from paying social contributions on earnings up to a level of about 60 per cent of the youth minimum wage.[25] Second, young people have been stimulated by youth unemployment policy to remain in school for another year; as students they may swell the ranks of labour supply interested in the small jobs (see second case study).

The decline in youth employment does not necessarily equate to dismissals. The number of dismissals since 2008Q2 has been substantial: witness the 88,000 youth inflows into unemployment benefit.[26] This amounts to 7 per cent of the number of all young employees, but if we disregard again

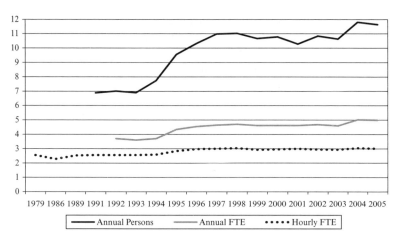

Source: See Table 9.6.

*Figure 9.8   9th–1st decile ratio for wage earnings, different approaches,
               Netherlands, 1979–2005*

the 40 per cent of small jobs discussed above the dismissal percentage
rises to 11 per cent, which is virtually identical to that of older workers.
In other words, young workers have been fired as often as the rest of the
work force. Of these dismissed youths, only a minority (40 per cent) left
unemployment benefit for a new job, surprisingly less than the 50 per cent
for older workers.

4.3   Wage Dispersion: Delaying Inequality Growth?

The effects of boom and bust on earnings inequality are as important as
those on employment. Naturally, the ultimate test of the effects would
be in the inequality of household incomes. To be sure, wage earnings are
the most important component for most households, but it falls outside
the present focus on the effects in the world of work to consider these
incomes.

A severe handicap in determining earnings effects is that no recent data
are available beyond 2005, let alone quarterly instead of annual data, and
that the data are also of lower quality than for employment.[27] It is important to consider, first, the definition of earnings for which inequality is
measured as results vary widely between definitions. Closest to household
incomes is total take-home pay over a year. This type of earnings shows
a very high inequality, with a 9th–1st decile ratio close to 12 in 2004 and
2005 and a steep rise from a level of around 7 in the early 1990s (Figure

9.8: Annual persons) which, however, partly reflects a break in the series. However, these annual earnings combine three effects: the hourly wage, the number of hours worked in a week, and the part of the year persons have worked. As a result, it incorporates to a considerable extent workers' voluntary choices of the number of weekly working hours and of the time in the year of labour market entry or exit.[28]

The level of inequality is much lower if we account for persons' weekly hours (annual FTE): the D9:D1 ratio is now around 5 in 2005. Part-time jobs are responsible for the large difference. This reflects their strong concentration at the lower end of the earnings distribution. For annual FTE earnings the increase in the inequality ratio over time is also more modest, up from 3.6 in the mid-1990s.

Correction for the third effect, which is that people may have earnings for only part of the year, follows from the distribution of hourly earnings: hourly FTE. The D9:D1 ratio is now lowered to a level of 3 in 2004–2005. Hourly FTE seems to be the best indicator of 'pure' wage inequality to the extent that it reflects exclusively the employer–employee wage negotiations and leaves out the choice of working hours. The availability of this indicator also enables covering the deep recession of the early 1980s. At first sight, its evolution shows comparatively little movement, neither up nor down. A closer look, however, reveals remarkable fluctuations. In particular, the D9:D1 inequality ratio fell by more than 10 per cent between 1979 and 1986, from 2.55 to 2.28,[29] a fall that exceeded any later decline. Interestingly, this occurred during the severe recession of the early 1980s and there seems to be something that we can learn for the current recession.

Opposite movements at bottom (upward) and the top (downward) of the earnings distribution together have lowered that inequality ratio. The opposing movements are the result of both labour market change and policymaking. Table 9.6 dissects the change along two dimensions: full-time versus part-time employment and public versus private sector, respectively.[30] The former affects primarily the bottom of the distribution. The share of part-time jobs in FTE employment increased by half between 1979 and 1986, from 9 per cent to 14 per cent, and this growth was strongly concentrated in the lower earnings bands. Its share in the earnings band of less than 5 euros per hour more than doubled, from 15 per cent to 32 per cent. The increased presence of part-time jobs with fewer hours implies that a smaller percentage of all hours worked are low paid. As a result, the bottom moves up and earnings inequality declines. Separate data show the low ranking of the additional part-time jobs (Panel A.1) in the earnings distribution. Their deciles fell substantially and the dispersion widened, in sharp contrast to full-time workers (Panel A.2). The change after 1979 – at the time the incidence of part-time employment was still limited – started

Table 9.6   FTE* hourly earnings: decile levels and decile ratios in parts of the economy, Netherlands, 1979 and 1986 compared

A. Decile levels (euros per hour)				B. Decile ratios			
	1979	1986	Change** (%)		1979	1986	Change (%)
A. Total, excluding agriculture***							
D1	4.30	5.48	−4	D9:D1	2.55	2.28	−11
D5	6.56	7.86	−9	D9:D5	1.68	1.59	−5
D9	10.99	12.50	−14	D5:D1	1.52	1.43	−6
A.1 Part-time							
D1	3.83	3.72	−26	D9:D1	2.47	2.74	11
D5	5.21	5.74	−17	D9:D5	1.81	1.78	−2
D9	9.45	10.20	−18	D5:D1	1.36	1.54	13
A.2 Full-time							
D1	4.38	5.93	2	D9:D1	2.53	2.74	−15
D5	6.18	8.06	−1	D9:D5	1.80	1.78	−12
D9	11.09	12.67	−13	D5:D1	1.41	1.54	−3
B. Private sector, excluding agriculture							
D1	4.06	5.08	−5	D9:D1	2.49	2.44	−2
D5	6.34	7.85	−6	D9:D5	1.59	1.58	−1
D9	10.11	12.37	−7	D5:D1	1.56	1.55	−1
C. Public sector: government, education, health care and social services							
D1	4.66	5.62	−8	D9:D1	2.58	2.26	−12
D5	7.19	7.89	−17	D9:D5	1.67	1.61	−4
D9	12.03	12.72	−20	D5:D1	1.54	1.40	−9

Notes:
* FTE approximated with rule of thumb as full-time numbers plus half of part-time numbers.
** Real change after deflation (32 per cent). A caveat is that D9 values above 25 (1979) and 26 (1986) are in the top band, which is supposed to have a width of 5 and 6 for 1979 and 1986, respectively.
*** Data underlying Figure 9.8 exclude agriculture for 1979, but include it for other years.

Source: Author's calculations on CBS, JLO and EWL statistics.

a general trend of a growing overlap between low-wage jobs and part-time jobs. Salverda (2008a, Figure 2.9) shows that, in 1979, 24 per cent of low-wage[31] jobs were part-time, which contrasts with 70 per cent in 2005. The shift towards part-time jobs during the financial crisis may have further boosted that trend.

By contrast, the public/private dimension is important for the top of the earnings distribution as public servants are overrepresented there, mainly because of their higher level of education. Government policies vis-à-vis the pay of employees in the broad public sector (government, education and health care) have exerted downward pressure on pay. In 1984, in the wake of the Wassenaar Agreement and long after the start of the 1980s recession, public employees' pay was nominally lowered by 3 per cent and frozen for most of the remainder of the 1980s.[32] Although the measure was uniform for all wage levels, it affected higher earnings more strongly because of the concentration of (well-educated) workers (Panel C). At the same time, wage inequality in the private sector (Panel B) hardly changed as real wages at all levels fell to a similar extent. As a result, the aggregate decline in earnings inequality (Panel A) is largely due to the changing treatment of the public sector.

After 1986, wage inequality rapidly returned to its initial level (Figure 9.8) but, unfortunately, that reversion cannot be decomposed similarly. In subsequent years, the inequality of hourly FTE wages again tended to decline somewhat in the initial stage of recessions (1991–1993, 2001–2003) but the declines were slight and always followed by new increases. The inference that can be drawn is that government pay policy can compress earnings inequality significantly. In many European countries including the Netherlands a freezing or lowering of public-sector pay is part of the austerity plans being developed and implemented. The compression of inequality seems an artificial effect which in due course may either be corrected by pay increases or lead to problems of labour supply to the public sector as competitive conditions deteriorate relative to the private sector.

5. CASE STUDIES

Two case studies provide an in-depth illustration of the current crisis and policymaking. First, I consider the role of the partial unemployment benefit. Second, I focus attention on the overlap between employment and education for youths, which is highly developed in the Netherlands and may help explain the relatively modest increase in unemployment during the financial crisis.

5.1 Partial Unemployment Benefit – Effective, but Mainly for Adult Men

5.1.1 General measures to reduce working hours
Several provisions can enhance the flexibility of working hours and may have contributed to mitigating the increase in observed unemployment.

First, full-time hours can be shifted to part-time.[33] The long-run trend of the shift and its acceleration during the financial crisis were highlighted above. Second, overtime hours can be reduced – unfortunately, no statistical data have been available since 2005. Third, individual working hours can be adapted with the help of personal working time accounts in the firm: during slack periods, people use the time savings accumulated from working more hours during the boom. Quantitative information is lacking for the Netherlands. Finally, a new option of partial unemployment benefit was (re-)introduced by the government in 2008/2009 under pressure from unions and employers – and will now end in July 2011. This new option is the focus of this first case study.

5.1.2 New part-time unemployment benefit

The sudden onset of the financial crisis led to a heated public debate in autumn 2008 involving the social partners, who urged the government to establish, first, a temporary Special Regulation (December 2008–March 2009) and then, in April 2009, the more general Ministerial Order for Part-time Unemployment Benefit for Retaining Skilled Employees. The justification was the retaining of skilled workers whose departure would damage a firm's prospects and investments in human capital. A similar measure had been in existence since 1945 and was very popular during the first two recessions: the ratio of applications relative to full dismissals reached an impressive 65 per cent in 1975 (180,000 applications) and 30 per cent in 1981 (100,000). However, admission conditions were drastically tightened in 1984, ruling out normal business risk. Problems were now defined as calamities surpassing normal business risk or an unusual accumulation of different types of business risks. Since 1984, the ratio to dismissals has hovered below 7 per cent – still showing some effect of the economic cycle (1993, 2001). In 2004, the rules were made more uniform but no application data have been available since then. Thus the new measures filled a gap.

According to the measure of April 2009, an employee's hours could be cut by a maximum of 50 per cent, which would then make the employee eligible for unemployment benefit. The employer was obliged to retain the employment relationship after expiry of the benefit for one-third of the weeks that the benefit had lasted, with a minimum of 13. He also had to provide training to the workers involved during the time of the benefit. Admission could be requested for a maximum of 13 weeks, and extended twice for 26 weeks each time, up to a maximum of 65 weeks.

The total use of the first measure, the Special Regulation of November 2008, concerned 850 firms and amounted to 1.5 million weekly hours or 40,000 full-time equivalents, twice as much as originally intended. The

Table 9.7 Applications of partial unemployment benefit by age and gender, Netherlands, 2009 and 2010

	2009-2*	2009-3	2010-1	2010-2	Total
Total number	34,095	19,154	14,072	4,132	71,453
Ratio to dismissals (%)					
Total	25.2	12.2	9.0	3.5	12.6
15–24	9.2	4.5	7.8	15.4	8.6
25–34	18.4	8.7	6.6	12.0	11.1
35–44	29.8	14.0	9.2	15.7	16.9
45–54	33.6	16.9	10.4	17.0	19.1
55–57.5	33.6	17.9	11.1	18.3	19.7
57.5+	30.5	15.7	14.0	21.4	19.8
Men	36.0	17.2	13.1	23.6	21.8
Women	10.1	5.0	2.4	4.5	5.4

Note: * Four-month periods.

Source: Derived from UWV, Kwantitatieve informatie (Viermaandsstatistieken), various issues.

intended spending will have doubled too, to 400 million euros. Almost half of the use concerned extensions of initial applications (in 325 firms) up to a maximum of 30 weeks. The number of firms that applied for the Ministerial Order of April 2009 was much larger and amounted to 6,700 up to April 2010 (Chkalova, 2010: 18).

For that second measure, Table 9.7 pictures the aggregate inflows. Close to 1 billion euros was spent on the benefits. It shows an immediate use of 34,000 full-time equivalents in the first period, differing little from the preceding Special Regulation. After the first phase, applications declined, although employment losses and dismissals grew. Thus, the bigger role for the second measure seems to rest primarily on its longer duration. On average, partial benefits amounted to 12.6 per cent of dismissal benefits. This concerns individual employees who may at best use the partial benefits for 50 per cent of their working time.

It is clear that the initial, short-lived effects of the two successive measures were comparable to the level reached during the 1980s crisis, but only relatively – as a ratio (25 per cent) to dismissal benefits – since the absolute number was only half as high. Also, the current eight high-application months are no match for the three-year period of 1981–1983. Evidently, current dismissal unemployment is also at half the level of the 1980s.[34]

Thus the absolute effect of the new measures seems modest. That conclusion was drawn by CPB (2009 and 2010) and especially by CPB directors van Ewijk and Teulings (2009: 121–123). However, for an adequate evaluation we need to go beyond the aggregate and account for the concentration of applications. These focused strongly on men in comparison to women, and older workers in comparison to young. For them, the mitigating effect on unemployment has been important, as shown by the ratio to dismissals. Those aged between 45 and 57.5 years attained a maximum ratio of one-third in the second four months of 2009. From other data,[35] it can be inferred that the older workers were mainly males: they made up 88 per cent of those aged 45 and over. This gives this group a ratio of benefits to dismissals of 26 per cent over the full year, and likely much higher during the initial phase of April–August 2009. Thus perhaps up to 40 per cent of older male unemployment was prevented during that period, and up to 25 per cent for younger men. On the employment side, assuming that older men work full-time, the partial benefit may have halved the decline in adult male full-time employment.[36] The effect for males contrasts sharply with that for women of all ages, where the effect may at best have been around 10 per cent. Larger firms were overrepresented in the first use, particularly in the metal and metalworking industry. One can speculate that by the time bigger firms began to perform better and small firms started to apply for the benefit the measure was terminated (cf. Chkalova 2010: 18).

Our first case study reported below concerns a larger metalworking firm, a typical participant in the measure. It indicates that – as long as the current economic upswing is maintained – the temporary measure has been fairly successful. It also illustrates the strong focus on older men found above. It makes clear that the training obligation was taken seriously and that this worked out to the benefit of both workers and firm.

The concentrated effect is fairly significant and is missed when only the aggregates are studied. Without it, the gender gap in labour market change would have been significantly more disadvantageous for men. At the same time, the strong focus on older men and the large role of bigger firms risks making the measure a form of labour hoarding tilted against female employees and small enterprises and making life more difficult for newcomers in the labour market – that is to say, in principle but probably not in practice, as otherwise the jobs concerned might have been lost entirely and not been available to newcomers. Clearly, the training effect also goes only so far and cannot be sustained indefinitely.

5.1.3   Partial unemployment benefits in a major truck-producing firm

The economic downturn took the firm entirely by surprise. Part of the explanation of that surprise must be sought in the fact that the firm is primarily a national assembly plant producing according to orders received from international headquarters, which have responsibility for sales. Thus, knowledge of market developments is absent at plant level. In early October 2008, the firm was planning an expansion of productive capacity, but less than two months later it had helped to lobby the government to introduce the Special Measure, and applied for virtually its entire permanent staff of up to 1,000 workers. Most applications were renewed twice under the official measure of April 2009. Some 80–100 employees were posted to other firms, and individual workers were taken out of the measure on a case-by-case basis, when needed.

The work force fully fits the category of older males, on whom applications have concentrated. The firm operates on a lean just-in-time basis, employing a considerable share of the work force on flexible contracts, hired through a temp agency office located at the plant. Not long before the start of the crisis, 60 of them had been offered a permanent position. Before December 2008, all 300–400 temp agency workers had been dismissed, although contacts with many were maintained with a view to rehiring.

This contrasts sharply with the situation at the time of the interviews. By then, operations were almost back to normal: the permanent staff had returned to working full-time and their original pay, while up to 600 temp agency workers had been hired, equivalent to one-third of the work force. Thus the partial benefit measure can be deemed a success for the temporary help it has offered to the firm, and the return of the employees to their jobs that it has enabled. It also improved the plant's competitive position for the flexible upsizing of production.

No permanent employees were dismissed, although a few found other jobs. All workers were deemed experts in the sense of the measure. They retained their employment relationship but paid a price nevertheless. The partial UI benefit would pay only 70 per cent of their basic salary for the working time lost. By agreement with the unions, this was supplemented by the firm up to 100 per cent. However, they did lose the 15 per cent shift allowance as production in two shifts terminated, and also the annual 13th-month bonus, while application of the wage increase stipulated in the collective labour agreement for the industry was postponed for a few months. The firm stopped existing subsidies for individual non-work-related training. A different type of cost to (older) workers was the need for training – they needed some convincing by, inter alia, the union.

On the firm side, significant costs were attached to the use of the measure. Immediately, in December 2008, the firm started a mobility centre to take care of the applications – all individual – and the administrative reporting of the activities undertaken, the posting of workers to

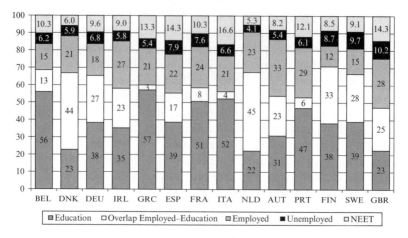

Source: Author's calculations from Eurostat, ELFS, and OECD, NEET statistics
(courtesy Thomas Manfredy).

*Figure 9.9   Youth (15–24 years) population by activity, 14 EU countries,
2007 (%)*

other firms, and the obligatory training of employees for whom benefit
was received. Training was indeed undertaken. Experienced workers
trained the less experienced and experiences were exchanged between the
two main types of work: logistics and assembly. Worker teams scrutinized
the set-up of the production process and suggested improvements, which
was considered an important advantage by the firm. Another advantage
accruing to the firm was improved access to the joint industry training
fund that subsidized some of the training. The firm also benefited from a
first-mover advantage. Being in the vanguard of the new measure it could
exert some influence on the measure's precise organization and it was
also ahead in the timely posting of workers. Finally, the firm also saved
on costs by cutting outsourcing and some of the work was insourced and
done by its own employees.[37]

5.2   Young People in Education and/or Employment: To Overlap or Not

5.2.1   Netherlands characterized by significant overlapping

As we have already seen, there is a substantial overlap for Dutch young
people between two different states: participating in education, on the one
hand, and being in employment, on the other. At 45 per cent of the young
population as a whole, this overlap is larger than in any other EU country,
although Denmark comes close (Figure 9.9). Despite this high level, the

overlap has kept increasing substantially in recent years, up from a level of 32 per cent in 1998. As already observed, the overlap largely concerns small jobs of up to 12 hours per week.

5.2.2 In the crisis, attempts to keep young people in education

The overlap suggests the possibility of significant coming-and-going between the two states, which may mitigate the severity of employment declines for young people as a result of the financial crisis. Certainly, the government has decided that it is a good idea to keep young people – below the age of 27[38] – in education longer. In spring 2009, when youth unemployment policy made a comeback on the policy agenda, the School Ex programme was started as part of the Action Plan Youth Unemployment. The programme aimed, first, to lure 10,000 fresh graduates of senior secondary vocational education (MBO) into staying in education for another year so as to improve their chances in the labour market. Second, graduates who turned down the offer would receive individual support from the employment office UWV for finding a job if they did not already have one. The government made available a significant subsidy of 200 million euros. Four questions can be asked: Did pupils actually stay? If so, was this due to the policy initiative? If so, was the additional year worth the while of these young people in terms of learning? Finally, what is the wider effect of this education policy?

5.2.3 Mixed results

To assist the policy, MBO schools surveyed their graduates, offering them the opportunity to stay on longer. In 2009, under great time pressure, 72,000 were reached and, at first glance, the target of 10,000 additional students was reached, as 15 per cent of the surveyed decided to stay. A government evaluation in October 2009 was positive (OCW, 2010).[39] However, more recent statistical data cast some doubt on the effect. The total number of pupils in MBO did grow by 10,000 (514,000 → 524,000) between 2008 and 2009, but only 3,600 were in the target age range below 27 years, while the remainder were above.[40] Naturally, that does not do away with the effect for the latter group, but that was not the purpose of the policy.[41]

Was the increase in fact due to the policy? In a historical perspective, this may be doubted. First, in times of higher unemployment young people have always decided to remain in education (Figure 9.10[42]). The current shift lags far behind previous occasions in the 1980s, 1990s and 2000s. Also more directly, the share of the young population participating in MBO rose in 2006 and 2007, but did not in 2009.[43]

For the third issue, our case study below of a school illustrates the learning effect.

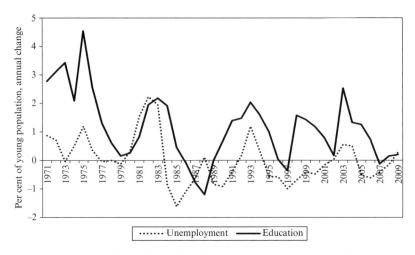

Source: Author's calculation from CBS, full-time education, population and registered unemployment statistics.

Figure 9.10   Participation in education (15–19 years) and unemployment–population ratio (15–24 years), annual changes in percentage points of respective population, Netherlands, 1971–2009

5.2.4   Example of School Ex programme at a major school of secondary vocational education[44]

The school, with some 26,000 students, aims to offer an attractive programme of education in competition with similar schools in the same part of the country. It has participated in the School Ex programme from the start. The programme's primary activity of asking students who just graduated to stay for another year or, alternatively, to agree to establishing contact with the public employment service for personal labour market advice, was organized at the national level. The school cooperated only as a conduit for implementing this.

No special programmes were developed for the stayers to follow. No need was seen for that as students who graduate from levels 1, 2 or 3 can continue within the existing programme, while those graduating at level 4 are expected to continue at the tertiary level at a polytechnic – if they choose to continue.

The school has not seen an increase in the number of students at MBO. It sees a shift, however, under the influence of the financial crisis from the enterprise-based type of vocational secondary education (BBL) towards the school-based type (BOL), and on a full-time basis. Part of the explanation is more structural as a higher status is attached to BOL, particularly by minority students. At the same time given labour market developments in recent years the effects of discrimination on minority pupils in BBL and graduates looking for employment have structurally diminished in the school's view.

The stagnating number of students implies that the additional funding promised by the government is also stagnating. The school is convinced that the part of the financial means originally promised for 2010–2011 will not be forthcoming.

The most important messages are that student numbers did not grow and no special programmes were introduced. The latter is not a problem for the young who decide to stay at their own initiative, as pictured in Figure 9.10, but one might expect more from a special policy measure aimed at convincing young people to study further.

5.2.5   Education policy: Wider effects

This leads us to answer our fourth question: what are the wider effects of this education policy? First and foremost, the downward effect on youth unemployment is largely once-only and concentrated in the first year. After that, each new cohort will replace the preceding one. In practice, the focus on the role of MBO schools tends to hide problems in BBL, which is part of the same secondary vocational educational system. Indeed, pupils below the age of 27 numbered almost 6,000 fewer in BBL in 2009 in comparison to 2008.[45] Third, the approach may reinforce diploma inflation and competition in the low-skill labour market, as there are more students who take an interest in small jobs. This can put pressure on the employment of the low-skilled and increase their unemployment rate, and also on the participation of young people in low-skill education as they become aware of the increasingly depressed prospects after finishing school. Both seem to have happened in 2009: the employment ratio fell by 5.0 percentage points, of which 2.1 percentage points were in the overlap with education; the participation rate in secondary education declined (–0.3 percentage points); the unemployment ratio crept up only slightly (data from de Jong et al. 2010). As a result, the main change was a 1.5 percentage points increase in the NEET share, up from 7 to 8.5 per cent. In other words, there is significant discouragement of young people, to which the stimulus of MBO participation has been unable to provide the answer.

6.   CONCLUSIONS

The overarching question is how the financial crisis compares to previous recessions – whether 'this time is really different' – and what that implies for inequalities arising in and from the world of work. Apparently, this might mean that in the current crisis economic recession or labour market decline, or both, differ from previous occasions, or from what might have been expected for the one or the other on the basis of previous experience. The obvious disparity in abruptness and depth in comparison to the dotcom crisis caused us to extend the comparison to include the three preceding recessions of the 1970s, 1980s and 1990s. The evolution of (deflated) investment instead of GDP was taken as the starting point – on a per capita basis as population growth has diminished radically. Both choices were borne out by the study: the evolution of investment mirrors the depth and duration of labour market problems much better than GDP, and the financial crisis resembles the crisis of the 1980s much more closely than the dotcom crisis of the early 2000s. GDP and investment fell as much as before, and at a much faster pace. At the same time, important economic differences were found, to the disadvantage of the financial crisis: prices tended towards deflation, international trade suffered and savings got a battering as never before. Only a faster-than-ever increase in government consumption prevented disaster.

The examination of labour market differences was more complex. Of prime importance is the divergence between the number of persons in work and the number of hours worked (FTE). Two years into the crisis – from the second quarter of 2008 to that of 2010 – the number in work has declined only a little (−1 per cent), which might explain the popular feeling that the effects of the crisis are benign, but hours of work have decreased by more than 5 per cent, equalling the 1980s recession. The relative increase in the number of unemployed persons per capita has exceeded that of the 1980s, but as this started from a very low level the unemployment rate still seems surprisingly low. In particular, full-time employment fell while part-time employment increased, reinforcing a long-term trend. The effect of the full-time to part-time shift was complemented by the increasing contractual flexibility of the work force and the (temporary) introduction of partial unemployment benefit aimed at retaining people in employment, although the aggregate effect was modest. Dutch FTE employment trends resembled the American and the British more than the German or the French.

On the earnings side, the Dutch tradition of wage moderation stumbled over the very abrupt economic decline. Initially, the increase in real wages was higher than it had been for many years and a strong rise in unit labour costs was a major difference in relation to previous recessions.

For the effects on inequalities a distinction was made between employment chances and earnings outcomes. The former showed strong divergences by age and gender, and a concomitant divergence by full-time and part-time jobs. The moderate decline in the aggregate employment rate and labour-force participation rate hides a strong decline for young people and a significant increase for older workers, with a smaller decline for the prime-age group in between. In particular, up to 25 per cent of low- and medium-educated young workers lost their full-time jobs. The high overlap between education and employment that is the hallmark of the Dutch youth labour market shrank as employment fell and education stalled. On balance, young people withdrew from education, training and employment into inactivity in 2009. Minorities suffered more than anyone else and showed significant withdrawals from the labour market into non-participation. Educational differences are clearly visible in that the low, medium and high skilled all suffered a decline in full-time employment numbers while only the medium and high skilled found some compensation in rising part-time numbers. However, the negative effects on hours worked were more similar between the three levels because of the shift towards fewer hours on the job.

The scrutiny of effects on earnings inequality had to overcome major data problems. Focusing on the full-time equivalent-based dispersion of hourly earnings the tentative conclusion is that the initial effect of recessions is to reduce inequality, but only modestly and temporarily. During the 1980s recession, the decline in inequality was significantly reinforced by the government policy of lowering public-sector pay. This may tell us a lesson for the current situation where many countries implement or ponder austerity plans including strong reductions in pay – the Netherlands was virtually alone in this respect in the 1980s.

The second year of the crisis has improved little on the first. The decline in hours worked was unchanged. Improvements may be temporary, as has been the case before during recessions. Given the excessive fall in investment and the threat of austerity policies, which will take away the government spending that just saved the economy, there is little room for optimism about the future of economy and employment. This will tend to reinforce age and gender differences and further diminish the role of full-time jobs. However, if austerity policy also succeeds in putting pressure on public-sector pay, earnings inequality may be artificially reduced in the aggregate and the short run, but, as the 1980s can teach us, probably not in the private sector.

NOTES

1. CBS (2010: 7).
2. That job growth lags behind population growth is currently a matter of great political concern in the US.
3. Apart from population and productivity growth.
4. Naturally, peak-to-trough information still has an importance of its own and will also be accounted for below.
5. Compare, for example, *Financial Times* (7/12/2010) on unabated corporate reluctance to invest.
6. Private non-residential gross fixed capital formation.
7. See note 1. The decline is 4.1 per cent on a per capita basis.
8. Note that I generally use the OECD Economic Outlook database (No. 87 of May 2010) because no full set of quarterly economic data is available from CBS before 2001 and in order to enhance international comparability. Only the data for the current crisis are from CBS, as they are more up-to-date and enable coverage up to the second quarter of 2010 – two full years into the financial crisis. If data are not available with seasonal correction, corresponding quarters will be compared to mitigate seasonal effects. These effects are finally established only at the end of the calendar year, implying that the adjustments for 2010 are still provisional. More detail (particularly for Tables 9.1 and 9.2) is available in Salverda (2011).
9. Note, however, that investment is a much smaller quantity than GDP and statistically sensitive to individual large-scale investments, which may account for some of the quarterly volatility.
10. After correction for re-exports which, in volume terms, have grown from one quarter of exports and imports in 1996 to about half now.
11. One part of the much discussed global imbalances in trade and production.
12. 'Germany on a Roll', *Financial Times*, 15 August 2010.
13. The hours-count employment rate is defined on a full-time equivalent FTE basis, one FTE being equal to 1,840 hours of work annually, or 35 hours per week; it can be considered a standardized definition of full-time work.
14. Based on the legal definition of the full-time labour contract. Derived from CBS *Labour Accounts*, assuming that before 1987 all full-time jobs were statistically observed and that no full-time worker holds a second job.
15. Part-time is defined here not contractually but as less than 35 hours of work per week.
16. People increasingly hold a second job: 44 per cent or 200,000 more now than at the start of the century. The share has remained unchanged, at 7.5 per cent or one in every 14 employees, over the past two years.
17. The number of full-time job seekers grew by 143 per cent, while full-time employment fell by 5 per cent over 2001Q1–2005Q1 (Dutch LFS).
18. Salverda (2009) discusses the role of CPB forecasts in Dutch wage bargaining.
19. For example, in May 2008 the CPB predicted GDP growth for 2009 at +1.75 per cent but this turned out to be −4 per cent, close to a 6 percentage-point difference.
20. CBS/Statline, Nationale Enquête Arbeidsomstandigheden. Based on a workplace survey by TNO.
21. One implication is that, as a result of sorting, the present low skilled may be a very different sample from the large numbers present at the beginning of the period covered here.
22. FTE figures are a rough approximation using the mid-points of four hours-bands. Declines can result from both lower employment rates and a compositional shift towards lower bands, including between the three bands of part-time jobs ranging from less than 12 hours per week to 20–35 hours.
23. Note the definitional difference from nationality: minorities include the next, Dutch-born generation of immigrants.
24. In 2009 25 per cent of working-age non-western minorities were aged 15 to 25 and

almost 50 per cent were low skilled, while roughly 15 per cent of all youths or low skilled were non-western minorities.

25. Small-jobs Ruling, introduced for 2010 and extended to 2011.
26. Part-time dismissal also entitles people to unemployment benefit, so not all inflows necessarily represent full dismissals.
27. The earnings presented here had to be derived from tabulated data, applying linear interpolation in earnings bands and capping the upper band, and using means of bands of working hours for arriving at FTE measures. Results should be interpreted with care. Even more so, because of a series break around 1995 which, unfortunately, cannot be pinned down exactly but has primarily expanded coverage of low-paid, small part-time jobs and thus increased dispersion (especially for head-count) and may be responsible for a significant part of the increase between 1994 and 1997 (Figure 9.8).
28. In principle, also labour market exit, but that is not applicable as people are mostly observed to be in work at a particular moment in time.
29. Correcting for the non-coverage of the agricultural sector in 1979.
30. See Salverda (1998) for a more general analysis attributing changes in inequality between 1979, 1985 and 1989 to changes in pay differentials and other effects, including employment composition, and making a comparison to US evolution.
31. Following the OECD and EU definition as below two-thirds of the median hourly wage.
32. Note that this concerned pay scales in collective agreements; individual pay could still rise because of seniority in the scales.
33. Employees can receive part-time unemployment benefit as a normal UI option for given for a part-time dismissal without return to the same employer. It is confusing that the measure studied here is called part-time UI in Dutch instead of partial.
34. Note that an important reason for the much lower inflows is the dramatic reduction of entitlements for young workers. Their inflows fell from an annual average of 136,000 over 1987–1996, with a maximum of 160,000 in 1993–1994, to 47,000 over 1997–2009, with a maximum of 60,000 in 2003–2004.
35. Chkalova (2010) presents cross-tabulated data with a somewhat different age break-down over the full year April 2009 to March 2010.
36. Assuming respondents consider their partial benefit as temporary and mention their full-time hours as 'usual' working hours, which is the question asked for determining full-time employment in the ELFS.
37. Interviews with firm and union officials in September–October 2010 are gratefully acknowledged.
38. Recently, this age threshold was adopted in a law obliging young people to be either in employment, an apprenticeship or education.
39. Datawise, it is too early to pin down whether it was fresh graduates who stayed; evaluation has to make do with the total number of pupils. Also, we do not know whether they actually finished the full additional year of education.
40. CBS/Statline, MBO deelnemers naar leeftijd. The number remained unchanged as a percentage of the relevant population.
41. The new government intends to discontinue paying for the education in MBO of those aged 30 and over, who now number 60,000 (a figure which is rapidly increasing).
42. The correlation is $y = 0.7333x + 1.1466$ (y education, x unemployment; $R^2 = 0.2605$). This concerns all types of education, not only MBO.
43. By contrast participation in tertiary vocational education grew significantly.
44. Interview with members of the Board in November 2010 is gratefully acknowledged.
45. Consequently, the number in the relevant age range up to 27 years that were in the school part of the system did increase by 10,000.

BIBLIOGRAPHY

CBS (Statistics Netherlands) (2010) *De Nederlandse Economie 2009*. The Hague.
Chkalova, K. (2010) 'Deeltijd-WW in beeld', *Sociaal-economische Trends*, No. 3: 15–20. The Hague: CBS.
CPB (2009) *Macro-economische Verkenning 2010*. The Hague: CPB.
CPB (2010) *Centraal Economisch Plan 2010*. The Hague: CPB.
de Jong, W., P. van den Berg and M. Geerdinck (2010) *Tijdsbesteding van Jongeren: Historische reeks 2004–2009*. The Hague: CBS.
Krueger, A. and J.-S. Pischke (1997) 'Observations and Conjectures on the US Employment Miracle'. NBER working paper no. 6147. Cambridge MA.
OCW (2010) Letter of State Secretary Bijsterveldt to Parliament of 10 February. The Hague: Ministry of Education, Culture and Science.
OECD (2005) *Ageing and Employment Policies – the Netherlands*. Paris: OECD.
OECD (2010) *Education at a Glance 2010*. Paris: OECD.
TNO (2010) *NEA 2009: Vinger aande Pols van Werkend Nederlands*. Hoofddorp: TNO.
Salverda, W. (1992) *Youth Unemployment; Dynamics of the Dutch Labour Market 1955–1988*. Groningen: Wolters Noordhoff.
Salverda, W. (1998) 'Incidence and Evolution of Low-wage Employment in the Netherlands and the United States 1979–1989', in S. Bazen, M. Gregory and W. Salverda (eds), *Low-Wage Employment in Europe*, 25–62. Cheltenham, UK and Northampton, MA, USA: Edward Elgar.
Salverda, W. (2008a) 'Low-wage Work and the Economy', in W. Salverda, M. Van Klaveren and M. Van der Meer (eds), *Low-Wage Work in The Netherlands*, 32–62. New York: Russell Sage.
Salverda, W. (2008b) 'Labor Market Institutions, Low-Wage Work, and Job Quality', in W. Salverda, M. Van Klaveren and M. Van der Meer (eds), *Low-Wage Work in The Netherlands*, 63–131. New York: Russell Sage.
Salverda, W. (2009) 'The Bite and Effects of Wage Bargaining in the Netherlands 1995–2005', in M. Keune and B. Galgóczi (eds), *Wages and Wage Bargaining in Europe: Developments since the mid-1990s*, 225–254. Brussels: ETUI.
Salverda, W. (2010) 'The Dutch Minimum Wage: Minimum Wage Fall Shifts Focus to Part-time Jobs', in Daniel Vaughan-Whitehead (ed.), *The Minimum Wage Revisited in the Enlarged EU: Issues and Challenges*, 229–339. Cheltenham, UK and Northampton, MA, USA: Edward Elgar.
Salverda, W. (2011) 'This Time is Different?! The Depth of the Financial Crisis and its Effects in the Netherlands', Working Paper, Amsterdam Institute for Advanced Labour Studies. Available at: www.uva-aias.net.
Salverda, W., B. Nolan, B. Maitre and P. Mühlau (2001) *Benchmarking Low-Wage and High-Wage Employment in Europe and the United States*. Report to the European Commission DG Employment and Social Affairs. Available at: http://www.uva-aias.net/uploaded_files/regular/draftdef0-1-1.pdf.
van Ewijk, C. and C. Teulings (2009) *De Grote Recessie. Het Centraal Planbureau over de kredietcrisis*. Amsterdam: Balans.

APPENDIX

Table 9A.1   Summary of 'anti-crisis' policy measures, the Netherlands, 2008–10

Assistance for the financial system	• Capital injections (at a return) to banks and insurance companies in the amount of 33 billion euros: ING Bank (10 billion), AEGON insurance (3 billion), SNS Reaal Bank (0.75 billion) and ABN AMRO/Fortis full takeover (17 + 2.5 billion) • State loans to ABN AMRO/Fortis: 34 billion euros short-term + 16 billion euros long-term • State coverage of part of US mortgage portfolio of ING Bank: the Illiquid Assets Back-up Facility (IABF): 24 billion euros • State guarantees (for a fee) for bank loans in capital markets: up to 200 billion euros available, actually used for issues of 50 billion euros (of varying maturities): ING 13 billion euros, Fortis 19 billion euros, SNS Reaal 4 billion euros (together 70% of the total) • Deposit guarantees on individual bank accounts increased from 40,000 euros to 100,000 euros per account (note that this is an obligatory guarantee provided by the collective of banks measured by their size, and not by the state)
Autonomous growth of government spending (see Table 9.2)	Composed of: automatic stabilizers (= social security – for UI financed from dissavings of the UI Fund), spending moratoriums (especially health care) and some investment
Special government spending related to the crisis	• Action plan for youth unemployment (see Section 5.2 for details and evaluation) • Special activation measures (0.75 billion euros over 3 years) • Partial unemployment benefit (see Section 5.1 for details) • Training: (i) temporary subsidy to employers of 50% of costs for individual workers up to a maximum of 2,500 euros for new hires after 1 January 2009, depending on the person's previous position; (ii) permission to receive unemployment benefit and training simultaneously • Intensification of unemployment mediation with the help of labour mobility centres • Stimulus to building trade: additional state investment and maintenance (0.64 billion euros over 2 years),

Table 9A.1   (continued)

VAT cut on maintenance, augmentation of mortgage guarantee from 265,000 euros to 350,000 euros, enhancement of income tax deductibility of mortgage interest

- Continuation of high-tech projects and retaining of knowledge workers (0.28 billion euros)
- Regulation on limited financial support for enterprise, up to 500,000 euros maximum, given as a subsidy
- Tax measures: temporary extension of corporate loss compensation from one to three years, augmentation of profit exemption for SMEs from 10 to 12%; exemption of employers' contributions for small jobs for up to 50% of youth minimum wage

10. From the highest employment growth to the deepest fall: Economic crisis and labour inequalities in Spain

Rafael Muñoz de Bustillo Llorente and José-Ignacio Antón Pérez

1. PECULIARITIES OF THE SPANISH ECONOMIC BOOM

The motto *Spain is different*, developed in the 1960s as a trademark of the then newborn national tourism industry, became for many decades – for better or worse – a good summary of one stereotype of Spanish society. Spain's democratization at the end of the 1970s, the late development of a welfare state (even if Mediterranean in nature) and accession to the EU in 1986 led to a process of economic and social change that was expected to turn Spain into a different nation, setting the country on a path of convergence with its European neighbours. But it seems that 30 years of change have not been enough to shake off the cliché that Spain is different. In fact, Spain displayed very different behaviour over the previous economic boom in comparison with the rest of the EU and, unfortunately, also very different behaviour in these times of crisis.

Figure 10.1 depicts the evolution of employment in Spain in comparison with the rest of the EU-15 and the EU-27. The numbers require little comment. While in 1998 Spain contributed 9 per cent of total EU employment, in none of the following years until 2006 did Spain's contribution to total EU employment growth fall below 20 per cent, reaching 46.5 per cent in 2004 (and averaging 30 per cent for the period 1998–2007).

The high employment creation of the Spanish economy during the boom years allowed for a considerable reduction in the unemployment rate, even in a context of high labour force growth due to the increase in the female labour force participation rate (from 37 per cent in 1996 to 66 per cent in 2009, an increase of 3.9 million) and an unprecedented rise

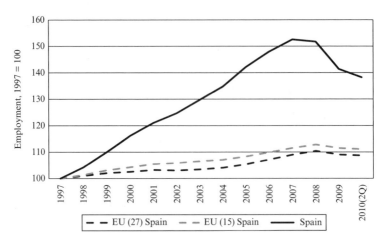

Source: Authors' analysis from European LFS.

*Figure 10.1   Evolution of employment in Spain vis-à-vis the EU,
1997–2010 (2nd quarter)*

in the immigration rate (Figure 10.2). In this respect, in a little under a
decade Spain changed from a country with almost no immigrants into a
country with immigration rates higher than classic immigration countries,
such as Germany, Belgium and the Netherlands.

Spanish economic growth relied heavily on the construction sector,
whose size in GDP terms rose from 7.2 per cent in 1997 to 12.1 per cent ten
years later, well above the EU average (6.2 per cent).[1] In fact, from 1996
to 2007, one out of every five jobs created in Spain was in the construction
sector. This element, along with a corporate culture of temporary employment (at the start of the crisis almost one-third of employment involved
temporary contracts), led in 2008 to the complete reversal of the picture
shown in Figure 10.2: while before the crisis Spain had a major role in
European employment growth, after 2008 Spain became the leading actor
in the European employment debacle (accounting for 29 per cent of the
EU employment losses from 2008/3 to 2009/3).

It is important to stress that, both during the boom and during the
crisis – but especially in the former – the special behaviour of the Spanish
economy is mainly related to the high elasticity of employment to changes
in GDP, and it is less related to the higher intensity of the Spanish recession in terms of lost GDP, because Spain has not suffered a particularly
intense recession in terms of GDP. In fact, in 2009 the fall in GDP in Spain
(–3.7 per cent) was lower than the EU average (–4.1 per cent). Cyprus,

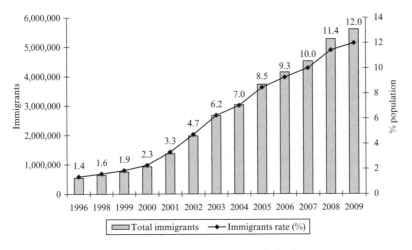

Source: Authors' analysis from local population registers in Spain.

Figure 10.2   *Foreign population in Spain, 1996–2009 (total and percentage of total population)*

Greece, France, Malta, Portugal, Belgium and Luxembourg have all experienced smaller GDP reductions (and Poland's GDP even increased in 2008–2009), while Germany (–4.7 per cent) and Ireland (–7.6 per cent) have been particularly hard hit. Nevertheless, the Spanish labour market has shown an astonishing capacity to shed redundant labour, reducing employment at a much faster pace than its European counterparts. The differences in GDP growth elasticity of employment (percentage change in employment divided by percentage change in real GDP) reproduced in Chapter 1 are eloquent testimony to this: the reaction in terms of employment lost for each percentage point of reduction in GDP was four times higher in Spain compared to the EU average.

The aim of this chapter is to review the main implications of the crisis in terms of inequalities in the Spanish labour market and society as a whole. In order to do so, in Section 2 we study how the crisis has affected workers in terms of unemployment, wages and income, and other working conditions. This section has a twofold goal: first, to see how the crisis has affected the employment and working conditions of different groups of workers; second, to explore whether there have been trade-offs between changes in different job characteristics and employment. In this respect, we can assert that, according to the aggregate data presented above, in macroeconomic terms Spain is a paradigmatic example of quantity adjustment as a strategy for coping with a reduction in demand. Section

3 presents a summary of economic policy measures, dealing also with the potential impact of the crisis in terms of future budget cuts to deal with the growing public deficit produced by the crisis and the role played by social dialogue in the management of the crisis and the post-crisis. To complement this analysis, in Section 4 we present two case studies of how the crisis has affected a specific sector and enterprise and its impact on the workers. Section 5 summarizes the major conclusions.

2. AREAS OF WORK MOST AFFECTED BY THE CRISIS

As already mentioned, employment reduction has been the major instrument of adjustment deployed by Spanish firms in the crisis, leading to a huge increase in the unemployment rate of 10 percentage points in two years: from 8 per cent in 2007 (third quarter) to 18 per cent two years later, stabilizing at around 20 per cent by the end of 2010. Nevertheless, it is important to keep in mind that, along with the dismissal of workers and the non-renewal of labour contracts, unemployment also increased due to the increase in the size of the labour force until the first quarter of 2009, when the crisis was well established in Spain. Altogether, the Spanish labour force grew by 0.7 million (equivalent to 3 percentage points of unemployment) after the start of the crisis.

Obviously, especially in Spain, the first source of inequality due to the crisis is related to the differential impact of unemployment among workers. But before analysing the distribution of unemployment it is important to put these numbers in the specific historical context of the Spanish labour market. We would like to focus here on two questions, illustrated by Figure 10.3 panels a and b. First, as we can see in Figure 10.3a, the high rates of unemployment experienced by the Spanish economy, while unusual in the EU context, are not unknown in Spain. In fact, the unemployment rate is still below the levels reached in the mid-1990s, particularly for women. Second (Figure 10.3b), the reduction of employment, as significant as it has been, has only brought the employment level of the Spanish economy back to the 2005 level. In terms of total employment rate (employment/total population), in the third quarter of 2009 the rate was 41.3 per cent, more than four points below the maximum reached in 2007 but still well above the 32 per cent of the mid-1990s. That is, from a historical perspective we can say that the employment level of the Spanish economy is still very high. It is also interesting that the destruction of employment due to the crisis, as important as it is, explains only 43 per cent of total unemployment in the first quarter of 2010. Another 9 per cent, as already mentioned,

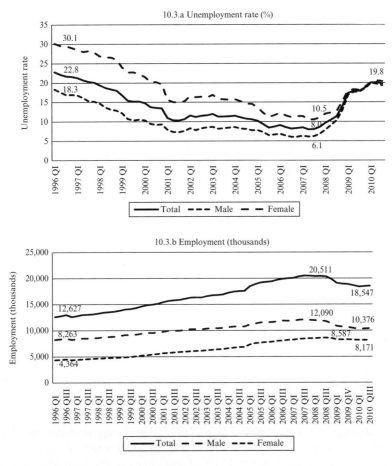

Source: Authors' analysis from Spanish LFS.

Figure 10.3   *Evolution of employment and unemployment rate by gender,*
            Spain, 1996–2010, 3rd quarter

is explained by the increase in the labour force during the period, while the
remaining and larger part – 47 per cent – is related to the unemployment
existing before the start of the crisis.

2.1   The Unequal Impact of the Crisis on Employment

Unemployment is a source of inequality in itself and an indirect source of
inequality in terms of present and future income. Although this last effect

Work inequalities in the crisis

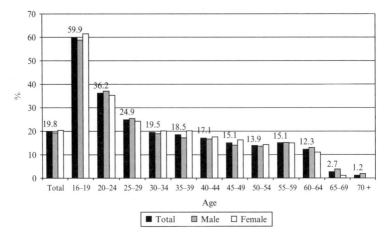

Source: Authors' analysis from Spanish LFS.

Figure 10.4   Unemployment rate by age, Spain, 2010 (3rd quarter)

can be mitigated, at least in the short term, by unemployment compensation, it has been well established by the social science, medical and psychological literature that the impact of unemployment on well-being goes far beyond its financial implications.[2]

The economic crisis has thrown some people into unemployment, while the majority have remained in work; this is obviously the most open inequality produced by the crisis. In the presence of a demand crisis, labour adjustment by firms often follows the last-in–first-out principle. This means that young workers have a higher risk of losing their jobs. Also, among workers with different kinds of labour contract – temporary versus open-ended, entailing different dismissal costs (lower in the former case) – the risk to temporary workers of losing their job is also higher. These two risk groups overlap to a considerable extent, as temporary contracts are much more common among young workers.

That is exactly what has happened in Spain. As can be seen in Figure 10.4, youth unemployment rates have skyrocketed, surpassing 20 per cent, the average for those aged 25–29, and 30 per cent for those aged 20–24. Nevertheless, that does not mean that unemployment in Spain has affected only young workers: in relative terms, the unemployment rates of all cohorts have grown at a similar pace, multiplying by 2.1 for those less affected (54–59 year olds) and 2.49 for those more affected (25–29 year olds).[3]

Being employed on a temporary contract, as argued in Muñoz de Bustillo (2007a), has proved to be a major risk factor. In aggregate terms, at the height of the crisis all the adjustment in employment has so far fallen upon temporary workers: from 2007 to 2009 (third quarter) temporary employment decreased by 1.34 million, while open-ended employment increased by more than 100,000, pushing the temporary rate down from 31.9 per cent to 25.9 per cent. Most of the adjustment fell on workers from 20 to 29 years old, who absorbed 75 per cent of the employment decrease.[4] Although the most recent phase of the crisis has also engulfed permanent workers in growing proportions, if we take the whole period of employment destruction finishing in the third quarter of 2010, 82 per cent of the employment adjustment fell on temporary workers.

In this context of employment destruction, and for the first time in modern history, the crisis has largely spared women's employment, at least in relative terms. As we can see in Figure 10.4, although female unemployment has increased, the female unemployment rate is now almost identical to the male unemployment rate. In fact, female employment has remained stable since the peak of the cycle in 2007, with a comparatively small reduction of less than 300,000 (13 per cent of total employment destruction). The increase in the female unemployment rate is largely the result of an increase in the female labour force participation rate.[5] This result can be explained by the differential impact of the economic crisis on economic sectors, as the recession has affected mostly construction (loss of one million jobs) and, to a lesser extent, industry (loss of 0.7 million jobs), traditionally male-dominated sectors.[6] In contrast, the service sector, which employs 85 per cent of Spanish women, has largely been spared by the crisis in terms of employment. From a different but related perspective, part-time employment – not very important in Spain but still comprising 12 per cent of total employment – has shown much greater resilience to the crisis. As part-time employment mostly involves women, this helps to explain the comparatively better performance of female workers.

Within the at-risk group of young workers, those with lower educational levels face a higher risk of unemployment and worse prospects for employment in the future. This is especially true of the group of early school leavers. In this respect Spain, with a rate of early school leavers of 31 per cent (the third largest in the EU, after Malta and Portugal, compared to an EU27 average of 16.4 per cent), faces a significant educational deficit, with major implications for the future working life of those affected. According to a recent analysis by Muñoz de Bustillo et al. (2009a), early school leavers have more difficulty getting their first job, experience a higher inactivity rate and receive lower wages (completing secondary education is associated with a 20 per cent earnings increase for men and 16 per cent for women). Furthermore, in the long term, early school leavers have a higher probability of being trapped in unemployment or low wage employment.

Finally, they have a lower probability of pursuing lifelong learning: therefore, the educational handicap of this group grows over time. It is worth pointing out that such a high rate of early school leaving is partly explained by the growth model based on low-skilled labour followed by the Spanish economy (a major determinant of the risk of leaving the school system early for boys is having a father working in construction).

The last vulnerable group of workers in terms of unemployment risk is the immigrant workforce. Once again, several risk factors converge in this group. First, they are highly concentrated in construction (39.7 per cent of male immigrants compared to 17.7 per cent of male nationals in 2008) and they have lower educational attainment (especially among young workers) and a higher probability of being on a temporary contract. Furthermore, according to our own analysis of the probability of being employed by country of origin, controlling for observable socio-demographic characteristics, immigrants face a lower probability of being employed (Antón et al. 2010). Although this lower probability of employment among immigrants is often explained by economists in terms of the non-transferability of immigrants' skills, we cannot rule out the existence of discrimination in the labour market against this population group, which has been proved to be significant in other contexts in Spain, such as the rental housing market (Bosch et al., 2010). In fact, the existence of discrimination in the labour market due to (among other reasons) workers' ethnicity was shown recently by Eurobarometer 71.2 (2009) in *Eurobarometer Survey on Poverty and Social Exclusion*. According to this source, 66 per cent of respondents in Spain consider that this type of discrimination is fairly or very widespread (compared to an EU average of 61 per cent). What is more important from the perspective of this book is that 74 per cent consider that the economic crisis will only exacerbate discrimination in the labour market on the basis of ethnic origin (57 per cent EU average). Spain is a fairly homogeneous country in terms of ethnicity (with the exception of the Roma community), and so discrimination in terms of ethnicity is explained almost entirely by workers' place of birth.

The high vulnerability of immigrants to the crisis is revealed by the existence of an important differential in the immigrant unemployment rate: 24 per cent among EU immigrants (mostly Romanian and Bulgarian) and 30 per cent among non-EU immigrants, compared to 15 per cent among nationals. Furthermore, the impact of the higher unemployment rate of immigrants on their well-being is much higher than in the case of locals for several reasons: (i) their often recent arrival in the country and their shorter employment record put them in a weaker position in terms of receiving unemployment benefits;[7] (ii) lack of (or lower) family income support; and (iii) lower savings, related both to the lower than average wages received

Table 10.1   Growth in the unemployment rate of different types of workers, Spain, 2007–2009

	Change (ppt)	3rd Quarter 2007	4th Quarter 2009	Change (%)
Immigrant women with elementary or basic education	14.5	15.3	29.8	94.8
Spanish women with elementary or basic education	11.3	13.3	24.6	85.0
Immigrant men with elementary or basic education	30.0	10.4	40.4	288.5
Spanish men with elementary or basic education	14.6	6.9	21.5	211.6
Immigrant women	11.9	14.1	26.0	84.4
Spanish women	8.1	9.8	17.9	82.7
Immigrant men	23.6	9.7	33.3	243.3
Spanish men	10.6	5.6	16.3	191.1
Young women with elementary or basic education	15.7	19.6	35.3	80.1
Young men with elementary or basic education	26.0	12.2	38.3	213.9
Women with elementary or basic education	11.7	13.6	25.3	86.0
Men with elementary or basic education	16.7	7.3	24.0	228.8
Women with elementary education	16.7	19.0	35.7	87.9
Men with elementary education	24.0	11.9	35.9	201.7
Women with higher education	3.7	6.1	9.8	60.7
Men with higher education	3.8	3.8	7.6	100.0
Women	8.5	10.5	19.1	81.9
Men	12.4	6.2	18.6	200.0
All	10.8	8.0	18.8	135.0

Source: Authors' analysis from LFS micro-data.

and to the remittances they send to their families back home. This can be seen in the higher loan default rate of foreigners (12.5 per cent) compared to nationals (1.6 per cent) (Banco de España, 2008), among other things.

To sum up the unequal impact of unemployment on different workers, we present in Table 10.1 the growth in the unemployment rate (in relative terms and in percentage points) from the start of the crisis to the fourth quarter of 2009 for different types of workers.

Work inequalities in the crisis

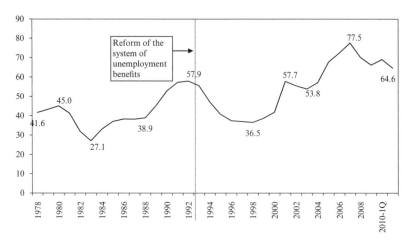

Source: Authors' analysis based on Spanish LFS and INEM.

*Figure 10.5   Percentage of unemployed workers receiving unemployment
            benefits, Spain, 1978–2010 (3rd quarter)*

Work is not only a way of earning a living, it is also a crucial part of life
itself and the main system of integration in society for men and women.
Therefore, it would be a simplification to reduce the impact of unemployment to its effects in terms of earnings. Nevertheless, that does not mean
that the implications of unemployment in terms of the reduction in income
are secondary to the worries of the unemployed and their families. Until
the crisis Spain had an unemployment protection system composed of
two pillars. The first is contributory in nature and protects all those previously employed for a minimum of 360 days. Its duration is related to
the employment record of the worker (from a minimum of 120 days to a
maximum of 720 days). Once used up, under certain circumstances unemployed workers might qualify for a second, less generous welfare scheme,
for a maximum of 18 months and a flat amount equivalent in 2009 to 67
per cent of the minimum wage. The enormous increase in unemployment
associated with the crisis, the lack of prospects of improvement in the
labour market in the short term and the corresponding increase in long-
term unemployment (43 per cent in the third quarter of 2010), led to the
ad hoc creation in August 2009 of a third flat-rate temporary pillar of 426
euros, available, under certain restrictions, to unemployed workers after
their right to the two first pillars of unemployment protection has ended.

In this respect, as we can see in Figure 10.5, the behaviour of the government and, subsequently, the coverage of unemployment benefits in

the present and the previous economic crisis of 1992, have been markedly different. While in 1992 the public authorities, confronted by an increase in the proportion of workers receiving unemployment benefits, opted to tighten the requirements for receiving such benefits, this time the response has been to extend the duration of benefits, although with a reduction in their amount. Furthermore, as the present crisis was preceded by a long period of employment growth, workers now face their potential or actual job losses with longer accumulated rights to unemployment benefits. This has allowed the government to maintain a comparatively high level of social protection among unemployed workers. From a gender perspective, the protection gap in favour of men at the beginning of the decade (in terms of a higher percentage of unemployed receiving unemployment benefit) has been greatly reduced, from 10 percentage points in 2000 to slightly more than 2 in 2010 (first semester).[8] The same applies to the gender gap in terms of the 'generosity' of the benefits, reduced in the same period from 20.8 per cent to 15.5 per cent (for the contributory tier).

This combination of high unemployment protection rate (much higher than in the previous crisis), high concentration of unemployment among young people, the late emancipation of Spanish youth and the higher employment density (once again compared to the previous crisis) explains the existence of a gap between the high growth in unemployment, the much lower growth in the number of households with all active workers unemployed and the still lower growth in the number of households with no income. In 2010, in 7.6 per cent of households all active workers were unemployed (at the other end of the spectrum, in 78 per cent of households all active workers were employed), but only 2.6 per cent of total households did not have any income whatsoever. It is interesting to note that, in 2007, when employment reached its all time maximum, the figure was 2.1 per cent. This means than the system of protection (public and private, intra-family) has, so far, reduced the social impact of the unemployment crisis. These data also point to the existence of an important duality in terms of the impact of the crisis: a large percentage of the population is largely unaffected (the 78 per cent of households in which all the active workers are employed) and a sizeable proportion, 7.6 per cent, in which all active members are unemployed.

From a different perspective, it is interesting to know where unemployment is located in terms of the distribution of income. Obviously, the social impact of unemployment will be different if it is concentrated in the lowest strata of the population in terms of income, with lower savings and lower chances of cross-insurance within the family unit, or in the upper-middle, upper-high classes. Unfortunately, this is a tricky question to answer, because as the newly unemployed see their income diminish, partially (if they receive unemployment benefits) or totally, they would automatically

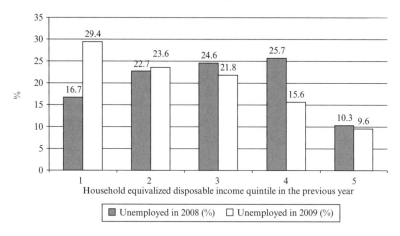

Source: Authors' analysis from SILC micro-data.

*Figure 10.6   Distribution of unemployment, by income quintile previous
            year, Spain, 2008 and 2009*

move to lower income deciles. In order to address this problem we have
calculated the distribution of unemployment in 2008 and 2009 by income
quintile in previous year (on condition that they were working in the previous year). Figure 10.6 displays the results of our analysis. In terms of quintiles, only around 10 per cent of the unemployed belonged to the upper 20
per cent income quintile, while the first and second quintiles accounted
for more than 50 per cent of total unemployment in the second year of the
crisis. In conclusion, the growth in unemployment seems to have affected
more the lower quintiles in terms of income distribution.

2.2   Changes in Working Time: Minimal Adjustments

Other possible strategies for adapting the workforce to lower demand
include working time reductions and work-sharing. This question is
especially relevant given that, in some countries, such as Germany,
such devices have already been introduced during the crisis, resulting
in minimum levels of job destruction (Bosch, 2010). The application of
these mechanisms usually involves a working time reduction, followed
by a pay reduction which is at least partially compensated by government subsidies. In this way, the impact of the crisis on the labour market
is shared by employers, employees and taxpayers.[9] In the case of Spain,
the large increase in unemployment seems to indicate that such strategies
have not been operating on the right scale. In order to formally assess

this issue, we have studied working time from a twofold perspective: first, using the Spanish Labour Force Survey, we have focused on the evolution of working time and overtime from the workers' point of view; second, by using a panel of firms (the Survey of Economic Trends – Encuesta de Coyuntura Laboral) we have monitored the behaviour of firms that have experienced a fall in activity levels during the crisis in terms of both employment and average working time per worker.

Focusing first on the workers' perspective, aggregate data (Table 10.2) show that both contractually agreed and standard weekly working hours have not undergone important changes since the beginning of the crisis, with changes of less than one hour a week. In turn, effective working hours have even increased slightly contrary to what happened in most other European countries (see Chapter 1). In addition, the dispersion – measured in terms of the standard deviation – does not suggest a relevant increase in the variability of working time arrangements. Finally, there is a reduction of 2 percentage points in the proportion of employees working overtime, although the share of workers in this situation is remarkably low (6.8 per cent at the peak of the boom).

The second, and perhaps the most interesting, perspective looks at the evolution of the relationship between working time and employment at the firm level. Using the Survey of Economic Trends – a quarterly panel of firms reporting, among other information, their employment figures – we focus on the most acute period of the crisis in terms of job losses (third quarter of 2008–fourth quarter of 2009) in order to sort out how those firms that have experienced a reduction in total working hours (which might be taken as a measure of the change in their level of economic activity) have behaved in terms of jobs and average working time per employee. The database comprises around 6,000 firms. In this respect, Figure 10.7 (panels a and b) shows, first, the relationship between the change in activity (proxied by the percentage variation of working hours at firm level) and the percentage variation of the number of employees of the firm and, second, the relationship between the percentage variation of the former variable and the percentage variation of weekly working hours per worker at firm level. Both relationships, which are computed at firm level, suggest that, on average and in most cases, the impact of the crisis was almost completely translated into a reduction in the number of jobs, while the significance of average working hours in the adjustment was trivial.

2.3 Inequalities in Wage Adjustments to the Crisis

As already mentioned, the first inequality produced by the crisis is between those able to keep their jobs and the unemployed. A second potential

Table 10.2 Selected indicators related to working time during the crisis, Spain, 2007–2010

	2007Q3	2007Q4	2008Q1	2008Q2	2008Q3	2008Q4	2009Q1	2009Q2	2009Q3	2009Q4	2010Q1
Contractually agreed working hours											
Mean	37.6	37.3	37.3	37.3	37.4	37.1	37.0	37.0	37.1	36.8	36.7
Standard deviation	8.2	8.4	8.5	8.5	8.2	8.7	8.8	9.0	8.7	9.2	9.2
Standard working hours											
Mean	38.7	38.4	38.3	38.3	38.5	38.0	37.9	37.9	38.0	37.7	37.5
Standard deviation	9.1	9.3	9.4	9.5	9.1	9.5	9.6	9.9	9.5	10.0	10.0
Effective working hours											
Mean	32.2	34.1	34.4	35.9	32.1	34.8	34.4	34.8	31.9	34.1	34.1
Standard deviation	16.9	14.2	14.1	13.2	16.8	13.9	13.7	13.6	16.8	14.0	13.8
Employees working overtime (%)	6.8	7.2	7.4	7.4	6.0	6.3	5.0	5.2	4.3	4.9	4.8

Source: Authors' analysis from Spanish LFS.

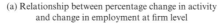

(a) Relationship between percentage change in activity
and change in employment at firm level

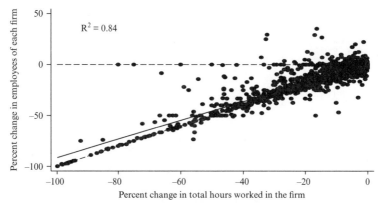

(b) Relationship between percent change in activity
and change in average working hours per employee at firm level

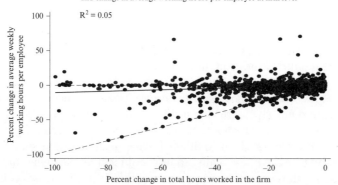

Source: Authors' analysis based on Survey of Labour Trends.

Figure 10.7 *Relationship between change in activity level and employment and average working hours by employee in firms affected by the crisis, Spain, 2008, Q3–2009 Q4)*

source of inequality is the unequal impact of the crisis on the factor distribution of income (between wages and profits) and on wage dispersion itself.

In order to address the second issue, and due to the peculiarities of the Spanish model, it is advisable to consider the evolution of wages and profits from a medium-term perspective: what was the evolution of factor income distribution like during the boom (2000–2007)? According to

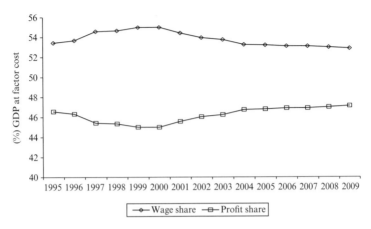

Source: Authors' analysis based on National Accounts data.

Figure 10.8   Wage share and profit share, Spain, 1995–2009

National Accounts data, as can be seen in Figure 10.8, for the first time in modern history (Muñoz de Bustillo, 2007b) in Spain the wage share did not increase during the economic boom.[10]

This reduction in wage share, a trend found in most European countries (see Chapter 5 of *Employment in Europe 2007*, European Commission, 2007), is particularly interesting in the Spanish case, as Spain has one of the lowest wage shares among the EU-15.[11] As we can see in Figure 10.9, the crisis has intensified this trend of further declining wage share, pointing to a first source of inequality in terms of income: the higher impact of the crisis on those receiving wage incomes.[12] In fact, the crisis has intensified the redistribution of income towards profits that can be observed in Spain since 2000.

Due to the shortcomings of the Spanish data on wages it is not possible to study in detail the impact of the crisis on wages. According to the OECD, in aggregate terms, during the crisis the growth of real wage compensation per employee in the private sector (unlike in the public sector, see Section 3) was higher than in previous years. In fact, in 2009, at the peak of the crisis, the estimated nominal wage growth (around 4 per cent) was in line with the growth of previous years, but the coincidence of such an increase in nominal terms with a period of deflation (minus 0.3 compared to 4.1 in 2008) led to an increase in real wages above 4 per cent, well over the meagre increases (or even decreases) of previous years (from 1 to 2 per cent depending on the years, with negative growth in 2005 and 2006, at –0.5 and –0.6 per cent, respectively). As we will see next, the

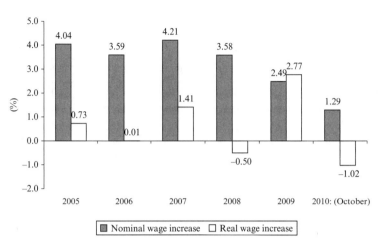

Note: In 2010 CPI October 2009–October 2010.

Source: Authors' analysis based on Spanish Ministry of Labour and Immigration data.

Figure 10.9   *Agreed wage increase in collective agreements, Spain, 2005–*
2010 (October) (private sector)

unequal impact of the crisis on different types of jobs explains part of such behaviour. In fact, according to the agreed wage increase in collective agreements (Figure 10.9), the resulting wage rise is much lower, decreasing in real terms (–1 per cent) by 2010.[13] As we will see in Section 3, public workers have also been affected by the crisis (in this case as a spin-off of the 'debt crisis') with an average reduction of 5 per cent in their nominal wage (7.3 per cent in real terms), starting in June 2010.[14] In contrast, executive pay has been largely unaffected by the crisis. According to a recent study of executive pay of 582 CEOs and high executives of the IBEX-35 (the 35 most important firms on the Spanish Stock Exchange) carried out by *El País* (16 May 2010), average pay in 2009 was 0.98 million euros (113 minimum wages compared to 98 in 2005).[15]

Turning now to the minimum wage, the crisis has led to a reduction in the increase of this wage floor planned by the current government. Spain has a relatively low minimum wage by EU standards. Furthermore, since 1980, the minimum wage has been losing ground in relation to the average wage, falling from 46 per cent of the average wage in 1980 to 32 per cent in 2004. The change of government in 2004 – from the Conservative to the Socialist Party – led to a change in this trend, and it reached 540.9 euros, around 34.5 per cent of the average wage, in January 2008. Under the current government (2008–2012), the electoral programme of the

Work inequalities in the crisis

*Table 10.3   Evolution of wage inequality and incidence of low-paid work,
            Spain, 2004–2009*

	2004	2005	2006	2007	2008	2009
Low paid I (percentage below 60% of the median hourly wage)	10.7	11.3	12.2	10.8	10.0	10.9
Low paid II (percentage below 2/3 of the median hourly wage)	15.8	17.3	17.4	16.6	15.5	16.4
Gini index	0.297	0.291	0.290	0.284	0.275	0.273
p90/p50	2.101	2.043	2.028	2.067	2.017	1.998
p50/p10	1.706	1.727	1.748	1.706	1.669	1.704

Source: Authors' analysis from SILC micro-data.

Spanish Socialist Party (PSOE) included an increase in the minimum wage to 800 euros. The economic crisis and the presumed negative employment impact of a sharp rise in the minimum wage in a recession have postponed *sine die* the minimum wage increase needed to reach the 800 euros target by 2012. Compared to the 7 per cent annual increase for the period 2008–2012 needed to meet that end, in 2008 the increase was 5.2 per cent and in 2009 4 per cent. In January 2010, the minimum wage was raised by only 1.5 per cent to 630.33 euros, well below the goal of 800 euros by 2012.

A final question that must be answered concerns the extent to which the crisis has affected wage distribution and its impact on low wage employment. According to the most recent data available (Statistics on Income and Living Conditions (SILC) 2009), the crisis, at least until 2009, has not had any significant impact on wage distribution. In fact, as is shown in Table 10.3, the Gini Index slightly decreased from 2004 to 2009. The same applies to low wage work, which decreased until 2008 and increased again as the Spanish economy got deeper into crisis in 2009.

Finally, according to official Spanish statistics on poverty risk (SILC), in 2009 the poverty rate reached 20.8 per cent, 1 percentage point higher than in 2007. In contrast, the poverty rate of those aged 65 and older decreased from 28.2 in 2007 to 24.6 in 2010. This decrease in the poverty rate in old age is explained by the combined effect of a decreasing poverty threshold due to the reduction in median GDP (the poverty line is defined as 60 per cent of median income, so a decrease in per capita GDP automatically produces a decrease in the poverty line) and growing average pensions in real terms (due to lower than expected inflation, the variable used to increase pensions at the start of the year). For people aged between 16 and 64 (the age group directly affected by the crisis), the poverty risk increased more sharply, from 16.8 per cent in 2007 to 19.1 per cent in 2009. This result is similar to the conclusions obtained from a follow up ad hoc survey addressed to vulnerable population groups conducted by FOESSA in 2007 and 2009 (Laparra, 2010).[16] This study distinguishes four different social situations: integrated, vulnerable inclusion, moderate exclusion and severe exclusion, depending on a number of indicators of exclusion including unemployment, consumption and education. The results point to a reduction from 2007 to 2009 in the percentage of integrated households (from 48.9 per cent to 35.2 per cent) and an increase in vulnerable inclusion (from 34.9 per cent to 46.3 per cent) and moderate exclusion (10.4 per cent to 12.9 per cent), the major driver of these changes being the increase in unemployment.

As already mentioned, the crisis may have an unexpected impact on the evolution of wages. If the crisis has an above average impact on high wage jobs, then, independently of the evolution of wages at the individual level, as high wage jobs are destroyed aggregate data will show a decrease in the average wage. In contrast, if the destruction of employment is concentrated at the bottom, we might get an overall wage rise. Therefore, it is important to ask what kinds of jobs have been most affected by the crisis in Spain. To this end, we have followed the methodology proposed by Fernández-Macías and Hurley (2008), which comprises four steps: (i) a job matrix of the Spanish economy combining activity and occupation must be defined (at the one-digit level, the level of detail offered by the Spanish Labour Force Survey). This process produces a matrix of nearly one hundred jobs. (ii) These jobs are ranked according to their average wage estimated using the 2006 Structure of Earnings Survey. (iii) In order to facilitate the analysis, the different jobs are placed (from the lowest to the highest wage) in five quintiles, from the lowest wages (first quintile) to the highest (fifth quintile). (iv) In each quintile, jobs are expressed in net terms (job created – job destroyed).

The creation and destruction of jobs is monitored according to their position in the five quintiles. In Figure 10.10, we can see the location of jobs destroyed (and created) in net terms, quarter by quarter, since the start of the crisis. Some important conclusions can be drawn from this analysis: (a) in terms of employment, high-quality jobs have been spared by the crisis; (b) job destruction is higher in the third and fourth quintiles, concentrating therefore in 'middle class jobs'. As a result, we can say that the crisis in Spain will produce a polarization of employment, in contrast to the general upgrading observed during the growth years (Fernández-Macías, 2010).

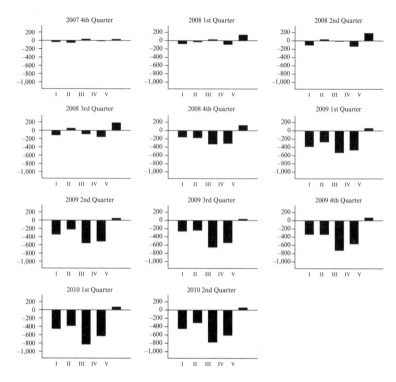

Source: Authors' analysis from Spanish EES 2006 and LFS.

Figure 10.10   Accumulated change in employment by job quintile, Spain, 2007 4th quarter–2010 2nd quarter (thousand workers)

The labour contract and, in general, the work relationship represent a compact that includes wage, working conditions, formal and on-the-job training, future prospects in the firm and so on. So far, we have focused on three major elements in this package: wages, working time and employment, but the crisis might have had an impact on other items of the compact, as well. It is obvious that job quality is determined by many more attributes than wages or working time, as supported by an extensive body of social science, health and medical literature. Therefore, in monitoring the evolution of employment, job quality matters.[17]

2.4   Impact on Working Conditions

It can be argued that the crisis can affect other items of the labour compact for different reasons and in different ways:

(i)   As a result of the crisis and the reduction in demand and profits, the firm might try to downgrade working conditions in order to reduce costs and/or increase productivity.[18]

(ii)   Unemployment growth will increase the leverage of employers with regard to employees, as now the opportunity cost of losing the job is higher. This might facilitate the deterioration of working conditions.

(iii)   The worsening of working conditions might be used as a trade-off to maintain employment and/or wages.

(iv)   From a different perspective, it can be argued that slack demand, if not fully compensated by a reduction in employment, might lead to a reduction of the workload and an improvement in working conditions.

In the last case, working conditions (at least some aspects) would follow a countercyclical pattern, improving during crises and deteriorating during economic booms. In the former cases working conditions would show a pro-cyclical pattern. Therefore, there is no reason to expect *ex ante* a positive or a negative impact of the crisis on working conditions, although there are more arguments in favour of the pro-cyclical behaviour – that is deteriorating – of at least some of the dimensions of working conditions. Furthermore, working conditions might show a time trend,[19] independently of changes in the economic cycle, so it could be that the changes we observe during the crisis are not connected at all with this juncture, responding to changes taking place in the long run.

In order to study the evolution of working conditions (other than wages) during the crisis, we have used the Spanish Quality of Work Life Survey for the years 2006 (the last wave before the crisis) and 2009 (which corresponds to the last available wave).[20] This database offers a large battery of variables associated with working quality for a representative sample of Spanish workers. Most of them are measured from the worker's own perspective, as in almost all cases – with the exception of being involuntarily part-time employed (a binary variable) – the worker has to report his or her satisfaction or valuation of a certain job attribute using a scale from 0 to 10. This exploration of the changes in working conditions during the crisis is limited to private-sector employees, excluding self-employed and public employees.

As different jobs are of different quality, it is clear that the focus should be on those changes in working conditions not driven by compositional effects in employment. In other words, if intrinsically high-quality jobs are being destroyed by an economic crisis, it is unavoidable that the working conditions of the workers will deteriorate. Assuming that a certain job can be defined by the occupational level and sector of activity (as was done in a previous subsection), it is reasonable to monitor the evolution of job quality controlling for these two variables in order to avoid any compositional effect. In this spirit, we carried out 140 regressions of each variable of working conditions on the following independent variables: sex, age, age squared, education, dummies for occupational level (considering four broad categories: high-skilled white-collar workers, low-skilled white-collar workers, high-skilled blue-collar workers and low-skilled blue-collar workers) and sector of activity (taking into account primary sector, industry, construction and services) and a dummy for 2009 to identify the impact of the crisis. We ran the analysis separately for the whole sample of private employees and for three usually disadvantaged groups: women, young workers and low-educated workers (those with elementary or basic education). The total sample considered here comprises almost 10,000 private-sector employees.[21]

Table 10.4 presents the main results of the 140 regressions. All the regressions have the same structure, the dependent variable being the change from 2006 to 2009 of the different indicators related to working conditions included in the survey. The coefficients reported in the table correspond to the coefficient for the dummy variable 2009 and represent the average change in certain job attributes between 2006 and 2009, other things being equal. Several points can be highlighted. First, according to the overall result we cannot distinguish the period of economic crisis as a generalized worsening of working conditions, even for particular groups of workers, such as women, young people or low-educated employees. Secondly, in particular, the evolution of most of the variables associated with working conditions is remarkably positive in almost all cases. In fact, in the aggregate, on the negative side there is only a decrease in satisfaction with wages, job stability and working time flexibility and an increase in the level of effort and perceived ethnic discrimination and bullying or harassment at the workplace. Third, in general, there are no backward steps in any dimension for any of the particular groups analysed (women, young people and low-educated workers), with some exceptions. For instance, confidence in colleagues at the same level decreases (maybe as a result of an increase in competition between colleagues to retain the job), perceived sexual harassment at the workplace increases in the case of low-educated workers and women perceive a higher level of discrimination against disabled employees. It is also true that, in many cases, the positive general trend does not translate into advancement for women, the young and the low-educated. Nevertheless, one should be cautious in interpreting these results insofar as the available sample becomes smaller when analysing these particular groups.

Finally, comparison of the results of Table 10.4 with the mean and standard deviation of working conditions in 2006, before the beginning of the crisis (not included in the table), suggest that, even in the cases where the economic crisis has brought about statistically significant changes in working conditions, the quantitative relevance of negative impacts is remarkably low. For instance, in the worst case, the decrease in satisfaction with wages among young employees, the negative effect (–0.424) represents less than 7 per cent of the sample mean and less than 0.2 standard deviations.

It is important to stress that the analysis presented above is valid only for regular workers, and not for informal or underground workers not covered by labour contracts and health and safety standards. To the extent that the crisis leads to an increase in informal and undeclared work (as a more favourable alternative to being fully idle), it can be argued than most of the deterioration in working conditions (including wages) will be invisible to a survey addressed to standard workers. Unfortunately, aside from some indirect and anecdotal evidence about the increase in the underground economy and undeclared work, it is very difficult to present a serious estimate on the increase in this type of work. Nevertheless, the review of the literature on the issue, both at aggregate and regional level (Colectivo Ioé, 2008), shows that informal work follows a clear anti-cyclical pattern, decreasing during economic booms and increasing during recessions. Thus we should expect an increase in the level of informal work, especially among immigrants with fewer alternatives for survival and less bargaining power.

From a different perspective, the reduction in economic activity, especially in high-accident-risk sectors, such as construction (27 per cent of all accidents with more than three days lost in 2007), has contributed positively to the existing downward trend in the rate of accidents at work, both fatal and total. In the former case, the number of fatal accidents at work (including *in itinere*) went down from 1,575 in 2000 to 826 in 2009 (a rate per 1,000 workers of 0.044 in 2009 compared to 0.102 in 2000). The same result arises when we look at the total number (and rates per 1,000 workers) of total accidents (with more than three days of work lost), although with an important difference: while the reduction in fatal (and serious) accidents starts in 2000, the reduction in the number and rate of total accidents is concentrated in 2008 and 2009, and is mainly explained by the reduction in the more common category of 'less serious' accidents. This intensification of the decrease in less serious accidents might be related to the reduction in the workers' propensity to take days off in case of minor accidents in a context of high unemployment (and higher risk of being fired) in comparison to the boom years. This circumstance, going to work in poor health to reduce the chances of being fired, can be interpreted

Table 10.4 Average changes in working conditions, Spain, 2006–2009 (OLS estimates)

	Total	Women	Youth	Low-educated workers
Overall job satisfaction	0.076	0.135	-0.049	0.068***
Satisfaction with wage	-0.326***	-0.285***	-0.424***	-0.395
Work organization				
Stress	-0.098	0.097	-0.255	-0.147
Monotony	0.026	0.081	-0.002	0.066
Physical effort	0.281***	0.193	0.220	0.373
Satisfaction with work activity	-0.019	0.035	-0.157	-0.035*
Satisfaction with self-fulfilment	0.192***	0.297***	-0.008	0.139
Satisfaction with autonomy/independence	0.219***	0.242**	0.137	0.083
Satisfaction with participation in decision-making	0.134*	0.205*	0.173	-0.006
Work environment				
Satisfaction with air conditioning	0.469***	0.437***	0.460***	0.358**
Satisfaction with heating	0.208**	0.187	0.133	0.097
Satisfaction with ventilation	0.095	-0.006	0.135	0.042
Satisfaction with noise	0.228**	0.297**	0.141	0.113*
Satisfaction with lighting	0.125***	0.105	0.135	0.165**
Satisfaction with space	0.237***	0.216**	0.217	0.207
Labour relations				
Relations with bosses	0.100	0.055	0.077	0.057
Trust in bosses	0.124*	0.161	0.201	-0.004**
Trust in same level colleagues	-0.072	-0.075	-0.046	-0.158
Trust in subordinates	0.100	0.188	-0.212	0.087

Sex discrimination at work	-0.001	0.096	-0.048	0.068
Age discrimination at work	-0.040	0.039	-0.077	0.001***
Ethnic discrimination at work	0.090*	0.128*	-0.083	0.162
Disability discrimination at work	0.064	0.149**	0.091	0.091***
Bullying	0.130**	0.087	0.145	0.187*
Sexual harassment	0.040	0.060	0.068	0.064*
Working time arrangements				
Involuntary part-time (probability)	0.020**	0.031*	0.050**	0.021**
Satisfaction with working time	0.144**	0.029	0.040	0.154
Satisfaction with working time flexibility	-0.176**	-0.212	-0.293	-0.175
Satisfaction with breaks	0.147*	0.254*	-0.066	0.109
Satisfaction with holidays	0.230***	0.282**	0.153	0.119***
Satisfaction with job stability	-0.205***	-0.136	-0.411**	-0.301
Health and safety conditions				
Risk at work	0.088	0.212*	0.326	0.065
Satisfaction with health and safety facilities	0.505***	0.477***	0.291	0.517***
Satisfaction with health and safety conditions	-0.021	-0.129	-0.224	-0.111
Training				
Hours of training received last year	3.427***	5.635***	6.201*	0.545

Notes: The table shows the coefficients obtained by regressing each variable on a dummy for 2009 controlling for sex, age, age squared, education, occupational level and sector of activity.

* significant at 10% level; ** significant at 5% level; *** significant at 1% level.

Source: Authors' analysis from Quality of Work Life Survey 2006–2009.

as a deterioration of working conditions. This interpretation of the data is supported by some direct evidence obtained on the shopfloor.[22]

Summing up, according to the data presented, there has been no major (negative) change in working conditions as a result of the crisis, at least not in the first part of it (until 2009).[23] It is probable that if the crisis continues, working conditions surveys will start to show some deterioration, especially in areas related to stress and, paradoxically, overwork, as the reduction in payroll (often more intense than the reduction in demand) ends up increasing the pressure on the remaining employees (a trend that we identified in some of the case studies presented in Section 4).

3.   THE POST-CRISIS AND THE GREAT U-TURN: IMPACT ON PUBLIC BUDGETS AND ON OTHER REFORMS

By the end of 2009 and in 2010 worries about the economic situation and the follies of the international financial system gave way to a growing concern about the impact of the crisis on public finances. In this context, the situation of Spanish public finances, with their relatively high dependency on foreign debt, was the subject of detailed attention from the international mass media. Even though in terms of debt and future debt cost Spain's situation is relatively comfortable (after a deficit of 11.1 per cent in 2009, total public debt as a proportion of GDP was 53.2 per cent, well under that of Ireland, at 64 per cent, the United Kingdom, at 68.1 per cent, Germany, at 76 per cent, Belgium, at 96.9 per cent or Italy, at 115.8 per cent), in 2010 the country was considered by the media and the markets in the same 'basket' group of Portugal and Greece, leading to an increase in financial instability and growing concerns about Spain's future ability to pay back its debts. By the end of April 2010, Standard & Poor's reduced the rating of Spanish public bonds to AA, based on their own estimates of the future growth of the Spanish economy, well below the estimates of the IMF, the European Commission and other research institutes, and frivolous opinion about the alleged 'rigidities' of the Spanish labour market. Already by the end of 2009, there was a U-turn in government priorities with regard to economic policy, putting the fight against the public deficit at the forefront of its concerns. The deficit reduction measures approved include a much criticized increase in VAT by June 2010 that could jeopardize the slow recovery of the Spanish economy.

In a first phase, the measures to reduce public deficit included: (i) a reduction of public employment: only 10 per cent of the vacancies will be covered; (ii) a virtual wage freeze for public employees (around 14 per cent of total employment), with an approved nominal increase in 2010 of 0.3 per cent – this increase implies a reduction in real wages of around 1 per cent; and (iii) a general reduction in expenditure, starting in the last quarter of 2009, leading to an increase in total public expenditure of only 0.8 per cent, compared to 4.1 per cent the previous quarter – in fact, the reduction in GDP in the fourth quarter (–3.1 per cent) is fully explained by the reduction in the compensatory increase of public expenditure.

As part of the government efforts to reduce public expenditure, President Zapatero, after his return from Davos, launched a proposal to increase the retirement age from 65 to 67. This initiative is interesting for several reasons: first, in practice, such an increase in the retirement age would not have any short- or medium-term impact on public expenditure. Second, the Spanish public pension system is in surplus, even during the crisis. Third, old age public expenditure in Spain – 9 per cent in 2007 – is lower than the EU average of 11.8 per cent, and is well under the 14.8 per cent of Italy. Finally, neither the legal (65 years) nor the actual (around 63 years) retirement ages of Spanish workers are especially low from a comparative perspective. What, then, is the reason for this proposal? We might speculate that the real reason for bringing this polemical and unpopular proposal to the forefront of the economic and political debate is to send a signal to the international financial markets of the will and strong commitment of the government to do whatever is needed to reduce public expenditure, even if it means taking unpopular measures.

By the end of spring 2010, the spread of the Spanish public bond in comparison to the German bond widened to 223 basis points. In order to counter these tensions and satisfy the Directorate General for Economic and Financial Affairs of the European Commission (Ecofin)'s demands for more aggressive deficit reduction, the Spanish government presented a second austerity plan and approved a package of labour market reforms. The 'highlights' of these measures, summarized in Table 10.5, contrast widely with the countercyclical measures of deficit expenditure taken in 2008 and 2009 (first part of the table), applauded at the time by both the markets and international financial institutions.

Overall, the plan is to reduce the public deficit of 11.2 per cent in 2009 by almost half (to 6 per cent) by 2011 in order to meet the limit of 3 per cent by 2013. From a Keynesian perspective it is difficult not to wonder whether such an intense reduction of the public deficit, in a context of extremely mild (if not negative) growth, will not result in double dip recession, exacerbating the unemployment crisis. Fortunately, the depreciation of the euro against the dollar and other currencies has allowed the partial compensation of the reduction in demand derived from the new fiscal policy by an increase in exports. Nevertheless, whether improvements in

Table 10.5 Economic policy in time of crisis: Major measures taken by the Spanish central government, cost and expected impact on inequality

Measure	Year	Description and purpose	Cost	Direct expected impact on inequality
		Pre-crisis		
Tax rebate of €400	2008	Increase private consumption in a situation of pre-crisis (and general elections)	€10,000 million in 2008–2009	Slight reduction of relative income inequality
Lump sum payment of €2,400 per newborn child (the so-called *cheque-bebé*)	2008	Contribution to family expenditure related to the birth of a child	€1250 million per year	Marginal reduction of relative income inequality
The crisis: **Plan Español para el Estímulo de la Economía y del Empleo (Plan E)** (Spanish Plan to Stimulate the Economy and Employment, €40 billion)				
Fondo Estatal de Inversión Local y Fondo Especial del Estado para la dinamización de la economía y el empleo	2009	Fiscal stimulus through small scale public works, mostly run by local government	€11,000 million	Reduction of inequality in employment
Fondo para la Adquisición de Activos Financieros	2009	Reduce the problems of financial institutions by the acquisition of part of their financial assets	Up to €50 billion	
Reduction of the corporate tax rate	2009	From 32.5% to 30%. Increase post-tax profits		Increase in inequality
Elimination of the property tax	2009		€1.8 billion	Increase in inequality

Measure	Year	Description	Amount	Effect
Increase in tax rate on savings income from 18% to 19% and 21% (after €6,000)	2009		€8 billion	Decrease in inequality
Different financing facilities for firms	2009			
Reduction of firms' social security contributions in specific cases	2009	To motivate permanent hiring of unemployed workers heads of households and temporary lay-offs instead of firing, etc.		Decrease in inequality
Automobile Plan E2000	2009	Subsidies for the purchase of new automobiles		
Subsidies to unemployed graduates to continue post-graduate education	2009	Facilitate post-graduate education for unemployed workers receiving unemployment benefits	€70 million	
Extension of unemployment benefits (6 months). Extended twice	2009	Flat rate of €426 per month for 6 months (under certain conditions)	€1.5 billion	Decrease in inequality
Fondo de Reestructuración Ordenada Bancaria	2009	Contribute to the orderly restructuring of banks and saving banks	€6.75 billion	
Automobile Plan E2000	2010	Subsidies for the purchase of new automobiles	€100 million	

Table 10.5 (continued)

Measure	Year	Description and purpose	Cost	Direct expected impact on inequality
		The post-crisis and the debt crisis		
Freeze on increase in retirement pensions in accordance with the CPI	2011	Exceptions: minimum and non-contributory pensions Reduction of public deficit	€1.53 billion	Increase inequality
Reduction of wages of public employees	2010	5% average reduction Reduction of public deficit	€6.8 billion in 2010–11	Increase inequality
Increase in VAT (from 6 to 8% and from 16 to 18%)	2010	Reduction of public deficit	€5.15 billion	Increase inequality
Elimination of the €400 tax rebate	2010	Reduction of public deficit	€5.7 billion	Slight reduction of relative income inequality
Reduction of 5 percentage points of social security contributions of SME	2010	Only if employment in the firm is constantly increasing	€700 million	
Reduction of public investment (infrastructure)	2010	Reduction of public deficit	€6.045 billion	
Reduction in ODA	2010–11	Reduction of public deficit	€800 million	Increase in overall inequality
Elimination of the *cheque-bebé*	2011	Reduction of public deficit	€1.25 billion	Marginal increase in relative income inequality
Tightening of the requirements for part-time retirement (already planned for 2013)	2010	New requirements: 61 years old, 30 years of contributions, the last 6 in the same firm Reduction of public deficit	€430 million	

No retroactivity of the recognition of dependency benefits	2010	Reduction of public deficit	€300 million	Increase inequality
Generalization of existing special open-ended contract (*contrato de fomento del empleo*)	2010	Labour market reform. Reduction of redundancy payments to a maximum of 33 days per year. Aimed at reducing temporary employment		Increase inequality
Limitation of the duration of temporary contracts to 3(+1) years and increase in redundancy payments after termination from 8 to 12 days per year	2010	Aimed at reducing temporary employment		Decrease in inequality

423

Table 10.5 (continued)

Measure	Year	Description and purpose	Cost	Direct expected impact on inequality
Clarification of the objective dismissal clauses (with a lower redundancy payment of 20 days per year)	2010	Reduction of 'judicial uncertainty' in the case of filing for objective dismissal due to economic, technical or organizational reasons		Increase inequality
New regulation on changes in agreed working conditions due to unexpected circumstances (including geographical mobility)	2010	Reduction of the existing restrictions on wages, working time and other forms of inner flexibility		
Non-applicability of collective agreements (above firm level) in relation to wages	2010	To facilitate the reduction of wages in case of crisis in order not to jeopardize employment levels in the firm		Increase inequality
Reduction of restrictions on temporary work agencies	2010			Increase inequality

Source: Compiled by the authors.

the foreign sector will be enough to compensate all of it, especially in a context of general and coordinated reduction of public deficits all across Europe, remains to be seen.

In relation to labour market reform, two things must be highlighted here. In the first place, the labour reform by decree (with the backing of the congress) came after the failure of a process of social dialogue between the major trade unions (CC.OO. and UGT) and the employer's association (CEOE). Although the government of President Zapatero is very fond of using social dialogue as a major tool for the implementation of policy, the lack of agreement between the social partners and the abovementioned pressure from European and international institutions to take measures to tackle the Spanish unemployment problem led to the unilateral approval of a labour reform, considered mild by the employers but meeting with fierce opposition from the trade union movement (including a general strike on 29 September 2010).

Secondly, the reform is the government's response to what is considered to be the major problem of the Spanish labour market, the abnormally high rate of temporary employment, that is normally explained by mainstream economists as the result of tight employment protection legislation and high dismissal costs for employees with open-ended contracts. According to the mainstream analysis of the faults of the Spanish labour market, the high level of employment protection enjoyed by employees with open-ended contracts is behind both the lack of flexibility of the labour market and its duality. The way to tackle the problem from this point of view is to create a new type of contract with lower redundancy payments, thereby reducing employment protection.

But this interpretation is subject to various critiques:

- As we have seen in previous sections, the main problem of the Spanish labour market is that it has too much flexibility, not too little.
- Such flexibility is the result of excessive resort to temporary employment. Even so, employees with open-ended contracts are not adequately protected from dismissal. According to our analysis of longitudinal data, in 2007, at the height of the economic boom, around 40 per cent of unemployed workers with previous work experience had had an open-ended contract in the past.[24] In other words, to have an open-ended contract does not isolate workers from the ups and downs of the market, although the main burden of adjustment falls on temporary workers. If we take the period 2008–2010 (third quarter), around 18 per cent of net job losses (excluding self-employed) were suffered by workers with open-ended contracts.

That means that open-ended contracts (as they should be called) are more stable than temporary contracts, but that does not make them fixed in any way.[25]

- Although much of the literature takes for granted the negative impact (in terms of employment performance) of Employment Protection Legislation,[26] the results of the second wave of empirical studies dealing with this issue do not support such a view (Fitoussi, 2003; Baker et al., 2005; Bassanini and Duval, 2006; Jaumotte, 2010).
- Dismissal costs in Spain, averaging 0.93 per cent of total labour costs in the period 2001–2009, are in line with the European average of 0.96 per cent in 2004. Obviously, the crisis has had an impact on total dismissal costs, which rose to 1.14 per cent in 2008 and 1.57 per cent in 2009.[27] Nevertheless, it is difficult to believe that such a small part of labour costs could have such a big impact on the functioning of the labour market.

Notwithstanding these arguments, the debate about the problems of the Spanish labour market has been monopolized by dismissal costs, and the core of the reform addresses this issue. The reform aims to facilitate the use of dismissal 'on objective grounds' for economic, organizational and technical reasons (with judicial approval), subject to lower dismissal costs (20 days compared to 42 or 33, depending on the type of contract). Furthermore, only 12 days' wages will be paid directly by the firm, while the remaining eight will be paid by FOGASA, a fund financed by firms. If this procedure is generalized, the dismissal costs for firms in the case of hiring on the basis of a temporary or open-ended contract would be the same, as the reform raises the dismissal costs of temporary workers at the end of their contracts from eight to 12 days (in 2015). The proposal also generalizes a special contract (*Contrato de Fomento del Empleo*) with lower redundancy payments in case of unfair dismissal (33 per year, instead of the 42 of standard contracts). Although it is still too early to know the impact of the reform, the available qualitative information points to a significant increase in the number of dismissals being processed using this cheaper and new alternative, dismissal on 'objective grounds'.[28]

4.   THE CRISIS: TWO ILLUSTRATIVE CASE STUDIES

In 2009, the Spanish economy lost almost 80,000 firms (excluding self-employed); 4.8 per cent of existing firms in 2008. This reduction was accompanied, as we have seen, by a huge reduction in employment at the surviving firms. Closures were much higher among the smallest firms: according to DIRCE, the Spanish national firm register, 93.5 per cent of all firms closed had between one and five employees. In contrast, in terms of the destruction of employment, the highest intensity of destruction has been concentrated in medium-sized firms of between 11 and 50 workers, with an index of employment destruction of 158 compared to 88 for smaller firms.[29] In what follows, we will present a snapshot of the crisis in two major sectors of the Spanish economy: the construction and automobile industries.

4.1 The Spanish Construction Sector: A Giant with Feet of Clay

Between 1996 and 2008, the Spanish economy created almost eight million jobs (net). Almost one in five new jobs was in construction. In 1996, construction contributed 9.2 per cent of total employment, whereas in 2008 it contributed 12.5 per cent, more than doubling the total number of jobs in the sector. But two years of crisis were enough to set back the sector's relative contribution to total employment to 9 per cent. The increase in construction activity and housing supply was accompanied by huge increases in house prices; according to data from the National Statistics Institute, taking 1996 as the base year (=100), prices rose to 295 in 2008. Apart from these price increases, cheap credit due to historically low interest rates and the expectation of future house price rises fuelled demand, and maintained the housing bubble until it burst with the advent of the crisis. Although the crisis led to a reduction in house prices, most of the adjustment has taken the form of a reduction in the construction of new buildings and an increase in the stock of unsold houses. In fact, at the end of 2009 the stock of unsold houses reached 0.7 million.[30] This excess of supply has produced an average decrease in housing prices (considered mild by many analysts)[31] of 8 per cent since 2007 (4 per cent in new construction and 15 per cent in used housing). Construction has been the sector hardest hit by the crisis in Spain. Figure 10.11 presents the contribution of the different sectors of the economy to the destruction of employment from the first quarter of 2008 to the first quarter of 2010. As we can see, half of the reduction of employment in the period is accounted for by construction alone (1 million jobs and 38 per cent of its employment since the beginning of 2008), 35.5 per cent by industry (0.7 million and 21 per cent of its employment since the beginning of 2008) and slightly less than 13 per cent by services.

In Spain, construction is characterized by:

- High employment intensity of output.
- A comparatively high level of self-employment. This dynamic has been exacerbated by the crisis: at the start of the crisis the

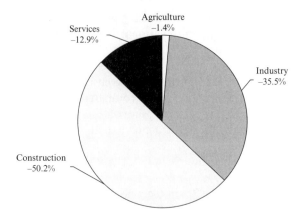

Source: Authors' analysis from Spanish LFS.

*Figure 10.11   Contribution of the different sectors of activity to job
destruction, Spain, 2008/2010*

    self-employment rate in the sector (20 per cent versus 17.5 per cent)
was 15 per cent higher than the national average; in 2010 it was 50
per cent higher (25 per cent versus 16.8 per cent).

- High rate of temporary employment: 49 per cent compared to 29 per
cent average in 2008.
- High proportion of immigrants. In the first quarter of 2008, 25
per cent of construction workers were immigrants. This group of
workers suffered a very strong employment adjustment, counting for
more than one-third of the total employment reduction in the sector.

The specific characteristics of the construction sector explain both the
sharp decline in production and the heavy impact of falling production
on employment. In this sector, most of the adjustment has taken the form
of non-renewal of temporary contracts on expiry and when building work
has been completed, or, in many cases, when the construction site was temporarily abandoned due to the bankruptcy of the firm or because it was
waiting for the economic climate to improve before finishing the building.

    A major source of illicit employment and fiscal fraud in the boom years
(Eurobarometer, 2007), the increase in unemployment is forcing many
once legally employed construction workers to offer their labour, often
on a self-employed basis, for lower wages. This is the situation of Mr A,
a Bolivian construction worker who, after years working in construction, first as an employee in a construction firm and later as a leader of
a subcontracted team with three other immigrants (until the firm started

to delay payments due to the crisis), is now unemployed and undertaking minor, undeclared private construction jobs in order to make ends meet.

Considering the huge drop in demand, it is difficult to imagine a scenario of adjustment in the construction labour market mostly or entirely related to wage reductions, especially because wages are only one – and not the most important – component of the cost of housing. In any case, although the review of the labour cost data (Quarterly Labour Cost Survey) does not indicate a major reduction in wages in the sector in 2008 and 2009, in 2010 there has been a sudden drop in wage rises. Other (not systematic) sources of information point to a significant reduction for various reasons. In some cases, such as bids in public tenders, the reduction is the product of the effect on wages of the lower bids needed to win in a context of increasing competition due to lack of activity in the sector. In one of our interviews, a manager of a medium-sized construction firm explained that he recently confronted his employees with the choice of accepting a lower wage in order to be able to make a winning offer or otherwise go home, as the payment of the prevailing wages would mean that the tender would not be successful. A representative of a conservative trade union, CSIF-construcción, told a local Valencia newspaper (*El Mercantil Valencianio*), an area with a large stock of unsold houses, that there had been an across-the-board wage reduction of up to 30 per cent in many cases. Such a reduction must be understood in terms of both the now much lower labour demand in the sector and the abnormally high wages existing in construction in the boom times (up to 3,000 euros a month for a foreman, well over the wages of a university lecturer, for example).

In the boom years, the combination of high wages and high demand for what was very often unskilled work acted as a powerful magnet, attracting very young workers to the sector, who in many cases even lacked minimum qualifications. In fact, 43 per cent of workers without even the lowest qualifications worked in construction in 2007: having a father working in the sector is a relevant statistical variable in explaining the risk of early school leaving among young males (Muñoz de Bustillo et al., 2009a). This makes the fall in employment in the sector especially dangerous, as the poor qualifications of the now unemployed workers leave them with poor prospects of transferring to other activities with a better long-term outlook.

Summing up, the adjustment in the construction sector to the abrupt and deep drop in housing demand (explained by the change in expectations concerning future house price increases, the credit crunch and increasing unemployment) has relied almost exclusively on the destruction of employment. Unemployment has, in particular, affected immigrants and early school leavers, thus increasing the social cost of the adjustment due to their lower access to unemployment benefits and their lower versatility in terms of skills. Since construction has a very high rate of temporary employment (51 per cent at the beginning of 2008), temporary employees suffered the most in terms of employment adjustment, but that does not mean that permanent employees have been spared by the crisis: they accounted for 35 per cent of total dependent employment lost in the sector. We could say that the construction sector exemplifies the liberal labour market strategy adopted by Spain based on temporary employment and a high reliance for such temporary jobs on migrant, unskilled workers. The crisis had a direct and immediate impact on inequalities among these categories of workers in terms of employment in the short run, but probably also in terms of wages and other working conditions in the future. Last but not least, the reliance on fixed-term employment considerably weakens the possibility of developing a robust system of social dialogue in the sector, making more difficult the use of other strategies of adapting to the crisis which are less costly from a social point of view, such as time sharing.

4.2　The Automobile Industry: Alternative Paths Through Social Dialogue

As we have seen, in Spain, in comparison to other countries – such as Germany – the bulk of the adjustment needed to counter the decline in effective demand generated by the crisis has taken the form of a reduction in employment. Spain is, therefore, a paradigmatic example of the danger of an employment system that relies almost exclusively on external numerical flexibility to meet changes in demand. Nevertheless, there are examples of firms that have used other mechanisms of adjustment, made possible by the Spanish regulations on collective dismissals (those affecting from 10 to 30 workers, depending on the size of the firm), alongside the so-called *Expediente de Regulación de Empleo* or ERE. When facing a situation of excess labour for economic (lower demand), technical (introduction of labour saving technologies) or organizational reasons, ERE allows firms to apply different mechanisms to adapt the labour force to the diminished needs of the firm, whether permanently, by layoffs, or temporarily, by different mechanisms of short-term suspension of working contracts or working time reductions. Table 10.6 depicts the intensity of use of the different types of EREs in the years prior to and during the crisis. As we can see, with the crisis there has been a significant increase in the number of EREs approved and a change in their type, from permanent termination of contracts to temporary suspension as a way of responding to a reduction in demand considered transitory. It is also important to note the marginal role of working time reduction as a means of confronting the reduction in demand.

Table 10.6   Workers affected and type of collective dismissal, Spain, 1999–2010

Year	Workers affected	Termination (%)	Temporary suspension (%)	Reduction in working time (%)	Agreed (%)
1999	77667	33.0	63.7	3.3	64.9
2000	60325	49.3	48.6	2.1	81.2
2001	122344	30.9	68.5	0.6	50.1
2002	71643	55.8	42.4	1.8	78.3
2003	83481	51.5	46.1	2.4	84.3
2004	60276	51.7	47.4	0.9	82.9
2005	72563	48.1	50.7	1.2	79.7
2006	51952	52.3	47.4	0.3	87.4
2007	58401	44.1	55.5	0.4	81.9
2008	148088	27.4	70.8	1.8	84.0
2009	549282	11.6	84.7	3.7	81.8
2010*	202919	18.8	73.4	7.8	87.8

Note: * January–September.

Source: Authors' analysis from MTIN.

The second of our case studies focuses on a sector that has used EREs more intensively, only partially based on the permanent reduction of the labour force: the automobile industry (and its auxiliaries). The use of this type of adjustment mechanism is a valuable example of the existence of alternatives to the stark dismissal of the redundant labour force and the role played in choosing this option by social dialogue, as EREs must be negotiated by trade unions and firms before being approved by the labour authority.

4.2.1   Core labour force also affected by the crisis

The motor vehicle industry is a major driver of manufacturing production in Spain. In 2007, at the peak of the boom, the sector contributed 4.9 per cent of GDP and 9 per cent of employment (both direct and indirect). More importantly, in a country with structural problems with regard to the balance of payments, the production of motor vehicles is clearly an export-oriented activity, exporting in 2007 the equivalent of 83 per cent of its production (86.8 per cent in 2009) and accounting for 13.3 per cent of total exports in 2006 (12.7 per cent in 2009). This percentage increases to 17.5 per cent (still in 2006) when we take into consideration the whole sector (including auxiliary industries).

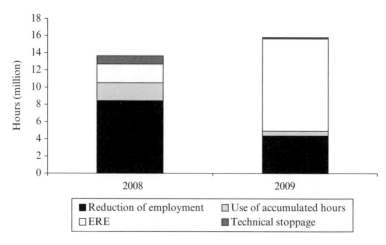

Note: Technical stoppage = stoppage of production in order to do maintenance work or other activities not compatible with the production process; use of accumulated hours = use of hours accumulated in time accounts by workers; ERE = temporary layoffs by an *Expediente de Regulación de Empleo*; reduction of employment: termination of temporary contracts and permanent layoffs.

Source: Authors' analysis based on ANFAC (2008 and 2009).

Figure 10.12   Importance of the different systems of reducing total working hours in the automobile sector, Spain (in millions)

In Spain, there are 10 motor vehicle manufacturing firms, all foreign-owned, with a total of 18 factories, located in different Spanish regions. Spain ranks eighth in world motor vehicle production, and is the second European producer after Germany.[32] The crisis has had a direct and profound impact on the sector: from 2007 to 2009, the production of motor vehicles decreased by 24.9 per cent and new registrations decreased by 44.6 per cent. In fact, at the beginning of the crisis the share of the Spanish market of 'Spanish' firms was 25 per cent, rising to 28 per cent in 2009.

In 2009, in order to incentivize sector demand, the government launched Plan 2000E, consisting of subsidies for the renewal of cars over 10 years old (with a budget of 140 million euros in 2009 and 100 million euros in 2010). According to ANFAC (2010), the plan has been fairly successful, producing an additional demand of 140,000 new car sales in 2009, mitigating the impact of the crisis on the sector.

Employment adjustment in the sector has taken the following form (Figure 10.12): (a) in the first year of the crisis, 2008, the reduction in demand was met mainly by a reduction in the labour force of 7 per cent. More than half of this reduction, 58 per cent, involved the non-renewal of temporary contracts; the rest involved the reduction of open-ended contracts, normally by means of early retirement and incentivized quits. The core labour force has therefore also been affected. These two mechanisms explain around 62 per cent of the adjustment. The rest was done mainly by the use of working hours saved in the past (15 per cent) and temporary layoffs (using ERE). (b) In the second year of the crisis, firms relied more intensively on temporary layoffs (two-thirds of the reduction in hours),[33] resorting to the reduction in employment for the rest (28 per cent), and only marginally to the use of accumulated hours, by then no longer available. On this occasion, all the reduction in employment was of permanent workers, in a process of substitution (sector-wise) of workers with open-ended contracts by temporary workers. This can be seen for the industrial sector as a whole, in which the temporary employment rate decreased from 22 to 15 per cent from the beginning of 2008 to the end of 2009, increasing again since then to 16.5 per cent in the third quarter of 2010.

In order to follow the details of the process of adjustment in the sector, we gathered detailed information on three important firms in the auxiliary sector (producers of components for the automobile industry).

4.2.2 Firm A: Trade unions limiting the scope of adjustments

Firm A is located in the south of Spain in a town in Andalusia (Jeréz de la Frontera) that for decades has struggled to maintain its level of manufacturing. With around 200 workers in 2007, at the time of writing (2010) the establishment had 122 workers as a result of the fall in demand in the automobile sector. The firm has tried to diversify its production – hitherto focused entirely on the production of components for automobiles – by entering a different sector of activity (related to alternative energy), but so far has not succeeded, in part because of the impact on the sector of the reduction of subsidies for the generation of solar energy. The process of adjustment has closely followed the stages reviewed above. First, the adjustment fell mostly on temporary workers, although in 2007 only 10 per cent of the labour force was on temporary contracts as the result of a union-backed policy of transformation of temporary into open-ended contracts during the years before the crisis (in 2005 the temporary employment rate was 23 per cent). The reduction in the workforce was accompanied by a paid reduction in working time of 116 hours per worker to be recovered in the next three years, if necessary due to an increase in demand (a kind of time savings account but in the other direction). In 2009 and 2010, two different EREs allowed the temporal suspension of work for 190 days and 120 days, respectively. These EREs affected the whole workforce except the managers, workers over 50 years old (in order not to affect their future pensions) and new employees without full rights to unemployment benefits. The firm complemented the unemployment benefits received by the suspended workers up to 84 per cent of their normal wages. In 2010, a new ERE was approved for the extinction of 42 jobs (plus 14 more depending on the evolution of the workload). In contrast to the previous EREs, this time the firm unilaterally decided which workers were to be affected by the termination of contracts, although most of them were production workers. According to the workers interviewed, the crisis had a profound impact on the level of trust both between employers and employees and among the workers themselves. It is also affecting levels of anxiety and stress. In some cases, workers put off visiting a doctor until they start their period of work suspension in order to avoid being blacklisted (making it a kind of 'presentism', as opposed to absenteeism).

4.2.3   Firm B: Time flexibility and ERE through social dialogue

The story of Firm B, in general, is very similar. Firm B is a large establishment of a transnational corporation, with around 1,000 workers in 2010. It is located in Catalonia, in a much more prosperous region than Firm A. The first measure taken by the firm and trade unions to address the increase in stock arising from the reduction of demand in the automobile industry was to negotiate, in 2008, an agreement on time flexibility, generating a time account of up to 29 days per worker, to be recouped (up to 80 per cent) once demand recovered. Together with this measure there was an ERE for the termination of 167 employees (older than 58) by means of early retirement, with partial compensation by the firm for income lost. In 2009, the firm asked for approval of an ERE for a suspension of work of up to 50 days for all production workers and 17 days for the rest. The firm complemented the unemployment benefits received by the employees, making them up to amount to 80 per cent of their wages. In 2010, another ERE, this time for the termination of 66 contracts, was approved. After negotiations with the firm, the ERE was implemented through incentivized quits and early retirements. The workers interviewed believe that, owing to the reduction of investment in maintenance, the crisis has degraded working conditions in some respects (high temperatures of above 32 degrees Celsius on the shopfloor due to the malfunctioning of the air conditioning system were given as an example). According to the trade union representative interviewed, the reduction of the workforce has increased the workload for the remaining workers, increasing the levels of stress and anxiety. The workers expect a very low increase in real wages in the future and greater pressure for higher functional and working time flexibility.

4.2.4 Firm C: Social dialogue agreement under threat of relocation

The third firm, Firm C, also a transnational company, belongs to the same sector, and is slightly larger, with around 1,200 workers in 2010 in different establishments in Spain. In this case, the impact of the crisis is tangled up with the decision of the company to relocate part of its production to the UK. This is common practice in the sector. In the opinion of many of the workers' representatives interviewed, the crisis is being used as an excuse to relocate to countries with lower costs or higher productivity. As in other cases, the first measure was to activate whatever sources of time flexibility were laid down in the collective agreement (reduction of working days), along with the changes in the timing of vacations, the internalization of activities previously outsourced (cleaning) and the closing of the head-quarters, moving the administration department to one of the firm's factories to save costs. This last measure, involving spatial mobility, affected 105 workers. In 2009, as part of a Europe-wide restructuring plan, there was a termination ERE affecting 122 workers, and another two suspension EREs in two different establishments affecting 12 workers for six months and 365 workers for 40 days. In 2010, three different extinction (that is, permanent layoffs) EREs were approved, two of them as a result of the total closure of the plant and the third due to the lack of demand leading to excess capacity. The proposed EREs finally affected fewer workers than intended by the firm. A significant proportion of the workers were hired by other establishments of the firm, with a commitment on the part of the firm to rehire other workers affected by the measure. Once again, the crisis is considered to have degraded working conditions, mainly in terms of increased levels of stress, anxiety and 'disenchantment', worsening relations between management and employees as the firm tries to maintain profits and competitiveness, putting more pressure on workers.

4.2.5 Role of social dialogue alongside a deterioration of working conditions

A review of the cases selected above points to the existence of a fairly complex system of industrial relations in the sector, far from the hire-and-fire mechanism that characterized other sectors of activity, such as construction. Often, in the process of negotiation conducted prior to the filing of an ERE, the demands of the firms are softened, leading to fewer dismissals (in the case of termination EREs) and better conditions for the workers ultimately affected. All these improvements are possible only due to the existence of social dialogue in the establishments, buttressed by the compulsory approval of the ERE by the labour authorities and the higher probability of their approval when the ERE has been agreed to by the labour representatives in the establishment. We have also detected a subtle deterioration in working conditions, especially in terms of higher stress and anxiety and a worsening of the working atmosphere. As seen in Section 2.3, these changes have not yet been captured by the standard surveys of working conditions carried out in 2009. This means that the impact of the crisis goes beyond the increase in unemployment and also affects other working conditions, although with a time lag. Finally, as in other sectors, the core labour force has also been affected by layoffs, although, thanks to the bargaining process involved in the approval of the EREs, often with better conditions than temporary workers, whose contracts are not renewed when they expire. In this respect, the idea of a core labour force of permanent workers embedded in firms immune to the crisis is only a caricature of the Spanish labour market.

5.   CONCLUSION

A review of the impact of the crisis on the working world in Spain points to the existence of major divides as the result of the unprecedented decrease in GDP in 2008–2009. In this respect, what is characteristic of Spain in the European context is not the intensity of the crisis in GDP terms but the impact of falling economic activity on unemployment.

Reversing the intense job growth experienced during most of the decade prior to the crisis, in which Spain contributed almost one-third of total EU employment growth, in less than a year Spain generated more than two million unemployed, multiplying its unemployment rate by 2.5. To a significant extent, these fluctuations of the Spanish labour market correspond to the real estate bubble experienced by the country during the past 15 years, which disproportionately increased the importance of construction in the Spanish economy. The crisis has also shown the weaknesses of the economic specialization of Spain in construction and also on a labour market model based on the employment of temporary workers without skills and often concentrated in low-paid low-quality jobs. Although the reasons behind this high sensitivity of employment to the ups and down of the market in Spain are still under discussion, the intensity of the adjustment highlights the first implication of the crisis in terms of the generation of inequalities in the world of work, namely between the employed and the unemployed.

In this respect, our analysis reveals the existence of several groups of workers hit especially hard by the employment crisis: (i) those on temporary contracts (a sizeable proportion in Spain, with a temporary employment rate before the crisis of 30 per cent, well above the European average); (ii) young workers, affected by the crisis twice over, due to their status as temporary workers and as newcomers in a flat labour market; (iii) immigrants, affected both by their status as temporary workers and their concentration in the sector most affected by the crisis: construction; and (iv) those with lower qualifications, who have not only been affected by the collapse in construction, but are also less prepared to compete in a labour market with excess supply.

In this context of very high unemployment, it must be acknowledged that the government, in contrast to previous crises, has responded reasonably well, extending unemployment benefits to allow the maintenance of a high rate of protection through different tiers of benefits. This element, along with the existence of intense intra-family transfers and a historically high – despite the crisis – level of employment, allowed the social impact of the crisis to be reduced. Whether these elements will maintain their capacity to protect in the case of a prolonged period of stagnation is still open to debate. In fact, the extension of the last pillar (and resort) of the system of unemployment protection will apply, in principle, only until February 2012. Obviously, maintaining unemployment protection is only a first step that will not be enough by itself to accelerate recovery in the presence, as in Spain, of a structural crisis related to the excessive and unsustainable growth in construction. It can be argued that, in order to successfully change the growth engine of the Spanish economy, more effort has to be made in retraining and recycling the now highly redundant (and low-skilled) construction labour force. In this field, reform of the training system is urgent in order to link it more efficiently with the (future) needs of the production system. A final observation with regard to inequality is that, so far, the crisis has been more benign in relation to female unemployment, eliminating the unemployment gap (equalizing male and female unemployment rates) and greatly reducing the existing gap in terms of unemployment protection. It remains to be seen whether this trend will continue in the future or if it is contingent on the role played in the crisis by construction, the paradigmatic male employment sector.

A first corollary of the story told so far is the failure of the strategy followed in Spain of radical labour market flexibilization through the universalization of fixed-term contracts. Probably, the availability of a relatively cheap way of adapting the workforce to the fluctuations of the market has made redundant other systems of flexibility with lower social costs, such as internal flexibility or working time adjustments. In fact, from a social perspective, when firms react to falling demand by not renewing temporary contracts, they in effect socialize the costs of the crisis, as the now unemployed workers are fully subsidized by public expenditure through unemployment benefits. Analysis of the crisis in the automobile and auxiliary sector proves that the system of collective bargaining in Spain is rich and complex enough to allow for other strategies to temporarily adapt the workforce to firms' reduced needs without resorting to dismissals.

In contrast to employed–unemployed inequality, the crisis has had a much weaker impact on other inequalities in the world of work. This chapter has documented how few firms have relied on, for example, working time reduction as a means of reducing productive capacity, therefore concentrating the impact of the crisis on the employees fired, instead of distributing them among the workforce by means of lower working hours (however compensated). The only variable affected is overtime, although this plays a minor role in aggregate working time. From a different perspective, it can be argued than the extreme response of firms to the reduction in demand will show up, sooner or later, in an increase in the workload of the remaining employees, leading to a deterioration in working conditions. The case study of the automobile industry points in that direction. The economic collapse has had a strange impact on real wages. It must be acknowledged that the unplanned increase in real wages in 2009, a byproduct of the unexpected deflation of –0.3 (compared to an inflation rate of 4.1 in the previous year), probably came at the worst possible moment, with firms facing a strong reduction in final demand. The Spanish wage system showed a lack of flexibility in the new situation, and it was not until 2010 that reductions in real wages started. It is debatable to what extent a prompt reduction in real wages would have reduced the intensity of employment adjustment, as, together with a reduction in labour costs for firms (with an alleged positive impact on employment), such a reduction would have translated into a reduction in effective domestic demand, with a negative impact on employment. Nevertheless, such wage increases were short-lived, since by 2010 the agreed real wage increase of the collective agreements signed was –0.5 per cent. For those on the minimum wage, the crisis led to a halt in the process of increasing it, far from the objective of 800 euros fixed by the government by the end of its mandate (2012). This change of plan might be behind the increase in low-wage work observed in 2009. Finally, as a result of the public debt crisis, a very conservative increase in the wages of public-sector employees, bargained in 2009, was converted into an average decrease of 5 per cent in 2010. As shown in the analysis of job quintiles, most of the destruction of employment has been concentrated in low and especially middle quintile jobs (in terms of wages), sparing the upper quintile of jobs in terms of wages; therefore, one should expect a growing polarization of the Spanish labour market in terms of wages as a result of the crisis.

As with other aspects of working conditions, analysis so far has not revealed any major effects of the crisis on working conditions, although there is decreasing satisfaction with job stability and wages, especially among young workers, and an increase in work effort that is confirmed by the case studies developed in the chapter. Considering the aggressiveness of the reaction of Spanish firms to the crisis in terms of employment reduction it is reasonable to expect an increase in the pressure on employees and an intensification of the work effort demanded by employers. If this is the case, workers will be caught between the Scylla of a growing risk of unemployment and the Charybdis of higher demands from their employers.

In terms of economic policy, there is a clear divide between the policies activated in the first part of the crisis, 2008–2009, and from 2010 on. In the first stage, all measures were aimed at compensating the negative impact of the crisis in both economic and social terms. The government embraced unreservedly the standard Keynesian countercyclical recipe with a social touch. As the result of such a policy (and the decrease in the tax base due to the crisis), the social and economic impacts of the crisis were reduced, but there was also a rapid growth in the public deficit (mostly because of the dramatic drop in tax revenues and the working of the automatic stabilizer and only secondarily due to the ad hoc expansive measures approved), from a surplus of 1.9 per cent in 2007 to a deficit of 11.2 per cent in 2009. The year 2010 witnessed a U-turn in economic policy, the emphasis shifting dramatically from an expansive counter-cyclical policy aimed at securing the end of the recession, to a policy of deficit reduction, this time following the dictum of the financial markets (and the EU) – the very same markets whose behaviour lies at the root of the crisis. This policy has resulted not only in a harsh reduction of public expenditure, but also in a major labour market reform aimed at decreasing employment protection and reducing dismissal costs that was contested by a General Strike on 29 September 2010, putting an end to several years of fruitful social bargaining between the trade union movement, the employers' organization and the government. The reduction of public expenditure in core social programmes (–8 per cent in social welfare, health and education, –5.5 per cent in ALMP and –20 per cent in housing), the increase in taxes and the labour reform will not only have significant implications in terms of growing inequalities (such as raising taxes by increasing VAT instead of direct taxes, with obviously different implications in terms of income distribution as direct taxes are generally considered more progressive than indirect taxes (Stiglitz, 2000)), but could also jeopardize Spain's sluggish economic recovery, delaying the reduction of unemployment. In this respect, according to a recent analysis by the IMF (2010), an institution that cannot be accused of being heterodox in economic matters, each GDP percentage point of fiscal consolidation produces an average reduction in GDP growth of 0.5 per cent due to the stagnation of demand.

NOTES

1. Only in Ireland, where construction accounted for 10.2 per cent of GDP in 2007, can we find a similar pattern.
2. For example, although the direction of the causal relationship is still an issue of debate, there is a strong association between job loss and health problems. See, among others, Morris and Cook (1991); Jin et al. (1995); Goldney (1997); Keefe et al. (2002); Browning et al. (2006); Eliason and Storrie (2009); and Kuhn et al. (2009).
3. The picture changes slightly when considering differences in gender, as the unemployment rate has increased more markedly among males: multiplying by 2.86 for the male average compared to 3.56 for males aged 35–39 years.
4. In fact, this cohort also suffered from a reduction in open-ended employment as there was a reduction in so-called permanent contracts for this population group by a quarter of a million, while this sort of employment for older workers increased by slightly over 400,000.
5. This stagnation in female employment nevertheless conceals a change in the age composition of employment, with an important decrease in employment corresponding to young cohorts (aged 16–29) and an increase in the employment of older cohorts.
6. In 2008, men made up 93 per cent and 75 per cent of the labour force in construction and industry, respectively.
7. In 2008, half of unemployed immigrants received unemployment benefits compared to 78 per cent of nationals (Tobes and Angoitia, 2010).
8. In terms of age, there has also been a reduction in the disparity of the unemployment benefit protection rate by age group, although this time less intense. As expected, the protection rate grows with the age group: 6 per cent for workers aged 16–19, one-third of workers aged 20–24, two-thirds of workers aged 25–54 and almost all workers over 55 (taking all pillars into consideration).
9. For a survey of the different systems of short-time working arrangements operating in the EU see Arpaia et al. (2010).
10. In fact, these data underestimate the intensity of the decrease in the wage share, because during the period under consideration there was a substantial reduction in self-employment (from 25 to 17 per cent of the labour force), whose mixed income is statistically considered as part of profits. The transformation of self-employment into dependent employment automatically reduces profits (the mixed income generated by the once self-employed) and increases wages, producing a spurious increase in the wage share in the sense that it is not the result of a change in income distribution towards wages but the product of a statistical convention.
11. The reduction has been especially intense in construction (10 percentage points) and in hotels and restaurants (9.6 percentage points), but also in financial intermediation (14 percentage points).
12. Obviously, this does not mean that profits have been spared by the crisis. According to the Bank of Spain, the profit rate for the sample of firms comprising the *Central de Balances* decreased from 8.9 per cent in 2007 to 5.6 per cent in the year ending in the third quarter of 2009 (Banco de España, 2009: 35).
13. In order not to hinder the creation of employment, in 2009 business organizations and trade unions signed a framework agreement (ANC) for 2010–2012 setting a wage increase guide for collective bargaining of 1 per cent for 2010, 2 per cent for 2011 and 1.5–2.5 per cent for 2012, including a safeguard clause for those firms unable, due to their economic situation, to meet the abovementioned wage increase.
14. Through most of the decade public employees received nominal wage increases roughly in line with inflation.
15. According to the report, compensation grouped around two different points: a first relatively small group of 83 very high average 'wages' of 2.3 million, and another of 201 persons with wages averaging 0.7 million.
16. The sample consisted of 1,683 households and 3,500 people interviewed.

17. On the relevance of measuring job quality see, for instance, the extensive literature review presented by Muñoz de Bustillo et al. (2009b).

18. The relationship between working conditions and productivity is not straightforward; it can be argued that improvements in working conditions might increase productivity. That is, for example, the type of relationship behind the efficient wage theory, or the rationale behind the use of incentives to improve labour performance.

19. Such a trend might be related to changes in labour legislation, the affiliation rate and the role of the trade unions, globalization and so on.

20. For information on methodology, sampling procedure and questionnaires, see http://www.mtin.es/estadisticas/.

21. The limitations of the analysis should be clear. First, the object of the study itself (workers' perception of or satisfaction with working conditions) is a matter of concern because of the low explanatory power of objective job attributes in job satisfaction, a fact associated, among other things, with the cognitive dissonance experienced by workers (Muñoz de Bustillo and Fernández-Macías, 2005). Second, and relatedly, it is possible that the crisis makes workers' judgements about their working conditions milder, insofar as, in a context of crisis, keeping a job is taken as the clearest signal of success in the labour market. For example, a poll by a national newspaper reported that the percentage of people satisfied or very satisfied with their employment had increased by almost 6 percentage points between October 2008 and November 2009 (*Público*, 16 November 2009). Third, and probably more important, as already mentioned, the analysis of the survey should be taken more as a description of the evolution of the outcomes of certain job characteristics than as a true causal analysis: we cannot determine whether the evolution of the variables considered here is the result of a trend or a causal effect of the crisis. Nevertheless, and within these limitations, we consider it worthwhile to look at the evolution of job attributes across the period of economic crisis.

22. Although the issue of absenteeism is high on the agenda of Spanish employers' organizations, according to Eurobarometer (2010), Spain is the EU Member State with the lowest index of absenteeism (0.3 average of days of work lost in the previous four weeks compared to the EU average of 1.1).

23. This conclusion is roughly in line with the preliminary results obtained for the EU27 according to the Fifth European Working Conditions Survey (Eurofound, 2010).

24. According to the *Muestra Continua de Vidas Laborales*, MCVL (Continuous Sample of Working Life), an administrative sample of social security registers, 42.3 per cent of unemployed workers on unemployment benefits and 42 per cent of those without unemployment benefits had a full-time permanent contract in the past (17 per cent had a part-time permanent contract).

25. According to Toharia and Cebrián (2007), 41 per cent of permanent contracts signed in 2004 were not still valid one year later, which shows that, even in periods of economic growth, open-ended contracts are not at all permanent.

26. Employment Protection Legislation (EPL) refers to all labour market regulations dealing with the hiring and firing of employees. For an introduction to the topic see 'Employment Protection Regulation and Labour Market Performance' (OECD, 2004).

27. According to the *Annual Labour Cost Survey*, relative costs are higher in industry and construction compared to services (2.5 per cent, 2 per cent and 1.3 per cent, respectively) and higher in medium-sized establishments (from 50 to 199 workers), at 2 per cent, compared to smaller or larger establishments (1.8 per cent and 1 per cent, respectively).

28. C. Sánchez-Silva, 'Los primeros despidos de la reforma', *El País* (22 August 2010).

29. The index is defined as percentage contribution to employment destruction/percentage of total employment in the firm size category × 100. Therefore, indexes lower than 100 mean that the firms included in such a category have destroyed employment less than proportionately (in relation to their contribution to employment). The equivalent index for firms with over 250 workers is 50, while firms with between 51 and 250 workers have contributed to employment destruction proportionately in relation to their contribution to total employment. The data were obtained from the *Survey of Economic Trends*.

30. Almost one million if we add the unfinished houses still unsold. Fifty per cent of the excess of supply is in three coastal regions, pointing to the existence of a sizeable stock of houses that were intended to be sold as second homes (in many cases to foreigners) (Ministerio de Vivienda, *Stock de viviendas nuevas a 31 de diciembre 2010*). The large time lag (two to four years or even more, depending on the type of building) from the moment when the production decision is taken to the delivery of the product also explains the large stock of vacant houses.
31. See, for example, 'Floor to ceiling', *The Economist*, 21 October 2010.
32. International Organization of Motor Vehicles Manufacturers, OICA, *Production Statistics 2009* (including light commercial vehicles).
33. All companies applied EREs in order to cope with the reduction in demand, with the exception of Volkswagen, with a single production site in Navarre, which benefited from the launch of a very successful new model. The EREs, of various magnitudes, affected 16 of the 18 existing plants.

BIBLIOGRAPHY

ANFAC (2008) *Memoria Anual*, Madrid.
ANFAC (2009) *Memoria Anual*, Madrid.
ANFAC (2010) *Memoria Anual*, Madrid.
Antón, J.-I., Muñoz de Bustillo, R. and Carrera, M. (2010) 'Raining stones? Female immigrants in the Spanish labour market', MPRA Paper 20582.
Arpaia A. et al. (2010) 'Short-term working arrangements as response to cyclical fluctuations', *European Economy*, Occasional Papers 64, June.
Baker, D., Glyn, A., Howell, D.R. and Schmitt, J. (2005) 'Labor market institutions and unemployment: a critical assessment of the cross-country evidence', in D.R. Howell (ed.), *Fighting Unemployment: The Limits of Free Market Orthodoxy*, Chapter 3, Oxford: Oxford University Press.
Banco de España (2008) *Informe de Estabilidad Financiera 2008*, Banco de España.
Banco de España (2009) *Boletín Económico Noviembre 2009*, Banco de España.
Bassanini, A. and Duval, R. (2006) 'Employment patterns in OECD countries: reassessing the role of policies and institutions', OECD Social, Employment and Migration Working Paper No. 35, and OECD Economics Department Working Paper No. 486, Paris.
Bosch, G. (2010) 'Reducción de horas, no de plantilla: el trabajo compartido durante la crisis económica', *Principios Estudios de Economía Política*, 17: 29–51.
Bosch, M., Farré, L. and Carnero, M.Á. (2010) 'Information and discrimination in the rental housing market: evidence from a field experiment', *Regional Science and Urban Economics*, 40(1): 11–19.
Browning, M., Dano, A.M. and Heinesen, E. (2006) 'Job displacement and stress-related health outcomes', *Health Economics*, 15(10): 1061–1075.
Colectivo Ioé (2008) *Trabajo Sumergido, Precariedad e Inmigración en Catalunya. Una Primera Aproximación*, Fundación Jaume Bofill.
Eliason, M. and Storrie, D. (2009) 'Does job loss shorten life?', *Journal of Human Resources*, 44(2): 277–302.
Eurobarometer (2007) *Undeclared work in the European Union*, Special Eurobarometer 67.3, Luxembourg: European Commission.
Eurobarometer (2009) *Eurobarometer Survey on Poverty and Social Exclusion*, Luxembourg: European Commission.

Eurobarometer (2010) *Mental Health, Special Eurobarometer* 73.2, Luxembourg: European Commission.

Eurofound (2010) *Changes over Time – First Findings from the Fifth European Working Conditions Survey*, European Foundation for the Improvement of Working and Living Conditions, Dublin.

European Commission (2007) *Employment in Europe 2007*, Brussels: European Commission.

Fernández-Macías, Enrique (2010) 'Changes in the structure of employment and job quality in Europe, 1995–2007', PhD Dissertation, University of Salamanca Department of Sociology and Communication.

Fernández-Macías, E. and Hurley, J. (2008) 'More and better jobs: patterns of employment expansion in Europe', *European Restructuring Monitor Report 2008*, European Foundation for the Study of Living and Working Conditions.

Fitoussi, J.P. (2003) 'Comments on Nickell, Nunziata, Ochel, and Quintini', in P. Aghion, R, Frydman, J. Stiglitz and M. Woodford (eds), *Knowledge, Information, and Expectations in Modern Macroeconomics: In Honor of Edmund S. Phelps*, Princeton: Princeton University Press.

Goldney, R.D. (1997) 'Unemployment and health: a re-appraisal', *International Archives of Occupational and Environmental Health*, 70(3): 145–147.

IMF (2010) *World Economic Outlook (WEO): Recovery, Risk, and Rebalancing, October 2010*. Washington.

Jaumotte, F. (2010) 'The Spanish Labor Market in a Cross-Country Perspective', forthcoming IMF Working Paper.

Jin, R.L, Shah, C.P. and Svoboda, T.J. (1995) 'The impact of unemployment on health: a review of the evidence', *Canadian Medical Association Journal*, 153: 529–540.

Keefe, V., Reid, P., Ormsby, C., Robson, B., Purdie, G., Baxter, J. and Ngäti Kahungunu Iwi Incorporated (2002) 'Serious health events following involuntary job loss in New Zealand meat processing workers', *International Journal of Epidemiology*, 31(6): 1155–1161.

Kuhn, A., Lalive, R. and Zweimüller, J. (2009) 'The public health costs of job loss', Institute for Empirical Research in Economics, University of Zurich, Working Paper 424.

Laparra, M. (2010) *El Primer Impacto de la Crisis en la Cohesión Social en España. Un Análisis Provisional de las Encuestas Foessa 2007–2009*, Fundación Madrid: FOESSA.

Morris, J.K. and Cook, D.G. (1991) 'A critical review of the effect of factory closures on health', *British Journal of Industrial Medicine*, 48(1): 1–8.

Muñoz de Bustillo, R. (2007a) 'Spain: The paradox of job insecurity alongside high employment growth', in François Eyraud and Daniel Vaughan-Whitehead (eds), *The Evolving World of Work in the Enlarged EU. Progress and Vulnerability*, Geneva: International Labour Office, 439–480.

Muñoz de Bustillo, R. (2007b) 'La distribución funcional de la renta en España. Una visión desde la perspectiva del largo plazo', *Gaceta Sindical. Reflexión y debate* (nueva etapa), 9: 93–107.

Muñoz de Bustillo, R. and Fernández-Macías, E. (2005) 'Job satisfaction as indicator of the quality of work', *Journal of Socio-Economics*, 34(5): 656–673.

Muñoz de Bustillo, R., Antón, J.I., Braña, F.J. and Fernández-Macías, E. (2009a) *Abandono escolar y mercado de trabajo in España*, Madrid: Ministerio di Trabajo e Inmigración.

Muñoz de Bustillo, R., Fernández-Macías, E., Antón, J.-I. and Esteve, F. (2009b) 'Indicators of job quality in the European Union', study prepared for the Department of Employment and Social Affairs of the European Parliament (PE.429.972).

OECD (2004) *Employment Outlook 2004*, Paris: OECD.

Stiglitz, J.E. (2000) *The Economics of the Public Sector*, 3rd edition, New York: W.W. Norton & Company.

Tobes, P. and Angoitia, M. (2010) 'La cobertura de los inmigrantes ante el desempleo', *Información Comercial Española*, 854: 73–84.

Toharia, L. and Cebrián, I. (2007) *La Temporalidad en el Empleo. Situación y Trayectorias*, Madrid: Ministerio de Trabajo y Asuntos Sociales.

11. Negotiated flexibility in Sweden: A more egalitarian response to the crisis?

Dominique Anxo

1. INTRODUCTION

The Swedish model is based on a strong political commitment to the goal of full employment (see Anxo and Niklasson 2006). In contrast to other EU Member States such as France and Germany, economic downturns and structural changes have seldom been accommodated by public measures aimed at maintaining employment and favouring labour hoarding, for example by reducing working time, short-time working or work sharing. Traditionally, employment adjustments in Sweden have taken the form of external numerical flexibility, combined with active labour market policy and relatively generous income support. In line with this tradition, when confronted by the severe deterioration of the situation in the labour market, and in order to mitigate the impact of the crisis on income development and employment, the Swedish Government in 2008–2009 implemented a package of recovery and countercyclical measures, ranging from expansive fiscal and monetary policy to active labour market and educational policy.

The main objective of this chapter is to describe the patterns of employment adjustment during the current economic downturns and the role played by the Government and the two sides of industry in this adjustment process. The distinct feature of the Swedish industrial relations system and the contractual nature of labour market regulation create a favourable institutional environment for the emergence of negotiated compromises aimed at balancing flexibility and security. Sweden therefore represents a good illustration of a regime of flexicurity and negotiated flexibility, where the social partners are heavily involved not only in the shaping of labour market regulations and working conditions at the industry and local level, but also in the restructuring process during economic downturns. The second objective of this chapter is to identify and

analyse the impacts of the economic crisis on employment, unemployment, working conditions and income inequalities among various socio-
economic groups, with particular emphasis on education and skill level,
age, gender and ethnicity.

This chapter is structured as follows. Section 2 presents the main characteristics of the current recession and the specificity of the employment
adjustment process. Section 3 investigates the policy responses and the
role played by the social partners in mitigating the impact of the crisis
on employment and income development. We then analyse the impact
of the crisis for different age groups and gender and between natives and
foreign-born people (Section 4), and the impact of the crisis on wages,
income development and inequalities (Section 5). Section 6 presents
the results from two case studies. Two export-oriented manufacturing
companies were selected to illustrate the role played by the two sides
of industry in the downsizing and restructuring process during the economic crisis. Section 7 summarizes the main findings and provides some
concluding remarks.

2.   THE IMPACT OF THE GLOBAL CRISIS ON THE SWEDISH ECONOMY – MAIN CHARACTERISTICS OF THE 2008–2009 RECESSION

In the wake of the global financial and economic crisis, the Swedish
economy started to deteriorate rapidly in the second half of 2008. In
2009, Sweden's GDP decreased by 5.1 per cent, the worst deterioration
since the Second World War. With the severe drop in output and aggregate demand, employment has declined sharply over the past two years.
According to the most recent economic forecast by the National Institute
of Economic Research (NIER 2010), despite some recent signs of recovery[1] and a tendency for employment to increase, the overall unemployment rate is expected to remain at 8 per cent in 2011, a level much higher
than the Swedish equilibrium rate of unemployment (estimated at around
5–6 per cent).

As shown by Table 11.1, the decline of employment during 2009 was less
than the fall in output, implying that part of the adjustment took the form
of labour hoarding at the company level and reductions of working hours
instead of dismissals, but as developed in more detail in the following
section adjustment through a reduction of working time or other labour
hoarding measures has been limited.

Sweden is a small, open economy, highly dependent on exports and

Table 11.1   Economic indicators, Sweden, 2007–2011 (forecast)

	2007	2008	2009	2010	2011
GDP, market price	2.5	–0.2	–5.1	4.3	3.4
Hours of work	3.5	1.0	–2.6	1.7	1.0
Employment	2.4	0.9	–2.3	1.0	1.2
Employment rates (16–64)	75.6	75.7	73.3	73.8	74.5
Unemployment (ILO definition)	6.2	6.1	8.4	8.5	8.2
Unemployment duration (weeks)	25.9	25.3	27.9	–	–
Number of participants in ALMP	1.9	1.8	2.7	3.8	3.7
Hourly wage, business sector	3.4	4.0	3.2	2.3	2.6
Productivity, business sector	–0.9	–2.4	–3.6	2.8	2.5
Inflation	2.2	2.7	–0.3	1.1	1.6
Interest rate	4.0	2.0	0.25	1.0	2.75

Note: Annual percentage change and percentage, respectively.

Source: NIER (2010).

therefore very sensitive to variations in global demand. Sweden therefore exhibited some signs of a downturn in early autumn 2008, with a significant decline in newly reported vacancies, while layoff notices increased dramatically (from an average of 30,000 in 2007 to more than 115,000 in 2009). Not surprisingly, the increase in notified redundancies was particularly significant in export-oriented manufacturing industries, such as wood and wood products, machinery and motor vehicles. The financial crisis also affected insurance and real estate and financial activities, where layoff notices increased significantly (see Arbetsförmedlingen 2010).

Between 2007 and 2009, employment decreased by more than 100,000, while the unemployment rate increased from 6.2 per cent to 8.4 per cent. The fall in output and employment was particularly marked in manufacturing, with decreases of 25 and 20 per cent, respectively (see Figure 11.1), while employment increased by almost 10 per cent in the private service sector and in construction. As also shown by Figure 11.1, employment declined significantly in the female-dominated public sector, in particular at the municipality and county levels, which are responsible for social services, health and education.

With regard to Swedish manufacturing, the fall in employment (see Figure 11.2) has been particularly marked in export-oriented industries, in particular basic metal (–32 per cent), machinery and equipment (–23 per cent), manufacture of wood products (–22 per cent) and automotive (–18 per cent).

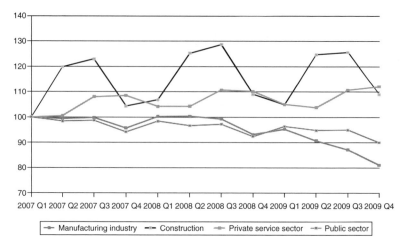

Source: Statistics Sweden (2010a).

Figure 11.1   *Employment trends by broad sectors, Sweden, 2007–2009*
             (2007Q1=100)

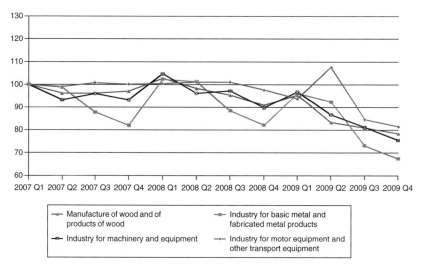

Source: Statistics Sweden (2010a).

Figure 11.2   *Largest declines in employment in manufacturing industries,*
             Sweden, 2007–2009 (2007Q1=100)

3. POLICY RESPONSES AND RECOVERY MEASURES

3.1 Macroeconomic Policy and Labour Market and Education Measures

Over the past two years, the Swedish Government has implemented a set of measures to mitigate the effects of the financial and economic crisis on the Swedish economy. Swedish fiscal policy since the end of 2008 has taken a clearer and stronger expansionary stance. In contrast to the 1990s crisis, when the bulk of countercyclical measures essentially took the form of an increase in the number of participants in various active labour market policy programmes (ALMP), the Swedish Government has relied to a greater extent on expansionary fiscal and monetary policy to counteract the current economic recession. It is also clear that, in comparison to the 1990s crisis, the room for manoeuvre in which to conduct a more expansive macroeconomic policy was larger than previously, due to healthier public finances at the start of the economic downturn. Globally, the package of measures adopted and implemented since autumn 2008 to counteract the effects of the global crisis amounts to SEK 83 billion, corresponding to 2.7 per cent of GDP.[2]

3.1.1 Developments autumn 2008–December 2009

The package of measures agreed on in the 2009 Autumn Budget Bill[3] was not aimed at combating the economic crisis, but was part of an overall economic policy aimed at increasing the level of employment in the long run through essentially labour supply-oriented measures, such as tax cuts and reforms of the social protection system (unemployment benefit, sickness insurance and disability pension). In the face of the drastic worsening of the economic situation, as well as the growing awareness that Sweden will experience a much more dramatic drop in output and employment, at the end of 2008 and the first half of 2009 the Government took further financial and fiscal stimuli measures. In particular, extensive investments in the maintenance and operation of the road and rail networks were decided on, in addition to the measures already announced in December 2008.[4] As far as the crisis of the financial system is concerned, at the end of October 2008 the Government launched a guarantee programme,[5] aimed at securing the medium-term borrowing of banks and mortgage institutions and lowering the cost of borrowing for households and companies. To protect Swedish savers, the bank deposit guarantee was raised from SEK 250,000 to SEK 500,000 in December 2008. In January 2009, the Government proposed, in order to stimulate activity and maintain labour demand in the construction sector, that work in the form of repairs, maintenance and improvement

of one-family houses and tenant housing be brought under the system
of tax credits for household work.[6] The Government also presented at
this time a number of measures to address the crisis in the automotive
sector and facilitate more rapid development of green technology.[7] In the
Supplementary Spring Budget presented in April 2009 and voted on by
the Swedish Parliament in June 2009, the Government announced further
countercyclical expansive fiscal measures to combat the crisis. These new
fiscal measures covered mainly two areas: increased Government grants to
municipalities and county councils and more resources for active labour
market policy.[8] In the 2010 Autumn Budget Bill, in September 2009 the
Government presented further measures to mitigate the impact of the
global crisis on employment. It decided on a further increase of SEK 10
billion in the central government grant to municipalities and county councils in 2010, as well as further investment in infrastructure (SEK 1 billion)
in order to maintain and secure employment in the public sector. As far as
tax policy is concerned, the Government also decided on the introduction
of a fourth step in the already implemented in-work tax credit (SEK 10
billion),[9] a reduction in social security contributions for the self-employed,
[10] a further reduction in income taxes for low income pensioners and an
increase in housing benefit for people on long-term sickness and activity
guarantees.

As far as ALMP measures are concerned, the volume of participants
in the various ALMP programmes was gradually increased, but never
attained the number of participants enrolled during the last severe recession in the early 1990s (see Figure 11.3). The difference concerns not only
the number of participants, but also the composition of ALMP measures.
Compared to the previous crisis, the current Government has focused
more on matching measures and/or work experience and trainee schemes.
Hence, the extra resources decided on in 2009 essentially took the form of
labour supply-oriented measures (matching measures, job search assistance, coaching and work experience and trainee schemes). The number
of participants in traditional labour market training was also slightly
increased, but much less than in the previous recession.

As far as measures aimed at stimulating labour demand are concerned
(job subsidies and social contribution reductions), most were planned
or already implemented and would have been initiated even without the
crisis and therefore cannot be considered per se as a response to the crisis.
However, the funds allocated to these wage subsidies have been increased.
Two exceptions are worth noting, however: the reduction of employers'
social security contributions, targeted at young people,[11] and the increase
in the compensation level of the already implemented New Start Jobs.[12]

All in all, the number of participants in labour market policy

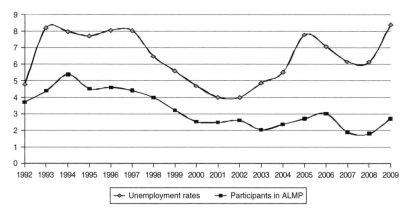

Source: NIER (2010).

Figure 11.3 *Unemployment rates and participants in active labour market policy measures, as a percentage of the labour force, Sweden, 1992–2009*

programmes has increased and is expected to further increase during 2010 but, as already mentioned, less than during the previous economic crisis in the early 1990s. It should also be noted that public sector job creation has not been used in connection to the crisis, but the increase of central government grants to local governments has certainly had an effect in maintaining or limiting the fall of employment in the female-dominated public sector.

Regarding education and training policy, the Government decided to temporarily increase the number of places in post-secondary vocational training, local authority upper secondary education for adults and universities and colleges.[13] To encourage more people to apply for secondary adult vocational education programmes, the Government's proposal of a temporary increase in opportunities for unemployed people over the age of 25, regardless of previous education, to obtain a higher level of post-secondary student aid in 2009 and 2010 was also adopted by the Swedish Parliament in December 2009.[14] As far as youth education measures are concerned, drop-outs from secondary school now have the opportunity, within the framework of the Youth Job Guarantee Programme,[15] to complete their studies. In the 2010 Autumn Budget Bill, the Government therefore announced an increase of 1,000 slots in adult colleges.

As far as the unemployment insurance system (UI) is concerned, individual unemployment contributions were reduced by about SEK 50 a month, as of 1 July 2009. The Government also amended membership requirements temporarily so that members of an unemployment insurance fund in 2009 would be able to count one month extra for each month of membership in 2009. In order to further facilitate joining an unemployment insurance fund, the Government simplified the admission requirements. The requirement of having worked a certain time in order to join a fund was abolished in July 2009. Another change introduced is that the unemployment contribution is now tax deductible for employed members. All these measures were aimed at reducing the negative impact of the reform of the UI system introduced in 2007. This reform implied, among other things, a worsening of the income replacement rate and an upper limit for benefit duration (300 days). Furthermore, individual contributions to the UI protection system were increased dramatically, entailing both a massive exit from the UI system during 2007 and also a decline in union membership (see Eliasson 2008; Kjellberg 2010; and Section 5).

3.2 Involvement of Social Partners in Mitigating the Impact of the Economic Crisis

The bulk of labour market regulations, working conditions and wage setting in Sweden are determined and regulated by collective agreements, and an analysis of measures initiated to combat the impact of the economic crisis on employment cannot be limited to government action. Compared to other Member States, such as France and Germany, no government recovery measures for maintaining employment by means of short-time working have been implemented in Sweden. The initiatives came instead from the two sides of industry. By way of illustration: the trade union federation IF Metall and the Association of Swedish Engineering Industries concluded a framework agreement on temporary layoffs, wage adjustments and training in March 2009. The agreement was valid until 31 March 2010, with a three-month notice period. To be valid, an arrangement had to be based on a local agreement between the employer and the union. Under the agreement, a person temporarily laid off from work must receive at least 80 per cent of their usual monthly wage. The Swedish Industrial and Chemical Employers' Association, the Employers' Association of the Steel and Metal Industry, the Employers' Association of Swedish Mine Owners, the Employers' Federation of Welding Engineering and IF Metall signed a temporary redundancy pay agreement on 2 March 2009, enabling local partners at the firm level to conclude agreements on temporary layoffs. This agreement is similar to the agreement between IF Metall and the employers in the Association of Swedish Engineering Industries. Some 400 companies affiliated to the Association of Swedish Engineering Industries have concluded such agreements. Most of them cover both manual and non-manual workers. On average, these short-time working agreements included an 18 per cent reduction in working hours and a 13 per cent reduction in wages. The average duration of these agreements was slightly over six months.

As for wage setting, experience from the deep economic crisis of the early 1990s shows that wage moderation characterized wage developments during the second half of the 1990s and early 2000s. There were therefore strong reasons to expect that, in the wake of the current severe economic and financial crisis, wage agreements would also be concluded to preserve employment stability and limit further increases in unemployment. The outcome of the 2009 and 2010 bargaining round seems to indicate that wage moderation has prevailed in Sweden (see Section 5 for details).

As described in Anxo (2009), in cases of collective redundancy due to restructuring or individual notice due to a shortage of work, the Swedish social partners have, since the early 1970s, negotiated security/adjustment agreements to help workers to find new jobs quickly, by way of adjustment measures and financial support. These support programmes are administered by bipartite organizations: the so-called Job Security Councils (*Trygghetsråd*) and Job Security Foundations (*Trygghetsstiftelser*), specially designed for this purpose. By supplementing the role of public employment agencies, these agreements, covering about half the labour force, contribute to improving the security of employees and to enhancing matching efficiency and have played an important role in accommodating the current deep recession. Worth noticing also is that, in order to alleviate the individual consequences of layoffs and plant closures, the Government set up a plan for enhancing and promoting cooperation between stakeholders, such as the Public Employment Service, the Social Insurance Agency, the abovementioned Job Security Councils and Job Security Foundations, the European Social Funds, municipalities, companies, non-profit organizations and trade unions.

4. DIMENSIONS OF INEQUALITY IN THE CRISIS

4.1 Employment Contracts, Working Time and Education/Skill Levels

In the early phase of the recession, adjustment essentially took the form of a reduction of overtime (see Figure 11.4, upper panel) and a dramatic reduction in the number of agency workers and temporary contracts, in particular among male employees (see Figure 11.4, lower panel).

Compared to the significant drop in the overall employment level, the crisis had a limited impact on average weekly working time. Weekly

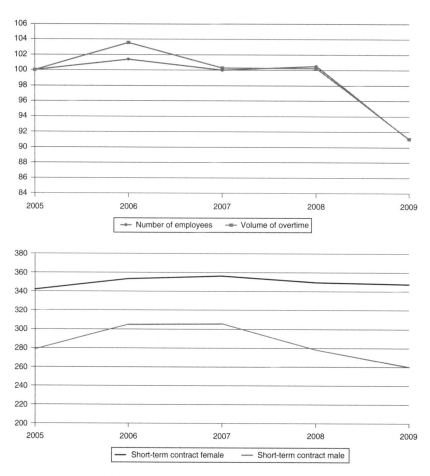

Source: Statistics Sweden (2010a).

Figure 11.4   *Trends in overtime and number of dependent employees*
            with overtime (upper panel, 2007=100) and in short-term
            contracts by gender (lower panel, in thousands), Sweden,
            2005–2009

working time in the manufacturing industry was reduced by 1.5 per cent
between 2008 and 2009, implying that employment adjustment in manufacturing essentially took the form of dismissals rather than reductions in
average working time among dependent employees. Both the volume of
overtime and the proportion of dependent employees working overtime
declined during the economic downturn, however, especially among male

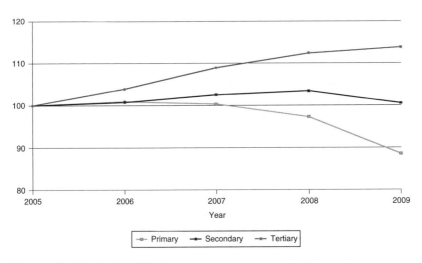

Source: Statistics Sweden (2010a).

Figure 11.5 Employment trends by educational attainment, Sweden, 2005–2009

employees. Furthermore, the share of male part-timers also increased (from a low level), explaining part of the slight decline in men's working time between 2008 and 2009. On the other hand, average weekly working time in the female-dominated public sector increased slightly during the recession. The lengthening of working time in the public sector is partly related to the decrease in the proportion of female part-timers and also to a reduction in absenteeism.

Unfortunately, we cannot assess whether this increase in working time is due to a modification of the distribution of working time in the public sector (increase in the share of full-timers among the remaining employees, that is, a lengthening of working time) or the fact that layoffs were concentrated on female employees with part-time contracts.

As also shown by Figure 11.5, the employment decline has also been particularly dramatic among low-educated and low-skilled workers, while employment among employees with a high level of education was only slightly affected and even increased among high-skilled employees.

4.2 Age, Gender and Ethnicity

Youth unemployment, as well as unemployment among non-natives, is more sensitive to fluctuations in the business cycle and the employment prospects of young people and foreign-born people[16] has worsened significantly since the end of 2008. In the fourth quarter of 2009, youth unemployment rates reached 29 per cent[17] and those for foreign-born people 16.4 per cent (compared to 7.8 per cent for natives). The dramatic increase in youth unemployment might be ascribed to several factors: first, a significant increase in the youth labour supply, a relatively larger cohort of young people entering the labour market when the recession started; second, the incidence of temporary contracts is high among young people; and third, the Swedish Employment Protection Act – more specifically, the application of the seniority principle (last in, first out) – favours workers with long seniority in the redundancy process. While the labour supply of people with an immigrant background was unchanged, the increase of unemployment among non-natives is also related to their weak embedding in the Swedish labour market (higher incidence of temporary contracts, lower work experience and concentration in the low skill segment of the manufacturing industry and service sector).

As shown by Figures 11.6 and 11.7, the impact of the crisis, in terms of relative unemployment, has been evenly distributed between the usual socio-economic groups, for example, based on gender, age and origin. This is due to the massive impact of the crisis on employment: all socio-economic categories were affected by the deep recession.

As far as gender is concerned, the relatively stronger impact of the crisis on male unemployment is related to the abovementioned decline of employment in the male-dominated export-oriented manufacturing sector, but compared to the previous crisis (1993) the gender gap in unemployment has remained much lower (see Figure 11.8). There are strong reasons to believe that this is related to the more rapid decline in employment in the public sector at the local and regional levels due to severe budget cuts, despite the additional appropriations to local government by the Swedish Government.

Regarding older workers, Swedish companies seem to have used early retirement to accommodate the recession much less than in previous economic downturns. The employment rate of senior workers (55–64 years of age) has, to date, remained almost unchanged (see Figure 11.9), while unemployment increased only slightly, from 3.2 per cent in 2008 to 5.2 per cent in 2009.

The fact that the youth and immigrant relative unemployment rates have not increased can also be explained partly by the abovementioned active labour market measures targeted on these two groups and implemented in the second half of 2008, as well as the education measures implemented in 2009.

The long-term consequences of high youth unemployment and the

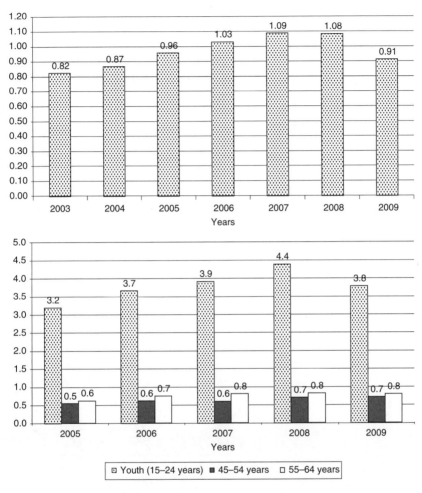

Source: Statistics Sweden (2010a).

Figure 11.6 *Relative unemployment rates by gender (female relative to male, upper panel) and age (relative to prime adult 25–44 years, lower panel), Sweden, 2005–2009*

deterioration of the labour market for people with an immigrant background are worrying. Several Swedish empirical studies (for example, Nordström-Skans 2004) have shown that an early period of unemployment can have lasting negative effects on subsequent employment performance and income development. These studies have identified significant 'scarring' effects of unemployment. Furthermore, an early period

Work inequalities in the crisis

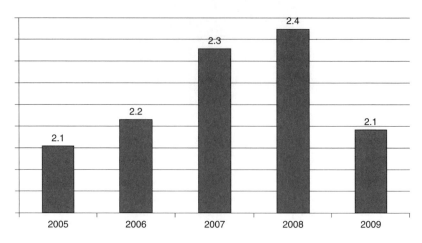

Source: Statistics Sweden (2010a).

*Figure 11.7   Relative unemployment rate of people with an immigrant
background, Sweden, 2005–2009*

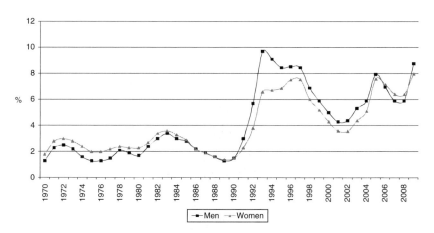

Source: Statistics Sweden (2010a).

*Figure 11.8   Unemployment rates by gender, Sweden, 1970–2009
(percentage of the labour force)*

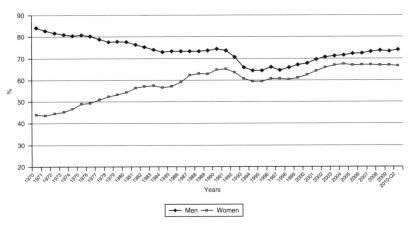

Source: Statistics Sweden (2010b).

Figure 11.9 *Trends in senior employment rates (55–64 years old), Sweden, 1970–2010Q2*

of unemployment may affect the timing of other transitions and events over the life cycle: the transition from school to work;[18] exit from the original family and the constitution of an independent household; access to housing; parenthood (increase of the median age at first birth and risk of a decline in overall fertility); career opportunities and wage development; as well as exit patterns from the labour force at the end of a person's career (see Anxo et al. 2010).

5. WAGES, EARNINGS DEVELOPMENT AND EARNINGS INEQUALITIES

As mentioned previously, experience from the deep economic crisis of the early 1990s shows that wage moderation characterized wage developments during the second half of the 1990s. The 2009 bargaining round covered few agreements and relatively few employees.[19] Only 30 of the 650 collective agreements were the subject of negotiation. In 2009, the negotiated pay increase was 3.4 per cent for manual workers in the private sector and 2.9 per cent for non-manual workers. In the first half of 2010, around 530 new collective agreements were concluded, covering around 1.4 million dependent employees. Most agreements cover the period from spring 2010 to spring 2012. The moderate outcome in terms of negotiated pay settlements during the last round of collective bargaining, coupled with the

Table 11.2   Wage development by industry, Sweden, 2000–2009

	2000	2005	2006	2007	2008	2009
Manufacturing	4.1	3.1	3.2	3.7	4.4	2.9
Construction	3.9	3.1	3.4	2.6	4.5	3.5
Business sector	3.7	3.2	3.1	3.4	4.0	3.1
Local authorities	3.6	2.8	2.8	3.0	5.0	3.9
State	4.8	3.3	3.4	3.8	3.9	3.8
All	3.7	3.1	3.1	3.3	4.3	3.3

Source: Mediation Office (2010).

weak situation in the labour market, imply that wages are expected to rise moderately during 2010 and 2011 (2.3 per cent in 2010 and 2.6 per cent in 2011), limiting also labour cost increases.

According to short-term wage statistics from the Swedish Mediation Office (2010), the rate of wage increases in 2009 was 3.3 per cent for the economy as a whole (see Table 11.2). For the private business sector, the rate was slightly lower, at 3.1 per cent. The highest rate of increase, 3.9 per cent, was recorded in the public sector at the regional level (county councils). As shown by Table 11.2, pay rises for 2009 were significantly below those recorded in 2008. To a considerable extent, this reflects the impact of the deterioration in the labour market on wage increases in 2009. Real wage growth – which averaged 2.5 per cent a year between 1995 and 2008 – was 3.5–4 per cent in 2009, primarily due to the negative average rate of inflation.

Wage dispersion (P90/P10) in Sweden has been increasing since the early 1990s, rising from around 1.80 in 1992 to around 2.00 in 2009. Even though it is too early to assess accurately the impact of the global economic crisis on wage distribution, it seems that, to date, this impact has been limited, with contrasting developments by gender.[20] As shown by Table 11.3, between 1996 and 2009 the increase of wage inequality was higher for women than for men, except for blue-collar workers in the private sector. The increase in wage inequality for women was particularly marked among white-collar employees in the private sector (an increase of almost 21 per cent) but also in the state sector (+15 per cent). Part of the increase in female wage dispersion might be ascribed to a compositional effect, that is, the increase of the share of females working in the private sector (in particular in white-collar jobs) and also to a tendency toward individualization of wage setting, in particular in the female-dominated public sector, implying greater wage differentiation.

According to a recent study (Ekberg and Holmlund 2010), Sweden also

Table 11.3   Wage dispersion by broad sector, P90/P10, Sweden, 1996–2009

Sector	Women			Men		
	1996	2002	2009	1996	2002	2009
Private sector (blue-collar)	1.54	1.50	1.53	1.63	1.54	1.56
Private sector (white-collar)	1.73	2.03	2.09	2.21	2.53	2.50
Local authorities	1.50	1.58	1.51	1.72	1.74	1.71
County councils	1.53	1.70	1.73	2.97	3.18	3.09
State/central administration	1.61	1.75	1.86	1.93	2.05	2.12

Source: Mediation Office (2010).

experienced a reduction in the gender wage gap between 2005 and 2009.[21] The reduction in the gender pay gap affects all industries but was particularly important in the public sector. The reduction in the gender wage gap might be ascribed to a relative increase of female educational attainment, the deregulation and privatization of part of the public sector and also the increase in the share of women in managerial positions.[22]

Looking at the development of the earnings distribution in the long run, the dispersion of disposable income has also increased. Although Sweden belongs to the set of countries with the lowest earnings inequalities, the Gini coefficient increased by 26 per cent between 1991 and 2008 (see Figure 11.10). However, as also shown by Figure 11.10, the Gini coefficient decreased between 2007 and 2009. The recent decrease of the Swedish Gini coefficient might be ascribed principally to the fall in capital income among high earners.

As shown by Figure 11.10, the reduction in disposable income has been particularly marked at the two ends of the income distribution. Low and high earners both experienced a significant decline in disposable income between 2007 and 2009. There are good reasons to believe that the deterioration among low earners (first decile) might be ascribed to the conjunction of several factors: the increase in unemployment, particularly among low skilled and low paid workers, the dramatic increase in youth unemployment (new entrants into the labour market not covered by the UI system), and the UI reform initiated in 2007 (see above). Regarding the last factor, the reform of the UI system resulted in a significant change in the generosity of the Swedish UI system, the income replacement rate being reduced to 70 per cent after 200 days of unemployment and the maximum duration for receiving unemployment benefits reduced to 300 days. Furthermore, the financing of the UI was modified: the contributions

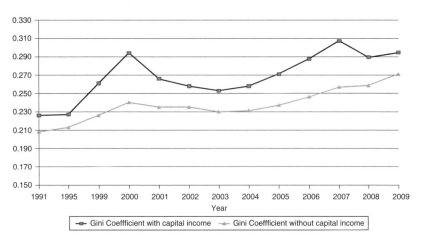

Source: Statistics Sweden (2010b).

Figure 11.10   *Gini coefficient, disposable income per consumption unit,*
with capital income and without capital income, Sweden,
1991–2009

of the various unemployment funds administered by the trade unions (the
Ghent system) were differentiated according to the unemployment level
in the sector/industry concerned. This reform entailed a large increase in
individual contributions; in some cases, UI fees tripled. The consequence
was both a large decrease in union membership[23] and a dramatic decline
in the number of dependent employees covered by the UI system: around
500,000 employees left the UI system between 2007 and 2008. Although
the Government again changed the qualification rules in 2009 (see Section
3) and introduced a ceiling on individual contributions, there is reason to
believe that a significant part of the decline in average disposable income
in the first decile is a consequence of this reform. There is also evidence
to indicate that the bulk of the reduction in capital income among low
earners is related to the deterioration of the financial and stock market,
which had a negative impact on pension benefit.

As also shown by Figure 11.11, the reduction in disposable income
among high earners (D10) is due essentially to the reduction in capital
income in connection to the financial crisis. As a consequence of this
development, to date the crisis has slightly reduced earnings inequalities
in Sweden.

During the period 2007–2009, average disposable income declined
slightly (–1.0 per cent), while the median disposable income by consumption unit actually increased by above 3 per cent. The impact of the crisis on

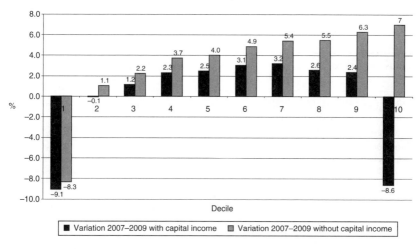

Source: Statistics Sweden (2010b).

Figure 11.11 Annual variation (2007–2009) of disposable income per consumption unit by decile, Sweden

the development of disposable earnings was not independent of the extent and generosity of the social protection and transfer systems (economic stabilizers), which remain high in Sweden, by international standards. Furthermore, the reforms of the tax system, which entailed a reduction in both average and marginal income tax, and the Government's countercyclical measures, such as the increase in the number of participants in ALMP, may partly explain the fact that disposable income has, to date, not been severely affected by the crisis.[24] Looking at different household types, the decline in disposable median income by consumption unit has been concentrated among single parents; the other categories, on the contrary, experienced an increase in disposable median income (see Table 11.4).

As shown by Figure 11.12, the share of people with low disposable income (poverty rate, 60 per cent of median income) among those 20 years of age and over has slightly increased during the crisis. Not surprisingly, the largest increase in the poverty rate is found among young singles without children (20–29 years old) who have been particularly hard hit by the crisis. In order to reduce the negative impact of the crisis on low income households and poverty, the Government also reduced income tax for pensioners and improved the situation of single parents and low income parents by increasing housing benefit. As shown by Figure 11.12, these measures seem to have stopped the increase of poverty among lone

Table 11.4   Variation of median disposable income by consumption unit, Sweden, 2007–2008

Household types	Variation of disposable income, 2007–2008 in %
Single persons without children	7.4
Single persons with children	–2.4
Married or cohabiting without children	1.4
Married or cohabiting with children	6.9
All persons aged 18 years or older	4.0

Source: Statistics Sweden (2010b).

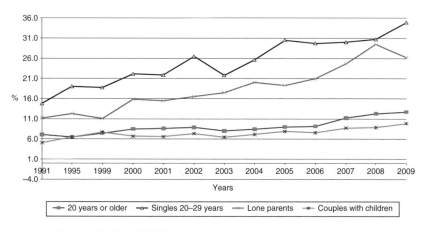

Source: Statistics Sweden (2010b).

Figure 11.12   Share of persons by type of household with low disposable income, Sweden, 1991, 1995, 1999–2009 (60 per cent of median income)

parents. By the same token, the share of older people (65 + years) on low incomes also declined between 2008 and 2009.

6.   CASE STUDIES

In order to illustrate the adjustment process during the recession we have chosen two companies from the export-oriented manufacturing sector:

one in the automobile sector, the other in the aluminium industry. These two industries were particularly affected by the economic downturn. The two case studies are also a good illustration of Swedish patterns of employment adjustment, namely a combination of negotiated external numerical and internal flexibility and the role played by the two sides of industry in downsizing and restructuring.

6.1 Flexicurity, the Swedish Way: The Volvo Cars Corporation (Göteborg)

The downturn in the global economy in the aftermath of the financial crisis hit the automotive industry in Sweden severely. It should be noted, however, that the two 'Swedish' car producers, Volvo Cars and Saab Automobile, owned up to the end of 2009[25] by Ford and General Motors, respectively, were experiencing serious profitability problems long before the start of the recession. In order to cope with the dramatic decline in orders and sales in connection to the crisis, the management at Volvo Cars (Swedish headquarters, Göteborg), in close cooperation with the trade unions, set up a comprehensive 'work sharing' and cost reduction programme,[26] with components such as: staff reductions and dismissals, temporary layoffs, short-time working and wage freezes, as well as early retirement schemes.

In early 2008, 6,000 employees were given notice. Around 4,600 of these were actually dismissed, corresponding to 17 per cent of the workforce. A significant proportion of these dismissed workers were agency workers and employees on temporary contracts, but a majority had tenured positions at Volvo (open-ended contracts). The company, of course, followed the regulations of the Swedish Employment Protection Act (LAS) regarding the seniority principle, but also strove to retain employees with the skills needed for future production. Bargaining with the various local trade unions made it possible to safeguard most of the personnel with key competencies.

During the layoff process, Volvo Cars also cooperated closely with two Job Security Councils[27] in order to accommodate the restructuring process and help the dismissed workers to rapidly find new job alternatives or training programmes. Furthermore, a special and temporary local public employment agency office was opened at the Volvo site in Göteborg to provide coaching, advice and support to the dismissed workers.

Employees at Volvo were also affected by temporary layoffs. The duration of temporary layoffs ranged between 8 and 45 days, depending on the job category, with a wage reduction of 15 per cent. According to Volvo's human resource manager, the absence of state subsidized short-time working schemes in Sweden explains the larger number of redundancies compared to the Volvo plant in Belgium where such a state subsidized scheme was implemented. In other words, in its Belgium plant, Volvo could accommodate the decline in production and sales by keeping on its workforce, while the adjustment in Sweden essentially took the form of layoffs and external numerical flexibility.

In addition, Volvo, in agreement with the local unions, decided to freeze the wages of blue-collar workers in 2009. White-collar workers also experienced salary cuts, ranging between 3 and 5 per cent. Overtime payments were stopped and no bonus payments were made during the restructuring process.

Around 400 older employees who, according to the human resource manager, did not meet future requirements, were offered an early retirement package. If the employees were older than 60, Volvo paid 70 per cent of their wage until the normal retirement age (65 in Sweden).

The human resource manager we interviewed believes that the financial crisis and the global economic downturn have led many Swedish companies to change their recruitment strategies, implying that in the future they will be more reluctant to increase their workforces on the basis of open-ended contracts (tenure). There are therefore strong reasons to believe that, in future, there will be an increase in the number of temporary employment agencies and short-term contracts. Two reasons may be put forward for this: (1) to create the conditions for greater external numerical flexibility to cope with up- and downturns; and (2) to provide companies with the option of adjusting labour costs more rapidly across the business cycle.

6.2   Negotiated External and Internal Numerical Flexibility: Profilgruppen

Created in 1981, the company Profilgruppen is a supplier of custom-designed profiles and refined aluminium components. The enterprise covers a variety of market segments and customers range from automotive industries (25 per cent of total production volume), interior design and construction, health care equipment and telecom/electronics to general engineering. Approximately 50 per cent of the company's production goes for export. Today (June 2010), Profilgruppen employs 387 employees, 75 per cent of them production workers. In June 2008, 490 persons were employed at the company. In the aftermath of the financial crisis and economic downturn the company experienced serious difficulties and was obliged to lay off 133 employees (120 manual and 13 white-collar workers, 27 per cent of the workforce). Fortunately, the relatively wide range of customers meant that the impact of the crisis was spread over a relatively long period. While the automotive industry was quickly affected by the recession it took longer for it to reach the company's other industrial segments. Despite the variation in the timing of the crisis across industries, Profilgruppen was severely hit by the crisis, both in the domestic and export markets. Orders and production levels declined rapidly after summer 2008 and around 133 employees were given notice during autumn 2008. Negotiations regarding the layoff process got under way rapidly with the various local trade union representatives. The main bargaining issues concerned which workers (with key competences, such as mechanics and electricians) could be exempted from the seniority rule (last in, first out, according to the Swedish Employment Act). The bulk of layoffs were therefore concentrated on low-skilled workers (mainly operators) and among them the seniority rule was scrupulously followed. Consequently, layoffs mainly affected young people (25–30 years of age) and/or employees with short tenure. The average age of employees at the company therefore increased. As far as temporary workers are concerned, at the start of the downturn the company counted only 17 employees on short-term contracts. These employees were dismissed first.

In the early stages of the dismissal process the firm could not use the short-time working agreement concluded at the branch level between the trade union IF Metall and the Association of Swedish Engineering Industries, since the agreement was not concluded before March 2009 (see above), that is, after the company initiated the redundancy process. On the other hand, during 2009 and in order to avoid laying off white-collar workers and retaining key competences within the firm, the company introduced a four-day week for a period of seven months. Short-time working was the outcome of a bargaining process and collective agreement with the local trade unions. This local agreement follows the disposition of the abovementioned collective agreement at the branch level and involved a reduction of 20 per cent in working time and a 10 per cent wage reduction. The local agreement covered both production workers and white-collar workers but, due to the large redundancies among production workers, short-time working was mainly implemented among white-collar workers.

In contrast to Volvo, the company did not make use of a wage freeze or early retirement to accommodate the decline in activity.[28] According to the company, the use of early retirement was considered too expensive.

As at Volvo Cars, Profilgruppen cooperated closely with two Job Security Councils[29] to help redundant employees (both white-collar and production workers) to return to the labour market as soon as possible. The support for the dismissed employees took the form of tailored individual plans, coaching and labour market training. It should also be noted that the intervention of the Job Security Councils started in the earliest phase of the redundancy process.

Some of the dismissed workers, who prior to the recession had open-ended contracts, have now been re-employed, but on a short-term contract.[30] According to the human resource manager, the fear of a double-dip is the main reason for recruiting on short-term contracts. Although the company has not yet made use of temporary agency workers and/or short-term contracts as a means of short-term adjustment over the business cycle, the human resource manager indicates that it cannot be ruled out that the company, like Volvo Cars, will in the future rely on external numerical flexibility – a larger proportion of short-term contracts – to a larger extent than today.

6.3   Lessons from the Case Studies

The two case studies constitute a good example of the Swedish adjustment process in operation during the current crisis, namely a mix of negotiated numerical flexibility and active support of dismissed workers through active labour market policy measures and/or negotiated agreements helping redundant workers to find a new job rapidly or to enhance their employability. These two examples therefore constitute, in our view, a good illustration of flexicurity '*à la Suédoise*' and stress the importance of social dialogue at the company level during the restructuring process.

The agreements on temporary wage freezes are also a good reflection of the overall tendency toward wage moderation in Sweden during a recession, and the willingness of the two sides of industry to share equally the burden of the crisis and limit the potential impact of the recession on wage structure and inequalities.

Even though, at the policy level, the various Swedish governments have been reluctant to use work sharing and short-time working to accommodate the crisis, our two case studies are also a good illustration of the use of a temporary reduction of working time to keep key competencies in the company and limit adjustment and transaction costs for high-skilled workers.

In contrast to other countries, with weaker industrial relations systems and unbalanced bargaining power between the two sides of industry, the specificity of the Swedish industrial relations system implies a more balanced sharing of the cost of the crisis in terms of both working conditions and inequalities at work.

It should, however, be noted that the significant increase in the incidence of short-term contracts coincided with the deep economic crisis of the early 1990s. Our two case studies tend also to show that the current crisis might in future lead to an increase in the share of temporary contracts and agency workers, implying the risk of deepening labour market segmentation. Furthermore, Swedish employment protection law – in particular the application of the seniority rule – explains largely why young cohorts have disproportionally borne the burden of the crisis, with potential long-lasting negative effects on subsequent careers and income development.

7. CONCLUSION

Traditionally, and in line with the core elements of the Swedish model, economic downturns and structural changes have seldom been accommodated by measures aiming at maintaining the level of employment. In contrast to other European Member States, public policies aimed at reducing working time (work sharing) or facilitating temporary layoffs have not been favoured in Sweden. During the current recession, employment adjustments in Sweden therefore essentially took the form of external numerical flexibility, combined with active labour market policy and relatively generous income support. Low-skilled workers in the export-oriented manufacturing industries were particularly hard hit by the crisis and in the initial phase of the economic downturn the brunt of adjustment was concentrated on agency workers and on workers with temporary contracts. Young people were also particularly affected by the economic crisis and unemployment among young people increased dramatically. The rise in youth unemployment can be ascribed to several factors: an increase in youth labour supply (cohort effect), the large incidence of temporary contracts among young people and the consequences of the application of the seniority principle. Compared to the severe economic downturn of the early 1990s, women's unemployment also increased rapidly during the current recession. Despite the increased state support for local authorities in 2009, the reduction in tax revenue at the local level led to severe budget cuts that translated into a reduction of employment in the female-dominated public sector.

Since the late 1950s, active labour market policy (ALMP) has played a vital role in Swedish stabilization policies. The preference for the principle of employment promotion (work-first principle) has always dominated over benefit options for the unemployed. In contrast to previous economic downturns, where the bulk of countercyclical measures essentially took the form of an increase in the number of participants in various active labour market policy programmes, during the current recession the Swedish Government has to a larger extent than before relied on expansionary fiscal and monetary policy. Faced by a deterioration of the situation in the labour market the Government gradually increased the number of participants in various ALMP programmes, however. Labour supply and matching measures have been emphasized and the extra resources have to a greater extent been targeted on individuals most in need of support. In this context, several active ALMPs have been targeted and tailored toward youth, immigrants and the long-term unemployed. In the aftermath of the global economic crisis, the Government has also temporarily increased the number of places in post-secondary vocational training and in local authority upper secondary education for adults, as well as the number of places in universities and colleges.

As far as wage development is concerned, the Swedish industrial relations system has favoured wage adjustments in line with productivity development. In order to preserve employment stability and limit further increases in unemployment, wage moderation has characterized the last round of collective bargaining. The outcome in terms of negotiated pay settlements, coupled with the weak situation in the labour market, implies that wages will rise moderately during the two coming years.

Even though it is too early to assess accurately the impact of the global economic crisis on wage distribution, it seems that, to date, this impact has been limited. The impact of the crisis on the development of disposable earnings and income inequalities is not independent of the extent and generosity of the social protection and transfer systems, which remain high in Sweden by international standards. Sweden, therefore, has comparatively powerful automatic stabilizers that dampened the fall in aggregate demand. Furthermore, both the countercyclical crisis measures implemented helped to reduce the effects of the crisis on household disposable incomes and to moderate the fall in public employment. In particular, the reforms of the tax system imply a reduction in both average and marginal income tax, and the countercyclical measures – such as the increase in the number of participants in ALMP – may partly explain why disposable income has so far not been severely affected by the crisis.

If the policy conducted by the Swedish Government helped to absorb and limit the negative impact of the crisis on employment and income inequalities in the short term, it should be stressed that the long-term consequences of the crisis might be significant. As shown by the case studies, we may not rule out that the current crisis, like the deep recession of the early 1990s, implies that, in future, a growing share of Swedish companies will rely increasingly on external numerical flexibility with a rise in the use of short-term contracts and agency workers. If this is the case, this development may worsen the duality in the labour market between insiders and outsiders, alter the conditions of entry into the labour market and delay the acquisition of a permanent and stable job. As also shown by previous developments, the crisis hit young people hard, especially young people with an immigrant background. The potential scarring effects of an early period of unemployment may have a long-lasting negative influence on subsequent employment performance and income development across the life course. Furthermore, an early period of unemployment may affect the timing of other critical transitions and events over the life course, such as the transition from school to work and the constitution of an independent household, as well as access to housing, parenthood and fertility patterns, career opportunities and wage development.

NOTES

1. The recent improvement in the Swedish economy is related to the strong expansionary fiscal and monetary policies, including tax cuts and low interest rates. Compared to previous economic downturns, Swedish economic growth has been, between 2009 and early 2010, driven less by increases in exports than by an increase in public and private consumption, due both to increases in disposable household income and the additional appropriations to local government decided on in autumn 2009 and the Spring Budget Bill (see Section 3).
2. SEK 48 billion in 2009 (corresponding to 1.6 per cent of GDP) and a further SEK 35 billion for 2010 (1.1 per cent of GDP). 1 SEK = 0.097 euro, 1 SEK = 0.14 dollar in 2009.
3. Approved by the Swedish Parliament (Riksdag) in November 2008.
4. In addition to the already increased funding in infrastructure adopted in the 2009 Autumn Budget Bill (SEK 10 billion), it was decided that a further SEK 1 billion would be invested in infrastructure (operation and maintenance of roads and railways).
5. The State will initially guarantee up to SEK 1,500 billion of debt instruments. Of this, a maximum of SEK 500 billion can be used to guarantee covered bonds with a maturity of between three and five years.
6. This measure implied a reduction of tax revenue by around SEK 3.6 billion.
7. A new limited company was formed and received SEK 3 billion to conduct research and development in the automotive sector. Furthermore, the Government secured the possibility of making available state credit guarantees of up to SEK 20 billion to companies in the automotive sector to guarantee the loans they take out from the European Investment Bank. The Government also has the possibility of providing rescue loans to companies in the automotive sector that are in financial difficulties, in exchange for adequate security.
8. This corresponded to about 0.3 per cent of GDP in 2009.
9. This first step implies a reduction of marginal tax by 1–1.5 percentage points for low and medium income earners.
10. By 5 percentage points, up to a ceiling of SEK 10,000 per year.
11. In January 2009, the total employers' social security contribution for young people was lowered to 15.49 per cent. The reduction means that employers' contributions have been halved. The age group has also been broadened to cover everyone under the age of 26.
12. The New Start Job was introduced in January 2007. In relation to the crisis and in order to limit the development of long-term unemployment, the Government increased the compensation given to employers who recruit a person to a 'new start job'. The initial compensation amounted to the employer's social insurance contribution for a person who was entitled to such a job (that is, they had been unemployed or sick for more than a year). From 1 January 2009, the employer received twice that level of compensation.

13. Around 10,000 more slots for universities and colleges, 3,000 more slots in post-secondary vocational training and 10,000 more slots per year in adult vocational training.
14. The Government has also decided to increase compensation in the general study grant and loan system (Studiemedel) by SEK 431 per month.
15. The aim of the Youth Job Guarantee is to help young unemployed people (20 years of age or over) to find jobs or enrol in the regular education system through intensified employment services, activation measures, traineeships and stronger incentives to study.
16. In particular, for those born outside Europe.
17. One of the highest in Europe, after Spain.
18. And possibly some overinvestment in human capital related to a postponement of their exit from the education system due to poor employment prospects.
19. All in all, the 2009 bargaining round affected 175,000 employees, of whom 70,000 belonged to the Building Workers' Union.
20. According to the Mediation Office (2010) the overall wage dispersion (P90/P10) decreases slightly between 2008 and 2009.
21. Between 2005 and 2009 the non-standardized gender wage gap decreased by 1.5 percentage points from 16.3 per cent to 14.8 per cent. During the same period the standardized gender wage gap decreased by 0.8 percentage point from 6.8 per cent to 6.0 per cent. Between 2008 and 2009 the standardized wage gap for the economy as a whole was reduced by 0.3 percentage point from 5.8 per cent to 5.5 per cent.
22. Between 2005 and 2009, the share of women in managerial positions increased by 60 per cent (managers, chief executives etc.) from 8 to 13 per cent.
23. Union membership declined by 11 per cent for blue-collar workers (Swedish Trade Union Confederation, LO) and by 7 per cent for white-collar workers (Swedish Confederation for Professional Employees, TCO), see Kjellberg (2010).
24. In a context of low labour demand and high unemployment the short-term positive impacts of a tax cut on work incentives and labour supply, both at the intensive and the extensive margins, might be questioned. On the other hand, the tax credit results in higher disposable income for households with low or average income. These households can be expected to have a higher propensity to consume, which might contribute to higher aggregate consumption and demand and, through a multiplier effect, have a positive impact on the employment level.
25. Early in 2010, the Ford Motor Company sold the Volvo Car Corporation to Geely Automobile Holdings Limited.
26. The package of measures discussed in this chapter was implemented only in Sweden. In Belgium, Volvo Cars exploited other cost and work sharing mechanisms, such as a system of state subsidized short-time working.
27. The Job Council *Startkraft* provided support for the dismissed production workers, while the Job Council *Tryggetsråd* (TRR) provided advice and support for white-collar employees, management and union representatives.
28. With the exception of three employees older than 63 years of age.
29. The Job Council *Arbetslivsressours* provided support for the dismissed production workers, while *Tryggetsråd* (TRR) provided advice and support for white-collar employees, management and union representatives.
30. It should also be noted that, according to the Swedish Employment Protection Act, the dismissed workers have priority during the re-employment phase.

BIBLIOGRAPHY

Anxo, D. (2009) 'Job security councils and job security foundations', *European Employment Observatory, Spring Review*, European Commission, Brussels.

Anxo, D. and H. Niklasson (2006) 'The Swedish model in turbulent times: Decline or renaissance?', *International Labour Review*, Vol. 145, No. 4, Geneva.

Anxo, D., G. Bosch and J. Rubery (2010) *The Welfare State and Life Transitions: A European Perspective*, Cheltenham, UK and Northampton, MA, USA: Edward Elgar.

Arbetsförmedlingen (2010) *Statistics on Vacancies and Lay-off Notices*, Stockholm. Available at: http://www.arbetsformedlingen.se/Om-oss/Statistik-prognoser. html.

Ekberg, J. and L. Holmlund (2010) *Vad säger den officiella lönestatistiken om löneskillnaden mellan kvinnor och män 2009?*, Swedish Mediation Office, Stockholm.

Eliasson, K. (2008) 'En arbetslöshetsförsäkring för de som har råd' (An unemployment insurance system for those that can afford it?), Luleå tekniska universitet, institutionen för Arbetsvetenskap. Available at: http://epubl.ltu. se/1402-1781/2008/18/index.html.

Kjellberg, A. (2010) 'Kollektivsavtal täckningsgrad samt organisationsgrad hos arbetgivarförbund och fackförbund', Working Paper, Department of Sociology, Lund University, Lund.

Mediation Office (2010) *National Report 2010* and *Wage Statistics*, various years, Stockholm. Available at: http://www.mi.se/inenglish/menu_eng_annualreport. html.

National Institute of Economic Research (NIER) (2010) *The Swedish Economy, September 2010*, Konjunkturinstitutet, Stockholm.

Nordström-Skans (2004) 'Scarring effect of the first labour market experience: A sibling based analysis', Institute for Labour Market Policy Evaluation Working Paper 1004:14. Stockholm.

Statistics Sweden (2010a) *Labour Force Survey*, various years, Stockholm.

Statistics Sweden (2010b) *Undersökning av hushållsekonomi* (Survey of household economic situation), Stockholm.

APPENDIX

Table 11A.1   Policy responses: recovery measures, active labour market policy and education measures, Sweden, fourth quarter 2008–fourth quarter 2009

Policy area	Description of measure(s) taken	Implemen-tation	Objectives
Increasing aggregate demand	Increased investment in infrastructure and repair and maintenance (SEK 1 billion)	In force since early 2009	Sustain employment in the public and construction sectors
	Tax credit in the construction sector. Work in the form of repairs, maintenance and improvement of one-family houses and tenant housing included in the existing tax credits for household work	In force since early 2009	
	Expansive finance policy: increased resources for local government. Globally, the package of measures adopted and implemented since summer 2008 amounts to: SEK 83 billion, corresponding to 2.7% of GDP, SEK 48 billion in 2009 (corresponding to 1.7% of GDP) and a further SEK 35 billion for 2010 (1.1% of GDP)	Second half of 2008–	Sustain aggregate demand. Maintain employment in the public sector (local authorities in charge of education and health)
Increasing labour demand (ALMP)	Wage subsidies: new start job (first introduced in 2007). The Government has doubled the deduction to employers that recruit a person for a new start job, implying that the employer will pay about half the cost of the current wage	January 2009–	Countercyclical employment measure
Youth measures	Reduction of employers' social security contributions for young people. The total reduction means almost a halving of employers' contributions. The age group has also been broadened to cover everyone under the age of 26	January 2009–	Reduce youth unemployment

Table 11A.1   (continued)

Policy area	Description of measure(s) taken	Implementation	Objectives
Maintaining labour demand	Agreement on temporary layoffs/short-time working, wage adjustments, and training between IF Metall and the employers' federations in engineering, metals and industry and chemicals	March 2009– March 2010	Maintain employment
Offering social protection, strengthening social cohesion	Temporary amendment of membership requirements of Unemployment Benefit Funds Members of unemployment insurance (UI) funds in 2009 will be able to count one month extra for each month of membership in 2009 Extension of sickness benefit for those not able to work. Increase of housing allowance Measures to increase income for low income groups, such as the reduction of pensioners' taxes and housing allowance for low income families and lone parents	2009–2013 2009–	Reduce the risk of social exclusion and poverty
Increasing labour supply. Making work pay	Extension of the already implemented in-work tax credit	2008–	Enhance work incentives and increase labour supply at the extensive (participation) and intensive margins (working hours). But also sustain aggregate demand
Improving labour market matching	The administrative appropriation to the Swedish Public Employment Service has been raised for both 2009 and 2010 in order to expand its matching services and provide early and individual support to people who have lost their job. The coaching support and wage subsidy programme (New Start Up) has also been extended to young people	2009–	Improve the matching process and control of search activities

Table 11A.1   (continued)

Policy area	Description of measure(s) taken	Implemen-tation	Objectives
Investment in human capital	Temporary increase of the number of slots in post-secondary vocational training and local authority upper secondary education for adults, as well as universities and colleges (10,000 more slots for universities and colleges, 3,000 more slots in post-secondary vocational training and 10,000 more slots per year in adult vocational training)	2009–2011	Skill upgrading measures
Adaptability of education and training	Increase of the number of participants in traditional labour market training (1,000 places) Possibility for unemployed people over the age of 25, regardless of previous education, to obtain a higher level of post-secondary student aid in 2009 and 2010 Drop-outs from high school will have the opportunity, within the framework of the Youth Job Guarantee, to complete their studies	2009–	Skill upgrading measures

12. Crisis in Turkey: Aggravating a segmented labour market and creating new inequalities

Seyhan Erdoğdu

1. INTRODUCTION

Even before the global crisis began to exert its effects on Turkey – more specifically, from 2005 – the country was already experiencing constraints on economic growth. With falling rates of growth and high rates of unemployment, Turkey was facing economic problems well before the outbreak of the recent crisis. Some employment measures to tackle the problem of rising unemployment in Turkey were launched in early 2008.

Meanwhile, Turkey has been undergoing structural change in terms of social policy and public administration, which gained pace in particular after 2006. The new system introduced by the Law on Social Security and General Health Insurance of 2006, and the amendments to this Law in 2007 and 2008, reflect the most significant recent changes in the domain of health and social security (SGK 2010). Public administration is another domain which is undergoing structural transformation. Important changes are taking place in the missions and functioning of labour administration at both central and local levels. The effects of the global crisis have combined with the impact of the changes in social policy and public administration which took effect prior to the crisis.

This combination of pre-crisis changes at the economic, social and administrative levels with changes triggered by the crisis makes it very difficult to distinguish the effects of the crisis.

Another constraint is the fact that the global crisis is continuing and it is impossible to fully anticipate its future depth, duration and scale. Economists vacillate between maintaining that the 'worst is over' and that 'the worst is yet to come'. While the crisis persists in some countries, its internal phases and the effects of the monetary and financial measures adopted are resulting in short-term changes in the economic and social effects of the crisis. Quarterly changes in data on growth, employment, fiscal balances and trade deficits all influence assessments regarding the trajectory of the crisis and thus the measures adopted and being considered for adoption.

The chapter is organized as follows. Section 2 examines the effects of the global crisis on the world of work in Turkey. Section 3 looks at measures taken against the crisis in Turkey in relation to working life. For this section, in addition to a review of related legal and institutional documents (ÇSGB 2010a; İş Teftiş Kurulu 2010; SGK 2010; SYDGM 2010; İŞKUR 2010), interviews were undertaken with representatives of the Ministry of Labour and Social Security (MLSS), the Labour Inspection Board, the Public Employment Agency (İŞKUR) and the Social Security Institution (SSI) in 2009 and 2010. In Section 4, the views and activities of the social partners with regard to the global crisis and the anti-crisis measures are examined. To this end, semi-structured interviews were conducted with representatives of the workers, civil servants and employers' confederations in 2009 and 2010, as well as a review of the documents and periodicals of these Confederations published in 2008–2010. This section also explains the anti-crisis measures adopted by the trade unions and employers at the enterprise level, relying on the information and documents provided by the trade unions in response to our questionnaire in 2010. In Section 5, which is a case study, the effects of the economic crisis on enterprises in the city of Bursa and the anti-crisis measures at the local level are examined. The section draws on the findings of the group interview with representatives of government, trade unions and employers' organizations at the local level, as well as interviews with workers and employers at the firm level, all conducted in 2009.

2. EFFECTS OF THE GLOBAL CRISIS ON WORKING LIFE IN TURKEY

2.1 Impact Channels of the Global Crisis in Turkey

Turkey went into the global crisis with a high current account deficit, an import-dependent industry, a heavy external debt burden and high rates of unemployment. All this made Turkey particularly vulnerable (BSB 2008, 2009; Boratav 2009; Durmuş 2009; Eğilmez 2009; Sönmez 2009; UNCTAD 2008).

The impact of the global crisis on Turkey has been shaped through the channels of foreign trade, capital flows and expectations.

Close to 50 per cent of Turkey's exports are to the EU. In parallel to the effects of the global crisis on the real economy of the EU, Turkey experienced shrinking foreign demand. Starting from November 2008, Turkey's total exports fell, which was reflected in both production and employment (UNCTAD 2009: 6).

In association with the repercussions of the global crisis, Turkey experienced net capital outflows starting from October 2008 and the real economy began to face difficulties in external financing. In addition to the constraints in international capital markets, the high leverage ratios of private corporations and the expectations of a decline in future profits due to continuing economic uncertainties caused the banking sector to become reluctant to lend to the real sector. This played a major role in the significant decline of private investments. The rate of medium- and long-term debt servicing of the non-banking private sector, which was 191 per cent in 2008, decreased to 73 per cent in the first seven months of 2009 (DPT 2009a: 5). The privatization of the banking system to foreign banks played a role in the closing of credit lines to the domestic market. The inactivity of credit channels affected small and medium-sized enterprises to an even greater extent (SPO 2009a: 12).

The global crisis had a negative effect on public finances. Tax revenues fell in parallel with declining growth, due to several tax and social security contribution reductions and exemptions introduced to revive the real economy, leaving them well below the original budget estimates. Lowered social security contributions, the high cost of the transformation of the health care system and increases in various items of public spending augmented the budget deficit and the debt burden. The central government budget deficit for 2009, which had been projected as 10.4 billion lira at the beginning of 2009, reached 52 billion lira at the end of the year and the primary balance, which had originally been envisaged to yield a surplus of 29.8 billion lira, was in deficit in the amount of 14 billion lira (Undersecretariat of the Treasury 2010).

All of these developments increased uncertainties and thus undermined confidence and expectations. While consumers suspended certain spending decisions, investors did the same with intended investments, which combined to generate economic stagnation.

2.2 The Economy: Decline and Contraction

The impact of the global crisis on Turkey echoed the previous crisis. Following the financial crisis of 2001, the Turkish economy experienced a fairly rapid recovery, with the remobilization of capacity which had lain idle during the crisis and also due to favourable trends in international markets: average growth in 2002–2007 was 6.8 per cent. As shown in Figure 12.1, within this period, the highest rate of growth was in 2004, at 9.4 per cent. After 2004, which was the last year of cyclical growth, the rate of growth started to fall in relative terms; the rates of growth for 2005,

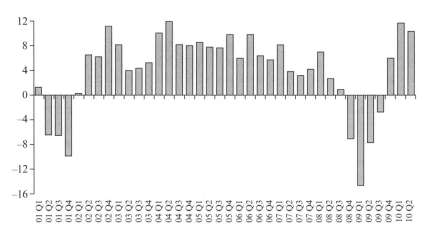

Source: TURKSTAT, Treasury.

Figure 12.1   GDP growth rates, Turkey, 2001–2010 (%, year-on-year)

2006 and 2007 were 8.4 per cent, 6.9 per cent and 4.7 per cent, respectively. In the last quarter of 2008, GDP shrank by 6.5 per cent and the rate of growth over the year was 0.9 per cent.

A similar course can be observed in manufacturing, which is the driving force of growth. The contribution of an increasing rate of capacity utilization in the manufacturing industry to growth in production disappeared after 2005 and rates of output growth also slowed. Output growth in manufacturing which had climbed to 11.9 per cent in 2004, later declined to 8.2 per cent, 8.4 per cent and 5.6 per cent in 2005, 2006 and 2007, respectively. The decline of 10.8 per cent in the manufacturing industry observed in the last quarter of 2008 pulled down the average annual growth rate of this sector to 0.8 per cent.

As the effects of the global crisis began to be felt more deeply in Turkey, the decrease in the growth rate observed before the crisis turned into a contraction, beginning with the last quarter of 2008 (DPT 2009a, 2009b; İSO 2009; Türkiye Kalkınma Bankası 2009a, 2009b).

Leaving aside agriculture, financial institutions and some public services, significant contractions were observed in almost all sectors and GDP contracted by –4.7 per cent in 2009.

2.3   Direct Employment Effects

The employment effects of the crisis began to be felt strongly from the third quarter of 2008, becoming milder towards the end of 2009.

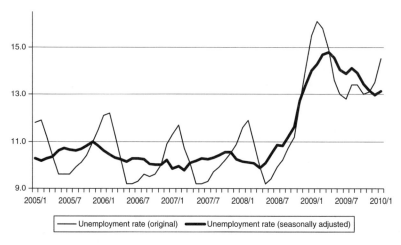

Source: TURKSTAT.

Figure 12.2   Unemployment rate, Turkey, 2005–2010 (%)

As shown in Figure 12.2, the first direct effect of the economic contraction in the Turkish economy on the world of work concerned employment; Turkey was confronted with the problem of the economic crisis turning into an employment crisis.

Like many other developing countries that cannot generate quality jobs even with high rates of growth, Turkey was facing a serious problem of unemployment and idle labour prior to the crisis. An important characteristic of the period 2002–2007 was the existence of 'jobless growth'. While the average annual rate of growth in 2004–2007 was 7.3 per cent, the average annual growth in employment, according to data revised on the basis of new population projections, remained at 1.4 per cent. Jobless growth was more salient in import-dependent manufacturing. Thus, despite the strong growth performances that followed the 2001 crisis and some expansion in employment associated with this growth, unemployment rates climbed by 3 percentage points above the pre-crisis period, reaching 10 per cent.

In the crisis year of 2009, this 10 per cent band increased by 4 percentage points, settling around 14 per cent. The non-agricultural unemployment rate was 17.4 per cent with a 3.8 percentage point increase in comparison to 2008. This rate was 16 per cent for males, with a 3.7 percentage point increase, and 21.9 per cent for females, with a 3.8 percentage point increase.

During the first quarter of 2009, as the unemployment rate rose to 16

Table 12.1 Labour market indicators: urban–rural differences, Turkey, 2005–2010

Years	Labour force participation rate (%)	Unemployment rate (%)	Employment rate (%)	Population not in labour force (000s)
Urban				
2005	44.1	12.8	38.5	19092
2006	44.2	12.2	38.9	19396
2007	44.3	12.0	39.0	19640
2008	45.0	12.8	39.2	19634
2009	45.8	16.6	38.2	19611
2010	46.6	14.9	39.7	19479
Rural				
2005	52.1	6.3	48.8	6812
2006	51.2	6.2	48.0	7027
2007	50.8	6.8	47.4	7240
2008	51.4	7.2	47.7	7332
2009	52.7	8.9	48.0	7326
2010	53.0	8.3	48.7	7434

Source: TURKSTAT (2010: January–June).

per cent and the rate of non-agricultural unemployment to 19 per cent, there were concerns that the country was heading for a serious social crisis. As of February 2009, the overall rate of open unemployment was 16.1 per cent. Adding to this the underemployed and those not looking for a job but ready to work, the actual rate of unemployment in February 2009 climbed to 29.2 per cent.

2.3.1 Urban–rural differences

Table 12.1 shows that in the pre-crisis period, Turkey was confronted by the problem of low and steadily falling labour force participation and employment rates. However, during the crisis the labour force participation rate (2008–2009 seasonally adjusted) increased from 46.7 per cent to 47.3 per cent and the employment rate fell from 42.1 per cent to 40.3 per cent.

Looking more closely at the picture of urban–rural differences in Turkey, it becomes clear that the labour force participation rate increased more in rural areas during the crisis period of 2008–2009 in comparison to the urban areas. As for the employment rate, the reverse holds true: while the change in the employment rate in the rural areas was positive,

Table 12.2   Labour market indicators: gender aspects, Turkey, 2005–2010

Years	Labour force participation rate (%)	Unemploy- ment rate (%)	Non- agricultural unemploy- ment rate (%)	Employ- ment rate (%)	Population not in labour force (000s)
Female 15+					
2005	23.3	11.2	18.7	20.7	18 935
2006	23.6	11.1	17.9	21.0	19 164
2007	23.6	11.0	17.3	21.0	19 464
2008	24.5	11.6	18.1	21.6	19 526
2009	26.0	14.3	21.9	22.3	19 466
2010	27.3	13.2	20.1	23.7	19 355
Male 15+					
2005	70.6	10.5	12.2	63.2	6 969
2006	69.9	9.9	11.3	62.9	7 258
2007	69.8	10.0	11.4	62.7	7 415
2008	70.1	10.7	12.3	62.6	7 441
2009	70.5	13.9	16.0	60.7	7 471
2010	70.6	12.4	14.3	61.8	7 558

Source: TURKSTAT (2010: January–June).

the change in the employment rate in the urban areas was negative (–1). This difference is explained by the fact that some of the new entrants to the labour force and some of the unemployed unable to find urban jobs returned to rural areas. This tendency is in the opposite direction to labour market trends in Turkey, which are characterized by a continuous and marked rural to urban migration, which entails changing sectoral employment patterns from agriculture to industry and, over the past decade, to services. It also indicates that in the crisis period, while industrial full-time jobs were lost in the urban areas, employment creation in the rural areas mitigated the effects of the crisis, with job creation for persons becoming self-employed and among unpaid family workers.

2.3.2   Gender dimension

One other dimension that deserves attention is male and female differences in labour market performance under crisis conditions. As shown in Table 12.2 the Turkish labour market has always been very much segregated on a gender basis. The labour force participation rate for women has been on the rise (from 23.3 per cent in 2005 to 26 per cent in 2009), but is still much less than that of men (70.5 per cent in 2009). Women have low employment rates and higher unemployment rates, notably in non-agricultural sectors. Behind women's low labour market participation, there are a number of socio-cultural factors which assign women to the position of housewife. Furthermore, the neoliberal agricultural policies pursued in Turkey accelerated the decline in rural employment, with closely associated falling rates of employment. Since female employment is concentrated mainly in agriculture, any shrinkage in this sector will leave women out of work. Women ejected from agriculture en masse would not have employment opportunities, even in labour-intensive manufacturing. While falling employment in agriculture led to the shift of the male labour force to informal employment in the form of waged work, own-account working or small family enterprises in industry and services, females tended to leave the labour force and become economically inactive (Toksöz 2009).

On closer scrutiny, we see that during the crisis year of 2009, labour force participation rates for men increased by 0.4 percentage points and those for women by 1.5 points. Thus the crisis helped to continue the long-term reduction in the gender gap that had started before the crisis. In 2009, the employment rate for women in both urban and rural areas increased by 0.4 and 1.4 percentage points, respectively, while it decreased for men by –2.3 percentage points in urban and –1.1 points in rural areas. These figures reflect the added worker effect observed in most countries during crisis periods (temporary increase in the labour supply of women due to the unemployment of male breadwinners).

2.3.3 Change in the sectoral distribution of employment

The sectoral breakdown of post-2001 crisis employment patterns reveals massive depopulation in the rural economy. Agricultural employment was reduced by just over 3 million workers between 2001 and 2008. In the 2008–2009 crisis, this pattern was interrupted and the share of agricultural employment increased, while that of industry declined. Employment in agriculture increased by 1 percentage point and services increased by 0.5 percentage points, while that of industry decreased by 1.6 and the share of construction did not change (Figure 12.3). As in the 2001 crisis, it was industry which was most affected by shrinking external demand. The increase in agricultural employment reflected the increase in female employment in agriculture as unpaid family labour, while the decrease in industry meant a decrease in male employment. The increase in service sector employment was mostly in small-scale, family-owned services, with low productivity and insecurity of employment.

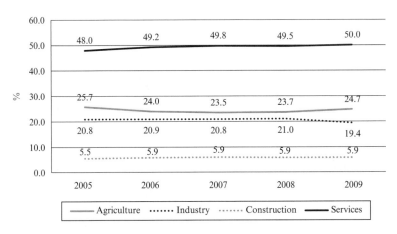

Source: TURKSTAT.

Figure 12.3 Sectoral distribution of employment, Turkey, 2005–2009 (%)

2.3.4 Change in employment status

With the shift in the sectoral distribution of employment towards agriculture and away from industry, the work status of the employed also shifted from wage work towards own-account and unpaid family work. Turkey experienced a continuous commodification of labour during the post-crisis period of 2001–2007. However, in the global crisis we saw, for the first time in years, the reversal of this trend as the share of wage and salary earners in total employment decreased. Potential wage earners in urban areas were either transferred to own-account work, still in urban areas, or returned to agriculture to work on family land as self-employed or unpaid family labour. In both cases, the transformation took the form of informalization (Figure 12.4).

2.3.5 Young and unqualified workers hit harder

As shown in Figure 12.5, one critical development has been in the rate of youth unemployment. Between 2008 and 2009, youth unemployment increased from an already very high rate of 20.3 per cent to 25.3 per cent. In urban areas, it increased by 5.6 points from 22.6 per cent to 28.2 per cent. In rural areas, it increased by 3.4 points from 15.5 per cent to 18.9 per cent. The toll of unemployment in the crisis has been particularly heavy for urban youth (15–19 years, from 22.8 per cent in 2008 to 27.5 in 2009, and 20–24 years, from 22.5 per cent in 2008 to 28.5 in 2009). As unemployment increased and took its toll on young people the relative weight of long-term unemployment in total unemployment diminished.

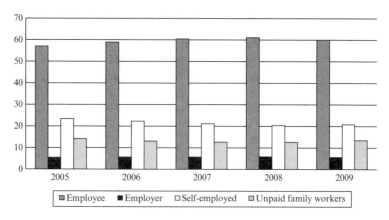

Source: TURKSTAT.

Figure 12.4   Employment status, Turkey, 2005–2009 (%)

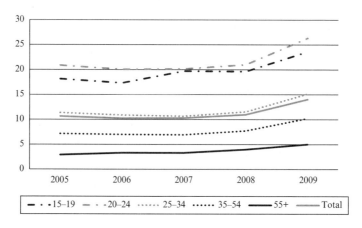

Source: TURKSTAT.

Figure 12.5   Unemployment rates of wider age groups, Turkey, 2005–2009 (%)

Employers chose to release unqualified workers and preferred to retain qualified workers during the crisis. Short-time working helped in this. Consequently, as shown in Table 12.3, the unemployment rates of less educated and secondary school graduates increased more than those of vocational graduates and those with a higher education.

*Table 12.3   Unemployment rates by educational status, Turkey,
2005–2009 (2005=100)*

	Illiterate	Literate but no school completed	Primary school	Junior high or equivalent vocational school	Lycee	Vocational lycee	University
2005	100.0	100.0	100.0	100.0	100.0	100.0	100.0
2006	97.8	96.7	96.6	91.5	101.4	87.2	93.1
2007	115.6	116.5	97.8	86.4	100.7	90.2	95.1
2008	140.0	133.0	105.6	92.4	102.2	88.0	101.0
2009	177.8	168.1	137.1	118.6	130.4	117.3	118.6

Source: TURKSTAT, author's calculations.

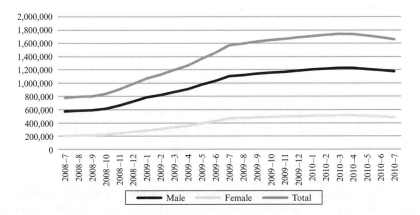

Source: İŞKUR.

Figure 12.6   Number of registered unemployed, Turkey, 2008–2010

2.3.6   The rise in the number of registered unemployed

In December 2009, the number of unemployed registered with İŞKUR (Public Employment Agency) increased by 71.01 per cent over the same month of the previous year, reaching 1,689,349 persons. Of these registered unemployed, 35 per cent were secondary school graduates and graduates of equivalent institutions and 15 per cent were university graduates; 30 per cent of the registered unemployed were women (İŞKUR 2009). Overall, registered unemployed decreased by –11.6 per cent between November 2009 and November 2010 (Figure 12.6).

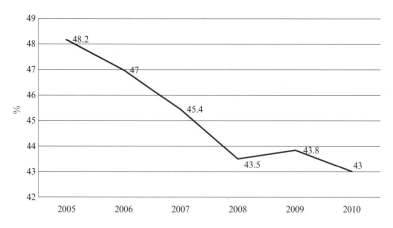

Source: TURKSTAT.

*Figure 12.7   Unregistered employment as a percentage of total
employment, Turkey, 2005–2010*

2.3.7   Increase in informality and undeclared work

An important point which needs to be addressed in relation to Turkey's
pre-crisis employment composition is the proportional weight of unregistered employment. From 2004 to 2008, the share of unregistered employment decreased from 50.1 per cent to 43.5 per cent.

However, the same declining trend is not observed in the crisis period of
2008–2009. Despite all the measures taken to tackle undeclared work, the
proportion of working people not covered by any security scheme increased
by 0.3 points to 43.8 per cent in 2009 (Figure 12.7). According to the observations of labour inspectors, undeclared work tends to spread during a
crisis. In some workplaces, social security registration of workers was withdrawn as if their work contracts had been terminated while they continued
working. As one labour inspector put it during our interview in 2009: 'In
May 2009 we went to Konya without prior notification to examine the
workplace conditions for short-time working requests. These requests were
mostly from the metal industry and its suppliers in Konya and Aksaray.
There was a significant shift to informal status, especially in casting.'

The Social Security Institution (SSI) statistics also suggest that the
number of workers covered by social security decreased significantly in
May 2009 over the same month of 2008 (–10.6 per cent), starting to rise
only at the beginning of 2010 (Figure 12.8).

The decrease in the number of self-employed persons covered under
social security is even more marked and did not improve even after 2009

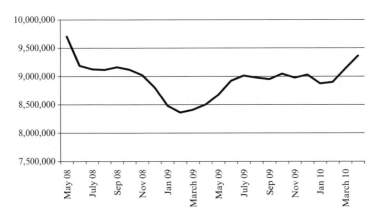

Source: SSI.

Figure 12.8 *Number of insured wage and salary earners under compulsory schemes, Turkey, 2008–2010*

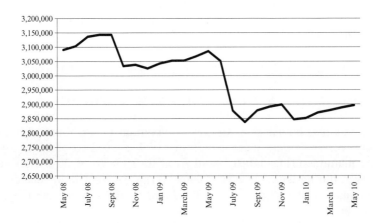

Source: SSI.

Figure 12.9 *Number of insured persons, Turkey, 2008–2010 (self-employed)*

(Figure 12.9). Workers' insurance contributions are deducted at source and transferred to the Social Security Institution (SSI) by the employers, whereas the self-employed pay their insurance contributions themselves. Under the severe conditions of recession many of the self-employed were unable to pay and shifted to undeclared/informal employment. However,

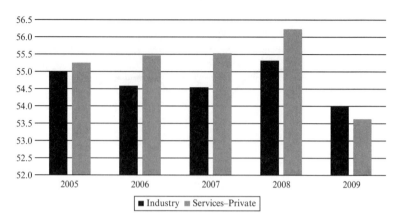

Source: TURKSTAT.

Figure 12.10   Average weekly working hours, Turkey, 2005–2009

the total number of self-employed increased in the crisis period, which may reflect the move away from waged work in industry to self-employment in agriculture and services.

2.4   Working Time Reduction: A Policy Alternative Used in the Crisis

According to TURKSTAT data, for 2008, the average weekly working time for a worker in the manufacturing industry was 55.32 hours which is considerably higher than the legal maximum of 45 hours. Average weekly working hours increased from 51.79 in 2002 to 55.32 in 2008 in the manufacturing industry and from to 55.38 to 56.20 in services. However, during the crisis year of 2009 average working hours decreased in the manufacturing industry to 53.99 and to 53.63 in services (Figure 12.10).

The industrial hours worked index in industry as a whole also decreased by 11 points from 2008 to 2009 (Figure 12.11), the decline being more pronounced in the export sectors of textiles, apparel, machinery and motor vehicles.

However, while changes in average working time have been an adjustment variable, labour adjustment by firms in response to the crisis took place mainly through changes in employment. According to calculations by Taymaz (2010), employment losses account for most of the decline in total hours worked in Turkey (79 per cent in manufacturing and 75 per cent in motor vehicles) (Table 12.4). The short-time working scheme and voluntary agreements between employers and trade unions for part-time

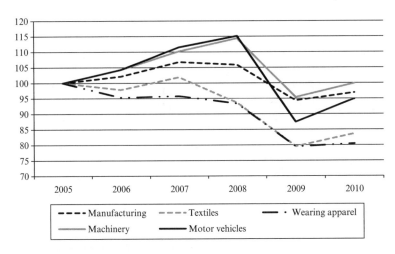

Source: TURKSTAT, author's calculations.

Figure 12.11 Industrial hours worked, Turkey, 2005–2010 (annual average)

Table 12.4 Changes in hours worked in manufacturing and motor vehicles, Turkey, 2008Q3–2009Q3

	Manufacturing industry (%)	Motor vehicles industry (%)
I. Number of employees	–7.5	–16.3
II. Average working time	–2.0	–5.5
III. Total hours worked (I + II)	–9.5	–21.9
Contribution of employment change (I/III)	78.9	74.6

Source: Taymaz (2010).

work or compulsory leave were not sufficiently widespread to dominate labour adjustment through reductions in working hours. Reduced working hours by means of short-time working or voluntary agreements between employers and trade unions took place in the primary sector, while secondary sector workers faced layoffs, in many cases without severance pay. This reinforced the dual structure of the labour market, leaving the secondary market workers more disadvantaged in the crisis period (TURKSTAT, *Quarterly Industrial Employment Surveys*, 2005–2009).

Table 12.5   Real gross wages, Turkey, 2005–2009 (2005=100)

Years	Industry	Construction	Trade–Services
2005	100.0	100.0	100.0
2006	103.3	117.0	110.0
2007	109.1	118.1	116.3
2008	109.5	118.4	120.2
2009	100.3	103.1	119.5

Source: TURKSTAT, Quarterly Industrial Employment Survey, author's calculations.

2.5   A Substantial Effect on Real Wages

The 2001 crisis in Turkey caused substantial real wage losses. Even though there was some increase in real wages after 2002, the previous real wage losses were not recovered and wage increases lagged considerably behind rising productivity in the period 2001–2007.

In 2008, led by the wages of unionized workers, real wages remained stable. According to information provided by TİSK, the employers' organization, in unionized private enterprises wage increases arising from collective agreements signed in 2008 remained moderate, only slightly above inflation. In some cases, there was even a wage freeze due to the difficulties enterprises were facing under crisis conditions.

In 2009, the effects of the present crisis hit hard and real wages fell sharply. The decline was felt in particular in industry and construction, while workers in services were less affected (Table 12.5).

Figure 12.12 depicts the sharp decline in the unit wage index. A decade ago, high inflation rates and high devaluations in the crisis period in Asia and Latin America facilitated sharp declines in real wages. In the global crisis of 2008–2009, many countries experienced limited price and currency fluctuations, implying that dramatic real wage decreases would be difficult. Moreover, in times of crisis, downward adaptation of wages is slow in comparison to the changes in other economic variables (ILO 2009). In contrast to these findings, in the 2008–2009 crisis period, Turkey witnessed a significant decrease in real wages (Figure 12.12). The overall decline in the textile and garment sectors in Turkey started well before 2008–2009 under pressure from global market competition, quotas imposed on textiles and garments and the overvalued Turkish lira. Employers unable to lower other production costs resorted to economizing on labour costs as a survival strategy; some even moving their enterprises to North Africa and Central Asia. There was a marginal revival of the sector in 2007, but it was

Source: TURKSTAT, Treasury.

Figure 12.12   Productivity and real wages in the industrial sector, Turkey, 2005–2010 (per hour worked)

short-lived. In the crisis period, layoffs in the textile sector were massive, and some employers even went bankrupt. The employment index in the textile and garment sectors went down from 94 to 80 and from 94 to 81, respectively (2005 = 100). Real wages were further depressed and in 2009 fell to record lows in textiles by –15 per cent, and in apparel by –13 per cent.

Closer scrutiny reveals that, in addition to wages in labour-intensive sectors, wages in capital-intensive sectors were also squeezed in the crisis. Wages in the more capital-intensive sectors of manufacturing were not declining in the pre-crisis period. In fact, real wages improved in sectors such as the manufacturing of machinery and equipment and the auto-motive industry. In 2009, the contraction of foreign demand hit these sectors very hard. For example, within the first eight months of 2009, the number of vehicles produced by the automotive industry declined by 21.6 per cent and exports by 33.6 per cent, compared to the same period in the previous year. Firms started to lay off workers and negotiated lower wages where unions existed or simply lowered wages in non-unionized sectors. It was in the capital-intensive manufacturing sectors that larger enterprises applied for the short-time working schemes offered by the Government. But these practices did not solve the problem of layoffs in the sector as a whole, and small firms which produced parts for larger companies as subcontractors mainly adjusted by means of layoffs, drag-ging down the sector's employment index dramatically, from 122 to 98

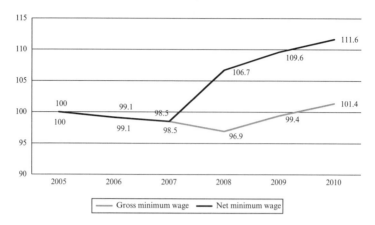

Source: MLSS, author's calculations.

Figure 12.13   Real Gross and Net minimum wages, Turkey, 2005–2010

(2005 = 100). Real wages were also depressed in the capital-intensive sectors, an example being motor vehicle manufacturing with a wage fall of –16 per cent (TURKSTAT, *Quarterly Industrial Employment Surveys*, 2005–2009).

2.6   Minimum Wages: Not Used as the Adjustment Variable

According to the 2006 data provided by the SSI (2006), 52 per cent of workers employed in the private sector have wage earnings at the level of the minimum wage. This proportion is higher in labour-intensive sub-sectors of the manufacturing industry, such as textiles. The minimum wage is not only important for employees paid at this level, but also as a reference point that affects the overall level of wages.

Figure 12.13 shows that gross minimum wages fell by 3.1 points between 2005 and 2008. In 2008, gross minimum wages continued to fall, however there was an increase of 8.2 points in net minimum wages as a result of lower taxes. In 2009 and 2010, gross minimum wages increased by 2.9 and 2.5 points, respectively. But these increases were able to bring the minimum wage only to its pre-crisis level. In the crisis period it seems that, while the legal minimum wage – as the minimum labour cost – was kept almost crisis-neutral, thanks to the decrease in 2008 of the tax wedge on the minimum wage, especially for workers with families, the real value of the net minimum wage increased (ÇSGB 2010b).

2.7 Increase in Unfair Working Conditions Not Adequately Dealt with by Labour Inspectorate

During the crisis period complaints to the MLSS increased significantly with regard to such problems as delays in the payment of wages, unfair dismissals, non-payment of severance pay and health and safety violations.

This situation increased the burden of the Labour Inspection Board and labour inspectors, as the unit in the Ministry in charge of examining such complaints. In the face of ever-increasing complaints, the Labour Inspection Board could not achieve its aim of reducing the share of labour inspections associated with complaints within total inspections.

As one of the most important anti-crisis measures adopted by the Government, short-time working also increased the burden of inspectors. According to Article 5 of the Regulation on this practice, the eligibility of applications by employers to benefit from this scheme is examined by labour inspectors, who also prepare the final reports. According to information supplied by the Ministry, labour inspectors had examined crisis-related short-time working applications from 4,879 enterprises as of September 2009. Workers' complaints which had been a priority before the crisis were replaced by short-time working applications during the crisis period. Having to spare more time for such applications, which had been increasing since November 2008 and reached their peak in March 2009, labour inspectors had to reduce the time spent on examining other crisis-related complaints and postpone a number of field inspections. Consequently, the average time it took to examine and bring to a conclusion one worker complaint increased from 78.18 days in 2007 to 91.38 days in 2008.

Tables 12.6 and 12.7 show the declining number of inspections during the crisis in terms of both working conditions and workers' health and safety and the increasing share of inspections based on complaints.

2.8 Poverty Increasing

During the global crisis, per capita GDP in Turkey fell from 10,440 US dollars to 8,578 US dollars. The estimates for 2011 and 2012 indicate that Turkey will not be able to recover its pre-crisis level of GDP per capita even with robust projected growth rates for 2010–2012 (Figure 12.14).

TURKSTAT poverty data for 2002–2007 suggest that, in urban areas, the rates of both food and non-food poverty and relative poverty (based on 50 per cent of equivalized median consumption expenditure) have fallen. In rural areas, food and non-food poverty remained above the urban rate throughout the period without showing any significant fall. In

Table 12.6   Inspection statistics relating to working conditions, Turkey, 2005–2009

	Overall inspections	Control inspections	Investigative inspections (based on complaints) (labour law)	Total inspections
2005	7 220	1 130	26 645	34 995
2006	5 897	871	27 728	34 496
2007	4 902	1 038	35 724	42 044
2008	3 691	839	34 589	39 119
2009	592	488	35 306	36 386

Source: MLSS.

Table 12.7   Inspection statistics relating to workers' health and safety, Turkey, 2005–2009

	Overall inspections	Control inspections	Total inspections	Total number of workers
2005	17 378	4 181	27 374	1 178 264
2006	16 245	4 196	26 615	1 158 372
2008	14 141	1 496	23 443	875 186
2009	6 082	1 011	19 709	867 605

Source: MLSS.

rural areas, the spending-based relative rate of poverty increased during the same period.

In 2008, the first year of the crisis, on the other hand, it appears that urban food poverty and spending-based relative poverty in rural areas both increased. In 2009, there was a fall in urban food poverty which might be attributed to various social assistance programmes. But rural food and non-food poverty, as well as rural relative poverty, increased (from 1.18 to 1.42 per cent, from 34.62 to 38.69 per cent and from 31 to 34.20 per cent, respectively).

A survey supported by TEPAV (Economic Policy Research Foundation of Turkey), UNICEF and the World Bank covering living conditions in five large provincial centres (Adana, Ankara, İstanbul, İzmir and Kocaeli) showed that three-quarters of families reported a fall in their incomes in the period October 2008–June 2009 (TEPAV 2009). According to the survey, the incomes of over 90 per cent of the poorest households have fallen. A fall in income was associated not only with unemployment; even

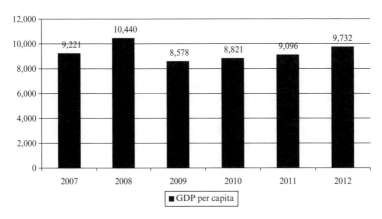

Source: TURKSTAT.

Figure 12.14   GDP per capita, Turkey, 2007–2012 (US dollars), 2010–2012 projected

when jobs were maintained, wage earnings and returns to self-employment fell for the lowest quintile. For informal workers, this fall was relatively higher. Families stated that family incomes, rental revenues and other supporting income all stagnated during the crisis. One-third of the poorest families declared their inability to pay for utilities and 9 per cent had their electricity cut off occasionally.

In response to this situation, families adopted the strategy of reducing their food expenditure to cover other essential needs. The urban poor had to adjust the most. Among the poorest 20 per cent of families in the urban centres, 75 per cent reported that they had reduced food consumption and 50 per cent said they had reduced the level of food consumed by their children. Also, 29 per cent of the poorest population reported a reduced resort to health services.

Survey results indicate that 10 per cent of the poorest urban households had access to public social assistance programmes, such as cash payments or fuel or food support, which accounted for 7 per cent of poor households' income.

Informal mechanisms of solidarity in the form of borrowing from neighbours, friends and relatives were used during the crisis and applications for assistance provided by the Social Assistance and Solidarity Foundations and local governments increased. Borrowing amounted to half of total income for poor and middle income households. However, despite these channels, one-fifth of the poorest families still stated that they could find no support at all during the crisis period.

3. MEASURES RELATED TO WORKING LIFE TAKEN IN RESPONSE TO THE CRISIS

3.1 Anti-crisis Measures

In Turkey, the Government adopted a series of measures collected under the heading of 'anti-crisis packages' which aimed at boosting domestic demand and exports, encouraging capital inflows and opening up domestic credit channels (SEDEFED 2009).

The Undersecretariat of the Treasury classifies the measures adopted by both the Government and the Central Bank as follows: 'liquidity support', which includes measures related to the banking sector to facilitate money flows to the markets; 'tax support', designed to reduce rates of VAT and special consumption tax (SCT); 'investment support', 'credit and guarantee support for production and exports', 'arrangements concerning credit use and credit cards', 'research and development support' and 'employment support' (T.C. Hazine Müsteşarlığı 2009). It is estimated that the cost of these support packages constituted 0.8 per cent, 2.1 per cent and 1.6 per cent of GDP in 2008, 2009 and 2010, respectively (DPT 2009a).

As can be seen from this list, which is revised on a monthly basis, anti-crisis measures in Turkey are essentially based on the idea of transferring resources to financial and industrial capital and boosting domestic demand by reducing the prices of durable goods.

In the context of mitigating the effects of the economic crisis on employment, the Government adopted both active and passive labour market policies. Among its active labour market policies, employment incentives provided to employers and vocational training and community work provided by İŞKUR, Turkey's Public Employment Agency, were at the fore.

Passive labour market policies included the short working allowance and the wage guarantee fund. There was a minor improvement in the amount of unemployment benefit, but the conditions of eligibility and terms of entitlement to unemployment benefits remained extremely restrictive and were not alleviated during the crisis period.

3.2 Active Labour Market Policies

The Government adopted three major legislative acts to promote employment and counteract the effects of the global crisis. The first one, commonly known as the 'employment package', was adopted on 15 May 2008, well before the full effects of the global crisis were felt in Turkey. The second one was adopted on 18 February 2009, which introduced amendments to existing legislation. The last one, dated 11 August 2009, amended existing unemployment insurance, social security and health insurance legislation.

The measures introduced by the 2008 employment package to boost demand for labour by reducing labour costs were centred on decreasing the tax wedge on employment of certain groups, such as women, young people and the disabled, who are more vulnerable to the effects of the crisis. The employer's share of social security contributions for disabled persons employed under compulsory employment legislation was henceforth to be covered by the Treasury, while at the same time the quota for compulsory employment was reduced from 6 per cent to 3 per cent for private sector employers. The employers' share of the social security contributions of women recruited in addition to existing employees, as well as of young persons aged 18–29, will be covered retrogressively for a period of five years by the Unemployment Insurance Fund. The number of jobs created by means of these incentives totalled 53,296 in 2009, 27,322 of them for women. In 2009, 81 million lira were transferred from the Unemployment Insurance Fund to the Social Security Institute to cover these incentives. Starting from October 2008, the employers' share in employees' disability, old age and death insurance were to be covered by the Treasury.

On 11 August 2009, further employment incentive measures were introduced to promote the employment of persons receiving unemployment benefits. However, these employment incentives were conditional on employers not being in arrears in their social insurance contributions. In 2009, 55,093 jobless people benefited from this incentive, 16,690 of them women. Another incentive was for new employment, applying to all workers hired in addition to those on the company payroll between April 2009 and December 2009 and in employment at the time of the application: the employer's share of social insurance contributions calculated at the minimum earnings level could be covered from the Unemployment Insurance Fund for six months.

On 14 July 2009, the Council of Ministers announced its new system of incentives for new investments. With regard to employment incentives, the system provided for state coverage of the employers' share of the social security contributions of newly recruited workers for two to seven years, differentiated on a regional basis. The second group of measures within the context of active labour market policies are intended to increase demand for labour by increasing productivity. Again, the employment package of 2008 introduced the basic changes in this regard.

Both new labour market entrants and other unemployed shall be covered by the Unemployment Insurance Scheme in the context of active labour market policies. Thus, the scheme has been given a wider scope and arrangements have been made to use the Unemployment Insurance Fund to finance job placement, counselling, vocational training, labour force adaptation, community work and similar services for all unemployed, whether or not they have paid contributions to the Fund, as well as labour market research and planning efforts.

A total of 30 per cent of the state share transferred to the fund as unemployment insurance contributions will be allocated to financing such services as extending training services to all unemployed persons, labour force adaptation, labour market research and planning and training and counselling. The Council of Ministers was authorized to raise this amount to 50 per cent, which it did.

With this facility, in 2009 and 2010 İŞKUR launched a vocational training initiative. Programmes implemented in 2009 were attended by 213,852 trainees (120,099 males and 93,753 females). The amount transferred in 2009 was 595 million lira. Planned funding for 2010 is also 595 million lira. This means that within two years İŞKUR will have expended more than 1 billion lira in its active employment programmes, for which it procures services from vocational training institutions.

In addition to the advantages that might be obtained from being awarded a certificate, another reason for the popularity of vocational training courses was the 15 lira allowance given to participants. Some of these courses come with an employment guarantee; however, employment created through this channel remains relatively limited (in 2009, only 15,000). Community work, where a minimum wage is paid for six months' manual employment in public schools or other public services, provided employment for 45,000 people after brief training in 2009.

İŞKUR's internship programme, under which interns are paid 15 lira per day, fell well below the target: only 1,285 interns were taken on by companies. The same is true of the business training programme, from which only 19 people benefited.

While İŞKUR monitors the labour market positions of its course attendants, no impact analysis has yet been carried out (İŞKUR, Interview 2009).

3.3   Passive Labour Market Policies

The 2008 employment package introduced reorganization of the Wage Guarantee Fund and short-time working allowances, given the likelihood that there would be more call for them during the crisis. The scope of the Wage Guarantee Fund was expanded: eligibility now also included cases in which workers cannot be paid due to the insolvency of their employers. Also, limitations on the period of payment were lifted. The number

Table 12.8   Payments from the Wage Guarantee Fund, Turkey, 2005–2010

Years	Number of Persons	Total Amount Paid, TL
2005	1 269	3 352 330
2006	1 134	1 640 989
2007	2 223	3 602 134
2008	827	1 071 806
2009	12 371	22 338 534
2010 January–July	10 590	16 497 184

Source: İŞKUR, Unemployment Insurance Fund Bulletins.

of beneficiaries and the amount paid from the Wage Guarantee Fund increased considerably in 2009 (Table 12.8).

Law no. 5838, adopted on 18 February 2009, improved the conditions under which it was possible to benefit from short-time working arrangements.

Under the original short-time work measure provided for first by the Labour Law and then by the Law on Unemployment Insurance, if the employer, in conditions of an overall economic crisis or other compelling factors, temporarily shortened weekly working hours (shorter work) or suspended enterprise activities partly or fully, he could then provide a short-time allowance for employees eligible for unemployment benefits, as long as the Public Employment Agency İŞKUR was duly informed about the situation and the approval of the Ministry of Labour was obtained. In such conditions, workers would be paid from the unemployment insurance fund for the period they were out of work for a maximum of three months. The daily allowance was equivalent to unemployment benefit. If short-time beneficiaries lost their jobs permanently, the period during which they received short-time allowance would be deducted from the period during which they would be eligible for unemployment benefits. In other words, this arrangement brought employees nothing in addition to unemployment benefits. Indeed, as a result of these strict limitations no person could benefit from this scheme in 2008, which was a crisis year.

Later, however, with Law no. 5838, dated 18 February 2009, the period envisaged for the short-time allowance was extended to six months and the amount of the allowance was increased by 50 per cent. Furthermore, in case of permanent job loss, the period of short-time payments will not be deducted from the period of eligibility for unemployment benefits.

As shown in Table 12.9, after these improvements in the regulations on short-time working, applications for short-time allowances increased

Table 12.9   Short-time working payments, Turkey, 2005–2010

Years	Number of Persons	Total Amount Paid TL
2005	21	10 566
2006	217	64 398
2007	40	22 051
2008	650	70 639
2009	190 223	162 506 260
2010 Jan-July	22 945	34 251 635

Source: İŞKUR, Unemployment Insurance Bulletins.

rapidly. In 2009, the number of persons who benefited from the scheme was 190,223. However, even with this rapid increase, the proportion of short-term beneficiaries was less than 2 per cent of registered employees in 2009. This explains the limited impact of the short-time working scheme on labour adjustment, as mentioned in Section 2.4.

The short-time working scheme is aimed at protecting jobs in order to maintain workforce attachment during the crisis. As such, it is used mainly to preserve the employment of skilled workers. It also helps employers to reduce the costs of shedding workers (particularly severance pay), which can be high for skilled workers on regular employment contracts who have been at the same firm for a long period. These workers also constitute the backbone of unions in Turkey, who prefer working time adjustment to labour adjustment. However, unskilled workers employed in small enterprises or through subcontractors within the framework of flexible and sometimes unregistered employment relations are more likely to be laid off during crises instead of being subjected to lengthy short-time arrangements. Furthermore, such workplaces are almost all 'union free' in Turkey. The relative narrowness of the primary sector and the generality of flexible and/or unprotected working arrangements in many enterprises in Turkey explains the limited number of beneficiaries of short-time working. Strengthening both labour market institutions and the trade unions would result in better use of the current system and allow for more efficient use of internal flexibility.

During the crisis period there was only one minor improvement concerning unemployment benefits. The amendment to Article 3 of Unemployment Insurance Law no. 4477 provides that, in calculating unemployment benefits, not the net but the gross amount of the minimum wage will be taken as the base, which increases the level of payment, to some extent, without any alleviation of the conditions of eligibility and terms of entitlement to unemployment benefits.

*Table 12.10   Unemployment Insurance Fund income and expenditure,
Turkey, 2007–2010 (current prices, million lira)*

	2007	2008	2009 (est.)	2010 (est.)
I: Revenue	7 390	9 587	9 382	9 054
Contributions	2 413	3 090	2 919	3 320
State contribution	814	1 022	986	1 107
Interest	4 100	5 367	5 389	4 531
II: Expenditure	404	1 940	6 290	5 011
Insurance expenditure	324	475	1 328	883
Other expenditure	81	1 464	4 961	4 128
III: Balance	6 986	7 647	3 092	4 043
IV: Total fund assets	30 712	38 359	41 451	45 494

Source: SPO.

3.4   Transfer of Revenues from the Unemployment Insurance Fund to the Budget

One controversial arrangement introduced by the Employment Package is the permission given to the Government to transfer revenues from the Unemployment Insurance Fund to the budget. According to this arrangement (dated 2008), in 2008 an amount totalling 1.3 billion TL was transferred and in the period 2009–2012 one-quarter of the Fund's interest revenues will be transferred, on the decision of the Higher Planning Board, to relevant institutions and agencies, to be used in 'investments in the context of the South-eastern Anatolia Project (GAP) and in other investments for regional economic and social development'. This arrangement was later expanded by Law no. 5921. Instead of one-quarter of the Fund's interest revenues, now three-quarters will be transferred to the general budget for 2009 and 2010, the ratio decreasing to one-quarter again in 2011 and 2012.

With this amendment, an amount totalling 4.2 billion TL was transferred from the Fund to the budget in 2009 and 3.6 billion TL in 2010. These investments and their employment effects have not been accounted for.

Both workers' and employers' organizations opposed the transfer of Fund revenues to the general budget. Trade Union Confederations TÜRK-İŞ and DİSK further accused the Government of financing the budget deficit with Fund revenues which instead should have been used for the unemployed.

Table 12.10 shows that as a result of this transfer, the ratio between Other Expenditure and Insurance Expenditure which was 1 to 4 in 2007, was reversed in the crisis period to 4 to 1.

Table 12.11   Public sector social expenditure (real), Turkey, 2007–2010 (2007=100)

	2007	2008	2009	2010
Education	100	108	114	120
Health	100	112	117	118
Social protection	100	100	108	113
Pensions and other expenditures	100	100	107	111
Social aids and unfunded expenditures	100	127	176	181
Direct income support payments	100	69	36	64
Total	100	105	112	116

Source: SPO, 2009 estimate, 2010 projected. Author's calculations.

3.5   Social Protection During the Crisis

In the Treasury list of anti-crisis measures no mention is made of additional social protection measures during the crisis period. However, using the social protection statistics we can discover something about social protection trends during the crisis.

The State Planning Organization (SPO) groups public sector social spending under three headings: education, health and social protection. Social protection spending comprises three main components: (i) pensions and other expenditure, (ii) social assistance and unfunded expenditure and (iii) direct income support payments (SPO 2009b).

The ratio of public sector social spending to GDP was 14.65 per cent in 2007, 15.08 per cent in 2008, 17.1 per cent in 2009 (estimated) and 17.58 per cent in 2010 (projected). However, given the contraction in GDP in the crisis period, the evolution of total real social spending and its components would better reflect trends in social protection. As shown in Table 12.11 the index score of total real social spending (2007 = 100) rose to 105 and 112 for 2008 and 2009, respectively.[1] The increase in social expenditure manifests itself mainly in the massive expansion of social assistance programmes implemented via poorly coordinated means tested programmes. The index score of the real value of social assistance and unfunded expenditure increased to 127 in 2008, 176 in 2009 (estimated) and 181 in 2010 (projected). The expansion of cash and in-kind transfers was not specifically designed to counteract the social impact of the crisis, but rather functioned as built-in protection measures.

4. SOCIAL PARTNERS ON THE GLOBAL CRISIS AND ANTI-CRISIS MEASURES

4.1 Social Dialogue Mechanisms During the Crisis[2]

During the economic crisis, a number of initiatives were launched to assign a different role to social dialogue mechanisms and to reach consensus through these mechanisms on measures to be adopted to counter the effects of the crisis.

The Economic and Social Council under the Ministry of Labour and Social Security, the Tripartite Advisory Board, İŞKUR, SSI and other institutions in which the social partners are represented, including provincial employment and vocational training boards at local level were brought to the fore as arenas for social dialogue.

A social dialogue arena independent of the Ministry of Labour and Social Security was created on 3 November 2008 when the Economic Coordination Board met under the chairmanship of the Prime Minister with the participation of key ministers. The Board included the crisis on its agenda and invited the social partners and NGOs to the meeting. TÜRK-İŞ, HAK-İŞ, DİSK, KAMU-SEN, KESK, MEMUR-SEN (trade unions), and TİSK, TESK, TZOB, TÜDEF, KEİG, the Community Volunteers Foundation, TOBB, the Women Entrepreneurs Board, KAGİDER and the Association of Private Employment Agencies also participated in the meeting, at which employers' and employees' organizations presented reports containing their remarks and suggestions on the crisis.[3]

At its January 2009 meeting, the Tripartite Advisory Board decided to meet every month to work on the crisis. At this meeting the social partners also submitted their reports on the crisis, containing their suggestions.

The Economic and Social Council, another mechanism for social dialogue, met on 5 February 2009 with the economic crisis on the agenda. The social partners shared their suggestions on anti-crisis measures with the Prime Minister, as well as other ministers and top-level bureaucrats.

In addition to the abovementioned national social dialogue during the crisis period, efforts were made to promote social dialogue also at the local level through the local employment and vocational training boards.

4.2 A Process Interrupted at the Peak of the Crisis

The efforts made at the inception of the crisis to create an environment conducive to social dialogue at the national level came to an end towards the end of 2009. During the İŞKUR General Assembly meeting on 23 November 2009, the Minister of Labour and Social Security directed criticisms towards the trade unions, accusing them of 'irresponsibility and a lack of vision'. In response to these accusations, in a joint declaration, both the employers' and the workers' organizations – TİSK, TÜRK-İŞ, HAK-İŞ and DİSK – described these criticisms as an expression of a 'conflict-based culture biased against the unions' (TİSK 2009a). After the joint protests of the social partners at İŞKUR's General Congress, workers' confederations issued another declaration and stated that they would not be participating at the meeting of the Tripartite Advisory Board planned for 25 November 2009 since they did not expect that a fruitful dialogue would be possible after the Minister's heavy criticism of the trade unions (TÜRK-İŞ 2009a). It seems that towards the end of 2009, a climate of conflict rather than dialogue prevailed between the Government and the social partners (TİSK 2009a).

4.3 Elements of Divergence

The trade unions have many points in common with regard to their demands within the framework of the social dialogue, which call mainly for increases in wages, pensions and other benefits and tax and price abatements in public services.

Such employer demands as short-time working, reductions in VAT, the Special Consumption Tax and employment taxes were supported by the trade unions, while they rejected other suggestions, including the introduction of further flexibility in labour markets, particularly temporary agency work, limitations on severance pay and maintaining the IMF anchor.

The Minimum Wage Commission is one of the most important social dialogue platforms in Turkey. It is interesting that the decisions taken in the crisis era were not based on consensus.

One point that both employers' and workers' organizations agreed on in the context of anti-crisis measures was the need to boost domestic demand. However, the two sides differed when it came to specific measures for that purpose. The employers suggested capital-focused measures, most of which were geared to boosting spending on investment and automotive and consumer durables. To be more specific, the private sector proposed the following, considering itself the main agent in each: boosting public investment in infrastructure, including railways, ports, irrigation and housing; reintroducing investment discounts and incentives; exempting both domestic and foreign investors from all taxes for a period of 10 years; credit allocation on favourable terms; free investment sites; and reducing the tax burden on energy. Employers also asked for further tax reductions in the sub-sectors of automotive and durable consumer goods, in which the effects of the crisis were more acute.

Workers' organizations proposed the following to increase domestic demand: increasing wages and benefits; raising the level of the minimum wage; expanding the coverage of collective bargaining; increasing retirement pensions; more favourable conditions for eligibility for unemployment benefits; introducing minimum income support; improving short-time working arrangements and strengthening of collective agreements.

One issue on which the parties had completely opposed stances was the introduction of new forms of flexibility in the Labour Code. While the employers wanted, for example, temporary employment through private employment agencies, the trade union organizations strongly rejected it.

4.4 Bilateral Anti-crisis Agreements

In the crisis period, action was also taken by trade unions and employers at the enterprise level, mainly by means of protocols and agreements on wages, social benefits and working time. On the part of the trade unions, the obvious aim of the protocols was to protect employment, especially in the textile/garments and automotive sectors, which were hit hard by the global crisis.

TEKSİF (Textile, Knitwear and Garment Workers' Union of Turkey), an affiliate of TÜRK-İŞ, and TTSİS (Textile Industry Employers' Association of Turkey) agreed a protocol regulating working time under crisis conditions. The protocol, signed concurrently with the 21st Session Group Collective Agreements of 2008 and valid until 1 December 2008 for the first group of enterprises, and 2 July 2009 for the second group of enterprises, suspended the implementation of the clauses of the collective agreement regulating overtime and weekend work payments for 60 enterprises. With the protocol, the level of overtime wages was decreased from 100 per cent to the legal minimum of 50 per cent, and the payment of two additional daily wages in the case of weekend working was reduced to 1.5 additional daily wages. A new protocol signed between TEKSİF and TTSİS extended the period of application of the first protocol until 31 March 2010, which is the expiry date of the 2008 collective agreement.

The Textile Workers' Union, an affiliate of DİSK (Confederation of Progressive Workers' Unions), and Coats Corporation Turkey – one of the signatories of the group collective agreement – also signed a protocol, based on the group collective agreement clauses regulating short-time working, on 9 February 2009. This protocol includes the implementation of a four-month period of short-time working in 2009. According to the protocol, unpaid leave of 7.5 hours a week was agreed, reducing weekly working hours from 45 to 37.5 and suspending Saturday working. An additional protocol signed on 17 April 2009 extended the validity of the agreements until 30 June 2009.

In the metal sector, which was also hit hard by the crisis, a 35 per cent wage decrease for a 16-month period was agreed by a protocol signed on 21 April 2009 between the Turkish Metal Union, an affiliate of TÜRK-İŞ, and Erdemir Corporation. Other contractual rights were preserved. The agreement on the wage cut applied to 5,224 members of the Turkish Metal Union and to 1,806 other employees, mainly managers and white-collar workers. According to the protocol, workers would resume receiving their regular wages and other rights based on wages without any deductions at the end of August 2009, the expiry date of the protocol, and payments would be made in accordance with the existing collective agreement.

Another protocol which modified certain clauses of the 2008 collective agreement was signed on 20 January 2009 between PETROL-İŞ (Union of Petroleum, Chemical and Rubber Workers), an affiliate of TÜRK-İŞ, and SODAŞ Sodium Corporation. The protocol froze wages for the first six months of 2009 at their 2008 levels, suspending the 3.87 per cent wage increase stipulated in the collective agreement. It also froze social benefits at their 2008 levels.

Similar actions have been taken by other unions and employers' organizations through collective agreements, agreements on short-time working and written or verbal protocols concerning wages, social benefits and working time. The temporary provision in the collective agreement between the Sugar Workers' Union and the Employers' Organization of the Sugar Industry covering the period 10 February 2009–31 January 2011 provided for lower wages if seasonal and fixed-term workers were transferred to permanent jobs. AGAC-İŞ, the Wood Workers' Union, agreed to unpaid leave and the postponement of wage increases and bonus payments stipulated in the collective agreements with Samedoglu Forest Products, Domsan Furniture and Agacoglu Forest Products. TES-İŞ, the Energy Workers' Union, agreed to lower the entry-level wages, bonuses and social benefits for workers to be taken on by the Baskent, Sakarya, Aydem and Kayseri Electric companies for the collective agreements covering 2009–2010.

5.   CASE STUDY: EVOLVING WORK PRACTICES IN THE CRISIS

To illustrate working conditions in the crisis and their effects on inequalities we present here what has been happening in one province hit

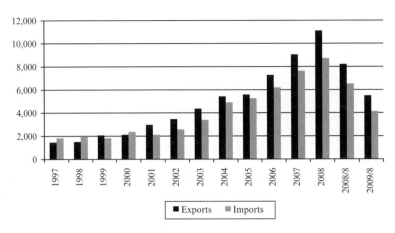

Source: BTSO (2009a).

Figure 12.15 Exports and imports, Bursa, Turkey, 1997–2009 (million US dollars)

particularly hard by the crisis, Bursa, and the adjustment policies put in place at the local level, notably through social dialogue.

5.1 Bursa: A City in Crisis

According to TURKSTAT's 2008 Regional Indicators, the population of Bursa Province is 2,507,963, with 88 per cent living in urban areas and 12 per cent in rural areas. Bursa is above the national average with regard to the rate of urbanization, the annual rate of population growth, per capita GDP and the share of industrial employment in total employment. The Province of Bursa occupies an important position in the automotive, machinery, textile and food industries.

Bursa was hard hit by the global crisis in 2008 and its effects only grew worse in 2009. This can be explained by the fact that exports play a significant role in the provincial economy: indeed, they accounted for 9 per cent of all Turkish exports in 2009. During the first seven months of 2009, when Turkey's exports fell by 30.5 per cent in comparison to the same period of the previous year, the figure was 31.6 per cent for Bursa. Looking at the import figures we see that Bursa's share in Turkey's total imports was 4.7 per cent and that imports to Bursa declined by 36.6 per cent in the first eight months of 2009 in comparison to the same period in 2008 (Figure 12.15).

It applies not only to Bursa but also to Turkey as a whole that provinces in which production is mainly export-oriented have been harder hit by the crisis as a result of falling foreign demand. But what makes Bursa more prone to the effects of the crisis is that exports from this province are mainly to EU countries, where the contraction in demand has been more pronounced than in other regions of the world (Kalkan and Başdaş 2009a, 2009b).

Looking at the regional distribution of exports from Bursa, it seems that the share of EU countries gradually increased from 69.7 per cent in 2004 to 75.1 per cent in 2009. On the other hand, the share of Middle Eastern and Northern European countries increased very little: from 9.4 per cent in 2004 to 10.6 per cent in 2009 (BTSO 2009a).

The automotive industry (including support industries), textiles and clothing, machinery and metal processing constitute the province's export base and have been seriously affected by the crisis.[4] Textiles and clothing were under pressure even before the 2008 crisis. According to a survey by the Chamber of Industry and Commerce (BTSO 2008) covering the 250 largest firms in Bursa, the number of firms from the textile sector in that sample has been falling continuously since 1997. Turkish textiles and clothing firms trying to engage in price competition in export markets did not perform well against competitors while the value of the lira continued to appreciate under the economic policy of financing the current account by attracting speculative capital to Turkey. These firms found it difficult to cope with global competition in the domestic market as well. In fact, representatives of the social partners in Bursa said that many investors were pessimistic about the future of this sector and consequently had shifted to other sectors, including construction and tourism. Thus, the contraction in the textiles and clothing sector in Bursa should not be associated with the current crisis alone. The falling trend already evident before the crisis was only exacerbated.

The same cannot be said for the automotive sector and its support industries. In Bursa, they experienced growth until 2008, making the province the leading centre in Turkey in terms of exports and employment (BTSO 2009b). In 2008, Bursa's share of all vehicles produced in Turkey was 49.3 per cent. Such major concerns as TOFAŞ-FIAT, OYAK-RENAULT and KARSAN-PEUGEOT all have their facilities in Bursa. In the province there are also many firms engaged in the production of parts and spare parts for motor vehicles. During the 2001 crisis, automotive enterprises in Bursa managed to compensate for the fall in domestic demand by shifting to foreign markets. While the sector felt the effects of the crisis in 2008 and suffered some stagnancy, there was no significant downturn in terms of exports and employment. This situation completely changed in 2009, however, and as a result of contracting foreign demand due to the global crisis, automotive industry indicators turned negative. Within the first eight months of 2009, the number of vehicles produced by the industry declined by 21.6 per cent and exports fell by 33.6 per cent compared to the same period in the previous year (BTSO 2009a).

Food is another major sector providing employment in Bursa. Bursa has a notable share in the production and export of fruit juices, soft beverages, canned food, tomato paste, processed food items, milk products and frozen foodstuffs in Turkey. During the crisis period of 2009, this sector too fell back in terms of output, exports, employment and profitability (BTSO 2009b). Between August 2008 and August 2009, the export of food and beverages fell by 22.8 per cent.

5.2 Job Losses High in Bursa

Heavily dependent on exports and EU markets which were deeply affected by the crisis, Bursa started to face serious problems, with increased unemployment and informalization. Furthermore, the contraction in exports had backward linkages to overall economic activities in the province, leading to a contraction in the domestic market oriented activities of firms and small enterprises.

According to data provided by the Social Security Institution for Bursa, the number of workers with insurance coverage decreased by 16 per cent in the period June 2008–June 2009, while the decrease for the insured self-employed was 22 per cent. As of September 2009, this falling trend had slowed down: there was a 13.5 per cent decrease in the period June 2008–September 2009. However, the decrease in the number of insured self-employed continued, rising to 23.5 per cent for the period 2008 June–2009 September. This fall in the number of insured wage earners and self-employed reflected increasing unemployment, on the one hand, and expanding informal employment, on the other.

Observations by İŞKUR confirmed the adverse affects of the crisis on employment in Bursa. The İŞKUR representative noted that firms applied the seniority principle in implementing dismissals, which thereby affected mainly younger workers. Other priority groups with regard to dismissals included workers with retirement rights or working while retired and younger workers about to be recruited to the military. There were dismissals not only of blue-collar workers but also of middle-ranking and top managers. According to the Regional Director of the Ministry of Labour and Social Security in Bursa, while the placement of blue-collar workers in new jobs was relatively easy, even in the crisis period, it could be difficult for white-collar workers.

5.3   Anti-crisis Measures and Local Reactions of the Social Partners

As the pressures of the crisis began to be felt more acutely, employers' and workers' organizations started to think about what could be done at the local level. The measures contemplated were mostly macro-level, and thus it was expected that central government would take responsibility. As measures to ease in particular the automotive sector, SCT reductions were considered and suggestions to lower consumption taxes were conveyed to the Government.

The automotive sector was in deep crisis by the first quarter of 2009 and in March 2009, the Government finally introduced special consumption tax reductions on a number of products, including motor vehicles. The SCT rate was reduced from 6.7 per cent to zero on white goods and electronic household goods; from 10 per cent to 1 per cent on commercial vehicles; from 37 per cent to 18 per cent on cars with an engine capacity not exceeding 1600 cm^3; from 4 per cent to 1 per cent on lorries and buses; and from 22 per cent to 11 per cent on motorcycles with an engine capacity not exceeding 250 cm^3. The reductions remained in place until 30 September 2009; the highest SCT reduction was on passenger cars.

Local representatives in Bursa affirmed the Government's SCT reductions as a positive measure since demand for passenger cars, in particular, was stimulated. But they added that these measures came too late and were not very effective from an employment point of view since firms made their sales mainly from inventories, and SCT reductions also benefited motor vehicle imports. Taymaz (2010), in his study of the effects of the crisis on the automotive industry, confirms that the impact on employment of the SCT reduction was limited: motor vehicle producers continued to lay off workers.

One other measure considered by the local social partners aimed at boosting the automotive industry and its support industries in Bursa was to offer consumers willing to exchange their old car for a new one various incentives, such as a 'scrappage discount', whereby the value of the abandoned car would be considered as advance payment before instalments. A scrappage discount has been in force since 2007, but limited to trucks, tankers, trailers, midi buses and buses and not tied to new purchases of motor vehicles. The Government extended its application several times in 2008 and 2009, but still excluded passenger cars and did not introduce the conditionality of a new purchase. Application therefore remained limited to around 15,000 vehicles and did not meet local expectations.

During the crisis, İŞKUR's Bursa Directorate increased considerably in importance (Table 12.12). According to monthly İŞKUR data for 2008, 17,846 persons were applying for unemployment benefits in Bursa as of September 2008. The number was 38,729 in 2009.

Table 12.12   Activities of İŞKUR's Bursa Directorate, 2007–2009

	Applications	Vacancies	Placements	Registered unemployed
2007	36 264	9 861	6 839	36 419
2009	61 382	5 703	3 696	86 274

Source: İŞKUR Bursa Directorate.

İŞKUR Bursa became very active in the crisis period, carrying out most of the work of Provincial Employment and Vocational Training Boards. Participation in vocational training courses organized by İŞKUR Bursa increased particularly in 2009, the daily payment of 15 lira to each participating trainee making the courses attractive, despite the lack of an employment guarantee in most schemes. In 2008, 2,768 trainees participated in 73 courses. In 2009, 455 courses were opened and 9,244 trainees took part, 46 per cent of them women.

Active labour market policies also included public works. The TİSK representative said that 800 persons were temporarily placed in jobs in 120 schools. However, he continued, this is not actually employment creation, but merely finding an excuse to pay such people wages. These measures were considered mere window-dressing and the social partners maintained that such measures would not represent a sustainable solution unless productive work opportunities were introduced.

According to İŞKUR, 649 firms had applied for the short-time working scheme as of 30 September 2009, covering 62,303 employees.

6. CONCLUSION

In common with many other developing countries that cannot generate decent jobs even with high rates of growth, Turkey was facing a serious problem of unemployment and idle labour even before the global crisis. Despite the high growth rates experienced in the aftermath of the 2001 crisis in Turkey, job creation was not adequate and the official unemployment rate settled at around 10 per cent for all sectors and around 13 per cent excluding agriculture. The global crisis further deepened this employment crisis. By the end of 2009, the unemployment rate had increased to 14 per cent for all sectors and to 16.6 per cent excluding agriculture.

In the crisis period, while full-time jobs in industry were lost in the urban areas, employment creation in the rural areas mitigated the effects of the crisis, with job creation for persons becoming self-employed and among unpaid family workers.

During the crisis year of 2009, labour force participation rates for women increased by 0.4 percentage points and those for men decreased by 1.5 points. In 2009, the employment rate for women in both urban and rural areas rose by 0.4 and 1.4 percentage points, respectively, while it decreased for men by –2.3 percentage points in urban and by –1.1 points in rural areas. These figures reflect the added worker effect observed in most countries during crisis periods.

As in the 2001 crisis, industry was most affected by shrinking external demand. The increase in agricultural employment reflected the increase in female employment in agriculture in the form of unpaid family labour, while the troubles of industry resulted in a decrease in male employment. The increase in service sector employment was mostly in small-scale, family-owned services, with low productivity and no security of employment.

The work status of the employed shifted from wage work towards own-account and unpaid family work, and the share of wage and salary earners in total employment decreased. Potential wage earners in urban areas were either transferred to own-account work, still in urban areas, or returned to agriculture to work on family land as self-employed or unpaid family labour. In both cases, the transformation manifested itself as informalization.

The toll of unemployment effects in the crisis has been particularly heavy for urban youth. As unemployment increased and young people bore the brunt of it, the relative weight of long-term unemployment in total unemployment diminished.

Employers chose to release unskilled workers, preferring to retain skilled workers during the crisis. Short-time working helped in this. Consequently, the unemployment rates of less educated (for example, secondary school graduates) increased more than those of vocational graduates and those with a higher education.

The declining trend with regard to undeclared work is not observed in the crisis period of 2008–2009. Despite all the measures taken to tackle undeclared work, the proportion of working people not covered by any social security scheme increased by 0.3 points to 43.8 per cent in 2009.

In some workplaces, social security registration of workers was withdrawn, with the same effect as if their work contracts had been terminated, although they continued working. Social Security Institution (SSI) statistics suggest that the number of workers covered by social security decreased significantly in 2009. The decrease in the number of self-employed persons covered by social security is even more pronounced.

During the crisis year of 2009, average working hours decreased to 53.9 in manufacturing industry and to 53.6 in services. However, while changes in average working time have served as an adjustment variable, labour adjustment by firms in response to the crisis took place mainly through changes in employment,

The short-time working scheme and voluntary agreements between employers and trade unions for part-time work or compulsory leave were not sufficiently widespread to dominate labour adjustment through reductions in working hours. Reduced working hours through short-time working or voluntary agreements between employers and trade unions took place in the primary sector, while secondary sector workers were faced with layoffs, in many cases without severance pay. This reinforced the dual structure of the labour market, leaving secondary sector workers more disadvantaged in the crisis period.

In 2009, the effects of the present crisis hit hard and real wages fell sharply. The decline was felt in particular in industry and construction, while workers in services were less affected. In addition to wages in labour-intensive sectors, wages in capital-intensive sectors were also squeezed in the crisis.

During the crisis, complaints to the MLSS increased significantly with regard to such problems as delays in the payment of wages, unfair dismissals, non-payment of severance pay and health and safety violations.

Three-quarters of families experienced a fall in their incomes in the period October 2008–June 2009 (TEPAV 2009). Falls in income were associated not only with unemployment; even when jobs were maintained, wage earnings fell for the lowest quintile. For informal workers, this fall was relatively higher.

Social spending increased in the crisis period, considerably mitigating its effects on the most vulnerable. However, despite various support channels, one-fifth of the poorest families could find no support at all during the crisis period.

In the context of mitigating the effects of the economic crisis on employment, the Government adopted both active and passive labour market policies. Its active labour market policies included employment incentives to employers, and vocational training and community work provided by İŞKUR, the Public Employment Agency, came to the fore. Passive labour market policies include the short-time working allowance and the Wage Guarantee Fund. There was a minor increase in unemployment benefit, but the extremely restrictive conditions of eligibility and terms of entitlement to unemployment benefit were not amended in the crisis period.

Even though there was recourse to tripartite social dialogue in the adoption of the crisis prevention packages, workers' and civil servants' trade union confederations stated that social dialogue remained just a talking shop. In the crisis period, action was also taken by trade unions and employers at the enterprise level, mainly through protocols and agreements on wages, social benefits and working time.

Turkey's employment crisis and the vulnerability of large sections of its segmented labour market pre-existed the global crisis. With the deepening of the employment crisis during the global financial crisis, new tendencies emerged with regard to inequality. Some of these tendencies will be short-lived, but some will be permanent, exacerbating existing structural problems.

NOTES

1. Index values for the per capita increase in total social spending (2007 = 100) are 103.6 and 109 for 2008 and 2009, respectively.
2. There are three trade union confederations in Turkey: TÜRK-İŞ, the Confederation of Workers' Trade Unions in Turkey, was founded in 1952 and is the oldest. The Confederation of Progressive Workers' Trade Unions of Turkey, DİSK, split from TÜRK-İŞ in 1967, while the Confederation of Turkish Workers' Unions HAK-İŞ was founded in 1976. A small number of unions remain independent. There are three civil servants' confederations in Turkey: the Confederation of Public Employees' Trade Unions KESK was founded in 1995; the Confederation of Public Employees' Trade Unions of Turkey TÜRKİYE KAMU-SEN was founded in 1992; and the Confederation of Civil Servants' Trade Unions MEMUR-SEN was founded in 1995. The differences between the three confederations are mainly political. A small number of unions belong to other confederations. The Turkish Confederation of Employers' Associations TİSK, which represents the employers in tripartite bodies, was founded in 1962. TİSK has 23 members, four of which are public sector employers' organizations.
3. For the social partners' responses to the crises, see TÜRK-İŞ (2008, 2009a, 2009b, 2009c, 2009d, 2009e and 2009f); DİSK (2008a, 2008b, 2008c, 2009a and 2009b); HAK-İŞ (2008 and 2009); TİSK (2008, 2009a, 2009b, 2009c and 2009d); Kutadgobilik (2008a and 2008b) and Kumlu (2009).
4. The machinery sector produces and exports textile machinery, packing machines, CNC hydraulic presses and heavy machinery. The metal sector processes office equipment, industrial equipment and automotive industry products.

BIBLIOGRAPHY

Bağımsız Sosyal Bilimciler (BSB) (2008) *2008 Kavşağında Türkiye*, İstanbul: Yordam Kitap.

Bağımsız Sosyal Bilimciler (BSB) (2009) *Türkiye'de ve Dünya'da Ekonomik Bunalım, 2008–2009*, İstanbul: Yordam Kitap.

Boratav, K. (2009) Bunalım Ortamında Çevre Ekonomileri. Available at: http:// haber. sol.org.tr/yazarlar/13560.html.

Bursa Ticaret ve Sanayi Odası (BTSO) (2008) *Bursa'daki 250 Büyük Firma Araştırması, 2008 Yılı Sonuçları*, Bursa: BTSO.

Bursa Ticaret ve Sanayi Odası (BTSO) (2009a) *Bursa'nın Türk Ekonomisindeki Yeri ve Önemi*, Bursa: BTSO Bilgi Notu (unpublished).

Bursa Ticaret ve Sanayi Odası (BTSO) (2009b) *Bursa'daki 250 Büyük Firma Araştırması, 2009 Yılı Sonuçları*, Bursa: BTSO.

Çalışma ve Sosyal Güvenlik Bakanlığı (ÇSGB) (2010a) Hizmetlerimiz Yayın ve Raporlar. Available at: http://www.csgb.gov.tr/csgbPortal/csgb.portal?page=yayinveraporlar.

Çalışma ve Sosyal Güvenlik Bakanlığı (ÇSGB) (2010b) Yıllara Göre Asgari Ücretler. Available at: http://www.csgb.gov.tr/csgbPortal/csgb.portal?page=ist atistikler&id=asgariucret.

Devlet Planlama Teşkilatı (DPT) (2009a) Genel Ekonomik Hedefler ve Yatırımlar, 2010. Available at: http://www.dpt.gov.tr/PortalDesign/PortalControls/WebI cerik-Gosterim.aspx?Enc=83D5A6FF03C7B4FC9F38684094BC4B9B.

Devlet Planlama Teşkilatı (DPT) (2009b) Ekonomik Gelişmeler Eylül 2009. Available at: http://ekutup.dpt.gov.tr/tg/index.asp?yayin=eg&yil=0&ay=0 Turkey 521.

Devrimci İşçi Sendikaları Konfederasyonu (DİSK) (2008a) Krizden Çıkış İçin, Sosyal Dayanışma ve Demokratikleşme, DİSK Basın Açıklamaları. Available at: http://www.disk.org.tr/default.asp?Page=Content&ContentId=607.

Devrimci İşçi Sendikaları Konfederasyonu (DİSK) (2008b) Küresel Kriz ve Türkiye, DİSK Basın Açıklamaları. Available at: http://www.disk.org.tr/default.asp?Page=Content&ContentId=608.

Devrimci İşçi Sendikaları Konfederasyonu (DİSK) (2008c) DİSK Genişletilmiş Başkanlar Kurulu Sonuç Bildirgesi. Available at: http://www.disk.org.tr/default.asp?Page=Content&ContentId=627&Highlight=acil+müdahale+programı.

Devrimci İşçi Sendikaları Konfederasyonu (DİSK) (2009a) İşsizliği ve İstihdamı Öncelikli Sorun Olarak Görmeyen Bir Tedbir Paketi, DİSK Basın Açıklamaları. Available at: http://www.disk.org.tr/default.asp?Page=Content&ContentId=79 3&Highlight=teşvik+ve+kriz+paketi.

Devrimci İşçi Sendikaları Konfederasyonu (DİSK) (2009b) DİSK'in 'Özel İstihdam Büroları'nın Mesleki Faaliyet Olarak Geçici İş İlişkisi Kurabilmesi' Hakkında Kanun Değişikliğine İlişkin Görüşleri, DİSK Basın Açıklamaları. Available at: http:// www.disk.org.tr/default.asp?Page=Content&ContentId=800.

Durmuş, M. (2009) *Kapitalizmin Krizi, 2008 Krizinin Eleştirel bir Çözümlemesi*, Ankara: Tan Kitabevi Yayınları.

Eğilmez, M. (2009) *Küresel Finans Krizi*, İstanbul: Remzi Kitabevi.

HAK-İŞ Konfederasyonu (2008) Küresel Krizin Ülkemize Olası Etkilerini Azaltmak İçin Alınması Gereken Önlemler, HAK-İŞ Raporu-2. Available at: http://www.hakis. org.tr/raporlar/krize_rapor-2.pdf (accessed on 7 October 2009).

HAK-İŞ Konfederasyonu (2009) *Sosyal Model Önerisi, Üçlü Danışma Kurulu Toplantısına Sunulan HAK-İŞ Raporu*, Ankara: HAK-İŞ.

International Labour Office (ILO) (2009) *Tackling the Global Jobs Crisis*, Report of the Director General, International Labour Conference, 98th Session, Report I (A), Geneva: International Labour Office.

İstanbul Sanayi Odası (İSO) (2009) Krize Karşı Mücadelemize Var Gücümüzle Devam Edeceğiz. Available at: http://www.iso.org.tr/tr/web/statiksayfalar/index.aspx?ref=0.

İş Teftiş Kurulu Başkanlığı (2010), Yayınlar. Available at: http://www.csgb.gov.tr/csgbPortal/itkb.portal?page=yayinlar.

Kalkan, S. and Ü. Başdaş (2009a) Kriz döneminde ihracat yapısının işsizlik üzerindeki etkileri, TEPAV Politika Notu. Available at: http://www.tepav.org. tr/tur/index.php?type=policynotes.

Kalkan, S. and Ü. Başdaş (2009b) İşletme büyüklüğü ve bölgesel farklılıkların kriz döneminde istihdam kayıpları üzerindeki etkileri, TEPAV Politika Notu. Available at: http://www.tepav.org.tr/tur/index.php?type=policynotes.

Kumlu, M. (2009) 'Eylemlerimiz İnat Kırdı', *TÜRK-İŞ Dergisi*, Sayı 384, p. 40.

Kutadgobilik, T. (2008a) 'Kriz Derinleşirken', *İŞVEREN*, Sayı 2, Cilt 47.

Kutadgobilik, T. (2008b) 'İşsizliğe Dikkat', *İŞVEREN*, Sayı 3, Cilt 47.

Sektörel Dernekler Federasyonu (SEDEFED) (2009) Kronolojik Olarak Önlem Paketleri. Available at: http://www.sedefed.org/default.aspx?pid= 60978&nid=57158.

Social Security Institution (SSI) (various years) http://www.sgk.gov.tr.

Sönmez, M. (2009) *Küresel Kriz ve Türkiye*, İstanbul: Alan Yayıncılık.

Sosyal Güvenlik Kurumu (SGK) (2010) *Social Insurance and Universal Health Insurance Law* (English version). Available at: http://www.sgk.gov.tr/wps/ portal/!ut/p/c1.

Sosyal Sigortalar Kurumu (SSK) (2006) *2006 Yılı İstatistik Yıllığı*, Ankara: SSK.

Sosyal Yardım ve Dayanışma Genel Müdürlüğü (SYDGM) (2010) Faaliyetlerimiz. Available at: http://www.sydgm.gov.tr/tr/.

State Planning Organization (SPO) (2009a) *Medium Term Programme, 2010–2012.* Available at: http://www.dpt.gov.tr/PortalDesign/PortalControls/WebI cerikGosterim.aspx?Enc=83D5A6FF03C7B4FC604230EE1496D705.

State Planning Organization (SPO) (2009b) *Public Sector Social Spending Statistics.* Available at: http://www.dpt.gov.tr/DocObjects/Download/7643/ Kamu_Kesimi_Sosyal_ Harcama_Istatistikleri.pdf.

Taymaz, E. (2010) The Effectiveness of Crisis Measures: The Case of the Motor Vehicles Industry, Paper presented at the Final Conference on Impact Analysis of the Crisis Response and Lessons Learned for the Way Forward, 22 October 2010, Ankara.

T.C. Hazine Müsteşarlığı (2009) Küresel Mali Krize Karşı Politika Tedbirleri, 10 Ağustos. Available at: http://www.hazine.gov.tr/doc/Guncel/Politika_ Tedbirleri.pdf.

TEPAV Economic Policy Research Foundation of Turkey (2009) *Economic Crisis Affecting the Welfare of Families in Turkey.* Available at: http://www.tepav.org. tr/upload/files/1265880052r3328.Household_Survey.pdf.

Toksöz, G. (2009) Labour Markets in Crisis Conditions from a Gender Perspective, Unpublished Report for the ILO, Ankara, Turkey.

Türkan, E. (2005) *Türkiye'de İşgücünün Yapı ve Nitelikleri: Gelişme ve Değerlendirmeler*, Ankara: Türkiye Cumhuriyet Merkez Bankası.

Turkish Statistical Institute (TURKSTAT) (various years) http://www.turkstat. gov.tr.

Türkiye İş Kurumu (İŞKUR) (2009) *İstatistikler*. Available at: http://www.iskur. gov.tr/LoadExternalPage.aspx?uicode=statikistatistikindex.

Türkiye İş Kurumu (İŞKUR) (2010) *Rapor ve Bültenler*. Available at: http://www. iskur.gov.tr/.

Türkiye İşçi Sendikaları Konfederasyonu (TÜRK-İŞ) (2008) 'Dosya: Kriz ve Yansımaları', *TÜRK-İŞ Dergisi*, Sayı: 382, Kasım-Aralık.

Türkiye İşçi Sendikaları Konfederasyonu (TÜRK-İŞ) (2009a) 'TÜRK-İŞ, HAK-İŞ, DİSK Üçlü Danışma Kurulu toplantısına katılmıyor', *Haberler ve Duyurular*.

Available at: http://www. turkis.org.tr/index.dyn?wapp=haberdetay0&did=537
23F36-45B4-4852-852EC13B77C32B61.

Türkiye İşçi Sendikaları Konfederasyonu (TÜRK-İŞ) (2009b) 'TÜRK-İŞ SGK
Genel Kuruluna Katılmıyor', *Haberler ve Duyurular*. Available at: http://www.
turkis.org.tr/index.dyn?wapp=haberdetay0&did=6C6EDEDF-3146-45FA-9B
C1-DA2E67DF9DE3.

Türkiye İşçi Sendikaları Konfederasyonu (TÜRK-İŞ) (2009c) 'TÜRK-İŞ Asgari
Ücret Komisyonunu Terketti', *Haberler ve Duyurular*. Available at: http://
www.turkis.org.tr/index.dyn?wapp=haberdetay0&did=BCB0F19E-3B94-490F
-8C57-E74ABD86DB5C.

Türkiye İşçi Sendikaları Konfederasyonu (TÜRK-İŞ) (2009d) *TÜRK-İŞ Dergisi*,
Sayı 383, Ocak-Şubat.

Türkiye İşçi Sendikaları Konfederasyonu (TÜRK-İŞ) (2009e) *TÜRK-İŞ Dergisi*,
Sayı 384, Mart-Haziran.

Türkiye İşçi Sendikaları Konfederasyonu (TÜRK-İŞ) (2009f) *TÜRK-İŞ Dergisi*,
Sayı 385, Temmuz-Ağustos.

Türkiye İşveren Sendikaları Konfederasyonu (TİSK) (2008) 'Küresel Krize Karşı
Alınması Gereken Tedbirler Raporu Hükümete Sunuldu', *İŞVEREN*, Sayı 2,
Cilt 47, Kasım, pp. 8–9.

Türkiye İşveren Sendikaları Konfederasyonu (TİSK) (2009a) 'Ortak Açıklama',
İŞVEREN, Sayı 3, Cilt 48. Kasım. Available at: http://www.tisk.org.tr/isveren_
sayfa.asp?yazi_id=2569&id=.

Türkiye İşveren Sendikaları Konfederasyonu (TİSK) (2009b) 'Kriz Döneminde
Endüstri İlişkileri', *Özel Ek, İŞVEREN*, Sayı 4, Cilt 47.

Türkiye İşveren Sendikaları Konfederasyonu (TİSK) (2009c) 'ESK İşsizlik
Gündemiyle Toplandı', *İŞVEREN*, Sayı 5, Cilt 47, Şubat, pp. 13–16.

Türkiye İşveren Sendikaları Konfederasyonu (TİSK) (2009d) 'Küresel Krize Karşı
Alınması Gereken Tedbirler', *Özel Ek, İŞVEREN*, Sayı 5, Cilt 47.

Türkiye Kalkınma Bankası A.Ş. (2009a) *Ekonomik Gelişmeler Özet Değerlendirme
Raporu*, M. Şimşek, F. Bayraktar and M. Tosun. Available at: http://www.
kalkinma.com.tr/data/fi le/raporlar/ESA/EG/EG-10-01-09_Ekonomik_Gelism
eler.

Türkiye Kalkınma Bankası A.Ş. (2009b) *Küresel Mali Kriz ve Reel Sektöre
Muhtemel Etkileri*. Available at: http://www.kalkinma.com/data/file/raporlar/
ESA/GA/2008GA/Kuresel_Mali_Kriz_ve_Reel_Sektore_Muhtemel_Etkileri.
pdf.

Undersecretariat of Treasury (2010) *Turkish Economy*. Available at: http://
www.treasury.gov.tr/irj/go/km/docs/documents/Treasury%20Web/Statistics/Eco
nomic%20Indicators/egosterge/Sunumlar/Ekonomi_Sunumu_ENG.pdf.

United Nations Conference on Trade and Development (UNCTAD) (2008) Will
We Never Learn? UNCTAD Policy Briefs. Available at: http://www.unctad.
org/en/ docs/presspb20085_en.pdf.

United Nations Conference on Trade and Development (UNCTAD) (2009) *Trade
and Development Report 2009*, New York and Geneva: United Nations.

APPENDIX

Table 12A.1   Overview of the main anti-crisis measures, Turkey, 2008–2010

	Years	Estimated fiscal cost, million TL	
Revenue measures		5855	
Tax on individuals	2009–2010	−1289	Revenues in the context of the law on assets of 13 November 2008 which introduced tax benefits for taxpayers who repatriate or declare their unrecorded assets, including cash, foreign currency, securities and other capital market instruments, as well as real estate
	2008–2010	197	The 10% withholding tax on gains from equities was reduced to zero per cent for domestic investors
	2008–2010	–	Payment of overdue taxes as of 31 October 2008 by instalments every 18 months at 3 per cent interest
Business taxes	2009–2010	1433	Within the scope of the new incentive system an arrangement was made towards reducing corporate tax rates
	2009–2010	105	Reduction in corporate tax facilitated for mergers
	2009–2010	328	Implementation period of Incentive Law 5084 was extended for another year (withholding support for income taxes)
Consumption taxes on specific goods and services	2009–2010	212	Special Communication Tax on the Internet was lowered to 5% from 15%
	2009–2010	1060	Temporary reduction in special consumption tax for motor vehicles
	2009–2010	165	Temporary reduction in special consumption tax for white goods and electronic household goods from 6.7% to 0%

Table 12A.1 (continued)

	Years	Estimated fiscal cost, million TL	
	2009–2010	340	VAT reduction on new home sales above 150 m², from 18% to 8% for three months
	2009–2010	135	VAT reduction on new office sales from 18% to 8% for three months
	2009–2010	560	Temporary VAT reduction on furniture from 18% to 8%
	2009–2010	85	VAT reduction on IT products from 18% to 8% for three months
	2009–2010	150	VAT reduction on machinery 18% to 8% for three months
Other revenue measures	2009–2010	51	Removal of motor vehicle tax and fines for old vehicles to be scrapped
	2009–2010	1 690	Resource Utilization Support Fund deduction taken from consumer loans reduced from 15% to 10% on condition that loans will be used for commercial purposes by banks and financial institutions
	2009–2010	320	Fee from real estate sales reduced from 1.5% to 0.5% for three months
	2009–2010	313	Reduction in real estate transaction fee (permanent)
Expenditure measures		34 703	
	2008–2010	14 775	The government will invest an additional 20.8 billion Turkish lira between 2008 and 2012 for the south-eastern Anatolia Project GAP and other projects for developing infrastructure and irrigation
Measures to reduce labour costs	2009–2010	7 531	From October 2008 in order to reduce labour costs employers' social security contributions were reduced by 5 percentage points, which will be paid by the Treasury
	2009–2010	292	5 percentage points of employer social security contributions will be paid by the Treasury to funds within the scope of Temporary Article 20 of Law No. 506

Table 12A.1   (continued)

Years	Estimated fiscal cost, million TL	
2008–2010	219	Within the context of the Employment Package from May 2008 social security contributions for young and female workers were reduced and will be paid by the Unemployment Insurance Fund
2008–2010	145	Within the context of the Employment Package employers' share of insurance premiums for disabled workers will be subsidized by the Treasury
2009–2010	268	The amount of short-term working allowances was increased by 50%. Moreover, its duration was increased from 3 months to 6 months
2009–2010	923	The application of Incentive Law 5084 which has already been implemented in 49 provinces ended in 31 December 2008. Its implementation period was extended for one year. (Insurance premium support for employers)
2009–2010	229	New job opportunities created through public works programmes
2009–2010	373	Activities related to vocational training on the part of İŞKUR were expanded
2009–2010	3	Entrepreneurship training and consultation service are provided to those who intend to set up their own business
2009–2010	102	First entrance to the labour market supported by internship training
2009–2010	102	Employer's premiums for new employees will be paid by the Unemployment Insurance Fund for 6 months on condition that new recruitment is in addition to those already employed before April 2009

Table 12A.1   (continued)

	Years	Estimated fiscal cost, million TL	
Transfers to households	2008–2010	246	Unemployment insurance payments will be calculated gross instead of net and so will increase by 11 per cent
Transfers to business	2009	150	Additional appropriation for Support and Price Stabilization Fund and Small and Medium Sized Industry Development Organization
	2009–2010	724	One year extension of Law No. 5084 on Incentives (energy support)
	2010	161	New incentive system: support for interest payments; cash support to firms to move to certain cities
Transfers to other public authorities	2008–2010	6962	Increase in transfers to local administration from central government
Other expenditure	2010	500	Regulation inserted in legislation regarding allocation of 1 billion TL to credit guarantee institute, IONS, which provides firms with credit
	2008–2009	1000	Paid-in capital of Eximbank increased from 1 billion TL to 2 billion TL
Fiscal measures with no direct immediate impact on fiscal balance		12773	
Guarantee and insurance schemes for financial institutions	2009	1700	Guarantee limit of the Treasury increased from 3 billion dollars to 4 billion dollars. The increment of 1 billion dollars will be mostly used to support exports and SMEs. Together with the limit for each company, EXİMBANK resources were increased from 10 million dollars to 20 million dollars

Table 12A.1 (continued)

	Years	Estimated fiscal cost, million TL	
	2009	5 100	The limit of export rediscount credit to be used by exporters has been increased from 500 million dollars to 1 billion dollars. In addition, the use of these credits has been rearranged and eased
Loans to enterprises	2008–2009	733	Small and Medium-Sized Industry Development Organization gave zero-interest loans to SMEs
	2008–2009	2 805	Small and Medium-Sized Industry Development Organization gave zero-interest loans to exporter SMEs
	2009	1 500	Under a protocol signed between the Turkish Union of Chambers and Commodity Exchanges (TOBB) and Halk Bank low-interest loans will be available. According to the protocol 800 million TL in cash and non-cash loans and 400 million dollars in export loans will be available
	2009	935	Under a protocol signed between the Turkish Textile Employers' Association and Ziraat Bank, association member SMEs can have access to loans at low interest
Total		53 331	
GDP share		5.4%	

Source: Republic of Turkey (2009), *Pre-Accession Economic Programme 2009*, Ankara: SPO.

13. Social impact of the crisis in the United Kingdom: Focus on gender and age inequalities

Damian Grimshaw and Anthony Rafferty*

1. INTRODUCTION

This chapter charts the inequalities in work and employment with a particular focus on gender and age inequalities resulting from the 2008–2009 recession in the United Kingdom. The reduction in GDP was the deepest and most prolonged for almost 30 years, unemployment increased to more than 8 per cent after a decade at 5–6 per cent and average real earnings fell. The consequences for men and women were strongly shaped by patterns of sex segregation, given the strong negative employment effects of the recession in the male-dominated sectors of construction and manufacturing and the economic shelter, at least until 2010, enjoyed by jobs in the female-dominated public sector. Also, unlike past recessions where women were more likely to have played the role of flexible buffer by working reduced hours, switching from full-time to part-time jobs or taking on temporary contracts, during this recession men shared hours reductions with women, experienced a similar rise in part-time employment and a higher rise in temporary work. However, women were penalized in three key respects: first, among the growing numbers of unemployed, women were only half as likely as men to claim unemployment benefits; second, women constitute the bulk of lone parent households which were subject to increasingly stringent job search tests to be eligible for benefits; and third, the recession marked a halt to a prior trend of rising relative pay for women in low paid work. The recession also had particularly negative consequences for different age groups. Young people experienced by far the largest drop in employment and by far the largest rise in unemployment, as well as a lower increase in pay. At the other end of the age spectrum, older workers were more likely than younger workers to become trapped in unemployment for longer periods.

Unlike other countries in Europe, the UK government implemented few policy measures during the recession that directly sought to offset the macroeconomic shock to employment and wage income (see also Clegg 2010). The emphasis has instead been indirect, through assisting companies with financial planning. Policy actions include, for example, options to defer tax payments (with some 60,000 companies deferring more than £1 billion by February 2009, including corporation tax, VAT and income tax payments[1]) and business loan schemes (such as the Enterprise Finance Guarantee that provided loans to small firms) (see Appendix for a complete listing). Moreover, the UK position changed in May 2010 with the election of a right-wing coalition government and a decision to speed up plans to correct the budget deficit (7.7 per cent of GDP in 2009–2010, up from 0.3 per cent of GDP in 2007–2008). Despite warnings from the IMF and the 2010 Nobel prize winner Pissarides,[2] among others, a set of new policies announced in the June and October budget statements during 2010 aim to reduce government spending by £85 billion (€101 billion[3]) over four years. Rather than raising taxes as a means of reducing the deficit, the decision to focus on public spending cuts chimes with the ideological position of the new right-wing government to reduce the size of government in its provision of social and welfare services. As such, the cuts are expected to lead to a deterioration in the income position of households on income support and to a loss of an estimated 490,000 jobs in public services (OBR 2010). The latter will almost certainly reverse the gender impact of job losses experienced during 2008–2009, with major job losses among women during the post-recession austerity crisis.

The chapter is organized as follows. Section 2 presents a general assessment of the recession in the UK labour market. Sections 3 and 4 investigate the implications for gender inequalities and for age inequalities, respectively, and more generally on work inequalities. Each section includes a wide-ranging interpretation of labour market effects that encompasses a conventional concern for labour market activity (employment, unemployment and inactivity) and earnings growth, as well as other indicators of inequality, such as employment contracts, access to benefits, working time and low pay. Section 5 presents the results from a case study of the security sector in order to illustrate the recession's effects in a male-dominated sector characterized by long working hours and low pay. Section 6 summarizes the main findings.

2. THE 2008–2009 RECESSION: DEEP AND WIDE-RANGING

2.1 The Employment Impact Compared to Previous Crises

The character of the UK recession of 2008–2009 is distinctive in comparison to those of the early 1980s and early 1990s, for two reasons: the drop in GDP was greater and more prolonged – six percentage points over six successive quarters from the second quarter of 2008 until the third quarter of 2009 – and the drop in employment relative to the drop in GDP was much more limited, at around 2 per cent.

Figure 13.1 shows that the relationship between the trend lines in employment and GDP are quite different in the recent recession compared to the previous two. The 1980s recession saw a drop in GDP of around 5 per cent over five quarters and an initial fall in employment of around 3 per cent (during the period of the recession). During the 1990s recession, employment losses exceeded the contraction in GDP, at 4 per cent and 2.5 per cent, respectively. By contrast, the 2008–2009 recession

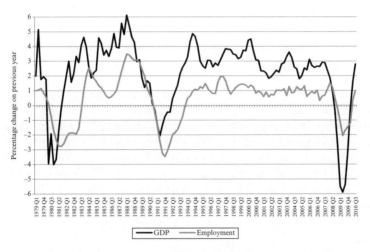

Note: Changes in GDP and employment on the same quarter in previous year. GDP at market prices, chained volume. Employment for all workers aged 16 years and over.

Source: ONS online published data accessed from Economic and Labour Market Review (October 2010) statistical tables, www.statistics.gov.uk/elmr/downloads/elmr2.pdf. Own calculations.

Figure 13.1   Annual change in GDP and employment, United Kingdom, 1979–2010

displays a much wider gap between GDP and employment trends: a fall in GDP over the six quarters of 6.3 per cent and a relatively small decline in employment of 1.9 per cent.

The second point of difference is that in the previous two recessions the employment decline continued long after the recovery of GDP; in the 1980s recession, quarterly falls in employment were sustained over 13 quarters and in the 1990s also over 13 quarters. What is significant about the 2008–2009 recession is that employment started to recover far more quickly. Comparing quarterly employment figures with the same quarter in the previous year, the decline started in September–November 2008 and continued for six quarters through to March–May 2010. Jobs data are similar, with falls in total jobs registered over seven quarters from June 2008 through to March 2010.[4] Overall, total employment fell by slightly more than 700,000 over the full period of employment decline. Nevertheless, there is a strong risk that the upturn in employment evident up to the latest available data for July–September 2010 will be short-lived. Forthcoming cuts to public spending are likely to have a major adverse impact on the ability of the UK economy to sustain and grow aggregate demand, with negative implications for the labour market. We explore this issue in detail in Section 2.2 below.

2.2   Rising Unemployment, Long-term Unemployment and Underemployment

The impact of the recession on unemployment follows a similar story. The unemployment rate increased sharply from 5.4 per cent to 7.9 per cent between the second quarter of 2008 and the last quarter of 2009 – a significant shock to a labour market that had experienced a rate of around 5–6 per cent during the previous decade (Figure 13.2). The lesson from previous recessions is to expect unemployment to continue to rise in the quarters following the return to GDP growth (Gregg and Wadsworth 2010: R67). However, available data up to July–September 2010 show that unemployment reached 8 per cent by the second quarter of 2009 and remained around this level.

Alongside the trend rise in unemployment there has also been a rapid increase in the share of unemployed in long-term unemployment. The six quarters of the recession drove numbers of people in unemployment for more than 12 months up by approximately 210,000. Because this was in line with the overall rise in unemployment the share of long-term unemployed initially remained around 23 per cent. However, since the third quarter of 2009, as flows into unemployment slowed, the share of the long-term unemployed has risen rapidly, up to 33 per cent by July–September 2010.

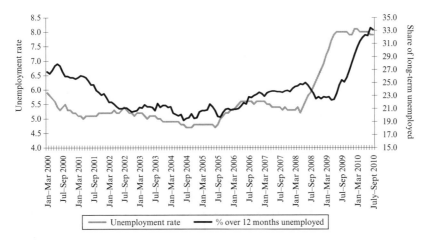

Source: UK Labour Force Survey (ELMR online data, October 2010); all aged 16–64.

Figure 13.2   Trends in the unemployment rate and the share of the long-term unemployed, UK, 2000–2010 (ILO definition[5])

Other measures of labour market participation provide alternative means of capturing the impact of the recession on the level of imposed non-participation in the labour market. One such measure is time-related underemployment. Following the US Bureau of Labor Statistics definition, the UK Office of National Statistics reports a measure of involuntary part-time employment that counts the number of people who wish to work full-time but currently work fewer than 35 hours per week. Reasons include the unavailability of full-time work or a drop in hours caused by a worsening of business conditions. Walling and Clancy (2010) report an increase from around 9 per cent to 13 per cent of part-time workers during the recession period – around 300,000 part-time workers (op. cit.: Figure 2). Extending the definition of underemployment to all workers (part-time and full-time) who wish to increase their weekly hours (whether in the same or a different job), the same study estimates that the number of underemployed increased sharply during the recession by approximately 590,000 to 2.8 million, from 6.8 per cent to 9.0 per cent of the active population (op. cit.: 20).

2.3   Sustained Fall in Real Wages

Another key indicator of the UK recession's impact on the labour market concerns earnings growth and wage inequality. Comparing average

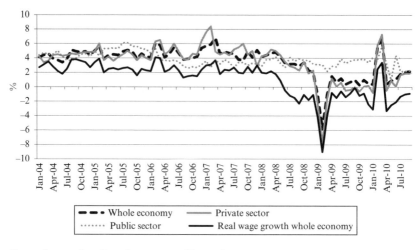

Note: Seasonally adjusted average weekly earnings.

Source: UK Labour Force Survey (ELMR online data, October 2010); all aged 16–64.

Figure 13.3   *Nominal wage growth (public and private sectors) and real wage growth, year-on-year at monthly intervals, UK, 2004–2010*

nominal weekly earnings growth for each month relative to weekly earnings in the same month the previous year shows a significant dip in earnings approximately halfway through the recession, from January to April 2009 (Figure 13.3). Compared to February 2008, average nominal weekly earnings in February 2009 were 5.8 per cent lower. Correcting for inflation, the drop in real wages at this point was 9.0 per cent. Nominal earnings growth recovered from the second quarter of 2009 but, year-on-year, real wages have continued to fall with the exception of February and March 2010. Had wages kept up with inflation during the period April 2008 to April 2010, weekly earnings would have risen from £437 to £464; instead, average weekly wages were just £446, a real cut in pay of 3.9 per cent over the two-year period.

Reflecting employment trends to date, the major divide in wage growth has been between the public and private sectors. Over the six quarters of the recession, private sector nominal wage growth averaged just 0.9 per cent and real wages fell by 2.1 per cent. In the public sector, nominal wages grew on average by 3.4 per cent and real wages remained flat with growth of 0.4 per cent. The divergent fortunes reversed the public–private sector wage gap; while before the recession public sector workers earned on average close to 2 per cent less than private sector workers, by the last quarter of 2009 there was a public sector wage premium of around 4 per cent.[6]

However, since the end of the GDP recession public sector workers have experienced falling real wages, while the downward trend has continued in the private sector. The reversal in public sector wage growth reflects the low pay settlements in 2010; for example, a rise of 2.25 per cent for health sector workers, 2.3 per cent for school teachers and a pay freeze for local government workers (following a 1 per cent rise in 2009). Prospects for public sector earnings are set to deteriorate further. The government has imposed a two-year pay freeze in 2011 and 2012 for public sector workers, defended by the Chancellor as 'the best way to protect your job during this difficult period'.[7] The pay freeze only applies to those earning above £21,000 (close to the median annual wage in 2010, equivalent to around €25,000), but media reports clarify that the freeze will also apply to part-time workers who earn less than £21,000 on a pro rata basis.[8]

Analysis of the earnings data up to April 2010 suggests that the 2008–2009 recession did not have an immediate adverse effect on wage inequality. The inter-decile measure of gross hourly earnings inequality among all employees (full-time and part-time) indicates very little change; in 2007 employees in the top decile (D9) earned 3.95 times those in the bottom decile, while in 2010 the multiple was 3.98. To put this change in context, the inter-decile ratio has fluctuated between 3.95 and 4.05 over the past decade with no clear trend direction. The recession also had limited effects on the gap between the middle and the highest paid and between the middle and the lowest paid: the ratio of the top decile pay level to the median wage changed from 2.26 to 2.24 between 2007 and 2010 and the ratio of the bottom decile to the median changed from 1.75 to 1.77. It would appear, therefore, that the recession's adverse impact on pay has been experienced by employees at all points of the pay distribution, such that the overall measure of wage inequality has changed very little. We consider trends in low pay in more detail in Sections 3 and 4 with regard to gender differences and age differences, respectively.

3. THE IMPACT ON MEN AND WOMEN

At first glance, the recession has had less adverse effects on women than on men. Until 2010, sex segregation in different sectors of the UK economy established a partial shelter for women from job losses. Moreover, men have been as likely as women to serve as a flexible buffer, with a fall in full-time jobs and increases in part-time and temporary jobs. Further

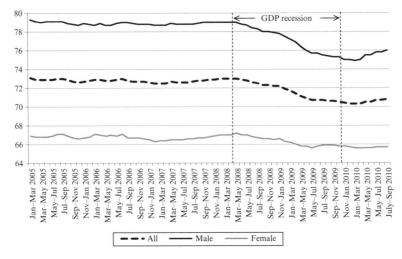

Source: UK Labour Force Survey (ELMR online data, October 2010); all aged 16–64.

*Figure 13.4   Trends in male and female employment rates, headcount, UK,
2005–2010*

investigation, however, reveals several dimensions of gender equality that
have worsened, or where past positive trends have been halted, as a result
of the recession. Particular issues include women's access to unemployment benefits, their household income status and risk of low pay.

3.1   Divergent Experiences of Job Losses

The employment decline among men was nearly three times the size of
that among women – approximately 640,000 and 220,000 (4.1 per cent and
1.7 per cent of the male and female workforce), respectively. The drop in
employment rates mirrors this pattern. Among the working-age population the male employment rate fell by more than four percentage points,
from 79.0 per cent to 74.9 per cent during March–May 2008 to January–
March 2010 and the female employment rate fell by around one and a
half points, from 67.0 per cent to 65.6 per cent (Figure 13.4).[9] However,
while the male employment rate picked up a little between the first and
third quarters of 2010 (up to 76.0 per cent by July–September 2010),
the female employment rate did not change – just 65.7 per cent by July–
September 2010. The failure of the female employment rate to improve
reflects the slowdown in public sector expenditure and widespread freezing of recruitment in important female-dominated areas of employment,

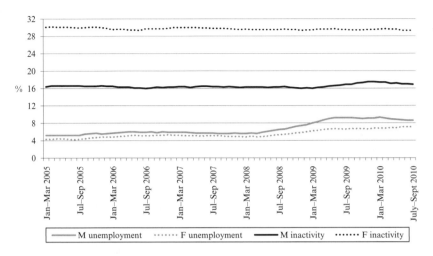

Source: UK Labour Force Survey (ELMR online data, October 2010); all aged 16–64. ILO unemployment definition.

Figure 13.5   *Unemployment and inactivity for men and women, UK, 2005–2010*

such as hospitals and local government. There is a high risk that women's employment will not recover its pre-recession level for some time, given the severity of the 2010–15 public spending cuts.

Unemployment trends for men and women mirror employment trends. The rate of unemployment (ILO definition) increased more sharply for men than women (Figure 13.5). Moreover, while in past recessions women may have moved from employment to the status of labour market inactivity rather than to unemployment, this did not occur during this recession. In fact, quite the opposite – women experienced no obvious impact on their rate of inactivity, while for men the recession caused a relatively rapid increase of inactivity. Overall, the male unemployment rate increased by around 3 percentage points, from 5.9 per cent to 9.0 per cent (from the second quarter of 2008 to the final quarter of 2009) and the female unemployment rate increased by slightly less than 2 percentage points, from 4.9 per cent to 6.7 per cent. The rise in male inactivity during the recession and the steady inactivity rate among women means that the gender gap in the inactivity rate that had been around 13–15 percentage points during the 2000s narrowed to 12 points. The explanation lies partly in women's increasing likelihood to be entitled to unemployment benefits (see Section 3.4), as well as the transfer of inactive female lone parents onto unemployment benefits.

Work inequalities in the crisis

Table 13.1   Job trends by sector for men and women, UK, 2008–2009

	% female share, 2008	Men				Women			
		Q1 2008	Q3 2009	Change	%	Q1 2008	Q3 2009	Change	%
Total	46.6	16 896	16 314	−582	−100	14 747	14 546	−201	−100
Agriculture and fishing	28.1	348	388	40	6.9	136	99	−37	−18.4
Energy and water	26.4	145	143	−2	−0.3	52	52	0	0.0
Manufacturing	25.1	2 363	2 128	−235	−40.4	791	712	−79	−39.3
Construction	10.9	2 004	1 855	−149	−25.6	246	240	−6	−3.0
Distribution, hotels and restaurants	50.5	3 494	3 382	−112	−19.2	3 559	3 449	−110	−54.7
Transport and communication	24.4	1 411	1 385	−26	−4.5	456	451	−5	−2.5
Finance and business services	43.9	3 743	3 579	−164	−28.2	2 926	2 796	−130	−64.7
Public administration, education, health	69.8	2 406	2 488	82	14.1	5 571	5 748	177	88.1
Other services	50.8	980	967	−13	−2.2	1 010	1 000	−10	−5.0

3.2   Sex Segregation by Industry

The reason is clear why men experienced greater job losses than women, namely sex segregation by industry. The negative employment effects of the recession were strongly felt in the male-dominated sectors of manufacturing and construction (female employment shares of 25 per cent and 11 per cent, respectively, in 2008), but also spread to the mixed male–female sectors of distribution, hotels and restaurants (51 per cent female employment share) and finance and business services (44 per cent) (see Table 13.1). Figure 13.6 (opposite) plots the quarterly change in jobs by industry from the first quarter of 2008 to the second quarter of 2010, separating out male-dominated industries from mixed and female-dominated industries. The sectors of agriculture and fishing and energy and water are also strongly male-dominated but are excluded here since they are relatively small.

Manufacturing jobs were already falling prior to the recession. The two-yearly average quarterly falls were around 1 per cent during 2000–02, 2002–04, 2004–06 and 2006–08,[10] but then the fall accelerated during the

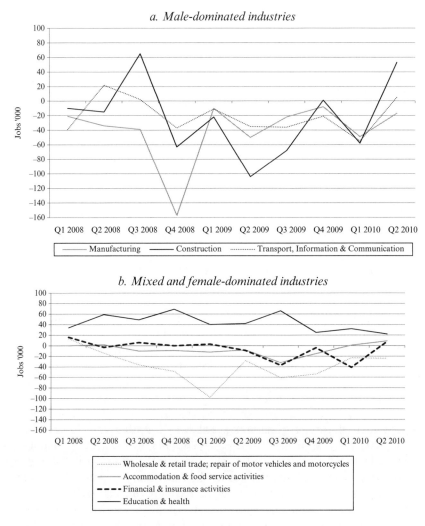

Source: UK Labour Force Survey (ELMR, online published tables). Authors' estimations.

Figure 13.6 Change in number of jobs by industry (1-digit), UK, 2008–2010

recession to an average quarterly drop of 1.5 per cent. Loss of construction jobs came around halfway through the recession, with significant losses registered during the first three quarters of 2009. The third major male-dominated industry, transport, information and communications,

suffered a net loss of 31,000 from the first quarter of 2008 to the third
quarter of 2009 (Figure 13.6a).

Among the mixed industries, job losses in the finance and insurance
sector (industry code K) came towards the end of the recession in the
second and third quarters of 2009 and during the recovery in the first
quarter of 2010. Like the accommodation and food services sector, overall
job losses in finance were smaller than in the male-dominated sectors
(Figure 13.6b). The scale of job losses in finance is surprisingly small
given that the recession was finance-led; job losses during the recession
amounted to 3.5 per cent of the finance and insurance workforce compared to losses of 2.7 per cent for the economy as a whole. The strongly
female-dominated wholesale and retail sector had previously expanded
during the early 2000s, reaching 5 million jobs by late 2007, but then lost
290,000 jobs during the six quarters of recession (5.7 per cent of jobs) and
a further 100,000 jobs from the third quarter of 2009 to the second quarter
of 2010 (Figure 13.6b).

As already mentioned, the one area that stands out is the strongly
female-dominated sectors of education and health (industry codes P and
Q). Both sectors expanded steadily from 1998 when the Labour government committed to increase public expenditure, with an emphasis on
education and health. There is no indication that the recession slowed job
growth in these sectors. Average quarterly job growth during the 2000s,
estimated over consecutive two-year periods, fluctuated at around 0.5 per
cent;[11] during 2008–2009 average quarterly job growth was 0.85 per cent
in the health sector and 0.61 per cent in education. Women in the workforce therefore benefited from the market shelter provided by public sector
employment during the recession (see also TUC 2010).

Because twice as many women as men work in the sectors of public
administration, education and health, women benefited twice as much
from the sustained job growth during the recession. As Table 13.1 shows,
women gained 177,000 jobs during the recession in this sector and men
82,000. Men and women lost jobs on an equal basis in the mixed sector
of distribution, hotels and restaurants and both witnessed significant
job losses of more than 100,000 in finance and business services. Overall,
therefore, it was men's job losses in manufacturing and construction and
their limited gains, compared to women, from job growth in the public
sector that explains the collapse in male employment.

Equally, women's over-representation in the public sector means they
will bear the brunt of public spending cuts. The government decision to
cut borrowing at a faster pace than that proposed by the previous Labour
government is forecast to lead to job losses of around 490,000 in the
public sector by the end of the four-year period, 2010–11 to 2014–2015.[12]

Taxes will also increase but their expected contribution to the overall reduction in borrowing is around one-third of that achieved from public spending cuts. While in a minority, several leading macroeconomists and labour economists describe the planned cuts as a mistake. For example, Britain's new Nobel prize-winning economist, Pissarides, warns against cutting welfare benefits because of the risk that people will sink into long-term poverty (see endnote 2). Also, one former member of the Monetary Policy Committee, Blanchflower, describes the austerity programme as 'the greatest macroeconomic mistake in a century'[13] and argues that the rigid four-year timetable for eliminating the structural deficit is both too short and too unresponsive. As Skidelsky put it in a recent column for the *Financial Times*, 'the budget balance should be dictated by economic circumstances, not by some arbitrary timetable: who knows what the situation will be in two, three, four years' time?' (14 October 2010).

3.3 Inequality in Hours and Contract Flexibility?

A second reason for women's distinctive experience may be because the employment data presented above refer to a simple headcount of numbers employed rather than volume of hours worked. Women might be expected to be more likely than men to act as a flexible buffer during the recession (Rubery 1988), working reduced hours in their full-time or part-time job, or switching from full-time to part-time work. The net effect would be a more significant contraction in the volume of hours worked by women rather than the numbers employed.

The data on average weekly working hours show that, in fact, men experienced a very similar level of reduction to women over the period of the recession. From the first quarter of 2008 to the last quarter of 2009 average weekly hours among men fell from 36.9 to 36.2 and among women from 26.6 to 26.2. In fact, as Table 13.2 shows, men experienced a drop in hours in full-time employment but a small rise in hours in part-time jobs. Women experienced a small decline in both full-time and part-time employment. Combined with the job loss data described above, men experienced a far greater reduction in total weekly hours worked – from 589 million hours to 556 million compared to limited change among women, from 354 to 353 million hours.

Similarly, employment trends for full-time and part-time jobs show that men were as likely as women, if not more so, to experience a fall in full-time employment and a rise in part-time employment. The trend in the part-time share of jobs for both men and women increased over the period of the recession, by close to 1 percentage point for men and women (Table 13.3). For men, this continued an upward trend registered during the two

Table 13.2   Average weekly hours among men and women, 2007–2010

	Men			Women		
	Full-time	Part-time	Second jobs	Full-time	Part-time	Second jobs
Q1 2007	39.1	15.6	10.1	34.0	15.7	8.8
Q2 2007	39.1	15.6	10.4	34.0	15.6	8.7
Q3 2007	39.0	15.3	10.7	34.0	15.7	8.7
Q4 2007	38.9	15.3	11.3	33.6	15.5	9.1
Q1 2008	39.3	15.3	11.0	34.0	15.7	8.8
Q2 2008	38.7	15.5	10.8	33.5	15.5	9.0
Q3 2008	38.9	15.5	10.9	34.0	15.7	8.8
Q4 2008	38.8	15.4	10.6	33.8	15.7	8.9
Q1 2009	38.3	15.4	10.7	33.6	15.5	8.9
Q2 2009	38.6	15.4	10.5	33.9	15.5	8.9
Q3 2009	38.6	15.5	10.5	33.5	15.4	8.9
Q4 2009	38.6	15.7	9.8	33.6	15.4	8.7
Q1 2010	38.8	15.6	10.9	33.8	15.5	9.1
Q2 2010	38.9	15.7	10.6	33.9	15.6	8.4
Q3 2010	38.9	15.7	11.1	33.8	15.7	8.7

Source: UK Labour Force Survey (ELMR, online published tables). Authors' estimations.

years prior to the recession, whereas for women it reversed a downward trend recorded since 2004 when women's part-time share reached a peak of 44.4 per cent. Figure 13.7 shows the relative employment trends of full-time and part-time employment for men and women over the recession. Indexing employment numbers to 100 for the period January–March 2008 we can see clearly that the widest discrepancy between trends in full-time and part-time employment occurred for men. The employment index for male full-time employment dropped by 12 points from 100.0 to 87.7, and for male part-time employment it rose 14 points to 113.8. The respective figures for female employment were a drop in full-time employment to 94.4 and an equivalent 6 point rise in part-time employment to 106.3. Moreover, there was a larger rise among men than women in the share of involuntary part-time workers, from 17 per cent to 25 per cent among men and from 7 per cent to 10 per cent among women. Of course, this representation of change in part-time employment overstates the trend for men since the numbers employed are small compared to numbers of female part-time workers. However, the actual increase in numbers of men employed in part-time jobs during the 2008–2009 period was close to the actual increase in numbers of female part-time workers – 85,000 and 102,000, respectively.

Table 13.3   Trends in female share and part-time shares of employment, UK, 2006–2009

	Female share of all employment	Part-time share of all employment	Part-time share of female employment	Part-time share of male employment
Q1 2006	46.2	25.3	42.5	10.6
Q2 2006	46.1	25.4	42.5	10.7
Q3 2006	46.0	25.5	42.7	10.9
Q4 2006	46.0	25.6	42.9	10.9
Q1 2007	45.9	25.5	42.6	11.0
Q2 2007	45.8	25.4	42.5	10.9
Q3 2007	45.9	25.3	42.2	11.1
Q4 2007	45.9	25.4	42.2	11.1
Q1 2008	45.9	25.4	42.1	11.2
Q2 2008	45.9	25.4	42.0	11.3
Q3 2008	46.0	25.5	41.8	11.6
Q4 2008	46.1	25.7	42.0	11.8
Q1 2009	46.2	25.8	42.3	11.7
Q2 2009	46.5	26.2	42.4	12.2
Q3 2009	46.7	26.5	43.1	12.0
Q4 2009	46.8	26.6	43.0	12.2

Source: Labour Force Survey (ONS ELMR); authors' calculations.

The data thus help to explain why women's employment rate changed little over the 24-month period; the drop in full-time jobs (135,000) was to a large extent offset by the rise in part-time jobs (102,000). For men, although the increase in part-time jobs was significant, it was far outweighed by the drop in full-time jobs (some 640,000).

Over the course of the recession, men also witnessed a stronger rise in temporary employment contracts than women, reflecting their over-representation in sectors subject to greater short-term financial pressures. Over the six quarters of the recession (from the second quarter of 2008 to the fourth quarter of 2009), the share of temporary employment among men increased from 4.7 per cent to 5.4 per cent, a rise of some 60,000 jobs. Among women there was no significant change, although the share remained at a higher level than among men, at 6.2 per cent (Table 13.4). One trend, however, was similar for both men and women; both experienced a significant rise in the share of temporary workers who could not find a permanent job – from 30 per cent to 39 per cent among men and from 22 per cent to 32 per cent among women.

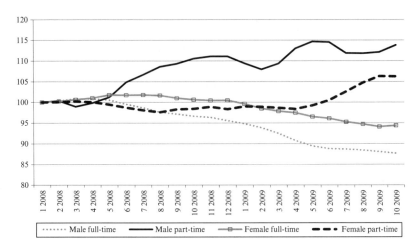

Source: UK Labour Force Survey (ONS, ELMR), online published tables. Authors' estimations.

Figure 13.7 Quarterly change in full-time and part-time employment by sex, UK, 2008–2009

Table 13.4 Change in shares of full-time, part-time and temporary jobs by sex, UK, Q2 2008, Q4 2009 and Q2 2010

	Q2 2008	Q4 2009	Q2 2010	Percentage point change in share 2008–2009
Men:				
Full-time	89.5%	88.7% (−575)	88.3% (+94)	−0.8
Part-time	10.5%	11.3% (+38)	11.7% (+74)	+0.8
Temporary	4.7%	5.4% (+61)	6.0% (+83)	+0.7
Women:				
Full-time	59.2%	58.0% (−227)	57.3% (−82)	−1.2
Part-time	40.8%	42.0% (+91)	42.7% (+88)	+1.2
Temporary	6.2%	6.2% (−5)	6.6% (+52)	0.0

Source: UK Labour Force Survey (ELMR online data). May–July 2008, Nov–Jan 2010 and May–July 2010. All employees aged 16 and over.

Table 13.5   *Share of the unemployed claiming benefits (Jobseeker's Allowance), United Kingdom, 2007–2009*

	2007	2008	2009	Change 2007–09
Men				
Not claiming	450 166	569 701	642 833	192 667
	58.6%	54.2%	48.3%	–10.2
JSA claimant	318 377	481 637	686 964	368 587
	41.4%	45.8%	51.7%	10.2
Total	768 543	1 051 338	1 329 797	561 254
Women				
Not claiming	491 757	541 112	604 143	112 386
	82.4%	78.3%	71.7%	–10.7
JSA claimant	105 112	149 743	238 831	133 719
	17.6%	21.7%	28.3%	10.7
Total	596 869	690 855	842 974	246 105

Source: Rubery and Rafferty (2010: table 4), UK Quarterly LFS data (October–December).

3.4   Inequality in Welfare and Household Income Status

Gender inequity is embedded in the UK system of welfare benefits. In common with several European countries, the UK system of unemployment benefits has traditionally encouraged women (indirectly) to withdraw from the labour market when they lose their job through restrictive eligibility criteria designed around a full-time, continuous employment model involving a minimum number of hours worked and earnings thresholds, as well as continuity of work experience. Women's over-representation in low wage jobs, part-time and temporary work means that such eligibility criteria have tended to exacerbate women's unequal access to benefits (Grimshaw and Rubery 1997).

In 2009, women in unemployment were indeed far less likely than unemployed men to claim Jobseeker's Allowance, the six-month fixed-sum benefit paid to the unemployed.[14] Among those unemployed, 28 per cent of women claimed unemployment benefits compared to 52 per cent of men. Nevertheless, women's relative position has improved compared to that prior to the recession. In 2007, just 18 per cent of unemployed women claimed benefits (and 41 per cent of men) (Table 13.5).

The reason for the increasing share of benefit claimants among both men and women is that job losses were almost entirely experienced by people in full-time employment who are more likely to meet eligibility criteria.

For example, the minimum annual earnings threshold for Jobseeker's Allowance is 25 times the weekly lower limit for social security (National Insurance) contributions – £97 (€116) per week in 2010–11; a woman made redundant from a short hours part-time job paid the minimum wage and working only during school terms might easily fail to meet this threshold, whereas a full-time worker employed for at least half the previous year is certain to be eligible.

The effects of the recession on employment, unemployment and inactivity patterns have been strongly shaped by welfare policy reforms that target particular household types. In 2008, lone parents (most of whom are women) with children above 10 years of age lost eligibility to Income Support and were moved on to Jobseeker's Allowance, which requires continuous job search. The government objective was to move lone parents out of inactivity into employment as part of its 'make work pay' initiative. However, no change in policy was countenanced in the face of difficult recessionary conditions. From October 2010, the policy extended to lone parents with children above 7 years of age and from October 2011 to lone parents whose youngest child is aged 5 years of age. The ability of lone parents to apply for welfare benefits from a position of inactivity is thus much diminished. Lone parents with children under 12 can in principle restrict their job search to school hours' jobs, but in practice this policy is likely to be unworkable, given the insufficient number of available jobs, not to mention family-friendly jobs.

3.5 Inequality in Pay Prospects?

A fifth issue for analysis is the impact of the recession on women's pay prospects. Given the over-representation of women in low wage work (and the relatively high share of low wage work in the United Kingdom compared to other European countries) and the strong sex segregation by industry and occupation, this section focuses on these two features.

Did the recession lead to a worsening of pay among men and women in low wage jobs? There are two ways of addressing this question. First, we can evaluate the relative position of employees employed in the lowest paid jobs, such as the bottom 10 per cent of jobs – that is, the bottom decile. In the years prior to the recession, Figure 13.8a shows that the bottom wage decile of female full-timers and of female part-timers registered steady improvement relative to male full-time median earnings. Then, during the 2008–2009 recession, it stagnated for both groups: the bottom decile of female part-timers rose from 0.40 to 0.45 during 2001–2007, then dropped to 0.44 during 2008–2009; and among female full-timers it increased from 0.49 to 0.51 and then dropped marginally. Among male full-timers there is

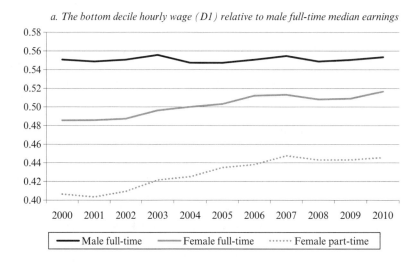

a. The bottom decile hourly wage (D1) relative to male full-time median earnings

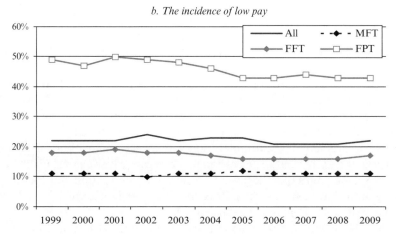

b. The incidence of low pay

Source: ASHE earnings database. Gross hourly earnings excluding overtime. Authors' compilation.

Figure 13.8 Trends in low wage work by sex and full-time/part-time, UK, 1999–2010

no evidence of a clear trend, either up or down; it is significant, however, that their bottom decile wage is a good deal higher than that of women, at around 0.55 of male full-time median hourly pay. Thus the recession clearly marked a halt to a six-year trend rise in wages for women in low paid work. The latest available data for 2010 suggest female full-timers have experienced a rise in their relative earnings, but little change is evident for female part-timers.

A second way to address what happened to low wage jobs is to assess the trend in the share of employees employed in low wage jobs. Defined as earnings less than two-thirds of the median for all employees, this measure has remained stubbornly high over the past decade at around 21–23 per cent of all employees (Figure 13.8b). Before and after the recession there has been a marginal increase, from 21.0 per cent in 2007 to 21.4 per cent in 2010. Among women in part-time work, who make up the bulk of low wage workers in the United Kingdom, there was no change in the incidence of low wage work before and after the recession, with around 43 per cent of female part-timers employed in low wage work during 2008 and 2009. The small rise in the overall incidence of low wage work appears to be the result of a rise among female full-time workers, from 16 to 18 per cent.

Further insight into the recession's impact on low wage employment can be revealed by the analysis of sectoral wage developments during 2008 and 2009. Were low wage, female-dominated sectors more likely to suffer below-average wage growth during the recession? Table 13.6 lists all those sectors (using the 3-digit SIC classification) for which the median hourly wage for all employees fell below the low wage threshold in 2009 (estimated at two-thirds of the median for all employees, £7.35 or €8.78). Of the 16 sectors listed, only five enjoyed above-average wage growth during 2008–2009.[15] Among those industries especially hard hit are the female-dominated low wage sectors of pre-primary education, residential nursing care activities and hotels and similar accommodation. It would appear, therefore, that the recession had a negative bias against many low wage sectors, reflecting the lower likelihood of unionization and collective bargaining coverage in these sectors and the more limited capacity for low wage workers to defend their rates of pay.

An important factor in understanding changes in pay in low wage sectors is the statutory national minimum wage. After several years of steady increases in the minimum wage (relative to the average and median wage), 2008 marked a halt. The minimum wage stood at 34 per cent of average earnings in 2001 (45 per cent of median pay) and rose to 40 per cent in 2007 (53 per cent of median pay), but then remained at 40 per cent during 2008, 2009 and 2010.[16] This trajectory is very helpful in explaining the changing relative pay of female part-time workers. Figure 13.9 plots the trend in average earnings of female part-timers and female full-timers relative to male full-time average pay, against a standardized point of 100 in 1999. As the minimum wage rises relative to median earnings during 2003–2007 there is a parallel rise in the

Table 13.6 Annual wage growth in low wage sectors, UK, 2008–2009, all employees

Description	Code	Number of jobs (thousand)	Median £	2008–2009 % change	% point wage change minus average
ALL Employees		24251	11.03	3.9	0.0
All Industries and Services		24236	11.04	3.9	0.0
All Index of Production Industries		2873	11.98	2.7	−1.1
All Manufacturing		2533	11.76	2.3	−1.6
All Service Industries		20269	10.84	4.4	0.6
Retail sale in non-specialized stores	471	1120	6.96	5.5	1.6
Retail sale of food, beverages and tobacco in specialized stores	472	87	6.50	4.8	1.0
Retail sale of cultural and recreation goods in specialized stores	476	113	6.43	3.2	−0.7
Retail sale of other goods in specialized stores	477	598	6.84	1.8	−2.1
Hotels and similar accommodation	551	205	6.60	0.5	−3.4
Holiday and other short stay accommodation	552	19	7.09	1.3	−2.6
Camping grounds, recreational vehicle parks and trailer parks	553	29	6.73	5.2	1.3
Restaurants and mobile food service activities	561	378	6.00	2.2	−1.6
Event catering and other food service activities	562	144	6.87	4.1	0.2
Beverage serving activities	563	244	6.00	2.6	−1.3
Cleaning activities	812	235	6.50	6.6	2.7
Pre-primary education	851	18	7.20	−3.2	−7.1
Residential nursing care activities	871	120	6.59	−2.1	−5.9
Amusement and recreation activities	932	28	6.72	1.1	−2.8
Washing and (dry-)cleaning of textile and fur products	9601	24	6.51	5.0	1.1
Hairdressing and other beauty treatment	9602	62	6.67	2.6	−1.2

Source: ASHE (2008 and 2009 online tables); authors' compilation.

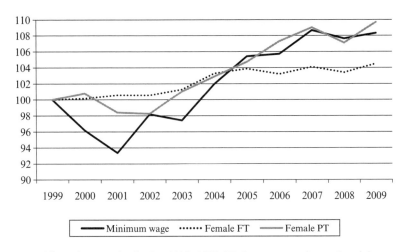

Notes: All earnings standardized to 100 in 1999. Minimum wage refers to the minimum wage relative to average earnings for all employees. Female part-time pay and female full-time pay are shown as a ratio of male full-time average pay.

Source: ASHE (online data, gross hourly pay excluding overtime); authors' calculations.

Figure 13.9   Trends in the minimum wage and female pay relative to average earnings, UK, 1999–2009

relative level of female part-timers' average pay. The decision to raise the minimum wage by just 1.2 per cent in October 2009 (from £5.73 to £5.80) was subsequently acknowledged as one of the lowest increases compared to other countries (LPC 2010: 194). The more generous 2010 uprating of 2.2 per cent reflected more optimistic expectations about pay settlements, with the median expected to be between 2 and 3 per cent during 2010 (op. cit.).

4.   THE IMPACT ON YOUNG AND OLD

There are many reasons why the current recession might be expected to impact on workers at different ends of the age spectrum in different ways. Job queue effects mean that young workers are at greater risk of job losses, whether because of customary last-in, first-out practices or over-representation among jobs designed around temporary contracts. At the same time, older workers who lose jobs are usually more likely than younger workers to become trapped in unemployment, whether because their accumulated firm-specific, or sector-specific, skills are less transferable, because of discrimination against hiring older workers or a tendency for lower geographical mobility. A further feature of unequal age effects concerns differences in workers' ability to sustain or negotiate pay rises during a recession, with younger workers potentially more likely to experience falling pay due to weaker pay bargaining power. There are also policy effects. Reforms in 2010 risk reducing the number of young people attending further and higher education, resulting in greater youth unemployment. We address each of these issues in turn in the following analysis.

4.1 Have Employment and Unemployment Trends Penalized Youth?

Young people experienced by far the largest decrease in employment as a result of this recession. During the six quarters of the recession (second quarter 2008 to final quarter 2009), employment rates for 16–17-year-olds dropped by 12 percentage points among men and 6 points among women, and rates for 18–24-year-olds were down 7 percentage points among men and 4 points among women (Figure 13.10). While youth employment rates had been steadily declining at least since the 1990s, reflecting increasing participation in full-time education, the recession speeded up this trend substantially through closing down employment opportunities for many young people.

During the recovery in 2010, employment rates among young men (both age groups) started to rise, but among women continued falling (16–17-year-olds) or remained flat (18–24-year-olds). The divergence of trends among 16–17-year-olds suggests alternative education choices among men and women.

Change in employment rates among core working-age groups was less substantial, especially for women. The largest decline was among men aged 25–34 who experienced a decline of around 4 percentage points. Older age groups similarly experienced little change and again this was especially the case among women (Figure 13.10).

In terms of unemployment, it is important to take into account the fact that young people were already experiencing a high and rising rate of unemployment for at least three years prior to 2008, making the subsequent increase much more damaging by comparison to older workers (Figure 13.11). Young people aged 16–17 years old experienced a rapid increase in unemployment, to a staggering 41 per cent among men and 30 per cent among women, by the end of 2009. Among the 18–24 age group, unemployment reached 21 per cent among men and 15 per cent among women.

Older workers saw a similar proportionate rise as young workers

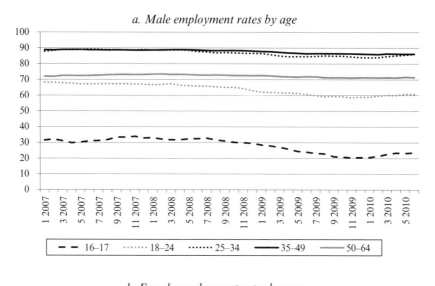

a. Male employment rates by age

b. Female employment rates by age

Source: Labour Force Survey (ONS, ELMR), online published tables, authors'
estimations.

Figure 13.10   Employment rates by age, male and female, UK, 2007–2010

(around 50 per cent), but from a far lower level. People aged 25–49 experienced an increase from 4.0 per cent to 6.2 per cent and the 50+ age group
from 2.9 per cent to 4.7 per cent.

Among young workers, those most affected are black and ethnic

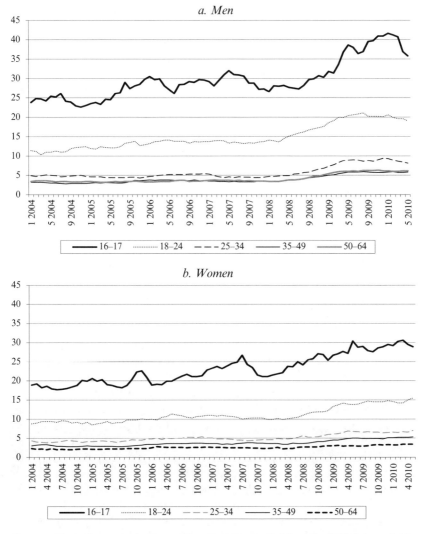

Source: Unemployment rates, seasonally adjusted, compiled from the ONS data available at www.statistics.gov.uk/statbase/product.asp?vlnk=8272.

Figure 13.11   Unemployment rates by age and sex, UK, 2004–2010

minority people. Analysis of third quarter 2009 data by the IPPR (2010a) finds that 48 per cent of black people aged 16–24 are unemployed and 35 per cent of all mixed ethnic groups, compared with 20 per cent of white people of the same age.

4.2   Are Older Workers More Likely to be Unemployed for Longer?

During this recession, while older workers were far more likely to remain unemployed for long periods than younger workers, trends among young men suggest a (negative) catch-up with older men.

According to the latest data for the third quarter of 2010, among men the share of long-term unemployed (more than 12 months using the ILO definition) was 44 per cent for older men (aged 50 years or more) and 33 per cent for younger men (aged 18–24). Among women, the respective shares were 40 per cent and 18 per cent. Older people are therefore clearly more at risk of long periods of unemployment.

In terms of numbers unemployed for more than 12 months, the impact of the recession was severe for older workers. At the start of the recession, some 84,000 older workers were estimated to have been unemployed for more than 12 months, but this more than doubled to 169,000 by the third quarter of 2010 (compared to an overall stock of older people unemployed of 394,000).

The situation is likely to be exacerbated by parallel changes in the welfare system as the result of government efforts to cut the deficit and an explicit redrawing of the ideological principles that define government's role in UK society (see Taylor-Gooby and Stoker 2011). Changes in entitlements to disability benefits (the 'employment support allowance') implemented in April 2011,[17] largely impacts older people since they are more likely than young people to be registered as disabled. With plans for more rigorous medical assessments and interviews, many people currently defined as disabled will be switched either to a 12-month work-related employment support benefit or the conventional six-month unemployment benefit ('Jobseeker's Allowance') while looking for work. Age UK, one of the leading charitable organizations in the UK protecting the interests of older people, estimates the policy reform will adversely impact 750,000 older people. Michelle Mitchell, Age UK director, said 'Before pushing people back into the recruitment arena or forcing them to work for longer, the government must lay the foundations of a better job market for older people with fairness and flexibility as cornerstones.'[18]

While older people are clearly at greater risk of long-term unemployment than younger cohorts, young men have experienced a rapid increase in their share of those unemployed for more than 12 months. With an overall rate of unemployment far higher than that among older people (three times higher among men and nearly five times higher among women), the upward trend in long-term unemployed among young men has impacted a substantial number of people. The share of young men unemployed more than 12 months has increased from 24 per cent to 33 per cent, compared to a fluctuating trend among older men from 42 per cent to 37 per cent to 44 per cent over the three periods shown in Figure 13.12. Numbers of young men in long-term unemployment have doubled over this period, from 74,000 to 138,000 in long-term unemployment, compared to a 38 per cent rise in overall unemployment among young men, from 307,000 to 424,000.

Analysis of the LFS shows that the risks for young people of being excluded from paid employment have increased significantly during the recession and the adverse impact is spread across all levels of education. The measure of so-called 'NEETs' – that is, 'not in employment, education or training' – increased for 16–24-year-olds for all levels of education, but especially for those with higher education. Table 13.7 shows that the percentage change in incidence of NEETs among young people is highest among those with a degree and higher education and lowest among those with no education.

Nevertheless, it is still the case that the overall incidence of NEETs is far higher among those with no education; more than one in three young people with no education (35 per cent) were defined as NEETs in the first quarter of 2010 compared to 11 per cent of young graduates. Prior to May 2010, the Labour government implemented policies to encourage young people aged 16–18 years old to stay on in education, including weekly payments in the form of the Education Maintenance Allowance. However, this policy was abolished by the new right-wing coalition government (with effect from January 2011) and as a result the incidence of NEETs is likely to rise further.

4.3 Have Young People Lost Out on Pay Increases?

As well as the differential age-related impacts of the recession on employment and unemployment, workers of different age groups also experienced diverse pay trends during the recession. This is not immediately apparent through investigation of trends in median pay among full-time employees. The increase in nominal median hourly pay for men and women in full-time jobs during 2008–2009 was quite similar among age groups, albeit with a slightly higher rise among the 40–49 age group in both cases (Figure 13.13).

However, women in part-time jobs witnessed a far more divided pattern of earnings growth by age. Young women in part-time jobs earned, on average, a 2.2 per cent rise (18–21 years of age) and a 2.4 per cent rise (22–29 years of age) in their median hourly pay, compared to average rises of 5.2 per cent among the 40–49 age group and 4.5 per cent among the 50–59 and 60+ age groups.

Work inequalities in the crisis

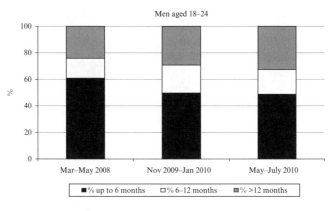

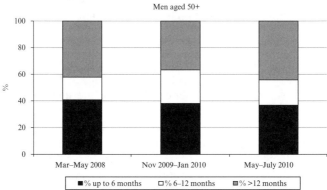

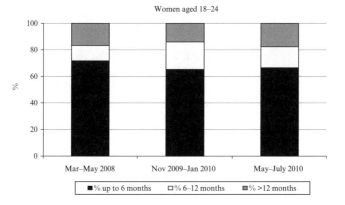

Women aged 50+

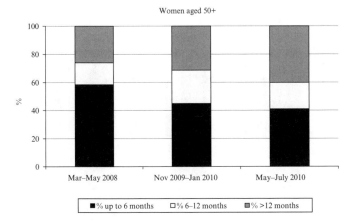

■ % up to 6 months   □ % 6–12 months   ▨ % >12 months

Source: Labour Force Survey (ONS, ELMR), online published tables, authors'
estimations.

*Figure 13.12   Share of unemployed by duration, by age and sex, UK, Q2
                 2008, Q4 2009, Q3 2010*

*Table 13.7   Incidence of NEETs by highest level of education, 16–24-year-
               olds, UK, 2008–2010*

	Q1 2008	Q1 2010	Percentage point change	% change
Degree	7.5	11.4	3.9	52
HE	7.9	12.9	5.0	63
Level 3	6.4	9.1	2.7	42
Level 2	14.0	16.1	2.1	15
None	34.6	36.1	1.5	4

Source: IPPR (2010b: table 1), Labour Force Survey data.

Young workers in low wage jobs also lost out compared to older
workers. Figure 13.13 includes details of 2008–2009 nominal pay growth
for the bottom decile (D1) and lowest quartile (D25). For all employees
the average pay rise for the bottom decile was lower for young workers
aged 18–21 years old than for core-age workers. Among male full-timers,
nominal pay for this group actually declined, by 0.2 per cent; this translates
as a reduction in real earnings of 2.5 per cent.[19] A drop in real earnings was
also experienced by 18–21-year-old women employed in the bottom decile
of full-time and part-time jobs for whom real average hourly pay fell by

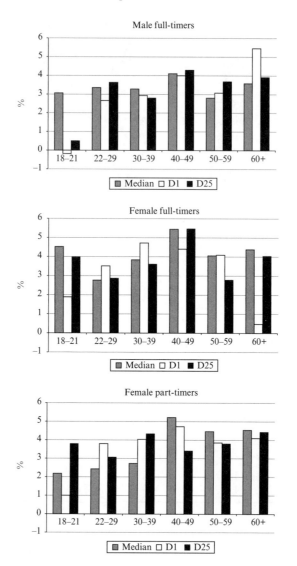

Source: Annual Survey of Hours and Earnings, authors' compilation. Average gross hourly earnings excluding overtime payments for all employees.

Figure 13.13 Change in hourly pay by age and sex, at the median, D1 and D25 wage points, UK, 2008–2009

0.5 per cent and 1.3 per cent, respectively (equivalent to rises in nominal hourly pay of 1.9 per cent and 1.0 per cent, respectively).

This adverse pattern for young people extends to the lowest quartile of the pay distribution among male full-time employees, for whom the nominal average pay rise was just 0.5 per cent. Low paid older workers fared relatively well with the one exception of women aged 60 years or more in full-time jobs whose bottom decile pay only increased by 0.5 per cent, a drop in real earnings of 1.8 per cent.

These divergent experiences among young and older workers point to a reinforcing of age divides in the wage structure. Young people are not only at the back of the job queue, but also less able to bargain for higher wages whether through concentration in non-unionized workplaces or lack of skills and qualifications. Overall, because the share of 18–21-year-olds constitutes a very small proportion of the total workforce, the trends are not picked up in our aggregate measures of wage inequality explored above.

5. HOW HAVE EMPLOYERS RESPONDED TO THE CRISIS IN AN UNDERREGULATED ENVIRONMENT? CASE STUDIES

5.1 The Context: A Lack of Policies to Assist Employment Adjustment

Unlike other countries in Europe, the UK has not implemented wide-ranging policies to assist the employment adjustment strategies of employers during the recession and recovery (see Appendix). Instead, employers are encouraged to exploit the guidance and advisory services of bodies, such as the CIPD (the Chartered Institute of Personnel and Development, the professional body for HR managers) and ACAS (the Advisory, Conciliation and Arbitration Service), as well as the government 'Business Link' body, which offer tips and training courses on managing redundancies, restructuring, working time change, and so on.

This means companies have been more likely to make employees redundant than in Germany, for example, where the national policy action on short working hours has encouraged less harmful adjustment strategies. A long list of high profile companies across all sectors of the economy have announced major job losses during the recession, including Corus (2,500 jobs, January 2009), Fujitsu (1,200 jobs, August 2008), Ford (850 jobs, February 2009[20]), AstraZeneca (250 jobs in November 2008 and 1,200 jobs in March 2010), BAE (200 jobs, November 2008) and ShopDirect (1,500 jobs, January 2010).

Table 13.8   Quarterly turnover in the security and cleaning sectors, UK, 2008–2010, £million

	Security and investigation services	Cleaning activities	All services	All manufacturing
2008 Q2	1 373	1 854	402 338	103 686
Q3	1 432	1 919	399 196	101 306
Q4	1 540	1 860	385 572	96 058
2009 Q1	1 490	1 842	349 549	86 735
Q2	1 485	1 857	346 943	87 618
Q3	1 484	1 815	358 379	88 781
Q4	1 560	1 795	386 789	93 889
2010 Q1	1 696	1 732	383 967	91 483
Q2	1 780	1 746	378 504	96 171
% Change from peak to trough	–3.6%	–9.7%	–13.8%	–16.3%

Source: Office of National Statistics (statistics.gov.uk). Not seasonally adjusted.

5.2   Case Study of a Male-dominated Sector: Low Skill, Long Hours Jobs in the Security Sector

Here we present a summary portrait of change in the security services sector, drawing on secondary output and employment data, plus interview data with managers at a medium-sized firm and a large, multinational firm with a strong presence in the United Kingdom. The choice of sector is largely motivated by a concern to illuminate changes affecting the male workforce. It also provides a glimpse into the restructuring of long hours working and low skill jobs. The fieldwork involved interviews with three HR managers at the large security firm (SecurityCo), one manager at the medium-sized firm (ProtectCo), one senior representative from the security trade association (BSIA) and one senior representative from the trade union (GMB) with members in the large security firm.

Table 13.8 shows that the security services sector did not fare too badly compared to other sectors of the UK economy. Quarterly turnover declined by around 4 per cent from a peak of £1,540 million to £1,484 (€1,775) million during 2008–2009. Declines in other low skill business services sectors, such as cleaning for example, were far greater, at close to 10 per cent. Moreover, falling turnover in the cleaning sector persisted for six quarters, compared to just three quarters in security.

The following analysis of case-study data addresses four interrelated themes concerning adjustment and responses to the recession in the security services sector (see Table 13.9):

1. intensification of price competition;
2. managing risk displacement from powerful client firms;
3. reduced working hours and the risk of reduced weekly earnings versus opportunity to raise the hourly rate; and
4. technology–labour substitution and the upgrading of jobs during the downturn.

5.3 Intensification of Price Competition

Like other business services sectors, the loss of one or two important contracts from major client organizations can have a significant adverse impact on the company whatever its size. Managers interviewed at the large and the medium-sized security companies pointed notably to a loss of contracts from clients in the construction and financial sectors, the two sectors that suffered most during this recession and which, as a result, are said to have become more cost-focused during the recession. Two senior HR managers from SecurityCo offered the following views:

> The main effect on us has been to reduce our costs and margins for our clients so [that] as they start to get pressured in terms of costs . . . it filters down the chain. (SecurityCo, HR manager1)
> I would say that the banks have been most aggressive with their pricing policies in recent years. (SecurityCo, HR manager 2)

The small firm ProtectCo experienced job losses amounting to 23 per cent of its pre-recession workforce, from 56 to 43 workers during 2008–2010. The redundancies were a direct result of losing contracts with construction firm clients, leading to a fall in managed construction sites from nine to just two and an associated cut in static guards (who remain at a fixed site while on patrol) from 21 to just four. Other clients in the retail and hospitality sectors were not affected and ProtectCo had managed to retain contracts with them.

Nevertheless, all clients were said to have exerted pressure on the case-study security firms 'to do more for less' (SecurityCo HR manager 1), ramping up the intensity of price competition in the bidding and re-bidding for contracts. Thus while SecurityCo did not experience a decline in revenues during the recession,[21] it did experience a narrowing of profit margins. The representative from the trade association, BSIA, confirmed that profits were squeezed across the sector and the trade union

Work inequalities in the crisis

Table 13.9   Summary of case-study findings

Challenges and firm responses:	SecurityCo (large firm)	ProtectCo (small-sized firm)	Impact on work inequalities
1. Intensified price competition	Clients more cost-focused; more aggressive pricing policies led to squeezed profit margins.	Loss of clients (construction), tighter profit margins on remaining contracts and resulting 23% job losses.	Squeezed profit margins restrict employers' ability to pay, dampening pay prospects.
2. Managing client pressures	Well developed strategy to work closely with clients – delivers cheaper basic services but also expands range of services on offer. Seeks to extend duration of contracts.	Aims to retain clients by delivering same service for a lower price. Seeks to extend duration of contract.	Downward pressure on pay settlements for manned guard services workers. Some potential for job upgrading but requires employer investment.
3. Pay and working hours time	Very long hours. Negotiating shorter hours in contracts with clients. Seeking to ensure a living wage.	Very long hours. Absence of trade union and limited evidence of employer efforts to address long hours culture.	General trend of reduced hours, but also reduced weekly pay packet, especially among low paid manned guards. Real decline in hourly pay in line with whole economy.
4. Technology–labour substitution and job upgrading	Implementation of 'security solutions', involving mobile guards and closed circuit television.	Implementation of 'security solutions', involving mobile guards and closed circuit television.	More job opportunities for better trained and better paid mobile security guards, but contingent upon client contracts.

representative highlighted the adverse implications for pay, which we demonstrate below.

Like other business services sectors (including cleaning, IT and temporary agencies) security firms target the public sector as an important source of outsourcing contracts, reflecting a longstanding government trend to shift activities to the private (and voluntary) sector (Grimshaw and Roper 2007). However, all interviewees expected conditions facing public sector clients to deteriorate in the forthcoming months because of the impending public sector spending cuts. Nevertheless, the common view was that this would in fact speed up the expansion of the lucrative public sector outsourcing market as public sector managers sought to make cost savings. Moreover, the benefits of contracting with a reliable public sector client – as one manager put it, 'you can always get your money from governments' (SecurityCo, HR manager 3) – outweighed the expected increased emphasis on costs.

> My view of next year would be that the government needs to cut costs and get value for money. And it's more likely to do that by outsourcing to the private sector. . . . So in actual fact I could see us having another year of growth next year. (SecurityCo, HR manager 2)

5.4 Managing Risk Displacement from Powerful Clients

Security firms are typically on the 'wrong end' of the subcontracting supply chain, providing services in a strongly price-led product market to a small number of better positioned client organizations. Both case-study firms had downsized the number of static guards during the recession and had to renegotiate several contracts with reduced margins. A common observation was that certain clients practised one approach to employment practices internally, but a different, more cost-focused approach with subcontracted workers.

Nevertheless, both security firms were actively pursuing diverse strategies to strengthen their position. A key strategy was to work more closely with the client organizations, to become more strongly embedded with the client in order both to improve the chances of retaining contracts and to expand revenue streams. And, as the manager at ProtectCo told us, success in retaining clients meant retaining workers. This was an especially well developed strategy at the larger firm SecurityCo:

> [SecurityCo strategy is to become] more involved with the client and delivering what we do and how we manage the client. It's about embedding yourself with the client to make sure they are achieving their aims and that way they are less likely to go outside [i.e. to another supplier] . . . Because if you lose a client then you have to take on another three to counteract it. (SecurityCo, HR manager 1)

While at the small-sized firm, ProtectCo, the strategy focused on delivering the same level of services at a cheaper overall price, at the larger firm, SecurityCo, the strategy involved expanding the range of services on offer. In addition to the conventional static guard services, other services offered include concierge/reception services, postroom services, travel services and risk assessments. At SecurityCo this was, on the one hand, a strategy to 'add more value for our customers' and, on the other, to reduce the share of revenues dependent on the 'easily traded commodity' of manned guard services (SecurityCo1). The type of contract – whether long or short duration, for example – was also perceived as critical to this strategy of embedding with the client. Both SecurityCo and ProtectCo sought to extend the duration of their contracts, up to five years where possible, a strategy welcomed by the union representative:

> The longer the contracts then the more stable the workforce, the better the pay, the better the terms and conditions, the better quality training, as they are also developing a broader and deeper relationship with their client. (GMB)

On the other hand, however, the firms' adjustment strategy of giving clients the same basic manned guard services for less carries obvious risks for work inequalities. In particular, it seems to have halted prospects for pay rises and skill development among employees undertaking manned guard duties in both firms. The risk is partly offset in the larger firm by its ability to offer higher value-added activities drawing on expertise in other divisions of the company.

5.5   Reduced Working Hours and the Impact on Pay and Wage Disparity

Across the sector, the recession caused a reduction in weekly working hours as clients sought to reduce costs by cutting hours of service provision. The median number of weekly hours, including overtime, in the sector dropped by nearly 3 per cent between 2008 and 2010. Among the lowest paid, the drop was much higher, from 46.3 hours to 43.3 hours, or 6.5 per cent. Nevertheless, long hours still characterize the service sector. Table 13.10 shows that the median weekly hours were 49.5 in 2010, nearly ten hours higher than the all economy median of 41.0 hours. At the large company, SecurityCo, average hours are 52–56 per week and typically involve four 12-hour night shifts and a Saturday morning of 4–8 hours for all employees delivering manguard security services.

The GMB union and SecurityCo employer positions on working time are divided. The trade union was leading a campaign to reduce working hours and sought to capitalize on the opportunities presented by the recession as clients negotiated reduced hours provision. Its long-term agenda

Table 13.10   *Change in hours and average earnings in the security sector*
(sector SIC 801), male full-time employees, UK, 2008–2010

	2010			% change in real earnings and hours, 2008–2010		
	D1	D5	D8	D1	D5	D8
Security sector:						
Weekly pay	£272.1	£404.7	£530.1	−7.8	−3.7	0.6
Hours worked	43.3	49.5	49.2	−6.5	−2.6	−2.8
Hourly pay	£6.29	£8.18	£10.78	−1.0	−1.0	3.7
All employees:						
Weekly pay	£295.3	£538.2	£833.7	−3.1	−2.8	−2.4
Hours worked	40.6	41.0	38.7	−0.2	−0.7	−1.0
Hourly pay	£7.27	£13.14	£21.56	−1.4	−1.8	−1.4

Source: Annual Survey of Hours and Earnings. Gross average hourly earnings including overtime. Percentage change in nominal earnings deflated by CPI for 2008 (3.6 per cent) and 2009 (2.2 per cent).

is to establish standard contracts of 40 hours per week 'at a decent rate of pay so that they [security guards] do not have to slog themselves to death to make ends meet' (GMB).

The risk is that the drop in weekly hours will not be offset by a rise in hourly pay, leading to a net fall in weekly earnings. We can see evidence of this across the sector. In terms of real earnings, weekly pay among the lowest paid male full-time workers (generally manned guard services workers) fell by almost 8 per cent between April 2008 and April 2010, far higher than the 3.1 per cent fall for the lowest paid in the whole economy.

In contrast to the union position, SecurityCo managers defend the UK opt-out from the European Working Time Directive as 'fundamental . . . so that they [workers] can earn a living wage' (SecurityCo, HR manager 2). However, the terms and conditions do not facilitate a living wage since despite its multinational, market leader status, SecurityCo pays neither an overtime premium nor a nightwork premium. Additional and unsocial hours are therefore paid at a basic rate of pay. Nevertheless, management efforts at SecurityCo went further than those at ProtectCo where the absence of a trade union reduced pressure on the employer to address the problem of long working hours.

Despite their differences, both union and company representatives were working together to renegotiate contracts with clients that reduced weekly hours, while also seeking to ensure a weekly living wage that would apply to a new weekly standard of 48 hours. The union representative was optimistic and argued the recession had had the effect of making security guards more aware of their poor pay and working hours conditions; 'Bizarrely, the recession has made people question more than they have done in the past their [hourly] rate of pay' (GMB). The union strategy was to lift the bottom rate of pay above the statutory national minimum wage and to ensure annual pay rises exceeded the minimum wage uprating in order to increase the pay gap between the lowest rate paid to security guards and the statutory minimum wage.

5.6   Low Skilled Labour Replaced with Technology and Up-skilling

A key component of employer strategies to protect against the adverse effects of the recession was the substitution of technology for low skilled labour. In bids to clients, managers at both case-study firms offered the alternative package of installation of closed-circuit television (CCTV) and mobile patrols – termed 'security solutions' by the industry body, the BSIA – instead of the usual continuous presence of static security guards. The option to use mobile guards could be presented as cheaper since the security firm could exercise greater flexibility in hours of guards provided. By contrast, static guards were a quasi-fixed cost with a set period of hours that had to be covered on the site. For SecurityCo and ProtectCo the aim was to reduce the share of labour costs and improve margins through greater utilization of surveillance technologies.

For the union, the strategy was also welcomed but only insofar as it encouraged greater investment in the more highly trained (and higher paid) mobile security guard or patrol officer. New contracts negotiated with clients were therefore linked to strategic decisions about training provision and staffing (SecurityCo HR manager 1) and offered the promise of general upgrading of jobs, skills and pay in the sector.

6.   CONCLUSION

The 2008–2009 UK recession had clear effects on inequalities in the world of work, notably differential effects on men and women, young and old. Men lost around three times as many jobs as women, largely because of their over-representation in the hard hit construction and manufacturing sectors and under-representation in the still expanding sectors of education and health, largely representative of the public sector. More surprisingly, men shared with women the role of flexible buffer, with a fall in average hours worked, a shift to more part-time employment and more temporary contracts. But women were penalized in ways that reflect the male-breadwinner model of the UK's welfare state (with a lower proportion of unemployed women claiming benefits), the stringent 'job first' approach to lone parent households (with a reduced share of lone parents able to claim income support without a job search requirement) and the gender bias in pay systems (with a halt in pre-recession improvements in the position of low paid female workers).

Among both men and women, young people were harder hit by this recession than the old. Possibly reflecting job queue effects, young people experienced by far the largest drop in employment during 2008–2009 and the largest rise in unemployment. Moreover, twelve months after the end of the GDP recession levels of unemployment among young people remain high, with a recent rise among women aged 18–24 years during summer 2010.

Older people were penalized with respect to long-term unemployment and were far less likely than younger unemployed people to move out of unemployment within six months, reflecting possible age discrimination in firms' hiring practices. A further cause for concern is the continuing rise in the share of young men in long-term unemployment, which suggests a growing number are failing to find work and joining the growing numbers of 'NEETs', those not in employment, education or training. The new government's decision to abolish the Young Person's Guarantee – introduced in 2009 by the previous Labour government – means a reversal of young people's fortunes is likely to be delayed. Moreover, young people in low wage jobs were far more likely than other groups of workers to experience a cut in real earnings during 2008–2009, reflecting their over-representation in non-unionized workplaces and weaker wage bargaining power given lower skills and qualifications than older workers in better paid jobs.

The way in which the employment consequences of the adverse economic conditions were mediated by business decisions is illustrated by the analysis of our case study, drawing on original interview data. Security firms suffered job losses during the recession, largely as the result of client organizations (especially in the construction, manufacturing and finance sectors) cancelling contracts. The squeeze on profits caused by more cost-focused client organizations was associated with four business strategies, each of which had clear consequences for work inequalities. First, security firms faced a squeeze on profit margins and/or a loss of client contracts during the recession. These pressures led directly to job losses and restricted the ability of the firm to award pay increases in line with inflation, evident in the sector-wide decline in real earnings. Second, both case-study security firms sought to displace product market risks by expanding the range of security services on offer to clients. While this did not address the problems of falling pay among the low paid manguard services workers, it did provide the potential for job upgrading, albeit contingent upon the agreement of new contracts with clients. Third, efforts by clients to reduce the contract price were married with a joint union–employer strategy at the larger security firm to reduce average weekly hours and upgrade hourly pay. This strategy is ongoing at the time of writing. However, sector-wide data point to the danger of achieving hours reductions without an offsetting rise in the rate of hourly pay. Moreover, no such strategy was visible at the non-unionized small firm investigated. Fourth, security firms were seeking to upgrade technologies and to substitute low skilled labour as part of a strategy (welcomed by the trade union) to reduce the share of fixed labour costs in contracts with clients and to upgrade jobs.

Whether or not these case-study findings translate into longer-term adjustments in the quality of work and inequality in the security sector remains to be seen. However, the news announced in September 2010 that the government intends to abolish the security industry licensing body, the Security Industry Authority, means there may be a radical shift in the composition of firms providing security services, with a falling share of employers willing to provide decent working conditions. Across the country, more generally, the combination of radical public spending cuts, an absence of constructive labour market intervention, restrictive welfare reforms and the abolition of many public bodies designed to coordinate the actions of the social partners is already laying down the foundations for a worsening of inequalities in UK society.

NOTES

*　Thanks are due to Claire Shepherd (EWERC) who assisted with the collection of interview data and to the representatives of the various organizations who agreed to participate in this study.

1. Williams (2009: 11).
2. In October 2010 Pissarides advised the government against cutting unemployment benefits, saying, 'The risk is essentially that people will sink into poverty. . . . When people get into poverty, they get disillusioned with their engagement in the labour force, they face longer periods of unemployment and it becomes much harder to get them back into the workforce. . . . Because the bill is very big, it looks very tempting to go and cut them, but I would be very concerned to see that happen in a recession' (http://uk.finance.yahoo.com/news/).
3. All currency conversions estimated on 10 December 2010.
4. Data available online at www.statistics.gov.uk/OnlineProducts/LMS_FR_HS.asp# economic (accessed October 2010).
5. The internationally agreed ILO definition of unemployment counts as unemployed a person who is either (a) without a job, wants a job, has actively sought work in the last four weeks and is available to start work in the next two weeks, or (b) is out of work,

has found a job and is waiting to start it in the next two weeks (see www.statistics.gov.
uk/downloads/theme_labour/unemployment.pdf).

6. The findings relate to average weekly wage data for the 12 months of 2007 and for the period October–December 2009, using the same dataset as Figure 13.3.

7. The new Chancellor of the coalition government said in the run-up to the election, 'You will see that whoever wins the election is going to have to ask from 2011 each part of the public sector to accept a one year pay freeze. We shouldn't include public servants earning less than £18,000 [€21,500]. Because I don't believe in balancing the budget on the backs of the poorest – and nor do you. . . . I know it is difficult to ask such hard working people to accept this freeze. But I want to be straight with you. A pay freeze of the scale I'm talking about is the equivalent to saving 100,000 public sector jobs. And I say to every public sector worker it is the best way to try to protect your job during this difficult period. We are all in this together.'

8. Workers with an annual full-time wage of less than £21,000 (equivalent to around €25,000) will receive a fixed annual sum of £250 (€298). But many part-time workers who earn less than £21,000 per year will have a pro rata salary greater than this level and therefore will also experience a pay freeze (www.bbc.co.uk – 'Fresh details about public sector pay freeze disclosed').

9. The male working-age population did rise slightly more than the female working-age population, but only marginally – a rise of around 0.21 million compared to 0.19 million over the period concerned.

10. The average quarter-on-quarter decline in manufacturing jobs for each successive 8-quarter period was 1.11 per cent (2000–02), 1.22 per cent (2002–04), 1.05 per cent (2004–06) and 0.60 per cent (2006–08) (LFS online data, authors' estimations).

11. The average quarter-on-quarter job growth in the health sector for each successive 8-quarter period was 0.76 per cent (2000–01), 0.67 per cent (2002–03), 0.77 per cent (2004–05), 0.17 per cent (2006–07) and 0.85 per cent (2008–09); and for the education sector, 0.19 per cent, 1.21 per cent, 0.56 per cent, 0.08 per cent and 0.61 per cent (LFS online data, authors' estimations).

12. Forecast based on estimates by the Office for Budget Responsibility (http://www.guard ian.co.uk/politics/ 2010/oct/19/spending-review-document-job-cuts).

13. Cited on the *Guardian* newspaper online website. Available at: www.guardian.co.uk/ business/2010/oct/18/ david-blanchflower-warns-against-spending-cuts.

14. It is worth noting just how low this benefit is – a weekly payment of £51.85 (approximately €62) to 18–24 year olds and £65.45 (€78) to persons aged 25 and over (2010); unemployed couples (or civil partners) receive £102.75 (€123). This compares to average weekly gross earnings of around £450 (€537). The individual gross replacement rate for a person of core working age is thus approximately just 14 per cent.

15. It is significant, however, that workers in 'retail sales in non-specialized stores' enjoyed average wage growth of 5.5 per cent, well above the average of 3.9 per cent for the economy, since this is the largest sector listed.

16. Increases in the national minimum wage were pitched at or below average earnings growth during these years in response to fears of job losses among members of the Low Pay Commission. The rate for October 2008 represented a 3.8 per cent rise (compared to average earnings growth in April 2008–April 2009 of 3.2 per cent), for October 2009 a 1.2 per cent rise (compared to 1.5 per cent average earnings growth in 2009–2010) and for October 2010 a 2.2 per cent rise compared to an as yet unknown average earnings rise.

17. This policy is preceded by the replacement of Incapacity Benefit with Employment Support Allowance for *new* claimants in October 2008.

18. Cited in a newspaper article by Mark King, 'Older workers "trapped in unemployment"', www.guardian.co.uk, 11 August 2010.

19. Adjustment using the CPI annual measure of inflation, estimated at 2.3 per cent April 2009, the month of earnings data collection.

20. This followed the move to a four-day week announced in October 2008 (timesonline, 01/10/08).

21. In fact, annual revenue at SecurityCo increased from £1,398m in 2008 to £1,629m (€1,946m) in 2009 (UK and Ireland data, company report).

BIBLIOGRAPHY

Brewer, M. (2009) 'How do income-support systems in the UK affect labour force participation?', Institute for Labour Market Policy Evaluation, Working Paper 2009: 27.

Clegg, D. (2010) 'Labour market policy and the crisis: Britain in comparative perspective', *Journal of Poverty and Social Justice*, 18 (1): 5–17.

Gregg, P. and Wadsworth, J. (2010) 'The UK labour market and the 2008–9 recession', *National Institute Economic Review*, No. 212, April.

Grimshaw, D. and Roper, I. (2007) 'Partnership: transforming the employment relationship in public services delivery', in P. Dibben, P. James, I. Roper and G. Wood (eds), *Modernising Work in Public Services: Redefining Roles and Relationships in Britain's Changing Workplace*, Basingstoke: Palgrave Macmillan.

Grimshaw, D. and Rubery, J. (1997) 'Workforce heterogeneity and unemployment benefits: the need for policy reassessment in the European Union', *Journal of European Social Policy*, 7 (4): 291–315.

IPPR (Institute for Public and Policy Research) (2010a) 'Youth unemployment and the recession', Technical Briefing. Available at: www.ippr.org.uk/upload edFiles/events/.

IPPR (2010b) 'Neets in numbers', *Youth Tracker*, Issue 4:9.

LPC (Low Pay Commission) (2010) *National Minimum Wage: Low Pay Commission Report 2010*, Cm 7823. London: The Stationery Office Ltd.

OBR (Office for Budget Responsibility) (2010) 'Pre-budget forecast, June 2010'. Available at http://budgetresponsibility.independent.gov.uk/d/pre budget forecast 140610.pdf.

Rubery, J. (ed.) (1988) *Women and Recession*, London: Routledge.

Rubery, J. and Rafferty, A. (2010) 'Women and recession', Paper for the UK Commission for Employment and Skills.

Taylor-Gooby, P. and Stoker, G. (2011) 'The coalition programme: a new vision for Britain or politics as usual?', *The Political Quarterly*, 82 (1): 4–15.

TUC (2010) 'Women and recession: one year on', TUC report. Available at: www.tuc.org.uk/extras/womenandrecession.pdf.

Walling, A. and Clancy, G. (2010) 'Underemployment in the UK labour market', *Economic and Labour Market Review*, 4 (2) February.

Williams, D. F. (2009) 'Companies, tax and the recession', KPMG Tax Business School, Discussion Paper. Available at www.kpmg.co.uk/pubs/Recession_accessible_March09.pdf.

APPENDIX

Table 13A.1   *Overview of main government policy measures implemented during the recession and those designed in response to the recession, UK, 2008–2009*

Policy area	Policy measure	Categories of workers/ households/firms targeted or affected
Public investment	£750 million Strategic Investment Fund (April 2009)	Workers in emerging technology sectors
Tax/ consumption	*Reduction in VAT from 17.5% to 15% for the period Dec. 2009– Jan. 2011 (from April 2010)*	All consumers
	New higher rate of income tax of 50% for earnings over £150,000	High paid workers
	Tax help for loss-making businesses to enable extension of three years of past tax losses relieved against previous year's income (April 2009)	Loss-making firms
	Temporary options to defer tax payments (Nov. 2008)	UK businesses
Unemployment and other welfare benefits	*Increased funding of £1.7 billion to Job Centre Plus to cope with the increased demand*	All workers
	Pre-recession reforms (since 2003) increased obligations on those on incapacity benefits to move into paid work; culminated in 2008 with a new benefit, Employment and Support Allowance, which is gradually replacing incapacity benefit and income support for people with a disability; new work assessment test	Targets non-employed people with disabilities
	Abolition of entitlement of non-employed lone parents to means-tested income support for those with children aged 7 years or over (phased in	Non-employed lone parents

Table 13A.1 (continued)

Policy area	Policy measure	Categories of workers/households/firms targeted or affected
	during 2008–2011), replaced by unemployment benefit which has a job-seeking requirement	
	Flexible New Deal (started October 2008) reforms unemployment benefits for young people, involving intensified job-search activity during months 6–12 of unemployment, then a referral for specialist help at month 12	Young unemployed people (aged 18–24)
	April 2010 temporary increase in child tax credits (until April 2011, cut for households with income over £40,000)	Households with children
Active labour market policy	*Future Jobs Fund policy during 2009–10 (abolished by new government) provided subsidies of up to £6,500 to employers (private, public, voluntary) to create new full-time jobs of at least 6 months duration and of benefit to the local community; results of successful employer bids usefully published on internet each month*	Funded approximately 75,000 new job starts for young people by Dec. 2010; also designed to provide 50,000 new jobs for long-term unemployed in areas of high unemployment
	Young Person's Guarantee operational from Jan 2010 (then abolished by new government) guaranteed all under-25s who have been unemployed for six months a chance of a job (including through the Jobs Fund), work-focused training or a work experience placement in the Community Task Force. From March 2010 take-up of this guarantee was made a condition of receipt of benefit	Targets long-term unemployed youth; opportunities for approximately 130,000 by Nov. 2010

Table 13A.1 (continued)

Policy area	Policy measure	Categories of workers/ households/firms targeted or affected
	Return to Work Credit (April 2008) for people coming off Employment Support Allowance of £40 per week (non-taxable) for first year of paid employment where gross annual earnings less than £15,000	UK businesses
	In Work Credit, payable up to 12 months, to lone parents who have left income support for a job of at least 16 hours per week, £40 per week non-taxable	Non-employed lone parents
	Supplement to Working Tax Credit for 12 months for people aged 50 or over who left an out-of-work benefit for a job involving more than 16 hours per week (up to £37 per week extra); abolished from April 2012	People aged 50 years or over
Redundancy policy	*Increased statutory redundancy pay from £350 to £380 per week (April 2009)*	All workers
Statutory minimum wage	1.2% increase Oct. 2008–Oct. 2009, compared to 1.3% rise in average earnings (including bonuses) and 2.1% inflation (CPI)	Low wage workers

Note: All measures specifically designed in response to the recession highlighted in italics.

Source: Brewer (2009); DWP statistics (available at research.dwp.gov.uk/asd/index. php?page=ypg).

Index